Oscar Gratitude . [illegible]
and Sour Grapes

Dustin Hoffman, after losing the first two t[illegible] inated: "Sure, I'd like to win an Academy Award. I realize that intellectually it doesn't really mean very much. But it is a means to more power, which in turn enables you to be choosy about your scripts. And it makes you more money—which you can put away toward the day when you won't be in such demand."

Glenda Jackson on looking back on her two Best Actress Oscars: "I felt disgusted, as though I was watching a public hanging. No one should have a chance to see so much desire, so much need for a prize, and so much pain when not given [it]."

Steven Spielberg on learning he had not been nominated as Best Director for *Jaws*: "I can't believe it. They went for Fellini instead of me."

Paul Newman on winning the Best Actor Oscar for *The Color of Money*, after losing on six previous nominations: "It's like chasing a beautiful woman for eighty years. Finally she relents and you say, 'I'm terribly sorry, I'm tired.'"

Kirk Douglas, reflecting on his failure to win after three nominations: "The Oscars have been more fair than most other awards. . . . How they could not give it to me was a bit of stupidity."

ANTHONY HOLDEN is the author of two biographies of the Prince of Wales, *Prince Charles* and *King Charles III*, as well as *Laurence Olivier* and *Of Presidents, Prime Ministers & Princes: A Decade in Fleet Street*. He lives in London.

Also by Anthony Holden

Greek Pastoral Poetry (1974)
Prince Charles (1979)
Of Presidents, Prime Ministers and Princes (1984)
Mozart's *Don Giovanni* (1987)
Laurence Olivier (1988)
King Charles III (1989)
Big Deal: *Confessions of a Professional Poker Player* (1990)

Behind the

OSCAR®

The Secret History of the Academy Awards

by

Anthony Holden

A PLUME BOOK

PLUME
Published by the Penguin Group
Penguin Books USA Inc., 375 Hudson Street, New York, New York 10014, U.S.A.
Penguin Books Ltd, 27 Wrights Lane, London W8 5TZ, England
Penguin Books Australia Ltd, Ringwood, Victoria, Australia
Penguin Books Canada Ltd, 10 Alcorn Avenue, Toronto, Ontario, Canada M4V 3B2
Penguin Books (N.Z.) Ltd, 182–190 Wairau Road, Auckland 10, New Zealand

Penguin Books Ltd, Registered Offices: Harmondsworth, Middlesex, England

Published by Plume, an imprint of Dutton Signet, a division of Penguin Books USA Inc.
This is an authorized reprint of a hardcover edition published by Simon & Schuster Inc.
For information address SIMON & SCHUSTER, Simon & Schuster Building, Rockefeller Center, 1230 Avenue of the Americas, New York, New York 10020.

First Plume Printing, February, 1994
10 9 8 7 6 5 4 3 2 1

PHOTO CREDITS

A/P Wide World Photos: 446.

© Copyright American Academy of Motion Picture Arts and Sciences: 14, 69 bottom, 82, 101 top, 111 top & bottom, 120 top & bottom, 150, 165, 276 top & bottom, 287 top & middle, 357 bottom right, 399 top & middle right & bottom, 483 bottom, 582 top & bottom, 592 top & bottom.

© 1991 Long Photography, Inc.: 14.

Courtesy American Academy of Motion Picture Arts and Sciences: 35 bottom, 276 middle, 287 bottom, 399 middle left.

Courtesy American Academy of Motion Picture Arts and Sciences & Columbia Pictures: *Guess Who's Coming to Dinner* copyrignt © 1967 Columbia Pictures Industries, Inc., 253 bottom left; *Taxi Driver* copyright © 1976 Columbia Pictures Industries, Inc., 330 top. & © 1960 The Alamo Company, 35 top. & © 1962 Associates and Aldrich Company, Inc. Renewed 1990 Warner Bros. Inc., 253 top. & Copyright 1969: Capital Cities/ABC, Inc., 288 bottom. & © 1990 Orion Pictures Corporation, 414 bottom. & © 1990 Reversal Films, Inc., 414 top. & © 1933 RKO Pictures, Inc., 120 middle; © 1934 RKO Pictures, Inc., 131; © 1941 RKO Pictures, Inc., 165 bottom. & © 1959 Turner Entertainment Co., 188 bottom left. & © 1977 United Artists Corporation, 317. & © 1966 Warner Bros. Inc., 253 middle; © 1982 Warner Bros. Inc., 357 top; © 1985 Warner Bros. Inc., 357 bottom left. & Island Pictures, Inc., 357 middle. & MCA Publishing Rights, a Division of MCA, Inc.: Copyright © by Universal Pictures, a Division of Universal City Studios, Inc., 188 bottom right, 330 bottom right. & Miramax Films, 22 bottom. & Turner Entertainment Co., still of Greta Garbo from MGM Collection, 483 top. & *Reds* Copyright © 1981 by Paramount Pictures, 330 bottom left. & *Patton* © 1970 Twentieth Century Fox Film Corporation, 69 top; *Seventh Heaven* © 1937 Twentieth Century Fox Film Corporation, 101 bottom left; *Street Angel* © 1927 Twentieth Century Fox Film Corporation, 101 bottom center; *Sunrise* © 1927 Twentieth Century Fox Film Corporation, 101 bottom right; *All About Eve* © 1950 Twentieth Century Fox Film Corporation, 217.

Photofest: 22 top, 188 top left & right, 288 top, 253 bottom right, 382.

UPI/Bettman Newsphotos: 52 top & bottom, 330 middle.

REGISTERED TRADEMARK—MARCA REGISTRADA

LIBRARY OF CONGRESS CATALOGING-IN-PUBLICATION DATA
Holden, Anthony, 1947–
Behind the Oscar : the secret history of the Academy Awards / by Anthony Holden.
p. cm.
Originally published: New York : Simon & Schuster, 1993.
ISBN 0-452-27131-2
1. Academy Awards (motion pictures) I. Title.
[PN1993.92.H65 1994]
791.43'079—dc20 93–32963
CIP

Printed in the United States of America
Designed by Levavi & Levavi, Inc.

For Sam

Here's looking at you, kid.

Contents

For Sam

Here's looking at you, kid.

Author's Note

The Academy Awards for any given year are presented in the following year; for example, the 1991 Oscar ceremony was held in March 1992. To avoid confusion throughout this book, the year cited is that of the film's release, and thus of the award rather than of the ceremony: e.g., 1991 for *The Silence of the Lambs*, although it was presented with its awards at the 1992 Oscar show. Discussion of the ceremony (or telecast) itself naturally uses the year in which it took place.

Behind the OSCAR®

The strain begins to show on the face of former Academy president Howard W. Koch, producer of the 1981 Oscar show, as cardboard replicas stand in for nominees at rehearsals for the big night.

1

Arrivals

It's the most exciting part of the industry, the night it all comes together and you get to see the movie stars.

—Meryl Streep, 1983

By midafternoon, from behind the tinted windows of a stretch limousine, the sun already seems to have set on downtown Los Angeles. Stepping out into fiercely bright light, on arrival at the Dorothy Chandler Pavilion, provokes the same guilty thrill as emerging from a daytime movie. In dark glasses, above evening dress worn since lunchtime, the evening begins on a surreal note that is not going to fade.

The show is not due to start until six PM, the optimum hour for coast-to-coast television. But guests traveling the ten miles from Beverly Hills have been advised to hit the road by three, so dense is the gridlock as eight hundred limos ferry the movie world to its annual orgy of self-congratulation.

Among the first to arrive, unnoticed by the screaming crowd on the bleachers, is the imposing figure of Frank Johnson, 55-year-old managing partner of the Los Angeles branch of the accountants Price Waterhouse. His briefcase chained to his wrist, Johnson is eager to rendezvous with his associate Dan Lyle. Aiming to converge at four PM precisely, the two executives have traveled the short distance from their downtown office in separate limousines, by separate routes.

Hijack, earthquake, limo gridlock—nothing, including acts of God, may endanger their annual mission. One day a year these two grave-faced accountants become the latter-day men from Wells Fargo. If one of them goes under, the other has to get through.

Each is clutching an identical case containing an identical set of twenty-two envelopes. Inside are the names of this year's Academy Award winners, to be announced in a couple of hours before a television audience of one billion people in one hundred countries worldwide.

Even their secretary, Michelle Morgan, is not privy to the contents. That morning she typed out a winner's card for each of the nominees in every category and handed them over to her bosses. After retrieving the results from a downtown bank vault, where they were locked over the weekend, Messrs. Johnson and Lyle then placed each winner's name in the relevant envelope and shredded the losers.

A team of six assistants had spent three days counting the ballots, but even they were sealed in separate rooms and sworn to secrecy. "We derandomize it so they don't know if they have a representative sample," says Lyle. Like members of a jury, Price Waterhouse staff are sworn not to discuss the results of the counting even among themselves. Would defiance be career-threatening? "Oh yes," says Lyle without hesitation. Which is no doubt why Bruce Davis, the Academy's executive director, has never even considered the clamor of other accountancy firms to collar the Academy's contract, in itself worth a mere $30,000 a year. "Price Waterhouse has never dropped the ball. They have treated it with the utmost seriousness."

And still do. At this stage these corporate accountants are the only two people in the world who know the names inside those envelopes. They have also committed them to memory. All morning, within the mighty portals of Price Waterhouse, the senior partners have been grilling each other on this year's Oscar results. Excitable or elderly presenters have been known, in the heat of the moment, to read out the wrong name. In such a crisis, it will fall to Johnson or Lyle to step onstage and see justice done.

Tonight is the climax of a process that has lasted three months, since the Oscar ballots first went out to Academy members in early January, along with a reminder list of eligible films. A month later, the returned ballots are solemnly carried under armed guard from the Academy's offices on Wilshire Boulevard to Price Waterhouse, where a team of six verify the secret coding designed to preclude forgery. The doors are then closed as Johnson, Lyle and their colleagues tally the nominations in all twenty-three categories.

Three days later, at 9 PM, they lead a four-man team over to the Academy's offices, where security guards lock the entrances behind them and shut down the telephone system. No one is allowed to leave the building for the rest of the night, as the Price Waterhouse team is sealed in the mail room with the photocopying machines. The list of nominees with which they emerge is handed over to a handpicked group of Academy personnel that proceeds to work through the night, preparing press releases and photographs for a predawn press conference.

By 5:30 AM, prime time for the East Coast breakfast shows, five hundred journalists are gathered in the Academy's private theater waiting for its president, with the assistance of last year's Supporting Role Oscar winners, to announce the names of this year's nominees. Each year a few surprises will draw gasps from the seasoned observers dragged so early from their beds. In February 1991, the nomination of *Ghost* as Best Picture and Julia Roberts as Best Actress moved one jaded publicist to mutter: "My God, they've thrown in everything but the *Teenage Mutant Ninja Turtles.*"

Alarm clocks all over Beverly Hills have aroused contenders to learn their fate. Within minutes the news is burning up telephone lines to movie locations around the country and the world. Two thousand miles away, it adds renewed purpose to a task force arriving for work at the Chicago factory of R. S. Owens, where this year's batch of one hundred Oscar statuettes has been in production since New Year's Day.

It may take decades to win an Academy Award, but making one is just five hours' work for a team of twelve at Owens. Each statuette is hand-cast from a steel mold kept in a high-security vault when not in use. The basic material is britannia metal, a pewterlike alloy of 90 percent tin and 10 percent antimony, more often used for tableware.

Each statuette is sanded and polished to a fine gleam, then plated successively in copper, nickel, silver and 24-karat gold, with each layer highly polished before the next one is applied. The finishing touch is a fine spray of epoxy lacquer, to protect the movie industry's most cherished icon from the ravages of time. "If you're lucky enough to win an Oscar," says Scott Siegel, the company's president, "never polish it with cleaning solvents. Dusting him off every now and then is all you need to do."

Each statuette is engraved with a serial number on the back of its base—Belgian black marble until 1945, these days made of brass. After a final inspection they are packed in custom-shaped Styrofoam containers, heavily insured, and transported by armored vehicle to the Academy's offices in Beverly Hills.

At the end of each Academy Awards show, it comes as something of a shock to the winners that the first thing they must do the next morning is hand their Oscar back to the Academy. Their names and categories are faxed to R. S. Owens, which makes brass nameplates in Chicago and sends them to Los Angeles to be affixed to the statuettes. The Oscars are returned to their anxious new owners, wherever they may be in the world, a week or so later.

R. S. Owens also manufactures the Emmy awards, Miss America statuettes, the National Football League's Most Valuable Player trophies and the Rock 'n' Roll Hall of Fame awards. But the Oscars, says Siegel, are their favorite product, and the team who make them get a big kick out of the telecast. "They get to watch all the top people in Hollywood weeping with joy or stunned or hysterical when they win an Oscar we made here at our factory. It's a real thrill." A lifetime maintenance program is also part of the Owens service. "Whether they're scratched or pitted or dented or tarnished, we make sure the Oscars return to Hollywood looking like winners."

Now the statuettes stand in gleaming ranks backstage, fifty per table on each side of the proscenium, as out front giant thirty-foot-high replicas beckon the presenters and potential winners who are beginning to arrive. In recent years the Oscar "arrivals" have become a permanent fixture of the telecast, the stars' five-figure outfits embodying the wealth and glamour of the industry at whose annual general meeting the paying public is privileged to peek. Female arrivals have been vetted in advance by the Oscars' official fashion coordinator, the Hollywood couturier Fred Hayman, who can help them obtain a free gown for the evening from designers in search of publicity. "We don't mind whose creation they wear," says Hayman, "so long as they are unique."

After stepping gingerly out of their limos, Hollywood's royalty parade down a red carpet between two blocks of bleachers crammed with fans who have waited as long as forty-eight hours for their seats, many camping overnight on the sidewalk. Arrayed along one side are serried banks of television cameras from all over the world, eager to catch every passing icon for what will look like an exclusive interview. Behind them, six deep, stand the press photographers, calling out the stars' names in hope of a personal-looking wave or smile.

It can take a "hot" name the best part of an hour to run this giant media gauntlet, waxing hopeful about the evening ahead, denying rumors about their personal lives, plugging their next project, time and time again. At its end, like Cerberus at the Gates of Hell, stands an elevated podium manned by Army Archerd, the *Variety* columnist who for thirty years has acted as the Oscars' outside emcee. Army is the stars' last port of call before taking their seats inside; a few words for the benefit of the folks on the bleachers, not to mention the watching millions, are a small price to pay for the right to spend the rest of the year in reclusive silence. But don't linger too long; the auditorium doors are firmly closed to all comers at 5:45 sharp.

The only line then still lingering outside is that of the "seat-fillers"—the volunteers in black tie and evening gowns who are shuffled in and out of the orchestra stalls as the celebs come and go. Both ABC and the Academy are intent that not one seat, at any time, shall be seen by the cameras to be empty.

Even back in the early forties, when this unique spectacle was half the size it is today, the whole experience proved too much for Raymond Chandler:

> If you can go past those awful idiot faces on the bleachers outside the theater without a sense of the collapse of the human intelligence; and if you can go out into the night and see half the police force of Los Angeles gathered to protect the golden ones from the mob in the free seats, but not from the awful moaning sound they give out, like

Cher's outrageous outfit stole the 1985 Oscar show as Don Ameche won a sentimental Oscar for Cocoon. Two years later, she would be named Best Actress for Moonstruck.

> destiny whistling through a hollow shell; if you can do these things and still feel the next morning that the picture business is worth the attention of one single intelligent, artistic mind, then in the picture business you certainly belong because this sort of vulgarity, the very vulgarity from which the Oscars are made, is the inevitable price Hollywood exacts from its serfs.

Chandler's pensées (rejected by the West Coast paper that commissioned them) were echoed forty years later, in the television age, by *The New York Times* critic Vincent Canby. "Why do we watch this nonsense with such rapt attention?" asked Canby in 1983. "More than any other program of its kind, the annual Oscar telecast epitomizes American show business, and where show business happens to be at that particular moment. . . . [The Oscar show] has to do not only with the movies, but also with television, with business and especially with the American civilization, as it is and as it wants to see itself."

Or to put it another way: "The Oscars are some sort of masturbatory fantasy. People think: an Academy Award—now if I get a parking ticket I don't have to pay it. I don't put the Award down. But, at my sanest, I would rather have a good three-man basketball game than sit here in my monkey suit." Thus spoke Elliot Gould, a nominee in 1969. The rebellious star of the recently released *M*A*S*H* nevertheless proved willing to be a presenter on that year's show, as did his then wife Barbra Streisand. Which rather proves Chandler's point. Even the cinema's antiheroes are seduced by the siren song of the Oscar.

However rich and famous movie stars may become, however admired and envied by audiences and colleagues alike, their cup will not actually run over until their name emerges from one of Frank Johnson's envelopes, and they can sob their way through an Oscar acceptance speech. Tonight's winners will bask in the glow of apparent immortality—the highest honor even Hollywood can confer—as well as boosting their fantastical fees. For those already in possession of most that this world can offer, it is a consummation devoutly to be wished—and a wish they will go to any lengths to consummate.

Wheelchair to wheelchair for the 1989 Best Actor award, both playing disabled heroes in bravura biopics, were **(ABOVE)** *Tom Cruise as the Vietnam veteran Ron Kovic and* **(LEFT)** *Daniel Day-Lewis as the Irish writer Christy Brown.*

2

Left Foot Forward

We want to thank all of you for watching us congratulate ourselves tonight.

—WARREN BEATTY, 1976

On the evening of February 7, 1990, the Hearing Room of the Hart Senate Building in Washington, D.C., was converted into a state-of-the-art cinema for the disabled. Broad aisles were cleared for wheelchairs; the film was captioned especially for deaf members of the audience; the blind were provided with earpieces carrying a radio description of what was happening onscreen. It was, in the words of one of those present, "an unlikely showing in an unlikely location." For the first time in movie history, a screening would be "universally accessible."

Over drinks before the picture, an excited cross section of the capital's disabled community found themselves mixing with politicians, movie moguls and film stars. As Senators Edward Kennedy and Robert Dole chatted with the British actor Daniel Day-Lewis, the usual news cameras were joined by those of television's *Entertainment Tonight.* Even the White House was present, in the shape of the president's counsel, C. Boyden Gray. A unique blend of Hollywood and Washington, the evening was billed as a "Reception and Celebration Supporting Legislation for Americans with Disabilities." To supporters of Congressman Steny Hoyer's Americans with Disabilities Act, it was just that. But to the representatives of Miramax, the movie distributors, it was a shrewd piece of Oscar campaigning.

The film to be screened was *My Left Foot,* a small-budget Irish biopic about the disabled writer Christy Brown, which few Americans had heard of—and even fewer seen—before Day-Lewis began monopolizing the acting awards handed out in the weeks preceding the Hollywood Oscars. Miramax seized the moment, and here in Washington was the reclusive British actor to deliver a short and moving speech to the capital's disabled community before the screening. He explained how he had spent two months in a Dublin hospital preparing for the role, meeting and studying victims of cerebral palsy, with which Christy Brown had been born. He had insisted on spending the entire filming period in a wheelchair—his body contorted, arms twisted, speech slurred, even when off the set. He thought he had begun to understand what this audience had to live through every day of their lives. As the lights went down to thunderous applause, the Irish-born actor concluded with a ringing pledge to toast the ADA in a Dublin pub.

Only one detail, one very Hollywood detail, went wrong. On every seat was placed a small white box, which turned out to contain a white chocolate left foot. Though perhaps more suited to a horror movie, the chocolate foot was a bonus no one had thought of a way to leave on wheelchairs. On an evening entirely geared to proving that the disabled should not be treated as second-class citizens, those without the use of their legs thus found themselves deprived of their custom-made candy.

Across the nation in its movie capital, Los Angeles, a more conventional Oscar campaign for *My Left Foot* was already under way. The film's producer and director, Noel Pearson and Jim Sheridan, were busy lobbying the film industry—and thus the Oscar electorate—at a long series of receptions and press conferences. "Noel and Jim really spent a lot of time in L.A. in December and January, just meeting people," said the executive vice-president of Miramax, Russell Schwarz. "We were in a unique position. There is a strong Irish community in L.A., which I didn't know about before. A lot of people wanted to shake hands." Several thousand videocassettes of the film were meanwhile mailed to the Academy's voting membership, to spare them the ordeal of going out to the movies.

Flesh-pressing was deemed unseemly for the elegant Day-Lewis, who anyway prefers the reclusive lifestyle of a male Garbo. "It's not the star's place to do parties," said Schwarz. But the actor gave interviews to the important magazines and television shows, stressing all the time that he would not be bothering but for the good he might be able to do the ADA in general and cerebral palsy in particular. Of the Washington reception, Schwarz ventured: "It wasn't too Hollywood, and it did create awareness." The key to such personalized promoting, he said, is "knowing when to push tactfully" and "having a film worthy of attention."

All this came as a surprise to Daniel Day-Lewis's British following, who had seen him undergo an all too public breakdown only months before. Haunted by the death of his father, Cecil, Britain's Poet Laureate, Day-Lewis had broken down while playing Hamlet at London's Royal National Theatre in the autumn of 1989, the very time of *My Left Foot*'s release. Halfway through a performance, unable to continue, he had dramatically quit the stage; the ghost of Hamlet's father had begun to turn into that of his own. In a rare interview with a London newspaper, he subsequently confessed that he might never act again, either on stage or on screen. He had lost the appetite.

Yet here he suddenly was in the United States, treading the talk-show circuit he supposedly eschewed, looking like a Renaissance angel as he traded gags with Arsenio Hall.

Cut six weeks to Oscar eve. Day-Lewis has already been spotted by paparazzi in the bar of the Four Seasons Hotel, wrapped around his inamorata, Isabelle Adjani, days before Tom Cruise slips into the Bel Air Hotel at the last possible minute. It is Saturday evening, March 23, and the polls for the 1989 Academy Awards have been closed for three days. Counted by the men from Price Waterhouse, the only people in the world who already know the Oscar results, the final tallies are now locked in a bank vault over the weekend. Most of the other nominees have been making themselves highly visible around town for a fortnight, trying to sway any floating voters; the word from the Cruise camp is that he has been too busy on location in Arizona for *Days of Thunder* to make all the goodwill appearances expected of Oscar hopefuls.

The truth was that Cruise was very apprehensive. Perennially tempted by low-grade movies, the young superstar might never have a better chance to win Best Actor; to do so, however, he would have to break some of Oscar's unwritten rules. With the possible exception of his supporting role in *Rain Man*—for which his costar, Dustin Hoffman, had been voted the previous year's Best Actor—Cruise's bravura performance in Oliver Stone's *Born on the Fourth of July* was his first movie role remotely worthy of Academy Award status. That this was his first nomination was in itself a negative; Oscar history stacks the odds against first-time male nominees. At 27, moreover, Cruise would have to become the youngest Best Actor ever—a distinction won in 1977 by 29-year-old Richard Dreyfuss for *The Goodbye Girl,* thus upholding the ancient Oscar tradition that the best actors tend to be honored for their worst pictures.

Hollywood punters were meanwhile relishing another, more cynical Oscar truism. From Ray Milland's alcoholic in *The Lost Weekend* (1945) to Cliff Robertson's retarded *Charly* (1968), actors seem to have had a hugely increased chance of winning an Oscar when playing physical or mental defectives. More recent examples abound, from Jack Nicholson's mental patient in *One Flew over the Cuckoo's Nest* (1975) to Hoffman's autistic savant in *Rain Man* (1988). Now the 1989 Best Actor contest saw Cruise's Ron Kovic wheelchair-to-wheelchair with Day-Lewis's Christy Brown.

Both, moreover, were playing real people, and the Oscar electorate has always shown a penchant for honoring the leading roles in biopics. A random sample over the years would include George Arliss as Disraeli (1929), Charles Laughton as Henry VIII (1932), Gary Cooper as Sergeant York (1941), Paul Scofield as Sir Thomas More (1966), George C. Scott as Patton (1970), Robert De Niro as Jake La Motta (1980), Ben Kingsley as Gandhi (1982), and F. Murray Abraham as Salieri (1984).

As Cruise lay low at the Bel Air, eating in the solitude of his room rather than join his fellow nominee Robin Williams and show host Billy Crystal in the hotel restaurant, his chances of a win seemed strong—largely because the opposition looked unusually weak. The other nominees, apart from Day-Lewis, were Morgan Freeman for *Driving Miss Daisy,* Robin Williams for *Dead Poets Society* and another little-known young Irishman, Kenneth Branagh, in the title role of a movie version of Shakespeare's *Henry V* that he had also produced and directed. Oscar history put them all at a distinct disadvantage.

Cruise's main asset in the Best Actor race was not so much his own superstardom—in Oscar terms, as much a liability as an asset—as the commercial and artistic success of the film for which he had won his nomination. The Oscar electorate, though suspicious of the biggest box-office stars, prefers to vote for box-office hits. *Born on the Fourth of July* had earned $60 million by the time of the Awards and had garnered seven other Oscar nominations—as useful to its producers in the Best Picture category as to its potential Best Actor in his. Cruise's own box-office takings in the previous seven years—the aggregate gross of all the films in which he had starred since 1982—had already exceeded an impressive $662 million, compared with $317 million for Robin Williams, $172 million for Morgan Freeman, $101 million for Daniel Day-Lewis and a mere $6.5 million for Kenneth Branagh.

Of the film awards that precede the Oscars, and wield a considerable influence upon the Academy members' votes, however, Cruise had won just one, the Golden Globe (Drama). Freeman had won two, the Golden Globe (Musical/Comedy) and the National Board of Review. Day-Lewis had won *nine,* including three U.S. "majors": the Los Angeles Film Critics, the National Society of Film Critics, and the New York Film Critics Circle. Neither Williams nor Branagh had won any—not even Cannes, traditionally regarded as upmarket and "arty," which had gone to James Spader of *sex, lies and videotape.*

Branagh looked the weakest runner from several points of view. He was the least well-known, and his film was the lowest-grossing nominee. He was at a further, usually terminal, disadvantage as the only Best Actor nominee whose film was not also nominated for Best Picture. He had won no other significant awards, and his film had taken only $4.9 million at the box office, even less than *My Left Foot.* At 29, though two years older than Cruise, he was probably still too young to win, especially at his first attempt.

Branagh had been shrewd enough to put himself on display on

the Los Angeles stage during the voting period,* starring in two of his own Shakespeare productions with the Renaissance Theatre Company, which he himself actor-managed. But his main Oscar asset was really the shadow of Laurence Olivier, with whom he was already earning handy comparisons. In 1946 *Henry V* had won the 39-year-old Olivier a Special Oscar for his "outstanding achievement" in bringing Shakespeare to the screen, despite unsuccessful nominations for Best Actor and Best Picture. Branagh, unlike Olivier, had secured a second nomination as Best Director—but he seemed even less likely to win that.

Robin Williams could also be confidently written off, primarily because of the Academy's traditional aversion to comedies and comedians—especially those who had made their names on television and were still regarded in the movie world as arrivistes. Comedies are perhaps the most popular movie genre to have won the fewest Oscars. Only three men have won the Best Actor award in overtly comedic roles: James Stewart in *The Philadelphia Story* (1940), Lee Marvin in *Cat Ballou* (1965) and Richard Dreyfuss in *The Goodbye Girl* (1977). None of the great names of screen comedy, from Charlie Chaplin and the Marx Brothers through Danny Kaye to Cary Grant ever won a single Oscar, while one of the greatest, Jack Lemmon, won his only Best Actor award for the earnest social drama *Save the Tiger,* not for *Some Like It Hot, The Apartment* or *The Odd Couple.* Woody Allen's *Annie Hall* (1977) was the only comedy to win Best Picture since Tony Richardson's *Tom Jones* in 1963.

W. C. Fields complained about this as early as 1936, when the Oscars were only nine years old: "Any actor knows that comedy is more difficult, requires more artistry. It is pretty easy to fool an audience with a little crepe hair and a dialect. It seems to me that a comedian who really makes people laugh should be as eligible for an award as a tragedian who makes people cry." But Robin Williams could take no more recent cheer from such examples as that of Steve

* This ploy had worked for several British Shakespeareans before him, notably Maggie Smith in 1969. Smith's performance in *The Prime of Miss Jean Brodie* had come and gone a year before the Oscars. But she had been appearing in *The Beaux' Stratagem* with Laurence Olivier's National Theatre company in L.A. in January, during voting for the Oscar nominations. "She received that adoration reserved for movie stars in the old days," wrote Nathan Cohen of the Toronto *Star.* "Los Angeles went wild about her." Of Smith's unexpected victory in the Best Actress stakes, the Academy's president, Gregory Peck, said: "This is great. Now you can see it's not rigged."

Martin, whose performance in *All of Me* won him two major 1984 awards, the New York Film Critics and the National Society of Film Critics—yet not even an Oscar nomination, despite a thin acting year, when the eventual winner was F. Murray Abraham for *Amadeus* over Jeff Bridges (*Starman*), Albert Finney (*Under the Volcano*), Tom Hulce (*Amadeus*) and Sam Waterston (*The Killing Fields*).

Could the Cruise–Day-Lewis face-off allow the popular Morgan Freeman to slide between them to victory? Statistics may not reflect social attitudes, but it was an undeniable fact facing Freeman's supporters that only once had a Leading Role Oscar gone to a black actor, Sidney Poitier for *Lilies of the Field* (1963). Since the 1970s the Oscar show had been regularly picketed by protesters bearing such banners as "Who Will Win Best White Actor and Best White Actress?" Only twice had black actors won the Supporting Oscar: Hattie McDaniel for *Gone With the Wind* (1939) and Louis Gossett, Jr., for *An Officer and a Gentleman* (1982). With Denzel Washington strongly fancied to become the third this year, for his role in *Glory*, the odds against a win for Morgan Freeman lengthened even more.

The only Oscar syndrome on Freeman's side, apart from one previous nomination, was a conspicuous display of his versatility. He was also on screen that year in *Lean on Me, Johnny Handsome* and *Glory*; and the voters have often displayed a tendency toward "body-of-work" awards. But another, more powerful factor was against him. Given the universal confidence that the Best Actress award would go to his *Driving Miss Daisy* costar, Jessica Tandy, Freeman was up against the fact that the two major acting awards had gone to the same film on only five occasions in sixty-two years: 1934 (Clark Gable and Claudette Colbert, *It Happened One Night*), 1975 (Jack Nicholson and Louise Fletcher, *One Flew over the Cuckoo's Nest*), 1976 (Peter Finch and Faye Dunaway, *Network*), 1978 (Jon Voight and Jane Fonda, *Coming Home*) and 1981 (Henry Fonda and Katharine Hepburn, *On Golden Pond*).

Almost as daunting for Day-Lewis and Branagh was the Academy's apparent isolationism. In sixty-two years of the Oscars, 75 percent of the awards had gone to Americans. The British may have been next in line, but only thirteen had previously won Best Actor—and only five of those in films, like both *My Left Foot* and *Henry V*, financed and made in the British Isles.

Cruise and Day-Lewis qualified for two other bonuses from the Oscar handicappers: playing out of character and wearing lots of makeup. Also going for Day-Lewis, despite his Irish passport, was the Academy's penchant for actors who put on accents. But beginner's luck, most unusually, could apply to any of the 1989 nominees. It was extremely rare for the five candidates to boast only two previous nominations among them—Williams for *Good Morning, Vietnam,* and Freeman for a supporting role in *Street Smart*, both in 1987.

Of the four main acting groups, Best Actors are statistically the least likely to win at their first nomination; less than half the Best Actor awards have gone to first-time nominees, compared with two-thirds for Best Actresses. In the 1970s only two of the male winners, Art Carney and Richard Dreyfuss, were first-time nominees, though the 1980s had seen a dramatic increase as Ben Kingsley, F. Murray Abraham, William Hurt and Michael Douglas began to reverse a fifty-year trend. But all were then well into their careers, and all had been familiar names and faces (onstage if not onscreen) for some years. Kingsley and Abraham, moreover, broke all the rules by winning in their first major picture.

But Oscar "rules," like any others, are there to be broken. This was the only consolation for the two second-time nominees, who otherwise had very little else going for them beyond their performances—the last consideration, all too often, to some of the electorate. Would this year see the Best Actor award, amid all this statistical confusion, find its way to the most outstanding performer? Could this be one of those years when one performance actually did stand out from the others? History suggested that Freeman might perhaps be helped by the clean sweep that seemed to be beckoning *Driving Miss Daisy*, Williams by the show-biz nuance that he had cohosted the awards show in 1985. As Branagh flew back from Japan for the ceremony, dozing in the back of his airport limo en route, he wondered if his tussle with international datelines had been worth it. "Of course," his executive producer, Stephen Evans, reassured him. "How else are they going to hear about *Henry V* in Middle America?"

A crew-cut Cruise, clutching the arm of his costar and future bride, Nicole Kidman, slid past the bleachers as quietly as possible, bypassing Army Archerd's television podium and lowering his head as he entered the auditorium. An extravagant Day-Lewis, by contrast, made an almost regal progress through the crowds, his Regency evening dress and shoulder-length hair worthy of Beau Brummel. He had shared his limousine downtown with his director, two producers and conominee Brenda Fricker; but he wasn't going to share his heady moment at the heart of the Hollywood razzmatazz.

Tonight would ensure a dramatic alteration to one of their lives. To both Cruise and Day-Lewis, whatever public platitudes they mumbled, the result mattered desperately. The ceremony ahead might be an unashamed piece of Hollywood propaganda, but it would offer its chosen ones every actor's dream in perpetuum: beyond the coveted respect of their peers, a further boost to their already prodigious paydays and the power to pick and choose among custom-built roles.

Even the most sanguine of performers, usually to their shame, find Oscar fever thrillingly irresistible.

Thanks to the Oscar, the American motion picture industry promotes its wares each year to more than a billion people in more than ninety countries worldwide—a larger audience than any global sporting event, any royal wedding—in a star-studded marathon television advertisement, good for at least three months of cunning advance buildup. The performers give their services free, and the Academy even profits from its own hype, deriving most of its income from the TV royalties.

Behind the smokescreen of glamour, schmaltz and supposed artistic achievement, Hollywood's Academy Awards are, of course, all about money. For performers, an Academy Award adds instant digits to the already huge fees they command, as well as conferring a distinct hint of immortality. For producers and distributors, a mere nomination is enough to wreathe a film and its makers in dollar signs. A win can double even a hit movie's box office.

Among recent Best Pictures, *The Last Emperor* grossed 68 percent of its $44 million *after* being nominated; *Platoon* 71 percent of $138 million, and *Rain Man* 41 percent of its $172 million. Even proven box-office hits, which tend to win Best Picture less often, can be given a new lease on commercial life by an Oscar: *Out of Africa*, for instance, added $37 million to its prenomination $50 million, and *Amadeus* more than doubled its $23.6 million. (See accompanying table.) A survey by one of the leading box-office data banks,

BEST PICTURE BOX-OFFICE MOMENTUM

	Before Nomination	Release Date	Nomination to Award	After Award	GRAND TOTAL	Box Office % Post-nomination
1987						
* *THE LAST EMPEROR*	14.0	Nov.	11.1	18.9	44.0	68%
Moonstruck	31.0	Dec.	28.2	21.0	80.0	62%
Fatal Attraction	143.0	Sep.	8.0	5.6	156.6	9%
Broadcast News	38.9	Dec.	9.0	2.8	50.7	23%
Hope and Glory	5.5	Oct.	4.1	0.4	10.0	45%
1986						
* *PLATOON*	40.0	Dec.	62.8	35.2	138.0	71%
Children of a Lesser God	22.0	Oct.	5.0	4.8	31.8	31%
A Room With a View	16.7	Mar.	2.4	1.9	21.0	20%
Hannah and Her Sisters	35.4	Feb.	3.1	1.5	40.0	12%
The Mission	11.0	Oct.	5.1	1.1	17.2	36%
1985						
* *OUT OF AFRICA*	50.0	Dec.	19.6	17.4	87.0	43%
The Color Purple	39.7	Dec.	37.7	16.7	94.1	58%
Kiss of the Spider Woman	12.7	Jul.	2.1	2.2	17.0	25%
Prizzi's Honor	26.0	Jun.	N/A	N/A	26.0	N/A
Witness	65.0	Feb.	N/A	N/A	65.0	N/A
1984						
* *AMADEUS*	23.6	Sep.	10.5	17.5	51.6	54%
The Killing Fields	7.6	Nov.	19.6	7.5	34.7	78%
A Passage to India	10.2	Dec.	14.6	2.3	27.1	62%
Places in the Heart	30.4	Sep.	2.7	1.8	34.9	13%
A Soldier's Story	18.7	Sep.	3.1	N/A	21.8	N/A

* = WINNER

Entertainment Data Inc. of Beverly Hills, suggests that the Best Picture winner goes on to earn an average of $30 million in postwin box office. This Oscar bonus is almost as much as the average *total* gross—$36 million—for all wide-release films.

Even losing Best Picture nominees do well out of their six-week run for their money. In 1988, all four losers jumped an average of 20 percent the week after the Oscar telecast; distributors are usually pleased by anything better than a 25 percent *decrease* in week-to-week box office. Over the past eight years, losing Best Picture nominees have gone on to earn an average of $6 million in post-Awards box office.

Even in Hollywood, nobody pretends that the Oscars are entirely about artistic merit. Originally launched to help repair the industry's tarnished image, they are now largely about what press agents call "positioning." A long list of apparent irrelevancies such as age, public image, previous track record, popularity within the industry and above all box-office bankability count for as much as the actual product or performance among many Oscar voters, who tend to be the older, often retired members of the film community. Their average age has been computed at sixty. "The nature of the Academy membership is elderly," as one director put it. "Everyone in it is as old as God and hasn't worked in twenty years."

"It's like the last vestige for somebody who used to be active in the business," says the *Hollywood Reporter*'s Robert Osborne, himself a veteran of the Oscar circuit and the Awards' official historian. Movie people who have seen better days "can still hang in there and feel like they're part of the raging tides going on because of the Oscars." Osborne professed himself surprised, on once glimpsing the membership list kept top secret by the Academy, to find it full of "lightweights": "There seemed to be a lot of Virginia Mayos." Robert Solo, the producer of *Colors*, has formed the same impression after years attending Academy screenings: "Sometimes I get the feeling that they sent the bus down to the Motion Picture Country Home and drove everybody into Beverly Hills to see a movie."

So what effect does this have on their voting habits? They may have liberal politics but their cinematic taste is distinctly conservative, as witnessed by such recent Best Picture choices as *Gandhi* over *E.T.*, *Ordinary People* over *Raging Bull* (voted by U.S. critics the finest film of the 1980s), and *Out of Africa* over *Prizzi's Honor*. As the same director puts it, "Institutions aren't the best judges of a work of art, just like the Académie des Beaux-Arts rejected the Impressionists."

The Oscar electorate is comprised of the 5,000-plus members of the thirteen branches of the Academy of Motion Picture Arts and Sciences, whose membership rules are not unlike those of a gentle-

In March 1992, membership of the Academy's branches broke down as follows:

Actors Branch	26.9%	1,341
Directors Branch	5.6%	282
Writers Branch	7.6%	377
Musicians Branch	4.7%	236
Art Directors Branch	5.8%	291
Cinematographers Branch	2.8%	142
Editors Branch	4.0%	202
Sound Technicians Branch	7.2%	360
Motion Picture Executives	7.4%	369
Producers Branch	8.1%	404
Public Relations Directors	6.6%	331
Short Subject Filmmakers	4.7%	237
Members-at-Large	8.4%	421
Total Voting Members		4,993
Nonvoting Associates		448
Total Membership		5,441

men's club. Oscar nominees are automatically invited to join; candidates must otherwise be proposed by two existing members, able to boast solo credits in at least two commercial or critical hits and approved by a subcommittee of the board of governors. Membership costs $150 a year.

It entitles cardholders to free screenings at the Samuel Goldwyn Theater, the Academy's private cinema within its plush Wilshire Boulevard headquarters, refurbished in 1990 to become the world's most sophisticated screening room. Members of the Oscar electorate, the crème de la crème of the motion picture industry, rarely watch films in the company of the moviegoing public, the people who pay their vast incomes—let alone knee-deep in popcorn, surrounded by screaming children. Megastars do not, of course, venture out even to the Academy's private cinema; they will assess the cinematography of, say, *Lawrence of Arabia* on the strength of a videocassette sent to their home.

John Wayne's Davy Crockett scours the horizon in vain for Oscars, despite the most shameless campaign in the awards' history for his patriotic epic, The Alamo. This trade paper advertisement (BELOW) *was typical of his publicist's excesses.*

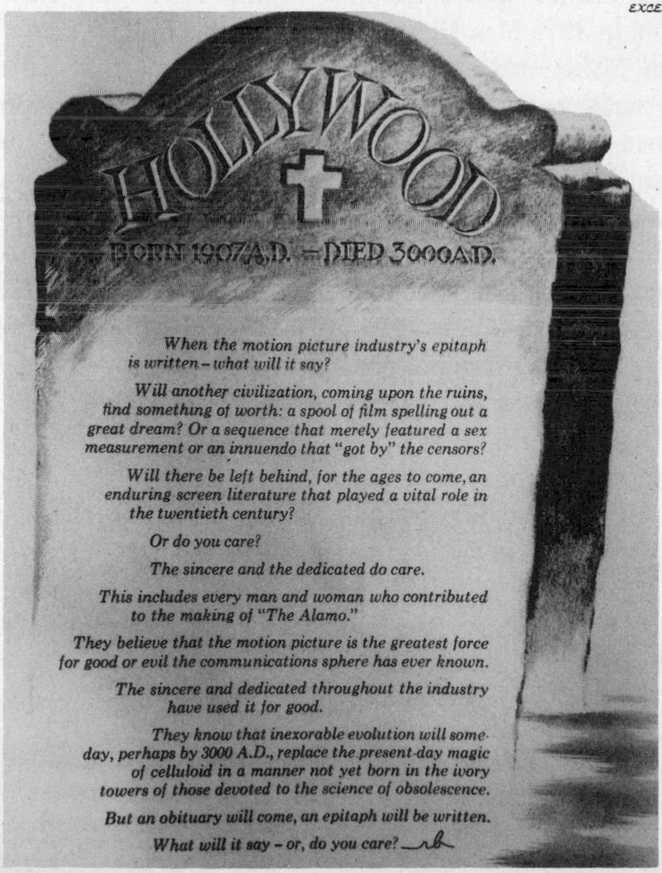

HOLLYWOOD
BORN 1907 A.D. – DIED 3000 A.D.
When the motion picture industry's epitaph is written – what will it say?
Will another civilization, coming upon the ruins, find something of worth: a spool of film spelling out a great dream? Or a sequence that merely featured a sex measurement or an innuendo that "got by" the censors?
Will there be left behind, for the ages to come, an enduring screen literature that played a vital role in the twentieth century?
Or do you care?
The sincere and the dedicated do care.
This includes every man and woman who contributed to the making of "The Alamo."
They believe that the motion picture is the greatest force for good or evil the communications sphere has ever known.
The sincere and dedicated throughout the industry have used it for good.
They know that inexorable evolution will someday, perhaps by 3000 A.D., replace the present-day magic of celluloid in a manner not yet born in the ivory towers of those devoted to the science of obsolescence.
But an obituary will come, an epitaph will be written.
What will it say – or, do you care? —rb

Members resident overseas enjoy similar privileges; in London, for instance, weekly private screenings are arranged by the Academy's U.K. representatives in a private cinema on Soho Square. Clearly, the committees choosing the films for screening wield considerable influence on the Oscar results—especially in Beverly Hills. Though their names, too, are jealously guarded, the Academy's theater operations coordinator, Candice Courtney, has confided that there are only eighty to a hundred slots per year—or roughly two per weekend. Many of the smaller independent films thus continue to go unnoticed. "Every year there are a number of movies that we'd like to screen, but don't have time," says Courtney. The Oscar electorate, in other words, sees pretty much the same mainstream movies as those favored by the middlebrow paying public—and has broadly similar tastes.

There is no guarantee, however, that this august group of voters will actually have *seen* the films they tick on the list of eligible candidates sent out to them each January. Busy moguls have been known to let their secretaries or mistresses mark their cards for them. In 1978 Mrs. Henry Fonda confessed to the *Chicago Tribune*'s Gene Siskel that she and another star's wife had filled out their husbands' ballot forms on a number of occasions—prompting a pained response from the Academy's then president, Howard W. Koch: "I'm sure this sort of thing happens on the rare occasion. Anyone who talks about it, however, is very foolish."

To be eligible for consideration, a film must run in at least one cinema in the Los Angeles area for a minimum of a week prior to midnight on New Year's Eve. Hence the timing of the release of most Oscar contenders, in mid-December, both to capitalize on the Christmas market and to be fresh in the minds of the Oscar electorate during the voting period. The one exception to this rule is Woody Allen, whose covert method of thumbing his nose at the whole process is to release his movies in February or March, the worst possible time in the Oscar cycle. Though the ceremony is held on a Monday night, when he is usually playing the clarinet at Michael's Pub in New York, Woody's indifference to the entire business has not stopped him winning Oscars.

Ballot papers go out in early January, with a reminder list of eligible films, their cast and personnel. The nominations are decided by the vote of members of the relevant branch: actors, in other words, vote for actors, directors for directors, writers for writers, and so on.

Much to the chagrin of Hollywood agents, who have for years been campaigning in vain to become a branch of the Academy, publicists too get in on the act. The only branch without its own award, the public relations fraternity may vote only for Best Picture. Once the nominations have been announced in mid-February, six weeks before the awards are presented, the winners in all categories are decided by a further vote of all members of the Academy, regardless of the branch to which they belong. Do set designers know much about music? Or sound men about editing? Or actors about cinematography? Not much more than the average moviegoer, but that's the way the system works.

The Academy never reveals voting figures, so no one apart from Price Waterhouse, the official scrutineers, knows what percentage of the electorate actually return their ballots—rumored to be less than half—or who beat whom by what margin. Nor does anyone know, given a secret ballot, who voted for whom, though everyone, of course, claims to have voted for the winner once the results are known. But there is no question, as is so often hinted, of foul play. Those two grave-looking men from Price Waterhouse, whose very grayness endows the show with both drama and authority, are the slickest public relations trick in the whole elaborate ritual.

"These two ritualistically dumpy men," in the words of the writer David Mamet (once a nominee, once a "backstage wife"), "reassure us that, in spite of the vast rewards to be gained by irregularity, our interests as a people are being protected. There still may be a surprise winner; God and the Devil still exist."

Apart from God and the devil, the main wild card in the complex equation that creates Oscar winners is hype. Ever since Joan Crawford bucked the studio system by hiring her own publicity agent in 1945, increasingly elaborate stunts have been devised to woo the Oscar votes of Academy members. The whole system approached crisis in 1960 when John Wayne and his costar in *The Alamo*, Chill Wills, went to extremes regarded even in Hollywood as tasteless (see pages 229–36). Gregory Peck's three-year presidency of the Academy, from 1967 to 1970, was distinguished by a sustained attempt to stifle the extraneous influences brought to bear on Oscar voters. Every year since, the annual Oscar mailshot to voters has been accompanied by a stern warning from the governors of the board of the Academy against "crude solicitations":

> This year, as in the past, you will be importuned by advertisements, promotional gifts and other lobbying tactics, in an attempt to solicit your vote. Each year, these crude and excessive solicitations embarrass the Academy, embarrass you and demean the significance of the Academy Award of Merit for outstanding achievement. All attempts by the Academy to discourage such promotions and advertisements have been in vain.
>
> We call upon each Academy member to disregard these attempts to influence your vote and we urge you to register your displeasure with those who, in an unrestrained and ambitious manner, attempt to do so. Excellence in filmmaking is the ONLY valid criterion for casting a vote for an Academy Award, and it is for your judgment of that excellence that the Academy has asked you to vote. No extraneous factors should be allowed to color your consideration of excellence.
>
> The Academy, the film industry and the world must trust your judgment.

For all the efforts of President Peck, it is now an accepted part of the annual "positioning" process that an expensive series of giant color advertisements are placed in trade magazines such as *Daily Variety* and the *Hollywood Reporter*, addressing themselves directly to the voters with the tasteful plea "For Your Consideration." Academy members are bombarded with literature about eligible films, reminders of screenings, video and audio cassettes—even bottles of champagne, dinner invitations and beguilingly chichi gifts. Though the Academy rules strictly forbid personal electioneering, that means little beyond a ban on direct solicitation of votes—or bribery.

Much of the pre-Oscar romancing is aimed at the Golden Globe awards, voted and presented by the Hollywood Foreign Press Association; these are the last major awards before the Oscars, announced just before the closing date for nominations, upon which they can wield a considerable influence. With fewer than a hundred members, and far less strict rules, the Foreign Press Association is a prime target for movie publicists in search of a shot at the Academy Awards.

The announcement of the Oscar nominations is the signal for a second round of hype that puts the first in the shade. For individual actors and directors, it is deemed okay to campaign for a nomination —but unseemly, once nominated, to campaign for the award. This is very much the province of the studios and their publicists, who now move in with big promotional budgets to pull out every stop ever invented. Any film gaining any nomination(s) will now be rereleased or see its distribution dramatically broadened. Producers of films nominated for Best Picture reckon to spend at least $500,000 on promotion during the six-week voting period from the announcement of nominations in mid-February to the close of final balloting in late March, during which all nominated films are screened in the Goldwyn Theater, as advertised by the Academy in a special handout to members. Nominees have even been known to hang around the Academy's headquarters during these screenings; one voter recalls being "extremely impressed" in 1988, on leaving a showing of *Stand and Deliver*, to find its nominated star, Edward James Olmos, waiting to shake his hand on the way out.

Overdoing all this, however, is thought somewhat vulgar, and can often prove counterproductive. "There are a lot of special mailers, but I don't think they're particularly effective," says Irwin Winkler, Oscar-winning producer of *Rocky*. "They are more annoying than anything else. All they show is that some people are so desperate that they will do anything to get a vote." Retired studio executives have been known to sell their mailing list of Academy members and their addresses for $3,000—plus postage.

Poor Pauline Collins, nominated in 1989 for an unwonted movie success in *Shirley Valentine,* was advised to hire herself a Hollywood press agent if she wanted to stand any chance of beating Michelle Pfeiffer, Isabelle Adjani and the two Jessicas, Tandy and Lange. When she telephoned one such "fixer" from London, she heard words to the effect of: "Thanks, but no thanks. You don't stand a snowflake's chance of winning. Just thank God for the nomination, get yourself over here for the celebrations, and have a good time." Collins quietly complied; it seemed the English thing to do.

The sixty-second Academy Awards, presented on March 26, 1990, marked an increasingly rare accolade for the British film industry: no fewer than ten Oscar nominations for British-financed films.

Taking on the might of Oliver Stone's *Born on the Fourth of July* and Bruce Beresford's *Driving Miss Daisy* were two low-budget movies made in the British Isles with British money, Branagh's audacious *Henry V* and Pearson and Sheridan's heroic *My Left Foot*, with eight nominations between them. Also nominated for acting awards were Pauline Collins, a surprise choice for the transfer of her stage success to the screen, and Day-Lewis's costar Brenda Fricker, for her performance as Christy Brown's long-suffering mother. All along, however, it was a British-born expatriate who looked the most likely to win; Hollywood sentiment seemed certain to ensure that her performance in the American-made *Driving Miss Daisy* would crown 80-year-old Jessica Tandy the oldest Oscar winner ever.

Though the Oscar fortunes of the British film industry have fluctuated over the years, its actors owe a comparatively high success rate to the exaggerated American reverence for the English stage. Even nine-times-nominated Meryl Streep has confessed to feeling "vastly intimidated" by English actors. "We American actors think we're just a bunch of slobs compared to them."

It was in only the third year of the Oscars that the first Briton, George Arliss, won Best Actor, though he set a long-term trend by doing so in an American film, *Disraeli* (1929–30). Of the twelve more Britons named Best Actor in the subsequent sixty years, only four won in British films, all of them biopics—Charles Laughton as Henry VIII, Laurence Olivier as Hamlet, Paul Scofield as Sir Thomas More in *A Man for All Seasons* and Ben Kingsley in the title role of *Gandhi*.

Eleven British-born actresses from Vivien Leigh and Greer Garson to Julie Andrews and Maggie Smith had meanwhile won Best Actress for American-made films, but only two in British films—Julie Christie (for *Darling*) and Glenda Jackson (*Women in Love*). Of the eight Britons to win Best Supporting Actor and the five to win Best Supporting Actress, only one of each were in British-made films: Sir John Mills and Dame Peggy Ashcroft in two David Lean pictures, *Ryan's Daughter* and *A Passage to India*.

Before the 1989 results, that made forty-three acting Oscars for Britain in sixty-one years—or a success rate of almost 20 percent. In terms of nominations, the statistics improve. Olivier's ten remains a male record, second only to Katharine Hepburn's all-time record of twelve. Two more Britons, Peter O'Toole and Richard Burton, hold the dubious distinction of the most nominations (seven each) without a single win.

A survey by Emanuel Levy,* professor of sociology and film at Columbia University, New York, showed that British representation had ranged from 11 percent in the 1950s to a high of 31 percent in the 1960s. In that dire decade for Hollywood, 40 percent of all acting nominees were non-American. In 1964 and 1983, no fewer than eight of the ten Best Actor nominees were British—though only one of them won, Rex Harrison in *My Fair Lady* in 1964, besting Peter Sellers, Richard Burton and Peter O'Toole. In 1983 the lone American nominee, Robert Duvall (playing against type, as a country-and-western singer, in *Tender Mercies*) prevailed over Michael Caine, Tom Conti, Tom Courtenay and Albert Finney.

A victory in 1990 for Branagh, Day-Lewis or any of their colleagues would thus defy history as well as the system. But above all it would cheer on the lonely handful of British producers still managing to raise their financing at home. The late 1980s had seen a dramatic decline in British film production; only twenty-seven feature films were made in Britain in 1989, compared with more than fifty the year before and an average of seventy in the mid-1980s.

These days, thanks to the box-office "brain drain," it was more common to see British talent at work in big-budget, big-revenue American films. Each of the previous two years had seen a British-born director, now working in Hollywood, nominated for an American film: Adrian Lyne for *Fatal Attraction* and Alan Parker for *Mississippi Burning.*

Among the 1989 nominations for Best Director, alongside Oliver Stone and Woody Allen, were two Irishmen (Branagh and Sheridan) and an Australian (Peter Weir, for *Dead Poets Society*). Highly conspicuous by his absence was another Australian, Bruce Beresford, who had directed the apparent front-runner for Best Picture, *Driving Miss Daisy.* Not since *Grand Hotel* sixty years before,

* *And the Winner Is . . .* (Continuum, New York, 1990).

at the fifth Academy Awards ceremony in 1931–32, had Best Picture gone to a film whose director had not even been nominated.

The five Best Picture nominees for the 1989 Academy Awards —chosen from 217 eligible feature-length films, the smallest total since 1982's all-time low of 175—all reflected what Hollywood likes to call the "humanistic" values notably absent from the year's top-grossing film, *Batman*. The odd man out was *Born on the Fourth of July*, which pulled out all the stops to sell audiences a still unpopular attitude toward Vietnam and its aftermath. The other four films were all what is known in the trade as "soft": that is, in the definition of the *Los Angeles Times*'s Sean Mitchell, "stories whose power does not depend on high body counts, special effects, elaborate plots, physical comedy or epic grandeur." Soft movies can be box-office poison; to the Academy, however, they tend to reflect what Mitchell calls "the film industry's sporadic attempts at high purpose atop its pudgy body of commerce."

The least likely to win was the least commercially successful, Ireland's *My Left Foot*, which had grossed a mere $14.4 million by the time of the awards, fully 80 percent of it (up from $2.8 million) since the announcement of its nomination. For Pearson and Sheridan, winning the nomination in itself looked enough of a victory against huge odds. The most commercially successful of the five, going into the awards, was *Dead Poets Society*, which had grossed $95.3 million, of which some $21 million postdated the nominations. *Field of Dreams* had grossed $63.4 million; but it had been released the previous April, generally too early to be a serious contender, and had thus added only $600,000 as a result of its nomination.

Touchstone Pictures had lost votes for *Dead Poets Society* by sending Academy members a videocassette featuring an intermittent "crawl" at the foot of the screen, listing the film's box-office figures, citing its Golden Globe nominations and quoting favorable reviews. "There's been a lot of grumbling about it," conceded an Academy official. "It would seem to have been counterproductive." Voters were also offended to receive a video of Disney's *The Little Mermaid*—part of its pitch for the music awards—punctuated by antipiracy warnings. Utterly wasted on Academy members were the plugs for the Universal Studios theme park that opened the *Field of Dreams* cassettes. Goldwyn's limited budget for promoting *Henry V* restricted them to mailing out copies of the trailer only, while Fox very shrewdly edited everything but the special effects out of *The Abyss.*

The clear front-runners for Best Picture of 1989 were *Born on the Fourth of July* and *Driving Miss Daisy*—polar opposites in their emotional and intellectual appeal both to moviegoers and to the Academy's voters. "The news is that there are people out there who want more than rapes and car chases and violence," rejoiced Richard D. Zanuck, producer of *Driving Miss Daisy*, a study of the relationship between a southern Jewish matron and her loyal black chauffeur. To Zanuck, the 1989 list was little different in kind from most other years, with the significant caveat that each producer had overcome great difficulties to get his movie made. "Each of these pictures represents the passions of filmmakers and not of the studios," he said. "But it's wonderful for us and other filmmakers to know that there's an audience out there that will embrace a story like *Driving Miss Daisy* that has no obvious elements going for it."

Oliver Stone considered his film "a liberal choice" by the Academy, especially after it had shut out two other controversial films, Spike Lee's *Do the Right Thing* (which had won the Los Angeles Film Critics award) and Michael Moore's angry documentary about General Motors, *Roger & Me.* "All five of the [Best Picture nominees] are aberrations, unconventional visions," said Stone. "*Dead Poets Society*—when was the last time there was a movie about poetry? Most people would probably assume *My Left Foot* is a downer, but you see it and realize it is very life-affirming." *Field of Dreams* reminded him of Spielberg's *E.T.* "I suppose *Driving Miss Daisy* is the least aberrant in that it was a play before being adapted."

The decisive difference between them was a brilliant Warner Bros. marketing campaign that saw *Driving Miss Daisy* ride into the voting period on a critical and box-office high. By the time of the Awards, each film had taken some $60 million at the box-office; but *Miss Daisy* had taken $27.4 million of that since the nominations, compared with only $11.4 million for *Fourth of July.* Warners had given Zanuck's film a very limited opening the previous December, to ensure Oscar eligibility while conserving its box-office energies until the voting period. As the rave reviews began to pile up, they stepped on the box-office gas, widening its distribution to 895 screens three weeks before the nominations and 1,397 as they were announced. Between mid-February and late March the film coasted on the strength of nine Oscar nominations; then, on winning Best Picture, Warners put their corporate foot to the floor to the widest point of release, at 1,668 screens nationwide. There followed a post-victory cruise of more than $30 million, past the magic $100 million mark—an extraordinary achievement for so rarefied a product.

The gradual expansion of *Driving Miss Daisy*'s release came after *Born on the Fourth of July* had peaked at the box office, and coincided with a political backlash against Stone's film. As the year began—even as late as mid-February, when it scooped eight nominations—Stone's powerful version of the memoirs of a paraplegic Vietnam vet, Ron Kovic, appeared to have all the ingredients of a certain winner. Yet *Driving Miss Daisy* beat it to Best Picture, and *Fourth of July* won only two Oscars—for Best Director and Editing. "I think the film is honest," said Stone backstage, visibly dismayed despite his own Oscar for direction. "It was attacked by a poorly motivated right wing. Because it is political, it made a lot of people angry."

Stone's constant politicizing in the press had taken its toll on some Academy members. They had already given multiple honors to his *Platoon*, three years before; they were wearied by the hectoring tone of his films, and dismayed to hear that *Born on the Fourth of July* was but the second of a planned Vietnam trilogy. The voters may also have gotten "tired," as one producer put it, "of hearing Ron Kovic say he was considering running for office." Said another insider: "It's a matter of timing in a campaign. *Platoon* was a big success on the same subject as *Born*. Academy members might have felt Oliver Stone had already been rewarded enough."

Warners' marketing strategy for *Driving Miss Daisy* opened other Oscar doors. As Stone's box office began to fall away during the voting period, *Miss Daisy* was turning into the year's fiscal Cinderella, giving the voters a perennially welcome opportunity to vote for a well-acted exponent of liberal moral values over a violent, blood-stained epic. Unlike *Born on the Fourth of July*, as one voter pointed out, *Driving Miss Daisy* "had no violence and no sex. . . . It's the kind of movie you wish Hollywood would make more of—one with decent values." With overwhelming public support on its side, *Daisy* started to feel like a winner. After the event, even the Academy's president, Karl Malden, dropped his supposed impartiality to comment: "*Driving Miss Daisy* is a real film about real people. That's why it won, and that's why it deserved to."

"Anything that tugs at your emotions has a good chance for a Best Picture award," said Zanuck. "I've worked on a lot of films, but it's rare to receive this much mail. Over a thousand letters saying 'My mother/grandmother is like her' poured in. Academy voters felt those same emotions." The producer also believed that the film's budget of $7.5 million, low by Hollywood standards, appealed to the industry, underlining the fact that movies did not need major stars to make money and win Oscars. "Nothing's automatic about the Oscars," said Zanuck, "but I felt all along that the actors had a real good shot at a nomination, especially Jessica Tandy."

At 80 years and 293 days, Jessica Tandy became the oldest actor or actress ever to win an Oscar (beating 1975's Best Supporting Actor, George Burns, by 224 days*). She was also only the seventh actress to have won the Leading Role Oscar at her first nomination, following Mary Pickford (*Coquette*, 1928–29), Ginger Rogers (*Kitty Foyle*, 1940), Judy Holliday (*Born Yesterday*, 1950), Shirley Booth (*Come Back, Little Sheba*, 1952), Louise Fletcher (*One Flew over the Cuckoo's Nest*, 1975) and Marlee Matlin (*Children of a Lesser God*, 1986).

"I'm on cloud nine," Tandy told the audience. Afterward, at the Governors Ball, she told Karl Malden: "Now we've all got one." For a moment, the Academy president couldn't think what his old friend meant. Then she explained: forty years on, she had at last joined the rest of the original Broadway cast of *A Streetcar Named Desire*—Malden, Marlon Brando and Kim Hunter—in winning an Oscar. "Brando, Kim and I found ourselves hired for the movie," Malden recalled. "But the studio wanted a big screen star for Jessica's role, Blanche Dubois, and of course the part went to Vivien Leigh—and won her her second Oscar. At the time, Jessica was none too pleased. Now, I guess she can afford to smile and forget."

The scandal of the 1989 Oscars, without precedent in sixty

* The oldest Best Actor winner was 76-year-old Henry Fonda for *On Golden Pond* in 1981. The oldest nominee was Eva Le Gallienne, aged 82 years and 79 days, for *Resurrection* in 1980; she was beaten by Mary Steenburgen in *Melvin and Howard*. See Appendix C, section B4.

years, was the omission from nomination of the Best Picture's director, Bruce Beresford. The show's host, Billy Crystal, acknowledged as much in front of the watching millions, by hailing *Driving Miss Daisy* as "the film which apparently directed itself." Comparisons were made with the great Oscar scandal of 1985, when Steven Spielberg's *The Color Purple* was nominated for Best Picture, but its director himself omitted. Although the Directors Guild taught the Academy some manners that year by handing Spielberg its top award, *The Color Purple* was doubly snubbed with no awards at all from its eleven nominations, as Sydney Pollack's *Out of Africa* swept the board.

"On paper, these two films have a lot in common," reflected the *Los Angeles Times*'s Jack Mathews. "Both are adapted from works by Southern writers looking at Southern racial issues and both were directed by white outsiders. On the screen, they were worlds apart—one stylistically aggressive, the other subdued. Just so were the reactions to the snubbing of their directors." Where Spielberg had wondered out loud what he had to do to win the Academy's favor, Beresford maintained a dignified silence.

Though his film had won four Oscars, including Best Picture, while Spielberg's had won nothing, Beresford's treatment at the hands of the Academy caused nothing like the same outcry as its snub to the home-grown wunderkind. But *Driving Miss Daisy* had not provoked racial controversy, as did *The Color Purple*. Beresford, moreover, was neither a Hollywood insider nor a proven blockbuster. The Australian's best previous films, *Breaker Morant* and *Tender Mercies*, had barely registered at the box office (although the latter had won a Best Actor award for Robert Duvall). And Beresford had failed to land a nomination from his peers in the Directors Guild, whose awards have a major influence on the Academy's.

Since the marriage consummated in 1952 between the Academy Awards and television—a shotgun wedding, at the time, between budding rivals—the garish character of the Oscar ceremony seems to have become an elemental part of its mass audience appeal. The overlong acceptance speech, the overblown production number, the over-the-top sets and costumes—all are now essential constituents of the viewing public's love-hate relationship with a show that has become a modern American institution. That the proceedings are irremediably tacky is now part of the fun. "It's a thrill," as one enthusiast wrote in 1990, "to be confronted with production numbers that are genuinely innocent in their awfulness; to see one contrived duo of celebrity presenters after another fumble their way through TelePrompTered shtick; and to see some of the most beloved actresses in the world try to outsequin each other for the honor of appearing in the worst-dressed columns of gossip writers everywhere."

But wasn't the Oscar telecast boring? "Nonsense. A few stretches may be tailor-made for a beer run . . . but these are mere interludes within an orgy of kitsch." The awards were "a chintzy exercise in movie-industry vanity, a terminally mediocre affair that continues to celebrate and define the lower-middlebrow aesthetic of mainstream Hollywood."

For their first fifteen years, the Academy Awards were presented at a private dinner, broadcast on local radio in Los Angeles as early as 1930, and (in part) nationally two years later. The show was first relayed nationally, in its entirety, in 1945—the year from which many date the Oscars' inexorable transformation into the international phenomenon they are today. But the Academy's governors had already waxed defensive about a rate of growth that would now make them purr. "Somewhat to the embarrassment of the traditional dignity of the Academy," said a rather arch statement in 1940, "the words 'Oscar' and 'Academy Awards' have slipped into the popular language like 'Sterling' and 'Nobel,' as recognized symbols of quality. . . ."

When the banquet was abandoned in favor of a presentation ceremony in 1944, for fear that conspicuous consumption would not look good in time of war, the national radio audience was fast approaching one hundred million. Fifteen years later, in 1959, as many were watching on television.

The show's costs, meanwhile, had soared. When the studios withdrew their financial support in 1948 (ostensibly because of the first Best Picture award to a non-American film, Olivier's *Hamlet*), it emerged that the show's basic costs were a mere $20,000, though studio contributions had run as high as $80,000. Four years later, in 1952, the television rights were sold for $100,000; by 1964, they had reached $1 million. Today ABC Television pays the Academy more than $2 million each year for the privilege of broadcasting the Awards; by the early 1990s, the network was in turn charging a record $10,000 dollars a second for commercials during the Oscar telecast. Part of the attraction for major corporate sponsors is a handsome allocation of tickets for executives and their guests, who attend the show in such numbers that hundreds of Academy members are turned away each year.

Though the first former film actor to become president of the United States, Ronald Reagan was not the first chief executive to offer the Academy Awards an official White House blessing. Fifty years before, in 1932, Vice-President Charles Curtis attended the ceremony to deliver a special tribute to the film industry, praising it for boosting national morale during the Depression. Franklin D. Roosevelt and Harry S Truman both anticipated Reagan by sending congratulatory messages, in 1941 and 1949, respectively—helping to sanctify the Academy Awards into an annual American festival as sacred as the Super Bowl or even Halloween. From the wheeling-on of tribal elders for ritual worship to the anointment of young new stars into the firmament, the Academy Awards ceremony is now an ancient rite familiar enough to make each year distinctive for its surprises or impromptu happenings.

In March 1990, the sixty-second Oscar show contained its share of unscripted dramas. Though merely introducing a film clip, Kim Basinger felt obliged to exploit her moment in the sun by departing from her script to protest the lack of Academy recognition for Spike Lee's *Do the Right Thing.* Come the time for the screenplay awards, a ramp was swiftly installed at stage-right—out of sight of the TV cameras—to accommodate Ron Kovic's wheelchair; on the aisle nearby, Kovic could be seen excitedly whispering to his companions, sure that it signified victory. When the name of *Driving Miss Daisy*'s author, Alfred Uhry, emerged from the envelope, Kovic's crashing disappointment was brutally compounded by the sight of the ramp being as swiftly removed. It was gone, along with Kovic's dreams of glory, before the winner had even made it to the stage.

But the high drama of the evening came with the arrival on-stage of the reigning Best Actress, Jodie Foster, to reveal the name of 1989's Best Actor in a Leading Role. To its many millions of devotees, the Oscar show's voyeuristic appeal lies in seeing their favorite film stars playing themselves, across a complex range of human emotions; four out of five nominees must conceal their dismay in tight, full-color close-up as they lead the ovation for the colleague who has frustrated their most cherished aspiration. For Tom Cruise, the moment symbolized his metamorphosis from teen idol and *Cocktail*-tosser to serious actor. ("Yes," as one critic put it, "but he's a *lousy* serious actor.") Cruise and Oliver Stone had chosen the Oscar high road of minimum personal input into a heavyweight product campaign. For Daniel Day-Lewis and his deceptively makeshift Irish bandwagon, in fact steered by the shrewd marketing minds of Miramax, this was the end of a carefully charted route winding back through that congressional hearing room in Washington D.C.

Those excruciating close-ups of the expectant nominees, reflected to them live via the giant screens beside the stage, showed Cruise in an agonized combination of hope and fear. When Foster grinned and called out Day-Lewis's name, Cruise was the first to smile and applaud; but he was also the first out of the building, out of the post-Oscar party circuit, and, indeed, out of town. Onstage, Day-Lewis pitched his thanks just right by envisaging "one hell of a weekend in Dublin."

Miss Daisy's stylish overhaul of the Stone juggernaut, and the political reaction against Stone's tamperings with Kovic's memoirs (see also page 77), appear to have cost Cruise an Oscar that would have lent some much-needed artistic credibility to his already huge box-office standing. Ballots are destroyed after the count, and local headcounts are scarcely scientific; but the available evidence suggests that the result would have been a very close call between Cruise and Freeman—had not both been unlucky enough to have come up against Day-Lewis, one of those maverick performers who command an unusual degree of open admiration from their peers. At the Governors Ball following the show, other film actors, from major commercial stars to more rarefied aesthetes, all testified that they voted for him because "I saw someone up there doing something I could not do myself." It is the highest compliment one of these titanic egos can pay another.

Day-Lewis was the fourteenth British actor in sixty-two years of the Oscars to carry off screen acting's ultimate accolade, only the fifth Briton ever to win Best Actor for a performance in a British film.* His popular victory also helped his costar, Brenda Fricker, beat Anjelica Huston and Julia Roberts to the lesser acting award; for once, the work of a genuine supporting actress was preferred to the claims of leading ladies in subsidiary roles. The gray area between leading and supporting roles—a vexed annual problem for both candidates and voters—saw Denzel Washington narrowly take the Supporting Oscar from Danny Aiello, Martin Landau and Dan Aykroyd, rewarded by *Miss Daisy*'s good vibes for a rare crossover from comedy to straight drama.

The fifth nominee was Marlon Brando, whose eighth Oscar nomination placed him on a plateau with Jack Lemmon and Geraldine Page behind Spencer Tracy, Jack Nicholson and Meryl Streep (nine each), Bette Davis and Laurence Olivier (ten) and the Oscar's all-time champion, Katharine Hepburn, with four wins from twelve nominations. Had his fellow actors' votes for Jack Nicholson's Joker in *Batman* not been split between Best Actor and Best Supporting Actor, so that he failed to be nominated as either, he would have joined Davis and Olivier at ten. Even on nine, however, he shares with Meryl Streep the distinction of being the most Oscar-nominated actors still very much at work.

Nineteen eighty-nine was one of those years when, for all the twists in the campaign trail, the Academy was deemed to have got it broadly right. The major awards all went to worthy winners for distinguished work, and only Bruce Beresford could legitimately claim unfair treatment. Trying to read movie trends into the results, however, was as futile an exercise as ever. "The Academy goes through phases," as one Oscar-winning writer put it. "A commercial picture that makes a lot of money gets rewarded, then people get tired of that and reward quirky, personal pictures. Films that are personal and felt come along all the time, but the awards mean nothing to the kind of pictures that get made next year. It never spills over because Hollywood doesn't change, the system doesn't change."

That, in Oliver Stone's phrase, is the nature of the beast.

* By the end of 1990 *My Left Foot,* made for just $2 million, had returned a rental in the United States and Canada of $7 million. (Rental is the share of a film's gross, usually between 40 and 50 percent, which is returned to the distributor.)

"There's always going to be the conservatives and the explorers," Stone mused. At the Academy Awards, as at the box office, both camps have discovered that winning is as much a matter of luck as judgment. But the rewards are hugely disproportionate. In sixty-four years only a Hollywood handful, chief among them Marlon Brando and George C. Scott, have found the Oscar an offer they could refuse.

Humphrey Bogart celebrates with his wife, Lauren Bacall, and their son Steven after winning the 1951 Best Actor award for The African Queen.

In 1954 Marlon Brando fooled around for the cameras with Bob Hope after winning his first Best Actor award in Elia Kazan's On the Waterfront. Eighteen years later he would reject the same Oscar for The Godfather.

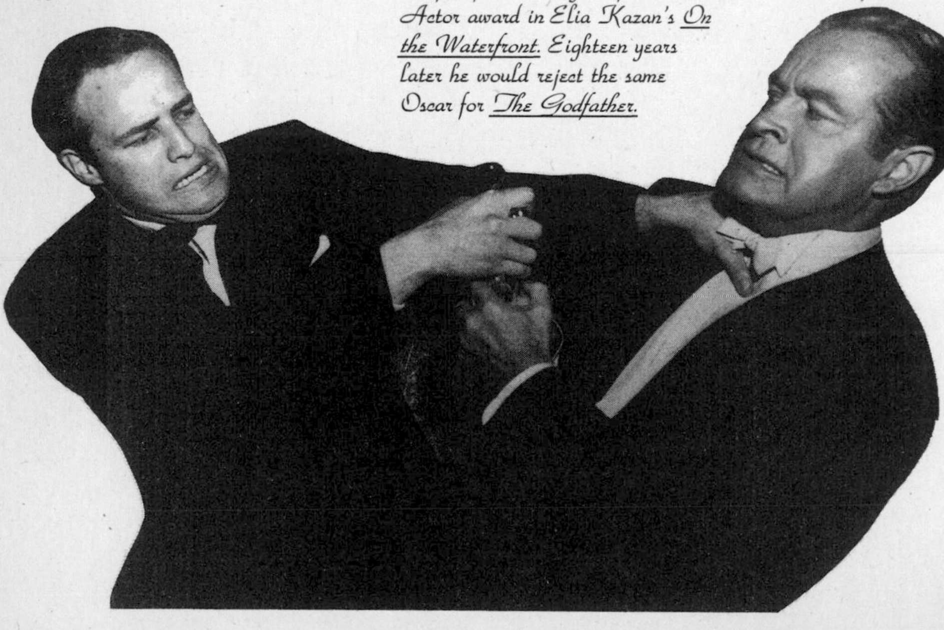

3

Bogie and the Art of Oscar Maintenance

The process was not something I could live comfortably with. I still can't.

—George C. Scott

It stands thirteen and a half inches tall, weighs eight and a half pounds and costs barely one hundred dollars to make. Yet the Oscar amounts to perhaps the most potent publicity gimmick any industry ever devised for itself. Along the way, it has also become the most coveted doorstop in the world.

In 1975 a Broadway role prevented Ellen Burstyn from going to Hollywood to accept her Best Actress award for *Alice Doesn't Live Here Anymore.* Two days later, Jack Lemmon and Walter Matthau turned up with her Oscar in a cardboard liquor box, which stood in the middle of the table as they dined together after the show. "What's really in that box, Walter?" Burstyn asked Matthau. "What does an Oscar mean?"

"Put it this way, Ellen," replied Matthau. "When you die, the newspaper obituaries will say, 'The Academy Award-winning actress Ellen Burstyn died today.' "

Across town, at much the same time, Robert De Niro was also

taking receipt of his first Oscar, and explaining to reporters why he hadn't bothered to turn up to collect it. "Well, lots of people who win the award don't deserve it, so it makes you a little cynical about how much it means. Did it mean that much to me? Well, I don't know. It changes your life like anything will change your life. People react to it. I mean, it's not bad, winning it."

Nineteen seventy-four was also the year that *Amarcord* won Federico Fellini his fourth Academy Award for Best Foreign Film. "It is, of course, a pleasure," said the distinguished Italian director, a cult figure to those "art-house" moviegoers who pay scant heed to Hollywood's annual Oscar orgy. "In the mythology of the cinema, the Oscar is the supreme prize."

How have Hollywood's Academy Awards attained their unique international power and preeminence? Acting awards are, by common consent, absurd. Any contest between actors is "meaningless," as Humphrey Bogart used to put it, "unless they play the same part." The only true test of ability, said Bogart, would be "to have all the nominees don black tights and recite *Hamlet.*" Bogie, who had yet to win his only Oscar for *The African Queen* in 1951, was quick to add that he would not be suggesting this "in any year I found myself up against Larry Olivier." He was, however, making a point that many actors privately endorse but few have the temerity to express in public—until they have an Oscar safely installed in their trophy cabinet. As the British director David Lean summed up: "If you have no hope of getting one, they're despised. But if you have, they're very important."

Bogart denounced the Academy Awards as "silly" and "all bunk," until he surprised both himself and the movie world by beating Marlon Brando to Best Actor in 1951. When Greer Garson read out his name, Bogart "jogged up onto the stage and took the Oscar as gently as though it were a newborn baby." For all his bravado, according to his wife, Lauren Bacall, he had really wanted to win. "When push came to shove, he did care and was stunned that it was such a popular victory. He had never felt people in the town liked him much and hadn't expected such universal joy when his name was called."

"It's a long way from the Belgian Congo [where he had filmed *The African Queen*] to the stage of the Pantages," Bogart told the audience. "It's nicer to be here." Just a year later, he was again displaying the public indifference expected of him by denouncing the awards as "fake." But all the indications are that winning mellowed even Bogart. In later years, he showed how seriously he took his Oscar when the young Richard Burton dared to argue with him about acting. "He stormed out of the room," recalled Burton, "and came back with his Oscar, which he thumped down on the table. 'You were saying . . . ?' he growled."

Bogart also became wise in the mysterious ways of the Academy and its Award. "The way to survive an Oscar," he announced, "is never to try to win another one. You've seen what happened to some Oscar winners. They spend the rest of their lives turning down scripts while searching for the great role to win another one. Hell, I hope I'm never nominated again. It's meat-and-potatoes roles for me from now on."

With the possible exception of Woody Allen—who, win or lose, has always displayed a fine disregard for release dates and awards ceremonies—Oscar history shows that the only people able to indulge in wholesale denunciations are past winners, sore losers, or those who have simply given up hope.

At one end of the scale stands the haughty Katharine Hepburn, Oscar's all-time champion with twelve nominations and four wins spanning fifty years. Hepburn's method of protesting while accepting was never to attend the awards show as a nominee. "Prizes are nothing. My prize is my work," she intoned in 1940, after failing to make it two wins out of three nominations. Forty years later her tune had not much changed: "Prizes are given. Prizes are won. They are the result of competition. Any way you want to look at it, from birth to death we are competing. . . . How does anyone know which performance? Which picture? It's an art. . . . Well, hell, let's face it. How does anyone know anything? It's our track meet. It's painful but it's thrilling."

In 1967 Hepburn filmed a greeting to mark the Oscars' fortieth anniversary; but she only once made a personal appearance at the Oscar show—in 1974, to present a Thalberg Award to her friend Lawrence Weingarten. "I'm very happy that I didn't hear anyone call out, 'It's about time,' " she said amid the standing ovation—adding, somewhat equivocally: "I'm living proof that someone can wait forty-one years to be unselfish."

That depends on your definition of unselfish. Hepburn was still not there in 1981, when she won her fourth Oscar—forty-nine years after she had won her first—for *On Golden Pond.* "I don't think there's anyone here or watching," said a diplomatic Jon Voight, "who doesn't appreciate the amount of love and gratitude represented by this Oscar selection tonight. We all send our love to Katharine." Asked why she had always refused to attend the awards, Hepburn mused: "It has to be because I'm afraid I'm not going to win. . . . If I were an honest person, which obviously I'm not, I would refuse to compete. I would make a statement and say, 'As I do not believe in Academy Awards'—and I don't believe in Academy Awards—'I do not wish to compete.' But I do say to myself, 'I wonder if I'm going to win it . . . ?' I mean, it's all false."

At her first nomination, for *The Deer Hunter* in 1978, Meryl Streep could afford to shoot her mouth off: "It's insane to have winners and losers in art. To say that one performance is better than another is just plain dumb. You wouldn't think of comparing two colors in a painting, would you? This blue is better than that blue?" Upon winning her first Leading Role statuette in 1982, however, having already won a supporting Oscar, her language was calmer. Confessing to feeling "freaked out," Streep likened the award to "a mantle visited on me that has no relation to what I do or what I am." Half of her seemed to be echoing the individualism of Hepburn, half speaking for a younger and more outspoken generation of actors, reluctant to be trapped into spotlit competition.

More typical is the posturing of a John Wayne, who for most of his career was given to such resigned cynicism as "You can't eat awards—nor, more to the point, drink 'em." All his life Wayne claimed that he had been nominated in 1948 for John Ford's *She Wore a Yellow Ribbon*, though the records show that the first of his two nominations came the following year as Sergeant Strycker in *The Sands of Iwo Jima*. "I always go to the Academy Awards each year," he shrugged, "in case one of my friends, who is out of town, wins an Oscar and I can accept on his behalf. I have received awards for Gary Cooper and John Ford. But no one—including me—ever has collected one for John Wayne. That doesn't keep me tossing in my bed at night." Then the real angst showed through: "Of course, the fellows who own and operate theaters don't know that I'm not much of an actor, as they have been foolish enough to pick me as the box-office champion of the year a couple of times."

Wayne definitively betrayed his hand in 1960, with the all-time shameless Oscar campaign for his patriotic brainchild, *The Alamo* (pp. 229–36). Gradually, throughout the ensuing decade, he began to wax more realistic: "My pictures don't call for the great dramatic range that wins Oscars." Then, in 1969, when the local enthusiasm for *True Grit* (not to mention his dramatic remission from cancer) suddenly seemed to bring him an unexpected chance of Oscar gold, he shut up altogether. After Hollywood sentiment had named him Best Actor over Richard Burton, Dustin Hoffman, Peter O'Toole and Jon Voight, it was a humbler "Duke" who drawled: "The Oscar is a beautiful thing to have. It's important to me. It symbolizes the appreciation of your peers."

Though this is the Oscar appeal most cited by candidates, rather than the millions it can add to their already absurd salaries, stars in the financial stratosphere can literally afford to ride the artistic derision of their peers. It will take something very unexpected for an Arnold Schwarzenegger or a Bruce Willis to add an Oscar to their box-office gold. But it is not impossible. Even a Sylvester Stallone can win an Oscar nomination for a film as successful as *Rocky*, which itself won Best Picture over *Network* and *Taxi Driver*, though the Academy's more high-minded members are unlikely to forgive him his *Rambo* series and the interminable *Rocky* sequels.

Success, to Hollywood, is not its own reward. Box-office returns have always counted with the Oscar electorate, which is showing increasing respect for sheer commercial clout in recent years by voting nominations to such films as *Ghost* and *Pretty Woman*. But a versatile actor like Harrison Ford, who has earned his Oscar spurs in such films as *Witness, Working Girl, Presumed Innocent* and *Regarding Henry* may still take some years to be forgiven for becoming the biggest box-office star of the 1980s in the *Star Wars* and *Indiana Jones* series. A Steve Martin, though honored by the New York critics for *All of Me*, will always be sniffed at by the Academy, as will a blockbuster star like a Bill Murray or a Dan Aykroyd—unless, as in Aykroyd's case, he takes on the kind of "serious" dramatic role that won him a Best Supporting nomination as Jessica Tandy's son in *Driving Miss Daisy*.

Bogart's seminal sentiments were eloquently paraphrased by Peter Bogdanovich, beaten as Best Director by William Friedkin in 1971: "The way I see it, there's only one place that does it right. Every year in Barcelona they give awards for poetry. The third prize is a silver rose. The second prize is a gold one. The first prize, the one for best poem of all, is a real rose."

The Oscars are about a different kind of romance, where hard steel and vicious infighting lurk perceptibly beneath the surface. To wide-eyed cinemagoers it may all be a game, but to those in the trade the Academy Awards are a matter of professional life and death. These days, the financing of an Oscar campaign is a standard clause in most major stars' movie contracts. Even Bogdanovich might eat his words if an Oscar were suddenly in prospect. He would not be the first.

Perhaps the most celebrated convert to Oscar-worship is Dustin Hoffman, who began his career a nervous critic. Nominated in 1967 for his first major film, *The Graduate*, Hoffman attended the ceremony in white tie and tails, but said he hoped he would not win. "I don't honestly believe I've earned it. It wasn't an important part, anyhow." He needn't have worried; Rod Steiger (*In the Heat of the Night*) won Best Actor over Hoffman, Warren Beatty (*Bonnie and Clyde*), Paul Newman (*Cool Hand Luke*) and the late Spencer Tracy (*Guess Who's Coming to Dinner*). "Thank God I didn't get the Oscar," said Hoffman afterward. "After I got the nomination, I thought, 'Okay, it's enough already for this one part.' God help me if it had all happened at 18."

After two more unsuccessful nominations (for *Midnight Cowboy* in 1969, and *Lenny* in 1974), for neither of which he showed up, Hoffman told an Oscar-night TV interviewer that the awards were "obscene, dirty and grotesque, no better than a beauty contest." Bob Hope opened that night's show by joking: "If Dustin Hoffman wins, he's going to have a friend pick it up—George C. Scott." Hoffman had given his tickets to his parents, who were duly embarrassed when Frank Sinatra publicly rebuked their wayward son: "Contrary to what Dustin Hoffman thinks, it is not an obscene evening. It is not garish and it is not embarrassing."

Five years later, Hoffman showed that he was not averse to

biting the hand that fed him. "I think that awards are very silly," he declared while accepting the 1979 Golden Globe for *Kramer vs. Kramer*. "They put very talented and good people against each other, and they hurt the hell out of the ones that lose." Awards, Hoffman asserted, "make more sense when they're given for a life achievement to a man like Mr. Fonda [who was receiving the Cecil B. de Mille Golden Globe for career achievements] and particularly to a man like Mr. Lemmon, who recently gave one of the great performances of his life [in *The China Syndrome*]."

There is no doubt that Hoffman spoke for many, winners and losers alike, in deploring the principle of a gladiatorial contest between actors, who are doing very different things in their own different ways. But he has never been inclined to refuse any awards that came his way. Accepting his first Oscar that same year, again for *Kramer vs. Kramer*, he began by playing the Hollywood game. Having kissed his entire family, plus Jack Lemmon for good measure, en route to the stage, Hoffman began by examining the Oscar and jesting: "He has no genitalia and he's holding a sword." He went on: "I'd like to thank my mother and father for not practicing birth control."

Then he began to get serious: "We are laughed at for thanking, but when you work on a film you discover that there are people who are giving that artistic part of themselves that goes beyond a paycheck, and they are never up here. . . . I'm up here with mixed feelings. I've been critical of the Academy, with reason. I'm deeply grateful for the opportunity to work. I refuse to believe that I beat Jack Lemmon, that I beat Al Pacino, that I beat Peter Sellers.*

"We are part of an artistic family. There are 60,000 actors in the Screen Actors Guild and probably 100,000 in Equity. Most actors don't work, and a few of us are so lucky to have the chance. . . . Because when you're a broke actor, you can't write and you can't paint. You have to practice accents while you're driving a taxicab. And to that artistic family that strives for excellence, none of you has ever lost, and I am proud to share this award with you."

Hoffman had become a tearful convert. Amid thunderous applause, Johnny Carson saw him offstage with: "I think we can all

* Tactlessly, he omitted to mention the fifth nominee, Roy Scheider.

agree that was beautifully said." The following year Hoffman presented the Best Actress Oscar, the traditional role of the previous year's Best Actor, with good grace; in 1986 he gushed extempore for two minutes and forty seconds, quoting tennis star Jimmy Connors on "giving a hundred fifteen percent," before presenting Best Picture to *Platoon*—one of only a handful of actors to offer wholesale endorsement to the system by accepting the honor of presenting the supreme award.

By his second Best Actor award, for *Rain Man* in 1988, Hoffman was a true veteran of Academy schmaltz. This time around the old opponent of acting contests had even found a cute way of acknowledging his fellow nominees: "I'm very honored, and I thank the Academy for your support. And I also thank Tom Hanks and Max von Sydow and James Olmos and my good friend Gene Hackman for their wonderful work, even if they didn't vote for me. . . . I didn't vote for you guys, either!"

Jane Fonda runs Hoffman a close second as a perennially confused critic/advocate of the system, schmaltz and all. Fonda has used the awards show as a platform for her already renowned political views, though never as outspokenly as her friend and *Julia* costar, Vanessa Redgrave. But only three sometime winners—George C. Scott, Marlon Brando and Woody Allen—have dared scoff openly at the system. Of these, Allen is really the only moviemaker in Oscar history to show genuine and consistent indifference to the entire process. Reexamination of the cases of Scott and Brando, the only two actors of the modern era to have turned down their Oscars, reveal inconsistency and muddled motives.

George C. Scott's celebrated attempt to reject his 1970 Oscar for *Patton* was not entirely the simple matter of principle it appeared. As he labeled the Oscar process "offensive, barbarous and innately corrupt," the roots of Scott's complaint could in fact be traced back to his first nomination in 1959, as Best Supporting Actor for the fine rage of his prosecuting attorney in Otto Preminger's *Anatomy of a Murder*. On that occasion, Scott had made no attempt to withdraw from what he later—after losing—called a "meat race." By general consent, he had been an unlucky loser to the British actor Hugh Griffith, a dubious beneficiary of the absurd *Ben-Hur* sweep.

According to Scott's friends at the time, he had desperately wanted the Oscar. Years later, he told his then wife, the actress Trish Van Devere, that he had learned an important lesson that night. "He said he wanted it so badly that he became almost completely wrapped up in it. When he didn't win, he took a hard look, and came to believe it wasn't healthy to want something so much." Scott vowed "never again to have anything to do with the Oscar."

When nominated again in the supporting category two years later, for *The Hustler*, Scott asked the Academy to withdraw his name—only to be refused by its president, Wendell Corey. "You were nominated by a vote of your fellow actors," Corey wrote him, "and the Academy cannot remove your name from the list of nominated performances. The Academy nominates and votes awards for performances and achievements as they appear on the screen. Therefore, any one person responsible for such a performance or achievement cannot decline the nomination after it is voted."

In his reply to the Academy, Scott argued that campaigning by actors and their agents had degraded the whole process. "It encourages the public to think that the award is more important to the actor than the work for which he was nominated," Scott told *The New York Times*, which quoted "a close friend" as saying that he disliked the whole Hollywood, back-patting atmosphere: "For the Oscar, you have to throw a few cocktail parties yourself and get people to screenings so they can take a look at you and that sort of thing." The Oscar facade was "against Scott's personal philosophy of life"; the Oscars were "just a way for the motion picture companies to make more money on the pictures, and have little other value."

Curiously, after his ringing defense of the system, Corey told Scott that he *could* refuse the award, if he were to win it. But the issue didn't arise. Scott was again an unlucky loser—to another freak "sweep" winner, George Chakiris in *West Side Story*.

Scott smoldered for another nine years: "Life isn't a race. It is a war of survival, and there are many who get crippled and injured on the way. And because it is not a race, I don't consider myself in competition with my fellow actors for awards or recognition." Then, in 1970, he received his first nomination as Best Actor, for the title role in *Patton*, and immediately tried to reject it. In a cable to the Academy from Spain, where he was filming, he said he would not be attending the awards ceremony, "nor will any legitimate representative of mine attend."

This time around Scott was at pains to give more courteous expression to his disdain. "Peculiar as it may seem, I mean no disrespect to the Academy," he said after being formally notified of his nomination. "I simply do not wish to be involved." The previous month, however, he had somewhat compromised his position, and further embarrassed the Academy, by accepting the New York Film Critics' Best Actor award for the same role. Accepting it on his behalf, another Mrs. Scott, the actress Colleen Dewhurst, told them: "George thinks this is the only film award worth having."

To a reporter who visited him in Spain, Scott explained: "I have no objection to awards as such. I would be perfectly willing to attend some function with the other actors where we would all accept awards and then take off for a drink." He had accepted the New York critics' award because he respected "the manner in which it is given." He did *not* respect "the hoopla, the publicity, the advertising" attached to the Oscar, which had "actors sitting in line like children waiting for the contents of the envelope to be announced." The "contrivance" of the whole affair disgusted him.

"Maybe he's scared he won't win, and he's trying to cop a plea now," 1960's Best Actor, Burt Lancaster, told *Newsweek*. But according to the Hollywood columnist Hank Grant, Scott would not accept the Oscar if he won it "because he doesn't like the way the Awards are handled. . . . This will make Scott a big hero with provincial pals in the East whose prime pastime is putting down Hollywood." More damagingly, Grant pointed out that Scott had waited until after the nominating ballot had closed to make his protest.

"Frankly, I resent being put on show like a buffoon," said Scott himself on national television, two days before the Awards ceremony. To win an Oscar required "a certain amount of wheeling and dealing, public relations, advertising, solicitation, phone calls, telegrams, threats, bribes." The ceremonies were "a two-hour meat parade, a public display . . . with contrived suspense . . . for economic reasons."

The suspense was all the greater in the Dorothy Chandler Pavilion on April 15, 1971, because rumor had it that Scott had been voted the winner. He was not, of course, present when the previous year's Best Supporting Actress, Goldie Hawn, came to the podium to open the envelope. Sensing a little diplomacy might be required of her, Hawn paused first to say that the term Best Actor was a "misnomer" and that "it is a specific achievement that is honored—a pertinent distinction." On opening the envelope her political savvy crumbled as she cried, "Oh, my God! The winner is George C. Scott!"

The eruption of approval around the hall signified the local interpretation of Scott's win: Hollywood loved a maverick, sure, but this was a sign that the Oscars were at last free of the studio manipulation that had dogged them for years, and from the arbitrary favoritism that often rendered the results laughable. In the year that a film like *Airport* could win ten nominations, however, this seemed a hasty conclusion to reach; and there were still suggestions that Scott's fulsome tirades against the Oscar were merely an alternative style of campaigning. Had he himself indulged in a personalized brand of the very "wheeling and dealing" he had denounced on TV two days before? Even before the Oscar telecast began, ABC's audience "warm-up" man had placed a sting in the tail of his traditional plea for brief acceptance speeches: "Keep it short. Make your speeches shorter than George C. Scott's rejection."

"I accept this award cheerfully, and under no duress," said *Patton*'s producer, Frank McCarthy, as he picked up Scott's Oscar and praised the Academy's choice. But the dissenting voices were soon making themselves heard. Ross Hunter, producer of *Airport*, one of *Patton*'s rivals for Best Picture, reneged on his threat to resign from the Academy if Scott won, but still protested that he was "ridiculing our Academy." Said a cooler David Niven: "It could be he just can't bear to hear someone else's name called out." And the first gag from the next presenter, Walter Matthau, openly acknowledged West Coast suspicion of Scott's tactics: "Next year I'm going to try the George C. Scott routine. . . . Did Goldie really say 'pertinent'?"

Next morning, as Scott told reporters he had watched a TV hockey game and gone to bed, Grant restated the Hollywood point of view, calling his conduct "public relations at its best, because his defiance was printed and aired all over the world, making him the most highly publicized nominee on the roster." Colleen Dewhurst stuck by her husband, despite her own more orthodox views: "George had to do what he did about the Oscar because that's the way he feels. Me? I want to win an award." Interviewed for the cover of *Time* magazine, Scott remained unrepentant: "I don't give a damn about [the Oscar]. I'm making too much money, anyway." His main objection, it emerged, was to the Awards ceremony itself, with its "phony suspense and the crying actor clutching the statue to his bosom and all of that crap."

Stung by the accusations of opportunism, however, Scott professed himself surprised at the scale of the furor he had created. If he were ever nominated in the future, he announced, he would accept. It was too much trouble not to. The sheer gracelessness of Scott's confused position was underlined the following year by Helen Hayes, who had won Best Supporting Actress in the year of *Patton*, and who began the 1972 ceremony with the words: "As George C. Scott didn't get around to saying last year, thank you."

Scott's real point was better made by his track record. Since those two contentious Supporting nominations, he had turned in a string of Oscar-level performances in such films as *Dr. Strangelove*, *The Flim-Flam Man* and *Petulia* without so much as a nod from the Academy. In 1964, for instance, the year of *Dr. Strangelove*, *Becket* and *Zorba the Greek*, all but one of the acting and directing Oscars went to *My Fair Lady*, *Mary Poppins* and *Topkapi*. What kind of a merit was being recognized *there*?

Only a month after refusing his Oscar, Scott rubbed salt in the Academy's wounds by *accepting* an Emmy award for his work in a television production of Arthur Miller's *The Price*—"because," he explained, "it's given by a blue ribbon jury of [my] peers and not as a general vote, like the Oscar." The following year, nevertheless, Scott's voting peers in the Academy showed that there were no hard feelings by again nominating him for Best Actor, for *The Hospital*. This time, sensibly, he stuck by his vow and said nothing, even when he lost out to Gene Hackman, and *The French Connection* won Best Picture and Best Director over *The Last Picture Show, A Clockwork Orange, Sunday, Bloody Sunday, Fiddler on the Roof* and *Nicholas and Alexandra*.

By the 1982 Awards, Scott was convert enough to call the Academy at the last minute to see if he could "scrounge" two tickets for the show; he happened to be in town with his wife, hustling for his new project *The Last Days of Patton*. En route to two hastily arranged seats at the back of the orchestra stalls, Scott bypassed the ritual public colloquy with Army Archerd, who called after him over the public address system: "Your Oscar is waiting for you at the Academy, Wilshire and Lapeer . . ."

The early 1970s proved heavy sledding for the Oscars. It was only two years after Scott's rejection, in 1972, that his open contempt for the Awards was duplicated by Marlon Brando, who sent what appeared to be an Apache maiden onstage to refuse his Best Actor award for *The Godfather*. Brushing aside the statuette proffered by a surprised Roger Moore, Sacheen Littlefeather launched into a speech on Brando's behalf protesting "the treatment of the American Indians by the film industry." After some boos, she gracefully offered apologies for her intrusion upon the proceedings and quit the stage to pass on Brando's lengthy statement to the press.

"What Marlon Brando did this year could signal the death of the Oscar as we know him," wailed Rona Barrett in a paid advertisement in the Hollywood trade papers. But she it was who subsequently discovered that Sacheen Littlefeather was in fact a bit-part actress named Maria Cruz, who had been elected Miss American Vampire of 1970—by which time Brando's stunt had already backfired on him in other ways.

As the *Hollywood Reporter* summed up, "The tragedy of Mr. Brando's act is that while he sought to serve the welfare of the American Indians, nothing was gained but ill will." His fellow nominee Michael Caine seemed to speak for the majority: "He should have been there himself. Doesn't he owe that town *anything*? He should treat the Oscar with the respect it deserves. Christ, if I had one, I know I would."

Backstage, as Littlefeather was confessing her terror to reporters ("I thought if I came out alive, I'd be lucky"), Charlton Heston predictably called Brando's gesture "childish." But Brando's producer, Albert S. Ruddy, stood staunchly by the man who had just helped him win Best Picture. "Where is the time and place for that kind of demonstration? It's whenever you have a moment that you would have the biggest audience. . . . It's something I may not have said myself, but I certainly back him in his right to say it."

Though he lost out to Joel Grey in *Cabaret*, Best Supporting Actor nominee Robert Duvall said of his *Godfather* costar's disdain for the Oscars: "I feel the people who give prizes in Hollywood are no more or less qualified than the New York Film Critics. I took a prize from them, so why not take one from Hollywood? It's all a lot of crap, but as long as it's there."

Brando himself remained silent. He had not refused his first Oscar eighteen years before, for *On the Waterfront*—nor the three consecutive nominations leading up to it, though already an outspoken critic of Hollywood and all its works. And the following year Hollywood, as with Scott, seemed determined to turn the other cheek by renominating him for *Last Tango in Paris*. As recently as 1989, the love-hate square dance continued with Brando's conspicuous absence from the Awards, after his eighth nomination (for *A Dry White Season*) over thirty-eight years.

In a rare television interview at the time, shortly before his public profile was reluctantly raised by his son's conviction for manslaughter, he told CBS-TV's Connie Chung: "That's a part of the sickness in America, that you have to think in terms of who wins, who loses, who's good, who's bad, who's best, who's worst. . . . I don't *like* to think that way. Everybody has their own value in different ways, and I don't like to think who is the best at this. I mean, what's the *point* of it?"

Even in the midst of a foulmouthed denunciation of the industry to which he owed so much, Brando nevertheless felt obliged to call the Oscars to his support: "What do I care? I've made all the money I need to make. I won a couple of Academy Awards if I ever cared about that. I've been nominated I don't know how many times and I'm in a position of respect and standing in my craft as an actor in this country. So what the hell, I don't need to gild the lily."

During the Great Brando Debate of 1972, it came as no surprise to hear his protest win support from Jane Fonda: "I thought what he did was wonderful." The previous year's Best Actress for *Klute*, Fonda had been openly disappointed by her failure to win at her first nomination, in 1969, for *They Shoot Horses, Don't They?* In this, the rebellious period of her several public lives, Fonda was wont to make such public pronouncements as: "I don't care about the Oscars. I make movies to support the causes I believe in, not for any honors."

But her radical left-wing politics had not prevented her meekly accepting the New York Film Critics award for *They Shoot Horses*: "It's the biggest accolade I've ever been given. One tries to be blasé about things, but now that it's happened, it's very nice." On being nominated for an Oscar, before losing turned her sour, she had managed to enthuse about the Academy Awards: "If you win an Oscar, what happens to your career is not to be believed. Your price goes up, you get offered all kinds of things," she gushed to Rex Reed. Then she blew it by rolling a joint and asking him, "You don't mind if I turn on, do you?" Reed noted that Jane, upon hearing her father return home, "leaped up and waved her arms to blow the pot smoke out of the room." Amid the ensuing furor, the veteran columnist Sidney Skolsky muttered: "I don't think the Academy will let her turn on."

Fonda's first appearance as an Oscar nominee had seen her climb out of her limousine, draped in mink over a Chanel gown, and greet the crowds with a clenched-fist Black Panthers salute. Next day, at a losers' party thrown by Elizabeth Taylor and Richard Burton, she persuaded Burton to sign a "sizable" check to the Panthers. Two years later, however, her acceptance speech on being named Best Actress for *Klute* could not have been more demure. Despite some boos when Walter Matthau called her name, she began by thanking "all of you who applauded." There followed a tense pause, when many thought she might launch into some heavy political statement. But she had thought better of it. "There's a lot I could say tonight, but this isn't the time or place. So I'll just say 'Thank you.' " Hollywood's relief was so intense that although Fonda skipped the Governors Ball, opting for a Japanese meal with Donald Sutherland, the *Hollywood Reporter* felt able to dub her "the little darling of the crowd."

Fonda had considered refusing the Academy Award, like Scott the year before and Brando the year after, as a protest against the war. But a friend changed her mind: "You're a frigging elite individual, Jane. It's really typical of the bourgeois middle-class family girl to want to refuse the Oscar." By accepting, she would have a unique chance to show "the masses" that she wasn't "some kind of freak or monster." Still under pressure from her comrades to turn the occasion to political advantage, Fonda sought the advice of her revered father, Henry, who "implored" her not to abuse the Academy's generosity; it was sheer bad manners, which would do her cause no good.

Fonda Sr. was, of course, right; by holding her peace, Jane won converts among the Hollywood hostile. But one wonders if she would have taken his advice had she known that her own father had not voted for her.

"I've been at too many private parties on Oscar night," he explained. "When the winner is announced, three quarters of the people in the room slap their foreheads and moan, 'Oh, *no*!' Well, I wouldn't want that to happen to me. I wouldn't want to walk up there thinking people all over Hollywood are saying, 'Henry Fonda? Oh, *no*!'

"Besides, I don't believe in that kind of artistic competition. Take the best performances of Laurence Olivier, Richard Burton, Jack Lemmon, Dustin Hoffman and Woody Allen, and you tell me how anyone can possibly pick the best one. It's an absolute impossibility." In later life, however, he made a distinction for Lifetime Achievement Awards: "I've always opposed competitions where one actor's performance is pitted against another's. When it comes to a body of work, that's different."

By 1976 Jane Fonda had mellowed enough to agree to cohost the Awards show; and by the following year, and her next nomination (for *Julia*), she found herself upstaged by the even more radical politics of her costar and conominee Vanessa Redgrave. Though she had enjoyed box-office success that year in a mindless satire called *Fun with Dick and Jane*, Fonda had meanwhile campaigned for the part of Lillian Hellman in *Julia*, and for her friend Redgrave to be cast in the title role of the story of a political friendship of Hellman's youth. It was, as producer Richard Roth put it, "perfect symmetry. The two most famous left-wing women of the seventies playing two left-wing women of the thirties. I liked it. Of course, the fact that Jane and Vanessa were both terrific actresses didn't hurt, either. Not to mention that they both agreed to work cheap."

Fonda had prepared for the role by visiting Lillian Hellman at her home on Martha's Vineyard—leading *Julia*'s anxious director, Fred Zinnemann, to ban politics from the set. When shooting was complete, he sighed: "If Lillian Hellman had been along with Vanessa and Jane, I don't think I could have handled it." In fact the two

George C. Scott called the Oscars "a meat parade, a public display with contrived suspense for economic reasons" and refused to accept the 1970 Oscar as Best Actor in the title role of Patton.

Sucheen Littlefeather prepares to protest the movies' treatment of the American Indian after rejecting, on Marlon Brando's behalf, the 1972 Best Actor award offered by Roger Moore and Liv Ullman.

actresses had managed to work so well together only by agreeing not to discuss politics; for Fonda, now a self-declared "progressive Democrat," there was the danger that Redgrave's hard-line Trotskyite views would make her seem almost right wing. She went so far as to distance herself from her costar by denying to *Newsweek* that she had named her own daughter (by Roger Vadim) Vanessa after her "political heroine."

By Awards night, Redgrave had managed to alienate most of the movie community by expressing strong anti-Israeli, pro-PLO sentiments in *The Palestinians*, an anti-Zionist TV documentary. The Jewish Defense League had picketed theaters showing *Julia*, demanding a statement from Twentieth Century Fox dissociating the studio from Redgrave's political views and undertaking never to hire her again. When this proved unforthcoming, the JDL unleashed a plague of white mice in theaters showing the film, and followed up with bomb threats. The studio resisted manfully: "While Fox as a company and the individuals who work there do not agree with Redgrave's political philosophy," said its statement, "we totally reject and we will not be blackmailed into supporting any policy of refusing to employ any person because of their political beliefs."

Stars arriving for this, the fiftieth-anniversary Awards show, had to fight their way through pickets from the League and pro-Redgrave supporters of Palestine, both studiously avoided by the television cameras. Redgrave herself arrived in an ambulance and was smuggled in a side entrance. There was high nervous anticipation in the air, as she was expected to win; a three-time Best Actress loser, for *Morgan, Isadora* and *Mary, Queen of Scots*, Redgrave's fine performance in *Julia* looked even better when set against her unusually weak opposition for Supporting Actress: Leslie Brown in *The Turning Point*, Quinn Cummings in *The Goodbye Girl*, Melinda Dillon in *Close Encounters of the Third Kind* and Tuesday Weld in *Looking for Mr. Goodbar*.

When Redgrave did indeed win, early in the proceedings, and went onstage to collect her Oscar from the distinctly apolitical figure of John Travolta, the Academy heaved a communal sigh when she began—as hoped—by expressing the depth of her commitment to *Julia*. "I think that Jane Fonda and I have done the best work of our lives," she said, "and I think this was in part due to our director,

Fred Zinnemann. And I also think it's in part because we believed in what we were expressing: two out of the millions who gave their lives and were prepared to sacrifice everything in the fight against fascist and racist Nazi Germany. . . ."

So far, so good. But Redgrave provoked horrified gasps around the Dorothy Chandler Pavilion when she continued: "And I salute you and I pay tribute to you and I think you should be very proud that in the last few weeks you have stood firm and you have refused to be intimidated by the threats of a small bunch of Zionist hoodlums"—now came some boos amid the gasps—"whose behavior is an insult to the stature of Jews all over the world and to their great and heroic record of struggle against fascism and oppression.

"And I salute that record, and I salute all of you for having stood firm and dealt a final blow against that period when Nixon and McCarthy launched a worldwide witch-hunt against those who tried to express in their lives and their work the truth that they believed. I salute you and I thank you and I pledge to you that I will continue to fight against anti-Semitism and fascism." Now dissent was drowned out by rousing applause as Redgrave embraced Travolta and walked offstage; outside, still unrecorded by the cameras, protesters were burning an effigy labeled VANESSA IS A MURDERER.

Though somewhat dented, the celebratory atmosphere of the fiftieth Oscar show was gradually restored until the screenwriter Paddy Chayefsky came onstage to present the writing awards. "If I expect to live with myself tomorrow morning," he began, "I would like—personal opinion, of course—to say that I'm sick and tired of people exploiting the occasion of the Academy Awards for the propagation of their own personal propaganda." To clamorous support he continued: "I would like to suggest to Miss Redgrave that her winning an Academy Award is not a pivotal moment in history, does not require a proclamation, and a simple 'Thank you' would have sufficed."

Chayefsky later revealed that he had been persuaded in the men's room, by a posse of producers led by Columbia's Dan Melnick, that someone had to reply to Redgrave. After the show he was "proud" of the fact that "she tried to speak to me and I cut her dead." When a reporter gave her a chance to answer Chayefsky, Redgrave replied that hers had not been a political speech. But it remained the topic of the evening, with the comedian Alan King speaking for the majority when he declared: "I am that Zionist hoodlum she was talking about. It's just a pity I wasn't on the platform tonight. I would have gone for the jugular."

At the Governors Ball, Academy president Howard Koch felt sorry for Redgrave: "She was sitting all alone with just her two bodyguards. It was her big night, and no one else would sit with her." But she did manage to get up and wander over to a few tables, exchanging greetings, causing Chayefsky to fume on: "This is disgusting. Vanessa thinks she can get away with anything. How can she have the nerve to come here and act like this?"

Redgrave's political activities have continued to conflict with her work ever since. The following year, when she was cast as an Auschwitz survivor in Arthur Miller's television adaptation of Fania Fenelon's memoirs, *Playing for Time*, one leading rabbi summarized the pained objections from the Jewish community: "It's like hiring J. Edgar Hoover to play Dr. Martin Luther King." Again the producers were obliged to dissociate themselves from her views, but to defend their right to hire performers regardless of their politics. In 1982 Redgrave successfully sued the Boston Symphony Orchestra after it had canceled performances of Stravinsky's *Oedipus Rex*, following protests that she was to participate. And as recently as February 1991, she felt obliged to buy a half page in *The New York Times* to clarify her position on Saddam Hussein and the Gulf War.

Redgrave's monopoly of the headlines in 1978 obscured the fact that those fiftieth Awards also marked the first time that the Academy was snubbed by Woody Allen. Ignoring the five nominations garnered by *Annie Hall*—including the fact that he himself was the first person to be nominated for Best Actor, Director and Screenplay since Orson Welles's *Citizen Kane* nearly forty years before—Woody stayed in New York, as usual, and played his clarinet at Michael's Pub before going to bed without even wondering whether his girlfriend Diane Keaton had won Best Actress.

On waking up the next day to find that she had, and that his brainchild had become the first comedy in twenty-five years to win Best Picture, Allen refused all comment. Only a year later, when nominated again for *Interiors*, did he break his silence. "I know it sounds horrible, but winning that Oscar for *Annie Hall* didn't mean anything to me."

Financially, Allen omitted to mention, it certainly did; on its post-Oscar rerelease, trumpeted as the year's Best Picture, *Annie Hall* grossed twice as much as it had the first time around. But Woody had loftier matters on his mind: "I have no regard for that kind of ceremony. I just don't think they know what they're doing. When you see who wins those things—or doesn't win them—you can see how meaningless this Oscar thing is." Allen has since won twelve nominations as writer, director and actor, but only one more Oscar, for the screenplay of *Hannah and her Sisters.*

"There are two things that bother me about the Academy Awards," Allen has said. "They're political and bought and negotiated for—although many worthy people have deservedly won—and the whole concept of awards is silly. I cannot abide by the judgment of other people, because if you accept it when they say you deserve an award, then you have to accept it when they say you don't. Also, it's hard not to get a slightly skewed feeling about the Academy Awards because apart from the ads and the campaigning and the studio loyalties, it's a popularity contest, really, because if the picture is not seen well or didn't do very well, its chances are hurt." After being nominated for *Crimes and Misdemeanors* in 1989, Allen conceded that he took "some pleasure," but added: "You have to be sure to keep it very much in perspective. You think it's nice at the time because it means more money for your film, but as soon as you let yourself start thinking that way, something happens to the quality of the work."

Jane Fonda, meanwhile, took seven more years to win her second Oscar, for the Vietnam War movie *Coming Home.* This time around her method of politicking was to campaign openly for the award, telling any interviewer who would listen: "This movie means more to me than any movie I've done so far." She also broke new ground by campaigning *against* that year's rival Vietnam movie, Michael Cimino's *The Deer Hunter*—even though, as she freely admitted, she hadn't seen it. Fonda made much of an alarmed phone call from her friend (and fellow left-wing activist) Julie Christie, who had led a walkout from *Deer Hunter* at the Berlin Film Festival.

Neither mentioned that Christie and her lover Warren Beatty were also in line for Oscars that year with *Heaven Can Wait*.

Like Hal Ashby's *Coming Home*, *The Deer Hunter* was, of course, antiwar; but it found itself accused of racism, exulting in its own violence, even representing the Pentagon's retrospective point of view. The film was attacked for portraying the Americans as innocent victims of an amoral rabble of an enemy, and failing to discuss the real issues behind the war. During the three weeks before the Oscar show, articles in *Harper's*, the *Los Angeles Times*, *Seven Days* and *L.A. Weekly* variously denounced the film as "a lie," "a criminal violation of the truth," and a "horrific history" in which all the non-Americans were "sweaty, crazy, vicious and debauched." Even *Izvestia*, the Soviet government newspaper, weighed in with the charge that it portrayed a war in which "the aggressors and the victims changed places."

Vietnam had proved a very different experience for Hollywood from World War II, when patriotic pro-Allies movies had gone into production while the war was still very much under way. Only one major pro–Vietnam War film was ever made, inevitably by John Wayne: *The Green Berets*, which appeared in 1968, the year of Nixon's election. It had taken ten more years for Hollywood to risk producing antiwar films, and the studios' anxieties about public response were rewarded with two box-office and critical hits. Universal's *The Deer Hunter* won five Oscars out of nine nominations, while United Artists scored three awards out of a possible eight for *Coming Home*, which dealt with the dilemma of Vietnam veterans returning to a hostile America, indifferent to their sacrifices.

"I may have lost my body, but I have gained my mind," the crippled Vietnam vet-turned-antiwar campaigner, Ron Kovic, had told Jane Fonda at an early seventies rally. The remark inspired her to plan *Coming Home*, in which she chose the politically approved Jon Voight to play her paraplegic lover. Both went nude for a graphic and necessarily inventive sex scene of which Kovic commented, according to Fonda, that it had "improved his sex life immeasurably." The wheelchair-bound Voight in *Coming Home* was thus a direct celluloid ancestor of the Ron Kovic who was to win Tom Cruise his first Oscar nomination—still more than a decade away—in Oliver Stone's *Born on the Fourth of July*. By some absurd irony, the star chosen by the Academy to present Best Picture for 1978, and thus pronounce the jury's final verdict between *Deer Hunter* and *Coming Home*, was one of the few who approved of neither: a dying John Wayne.

Come Oscar night, there were huge demonstrations outside the Dorothy Chandler Pavilion—some pro–*Coming Home*, most anti–*Deer Hunter*. Police arrested thirteen members of the Vietnam Veterans Against the War, who were protesting against *The Deer Hunter*'s "misinterpretation of reality." Another dissenting group, the Hell Won't Go Away Committee, condemned the film as "a racist attack on the Vietnamese people," denouncing its portrayal of the Vietnamese as a "viciously" violent people. Even "progressive" moviegoers, the group argued, seemed blinded by the power of the film's emotional impact: "They felt it was a great film despite its racism, despite its misinterpretation of history." Cimino professed himself "bewildered" by the animosity toward his picture, which he had intended to be "an antiwar statement."

Deer Hunter beat *Coming Home* for Best Picture, Best Director (Cimino over Ashby) and Best Supporting Actor (Christopher Walken over Bruce Dern), but Jon Voight and Jane Fonda collected the two main acting awards. "I accept this," said Voight, "for every guy in a wheelchair."

Fonda's curious method of making a point this time around was to start her acceptance speech in sign language. "While we were making the movie," she explained, "we all became more aware of the problems of the handicapped. Over fourteen million people are deaf. They are the invisible handicapped and can't share this evening, so this is my way of acknowledging them." She then thanked her two children, in the audience, for "being understanding and forgiving me my absences," and launched into the usual litany of gratitude to others associated with the film, ending with her then husband, the California politician Tom Hayden: "He helped me believe that besides being entertaining, movies can inspire and teach and even be healing." Afterward, referring to the demonstrators outside the theater as "my friends," she again dismissed *The Deer Hunter*: "I still haven't seen it, but ours is the best picture."

Fonda has since won three more nominations, for *The China Syndrome* (1979), *On Golden Pond* (1981) and *The Morning After*

(1986)—none of them successful. Her career tally thus stands at two wins for seven nominations. She was especially disappointed in 1989 that her eight-year struggle to produce and star in a film version of Carlos Fuentes's *Old Gringo* failed to win even a single nomination. By then Fonda had finally earned her Oscar spurs, dispelling the negative effects of her "Hanoi Jane" years by indulging in the appropriate Hollywood schmaltz on the night her dying father finally won his first Best Actor award, for *On Golden Pond.* "Oh, Dad," she trilled directly into the camera, on accepting it for him, "I'm so happy and proud for you. . . ." There followed ritualistic thanks to those involved in the film, for which she too had won a Supporting nomination, before she turned back to the camera to conclude: "Dad, me and the grandkids will be right over."

Hanoi Jane had finally become a Hollywood superbrat. Where once she had kept her Oscar for *Klute* on a dusty shelf in the cramped, conspicuously ascetic apartment she shared with Hayden, it now takes pride of place with her second one and sundry other awards—not in any of the sumptuous homes she shares with her latest husband, the television tycoon Ted Turner, but in her Los Angeles office. Hanoi Jane, indeed, would scarcely recognize the Jane Fonda of her mid-fifties—a multimillionaire businesswoman in her own right, thanks as much to her fitness books and videos as to her film production company, who not only admits to surgery for breast enlargement but wears Oscar-night gowns designed to show off the results.

Subsequent history, it should be said, has largely upheld Fonda's objections to *The Deer Hunter.* So effective was the Oscar campaign on the film's behalf by Allan Carr (detailed in Chapter 9), later to become producer of the Oscar show itself, that even on Awards night some of those associated with his "positioning" of the picture had begun to have doubts. There was "a rustle of embarrassment," said one journalist alert to industry nuances, when the award of Best Picture was announced: "Early on, we all thought the film was powerful but flawed. Now I think there have been a lot of second thoughts that emphasized the *flawed.* When the picture's name was read, it was as if you had proposed to a girl and were horrified that she had accepted. I had the peculiar feeling that, if the ballots had gone out one week later, *The Deer Hunter* wouldn't have won."

The most controversial—and memorable—scene in *The Deer Hunter* was a wholly invented one, in which the Vietcong force Robert De Niro and his companions to play Russian roulette. The central metaphor of the movie, as the war correspondent Peter Arnett put it in the *Los Angeles Times*, was "simply a bloody lie." Cimino defended the moment as a dramatic device which "symbolized nothing" but merely "moved the story along." Accused of "artistic irresponsibility" in distorting historical truth, he argued that *The Deer Hunter* was "a surrealistic, not realistic" film. He was not, he said, trying to rewrite history or recreate reality: "We're not doing newsreels. We're moviemakers."

The rewriting of history, especially in such sensitive areas of America's recent past, has since become a political undercurrent of the Oscars. The year of *The Deer Hunter* was also the year that a Best Screenplay Oscar was won by Oliver Stone for his adaptation of Billy Hayes's memoir, *Midnight Express.* Asked why the events in the film did not correspond with those in the book, Stone echoed Cimino: "We weren't making a documentary." The book, he continued, "didn't have the dramatic cohesion the film needed. For instance, the lunatic asylum was originally in the early part of the story. I moved it to the end because I felt things should keep getting worse, and that a lunatic asylum was the bottom line."

A more radical rewriting of Ron Kovic's memoirs, in which Stone invented the scene in which Tom Cruise visits the parents of a fellow G.I. he thinks he has killed, was to create a similar backlash against *Born on the Fourth of July*—and to cost Stone, as director and cowriter, a possible clean sweep of the 1989 Oscars.

Consistently erratic results are one reason the Oscars are perennially sneered at by critics and movie buffs who ought to know better. Accept the principle of singling out films for awards, and it is necessary to examine the methodology of those awards before denouncing them. In the case of the Oscars, it is the degree of sheer hype each year, combined with the spectacular awfulness of the Awards show itself, which blinds even the cognoscenti to the simple fact that these are internal awards just like any other industry's.

Most trades and professions, constantly reexamining their own navels, buoy their annual conferences with awards and citations of all shapes and sizes. The movie industry is no different—only smarter at self-publicity. Given the constitution of the electorate, the Oscars amount to votes of self-confidence distributed among themselves by workers anxious to keep their industry—and thus their jobs—in prime shape.

Oscars are voted not just by those actors, actresses and directors famous for having won them, but by the unknown carpenters, electricians and best boys, even extras, who earn a more mundane living from the movies. As John Gregory Dunne, an occasional Hollywood scriptwriter, has written:

> The Academy is essentially a trade union, a mixture of below-the-line sound men, special-effects men and PR people, film editors and set dressers, as well as above-the-line actors and directors, producers and writers. The awards are the awards of any union in any company town, a vote for jobs—and hits provide jobs, flops don't. If the New York film critics, most of whom work for union-organized publications, opened their membership to several thousand typesetters from the Typographical Union and projectionists from IATSE and secretaries from the Newspaper Guild, I suspect that the Academy's choices would seem a lot less moribund.

Hollywood's annual general meeting, televised to a billion fans in around one hundred countries, tends to get off to a woefully leaden start. Before any of those envelopes can be opened, there is the grim ordeal of sitting through a dreary sermon from whichever faceless bureaucrat happens to be the current president of the Academy of Motion Picture Arts and Sciences.

Not in 1990. "Thank God we've got an actor as president," one Hollywood producer was heard to whisper, and for once he wasn't talking about Ronald Reagan. As the lights went down, a dynamic figure strode purposefully forward and fired off an Oscar-worthy invocation, exhorting his audience to surrender to the spirit of the occasion as if they were Henry V's troops at Agincourt. Karl Malden, the first actor-president of the Academy since Gregory Peck twenty years before, was subsequently reelected to a second and third year in office. The veteran supporting star of such classic films as *On the Waterfront, Birdman of Alcatraz* and *The Cincinnati Kid*, himself an

Oscar winner in 1951 for *A Streetcar Named Desire*, Malden declared himself "a man with a mission."

Bouncing around the Academy's Beverly Hills headquarters with a vigor belying his 75 years, Malden was determined to make his mark as president of AMPAS. Where Peck is still remembered for his efforts to curb the less dignified aspects of Oscar campaigns, Malden had loftier, more educational ideals in mind. But his first presidential priority was to take the Awards show upmarket.

The previous year's debacle had brought hoots of derision even from Hollywood loyalists. Academy members still cringe at the memory of the opening ballad from Rob Lowe, the "bratpack" graduate, in a dance sequence with Snow White dire enough to bring a lawsuit from the Disney studios.

Malden hired his old friend Gil Cates, 55-year-old dean of the UCLA School of Theater, Film and Television, and a former head of the Directors Guild, to give the show some class. It was an unenviable assignment, in which Cates was generally thought to have succeeded. Dispensing with the old production numbers that embarrassed millions and exasperated the TV schedulers, he supervised a leaner, swifter-paced show, brought in a more sophisticated presenter, Billy Crystal—and, in 1990, satellite hookups around all five continents, Hollywood's gesture to a remarkable political year. Jack Lemmon's musings from Moscow were drowned in sonic feedback, and Crystal's mafioso jokes offended the Italian community, but otherwise the new format worked. The show was applauded on all sides as a refreshingly stylish display of what passes in Hollywood for restraint, and Cates was rehired to orchestrate the 1991 Awards.

With this first hurdle safely behind him, Malden declared it his next priority to show the world that the Academy does more than merely dish out its most famous awards. The Oscar telecast may be its main source of income, but AMPAS also functions year-round as a world center of film studies, training and education. Each summer, for instance, Malden presides at the presentation of the Academy's annual student film awards, contested by some three hundred aspirant filmmakers from all over the States. Then there is the task of sifting through some three thousand entries for the five $20,000 Nicholl Screenwriting Fellowships awarded each year.

The Academy also sponsors Visiting Artist programs at college campuses; mounts tributes, retrospectives and exhibitions; awards numerous other scholarships and grants in support of "film-related projects"; and publishes sundry works of reference, notably the *Academy Players Directory* and the *Annual Index of Motion Pictures*.

In addition to the Samuel Goldwyn Theater, its "state-of-the-art" private screening room for Academy members, AMPAS houses the world's largest archive of films, research material and other movie documents, freely available to researchers, scholars and writers. In 1990 some 14,000 people made use of the Margaret Herrick Library, named after the Academy's first executive director, which also dealt with 30,000 telephone reference questions.

Founded in 1931, and long rated the world's finest movie archive, the vast collection of screenplays, stills, production files and other movie memorabilia—some 100,000 files in all, over 70,000 of them biographical—has taken eleven years to catalogue. Thanks to a stream of legacies from celebrated members, the Academy boasts a unique collection of shooting scripts annotated by the directors themselves. When Steven Spielberg first visited, according to Malden, he couldn't believe that he was able to see—let alone touch—Fred Zinnemann's very own shooting script for *High Noon*, with all the director's marks in the margins. "Steven stood there and stroked it, dumbstruck."

Other famous movie names who bequeathed their personal archives to the Academy range from Cukor to Peckinpah, Huston to Hitchcock, Mary Pickford to Bette Davis. The Paramount Pictures collection alone contains scripts and pressbooks relating to 2,200 Paramount films spanning the years 1912 to 1965. Other production files cover 82,000 individual movies from the 1920s to the present day.

Under President Malden's auspices, this priceless collection was rehoused during 1990 in the old Beverly Hills Waterworks, a historic building stylishly and expensively converted for the purpose, and grandly rechristened the Center for Motion Picture Studies. Now the library, approached through the Bob Hope Lobby, is bigger and better than ever. "It is becoming a unique place of pilgrimage for students and lovers of film," says Malden. "But I'll go down in history as the man who spent all the Academy's money."

Toward the end of a long career as the supporting player par excellence, Malden was thriving in a leading role he had never sought, which was thrust upon him "by acclamation" after he had served six years representing actors on the Academy's board of governors. In the Academy's sixty-five-year history, only six actors before him have served as president: Douglas Fairbanks, Sr. (1927–29), Conrad Nagel (1932–33), Bette Davis (1941), Jean Hersholt (1945–49), Wendell R. Corey (1961–63) and Gregory Peck (1967–70).

But then the welfare of actors was the last thing on the minds of the Academy's founders back in 1926—as indeed was any suggestion that the Academy might hand out awards of merit.

Mary Pickford, the only actress among the Academy's founder-members, was the second winner of the Best Actress award, in 1928–29, for *Coquette.*

4

1926–1933

"A Pat on the Back"

It was just a small group getting together for a pat on the back.

—Janet Gaynor, first winner, Best Actress

In the summer of 1928 the newly founded Academy of Motion Picture Arts and Sciences paid an out-of-work artist named George Stanley five hundred dollars to model a statuette in clay, hand-cast it in bronze, and produce twelve 24-karat gold-plated copies for presentation as "awards of merit" at its annual dinner.

The design had originally been sketched out in the summer of 1926 by a bored committee chairman during one of the fledgling Academy's early meetings. As he listened to speeches about the need for a strong corporate image, Cedric Gibbons drew a naked knight plunging a crusader's sword into a reel of film, whose five slots he intended to represent the Academy's five original branches: producers, directors, actors, writers and technicians. Gibbons got his assistant, Fredric Hope, to design the base in detail, then handed over the statuette's manufacture to Stanley, under the supervision of Guido Nelli of the California Bronze Foundry.

It would be a few years before the statuette was christened

"Oscar," which turned out to be one of the most enduring and celebrated nicknames in the history of corporate logos. Bette Davis used to lay claim to this distinction. Upon winning her first statuette in 1935, she examined "the little gold-plated man in the palm of my hand"—"a Hollywood male and, of course, epicene"—and decided that his backside reminded her of that of her then husband, Harmon O. Nelson. "Since the O. in Harmon O. Nelson stood for Oscar, Oscar it has been ever since." But Davis's claim has been hotly disputed.

Though the Academy's extensive archives offer no conclusive evidence, insiders prefer the story that Margaret Herrick, the organization's first librarian (and subsequently its executive secretary), picked up a statuette on her first day at work in 1931 and mused that it reminded her of her uncle, Oscar Pierce. (Mr. Pierce, of Texas, was really Herrick's second cousin, but he was old enough for her to have always called him "Uncle.")

But the Hollywood columnist Sidney Skolsky also claimed that he was the first to use the word Oscar in 1933, irritated by Katharine Hepburn's Best Actress award for *Morning Glory:* "It wasn't a case of 'give our child a name.' I wasn't trying to make it legitimate. The snobbery of that particular Academy Award annoyed me. I wanted to make the gold statuette human." Searching for a name that would "erase the phony dignity," Skolsky fastened on the popular vaudeville routine in which comics would josh the orchestra leader in the pit: "Will you have a cigar, Oscar?"

The Academy archives reverentially record that Skolsky's column, supposedly the first official reference to the Academy Award as an "Oscar," was datelined Palm Springs, California, March 18, 1934. Movie folklore inevitably prefers the Bette Davis version. There is no dispute, however, about the provenance of a remark made around the same time by a sassy MGM screenwriter named Frances Marion: "The little gold-washed statuette was thought, by skeptics and art-lovers, a bit on the amateurish side. Still, I saw it as a perfect symbol of the picture business: a powerful athletic body clutching a gleaming sword with half of his head, that part which held his brains, completely sliced off."

For Guido Nelli's studio at the California Bronze Foundry, the vulgar clay statuette brought in by young George Stanley in 1928 was a costly diversion from their real artistic work. So the following year production passed to the Southern California Trophy Company, where it remained for half the history of the Academy Awards—from 1929, their second year, until 1960. SCT used to make fifty statuettes a year, at a charge to the Academy of $105 each. From 1960 to 1982, manufacture of the Oscars passed to the Dodge Trophy Company, and since 1982 has been the privilege of R. S. Owens & Co., of Chicago. Over the statuette's sixty-five-year history the five holes in the reel of film forming the base of the Oscar have expanded, along with the number of the Academy's branches, to twelve. But the design of the Academy Award—in its modest way a triumph for the durability of Art Deco—otherwise remains exactly the same today as that bored doodle made by Cedric Gibbons in 1926.

As the studio art director at MGM, and thus an underling of Louis B. Mayer, Gibbons had already been a key player in the unlikely sequence of events that had led, over the previous eighteen months, to the formation of the Academy and the entirely subsidiary afterthought that it might present annual awards of merit. The movie world might never have been blessed with the Oscar had it not been for a whim on Louis Mayer's part in the autumn of 1926. He would build his family a house at the beach.

Undisputed monarch of Hollywood, and eponymous boss of Metro-Goldwyn-Mayer, Mayer naturally called upon his studio's art director, that same Cedric Gibbons, to run him up a suitably regal design. When he then ordered a production manager to supervise its construction, however, Mayer made the unsettling discovery that his own MGM work force would be prohibitively expensive. It would be much cheaper, he was advised, to use outside labor.

The reason, already etched on Mayer's heart, was the Studio Basic Agreement, a contract signed in November 1926 by nine Hollywood studios and five labor unions, the climax of a ten-year struggle to unionize the craft side of the movie industry. Its implications had appalled the studio bosses, especially Mayer, even before he had wanted his beach house. Trouble had been brewing since a strike by studio craftsmen in 1918; growing labor discontent throughout the early twenties had led directly to the signing of the peace treaty eight years later. It provided contractual protection, as yet, for only stagehands, carpenters, electricians, painters and musicians; but it would surely not be long before the "talent"—the actors, writers and directors—would also be pressing for standardized contracts. Actors Equity was already trying to rally Hollywood's completely disorganized acting strength behind its union banner.

To Mayer, this was unthinkable. His studio's lucrative stranglehold on his employees was under threat. On New Year's Day 1927 he invited three influential members of the Hollywood community to dinner to talk it all over. It was no coincidence that two of the three were his minions, and that each represented a different branch of the industry: Conrad Nagel was one of Mayer's leading contract actors; Fred Niblo was director of one of MGM's biggest box-office hits, *Ben-Hur;* and Fred Beetson was head of the Association of Motion Picture Producers. There was no apparent agenda, but it did not take much for Mayer to steer the conversation toward the hot topic of the hour: the Studio Basic Agreement (SBA).

At the time, Hollywood was producing more than five hundred feature-length films a year for a weekly audience of one hundred million cinemagoers paying an average twenty-five cents each in twenty-three thousand theaters across the country. But there were problems beyond the SBA clouding its horizon. How much of a threat was posed to silent pictures by those studios dabbling in sound? One of the smaller outfits, Warner Bros., had bought the rights to a Broadway musical called *The Day of Atonement,* and was proposing to turn it into a sound movie renamed *The Jazz Singer.* Worse, as it then seemed, a series of domestic scandals involving movie stars, from the Fatty Arbuckle case to sundry unmarried cohabitations, was in danger of alienating the audience. The movie industry was undergoing a wave of criticism from church and parent-teacher groups.

Though the SBA had received less publicity, its implications were far more disturbing to the studio bosses. Over dinner that night, Mayer sowed in his guests' minds the notion of a "mutually beneficial" organization to unite the interests of the disparate groups who made up the movie industry. Behind the cigar smoke, it seemed more like a rearguard action to protect the studio bosses' muscle against rebellious technicians, and to keep the talent in its place. But Mayer made it sound like a private club for the film world's elite, and his handpicked guests endorsed the plan enthusiastically.

"The idea," in the words of Mayer's biographer, Bosley

Crowther, "seemed exciting, not to mention flattering." Mayer's guests duly proceeded "to spread it among important friends." Though his presence at the dinner has been disputed—he was not so obviously in Mayer's pocket as the other two guests—Beetson later wrote in the *Academy Bulletin* of his pride at being "one of the original four to discuss the value to the industry of forming an organization to benefit all in the industry." All present agreed to lobby support for a formal dinner to launch such an organization, to be held, at Mayer's expense, a week later.

Thus it came to pass, on January 11, 1927, at the Ambassador Hotel, Los Angeles, that the International Academy of Motion Picture Arts and Sciences was born (though the word "International" was subsequently dropped from its title). The thirty-six people who attended represented all the creative branches of the industry, and are now hallowed as the Academy's founder-members*—led, of course, by Mayer himself. Membership of the Academy, he said, was open to those who had contributed "in a distinguished way to the arts and sciences of motion picture production." Although he stressed the democratic nature of the new organization, it did not go unnoticed that the room contained a remarkably high percentage of producers; even Mary Pickford, the only actress among the founder-members, chose to join the producers' branch. Mayer ensured that he was elected chairman of a committee to define the Academy's "plan and scope," and suggested that two lawyers be co-opted as "special members" to draft a constitution and bylaws. These two lawyers—Edwin Loeb of Loeb, Walker and Loeb, and his partner George W. Cohen, known in Hollywood as "the father of motion picture contracts"—just happened to be Mayer's own.

Within two months the lawyers had drawn up articles of incorporation and submitted them to the state of California. Pending ratification of its status as a nonprofit organization, the Academy rented a three-room suite at 6912 Hollywood Boulevard and elected

* The Academy's thirty-six founder-members were: actors Richard Barthelmess, Douglas Fairbanks (Sr.), Jack Holt, Harold Lloyd, Conrad Nagel, Milton Sills; directors Cecil B. de Mille, Henry King, Frank Lloyd, Fred Niblo, John M. Stahl, Raoul Walsh; writers Joseph Farnham, Benjamin F. Glazer, Jeanie MacPherson, Bess Meredyth, Carey Wilson, Frank Woods; technicians J. Arthur Ball, Cedric Gibbons, Roy J. Pomeroy; producers Fred Beetson, Charles H. Christie, Sid Grauman, Milton E. Hoffman, Jesse L. Lasky, M. C. Levee, Louis B. Mayer, Mary Pickford, Harry Rapf, Joseph M. Schenck, John Stahl, Irving Thalberg, Harry Warner, Jack Warner; and lawyer Edwin Loeb.

its first officers. Fred Niblo, one of Mayer's original dinner guests, agreed to serve as vice-president under a more celebrated president, Douglas Fairbanks (Sr.); and the screenwriter Frank Woods, former film critic for the New York *Dramatic Mirror*, signed on as the Academy's first secretary. On May 4, 1927, the Academy was granted its charter as a legal corporation, and a week later an inaugural banquet was held at the Biltmore Hotel.

Three hundred people attended, two hundred and thirty-one of them swelling the Academy's funds that night by adding their names to its membership. According to Frank Woods's report of the occasion, Fairbanks reminded the gathering that "the screen and all its people were under a great and alarming cloud of public censure and contempt" and that "some constructive action seemed imperative to halt the attacks and establish the industry in the public mind as a legitimate institution, and its people as reputable individuals." Fairbanks also added—though no mention had previously been made of this—that among the Academy's functions would be the bestowing of "awards of merit for distinctive achievement."

The following month, on June 20, 1927, a statement of aims was published:

> The Academy will take aggressive action in meeting outside attacks that are unjust.
>
> It will promote harmony and solidarity among the membership and among the different branches.
>
> It will reconcile internal differences that may exist or arise.
>
> It will adopt such ways and means as are proper to further the welfare and protect the honor and good repute of the profession.
>
> It will encourage the improvement and advancement of the arts and sciences of the profession by the interchange of constructive ideas and by awards of merit for distinctive achievements.
>
> It will take steps to develop the greater power and influence of the screen.
>
> In a word, the Academy proposes to do for the motion picture profession in all its branches what other great national and international bodies have done for other arts and sciences and industries.

Buried away in paragraph five, sounding very much like an afterthought, lies the birth of the most potent instrument of publicity and self-promotion any industry ever devised for itself: the Oscar. In the words of one recent Hollywood historian, "Even the Oscar was just another way of striking filmmakers where they were most vulnerable—at their vanity." But the Academy's annual awards would not be so named for another few years yet, and it occurred to no one that these awards would one day be the only aspect of the Academy's work to be known to the moviegoing public—or, in the phrase of Charles Champlin, long-time entertainments editor of the *Los Angeles Times,* "the tail that wags the Academy." For the time being, Louis Mayer's brainchild remained a thinly disguised studio pressure group designed to keep further unionization at bay.

The Academy Awards were almost incidental. There was little interest or excitement even after the idea had been mooted in the statement of aims. Among the several committees formed in the wake of its publication, one was established under the name Awards of Merit, its original members being Sid Grauman (owner of Hollywood Boulevard's famous Chinese Theater), D. W. Griffith, Henry King, J. Stuart Blackton and Richard Barthelmess, under the chairmanship of that same Cedric Gibbons—a Mayer placeman, of course. An awards ceremony was apparently considered at its first meeting, but 1928 had already dawned when the *Academy Bulletin* reported that "a partial plan was worked out, but, in the press of other business, no definite action was taken by the Board." That pressing business was to prove rather more financial than honorific.

To Mary Pickford, the Academy was "the League of Nations for the motion picture industry," an "open forum where all branches can meet and discuss constructive solutions to problems with which each is confronted." But the real trick on Mayer's part was to ensure that the Academy represented a number of studios, and all the major talent groups, so that it could be perceived as a forum for the exchange of ideas and the settling of differences rather than the studio front organization it really was. To secure his cover, he ensured that the Academy was composed of separate branches for actors, directors, writers and technicians, as well as producers, and that three representatives from each branch made up the Board of Directors. With the benefit of a decade's hindsight, the earliest historian of Hollywood's labor struggle, Murray Ross, saw Mayer's aspirations rather differently:

> There was little exaggeration in Equity's claim that the producers controlled the destiny of the Academy. . . . The foundation members were charter members and a select few who were elected to the sacrosanct circle. Other Academy members were not eligible for election to the board of directors and could not amend the by-laws. The Academy was obviously never meant to be a thoroughly democratic organization. . . . The founding of the Academy was a master stroke of producer ingenuity; its successful operation resulted from actor acquiescence in its policies.

Or as another, much later study put it, "Studio owners, sensing a new era of labor militancy, threw down one of management's most dog-eared trumps—a company-formed union called the Academy of Motion Picture Arts and Sciences. . . . For all its limitations—most notably the lack of a binding enforcement procedure for its labor codes—[the Academy] managed to forestall serious labor organizing among the Hollywood artists for over five years."

As if to demonstrate what Mayer was up to, the Academy's first major challenge in the very summer of its foundation was to referee a dispute between studios and "talent groups" over the imposition of a 10 percent pay cut, supposedly demanded by the studios' New York bankers. When the talent threatened to strike, the studio bosses persuaded the producers' branch of the Academy to resolve things by negotiating cost cuts with other branches. In the terms of the announcement that followed, however, the producers laid the blame for rising motion picture costs squarely on their "fellow" branches. Thus the Academy was able to take the credit for resolving the dispute and averting the pay cut, but its "talent" branches felt double-crossed and never again showed much trust in the Academy's supposed neutrality. It was now openly labeled a "company union" —"precisely," as Bosley Crowther summed up, "what the gentleman who conceived it intended it to be."

As it became clear, meanwhile, that the "talkies" were here to stay, an increasing number of legitimate actors were traveling to Hollywood from Broadway, where the Actors Equity Association had maintained a closed shop since 1919. Determined that Equity should not now preempt its role as the natural representative of film actors, the Academy spent the autumn of 1927 negotiating a standard contract for freelance actors, the first such actor-producer agreement in the history of Hollywood. Equity would battle on for another couple of years, but the Academy had outmaneuvered them, as the failure of an Equity strike would prove in 1929.

By the early summer of 1928, recently installed in new offices in the Roosevelt Hotel, the Academy was in a mood to revive its original notion of annual awards—more to shore up its growing status in the movie community than to reward talent or excite the moviegoing public. By now *The Jazz Singer* had been released—to such popular excitement that the awards committee deemed it ineligible, on the dubious grounds that it would be "unfair" competition for silent pictures. In July it was announced that awards would be made in twelve categories: Production, Artistic Quality of Production, Actor, Actress, Director, Comedy Director, Cinematography, Interior Decoration, Engineering Effects and three writing awards: Adaptation, Original Story and Title Writing. The twelve months from August 1, 1927, to July 31, 1928, was declared the period of eligibility, and the studios were asked to produce a list of pictures released within those dates.

The Best Production award would honor "the most outstanding motion picture considering all elements that contribute to a picture's greatness." The Artistic Quality of Production award, by contrast, would salute "the Producing Company, or Producer, who produced the most artistic, unique and/or original motion picture without reference to cost or magnitude." The special award for Comedy Direction (which would survive only one year) was designed to assist those studios specializing in slapstick shorts, still the most lucrative of all celluloid products.

"Engineering Effects" was something of a cop-out by the Academy's technical branch, who could not agree how to categorize their different roles, separating only Cinematography and Interior Decoration from "the best achievement in producing effects of whatever character obtained by engineering or mechanical means." Title Writing—the art of composing captions for silent films—was an afterthought from the writers' branch, requiring the Academy to staple last-minute inserts into the ballot forms sent out to every member of the Academy along with the studio-inspired "reminder list" of eligible pictures, still an integral part of the Oscar process to this day.

In an attempt to offset its unpopularity with the talent groups, and ensure a healthy rate of returns, the Academy's rule book hyped the new awards into something that sounded worth winning: "All members of the Academy are urged as a special duty and privilege to fill in their nominations for the Academy Awards of Merit with full recognition of the importance and responsibility of the act. Academy Awards of Merit should be considered the highest distinction attainable in the motion picture profession and only by the impartial justice and wisdom displayed by the membership in making their nominations will this desired result be possible." Said Mayer of MGM, on the Academy's behalf: "The awards have a dual purpose. One is that we want to recognize fine achievements, and the other is that we want to inspire those others to give finer achievements tomorrow."

Nearly a thousand nominations were received from the general membership by the official deadline of August 15. Despite the reminder list, some members (notably fans of Charles Chaplin and Buster Keaton) had voted for films several years old, such as *Stella Dallas, The Gold Rush* and *The General,* all dating from 1925–26. These ballots were duly returned to be filled out again, delaying the whole process even further. A list of the ten candidates with the most votes in each category was then handed over to five boards of judges, one from each Academy branch, to whittle down to a "short list" of three. The winners and runners-up were then chosen by a Central Board of Judges, who consisted that first year of Alec Francis (representing the actors branch), Frank Lloyd (directors), Sid Grauman (producers), Tom Geraghty (writers) and A. George Volck (technicians). When they met for their final deliberations on February 15, 1929, to decide and announce the winners of the first Academy Awards, they found that they had been joined by Louis Mayer—who had come along, he explained, to "supervise" the voting.

At six AM next morning, less than an hour after the session finally broke up, King Vidor received a phone call from Sid Grauman, the producers' representative on the Central Board of Judges. The Central Board had voted Vidor's *The Crowd,* Grauman told him, winner of the Artistic Quality of Production award. Even though it was an MGM film, however, Mayer had protested the decision, and argued the merits of Fox's *Sunrise* deep into the night. Its director, F. W. Murnau, was an internationally respected artist who would bring kudos to the Academy; besides, a Fox victory would prove to the world that there was no collusion between the Academy, Mayer and MGM.

Mayer did not need to spell out his main reason for not wanting to see Vidor honored. "He wouldn't vote for it because it wasn't a big money-maker for MGM," Grauman told Vidor. Even in the Academy Awards' first year, Vidor reflected years later, "money mattered, though a win didn't earn an extra million dollars like it does now." Mayer also hated the picture, he thought, because "it was unglamorous, against the studio's image."

Stung by accusations that the Academy had become his private fiefdom, Mayer appears to have deprived several MGM employees besides Vidor that night of awards they might otherwise have received on merit. The only one of the first Academy Awards to go to Mayer's own studio was the least important: the writers' afterthought, Title Writing, to one Joseph Farnham for a film called *Telling the World.* Best Production and three other awards, including Best Actor, went to Paramount; Artistic Quality and four others, including Best Actress and Best Director, to Fox; Comedy Direction and Interior Decoration to United Artists. As well as statuettes to the winners, scrolls signifying an Honorable Mention were to be presented to all the other nominees.

The results were made public that morning, and printed in the *Academy Bulletin* two days later, though the awards would not be presented until the Academy's anniversary dinner at the Hollywood Roosevelt Hotel on May 16, 1929. "It was a private affair—no television, of course, no radio even—just a group of friends giving each other a party," recalled one of those present. Cary Grant later explained why the ceremonies remained almost coyly private through most of the thirties: "There is something embarrassing about all these wealthy people publicly congratulating each other. When it all began, we kidded ourselves and said: 'All right, Freddie March, we know you're making a million dollars. Now come on up and get your little medal for it.' "

According to Janet Gaynor, who that night became the first woman to be voted Best Actress—and, at 22, remained for sixty years the youngest ever to win the award*—the first Academy Awards ceremony "was just a small group getting together for a pat on the back."

Gloria Swanson, one of the nominees (for *Sadie Thompson*), had been hoping "with the utmost sincerity" that Gaynor would beat her. According to Frances Marion, "there was neither jealousy nor persiflage in Gloria's make-up." She said of Gaynor: "She's standing there on top of this shaky ladder. With all my heart I want her to win."

Unlike Swanson, the prototype Hollywood siren thrice married in her twenties, Janet Gaynor was the archetypal virgin-heroine off-screen as well as on—a Quaker who lived at home with her mother. But Gaynor was the only female star of the year to challenge Swanson's predominance at the box office. As well as Murnau's *Sunrise*, in which her murder was cruelly plotted by an unfaithful husband, Gaynor had made two big box-office tearjerkers with Fox director Frank Borzage, *Seventh Heaven* and *Street Angel*. Swanson's *Sadie Thompson* had proved a big money-earner for United Artists; adapted from a Somerset Maugham short story, "Rain" (under which title it was remade in 1932 with Joan Crawford), the film had been coproduced by Swanson and her Svengali, Joseph P. Kennedy.

Hollywood's most admired male artist was Charlie Chaplin, whose recent release *The Circus* was eligible for the first Academy Awards. But the big box-office actor of the year was 32-year-old Richard Barthelmess, veteran of a decade of D. W. Griffith hits; a founder-member of the Academy, Barthelmess had starred in two eligible films, *The Noose* and *The Patent Leather Kid*, in both of which his characters rivaled Janet Gaynor's for displaying moral courage in the face of an ugly world. The third contender for Best Actor was Paramount's expensive German import Emil Jannings, hailed in the studio publicity as "the greatest actor in the world" following his success as a tragedian in a series of silent German epics. In *The Last Command* and *The Way of All Flesh*, his fellow European Josef von Sternberg and Hollywood's own Victor Fleming both cast

* Gaynor's record was not beaten until 1986, when *Children of a Lesser God*'s Marlee Matlin became the youngest ever Best Actress at the age of 21 years and 218 days. The youngest Supporting Actress was Tatum O'Neal, who won for *Paper Moon* in 1973 when just 10 years and 148 days old. The youngest person ever to receive an Oscar was Shirley Temple, presented with a Special Award in 1934, when she was 5 years and 10 months. See Appendix C, section B4.

Jannings in classic Aristotelian fashion as a great man brought low by cruel quirks of fate.

Well aware of his own limitations as an actor, Jannings was one of the first members of the Hollywood community to appreciate the threat posed to the likes of him by the arrival of sound. Though a master of disguise and a considerable screen presence, Jannings told his studio that he would be returning to his native Germany as soon as his contract expired in 1929. It was perhaps for this reason, as much as Mayer's ambition to give at least one of the first Academy Awards to a foreigner, that Emil Jannings earned an unlikely place in movie history as the first man to be voted Best Actor. So anxious was he to leave town that he asked the Academy to let him have his statuette right away, and paused only to pose for studio publicity pictures before heading home well in advance of the presentation dinner.

Janning's Oscar was the first thing he showed U.S. Army intelligence officers when they visited his Bavarian home in the aftermath of the Second World War. For running Hitler's anti-British films unit, taking his orders directly from Goebbels's Propaganda Ministry, he was blacklisted by the Allies and retired to Austria, where he died forgotten and unmourned in 1950. Janet Gaynor, by contrast, remained one of Hollywood's most secure stars for another decade, surviving the transition to sound and taking over Mary Pickford's role as "America's sweetheart." Rivaling Marie Dressler in early 1930s popularity polls, Gaynor topped the 1934 box-office ratings and won another Academy Award nomination in 1937 opposite Fredric March in the original version of *A Star Is Born*. A longer-lasting star even than Garbo, whose unpredictable temperament she came to share, Gaynor emerged from retirement in 1957 to play Pat Boone's mother in *Bernardine*; in the 1970s she could be spotted in an early episode of television's *The Love Boat*, and was to be found onstage (in the Chicago production of *On Golden Pond*) as late as 1981, three years before her death following a car accident.

Jannings, Gaynor and Murnau were the main beneficiaries of Mayer's determination to ensure that the Academy Awards won instant respectability. The fact that both the main acting awards went to nonmembers, one of them a foreigner, was much vaunted for many years as proof of the electorate's impartiality.

"It was more like a private party than a big public occasion," recalled Janet Gaynor of that first Academy Awards ceremony. "It wasn't open to anyone but Academy members, and as you danced you saw the most important people in Hollywood whirling past you." According to the Roosevelt Hotel's press release, "the Blossom Room was a gorgeous sight, with its soft lantern lights shedding rays and shadows on the brilliant gowns and gay blooms. Thirty-six tables with their scintillating glassware and long tapers, each table bearing a replica in waxed candy of the gold statuette award, filled the entire floor space of the room."

Under the chairmanship of William C. de Mille (brother of Cecil B.), the evening began with the first demonstration of Western Electric's portable talking projection system, via which Academy president Douglas Fairbanks could be seen presenting the Best Production Award—for *Wings*, a First World War air epic—to Adolph Zukor at Paramount's Astoria Studios in New York. The guests then dined on jumbo squab perigeaux, lobster Eugénie, Los Angeles salad, terrapin and fruit supreme before Fairbanks rose to ask the winners (with uncanny foresight) for brevity in their acceptance speeches, and hand out the prizes.

The Production Award won by *Wings* cited it as "the most outstanding picture production, considering all elements that contribute to a motion picture's greatness"; Murnau's *Sunrise* meanwhile received a second such award as "the most unique, artistic, worthy and original production, without reference to cost or magnitude." Combining the two awards the following year, the Academy retrospectively named *Wings* the first winner of the Academy Award for Best Picture, thus irritating *Sunrise* fans in perpetuity. Thirty years later the French film magazine *Cahiers du Cinéma* was still hailing it as "the greatest film of all time." In 1990 the Academy's official historian, Patrick Stockstill, doubted that *Sunrise* would ever be reinstated, because "that would be admitting the original decision was a mistake."

Two other controversies of the kind that would haunt subsequent Oscar ceremonies hung over that first awards dinner, both concerning the Best Actor category. Led by columnist Jimmy Starr, there was some feeling that Charles Farrell, Janet Gaynor's costar in *Seventh Heaven*, had been unfairly overlooked by the judges. Much more conspicuous, however, was the Academy's slight to Charles

Chaplin, who had been ignored in all four categories for which he was eligible: acting, writing, producing and comedy directing (which went to Lewis Milestone for a wartime farce entitled *Two Arabian Knights*).

During the three months between the announcement of the results and the awards dinner—a mistake the Academy would not make again—Chaplin was voted the first recipient of an Academy "Special Award" for "versatility and genius" in his work on *The Circus*. With Emil Jannings already back in Germany, both runners-up had stayed away from the dinner; Chaplin, like Academy founder-member Richard Barthelmess, was in New York, whence he graciously cabled his thanks for the honor, upon which de Mille stood up to remark: "I think he is the only one to whom the Academy has or ever will give a first award to one man for writing, directing, acting in and producing a picture. It takes us back to the old days."

A Special Award was also given to *The Jazz Singer*, as "the pioneer outstanding talking picture, which has revolutionized the industry." Accepting on behalf of Warner Bros., its head of production Darryl F. Zanuck dedicated the award to the late Sam Warner, who had died the day before *The Jazz Singer* opened, as "the man responsible for the successful usage of the medium." Speeches then became infectious, and the restraint of the winners was wasted in a spate of long and emotional tributes to the Academy, climaxing in paeans to and from Louis B. Mayer himself, before Al Jolson closed the proceedings with a song.

"Hollywood was just one big family then," said Janet Gaynor years later, "and this was a bouquet—thrown to me, I think, because I was new and because they thought I had a certain freshness. It was nothing then like it is now. My agent didn't call me up the next day with an offer to double my salary. I didn't find a pile of scripts at my door. Photographers weren't camped on my front lawn. I just got up at five AM and drove off to the studio—as always."

But William Randolph Hearst had other ideas, and instructed Louella Parsons, Hollywood gossip columnist for his papers, to lavish all the superlatives at her command on the Academy's new awards. On the assumption that he would be able to organize a future award for his mistress, Marion Davies, Hearst wanted them to become the industry's most sought-after prize. In the Awards' first year of life, therefore, Oscar fever began to grow. "The Academy's awards program," in the words of its 1929 annual report, "is its most conspicuous function in promoting the advancement of the arts and sciences of motion picture production. No activity of the Academy has attracted as wide public attention as this one." Or as Frances Marion put it: "There was more excitement than at a children's party when you played pin the tail on the donkey, and in a way it was not unlike the childhood game. The participants found themselves blindfolded, a little too eager to win the prize, a little too scared to hope."

Would Hollywood otherwise have cared about the Academy Awards? In their second year, the year in which many major movie stars were making a nervous transition to sound, it quickly became clear that the Awards would have a crucial role to play in their careers. While the talkies, for instance, were giving many former Broadway stars the chance to talk (or sing) their way into Hollywood firmament, they presented a real problem to established sirens of the silent screen like Mary Pickford, whose quest for her first speaking role had also become one for a completely new screen image.

As a cofounder of United Artists, Pickford was well placed to select and produce the vehicle for this transformation. On the advice of Lillian Gish, she went for *Coquette*, a Broadway hit written for Helen Hayes, about a flapper responsible for a long trail of broken hearts and lives. Pickford cut off her famous blonde curls and began filming with gritted teeth; she was determined to be "free of the shackles of playing cute little girls with curls" and to "give the performance of my career, and give it in my own way." But it worked only for the most devoted of Pickford fans. Other actresses such as Ruth Chatterton, Bessie Love, Jeanne Eagels and Betty Compson were already establishing livelier and more natural presences in the new medium of talking pictures. Given the intense competition for awards engendered by a feverish Hollywood production year, the Academy's judges were forced the second time around to spend all of six months in conclave.

Pickford's place in the Academy's heart (and its hierarchy) had been made strikingly clear in the previous year's annual report, which momentarily stepped out of its bureaucratic prose to assure readers that President Fairbanks would be back from New York in time for the ceremony—"with our beloved Mary." By now desperate to win Best Actress, she had reached the verge of panic: her latest venture into sound, an ambitious version of *The Taming of the Shrew* costarring her husband, had proved a disaster. What more natural than that she should now invite all five members of the Central Board of Judges to tea at Pickfair, the home she shared with Fairbanks, the Academy's founder-president? In only their second year, the Academy Awards had notched up their first overt piece of campaigning.

With sound pictures eligible for the first time, producers were asked to nominate "the best production, silent or talking, drama, comedy or musical production, with special reference to quality, public appeal, general excellence, and all elements that contribute to a motion picture's greatness." The actors branch was urged to listen for "speech and diction, if employed." The entire process was becoming much more complicated, and there were lessons to be learned from the mistakes of the first year. "The development of talking pictures has made individual achievements of artists much more difficult to judge," announced the Academy's secretary, Frank Woods. "Sound has brought in a new element of screen art and a host of new people."

Though they stuck to the same system of a Central Board of Judges, acting on nominations from the branches (and again supplemented by the guiding presence of Louis B. Mayer), this year's panel pared the awards to just seven. They dropped Comedy Direction and Engineering Effects, limited the writers to just one award (under the blanket heading of Writing Achievement) and rationalized the two Best Picture awards into Best Production. This year, furthermore, they would not be making the mistake of announcing the results before the awards dinner; nor would there be any scrolls for honorable mentions.

The second Academy Awards dinner was held on April 30, 1930, at the Coconut Grove of the Ambassador Hotel, Los Angeles. "If you looked around at the elegantly gowned women glittering with jewels," noted one of those present, "you could scarcely believe there had ever been a depression, and that outside this extravagant setting people were wandering about in dire need." Dinner was eaten before the presentation ceremonies, which began at 10:30 PM and were broadcast live by a local radio station. The Academy's new president, William C. de Mille, prefaced the proceedings with a wary-sounding explanation that each achievement was judged "with special reference to its value to the motion-picture industry and to the arts and sciences on which that industry rests. Each achievement was judged from all its aspects combined rather than on any single point of excellence."

De Mille was also the first Academy official to be specific about the "peer recognition" that has since become, within the Hollywood community, supposedly the most satisfying aspect of winning an Oscar. "The most valuable award a worker can get is to have the acknowledged praise of his fellow workers," he wrote in the *Academy Bulletin* that followed the second Awards. "It means a great deal more to us than just the acclaim of the public." Among the Awards' novelty value was the fact that they amounted to the first occasion in film history that "individual creative work has been recognized" and that "meritorious achievements have been passed upon by experts."

The first award, for Interior Decoration, went to Cedric Gibbons, the very man who had designed the statuette, for his work on MGM's *Bridge of San Luis Rey*. The Cinematography award then went to another MGM film, *White Shadows in the South Seas*; though it was billed as the studio's first sound picture, Mayer had in fact ordered the addition of music and sound effects (but no dialogue) to footage already expensively shot in the South Seas for a torrid, originally silent, love story. The directing statuette was won by Frank Lloyd, for a silent First National costume spectacular, *The Divine Lady*, before Louis B. Mayer himself accepted the Best Picture award for MGM's *Broadway Melody*.

A buzz around the room indicated that a pattern had not gone unnoticed: apart from a rash of wins by Mayer's MGM, all the awards had so far gone to founder-members of the Academy. There was therefore less surprise, but more seditious muttering, when Mary Pickford was named as Best Actress for *Coquette*. Though the film had done well at the box office—grossing more than $1.4 million domestically, making it her most successful picture ever—there was more to Pickford's award than met the eye. In the words of her most recent biographer, Scott Eyman: "Considering the caliber of her performance, the Oscar would have been incomprehensible were it not for her social position within Hollywood. Mary's Oscar for her inferior work for *Coquette* surely qualifies as the first Lifetime

The moving spirit behind the Academy, Louis B. Mayer (FRONT ROW, FAR LEFT), *poses with other founder-members at its first meeting in 1927.*

The Academy was proud that its first Best Actress award went to a nonmember, Janet Gaynor, for three 1927–28 roles, in (LEFT TO RIGHT) *Seventh Heaven, Street Angel and Sunrise.*

Achievement award to be handed out by the Academy." Pickford promptly founded a time-honored Academy tradition by bursting into tears and declaring that she had forgotten her prepared acceptance speech.

Only the final winner, Warner Baxter as Best Actor for *In Old Arizona*, was not one of the Academy's charter members. No Special Awards were made. For the first and only time in the history of the Academy Awards, no film had won more than one honor. But the subsequent whispering campaign grew so persistent, and the jokes about Mary Pickford so malicious, that the awards committee was pressured into a more than cosmetic rule change. For the third year of the Academy Awards (and, as it transpired, for the next five years), the selection process would be broadened, with nominations and final voting thrown open to the entire membership. The reason given in the Academy's annual report was the "rather complicated" nature of the previous voting system, But the truth was rather more devious.

One immediate result was a huge increase in membership, much to the delight of the Academy's treasurer. His report in the *Academy Bulletin* of May 12, 1929, had bemoaned its financial lot, with President de Mille wondering: "Should [the Academy] go on for years and years simply maintaining the life of its corporate body, merely existing and doing nothing, like an old gentleman who retires to a health resort and devotes eighteen years to studying life? Or should it function no matter what happens tomorrow?" The latter course was eased by the 1930 annual report, which showed a startling leap in membership over the previous two years:

	Nov. 1928	*Nov. 1929*	*Nov. 1930*	*Foundation*	*Academy*
Actors	93	89	246	99	147
Directors	77	79	85	79	6
Producers	54	61	66	63	3
Technicians	67	77	111	83	28
Writers	70	71	74	69	5
Special	8	12	19	16	3
	369	389	601	409	192

The two right-hand columns of the table show that 192 of the 212 new arrivals had joined in a new membership category cunningly designed to keep control of the Academy in the hands of its founding fathers. "In common with the activities of the Actors Branch, designed to promote the best possible relations between players and producers," in the silken words of its 1930 annual report, the Academy had amended its constitution to create a new subclass of member, to be known as Academy members, at a reduced rate of $15 plus $1 a month. Unlike Foundation members, who paid $100 to join and monthly dues of $5, mere Academy members would not be allowed "to hold office or participate in the government of the Academy." The vast majority of those who had chosen to join at the cheaper rate were, of course, actors. The Academy had taken open pride in its "neutral, hands-off" policy toward the 1929 Equity dispute; but it still felt a need to sweet-talk the talent and attract as much of it as possible into membership, against the likelihood of further storms ahead.

Against this background, it was perhaps fortunate for the third year of the Awards, 1929–30, that there was for the first time an outstanding film and at least one outstanding performance that would turn out to be unassailable victors. The competition was complicated by the first screen utterances to come from Greta Garbo—GARBO TALKS! was the only slogan required to ensure box-office success for MGM's version of Eugene O'Neill's *Anna Christie*—and the emergence of Ronald Colman as the first true star of the "talkies." Other studios went to other sources in search of sound-oriented talent. With the emphasis firmly on song, Paramount imported a French music-hall celebrity, Maurice Chevalier, for a Ruritanian operetta with Jeanette MacDonald entitled *The Love Parade* while MGM poached a leading light of New York's Metropolitan Opera, Lawrence Tibbett, and starred him in a Lehar rewrite called *The Rogue Song*.

But Carl Laemmle had far more ambitious ideas. Head of Universal, the only major studio not yet to have received a single Academy Award nomination, Laemmle went for broke: for a massive $1.2 million budget he would film Erich Maria Remarque's powerful antiwar novel, *All Quiet on the Western Front*, hiring Broadway's hottest writers, George Abbott and Maxwell Anderson, to supplement a Hollywood team led by the director Lewis Milestone with his own son, Carl Laemmle, Jr., as producer. Because it treated the enemy sympathetically—it portrays a group of ex-schoolboys' growing terror in the trenches—the film provoked great controversy, earning the threat of a boycott from the American Legion. But it was a critical and commercial hit. "Here exhibited is war as it is, butchery," wrote *Variety*. "The League of Nations could make no better investment than to buy up the master print, reproduce it in every language to be shown to every nation every year until the word war is taken out of the dictionaries." For the first time, concurred the *National Board of Review*, "the sound and image mediums blend as one, as a form of artistic expression that only the motion screen can give."

The first film of the period to remain a contemporary classic, *All Quiet on the Western Front* earned Universal four nominations, for Best Production, Direction, Writing and Cinematography. In the year it had faced antitrust suits, bankruptcy and eventually sale, the Fox company was missing from the nominations list, while MGM garnered fifteen, Paramount eleven, United Artists six and Warner Bros. four.

Even in the absence of the Honorable Mention for runners-up, the Academy was anxious to stress that nomination was in itself an achievement. Before the 1930 awards, the board seemed intent on emulating Baron Pierre de Coubertin's Olympic creed—surely a hopeless task—with its announcement in the *Academy Bulletin*: "Regardless of which ones of the selected nominees are finally chosen by the Academy to win the statuette trophies, there will be undeniable distinction in winning the preliminary nominations at the hands of their fellow workers." Though not intended to carry quite the same weight as the original scrolls, a certificate of nomination has ever since been conferred by the Academy, and still is to this day.

The third awards banquet was held barely seven months after the second—on November 5, 1930, again at the Ambassador Hotel—in an attempt to endow the awards schedule with a regular annual routine. Despite the introduction of a $10 charge to Academy members, the event was a sellout. This time the host was Conrad Nagel, one of the Academy's founding fathers; William C. de Mille was away on vacation, suggesting that the Academy Awards had not yet become the "must" social event they are for *le tout Hollywood* today. Even the evening's Lifetime Achievement honoree, Thomas Edison, appeared only via a "talking picture reel." But President de Mille did greet the nominees among the 650 guests with a cryptic telegram read out by Nagel: "Tell [the losers] that in a conflict between personality and ability it is impossible to say which will win."

Despite two nominations, Garbo did not bother to show up either; the same was true of the veteran British actor George Arliss, despite nominations for his performances as the British prime minister in *Disraeli* and a corrupt Indian potentate in *The Green Goddess*. It was a year of double nominations: Arliss, Colman and Chevalier had each won two in the male acting category, to one each for Wallace Beery and Lawrence Tibbett, the first screen star to be nominated for his first film; in the Best Actress stakes, Garbo and Norma Shearer also each won separate nominations for two different films.

Arliss's Disraeli won the day, giving Britain its first Academy Award and leaving indigenous actors to wonder whether Europe was going to dominate this category. But the third Awards were primarily a personal triumph for Carl Laemmle. *All Quiet on the Western Front* won Best Production and Best Director, while Universal also won the Interior Decoration award for *King of Jazz*. Laemmle had equaled Mayer's MGM with three awards each (including the year's only new category, Sound Recording). Mayer himself presented the Best Production award to Laemmle, graciously adding: "I hear there's talk that the motion picture we honor tonight may win a Nobel Peace Prize." For all the film's continuing stature in the subsequent history of war movies, that is a double Hollywood has yet to bring off.*

Best Actress was not Garbo or Nancy Carroll, nor second-time nominees Ruth Chatterton or Gloria Swanson (for whom Joe Kennedy was still trying to win an Oscar) but Norma Shearer, for *The Divorcée*. A rumor had been circulating that in this, the first year the awards were decided by the entire Academy membership, all MGM employees had been sent a memo urging them to vote for Shearer, wife of the studio's head of production, Irving Thalberg. The forerunner of many such rumors, it was never confirmed. But Joan

*The only Oscar winner to have also won a Nobel Prize is George Bernard Shaw, honored by the Academy for his screenplay for *Pygmalion* in 1938 (see page 141), thirteen years after his work had been recognized by the Nobel Committee.

Crawford, who would have to wait another fifteen years for her own Oscar, believed it. "What do you expect?" she famously said of Shearer. "She sleeps with the boss!"

The following year saw yet more rule changes, with the introduction of Scientific or Technical awards; the redivision of the writing awards into Adaptation and Original Story; and the renaming of Best Production as Best Picture, supposedly to deter voters from being overimpressed by sheer scale and logistics. Cinematographers were meanwhile growing restive that budgetary differences enabled silent films to monopolize lavish locations and ambitious visual effects, so their citation was reworded to honor "cinematography of a black-and-white picture photographed in America under normal production conditions." As if to prove the point at once, an ambitious and expensive RKO Western called *Cimarron,* chronicling the settlement of Oklahoma, swept Best Picture and two other awards, though its nominated actors (Richard Dix, Irene Dunne) and director (Wesley Ruggles) missed out. For sixty years, until Kevin Costner's *Dances with Wolves* in 1990, *Cimarron* remained the only Western to have won Best Picture.

Although herself a nominee again, Norma Shearer presented the Best Actress award to its least glamorous recipient yet: 60-year-old Marie Dressler, a large, self-styled "ugly duckling," whom Frances Marion described as wearing "an outfit that made her look like a circus horse." Like an old Model T, in her own words, Dressler had to be "cranked up" to collect her award, beating off emergent stars such as Dunne, Ann Harding and Hollywood's latest sensation, Marlene Dietrich—for what proved to be the only nomination she ever received, in *Morocco. (The Blue Angel,* though eligible that year, was completely overlooked by the Academy.)

For his performance in Irving Thalberg's latest vehicle for his wife, *A Free Soul,* which also featured the unknown Clark Gable as a minor hoodlum, another stage-turned-screen actor, Lionel Barrymore, beat such opposition as Fredric March and Adolphe Menjou—not to mention 10-year-old Jackie Cooper, still the youngest Best Actor nominee ever (Appendix C, section B4), whose winsomeness in *Skippy* helped win Best Director for his uncle, Norman Taurog.

Thus did Barrymore make movie history. Already nominated in 1928–29 as director of the Ruth Chatterton tearjerker *Madame X,* he now became the first film artist to win nominations in two different categories. In the 1940s his sister Ethel would win one Oscar in four nominations. But their distinguished and more celebrated brother, John, mainstay of the most famous theatrical family of its day, would join D. W. Griffith and Charlie Chaplin as the first of the Hollywood giants to find themselves conspicuously overlooked by the Academy.

On January 25, 1931, at the end of her first day's filming on *Grand Hotel,* Greta Garbo called together the entire cast, kissed her costar, John Barrymore, and purred: "You have no idea what it means to me to play opposite so perfect an artist." For the first time in her screen career, she then permitted photographers to take pictures of herself and Barrymore off the set. "I admired him greatly," she said in later years. "Barrymore was one of the very few who had that divine madness without which a great artist cannot work or live."

Hollywood's first "all-star" melodrama, *Grand Hotel* was to win Best Picture at the fifth Academy Awards ceremony in November 1932. But Best Picture had been the only nomination the film received. Neither Garbo nor Barrymore earned so much as a mention. Already nominated for *Anna Christie* and *Romance* (1929–30), Garbo would receive two more unsuccessful nominations (for *Camille* in 1937 and *Ninotchka* in 1939). But Barrymore would never receive a single nomination.

His next assignment after *Grand Hotel* was *A Bill of Divorcement* with the screen debutante Katharine Hepburn, a Broadway star signed by Selznick for RKO, whose fortunes were on the wane. Unlike Garbo, the stiff East Coast actress didn't get on with her leading man. At the end of the last day of filming, Hepburn said to Barrymore: "I'll never play another scene with you." Replied Barrymore: "But, my dear, you never have."

One of the most accomplished actors working in Hollywood in the early thirties, Barrymore undoubtedly turned in the best performances of 1932—in *Grand Hotel* and *Bill of Divorcement*—though Best Actor was shared that year by Wallace Beery and Fredric March. One of the great stage and screen talents of the century, Barrymore appears to have been the first distinguished victim of what was to become a familiar Oscar syndrome: Hollywood prudery, spiced with a dash of sexual envy.

"The studio bosses—most of them great lechers—fumed at Barrymore's easy conquests," in the judgment of the film historian Peter H. Brown. He further earned the enmity of the authorities by "refusing to conform to Hollywood's rules. . . . He drank too much, snickered at Hollywood's pretensions, and spurned the invitations to their dull weekend parties." The screenwriter Frances Marion, already an Academy Award winner in 1929–30 for MGM's *The Big House,* was but one Barrymore friend who chronicled "his hurt, his denials, the shame of being an object of ridicule, even his frustration at never once being recognized in Hollywood circles as a great artist, though he had always insisted he would toss 'that phony Oscar' into the ocean if he won it. Another small boy whistling in the dark—he really wanted an Oscar above any honor he had ever received."

Louis Mayer and his ilk exorcised their shameful treatment of Barrymore by persuading themselves that he wouldn't have wanted an Oscar, anyway, so sated was he with the acclaim of Broadway and London's West End. But Barrymore's biographer, Gene Fowler, confirmed Marion's evidence to the contrary. "You know, Gene," Barrymore told him shortly before his death, "I think they were afraid I'd come into the banquet drunk, embarrassing myself and them. But I wouldn't have, you know."

When Hollywood closes ranks, the effects on any filmmaker can be devastating. The same treatment would soon be meted out to another of Garbo's leading men, John Gilbert, and in later years to such figures as Alan Ladd and Marilyn Monroe. There is no evidence to suggest that the Academy Awards were yet having much influence upon the audience, and thus upon box-office receipts; in the early 1930s a Best Picture winner like *Cimarron* still managed to lose RKO Radio as huge a sum as $5.5 million. But the Barrymore saga vividly illustrates how important the Academy Awards, in their first decade of life, had already become within the profession.

That a man of his distinction could become so exercised about the awards in their pretelevision, even preradio era belies the received Hollywood wisdom that they were as yet of little significance. By the fifth Academy Awards in 1931–32, national network radio was interested enough to broadcast the climax of the awards dinner, and the results were clearly beginning to exert a hypnotic hold over Hollywood "talent" that has never since slackened.

The fifth Awards also saw the introduction of awards for Short Subjects, in three categories labeled Cartoon, Comedy and Novelty —recognition of the box-office drawing power of the shorts that were now standard fare on cinema menus. Since his arrival in Hollywood ten years before, and especially since the birth of Mickey Mouse in 1928, Walt Disney had already established a predominance in the cartoon field that would see him win an unapproachable record of thirty-two Oscars, ranging from twelve cartoon awards across such categories as Short Subjects, Documentaries, Special Effects and Honorary awards. That first year he and his brother Roy were among the judges, along with Stan Laurel and Oliver Hardy, Mack Sennett and Leon ("Looney Tunes") Schlesinger.

At a loss as to how to handle their new Short Subject category, the Academy had handed over the nominating process to the experts. Unsurprisingly, they simply nominated themselves; Disney's *Flowers and Trees* won the Cartoon award, against opposition from himself and Schlesinger; and Laurel and Hardy's *The Music Box* won the Comedy statuette for MGM. In the Novelty section, however, Mack Sennett was dismayed to learn that his *Wrestling Swordfish* had lost by just three votes to an MGM short called *Swing High*. When Sennett pointed out that a three-vote difference, under the Academy's then rules, was considered a tie, the executive secretary ducked his obligation to cast the deciding vote by decreeing that the entire Academy membership should vote again. The winner of the first Novelty Short Subject award duly turned out to be Mack Sennett.

Walt Disney that night became only the second person to be voted a Special Award by the Academy, "for the creation of Mickey Mouse"; it was due to be presented by the recipient of the first, Charlie Chaplin, who made clear his attitude toward the whole business by electing to stay home.

Another far more mainstream Hollywood figure also delivered himself of a ringing verdict in the wake of the fourth Awards ceremony. It was Irving Thalberg who had coaxed Helen Hayes toward her screen debut after she followed her husband, the writer Charles MacArthur, to Hollywood. But the best he could come up with was the melodramatic title role in *The Sin of Madelon Claudet*, the hackneyed saga of a fallen woman who makes all manner of sacrifices so that her illegitimate son can study to become a doctor. It was probably the screen community's supine respect for Hayes's status as a stage actress that saw her to Best Actress victory over Marie Dressler (in *Emma*) and Lynne Fontanne *(The Guardsman)*. But the next time Thalberg was pondering an equally stilted script, he decided to give it the go-ahead for one good reason: "Let's face it. We win Academy Awards with crap like *Madelon Claudet*."

These fifth Awards saw several previous winners among the nominees—Marie Dressler, for instance, director Frank Borzage and writer Frances Marion—obliging the Academy to fend off a petition for a new rule prohibiting repeat winners. But an even knottier, unprecedented problem was to present itself during the awards dinner. At the time, the votes were still tabulated in the room itself, under the scrutiny of the voting committee, giving candidates a chance to scrutinize the process—and disappointed ones to complain, even demand a recount. At the first few dinners, it was the usual practice to read the votes out at the end, thus embarrassing the losers yet further. It was some time after Mrs. Thalberg had presented Fredric March with the Best Actor statuette, for his versatile histrionics as *Dr. Jekyll and Mr. Hyde,* that a scrutineer preparing for this announcement noticed that Wallace Beery, nominated for MGM's *The Champ,* had lost by only one vote. Under the rules, as Mack Sennett had already made clear, anything less than three was a tie.

With Louis B. Mayer in the middle of his lengthy acceptance speech for the Best Picture award to *Grand Hotel,* the Voting Committee chairman, B. P. Schulberg of Paramount, had time to send for another statuette and summon President Nagel. When Mayer finally sat down, Nagel called Beery to the podium and announced that he had tied. According to the next day's *Los Angeles Times,* "The time lapse made the second award seem like a consolation prize, but Beery nevertheless accomplished a very grateful acceptance." Ties have ever since been unpopular with both the Academy and its audience, primarily because they rob the result of its winner-take-all poignancy. There has been only one since in Oscar history, when the accountants of Price Waterhouse could not separate Barbra Streisand and Katharine Hepburn in 1968.

The first Oscars were presented at the Academy's second anniversary banquet at the Hollywood Roosevelt Hotel on May 16, 1929.

Emil Jannings, winner of the first Best Actor award, was so daunted by the "talkies" that he went home to his native Germany before the presentation dinner. Jannings subsequently ran Hitler's anti-British film unit.

This first tie in a major category, however, was made the more memorable by a subsequent March witticism, drawing attention to the fact that both he and Beery had recently adopted children: "It seems a little odd that we were both given awards for the best male performance of the year."

Though talking pictures had helped the film industry survive the crash of 1929, the early thirties began to see the Depression prove too much for even the major Hollywood studios. Before the winter of 1932, when movie attendance suddenly plunged, the industry had done "surprisingly well," as Bosley Crowther put it, out of "the peculiarly melancholy fact that jobless people sought sanctuary in dark and comforting theaters—until they were completely out of funds." By the end of that winter RKO and Universal were both in receivership, Paramount bankrupt, and Fox in crisis. The crunch came on March 5, 1933, when the newly inaugurated President Roosevelt's declaration of a national Bank Holiday poleaxed the majors, most of which were living on borrowed money, dependent for cash flow on dollars the moviegoing public had now run out of.

Amid the suspension of production schedules and talk of studio closures, salaries were immediately frozen under the threat of a total shutdown. As president of the Association of Motion Picture Producers, Mayer joined forces with an emergency committee formed by the Academy in suggesting a dramatic, all-round 50 percent pay cut as a temporary solution. It was a slick piece of public relations, making Hollywood look as if it were imposing upon itself a decent sacrifice on behalf of the nation. After some initial enthusiasm, the labor unions inevitably protested, pointing out that it would be somewhat easier for Louis B. Mayer to survive on half his $8,000-a-week salary than for a $50-a-week technician.

By March 13, the issue reached an impasse when stagehands mounted a strike, closing down every studio in Hollywood. In emergency session with Mayer and the producers, the Academy's committee came up with an ingenious solution to help lower-income workers. Anyone earning $50 a week or less would not take a cut, while those earning above $50 would waive a percentage of their salaries, on a sliding scale, up to a maximum of 50 percent—and for a strictly temporary eight-week period, from March 6 to April 30.

Still Hollywood's most vociferous dissidents, the writers resigned en masse from the Academy to form their own Screen Writers Guild, whose history dates from April 6, 1933. After much agonizing, the bulk of the studios' other employees realized that they had little option but to go along with the pay cut for now. At the end of the two-month freeze, most salaries were immediately restored in full. But employees of Sam Goldwyn and Warner Bros. found themselves double-crossed, as both studios refused to abide by the Academy's deadline.

The crisis escalated when Darryl F. Zanuck—as Warners' vice president in charge of production, the executive who had personally promised his employees that the pay cut would be temporary—resigned his $5,000-a-week job in protest. Again the Academy intervened, still intent on proving itself a successful independent arbiter. Granted permission to inspect the studios' books, it called in the accountancy firm of Price Waterhouse—the beginning of a professional relationship that would become permanent three years later, when a voting furor saw Price Waterhouse hired to tabulate Oscar balloting, as they have ever since.

The audit revealed that the studios were now solvent. But continuing intransigence from Harry Warner now led to the resignation of Conrad Nagel as the Academy's president, amid further recrimination. There were conflicting theories about Nagel's role in the saga; despite his own claim that he had used his office to try to persuade Warner to accept the Academy's decision, it was leaked from an Academy meeting that he had been thrown out by a vote of no confidence after arguing Warner's case. The official Academy statement dodged the question, saying simply: "The intensive struggle within the industry in the last few weeks has resulted in many questions of Academy policy with which Mr. Nagel felt he could not agree."

The Academy had again survived a sustained political crisis—but only narrowly, for its reputation had been further eroded among the "talent" groups, with whom its salary-cut proposal had never been popular. They remained unconvinced by an Academy announcement that the "most heartening and inspiring result" of the emergency had been a determination among the studio bosses that "a horizontal industry salary cut will never again be attempted." On the contrary, in the judgment of Murray Ross, the whole episode "marked the beginning of the end of the usefulness of AMPAS in the labor relations field." The events of March 1933, agree later historians of the period, "finally shattered the Academy's moral and professional stature in the eyes of Hollywood artists." Many of the Academy's leading lights were openly advocating its removal from the political arena; but they still had Mayer and his original aspirations to reckon with.

Nagel's replacement as Academy president, J. Theodore Reed of Paramount, worked fast on a new constitution to reorganize the

Academy, and after less than a month in office sent an Open Letter to every member in which he outlined the changes. "Every effort has been made to guarantee that both the election system and the Academy as a whole will be free from politics and any taint of self-preservation in office."

That summer the Academy all but foundered on the rocks of Roosevelt's National Industrial Recovery Act, signed on June 16, 1933, which suspended antitrust laws and sanctioned industrial self-regulation through "codes of fair competition." Of more than six hundred codes drafted, the motion picture industry's was by far the longest and most complex. Though its president had been a member of the drafting committee, the Academy's continuing internal strife deprived it of the influence craved by the studio bosses, who saw the results as a government attempt to take control of their industry.

The talent groups, by contrast, feared that the new code would give producers even greater sway. Convinced that AMPAS was selling them out, a group of leading actors quit in July to form the Screen Actors Guild; they were proved right that autumn, when the details of the code were published, mandating ceilings on the salaries of writers, actors and directors—but not of studio executives. The code further stipulated that agents be licensed by the very producers with whom they would be negotiating; and it limited the freedom of artists with expired contracts, giving their studios renewal options before they could accept bids elsewhere. "The agency-licensing, salary-control and antiraiding provisions," as Murray Ross noted, " . . . aroused instant and widespread indignation. The knowledge that Reed, the president of the Academy, was a member of the committee which drafted the obnoxious provisions intensified the actors' resentment. The guild now had its issue."

Now the Academy began to hemorrhage actors. As Bosley Crowther points out, the real consequence of Mayer's maneuvering during the Bank Holiday crisis was "a spirit of rebellion toward the Academy that led to the genesis and strengthening of the Hollywood craft guilds." On October 4, 1933, at a meeting at the home of Frank Morgan (later to find fame as the Wizard of Oz), such prominent stars as George Bancroft, James Cagney, Gary Cooper, Ann Harding, Jeanette MacDonald, Fredric March, Adolphe Menjou, Robert Montgomery, Paul Muni and George Raft now agreed to resign en masse from the Academy and switch to the Screen Actors Guild. A mass meeting at the El Capitan Theatre on Hollywood Boulevard four days later resulted in a lengthy telegram to President Roosevelt complaining that "the motion picture companies have not been bankrupted by salaries to talent, but by the purchase and leasing of theaters at exorbitant prices, caused by the race for power of a few individuals desiring to get a stranglehold on the outlet of the industry, the box office."

By the following month membership had climbed to a thousand, and the SAG joined forces with a rejuvenated Screen Writers Guild. Jointly they published *The Screen Guilds Magazine*, whose editorial columns railed against the Academy, openly denouncing it as a company union. The Academy Award's reigning Best Actor, Fredric March, was elected SAG vice-president, as were former nominees Adolphe Menjou and Ann Harding. Groucho Marx, elected treasurer, claimed that he went straight to a brothel after being sworn in, on the thesis that "it was the only safe place to go."

The central issue was that of negotiating rights, and the freedom of actors to choose their own representative in contract dealings with the studios. "Hidden behind the mask of an arbiter of taste, and obscured under the cloak of research," as the Screen Actors Guild put it, "what the Academy is really trying to do is destroy the possibility of an honest actor organization—of, by and for actors." The Academy, in short, was trying to put the guild and all like it out of business. "The Academy cannot exist and claim jurisdiction over actors without throwing a constant harpoon into Guild efforts for betterment of actor conditions."

President Roosevelt himself became sufficiently alarmed to invite SAG's president, Eddie Cantor, to join him for the Thanksgiving weekend, during which he agreed to remove, by executive order, many of the code's antilabor provisions. Eighteen months later, in May 1935, the U.S. Supreme Court would declare the National Industrial Recovery Act unconstitutional anyway. But the Hollywood guilds had won a symbolic victory over their employers, and the Academy had been dealt wounds from which its political aspirations would never recover.

• • •

By the time of the sixth awards dinner at the Ambassador Hotel on March 16, 1934, the Academy had been severely shaken. It was perhaps just as well that there had been an unusually long delay of sixteen months since the last banquet. This was not merely due to the political turbulence that had lasted throughout 1933, but to a welcome attempt to stabilize the period of eligibility for awards. For four years, since the second awards, this had remained August 1 to July 31; now, with a switch to the more logical calendar year, the 1932–33 awards would cover the work of a year and a half (August 1, 1932, to December 1, 1933). But it was at least the end of the clumsy two-year dating system. Since 1934 the eligibility period has remained January 1 to December 31, with the stipulation that a film must be shown in at least one Los Angeles cinema for a full week before the expiry time of midnight on New Year's Eve. (The one current exception is the Foreign Language Film Award, whose eligibility year runs from November 1 to October 31.)

Despite eight months of political turmoil, there was a strong turnout for the sixth annual Academy Awards dinner, held in the Fiesta Room of the Ambassador Hotel. Louella Parsons, by now one of Hollywood's most powerful columnists, testified to the growing significance of the awards within the Hollywood community: "You'd be surprised how the greatest of stars who have won the coveted little bronze statues have them sitting in places of prominence in their homes."

Amid all the political strife, 1933 had seen the emergence of Katharine Hepburn as a major star for RKO, while MGM's whiz-kid head of production, the "Boy Wonder" Irving Thalberg, had succumbed to heart trouble and vanished to Europe to recuperate. In Thalberg's absence Mayer invited another whiz kid, his son-in-law David O. Selznick, to take charge of production at MGM. Selznick's first act was to hire George Cukor from RKO to make *Dinner at Eight*, another all-star adaptation of a Broadway play designed to emulate the success of *Grand Hotel*.

Busby Berkeley was meanwhile making a fortune for Warners with three hits in swift succession—*Forty-Second Street*, *Gold Diggers of 1933* and *Footlight Parade*, all starring Ruby Keeler and Dick Powell. The lack of Academy nominations for the latter two was an early sign of a now traditional resistance to both musicals and their stars. Fred Astaire and Ginger Rogers were already winning huge audiences for RKO; but neither would ever be nominated for their musical performances. Astaire finally received a nomination (as best supporting actor) in 1974 for *The Towering Inferno,* more out of nostalgia than anything else, while Rogers would be honored in 1940 for a rare success in a nonmusical, purely dramatic role, as Kitty Foyle. And Mae West, who was single-handedly keeping Paramount from going under, was of course nowhere near Academy respectability.

Two guild members found themselves nominated for 1932–33 awards despite their resignations from the Academy: Frances Marion for Original Story (*The Prizefighter and the Lady*) and Paul Muni as Best Actor for *I Am a Fugitive from a Chain Gang*. Both reluctantly decided to attend the dinner, despite Muni's conviction that he would not win because "Americans don't like American actors." Muni's chain gang stint—Hollywood's latest twist on the raw social themes explored by its highly lucrative gangster movies—saw him up against two British actors: the dashing Leslie Howard as an eighteenth-century time-traveler in Frank Lloyd's *Berkeley Square*, and Hollywood's unlikeliest new star, the rotund Charles Laughton, typecast as King Henry VIII.

Having been filmed in England, Alexander Korda's relish of the lusty King Hal encountered no problems from the Hays Office and other U.S. censorship pressures, thus offering American audiences a slice of the bawdiness they were missing in their own pictures. Audiences loved Laughton; and Thalberg's last act before succumbing to heart trouble had been to cast him opposite his own wife, Norma Shearer, in *The Barretts of Wimpole Street*—which would win Best Actress and Best Picture nominations the following year.

The only two nominees who didn't make it to the dinner were the two eventual winners: Laughton and Hepburn, both Hollywood outsiders, neither very popular choices among the resident community; local sentiment would apparently have favored May Robson and Leslie Howard. These sixth Academy Awards marked the first and only time in Oscar history that Louis B. Mayer went home empty-handed. Fox's Anglophile *Cavalcade* won Best Picture, moving one critic to remark: "If there is anything that moves the ordinary American to uncontrollable tears, it is the plight—the constant plight—

of dear old England." To Louella Parsons, Noel Coward's patriotic saga was "greater even than *Birth of a Nation*!"

But 1933 will be remembered as the year in which the Academy Award statuette finally acquired its celebrated nickname, hitherto used by jealous losers as a term of abuse. When the universally popular Walt Disney won Best Cartoon for *Three Little Pigs*, and affectionately referred to his award as "Oscar," the name passed securely into the language. Wrote Frances Marion: "Those who had never won the gold-plated honor referred to it disparagingly as the 'Oscar.' Since the arrival of the talkies, competition had become grueling and the sharp edge of jealousy had never worn off." But "when Walt referred to the 'Oscar,' that name took on a different meaning, now that we had heard it spoken with sincere appreciation."

Now that it could talk about "Oscar fever," Hollywood was quickly becoming obsessed with the whole business. Only six years after their birth, the Academy Awards were inspiring responses such as this from one of 1932–33's nominated directors:

> In the interim between the nominations and the final voting for the Oscars, I was shooting another comedy at Columbia, but my mind was on those Oscars. Day by day I kept persuading myself that I would win *four* awards. I looked up the records. No picture had ever won four major Oscars. It would set a record. Hot damn! I wrote and threw away dozens of acceptance speeches; practiced sly humility before the mirror; rehearsed emotional breaks in my voice at just the right spots. I ordered my first tuxedo—from a tailor, yet; rented a plush home in Beverly Hills—to be "seen," sway voters in bistros . . . I drove everyone nuts.

This fevered director was Frank Capra, who had won his first Oscar nomination for a Columbia comedy named *Lady for a Day*, an adaptation of a Damon Runyon story in which gangsters help an elderly apple seller pose as a rich lady when her daughter comes to visit. Up against Frank Lloyd for *Cavalcade* and George Cukor for *Little Women*, Capra took a table full of friends to the dinner and waited for the evening's host, Will Rogers, to announce the winner.

The first host to present all the awards himself, Rogers not unnaturally broke with traditional practice by making a big drama out of opening each envelope, thus inadvertently inaugurating another little bit of theater now at the heart of the Oscar ritual. After opening the directors' envelope, Rogers declared: "Well, well, well, what do you know. I've watched this young man for a long time. Saw him come up from the bottom, and I mean the bottom. It couldn't have happened to a nicer guy. Come on up and get it, Frank!"

Capra's table exploded into cheers. He himself has left us the best description of what happened next:

> It was a long way to the open dance floor, but I wedged through crowded tables, "Excuse me . . . excuse me . . . sorry . . . thank you . . . thank you . . . ," until I reached the open dance floor. The spotlight searched around trying to find me. "Over here!" I waved. Then it suddenly swept away from me—and picked up a flustered man standing on the *other* side of the dance floor—Frank Lloyd!

The applause was "deafening" as the spotlight escorted Lloyd onto the dance floor and up to the dais, where Rogers greeted him with a hug and a handshake. Capra stood "petrified in the dark, in utter disbelief, until an irate voice behind me shouted, 'Down in front.' "

Capra's walk back, through VIPs yelling "Sit down! Down in front! Sit down!" as he obstructed their view, was "the longest, saddest, most shattering walk in my life. I wished I could have crawled under the rug like a miserable worm. When I slumped in my chair I felt like one. All my friends at the table were crying."

The rest of the evening "compounded the hurt," as Hepburn beat May Robson to Best Actress, and *Cavalcade* squeezed *Lady for a Day* out of Best Picture. There followed hysterically drunken scenes at Capra's house, ending only when the host finally passed out. "Big *stupido*—running up to get an Oscar dying with excitement, only to crawl back dying with shame. Those crummy Academy voters; to hell with their lousy awards. If ever they *did* vote me one, I would never, never, NEVER show up to accept it!"

Frank Capra would renege on that vow only the following year, when his next film would achieve the first "clean sweep" of all the major Oscars—including, of course, Best Director. In the process, he would find himself cast as the potential savior of his beloved Academy Awards from a very real threat of premature extinction.

Among *Gone With the Wind's* eight Oscars in 1939 (from 13 nominations, a record which stood for twenty years) was Best Supporting Actress for Hattie McDaniel, the first black player to win an Academy Award.

The 1932–33 Best Actress, in *Morning Glory,* was Katharine Hepburn, who went on to become the Oscars' all-time champion, with four wins from twelve nominations.

Claudette Colbert won Best Actress for *It Happened One Night* (1934), the first film to sweep all the top honors, including Best Picture, Best Actor for Clark Gable and Best Director for Frank Capra, who became President of the Academy at its time of crisis.

5

1934–1940

The Capra Years

We had to do something.
The Academy was dying.
—Frank Capra, 1936

Frank Capra was six years old when his family left Sicily for California, where his father got a job as an orange picker. Young Frank, who would ever thereafter trade on his "Poverty Row" origins, proved bright enough to win himself a degree from the state Institute of Technology, though his sights were already set on the film industry. After service in World War I he took a series of menial laboratory jobs before graduating to gag writer—at first on the *Our Gang* silent comedies for Hal Roach, and then for Harry Langdon at the Mack Sennett studio.

Capra's direction of three short Langdon features brought him to the attention of Columbia's Harry Cohn, who offered him a deal that would radically alter both their fortunes. Cohn would pay Capra a mere $1,000 per film; in return, Capra would have the unheard-of right to script, direct and coproduce his pictures without any studio interference.

Though Capra's salary would rise precipitously, the terms of his contract never changed. Over the next thirteen years, the director's association with Columbia would not merely establish him as one of the dominant film talents of the day, but propel Cohn's small and struggling studio into Hollywood's major league. Capra, in the process, would make a lasting contribution to Hollywood history by pioneering the art of the small-scale film with which the mid-American moviegoer could identify, while most of his competitors played the usual Hollywood game of mounting ever bigger and more expensive spectaculars.

Capra's particular forte was the down-to-earth, small-town hero, the idealist who struggled against adversity in pursuit of quintessentially American dreams. *Lady for a Day,* the harmless hokum that had caused his 1933 Oscar night humiliation, was early evidence not just of a comic touch, but of an ability to orchestrate celluloid sentiment that had even hard-boiled intellectuals in tears. *Mr. Deeds Goes to Town* (1936), *You Can't Take It with You* (1938), *Mr. Smith Goes to Washington* (1939) and *Meet John Doe* (1941) were the highlights of a long list of movies, climaxing in 1946 with *It's a Wonderful Life,* which Americans cannot resist to this day. But his magic touch was first apparent in 1932, when Capra's next, even less promising film turned out to be the first of his timeless classics.

Killing time in a barber shop while scripting *Lady for a Day,* Capra had picked up *Cosmopolitan* magazine and found himself reading a short story by Samuel Hopkins Adams entitled "Night Bus." It had "the smell of novelty," and he got Columbia to buy the rights, which were available for "buttons." The project was forgotten during months of machinations between Cohn and Mayer, with Capra lent out to MGM for another movie that never got made. Back at Columbia, Capra resurrected "Night Bus," only to find Cohn resistant—"There are too many bus pictures"—and his first-choice cast playing hard to get.

Robert Montgomery turned down the lead primarily because it required him to travel on a bus. Having already stooped to this unglamorous mode of transport in a film called *Fugitive Lovers,* Montgomery decided once was enough. Clark Gable, on loan from Louis B. Mayer for "disciplinary" reasons—he had turned down too many custom-written MGM scripts—was reluctant to undertake the part for the same reason; riding on buses did not seem to Gable compatible with his image as a screen heartthrob. His eventual co-star, Claudette Colbert, was equally reluctant to cancel her ship to Europe for a bus to nowhere. Colbert was Columbia's fourth choice for the role; Myrna Loy, Margaret Sullavan and Constance Bennett had all turned down Capra and his script. Even Colbert agreed only when Columbia doubled her usual salary and guaranteed she would be free in time for Christmas: $50,000 for a month's work. Harry Cohn knew the path to Colbert's heart: "That French broad likes money." From this film on, her studio salary would triple to a stunning $350,000.

The transformation of a *Cosmopolitan* story into one of the big box-office movies of the day was due to a seminal piece of Hollywood thinking from a friend of Capra's named Myles Connolly. Adams's original story had a bohemian artist eloping—by bus—with a languid heiress. It was Connolly, an expert story editor, who pointed out the flaws in this scenario. It was easy, he told Capra, to see why so many stars were turning it down.

> Sure, you've got some good comedy routines, but your leading characters are non-sympathetic, non-interest-grabbing. People can't identify with them. Take your girl: a spoiled brat, a rich heiress. How many spoiled heiresses do you know? And how many give a damn what happens to them? She's a zero. Take your leading man: a long-haired, flowing-tie, Greenwich Village painter. I don't know any vagabond painters, and I doubt if you do. And the man I don't know is a man I'm apt to dislike, especially if he has no ideals, no worms, no dragons to slay. Another zero. And when zero meets zero you've got zero interest.
>
> Now. Your girl. Don't let her be a brat because she's an heiress, but because she's *bored* with being an heiress. More sympathetic. And the man. Forget that pantywaist painter. Make him a guy we all know and like. Maybe a tough, crusading reporter—at outs with his pig-headed editor. More sympathetic. And when he meets the spoiled heiress—well, it's *The Taming of the Shrew.* But the shrew must be worth taming, and the guy that tames her must be one of *us.*

Once the title too was changed, as a sop to Harry Cohn, *Night Bus* became *It Happened One Night,* and Capra had found a formula that would last him a decade. The film had opened in New York, to a subdued response, even before Capra's *Lady for a Day* embarrassment; but word-of-mouth endorsement turned it into the biggest box-office film of the year. Film critics kept going back to see, as Capra himself put it, "how such excitement could be generated by such routine material." The combination of rich and poor was a perfect diet for Americans still stunned by the Depression; the sight of Claudette Colbert showing a bit of leg to hitch a lift became a cinematic icon to anticipate Marilyn Monroe's windblown skirt in *Seven Year Itch.* "The only rule in filmmaking is that there are no rules," concluded Capra, "and the only prediction is that all predictions are by guess and by God until the film plays in theaters."

The film won 1934 Oscar nominations in five categories, one more than MGM's *The Thin Man.* The only serious opposition seemed to come from within. Following the success of MGM's *The Merry Widow,* Harry Cohn too grasped the significance of the celluloid operetta as the forerunner of the Hollywood musical, and signed the Metropolitan Opera star Grace Moore, whom Mayer had fired for being too fat. Commissioned to come up with a love story about an overweight opera star and her voice coach, Columbia's writers dreamed up *One Night of Love,* which proved one of the year's top money-makers, and garnered a total of six Oscar nominations—one more than *It Happened One Night.*

Bette Davis, according to *Life* magazine, had given "probably the best performance ever recorded on screen by a U.S. actress" in RKO's version of Somerset Maugham's *Of Human Bondage.* At its East Coast opening, audiences stood to applaud and cheer her as the credits rolled. But Hollywood had yet to warm to Davis, and Colbert's opponents for Best Actress were her Columbia stablemate Grace Moore and the perennial Mrs. Thalberg, Norma Shearer, this time for MGM's *The Barretts of Wimpole Street.*

Amid the continuing reverberations of the NRA dispute, the omission of Bette Davis gave the new guilds more ammunition with which to snipe at the Academy, which they had still not forgiven for taking the producers' side in their hour of need. Following the Screen Actors Guild's demand that its members resign from the Academy, there had been only ninety-five actors left to vote the 1934 nominations. Less popular than ever, and terrified that the growing furor over Davis might prove the demise of its awards, the Academy had little option but to give way to the flood of demands that the rules be changed to allow write-in votes. Nine days after the nominations had been announced, the Academy's new president, the writer Howard Estabrook, could only concede defeat: "With so many achievements of unquestioned merit each year, it is inevitable that certain differences of opinion should arise." But the awards committee had decided on a change of rules to allow write-in votes at the second stage of balloting, "despite the fact that the criticism fails to take into consideration that the nominations have been made by the unrestricted votes of each branch."

Now Bette Davis was the front-runner. When she announced that she would attend the dinner, scheduled for February 27 at the Biltmore Hotel, all three other Best Actress nominees decided that a Davis victory had become inevitable, and they would best conserve their dignity by staying away. By her own account, however, Davis herself was not so sure. As the day approached, "the air was thick with rumors. It seemed inevitable that I would receive the coveted award. The press, the public and the members of the Academy who did the voting were sure I would win! Surer than I!" Her main concern was that her employers, Warners, were doing nothing to promote her for the award. "It [*Of Human Bondage*] was an RKO picture, it is true; but I belonged to Warners, and it was to their profit if I won."

The Davis drama overshadowed the birth of a new award, for Film Editing, and the advent of one of the great Oscar sideshows: the Music awards, consistently entertaining down the years for the Academy's almost unerring instinct for honoring forgettable songs at the expense of future classics. That first year, the Best Song Oscar went to Con Conrad's "The Continental" (from *The Gay Divorcée*) over Vincent Youmans' "Carioca" *(Flying Down To Rio)* and Ralph Rainger's "Love in Bloom" *(She Loves Me Not)*.

For its first four years, the Scoring award was meanwhile handed to the studio's head of music rather than the relevant composer on his payroll; the lucky recipient in its first year was Louis Silvers, head of Columbia's music department, for music written for *One Night of Love* by Victor Schertzinger and Gus Kahn. The defeated nominees were both Max Steiner, head of RKO Radio's Music Dept., for music written for *The Gay Divorcée* by Kenneth Webb and

Samuel Hoffenstein and a score for *The Lost Patrol,* which he had actually written himself.

With a professional humorist, Irvin S. Cobb, in charge of the proceedings, it was inevitable that upon reaching Best Director he would simply say: "Come up and get it, Frank!" Capra had brought the same dinner guests as the previous year in the hope of exorcising his humiliation. The sweep continued when Best Actor went to Gable and Best Actress to Claudette Colbert. The Davis write-in campaign had flopped disastrously; the voting figures revealed that she had not even beaten either of the other two formal nominees. "It now appears," wrote *The New York Times*'s Hollywood correspondent, Douglas W. Churchill, "that the more fortunate candidates must have a Tammany-like organization behind them."

Davis blamed it all on Jack Warner, who had not wanted her to play the part of Maugham's "vicious bitch." Audiences would "hate it," he had argued; it would "ruin her career." But Davis, who had also missed out on Claudette Colbert's role in *It Happened One Night* because of Warners' intransigence, would not give up so easily this time. "I pestered him night and day to release me to RKO. . . . I begged and pleaded and finally he said, 'OK, go hang yourself.' " Now she claimed that, since her nomination, Warner had instructed his employees to vote for her opponents: "My bosses helped them by sending instructions to all their personnel to vote for somebody else."

The Davis scandal of 1934 was the first flagrantly public example of the major studios' cynical stranglehold on Oscar voting. "My failure to receive the award," she said, "created a scandal that gave me more publicity than if I had won it." Analysis of the awards' first seven years showed that Mayer's MGM had scored 155 nominations and 33 Oscars—twice as many as Warner Bros., three times as many as RKO and four times as many as Columbia—thanks entirely to menacing manipulation of the block votes at their command. Joan Crawford best summed up the dilemma of the contract stars: "You'd have to be some kind of ninny to vote against the studio that has your contract or produces your pictures. Your future depends on theirs . . . and if an Oscar means a better future, so be it."

As Davis fumed helplessly, an Academy flunky was persuading the Los Angeles railroad station to hold the Santa Fe Super Chief to New York so that a reluctant Claudette Colbert could disembark and dash back into town to pick up her award. She had left again by the time Cobb reached the envelope for Best Picture. "The winner is . . . you guessed it, it is something that . . ."—the audience finished his sentence for him—"happened one night!" Harry Cohn's triumph was complete. The Academy Award had confirmed its unique blessing on the studio, as well as the director, from "Poverty Row": Little Columbia had become Big Columbia.

It was the first "clean sweep" in Oscar history—Best Picture, Best Director, Best Actor and Best Actress—a feat that would remain unique for nearly forty years, emulated only by *One Flew over the Cuckoo's Nest* in 1975 and *The Silence of the Lambs* in 1991. *It Happened One Night,* wrote one critic of the day, was "something to revive your faith in a medium which could belong among the great arts." Forty years later, Pauline Kael of *The New Yorker* praised its ability to "make audiences happy in a way that only a few films in each era do. . . . It was the *Annie Hall* of its day—before the invention of anxiety." Across the Atlantic, *The Observer* called it "one of the most entertaining films that has ever been offered to the public."

To cap the success he had craved, and further exorcise the memory of those cries of "Down in front!," the boy from Poverty Row now found himself elected president of the Academy—an unenviable position in what turned out to be its year of greatest crisis, as the organization paid the price for a decade of misuse by Mayer and his cronies.

On January 15, 1936, six weeks before the eighth awards ceremony, dissident directors met at King Vidor's house and followed the actors and writers in forming their own breakaway guild. Double Oscar-winners Frank Borzage and Lewis Milestone were among those present. "No one can respect an organization with the high-sounding title of the Academy of Motion Picture Arts and Sciences which has failed in every single function it has assumed," said a statement printed in the guilds' joint newsletter. "The sooner it is destroyed and forgotten, the better for the industry."

Six weeks later, just three days before the Oscar banquet, the new guild sent telegrams to all its members urging them to boycott the occasion. According to the guild, producers were inviting their writers along as "a concerted move to make people think that Guild members are supporting the Academy," which was "definitely inimical to the best interests of the Guild." As James Cagney explained, "It was either that or give the group some tacit recognition. They were hoping that respect for the Oscar awards would help them keep the Academy in the labor business as a company guild."

Via its executive secretary, Donald Gledhill, the Academy swiftly professed itself "very much surprised by this sudden attack"; but it had decided to proceed regardless. "The awards are entirely nonpolitical, and have nothing to do with the labor problems. They are entirely based on achievement." But the guilds remained implacable, urging their members to have "nothing to do" with the Academy. To Capra, the new president, it seemed that "the odds were ten to one the Academy would fold" and the Oscar "acquire the patina of a collector's item." It was open war between the producing companies and the guilds. As Capra saw it, the leaders of the actors, writers and directors were out to undermine the Academy as a way to damage the studios commercially, by depriving them of the box-office value of the Oscars.

Academy membership had fallen from 600 to 40; its staff was down to just one, the redoubtable Margaret Herrick; and funds were low. Only its "dedicated but discouraged" board of governors stood between the ten-year-old organization and extinction. But Capra's attempts to defend it against the guilds were not helped by the fact that, "oddly enough, the shortsighted company heads couldn't care less. The Academy had failed them as an instrument of salary cuts during the bank-closing crisis." The studios withdrew their memberships and financial support, "leaving the derelict organization in the care of a few staunch Academy-oriented visionaries dedicated to the cultural advancement of the arts and sciences of filmmaking, and the continuance of the Awards"—to Capra, "the most valuable, but least expensive, item of worldwide public relations ever invented by *any* industry."

Among Capra's handful of "visionaries" who "crossed all economic battle lines" that year were Clark Gable and Frank Lloyd, both nominated, as director and actor, for Thalberg's latest $2 million brainchild, *Mutiny on the Bounty.* The 1935 contest otherwise centered again on Bette Davis, whose inevitable march toward Oscar status seemed to be foundering on her own contention that Katharine Hepburn had given the year's best performance in RKO's *Alice Adams.*

"A strikingly sensitive performance in a well-made bit of post-Pinero drama," enthused *The New York Times* of Bette Davis's dipsomaniac has-been actress, Joyce Heath, in *Dangerous.* Her leading man was a Mayer loan-out, Franchot Tone, who had made a name for himself opposite Jean Harlow and Joan Crawford (later his wife), and who had also managed to make his mark opposite Gable and Charles Laughton in *Mutiny on the Bounty,* MGM's most expensive venture since *Ben-Hur.* With the aloof Garbo again overlooked, despite her huge commercial success in *Anna Karenina,* RKO had high hopes of Hepburn and *Alice Adams*—and also of *The Informer,* their low-budget drama about a stool pigeon in the 1922 Irish rebellion, starring 49-year-old Victor McLaglen. Poor box office confirmed the studio's fears that its subject was too depressing, but the film garnered the kind of good reviews that impressed the Academy's voters.

Worried by such strong opposition, MGM had the bright idea of taking out advertisements in the trade press to solicit votes for *Ah, Wilderness,* a small-town Eugene O'Neill drama starring Wallace Beery, Lionel Barrymore and Mickey Rooney. Thus began a dubious Oscar tradition that has lasted to this day. The 1935 ads showed the film's title wrapped around an Oscar, about to be presented to MGM's Leo the Lion. But the film's main claim to fame would remain the fact that it sired the Andy Hardy series; Mayer's campaign failed to win it a single nomination.

With the studios still sulking, Capra and the Academy board were themselves obliged to pay for the 1935 statuettes. In the wake of the Bette Davis scandal, the new president also brought Price Waterhouse back in to ensure the "integrity" of the voting, which the same firm has done ever since. Voters were again allowed to ignore the nominations and write in any overlooked candidates of their choice. Jack Warner sent all Academy members among his employees a cable "suggesting" that they write in votes for Warners movies.*

Still fretting about the boycott threat, Capra had the bright last-minute idea of converting the awards banquet into a tribute to the director D. W. Griffith. It was a ruthlessly cynical move. To the

* For the first and only time in Oscar history, one write-in candidate actually won; the Cinematography award went to Hal Mohr for Warners' *Midsummer Night's Dream.* At home when he heard the news on the radio, the astonished winner quickly dressed up and rushed downtown to claim his prize.

studio bosses, Griffith was a has-been; the "father of American cinema," as he was already known, had long been denied Hollywood financing. But to Capra's delight, the great man was in the mood to make the trip; at 61 he had just married his fourth wife, and thought Hollywood might make a pleasant honeymoon destination.

Capra was mightily relieved. "We had to do something. The Academy was dying," he recalled. "And the upcoming Academy Awards banquet loomed dark and discouraging." Though Oscar history recorded its first standing ovation when Griffith entered the Biltmore ballroom, his prematurely aged features and snow-white hair merely underlined the opportunism of Capra's gesture. A decade of rejection by Hollywood had taken its toll on the movies' founding father. Even his presence could not give pause to the guilds, who subsequently declared their boycott a success, stating that only twenty members of the Actors Guild and thirteen of the Writers Guild had turned up.

Capra himself later claimed that the boycott had "fizzled," and that "most of the winners were there." But *Variety*'s impartial verdict at the time was that "there was not the galaxy of stars and celebs in director and writer groups which distinguished awards banquets of recent years. . . . Banquet tickets were liberally sprinkled to secretaries and others on the various lots as a result." Luckily for Capra the two most conspicuous winners, Victor McLaglen and Bette Davis, had indeed shown up. Her leading man, Franchot Tone, led a standing ovation as Davis picked up her award; all his new wife, Joan Crawford, could muster, however, was "Dear Bette, what a *lovely* frock!"

There was many a bitchy comment about the plain day dress Davis was wearing, having decided only at the last minute to attend the ceremony. Informed in the ladies' room by a fan magazine editor that her choice of dress "defiled the Academy," Davis hit back that it was "simple but very expensive," a "*dinner* dress"—and that her win was "a consolation prize" for the previous year's fiasco. "This nagged at me. It was true that even if the honor had been earned, it had been earned *last* year. There was no doubt that Hepburn's performance [in *Alice Adams*] deserved the award. These mistakes compound each other like the original lie that breeds like a bunny. Now she should get it next year when someone else may deserve it."

A 1934 write-in protest won Bette Davis a rule change—but no Oscar—for her performance opposite Leslie Howard in Pandro S. Berman's production of Somerset Maugham's <u>Of Human Bondage.</u>

Thalberg too was there to pick up the Best Picture award for *Mutiny on the Bounty*. But few other stars were on hand. *The Informer*'s John Ford and Dudley Nichols, who won Best Director and Best Screenplay, had stayed away.

Nichols now set an awkward precedent by refusing to accept his award—which spent the next few days winging back and forth between him and Capra. When the Academy sent his Oscar to his home the next day, Nichols sent it back with a note: "To accept it would be to turn my back on nearly a thousand members of the Writers Guild who ventured everything in a long-drawn-out fight for a genuine writers' organization." Capra stubbornly returned it with the reply: "The balloting does not in any way take into account the personal or economic views of the nominees nor the graciousness with which they may be expected to receive the recognition." But an implacable Nichols again returned it, and Capra was forced to admit defeat.

As treasurer of the Screen Directors Guild, would John Ford follow suit and spurn his Oscar? "I am proud to have the honor," said Ford. "If I had planned to refuse it, I would not have allowed my name to go in nomination." So why had he not turned up at the banquet? "Because I am not a member of the Academy." A few days later Ford accepted his statuette in an Academy ceremony carefully orchestrated by Capra, and was promptly voted out of office by the Directors Guild.

Thanks largely to D. W. Griffith, who was presented with a Special Award, Capra and the Academy had just survived. But urgent changes were clearly required before the 1936 awards, and Capra swiftly set about making them. While demanding of his board that the Academy finally vote itself out of the political arena, he tried to exorcise the awards' first chaotic decade by making the rules much more democratic.

For the ninth year of the Oscars, it was announced, nominations would be made by a special Awards Nominating Committee appointed by the president, consisting of fifty members from each of the five branches. The final vote was naturally to be retained by the full membership. The change came, said Capra, in response to criticism of the "allegedly political methods of choice. . . . We feel that this committee of fifty will be able to give the various achievements of the year more individual discussion and consideration than could be done by the old method."

Capra also dispensed with the isolationist wording of the Cinematography and Interior Decoration awards, which had hitherto insisted that all nominated films be made in the United States; and as an olive branch to the Screen Actors Guild, he introduced two further changes that would prove to be lasting. The number of acting nominees was increased from three to five, and a new category of awards was announced—Best Supporting Actor and Actress.

During the Oscars' first eight years, only three supporting performances had succeeded in winning acting nominations: Lewis Stone in *The Patriot* (1928–29), Frank Morgan in *The Affairs of Cellini* (1934) and Franchot Tone in *Mutiny on the Bounty*; all, unsurprisingly, had lost to leading players. Though the new categories were universally welcomed, even in their debut year they were marked by the kind of confusion and controversy that has dogged them ever since. After the studios had weighed up the opposition, Fox put forward Stuart Erwin, the leading player in its football comedy *Pigskin Parade*, for Best Supporting Actor, while MGM steered Spencer Tracy toward a Best Actor nomination for his supporting role in *San Francisco*.

But Capra's ingenuity had again paid off. In a message to all its members the Screen Actors Guild guardedly held out an olive branch by calling off its boycott:

> Last year the Screen Actors Guild asked its members to stay away from the Academy dinner. Despite the fact that the request was at the eleventh hour, it was almost uniformly honored. Since that time the Academy has largely kept out of producer-actor relations. It should do so entirely, since this is the function of the Guild—the organization chosen by the actors to represent them. The Guild this year intends to offer no objection to its members attending the dinner, reserving the right, however, to change its attitude in future years as the situation warrants.

The 1936 awards, however, had already been overshadowed by an event that shook the entire community. Norma Shearer had not made a film since the birth of her second child; ever the dutiful husband, Irving Thalberg had stage-managed her an upmarket return as Juliet to Leslie Howard's Romeo, directed by George Cukor. In the fall of 1936 Thalberg was busy preparing his next two projects

—Greta Garbo in *Camille* and Luise Rainer and Paul Muni in *The Good Earth*—when he collapsed and died at the age of 37. Though he had been plagued since childhood with heart trouble, the death of Mayer's "Boy Wonder" at the height of his powers caused universal grief; Shearer herself withdrew from society, not to reappear until the Academy Awards six months later, at which her Juliet naturally saw her nominated as Best Actress for a record fourth time.

The year's big hit was *The Great Ziegfeld,* a $2 million MGM musical extravaganza with William Powell in the title role, forging a partnership with the fresh new Viennese face of Luise Rainer, a former pupil of Max Reinhardt's. In what became the film's most celebrated scene, Rainer reduced audiences everywhere to tears as Ziegfeld's first wife, Anna Held, congratulating her ex-husband (by telephone) on his second marriage. The novelist Graham Greene, then film critic of the London *Spectator,* considered the three-hour extravaganza a "huge inflated gas-blown object," which "bobs into the critical view as irrelevantly as an airship advertising somebody's toothpaste." But Powell was strongly fancied for Best Actor, his main challenger being Paul Muni, who had finally persuaded Jack Warner to stop casting him in gangster movies, and turned in an admired portrait of the French chemist Louis Pasteur.

MGM employees made up the bulk of the voting membership, and seemed likely to offer Shearer a massive sympathy vote. Suggestions that the studio management wanted to make an Oscar star out of Rainer seemed doomed when Louis Mayer cursed her new husband, the playwright Clifford Odets, as "that lousy Communist." But some judicious horse-trading was usually enough to make Mayer overlook such minor details. The fact that Warners, with the second-largest block of voting members, had loaned him Muni for MGM's newly released *The Good Earth* was the key. Would Warners help MGM push *The Great Ziegfeld* for Best Picture if MGM helped their star to collar Best Actor?

That was just how it worked out at the Biltmore Hotel, on March 4, 1937. With Academy funds still at crisis level, Capra felt obliged to charge $5 for members and $10 for guests, with the best seats set at $25. It was nevertheless "a gay occasion," according to *The New York Times,* with more than a thousand seats sold, mostly via Mayer and Warner, whose joint power had sewn up the evening between them. The only real issue before the electorate, as the post-prandial announcements approached, was the intriguing contest between Shearer and Rainer for Best Actress.

One of the other nominees, Carole Lombard, had been led to believe she stood a good chance of victory. For all her recent widowhood, Norma Shearer already had an Oscar; and the voters figured Luise Rainer would be sure to win next year for *The Good Earth.* According to her biographer, Larry Swindell, Lombard possessed "good antennae for professional gossip. She intercepted a rumor that the smart money had switched to Carole Lombard. Soon a lot of people were saying they just *knew* she was going to win!" So Lombard went to the ceremony with her hopes high, reuniting for the evening with her ex-husband William Powell, also in nomination for *My Man Godfrey,* and making up a foursome with Clark Gable and Jean Harlow.

But Lombard learned her true fate by chance, when she and Harlow left the dinner to visit the powder room. The voting had ceased at five PM; although the results were not due to be announced until eleven, the press had been informed, under a strict embargo, at eight. The wait had proved too much for Gladys George, another Best Actress nominee for her "talkie" debut in a bit of Paramount nonsense called *Valiant Is the Word for Carrie.* A stroll through the pressroom had been enough for her to discover that Rainer had triumphed, after which she had withdrawn from the scene in tears. Mayer, she explained in a drunken slur, had decided to dump Shearer and build up Rainer's box-office appeal with an Oscar—or two.

Rainer was "going to win next year, too," sobbed George to Lombard and Harlow—prophetically, as it turned out. Rainer had recently garnered terrific reviews for *The Good Earth,* the late Thalberg's dream box-office bequest to Louis B. Mayer, a visionary pairing of tonight's Best Actor and Actress in one of next year's Oscar contenders. As most of the other Best Actress nominees comforted each other in the ladies' room, the source of their grief was the only one not to have turned up. MGM flacks, also privy to the secret, were even now at her home, with direct orders from the boss to "put on some makeup and get downtown." In vain did Rainer protest that she had just driven from San Francisco in an open car, and that her face was all red. Louis B. Mayer's orders were orders. Mr. and Mrs.

Odets duly arrived at the dinner at 10:30, just in time for the presentations.

Walt Disney had set another precedent by presenting an award to himself, his fifth successive Oscar. All Capra's efforts as Academy president were doubly rewarded with his second Best Director award, for *Mr. Deeds Goes to Town;* and the first Supporting awards—plaques, as yet, rather than statuettes—went to Walter Brennan and Gale Sondergaard. The Mayer-Warner plot was complete when Warners' *Anthony Adverse* walked off with four more Oscars. That the studios, especially Mayer's, seemed to have this thing under control did not go unnoticed. "The principal trouble with the Academy Awards," wrote *The New York Times*'s Churchill, "is the lurking suspicion of logrolling and political dealing."

Capra ended the evening by announcing the inception of the Irving G. Thalberg Memorial Award "for the most consistent high level of production achievement by an individual producer, based on pictures he has personally produced during the preceding year." The award, said Capra, was designed "to encourage the pride, the fortitude, the good taste and tolerance that put Thalberg into pictures. It is to keep permanent his message: The stars brighten the night, the laugher of children is a message to the ear. Irving would have liked that."

Irving would also have liked the 1937 Best Actress nominations, which pitched his two posthumous projects, Rainer in *The Good Earth* and Garbo in *Camille* against Irene Dunne *(The Awful Truth),* Barbara Stanwyck *(Stella Dallas)* and the first Oscar winner, Janet Gaynor, in the very first version of *A Star Is Born.* *

Postponed for a week by a freak flood, the tenth awards dinner at the Biltmore on March 10, 1938, marked a Capra-inspired rapprochement between the Academy and the guilds, each of whose presidents attended: nominee Robert Montgomery for the actors, King Vidor for the directors and Dudley Nichols for the writers. The truce had been most firmly signaled by Nichols's recent decision to accept the Oscar he had previously spurned for *The Informer*.

Capra's sense of theater continued to shape the Awards into an

* This "original" version of *A Star Is Born* was itself based in part on *What Price Hollywood?* (1932), produced by Pandro S. Berman and directed by George Cukor.

ever more spine-tingling event. This year, for the first time, the results would be kept secret even from the Academy's officials until the press was informed immediately before the dinner. Before presenting the first clutch of Oscars, Cecil B. de Mille's remark that the Academy was "now free of all labor struggles" seemed slightly compromised by the bestowal of the first Irving Thalberg Award on Darryl F. Zanuck, one of the Academy's staunchest supporters during those very struggles. Its perennial capacity to misjudge music was then confirmed by the award of Best Song to something called "Sweet Leilani," from a Bing Crosby musical called *Waikiki Wedding,* rather than Gershwin's "They Can't Take That Away from Me" (from Astaire and Rogers's *Shall We Dance*).

But the highlight of the evening, then as now, was the identity of the man who came up to accept Alice Brady's Oscar as Best Supporting Actress in *In Old Chicago.* Everyone knew Brady was at home with a broken ankle, but few knew the face of the supposed representative who graciously accepted the award on her behalf. He walked out of the dinner and was never heard of again. When Brady protested that she hadn't received her Oscar, they gave her another one at an informal ceremony two weeks later. The imposter was never found.

In his acceptance speech, Best Director Leo McCarey (for *The Awful Truth*) confirmed another emergent Oscar trend by acknowledging that it was a consolation prize for his failure, the previous year, to be nominated for *Make Way for Tomorrow.* "Thanks," he told the voters, "but you gave it to me for the wrong picture." Surely the Academy would now, for the same wrong reasons, reward Greta Garbo?

The main shock of the evening was Garbo's defeat by Rainer, who became the first player to win successive acting Oscars. Garbo, by contrast, had become the first great talent to pay the price of refusing to play the game by Hollywood's rules—she acted too aloof from Tinseltown ever to be taken to its bosom—and Rainer had set a trend by winning for sheer versatility. The previous year she had shone as a forlornly abandoned show business wife, this year in the unlikely guise of a Chinese farmer's wife, O-lan, in MGM's $3 million version of Pearl S. Buck's epic novel *The Good Earth.*

Rainer had enshrined playing against type as an Oscar bonus;

but she now found herself frozen out by Mayer. "The industry seemed to feel," she later testified, "that having an Academy Award winner on their hands was sufficient to overcome bad story material, which was often handed out afterwards to stars under long-term contract." Soon she found herself labeled temperamental. The Oscar had brought about "a change of one's image felt by others but not by oneself. One was acclaimed now; therefore one's doings, one's motives, one's every utterance seemed to have a greater dimension and therefore suddenly became suspect. It seemed harder to continue one's work quietly."

Within six years she had fled for the New York stage. In two interviews with Charles Champlin of the *Los Angeles Times,* fifty years later, she explained why. "I was in Hollywood too early, I think. Now actors can take only the roles they want to. When you were under contract, you had to do roles whether you liked them or not. I fought. I was not so much glamorous as clamorous. I was full of fire and enthusiasm and very hard on myself."

After eight films in three years, Rainer made a precipitous exit in 1941. "I'm leaving . . . after two difficult years," she told *Movie Mirror* magazine. "It isn't only that I've been working so hard. It is that I have felt I have had no vital contact with either life or reality in the past months." Though she had said she was leaving for six months, Rainer never returned to films. After her divorce from Odets —it had, she said, been a marriage with "Strindberg-scale troubles" —she married a London publisher, Robert Knitter, and allowed her career to slip into decline. "I was simply too young and unsophisticated to handle it."

Though she could never bear to watch her Oscar-winning movies—"All I can see is the pain in my eyes"—Rainer came to regret her precipitous decision to quit while ahead. She had made intermittent forays onto the stage, and found a second career as a painter, but she always felt she had wasted her talent: "I've always felt guilty about not having continued to work. I should have made fifty more pictures. . . . I loved the work, and I still deeply love the work, but nothing around it—the negotiations, the arguments, none of that.

"I feel like that song of Piaf. She dies and goes to heaven and St. Peter won't let her in. She says, 'Look at my hands,' and he looks and says, 'Come in.' He will look at me and say, 'You haven't even started. *Go back.*' "

Luise Rainer is now remembered as the first victim of the "Oscar curse." In her own words, "I won Academy Awards for my first and second pictures. Nothing worse could have happened to me." On a nostalgic visit to Hollywood in 1983, she asked the Academy to replace one of her Oscars, which she was rumored to have broken in a fit of pique. "Actually it wasn't broken at all," she protested. "I think it got so tired standing there holding that sword all those years, it just collapsed."

Paul Muni had got it wrong. Though nominated again, last year's winner had decamped for a European vacation, telling Jack Warner: "Nobody wins two years in a row." He was right about himself—though *The Life of Emile Zola,* in which he had played the title role, earned ten nominations and won Warner his first Best Picture award. But he was proved wrong by Rainer—and by Spencer Tracy, a beaten nominee the previous year for *San Francisco,* who now won the first of two successive Oscars.

Tracy had hated both his Portuguese accent and his curly hairdo for Manuel in *Captains Courageous,* which saw him beat Muni's Zola to Best Actor. Muni and Fredric March, also nominated, were the two Hollywood actors he most admired, besides Lionel Barrymore. Tracy was "surprised, even apologetic," according to Larry Swindell, when he heard of his nomination; he still considered his Manuel "a poor showing, and felt Lionel Barrymore should have been recognized instead."

Hospitalized after a hernia operation, Tracy burst into tears when his wife, Louise, telephoned to say he had won. He would have been even more moved had he heard the banquet tribute to his dedication from Barrymore, his colleague and mentor. Then Louis B. Mayer took to the stage—impromptu, proprietorially—to add his own unique point of view:

> I'd like to praise Spencer Tracy's sense of discipline. Tracy is a fine actor, but he is most important because he understands why it is necessary to take orders from the front office . . . because he understands why it is wise to obey directors . . . because he understands that when the publicity department asks him to cater to certain visitors, it is a necessary inconvenience.

When the studio head's words were relayed to him, Tracy asked whether they amounted to a compliment or a threat. He had already turned in the performance that would see him named Best Actor again the following year: the part of a real (and, at the time, still living) priest called Father Flanagan in *Boys Town,* the story of a correctional home of that name in Nebraska. Seventeen-year-old Mickey Rooney was given a Special Award for his role as a juvenile delinquent in the film. Tracy evidently had no use for a second Oscar. "If you have seen Father Flanagan through me," he said, "I thank you." Adding that the Oscar really belonged to Flanagan, with whom he had forged a strong friendship, he subsequently presented it to him, with the inscription:

> To Father Edward J. Flanagan, whose great human qualities, timely simplicity and inspiring courage were strong enough to shine through my humble effort.

Nineteen thirty-eight had meanwhile seen Frank Capra become the first director to have his name in lights alongside those of his stars—"above the title," as he proudly recalled in the title he gave his memoirs. Amid his continuing labors for the Academy, Capra had managed to make a huge box-office hit of a stage comedy, George S. Kaufman and Moss Hart's *You Can't Take It with You.* So thoroughly did Capra now dominate the Hollywood scene that the Directors Guild offered his work for the Academy an unexpected tribute: they elected him guild president as well.

Thrown in at the deep end, Capra soon found himself head-to-head with Joseph Schenck, boss of both Twentieth Century Fox and the Association of Motion Picture Producers. When Schenck refused to accord the Directors Guild sole negotiating rights for directors, Capra mobilized the directors to threaten a strike. More drastically, with the Academy Awards only a week away, he threatened to resign his presidency of the Academy and mount a boycott of the dinner.

Schenck quickly backed down, and Capra's triumph was redoubled with a Best Picture–Best Director double for *You Can't Take It with You.* The Academy had resisted the temptation to give Best Picture to a cartoon, Walt Disney's *Snow White and the Seven Dwarfs,* the year's most successful picture with a box-office gross exceeding $4 million. But Disney made it six out of six successive cartoon wins with *Ferdinand the Bull.* And he was given a Special Award for *Snow White*—doubly special in that it consisted of an Oscar plus seven dwarf Oscars. It was handed over, of course, by Shirley Temple.

Nineteen thirty-eight was also the year that Bob Hope's theme song, "Thanks for the Memory," won Best Song, and was then reprised as the perennial host graced the Awards show for the first time. It was perhaps as well for Hope's future career that one of the Best Screenplay nominees, George Bernard Shaw, had never had the slightest intention of showing up. Shaw's involvement with Hollywood had been trouble from the start.

"Not the least regard will be paid to American ideas, except to avoid them as much as possible," Shaw had said when commissioned by Gabriel Pascal to write a screen version of his play *Pygmalion.* What Shaw meant by this, according to his official biographer, Michael Holroyd, was that *Pygmalion* should have been advertised as an "all British film made by British methods without interference by American scriptwriters, no spurious dialogue but every word by the author, a revolution in the presentation of drama on film." This typically Shavian exaggeration, as Holroyd points out, "was soon spoken of as having lifted moviemaking from illiteracy to literacy, thus compelling Hollywood, at long last, to take on real writers."

In truth, GBS was protesting too much. For all Shaw's blustering, Pascal had persuaded the great man to change the ending, so that the professor (Leslie Howard) got the girl (Wendy Hiller) in true Hollywood style. Pascal was not the only director that year to have persuaded Mayer to let him soothe British sensibilities by filming in England; Robert Donat had fled from Hollywood after a grim time making *The Count of Monte Cristo,* and the only way King Vidor could persuade him to star in *The Citadel* was to take his cameras across the Atlantic. Howard, Hiller and Donat were all nominated, as were both films for Best Picture. But the only winner was Shaw for Best Screenplay. "It's an insult for them to offer me any honor," he responded, "as if they had never heard of me before—and it's likely they never have." The old curmudgeon was sent his statuette anyway, and sightings of it prominently displayed on his mantelpiece at Ayot St. Lawrence were reported over a period of many years by visitors from Mary Pickford to Wendy Hiller.

Fay Bainter had achieved a first by winning nominations as both Best Actress and Best Supporting Actress; though she lost the first to her costar in *Jezebel,* Bette Davis, she duly picked up the second. These were the only pleasures of an otherwise disappointing evening for Jack Warner, who had expected James Cagney *(Angels with Dirty Faces)* and John Garfield *(Four Daughters)* to complete a Warners sweep of the acting awards, with *The Adventures of Robin Hood* scooping Best Picture. Not even *Alexander's Ragtime Band* could prove a match, however, for Capra's latest triumph.

For Davis, her second Oscar meant enhanced status with Jack Warner, whom she had unsuccessfully tried to sue for higher pay and greater script control. When she met him again now, she was "no longer the spunky little colonial asking for more representation from His Highness"; she was "a sovereign state demanding my own tithe—a member of the Commonwealth. . . . I had never been able to keep my mouth shut, but now mine was a voice that couldn't be ignored."

Among future Oscar winners attending their first banquet that night was 20-year-old Joan Fontaine, who was horrified to overhear a publicist from Warner Bros., Davis's studio, saying: "This is the last time Davis will win if I have anything to say." What could Davis possibly have done to this woman? Perhaps, Fontaine surmised, Bette "had failed to send her a Christmas present that year, had not waved to her across the set with enough warmth." According to Frances Marion, jealousy "was understandable among the women, so the men said." This did indeed prove to be Davis's last Oscar—and the beginning of a bitter disillusionment with the studio system for Fontaine, whose own Oscar three years later was also to prove a mixed blessing.

The Best Picture category was as crowded as ever, with ten nominees jostling for votes, and the Hollywood extras still confounding the studios' best efforts to control them. After last year's Best Song fiasco, which was squarely laid at their door, the 4,500 extras were now deprived of their block vote in the music awards. But their local muscle ensured their continued involvement in Best Picture and the acting categories, where they would always favor stars who had worked their way up from their ranks. The limit of five nominees for each of the acting awards now seemed to be giving those categories some semblance of order, for all the backstage chicanery. But the Best Picture race would remain an overattended party for another few years yet.

Nineteen thirty-nine was the Academy Awards' *annus mirabilis.* Ten great films, any of which might have won in other years, were nominated for Best Picture. Though *Gone With the Wind* was a worthy victor, that year's losers included *The Wizard of Oz, Mr. Smith Goes to Washington, Stagecoach, Wuthering Heights, Goodbye, Mr. Chips, Ninotchka* and *Of Mice and Men.*

Most of these movies have stood the test of time as modern classics. But how would respectable films like *Love Affair* and *Dark Victory*, also nominated that year, have fared if the rules restricted nominations to just five pictures, as in the Academy's original rules, reapplied today? Just five films were nominated in the first four years of the Oscars, but the pressure was such that in 1931–32 it was increased to eight; the following year to ten; and to twelve in 1934 and 1935. For the next eight years (1936–43), ten films competed annually for Best Picture—which made for extremely fierce competition, but also split the voting with some eccentric results. Not until 1944 did Best Picture finally join all the other main categories on a limit of five nominations, which has remained in place ever since.

Nineteen thirty-nine had seen Garbo turn comedienne in *Ninotchka* and Dietrich revive her screen career in *Destry Rides Again.* But Dietrich got nowhere near any awards, and Garbo fared little better. Given the intense competition that year, it is interesting in retrospect to see the New York Film Critics splitting their votes four ways, giving Best Actor to James Stewart for *Mr. Smith,* Best Actress to Vivien Leigh for *Gone With the Wind,* and Best Director to John Ford for *Stagecoach.* No fewer than thirteen ballots failed to break a tie for Best Picture between *Mr. Smith* and *Gone With the Wind,* so the critics cut their losses and gave it to *Wuthering Heights.* The Academy's voters would reach different results in all but one case.

When Hollywood announced its nominations, David Selznick's *Gone With the Wind* stole an early march on the opposition, setting a record of thirteen (which would last eleven years). Fearful of an unseemly guerrilla war between the studios, the Academy issued a dictum pleading for "no electioneering or lobbying, as there has been in the past." But Selznick's opponents had targeted the Director category as their best shot for foiling a clean sweep for Selznick. John Ford's work on *Stagecoach,* went the word, was by contrast "a feat of supreme directorship in making an ordinary story into a great film." Victor Fleming, moreover, was but the last of three directors to have worked on *Gone With the Wind*, which was anyway recognized as primarily Selznick's achievement.

Not to be outsmarted, Fleming cunningly put it out on the grapevine that Selznick was taking too much credit for the film, thus turning himself into a directorial martyr worthy of his colleagues' heartfelt sympathy. It was enough to win him a narrow victory over Ford. Ironically enough, illness prevented Fleming from attending the awards banquet, and it fell to Selznick to collect his statuette for him. His film's dominance of the awards by now had him in good enough humor to pay his director a generous public tribute.

The real surprise of Vivien Leigh's win, as *Gone With the Wind*'s sweep of the 1939 awards gathered pace, was that she stopped Bette Davis making it two in a row and thus realizing her ambition to become the first actress to win three Oscars. Now universally acknowledged as the consummate screen actress, Davis was also big box office; voted the second most popular actress in the United States, behind only Shirley Temple, she had starred in four hits that year alone: *Dark Victory, Jezebel, The Old Maid* and *The Private Lives of Elizabeth and Essex.*

Sensing that all opposition was doomed, MGM had tried to win some late support for Garbo with the highly dubious suggestion that she was contemplating U.S. citizenship. As for Dietrich, an administrative error saw *Destry* released hours after the deadline. Vivien Leigh, moreover, was not hindered by the trills of delight that greeted a Best Actor nomination for her lover (not yet her husband), Laurence Olivier, in *Wuthering Heights.* Larry was to lose to his friend Bob Donat, and to face a tough few weeks swallowing his pride as Mr. Vivien Leigh throughout all the *Gone With the Wind* hoopla; ever the patriot, however, he had the consolation that for the first time both top acting awards had gone to Britain.

Donat's victory was very narrow—a matter of "only a few votes," according to *The New York Times*—and as much of a surprise as Leigh's. He too had beaten that year's number one U.S. box-office star, Mickey Rooney *(Babes in Arms),* as well as the very popular Jimmy Stewart *(Mr. Smith Goes to Washington)* and Clark Gable in *Gone With the Wind,* which permeated every aspect of every award. The film's blessing fell upon those of its players who had had time to make other films, such as Thomas Mitchell, who won Best Supporting Actor for *Stagecoach;* but its curse fell upon its writer, Sidney Howard, who was run down by a tractor on his Massachusetts farm between the nominations and the ceremony, thus becoming the first person to win a posthumous Oscar. *Gone With the Wind*'s Best Supporting Actress, Hattie McDaniel, was not merely the first black person to win an Oscar, but the first to attend an Academy banquet as a guest rather than a waitress.

Selznick had faced charges of racism from some quarters of the American left, typified by the verdict of the American Labor Party that *Gone With the Wind* constituted "an insult to President Abraham Lincoln and the Negro people." As the chances of an Oscar for Hattie McDaniel had grown, however, black newspapers swallowed their initial complaints in favor of hymns to the artistry of the film's black performers, above all McDaniel. When Frank Capra and Fay Bainter pulled her name from the envelope, there was scarcely a dry eye in the Ambassador Hotel's Coconut Grove ballroom as the first black Oscar-winner concluded her graceful acceptance speech: "I sincerely hope that I shall always be a credit to my race, and to the motion picture industry." Later, she told Louella Parsons: "I love Mammy [her character in GWTW]. I think I understood her because my own grandmother worked on a plantation not unlike Tara." McDaniel's award, wrote the *Atlanta Constitution,* delighted all "genuine" southern people; and the Academy was widely hailed for its display of liberalism, in stark contrast to the tide of world events.

With a total of ten statuettes—including a Special Award for "mood enhancement" to its production designer, William Cameron Menzies, and an otiose Irving Thalberg Award to Selznick—*Gone With the Wind* set an Oscar record that would last twenty years. "What a wonderful thing," cracked Bob Hope, "this benefit for Selznick." But the man himself was still not satisfied; far from congratulating his publicist, Russell Birdwell, as they drove together to the celebration party, the producer could only complain: "I don't know why we didn't get the Best Actor award for Gable. Somewhere you failed. You didn't put on the proper campaign. Otherwise Clark would have been sure to get it." Birdwell was so hurt that he stayed away from the studio until Selznick called to apologize: "I was a pig. I worked so hard and I waited so long, I got piggish and I wanted everything."

Capra himself directed a documentary of the 1939 Awards show, having aided the Academy's bank balance by selling the "short subject" rights to Warners for $30,000. After five years in office, he left the presidency on a high note. The Academy's political problems appeared solved. From now on it would concentrate on the Academy Awards, and develop its educational and research functions, leaving labor negotiations to the guilds. Capra affirmed as much in his farewell speech: "I believe the guilds should more or less conduct the operations and functions of the institution." By the following year his successor, Walter Wanger, struck a more modern note by declaring it his intent to concentrate on the Academy's public relations, ensuring that they "are maintained on the same level as the great steel, iron and motor industries." Capra's cameras caught first-time nominee Alfred Hitchcock, on the verge of his career as one of the Academy's most conspicuous omissions. napping during Wanger's speech.

Nineteen forty saw Selznick fighting to maintain his momentum. The hysteria he had created over the casting of Scarlett O'Hara had certainly been one of the keys to *Gone With the Wind*'s huge public success; but it was always a long shot to try recreating it over the casting of Hitchcock's *Rebecca,* opposite Olivier's Maxim de Winter. There was thus much local satire over the eventual choice of Joan Fontaine; Olivia de Havilland's younger sister, according to one Hollywood wit, was perfect because she would already have a built-in inferiority complex.

Rebecca's main competition in the Best Picture stakes appeared to come from John Ford's *Grapes of Wrath,* hailed by Otis Ferguson as "the most mature motion picture ever made," and Chaplin's first talkie, *The Great Dictator.* In a final, desperate bid for two successive Best Pictures—which was to work, setting another Oscar precedent—Selznick repremiered *Rebecca* during the voting period in a cinema on Hollywood Boulevard, which he persuaded the governor of

California and the mayor of Los Angeles to rename Rebecca Lane for the duration. His reward was eleven nominations for *Rebecca*—the second successive year that Selznick had led the field.

Back on Broadway, Katharine Hepburn had driven an unusually hard bargain for starring in *The Philadelphia Story:* on top of her usual salary, a percentage of the box office *plus* the film rights. Once it headed for Hollywood she was able to call in her favorite director, George Cukor. The result was to be another all-time classic, the inspiration for a popular musical version, *High Society*—and a third nomination, but no second Oscar, for Hepburn. The East Coast ice maiden was undismayed: "Prizes are nothing. My prize is my work."

Even in defeat, however, Hepburn's influence upon the Oscars, like *Gone With the Wind*'s, seemed all-pervasive. It was thanks to Hepburn's status as RKO's resident dramatic actress that Ginger Rogers had found herself locked throughout the 1930s in a chain of big box-office musicals and light comedies, and an immortal partnership with Fred Astaire. But now Hepburn decided that she didn't want to make "a soap opera about a shopgirl," and rejected the title role in *Kitty Foyle,* the tale of a white-collar career girl with a turbulent love life. Rogers was able to insist on it. "The most daring novel ever written by a man about a woman!" shrieked the billboards, and Ginger won rave reviews, hailing the "one-time Interstate Circuit hoofer" who had given "a spirited top-flight dramatic performance, the equal of anything seen on the screen in years." RKO parlayed the critical acclaim into a series of trade-press advertisements, and Ginger Rogers won the only Oscar of her career—adding weight to the theory that the Academy resists musical stars, and poignancy to its failure ever to vote an award to Fred Astaire.

After seeing *Kitty Foyle,* Astaire had written Rogers a letter she made public in 1991, after his death, which ended by saying that her "solid" performance "*should* bring you the highest honors anyone can win!" This, she said, was the letter she treasured from among the many that flowed in—including one from Katharine Hepburn: "I am very jealous, but most happy for you." All Hollywood was genuinely delighted by the success of the girl who had battled her way up from the chorus line—as David O. Selznick's own note to Ginger confirmed, even though she had beaten his own candidate, Joan Fontaine: "Throughout the industry there was great satisfaction and pleasure over your recognition, and also the charming way in which you received the honor."

Among the evening's more gracious losers—in retrospect, anyway—was Fontaine, who was neither "surprised nor sorry" to lose to her friend. "For me to have won it with my first good role would have been precipitous. The voters might well have thought Hitch was my Svengali—that after so many undistinguished performances in the past, surely it was Hitchcock who had mesmerized me into the performance I was nominated for." Fontaine would not have long to wait for her compensation, even if it was eventually to turn sour on her.

For Hitchcock, another of the night's losers, *Rebecca* would prove the first of five unsuccessful nominations over twenty years, even though it won Best Picture. For Chaplin, who had garnered two nominations for *The Circus* in the very first Academy Awards, his fruitless citations as actor and director for *The Great Dictator* would prove his last. Despite the honorary awards that inevitably came their way, both their names will always remain at the top of the list of Hollywood iconoclasts never voted an award by their peers (see Chapter 11).

Oscar history shows that versatility is often a cunning route to victory: play two very different roles in one season, and the heavier one's chances of nomination soar. As recently as 1990, Robert De Niro stole one of the year's runaway hits, *Goodfellas,* from its other stars, but it was *Awakenings,* in which he portrayed a victim of a brain disorder, that won him his fourth Best Actor nomination; the following year Nick Nolte's nomination for *The Prince of Tides* was due in part to a contrasting role opposite De Niro in the simultaneously released *Cape Fear.* Back in 1940, Henry Fonda latched on to the same idea, ensuring that his Oscar-caliber role in *The Grapes of Wrath* was cunningly followed by a comedy lead in Preston Sturges's *The Lady Eve.*

But James Stewart was also the only Best Actor nominee to turn up at the awards show—another, simpler way of gaining favor with the authorities. "I voted for Henry Fonda," revealed Stewart, "but of course I also voted for Alfred Landon and Wendell Wilkie." Fishing for marlin off Mexico with John Ford, Fonda declared himself "mighty pleased" that his friend Stewart carried the day, for *The*

Philadelphia Story, over Chaplin, Olivier's Maxim de Winter and Raymond Massey as Abe Lincoln. Poor Chaplin was even this year's victim of the perennial aberration of the extras; their block vote ensured the Best Supporting Actor award for one of their own graduates, Walter Brennan, over the popular Jack Oakie's remarkable performance as "Napaloni" (alias Mussolini) in *The Great Dictator.* The Supporting awards had been in existence a mere five years, but Brennan's Judge Roy Bean in Goldwyn's *The Westerner* saw him extend his monopoly to three wins out of three nominations.

But it was the *Los Angeles Times*'s breech of the previous year's results embargo that prompted the most significant innovation of the 1940 awards dinner: the introduction of those momentous sealed envelopes that are now so crucial a part of the Oscar ritual. By attempting to curb, even punish the excesses of the press, the Board of the Academy had inadvertently invented one of the keys to the phenomenal growth of their awards in subsequent decades. So potent was the new element of suspense that even the press could see that it was no use protesting. The Oscar phenomenon was taking shape.

An ambitious President Walter Wanger had invited his White House counterpart, Franklin D. Roosevelt, to grace the proceedings; though tempted, the president had been obliged to concede that the worsening situation in Europe required him to stay in the White House. He did, however, seize the chance to honor the Academy by beginning the awards banquet with a six-minute radio address, simultaneously broadcast to the nation. FDR praised Hollywood for its fund-raising efforts, and its filmmakers for sanctifying "the American way of life."

As Judy Garland sang "America" down the radio line back to the president, and to the listening nation, there was a sense that even the Oscars might soon have to adjust to war.

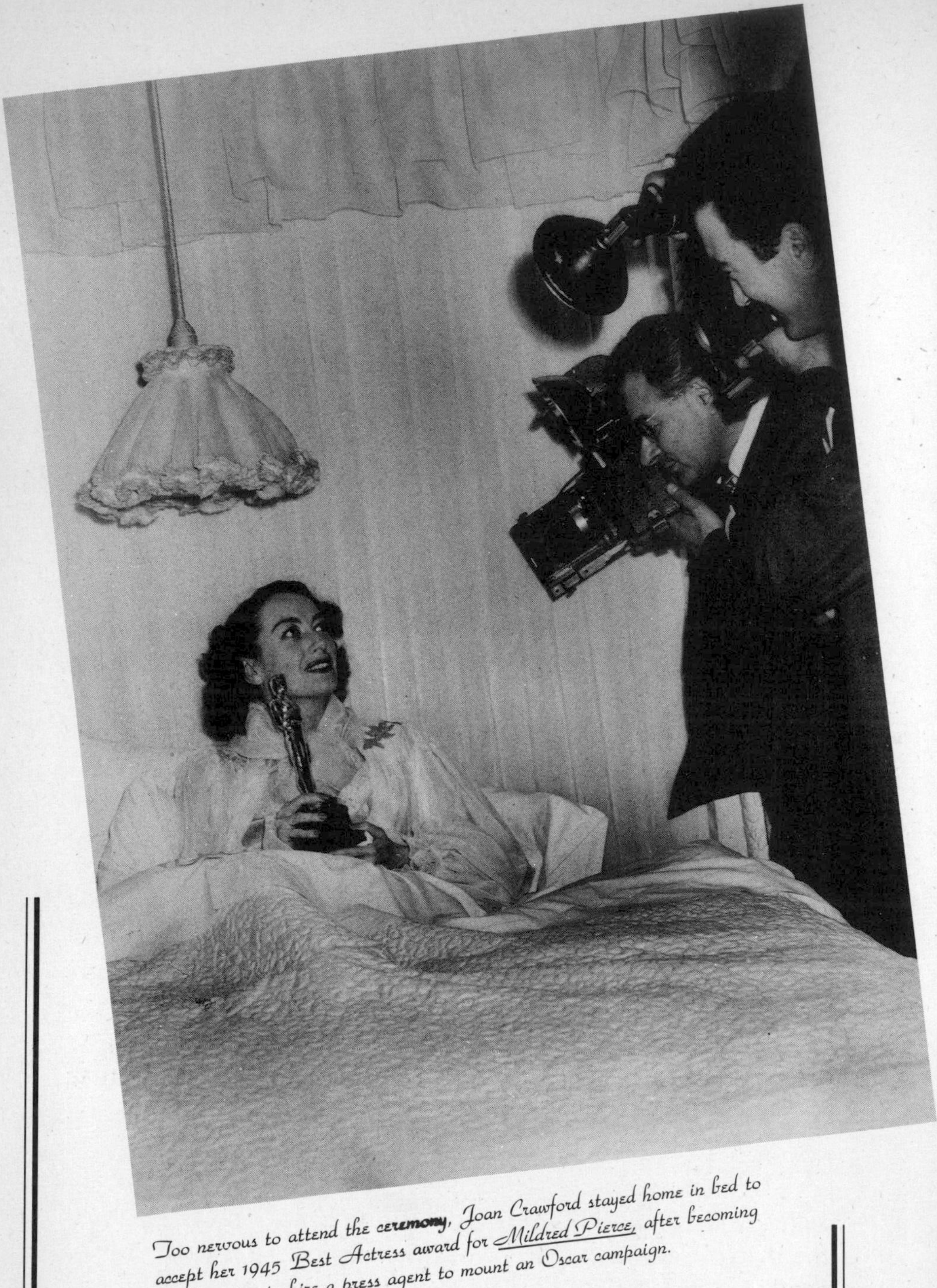

Too nervous to attend the **ceremony**, Joan Crawford stayed home in bed to accept her 1945 Best Actress award for Mildred Pierce, after becoming the first star to hire a press agent to mount an Oscar campaign.

6

1941–1947 The Oscars Go to War

That Oscar can be a jinx.
. . . It's an uneasy head
that wears the crown.

—Joan Fontaine

Ten months before Pearl Harbor, it was Hollywood showmanship that had seen the 1940 Technical awards presented by a producer listed in the program as Lieutenant-Colonel Darryl F. Zanuck. When war finally arrived, it fell to the unlikely figure of Bette Davis to show the way.

Davis was the newly elected president of the Academy, in succession to Walter Wanger. "I never imagined that I would hold this exalted post. As the only woman so honored, I was frankly proud." But she soon discovered that she was expected to be a supine figurehead—"on the face of their past experience with me, an unwise assumption."

Davis arrived at her first meeting with full knowledge of her rights of office. She had even studied the bylaws. "It became clear to me that this was a surprise. I was not supposed to preside intelligently." She felt like "an heiress at a deceased father's board of directors' meeting," but considered herself "quite capable of holding a gavel."

The board was "horrified," Davis recalled, by her first suggestion: that the usual sumptuous banquet would be inappropriate in time of war. Her alternative idea was that the awards be handed out at a ceremony held in a large public theater—at a cost of $25 a seat, with the proceeds donated to British War Relief. Davis went on to recommend that her friend Rosalind Russell (then Hollywood's leading organizer of charity events) be asked to stage-manage the occasion. Wanger, the outgoing president, eventually broke the silence by reminding Davis that she had won two Oscars, and asking her, "What have you got against the Academy?"

Given the blackouts required since Pearl Harbor, some adjustments did seem to be needed to a ceremony now accustomed to lighting up the California sky. But surely this was too drastic. The board's fears seemed to be confirmed by protests that a glitzy Oscar night was just what was required to take people's minds off the war. But it nevertheless voted for compromise.

In December came an official announcement that this year there would be no Oscar banquet. The awards would be presented in "a different format," as yet undecided. It was rumored that Davis was threatening resignation. When Zanuck heard, according to Davis, he told her that if she quit, she would "never work in this town again." Davis "took a chance and resigned anyway," with an official statement pleading ill health and pressure of work. That her protest had struck a chord with Academy members was soon demonstrated by her fifth Best Actress nomination, for *The Little Foxes.*

With Wanger back, filling the breach as acting president, the board announced at the end of January 1942 that it had changed its mind; it was reinstating the banquet, "to boost civil morale," but on a more modest scale. It would, for instance, be referred to as a "dinner"; tickets would be reduced from $25 to $10; there would be music, but no dancing; formal dress would not be worn; and ladies were requested not to wear flowers, but to donate the money they would have spent on them to the Red Cross.

Despite fears of a low turnout, a record 1,600 people attended the fourteenth Academy Awards ceremony at the Biltmore Hotel on February 26, 1942—among them many female stars who had blithely defied their orders not to dress up. American flags, rather than flowers, garlanded the entrance, and flags of the Allies decorated the hall. The guest of honor was Wendell Wilkie, the Republican presidential candidate defeated by Roosevelt in 1940, whose top table seat was overlooked by a giant American bald eagle.

Two of the evening's early results saw Oscar habits turn into Oscar traditions: that Walt Disney should receive at least one award every year; and that Best Song would always provoke a row or a joke result, or both. Nineteen forty-one proved no exception, with Disney notching his tenth Best Cartoon award for *Lend a Paw* as well as picking up two Honorary Oscars, one of them the Irving Thalberg award, for *Fantasia,* his first box-office flop—while his *Dumbo* also won Best Score. Meanwhile, the long-suffering extras again took the rap for giving Best Song to Jerome Kern's "The Last Time I Saw Paris"—which, as the losers pointed out, should not have been eligible since it was not written specifically for the movie in which it was featured, *Lady Be Good.* Even Kern himself, who had first published the song two years before, said as he collected his statuette that he had voted for Harold Arlen's "Blues in the Night."

But the central drama in the Biltmore that evening was the competition between the two volatile sisters nominated for Best Actress. Capitalizing on the success of *Rebecca,* Selznick had cast Joan Fontaine opposite Cary Grant in her second successful Hitchcock film, *Suspicion;* Paramount, meanwhile, had high hopes that Olivia de Havilland's strong performance in *Hold Back the Dawn,* as a teacher duped into a phony marriage by Charles Boyer, would remind the Academy of her gracious loss two years before to Hattie McDaniel.

Only later did de Havilland confess that it was not at first so gracious. For two weeks after losing to McDaniel, she confided, she had been "convinced there was no God." While realizing that McDaniel deserved the award, de Havilland had found on the night that she "couldn't stay at the table another minute. I had to be alone; so I wandered out to the kitchens and cried." It took a fortnight for her to be able to feel "very proud . . . that I belonged to a profession which honored a black woman who merited this, in a time when other groups had neither the honesty nor the courage to do the same sort of thing."

Would tonight make amends—or would her sister prove a second Hattie McDaniel? Joan Fontaine had not planned to attend the dinner, telling Jean Hersholt, the Academy's new president, that she was not in the habit of staying up so late; she had to be up at 6:30 the next morning, as usual, to be at the studio by eight. Hersholt enlisted her big sister Olivia, a staunch Academy member, to twist her arm: "You have to be there. Your absence would look odd." When Joan protested that she didn't have anything to wear, Olivia came around to her studio dressing-room "within an hour . . . with our usual saleslady from I. Magnin."

With both sisters seated at Selznick's table at the Biltmore Hotel that evening, the stage was set for a sibling rivalry saga to whet any producer's appetite. It fell to the reigning Best Actress, Ginger Rogers, to open the envelope and announce that the winner was the younger sister, Joan Fontaine, only 23. "I froze," recalled Fontaine, who stared across the table at de Havilland. "Get up there," whispered her sister. When she did, she burst into floods of tears. "All the animus we'd felt toward each other as children," Fontaine recalled, "the hair-pullings, the savage wrestling matches, the time Olivia fractured my collarbone, all came rushing back in kaleidoscopic imagery. My paralysis was total. . . . I felt age four, being confronted by my older sister. Damn it, I'd incurred her wrath again!"

Fontaine's Oscar was clearly a consolation prize for missing out to Ginger Rogers the previous year. This was her second and de Havilland's first nomination as Best Actress (though de Havilland had also lost out the previous year in the Supporting category). "It was a bittersweet moment," said Fontaine. "I was appalled that I'd won over my sister." But Olivia de Havilland would proceed to her revenge with two Best Actress Oscars, in 1946 and 1949, while her sister was to receive just one more (unsuccessful) nomination in 1943. De Havilland may have lost this battle, but she was determined to win the war.

For a contract star like Fontaine, Oscar success could be double-edged. In the Academy Awards' first three decades, it brought great financial rewards for the star's studio—which had, of course, helped manipulate the award—but little for the performer. In Fontaine's case, her official loan-out fee from Selznick International jumped from $25,000 to $100,000 after her first nomination, for *Rebecca,* and to $200,000 after she won Best Actress for *Suspicion.* Fontaine herself saw only a small percentage of this booty, remaining on her pre-Oscar contract of $13,000 a year, while being badgered by the studio to buy a large house with servants, several cars, maybe a yacht or a racehorse—all "necessary for the star's image."

From Selznick's point of view, the loan-out price increase maximized his asset, scaring off rival producers who might otherwise have hired her; from Fontaine's, it was a new twist on the old theme of the "Oscar jinx." After *Rebecca,* for which she was paid $250 a week, she never made another film for Selznick, who loaned her out throughout the rest of her seven-year contract. She was also obliged to miss out on "wonderful offers from Broadway" and "great possibilities at other studios" unless Selznick could get his asking price. If she tried to refuse a loan-out role, telegrams "as long as a roll of bathroom tissue" would arrive at her home telling her she was "ungrateful, arbitrary and temperamental," and threatening suspension—which could mean an unwelcome extension of the contract. In her memoirs, Fontaine gives due credit to her sister for a 1944 Supreme Court of California ruling known as the de Havilland decision, which released all contract players from having to serve time added to their contracts through suspensions.

In the contract era, when the studios held such a financial stranglehold on their stars, Oscar winners could benefit only when their terms came up for renegotiation. Even the first Best Actress, Janet Gaynor, said her salary tripled after the award; fifteen years later, his 1942 Oscar enabled the hard-bargaining James Cagney to up his worth from $140,000 to $360,000.

By the fifties, and the twilight of the contract system, individual stars could benefit much more directly from winning an Academy Award. As early as 1962, after his Oscar for *On the Waterfront,* Marlon Brando's fee leaped to $1.2 million for the commercially unsuccessful *Mutiny on the Bounty.* In 1951, he had turned in his first nominated role, in *A Streetcar Named Desire,* for a paltry $75,000.

For Fontaine, the Oscar curse took yet another form: typecasting. "One critic for the *Saturday Night Review* said I could only play simps. But my simping became suddenly more expensive. Selznick charged a lot more for my services." By the last role of her contract, *The Emperor Waltz* for Paramount, her loan-out fee was $225,000—of which she received $75,000—"minus my agent's commission."

As Selznick earned millions loaning out Fontaine, as a custom-built simp in movies like *Jane Eyre,* he fulfilled another of the Oscar's darker rules by claiming all the credit for her success. The man who had once described Fontaine as "the hardest woman in Hollywood to get a performance out of" was now saying: "She could have become a top star at no place else but Selznick. . . . I nurtured her."

So it was not only her lifelong feud with her sister that turned Joan Fontaine's Oscar triumph sour. She was the first leading actress since Luise Rainer to find the consequences of victory distinctly double-edged:

> Winning an Academy Award is undoubtedly a great accolade, supreme praise from one's peers, a recognition to be accepted gratefully and graciously. It can also damage irreparably one's relations with family, friends, co-workers, the press. In those days, winners of the Oscar seemed like minor members of royalty suddenly elevated to the throne. All eyes watched to see the slightest sign of arrogance, inflated ego, disdain. The press clamored for home sittings, still photos, any scrap or tidbit to fill the endless gossip columns, fan magazines, Sunday supplements. One suddenly had international recognition, the best table in restaurants, preferential treatment wherever one traveled. It was a fishbowl existence until the next year's awards, when a new winner would occupy the throne. Naturally, there was many a doubter, many a detractor, many an ill-wisher. It's an uneasy head that wears the crown.

If sibling rivalry had provided the main buzz of the 1941 awards, the fourteenth Oscars have since gone down in movie history as the night the Academy snubbed Orson Welles. In the more dramatic judgment of Pauline Kael, chronicler of *Citizen Kane,* February 26, 1942, was the night the Academy "destroyed" Orson Welles. "They failed in what they believed in; they gave in to the scandal and the business pressures. They couldn't yet know how much guilt they *should* feel: guilt that by their failure to support *Citizen Kane* at this crucial time—the last chance to make *Kane* a financial success—they had started the downward spiral of Orson Welles, who was to become perhaps the greatest loser in Hollywood history."

When he was still in his early twenties, Welles had been brought to Hollywood by RKO's George J. Schaefer on the urgings of Nelson Rockefeller, then the studio's president. With RKO in the doldrums, financially and artistically, Rockefeller had taken a more than passing interest in the national uproar caused on Halloween 1938 by Welles's radio broadcast of H. G. Wells's *The War of the Worlds;* so realistically had he adapted the story of a Martian landing into an apparently live radio news bulletin that thousands of Americans had fled their homes in terror. So committed was Welles to stage and radio drama, and so suspicious of Hollywood, that he was able to hold out against Schaefer's blandishments until offered a deal unprecedented for an *enfant terrible* with no movie experience at all: complete control of his own set, and everything that happened on it. After a few false starts with what he called "the biggest toy-train set any boy ever had," Welles made a movie no studio would normally have touched.

It was Herman Mankiewicz, an experienced Hollywood writer who had worked on some of Welles's *Mercury Theatre of the Air* radio scripts, who originally had the idea of a "prismatic" biopic. Intrigued by the idea of telling one man's life story from several different points of view, Welles jumped at it when "Mank" suggested a character almost openly modeled on William Randolph Hearst, the California-based proprietor of the world's largest newspaper empire. An immensely gifted writer, then in a downward spiral fueled mainly by alcohol, Mankiewicz had been a regular guest of Hearst and his mistress, Marion Davies, at San Simeon, their opulent castle in the California hills.

Mankiewicz, at the time, was recovering from a series of broken bones caused by his alcoholic accidents. To keep him sober while he worked on the script, Welles dispatched him to a rented house in Victorville, well out of harm's way, for the three months it took him to finish the first draft. Mankiewicz's nurse, a Mrs. Alexander (from whom the Marion Davies figure in the film, Susan Alexander, took her surname) doubled as the secretary to whom he would dictate each morning and evening, regaling her with stories of Hearst, Davies and San Simeon—Xanadu in the film—during their lunchtime and afternoon breaks.

Even before shooting was finished, Hearst had got wind of its contents, thanks to another drunken indiscretion by Mankiewicz, and was making threatening noises to the studio. RKO films were mentioned either unfavorably or not at all in the Hearst press; and Hollywood as a whole was made to feel that his wrath might spill over into the entire system. It was very much to Schaefer's credit, therefore, that he refused an offer made by Louis B. Mayer, acting on Hearst's behalf, of a cash payment of $842,000 if RKO would destroy the negative and all prints of *Citizen Kane.* As the film had cost only $686,000, this amount would also have covered a fair proportion of postproduction expenses.

But the fear Hearst had inspired throughout the movie industry ensured that RKO found very few outlets willing to show its film, which did poor business despite sensational reviews. Welles and his cameraman, Gregg Toland, had broken new ground in the art of filmmaking, pioneering the use of deep-focus camera techniques that have since passed into the cinematic language. The sheer dash and style with which Kane's story is told, pointedly eschewing the sentimentality typical of Hollywood's portraits of giant figures have rarely been matched. Since its release in 1941, *Citizen Kane* has consistently been voted number one in international film critics' annual lists of all-time great movies—and still is to this day. The film "marked a new epoch," wrote Archer Winsten of the *New York Post* at the time. "The most sensational film ever to come out of Hollywood," said Bosley Crowther in *The New York Times,* "a great motion picture . . . a few steps ahead of anything that has been made in pictures before." Orson Welles, predicted the *Film Daily,* could "prepare his mantel for a couple of Oscars."

Citizen Kane swept the New York critics' awards and earned nine Oscar nominations, as against ten for John Ford's *How Green Was My Valley* and eleven for Howard Hawks's *Sergeant York.* Ford's childhood memoirs of a Welsh mining village earned acting nominations only in the Supporting categories; but Hawks's timely slice of Americana, the true tale of a simple hillbilly who became a World War I hero, won Gary Cooper his second shot at Best Actor. All three were on the list of ten films slated for Best Picture; nominated as *Citizen Kane*'s sole producer, Welles himself was also up for Best Actor, Director and Writer—a feat to remain unique until Warren Beatty's *Heaven Can Wait* in 1981.*

* In 1977 Woody Allen was nominated as Best Actor, Director and Writer for *Annie Hall,* but he was not the film's producer. *Annie Hall* did win Best Picture for its producer, Charles H. Joffe (and Best Actress for Diane Keaton). In 1981 Beatty again received all four major nominations, for *Reds.* In 1990 *Dances with Wolves* won Best Picture for Kevin Costner, who was also nominated for acting and directing; it also won the Screenplay Oscar for Michael Blake.

Welles's joint nomination for Original Screenplay was the only Oscar he won that night, or any other Oscar night to come, and it was probably the only one that he did not deserve. Minute investigation into the genesis of *Citizen Kane*—one of the perils of making a cult movie—casts doubt on Welles's right to have claimed even joint authorship with Mankiewicz. The definitive inquiry into the authorship (and many other aspects) of *Citizen Kane* was conducted for *The New Yorker* in 1971 by its film critic Pauline Kael, who concluded that "Welles could do so many different things in those days that it must have seemed almost accidental when he didn't do the things he claimed to. . . . If ever there was a young man who didn't need unearned credits, it was Orson Welles."

But to those who worked with Welles, as with so many other directors, this was nothing new. "Directors, in the theatre and the movies," as Kael put it, "are . . . cavalier towards other people's work, and Welles was so much more talented and magnetic than most directors—and so much younger, too—that people he robbed of credit went on working with him for years." Besides, his contract with RKO stated that "the screenplay for each picture shall be written by Mr. Orson Welles." In Kael's view, Welles took this stipulation as no more than his due—a necessity of his station. "He probably accepted the work that others did for him the way modern Presidents accept the work of speechwriters."

Kael's research shows that Welles "made suggestions" in his early conversations with Mankiewicz, "received copies of the work weekly while it was in progress at Victorville," and "may have given advice by phone or letter." He certainly made suggestions for later cuts that helped Mankiewicz "hammer the script into tighter form," and he is known to have made a few changes on the set. But the evidence of Mrs. Alexander—who took the dictation from Mankiewicz "from the first paragraph to the last," continued her secretarial work on the revision of the first draft, and remained in charge of the script at the studio until after the film was shot—was damning: "Welles didn't write (or dictate) one line of the shooting script of *Citizen Kane.*"

One of Welles's biographers, Frank Brady, has more recently defended Welles's "legal, artistic and moral right" to be listed as one of the film's writers. Brady argues that Welles was concerned about the stipulation in his contract that he write his own screenplays. Besides, according to Brady, "all the people who worked on the film have since confirmed that Welles did substantial writing and editing of the script; the RKO corporate ledgers also list Welles as having worked no less than 111 days on the script alone."

The first of these two claims is unconvincingly vague; and the second may, of course, be based on figures disguised by Welles because of his concern over his contract. But Brady also disputes Kael's claim that Mankiewicz would have got no credit at all had he not been proud enough of his work to appeal to the Screen Writers Guild for help. Brady quotes the guild's attorneys as saying that the matter was beyond their jurisdiction, while Kael suggests that it was the guild that finally won Mankiewicz the right to prior billing over Welles as author of the original screenplay. Kael also believes that "it is unlikely, under the present rules of the Writers Guild, that Welles would have been entitled to any writing credit at all."

Now that all the relevant parties are dead, it is equally unlikely that the vexed issue of the authorship of the *Citizen Kane* shooting script will ever be satisfactorily resolved. One key player who could have helped, Joseph Cotten, merely testified with a sigh: "More works of conjecture have been written on the screenplay of *Citizen Kane* than Orson and Herman were ever able to cram between those blue covers." Brady attacks Kael's essay as "a virtual tome" that aspired "to elevate Mankiewicz's position as the principal screenwriter on the film." But he cites merely "some people" as suggesting that "it was Mankiewicz, not Welles, who acted as the disreputable one in this legendary controversy."

The New Yorker's critic was being cruel only to be kind. Kael went to such detailed lengths in her essay, "Raising Kane," because of her belief that Welles was otherwise robbed of his due, his potential, and the rest of a uniquely promising career by the political troubles that beset the release of *Citizen Kane*—and because Hollywood's timid self-interest, combined with its jealousy of Welles's youthful success and talent, caused the film industry to abandon him to his fate.

"Had it not been for the delays and nervous atmosphere that made the picture *seem* unpopular and so *become* unpopular, it might have swept the Academy Awards. It had taken the New York Film

Critics awards with ease, but early in 1942, when the 1941 Academy Awards were given, the picture had the aroma of box-office failure—an aroma that frightens off awards in Hollywood." At the ceremony, each time the title or Orson Welles's name was read, "there were hisses or loud boos. . . . The prize for the Original Screenplay was partly a love gesture to Herman Mankiewicz, one of their own; the film community had closed ranks against Orson Welles."

The night that Joan Fontaine triumphed over her sister was thus also the night that Gary Cooper, John Ford and *How Green Was My Valley* completed a shameful triple over Orson Welles and *Citizen Kane*—which will always rate top of the long list of distinguished films to have been bypassed, for whatever arcane or passing reason, by an Academy aberration.

"Like most of the films of the sound era that are called masterpieces," as Kael concludes, "*Citizen Kane* has reached its audience gradually over the years rather than at the time of its release." But Welles had directed "what is almost universally acclaimed as the greatest American film of the sound era." Had it not been for his rejection by Hollywood, he "might have become the greatest all-around American director of that era"; instead, "in his inability to realize all his artistic potentialities, he is the greatest symbolic figure in American film since Griffith." Kael lays the blame squarely on the movie industry itself, with the withering indictment that it is "always frightened, and is proudest of films that celebrate courage."

Neither Welles nor Mankiewicz was on hand to pick up his statuette. Welles was said to be scouting South American locations (for a movie that never materialized), while Mankiewicz had stayed home because, according to his wife, "he did not want to be humiliated. He thought he'd get mad and do something drastic when he didn't win." Whether or not the two men had already fallen out—opinions, again, differ—the record shows that they never worked together again.

Bette Davis and *The Little Foxes* were also overlooked that night, as Ford and his saga of the Welsh valleys became the mass beneficiary of the anti-Welles backlash. *How Green Was My Valley,* which won Darryl F. Zanuck his first Best Picture award, was the last of the nominated films to be released, prompting *Variety* to suggest that it was simply "short memories" which had shut out the year's other great films, which included John Huston's *The Maltese Falcon.* Rumor again had it that those hapless extras had done in Welles, leading *Variety* to conclude: "To them a genius can't be a good guy." The sentiment was echoed by Alva Johnston in a 1942 restrospect on the whole affair in the *Saturday Evening Post.* "Genius," he concluded, "got a bad name on account of Orson Welles."

As befitted the first full year of America's war, the Academy's board of directors decreed that the Oscars would be made of plaster for the duration, all metal being needed for the war effort.

At the next awards dinner at the Ambassador Hotel on March 4, 1943, Private Tyrone Power and Private Alan Ladd unfurled a giant flag bearing the names of 27,677 of Hollywood's own who had "answered Uncle Sam's call." Colonel Frank Capra was on hand to present the Director's award and to receive one for a documentary he had made about the U.S. Army. A message from President Roosevelt congratulated Hollywood on "turning the tremendous power of the motion picture into an effective war instrument without the slightest resort to the totalitarian methods of our enemies."

The president was too tactful to mention that war was also proving big box office and helping the studios back into their best financial shape since the 1929 crisis. Patriotism being the theme of the year, its most successful products were Warners' *Yankee Doodle Dandy,* starring an all-singing, all-dancing James Cagney as the showman George M. Cohan, and Louis B. Mayer's weepie about an English war widow, *Mrs. Miniver.* Once Mayer had seen due publicity accorded a letter he received from Winston Churchill, describing *Mrs. Miniver* as "propaganda worth a hundred battleships," MGM's box-office winner also became a surefire Oscar favorite. Among its twelve nominations was Best Screenplay for the writing team that adapted Jan Struther's best-selling collection of short stories, reaching its crescendo with a climactic sermon preached in a bombed church by Henry Wilcoxon:

> This is not only a war of soldiers in uniforms. It is a war of the people—of all the people—and it must be fought not only on the battlefield but in the cities and in the villages, in the factories and on

> the farms, in the home and in the heart of every man, woman and child who loves freedom. . . . We have buried our dead, but we shall not forget them. Instead, they will inspire us with an unbreakable determination to free ourselves and those who come after us from the tyranny and terror that threaten to strike us down. This is the people's war. It is our war. We are the fighters. Fight it, then. Fight it with all that is in us. And may God defend the right.

Set in a "rose-strewn English village, Hollywood variety," according to the English film historian Leslie Halliwell, *Mrs. Miniver* "provided a beacon of morale despite its false sentiment, absurd rural types and melodramatic situations. It is therefore beyond criticism, except that some of the people involved should have known better."

Mrs. Miniver won Best Picture for Mayer, Best Director for William Wyler (his first, at his fifth nomination) and Best Actress for Greer Garson, whose performance in the title role moved *Variety* to speak of her "knee-weakening smile." It also scooped a deserved Supporting Oscar for Teresa Wright; Cinematography for Joseph Ruttenberg; and Best Screenplay for the writing team, which included James Hilton, the English author drawn to Hollywood by the success of his novel *Goodbye, Mr. Chips.*

But for sheer flag-waving, the moist-eyed sentiments of *Mrs. Miniver* were small beer beside the patriotic fervor attending the premiere of *Yankee Doodle Dandy* at New York's Hollywood Theatre. Jack Warner charged seat prices as high as $25,000, making $5.75 million for the U.S. Treasury and plenty more for himself as the film became Warners' highest-ever grosser. Warners' writers, too, knew how to build a climax, which saw Cohan visiting the White House to accept the thanks of President Roosevelt for writing an alternative national anthem.

"Where else in the world," said Cagney's Cohan, "could a plain guy like me sit down and talk things over with the head man?"

"Well now, you know, Mr. Cohan," replied Captain Jack Young as the president, "that's as good a description of America as I've ever heard."

The part of Cohan—opposite his sister Jeanne as Cohan's sister Josie—wrought some kind of apotheosis for Cagney, exorcising a decade of Hollywood battles. Originally dismissed as "a little runt" by Howard Hughes, who threw out Zanuck's idea of casting him as Hildy Johnson in *The Front Page,* Cagney had proved perfect for the hot new genre of the early 1930s, the gangster movie. As a rising young actor he had grown accustomed to working long, hard hours for Warners until he finally made his name in *The Public Enemy*—the film in which he also won a lasting place in movie history by becoming the first man to hit a woman onscreen. Of the moment Cagney shoves a grapefruit into the face of his moll (Mae Clarke), Bosley Crowther wrote: "This was and remains one of the cruelest, most startling acts ever committed on film—not because it is especially painful, except to the woman's smidgen of pride, but because it shows such a hideous debasement of regard for another human being."

If Edward G. Robinson was gangsterism's number-one star on the strength of *Little Caesar, The Public Enemy* firmly installed Cagney as number two. When Warner Bros. brought them together in 1931 for *Smart Money,* Cagney had been dismayed to find that the title did not reflect his fortunes. His paycheck did not rise, as the studio had promised, now that his films had become commercial hits. Already known, in his own phrase, as a "professional againster," Cagney also believed he was working too hard and taking unnecessary physical risks. When the studio refused to acknowledge its promises, and threatened him with suspension, he simply walked out of Hollywood. In vain did the *Hollywood Reporter* publish an open letter urging him to think again.

After the success of a comedy called *Blonde Crazy,* however, Warners felt themselves obliged to take Cagney back at $1,000 a month. After three more commercial hits—*Taxi, The Crowd Roars* and *Winner Take All*—he still believed he was not earning enough. Some Warners stars, he knew, were making $100,000 a film. The studio was making millions, and Cagney thousands, out of his pictures. So out he walked again.

Late in 1932 the Academy called in Frank Capra (not yet its president) to negotiate a settlement. Cagney had agreed to a deal whereby he received $3,000 a week with increases that would bring him to $4,500 a week by 1935. He was also granted his demands for a maximum of four films a year, and top billing in all of them. Given that Dick Powell was on $6,000 a week, and Edward G. Robinson and

Sibling rivalry was a feature of 1941, as Joan Fontaine (ABOVE, in Hitchcock's *Suspicion*) beat her sister Olivia de Havilland (in *Hold Back the Dawn*) to the Best Actress award . . . and scandal, as Orson Welles (BELOW) became the first person to win nominations as actor, director, producer, and writer for *Citizen Kane*—but won only a share of the screenplay award.

Douglas Fairbanks on $4,000, Capra appeared to have won Warners a pretty good deal.

Cagney had also negotiated himself some dancing roles amid more gangsterdom. By 1935, however, he found himself clocking five films in twelve months, some of them with second billing, and staged his third walkout. It was quite unprecedented for an actor to lock horns with a major studio like this. Though Cagney won his case, making two $100,000 films for a rival studio while doing so, he was a proven enough money-maker for Warners to be keen to have him back. A new deal was struck guaranteeing him $150,000 a picture plus a percentage of profits, at a maximum work rate of two films per year. It was in one of these, for his Rocky Sullivan opposite Bogart and Pat O'Brien in *Angels with Dirty Faces,* that he had won his first Oscar nomination in 1938.

Yankee Doodle Dandy, which had begun filming the day after Pearl Harbor, was Cagney's last contract movie for Warners, freeing him to form his own production company with his brother William, who had produced it. His magnetic performance deservedly won him Best Actor over Ronald Colman *(Random Harvest),* Gary Cooper *(The Pride of the Yankees),* Walter Pidgeon *(Mrs. Miniver)* and Monty Woolley *(The Pied Piper).* Cagney accepted with Cohan's famous line from the film: "My mother thanks you, my father thanks you, my sister thanks you, and I thank you." Soon afterward he was elected president of the Screen Actors Guild, and found himself invited to the White House for real, to perform some numbers from the film at President Roosevelt's birthday party. Asked late in life which of his movies was his own favorite, Cagney replied: "I guess it'd have to be the Cohan picture."

The year's other notable war epic was Noel Coward's *In Which We Serve,* a naval drama based on the experiences of Lord Louis Mountbatten when his ship, HMS *Kelly,* was sunk beneath him. Coward, the film's star, producer, author, composer, scriptwriter and codirector (with the young David Lean), was consoled with a Special Oscar for being shut out of the awards by a last-minute rule change, which brought the eligibility deadline back from January 12 to December 31—"to allow eight weeks, rather than six, to consider nominations."

Nineteen forty-two was the year a cowboy star named Don Barry tried (in vain) to organize a write-in vote for a rising young actor named Ronald Reagan (in *Kings Row*). It was the year Irving Berlin followed Disney's precedent by opening the envelope to find that he must present the award to himself: Best Song for "White Christmas." ("This goes to a nice guy," said Berlin. "I've known him all my life.") It was the year Mary Pickford, one of its founder-members, resigned from the Academy because she was allocated a "lousy" seat at the back, "somewhere in Arizona." But it lingered in Hollywood's memory as the year of Greer Garson's acceptance speech: five-and-a-half interminable minutes that became legendary.

"I am practically unprepared," she began. "This is the most wonderful thing. I feel just like Alice in Wonderland." Born Enid Garson in Ireland's County Down, she proceeded to thank the Academy for honoring artists from overseas. "I may never win another statuette," she predicted (accurately). "But tonight is a memorable one—one that officially places the welcome mat for me. I shall cherish this evening and the kindness of my many friends here forever."

That would have been more than enough. It was almost one AM, and the evening had already been overloaded with political speeches. But Garson felt moved to unburden herself of some not unfamiliar views on the arbitrary nature of awards. She did not, she went on, consider acting a competition. "A nomination means that an actress had one of the five best roles and opportunities of the year, and that actress had met the challenge." And so she continued until well after one, prompting one unidentified member of the audience to earn himself an immortal place in Oscar folklore with the remark: "Her acceptance speech was longer than her part."

In later years Garson grew defensive about such jokes, arguing that her speech just *seemed* long "to a roomful of weary listeners at midnight," even that she could claim "to have triggered a needed overhaul of the Awards program," transforming it from a "rather loosely organized, informal dinner-dance . . . to a split-second, elaborately staged, spectacular gala for an audience of millions." There was indeed much criticism that night of the crush, the lack of space on the dance floor, and the tiresomeness of the speeches. Greer Garson's verbosity was the last straw. Walter Wanger ended the evening by reassuring the audience, perhaps by way of coded apology, that next year's format would be different.

• • •

And so it was. The sixteenth Oscar ceremony on March 2, 1944, took on a completely new look: staged at the 2,258-seat Grauman's Chinese Theatre on Hollywood Boulevard—and opened for the first time to members of the public, in the shape of the armed forces. Academy president Walter Wanger, who had been the first to condemn Bette Davis's ideas, now stole them as he canceled the award dinner, moved the awards to a public theater, and gave free passes to two hundred service personnel. Instead of the array of speakers who had caused such dismay the previous year, entertainment would be offered for the first time. As Wanger announced a "variety show" built around USO stars, "to let Hollywood see how its personalities entertained the boys abroad," he was midwifing the birth of the Oscar "show" as we know it today.

The buildup to the show also cemented some other modern trends. Jack Warner had been having such a good year—*Casablanca, Watch on the Rhine* and *This Is the Army* had earned him patriotic millions—that Louis Mayer felt obliged to run Oscar ads in the trade papers for the first time since before the war. Once Mayer's eight-page glossy promotion had predicted Oscars for MGM's *Madame Curie,* Fox followed suit with pullouts hailing *The Song of Bernadette,* adorned by a Norman Rockwell portrait of its new young star, Jennifer Jones. Though married with two young children, to the rising star Robert Walker, Jones was made out to be "eligible" by the studio's publicists, who also called *Bernadette* her screen debut, concealing the fact that she had already made a B movie with John Wayne for Republic under her real name of Phyllis Isley.

Three months before D-Day, patriotic war movies vied for the awards, as at the box office, with unashamedly heartwarming escapism. Adapted from Lillian Hellman's Broadway play by Dashiell Hammett, *Watch on the Rhine* gave Paul Lukas a showcase part as a German refugee pursued through Washington by Nazi agents. Following the awards of the New York critics, who named it Best Picture and Lukas Best Actor, Warner could afford to remain aloof from the pre-Oscar fray. For the first time ever, his studio led the Oscar nominations with a total of twenty-seven, though Fox's *Song of Bernadette* led the individual scores with twelve and Paramount's *For Whom the Bell Tolls* with nine.

The show did not seem the same without Bette Davis. This was the first time in six years that Davis had not won a nomination; yet Greer Garson, despite the running gags still satirizing her acceptance speech, secured her fourth in five years for MGM's *Madame Curie.* Ingrid Bergman, nominated opposite Gary Cooper in Sam Wood's film of Hemingway's *For Whom the Bell Tolls,* also had the immensely popular *Casablanca* going for her. But the run-up to the Oscars was permanently altered by the decision of Hollywood's Foreign Press Association to present its own awards, to be named the Golden Globes. The first went to Jennifer Jones for *Bernadette.*

As traffic chaos reigned outside the Chinese Theatre—for the first time in Oscar history, there were no hotel flunkies to take care of the stars' limousines—the curtain went up for the first time on another icon of the Awards' contemporary era: a giant Oscar, fully twelve feet high, butt of many a joke from Jack Benny, the host drafted to greet overseas forces in a radio version of the occasion. An early surprise came with the award of Best Director to Michael Curtiz for *Casablanca;* following a now hallowed director's tradition, Curtiz observed that he had expected to win in 1938 *(Angels with Dirty Faces, Four Daughters)* and 1942 *(Yankee Doodle Dandy);* this was the first time he had come without an acceptance speech in his pocket. Jennifer Jones's way of accepting Best Actress was to apologize publicly to Ingrid Bergman, whose gracious backstage reply to Jones was recorded for posterity: "No, Jennifer, your Bernadette was better than my Maria."

Those extras again wielded their disproportionate influence—but this time with welcome results. Too late did Fox realize that its "prestige" campaign for *Bernadette* was proving counterproductive; the film was still in "limited" release, with ticket prices so high that few extras had been able to afford to go. After the popular surprise that *Casablanca* had been voted Best Picture, a poll of extras revealed that barely 25 percent of them had yet seen *Bernadette,* while almost all had seen *Casablanca.*

The film's producer, Hal Wallis, declared himself aggrieved that his studio boss, Jack Warner, had beaten him up to the stage to pick up the Best Picture award. Hired as Zanuck's replacement, Wallis "couldn't believe it was happening" when Warner "ran to the stage ahead of me and took the award with a broad, flashing smile and a look of great satisfaction. . . . As the audience gasped, I tried to get out of the row of seats and into the aisle, but the entire Warner family sat blocking me. I had no alternative but to sit down again, humiliated and furious." Though the incident led him to leave Warner as soon as his contract expired, Wallis had the consolation that the five movies he produced in 1943—*Casablanca, Watch on the Rhine, Air Force, Princess O'Rourke* and *This Is the Army*—all won Oscars. *This Is the Army,* indeed, went on to become the second-biggest moneyspinner to date, behind only *Gone With the Wind.*

"Going public" at the Chinese Theatre met with a mixed response. To the audience, the appalling price of letting in the *hoi polloi* was that no drink could be served during the show. The *Hollywood Reporter* thought that it had been "a swell affair," but *Variety* missed the color and glamour of the star-studded banquets; the sixteenth awards show had been "just one of those things." Undeterred, the Academy announced that it had decided to maintain the new venue "for the foreseeable future" (which would turn out to mean the next three years).

Despite the embarrassment of a Hollywood labor strike, the 1944 Academy Awards show was the first to be broadcast in its entirety on the ABC radio network. The penultimate year of the war saw a heroic struggle between a light comedy typical of the era's sentimentality and a huge epic typical of its patriotic zeal. Thanks only to some deft casting did Paramount's producer-director Leo McCarey get away with the Irish blarney of *Going My Way,* which saw crooner-turned-actor Bing Crosby's Irish priest charming his way through the slums of New York. Over at Fox, Zanuck believed that he had excelled himself with *Wilson,* his massive, $3 million Technicolor study of the rise and fall of an American President, which gave Alexander Knox in the title role a celebrated 1,194 lines in 294 scenes.

Also on the grand scale, Selznick was still trying to recreate the sweep and success of *Gone With the Wind.* "This is the story of the unconquerable fortress, the American home" was how he prefaced his latest attempt, *Since You Went Away,* a sort of American *Mrs. Miniver* in which Claudette Colbert and Jennifer Jones wielded the stiffest of upper lips during the wartime absence of their husband/father. When *Going My Way* swept the New York awards, and *Wilson* won Zanuck an invitation to address the American Nobel committee, Selznick shrewdly abandoned all hope of Best Picture and shamelessly went after the acting awards.

Every day that January he took the back page of each trade paper to promote one of his stable of stars—even if they were in other people's movies. While he plugged Jones, Colbert and Shirley Temple in *Since You Went Away,* Selznick also hailed his contract actress Ingrid Bergman's work in MGM's *Gaslight,* a remake of the 1940 British version of Patrick Hamilton's hit stage play. Via his shell-shocked soldier in another Selznick wartime weepie, *I'll Be Seeing You,* he meanwhile reminded voters of the versatility of Joseph Cotten. The ploy won nominations for Bergman and Colbert—but not, alas, for Cotten, who would become another name on the list of fine actors never to win so much as an Oscar nomination.

Though far more successful at the box office, *Going My Way* found itself equaled by *Wilson* with ten Academy Award nominations. Conspicuous by her absence was Tallulah Bankhead, who had won the New York critics' award for her fine performance in Alfred Hitchcock's *Lifeboat* (from a story he commissioned from John Steinbeck). Ever the East Coast maverick, Bankhead had as little time for Hollywood as did the movie establishment for her. "Did I get an Academy Oscar?" she asked eight years later, in her memoirs. "No! The people who vote in that free-for-all know on which side their crepes suzette are buttered. I wasn't under contract to any of the major studios, hence was thought an outlaw."

In marked contrast was Crosby's costar Barry Fitzgerald, who achieved the unique—and seemingly impossible—feat of securing nominations for the same part in both the Best Actor and Best Supporting categories, eventually winning the latter. As a prompt rule change ensured that his perverse double could never be repeated, Fitzgerald equally promptly decapitated his Oscar while practicing his golf swing; once Paramount had coughed up ten dollars for a replacement, it was duly noted that he had in the end got two Oscars, after all.

Paramount officials had to drag a reluctant Bing Crosby off the golf course to head downtown for the awards ceremony, where he genially expressed his astonishment at winning. "This is the only country where an old broken-down crooner can win an Oscar for acting. It shows that everybody in this country has a chance to succeed." *Going My Way* also won Best Picture and Best Director for McCarey, who thus shut out *Since You Went Away* and *Gaslight,* Hitchcock and Billy Wilder (*Double Indemnity*)—as well as Zanuck's beloved *Wilson.* The producer's only consolation prize was to receive his second Irving Thalberg Award from the hands of Thalberg's widow, Norma Shearer, the first time she had presented it. Zanuck never fully forgave the Academy for overlooking *Wilson,* bearing grudges until his dying day.

Warner's *Mr. Skeffington* and MGM's *Mrs. Parkington* between them secured Bette Davis her seventh nomination and Greer Garson her fourth in a row. But it was *Gaslight* that won Ingrid Bergman the first of her three Academy awards. At the time she was working with Crosby and McCarey on *The Bells of St. Mary's,* a sequel to *Going My Way;** at six PM they had all wished each other good luck as they went home to change for the Oscars—where all of them wound up winners. "I'm afraid if I went on the set tomorrow without an Oscar," said Bergman upon clutching hers, "neither of them would speak to me."

With the end of the war, the 1945 awards saw the statuettes restored to their gold-plated splendor, and the guests to their white ties and glittering gowns, as Hollywood celebrated its contribution to Hitler's downfall. Again at the Chinese Theatre, the festivities began with the unfurling of a huge flag bearing the numbers 118 and 7,926—supposedly the numbers of movie personnel who had, respectively, died in action and made it back. No one had the bad taste to ask how the resulting total of 8,044 related to the 27,677 names unfurled by Privates Power and Ladd three years before.

Even before the envelopes were opened, 1945 had already gone down in Oscar history as the year Joan Crawford made an innovation that would permanently alter the character of the Academy Awards, by hiring her own personal press agent to press her claim for glory.

"Me direct that temperamental bitch! Not on your goddamn

* Today *The Bells of St. Mary's* would no doubt have been called *Going My Way II.* It is one of countless examples of sequels and/or remakes of successful films throughout Hollywood's "golden" period which disprove the notion that there is anything new about the contemporary producer's urge to remake his hits with a string of numbers on the end.

life!" raged the director Michael Curtiz when Bette Davis dropped out of his post-*Casablanca* project, *Mildred Pierce,* and Warners' Jerry Wald offered him Joan Crawford. Wald was indeed taking a chance. Twenty years since she had made her first silent, Crawford's career had been in the doldrums for a decade and more; since holding her own in *Grand Hotel,* opposite Garbo, Beery and the Barrymores, her brand of moody career girl had become box-office poison. After a series of commercial flops, punctuated only by the all-female comedy *The Women* in 1939, Mayer and MGM had finally dropped her. After a dangerous two-year absence from the screen, it was as if she had been waiting for the title role in *Mildred Pierce,* ideally suited to her specialty: the hard-done-by working woman who triumphs over impossible odds, graduating from rags in the first reel to triumphantly glitzy gowns in the last.

"She comes over here with her high-hat airs and her goddamn shoulder pads," complained Curtiz. "I won't work with her. She's through, washed up. Why should I waste my time directing a has-been?" But Crawford wanted the part so badly that she meekly submitted to the humiliation of a screen test, which convinced him that Wald might have a point. By the end of filming, which often proved tempestuous, even Curtiz was a convert. The breakthrough came, according to Crawford's biographer, Bob Thomas, when the ill-tempered Hungarian realized that Crawford "was not trying to proclaim her star status; she only wanted a good picture, which she desperately needed." By the wrap party he told the assembled cast and crew: "When I agreed to direct Miss Crawford, I felt she was going to be as stubborn as a mule and I made up my mind to be plenty hard on her. Now that I have learned how sweet she is, and how professional and how talented she is, I take back even thinking those things about her." Crawford then presented her newfound friend with a pair of her much-mocked shoulder pads.

Or so we are led to believe. Pushing stories like these around town was the job of Henry Rogers, whom Crawford had hired to keep her name alive after she was dumped by MGM. To help out his movie, producer Wald came in on the plot. While *Mildred Pierce* was still on the set, Wald telephoned Rogers with an idea—then original, now commonplace: "Call Hedda Hopper and tell her . . . I was raving to you about the great performance Joan Crawford was giving in

Mildred Pierce. Tell her that I am so impressed with her that I'm certain she is already a strong contender for an Academy Award. She will pay attention to what you tell her. She will telephone me for confirmation. I'll repeat to her what I just told you."

The very next day, Hopper's column proclaimed: "Insiders at Warner Bros. Studio are saying that Joan Crawford is giving such a great performance in the early stages of *Mildred Pierce* that she will be a strong contender for next year's Academy Award." This had Crawford summoning Rogers. "My telephone has been ringing since early this morning. Everyone is congratulating me on my performance. I didn't know what they were talking about until one of my friends told me to read Hedda Hopper's column in this morning's paper. Where did that story come from? What's going on?"

Rogers explained Wald's tactics, and sought Crawford's approval to start an Oscar campaign on her behalf. The ideas he put forward were without precedent. "If Hedda ran the kind of item she did this morning, I'm sure I can get other columnists to jump on the Joan Crawford bandwagon. You know as well as I do that members of the Academy vote emotionally. . . . I'm confident that people in our business can be influenced by what they read and what they hear."

Crawford remained cautious. "It could kick back. I could become a laughingstock if it ever got out that Joan Crawford's press agent was plugging her for an Academy Award." She also knew that she was one of the least popular members of the movie community. "People in Hollywood don't like me, and they've never regarded me as a good actress." Pacing up and down her dressing room, nervously smoking a cigarette, Crawford doubted it would work. She was also apprehensive about Rogers's bold determination—for security reasons—not to work with Warner Bros., not even to let the studio in on the secret. But he was so eager to give it a whirl that eventually she gave in. "Go ahead. Try it. We'll see what happens."

Next thing Wald knew, his fellow producer Hal Wallis was pulling him into a corner at one of his parties and saying: "Jerry, I hear that Joan Crawford is so sensational in *Mildred Pierce* that she will be a strong contender for the next Academy Award. If that's true, I'll certainly want to use her in my next production."

"It's true," said Wald. "But I'm curious as to where you heard about it."

"I don't know. I'm not quite sure," replied Wallis. "I guess I must have read it somewhere!"

Infected by Rogers's invisible campaign, which had now spread to other newspapers, Warners upgraded *Mildred Pierce* in their publicity schedule and began to promote it at a much earlier stage than usual, long before it opened. When the film finally premiered, to excellent reviews—both *Variety* and James Agee in *The Nation* hailed it as Crawford's finest performance—the studio capitalized in a trade paper campaign for a Crawford Oscar nomination, and set up special screenings for Academy members.

But her opposition was younger and more fashionable. Greer Garson, still America's favorite female star, won her fifth consecutive Best Actress nomination in MGM's *The Valley of Decision,* as an Irish housemaid who marries the boss's son, while Jennifer Jones was also milking a favorite Oscar theme as a female "victim"—a fetching amnesiac in Paramount's *Love Letters.* But above all the reigning Best Actress was riding high, and working hard, as three Ingrid Bergman vehicles opened coast-to-coast. Versatility was the name of her game as a fallen Creole woman in Warners' *Saratoga Trunk,* a bespectacled psychiatrist in Hitchcock's *Spellbound,* and a winsome nun in the *Going My Way* sequel, *The Bells of St. Mary's.* So popular did this last film become that Oscar fever extended to Bing Crosby: could he become the first actor to win successive Academy Awards in the same role?

In *Valley of Decision* and *Spellbound,* meanwhile, opposite Garson and Bergman, a new male star was born that year. Four years after deciding that one of Gregory Peck's early tests was "nothing to get excited about," Selznick reported to Neil Agnew, vice-president of his new production company, Vanguard, that "all the dames [were] 'oohing' and 'ahing' and gurgling" from the moment his name appeared in the opening credits, and weeping as his performances ended. Peck was "the new rage"; it was tough to keep the audience quiet while he was onscreen. With a third contrasting role as a Scottish missionary priest in Japan in *The Keys of the Kingdom,* Peck too seemed destined for the Oscar race in his first year onscreen.

But the movie making all the 1945 headlines was Paramount's *The Lost Weekend.* Billy Wilder's study of alcoholism founded a genre destined to exert a perennial pull on the Oscar electorate: the "social-problem movie." Shot on location in New York, around Third Avenue bars and Bellevue Hospital, the film won lavish enough praise for Paramount to tout it as "the Most Widely Acclaimed Motion Picture in the History of the Industry." At the center of all the attention, thanks to his tour-de-force performance as the dipsomaniac would-be writer, was a Welshman born Reginald Truscott-Jones; for ten years he had made no particular impact in Hollywood, thanks to a succession of mediocre scripts, under the name of Ray Milland.

The New York critics alarmed Crawford by voting Bergman their Best Actress, giving the rest to Wilder, Milland and *Lost Weekend*—which entered the Oscar running with seven nominations to eight for *Bells of St. Mary's.* With attention focused on Billy Wilder's determination not to lose out to Leo McCarey two years in a row, the surprise nominees were a new heartthrob, Cornel Wilde, for his portrayal of Chopin in Columbia's *A Song to Remember;* and MGM's *Anchors Aweigh,* which saw Gene Kelly an unlikely candidate for Best Actor.

By Oscar night, Milland had become the recipient of "more awards than I knew existed": apart from the New York critics, *Look* magazine, the Foreign Press award and a citation from Alcoholics Anonymous, "Unwed Mothers of America also got into the act . . . and there was a warm commendation from Joe's Bar and Grill." After the show he insisted on a detour en route to Paramount's celebration party. "When the car stopped at Hillcrest I got out and, with the golden Oscar in my hand, I walked to the edge of Sunset and looked down at the lights. They seemed very bright that night. After a few moments I quietly said, "Mr. Novarro, tonight they belong to me!"

Come Joan Crawford's Big Night, she couldn't face the tension. "Henry, I can't do it," she gasped down the phone to a dismayed Rogers. "I can't go to the Academy Awards."

"But you must!" Rogers told her. "It will be the biggest night of your life."

"Henry, I'm so frightened. I know I'm going to lose."

Besides, said an adamant Crawford, she was developing a nasty cold. Knowing her real complaint was cold feet, Rogers asked Jerry Wald to intervene, but he too failed to persuade her. So Rogers now stationed press photographers outside her home while Crawford summoned doctors and ran up a fever of 104 degrees. Tension mounted as she sat by the radio and heard Milland named Best Actor. When Charles Boyer opened the Best Actress envelope and read out her name, there was "an explosion of applause around the house" and Joan's health "seemed to improve dramatically," according to her daughter Christina. "She bounded out of bed and took a shower. She put on some makeup and her prettiest negligee with a satin bed jacket. She brushed her hair and waited for the photographers to arrive." By the time Henry Rogers arrived, she was sitting up in bed, "coiffed, perfumed, resplendent, radiant."

Michael Curtiz, who had picked up her statuette at the Chinese Theatre, soon arrived to present it in one of the more bizarre vignettes of Oscar history. Next morning's papers carried photos of a bed-bound Crawford, hugging her Oscar and purring: "This is the greatest moment of my life. . . . Usually I'm ready with the wise-cracks, but I can't say anything. My tears speak for me."

As Rogers testified years later: "Joan may have been afraid to attend the Oscar ceremonies that night, but she was also a great show-woman. The photo of her in bed clutching the Oscar pushed all the other winners off the front page. She was there all by herself."

Would Joan Crawford have won the Oscar without the invisible help of Henry Rogers? As Rogers himself says to this day: "We will never know." Impressed by what he had done for Crawford, however, Olivia de Havilland followed suit by herself hiring Rogers the following year, when she had to make a careful choice between two Oscar-potential roles. In Universal-International's *The Dark Mirror* she played contrasting twins enmeshed in a murder mystery; in Paramount's *To Each His Own* she aged thirty years as a woman who rediscovers her illegitimate son in wartime London. To promote both might split her vote, and halve her chances of a nomination; the more heart-warming role in *To Each His Own,* very much a woman's film, adjudged Rogers, gave her the better shot.

He proceeded accordingly, and *To Each His Own* soon had de Havilland pleading for votes in trade-paper ads amid a strong field led by Rosalind Russell, who broke all records with the number of pleas for votes she purchased on behalf of her polio-battling nurse in *Sister Kenny.* The opposition consisted of the British actress Celia Johnson in Noel Coward's *Brief Encounter,* and Gregory Peck's two latest leading ladies: Jennifer Jones in a torrid Selznick Western, *Duel in the Sun,* and Jane Wyman in an MGM animal weepy, *The Yearling.*

This time, it was de Havilland who prevailed; but poor Henry Rogers's moment of triumph became an action replay of the previous year's agonies when Joan Crawford again pleaded last-minute stage-fright and backed out of her traditional duty of presenting Best Actor. The breach was filled by Joan Fontaine, who was then publicly snubbed by her sister Olivia while trying to offer her congratulations. Once the scene had been captured by photographers for the next day's front pages, it fell to the hapless Rogers, who ought to have been celebrating a second successive Best Actress triumph, to explain: "The girls haven't spoken to each other for four months. This goes back for years and years, ever since they were children. They just don't have a great deal in common."

For Henry Rogers, the Fontaine–de Havilland feud was proof positive that no publicity is bad publicity. One of the Oscars' most astute observers over the years, Rogers years later revealed the psychological tactics he employed to win de Havilland her award. Shrewd enough to see the Oscars as "more of a popularity contest than a talent contest," his success was founded on the belief that the voters' choice came down to "a number of emotional and sometimes practical considerations, none of which have to do with the quality of the performance."

> A maelstrom of thoughts whir through the mind of the voter before he affixes his pencil to the ballot. . . . Best Actress? Who shall I vote for? I don't like Bette Davis so I'm not going to vote for her. Loretta Young? She snubbed me at that party the other night. Olivia de Havilland? Maybe she's the one. Her sister, Joan Fontaine, with whom she has often feuded, has been treating her abominably. I feel a little sorry for her. I've been reading about her a lot lately. I didn't like her as a person a few years ago, but she seems to have changed for the better recently. She's much nicer to everyone than she used to be. I heard that everyone on the set at Paramount was very impressed with her behavior on that last movie she did. Those were very interesting ads on her performance that have been running in the trade papers in the past few months. I like her image—and she certainly gave a fine performance in that movie, certainly as good as any of the other contenders.

Without realizing it, in other words, the voters' thought processes were subliminally influenced by press propaganda entirely stemming from Henry Rogers. He became "convinced that a publicity campaign, conceived and executed by the Henry Rogers publicity organization, could result in an Academy Award for my client. Who was the next person I would touch with my magic wand?"

Before the year was out, Henry Rogers was to drop that magic wand and learn "a lesson in humility."

Nineteen forty-six saw Selznick still looking for a blockbuster to rival *Gone With the Wind.* Inspired by the chemistry between Jennifer Jones and Gregory Peck, and the climactic, gory duel in which they died in each other's arms, he lavished an unprecedented $1 million on publicity—for a $7 million film—beginning fully eighteen months before *Duel in the Sun* opened. But Selznick's investment backfired on him. Thanks to his constant interference, the film had finally been part-directed by Josef von Sternberg, William Dieterle, Reaves Eason, Otto Brower and Selznick himself, as well as the credited King Vidor. Memorably dubbed "cornographic" by one London critic, it was outlawed by the Catholic Church after Archbishop John J. Cantwell of Los Angeles declared that no Catholic could see it "with a free conscience"; Jennifer Jones, who had won her Oscar playing the pious Bernadette, and whose cleavage was now the picture's best advertisement, was to the archbishop "unduly, if not indecently, exposed."

Darryl Zanuck had loftier aspirations with his adaptation of Somerset Maugham's *The Razor's Edge,* and hired Norman Rockwell to sanctify Tyrone Power and his costars for the trade-paper ads. But two quite different films had struck deep American chords. Frank Capra and Jimmy Stewart were back from the war with *It's a Wonderful Life,* the ultimate in Middle American sentimentality, which today remains standard fare on the nation's Christmas TV screens; and Sam Goldwyn was shrewdly celebrating the return of war veterans in *The Best Years of Our Lives.* Chronicling the mixed fortunes of the troops filtering back home, the film was a direct ancestor of Hal Ashby's *Coming Home*—which would stir different Oscar sentiments, after a very different war, thirty years later.

For the first time in Oscar history, however, there was a distinct danger of a mass European invasion of the Academy Awards. Italy and France were nosing their way into Oscar territory with two more hard-gestated products of wartime, Roberto Rossellini's *Open City* and Marcel Carné's *Children of Paradise.* But the main threat came from Britain, with David Lean's ten-Kleenex film of Coward's *Brief Encounter*—and *Henry V,* Olivier's master class in how to film Shakespeare in Technicolor. Though *The Best Years of Our Lives* won the New York critics' vote for Best Picture, Olivier and *Brief Encounter*'s Celia Johnson collared the acting awards; and Olivier again, this time with *Open City*'s Anna Magnani, carried the National Board of Review.

Henry V's British distributors had taken out only one, very tentative trade-paper advertisement of the kind by now obligatory for Oscar consideration. Yet the Hollywood grapevine won Olivier's film a Best Picture nomination alongside the offerings of Zanuck, Goldwyn, Mayer and Capra; and Olivier himself joined Stewart, Peck, *The Jolson Story*'s Larry Parks and *Best Years*'s Fredric March as a Best Actor candidate. With *Henry V* and *Brief Encounter* scoring eleven nominations between them, including the first ever British directing nomination for David Lean, *Variety*'s headline reflected Hollywood's anxieties: BIG THREAT FOR OSCARS BY BRITISH.

Sam Goldwyn's showmanship had helped him anticipate the challenge. Calling a news conference in his suite at the Sherry-Netherland Hotel, a few days before the New York opening of *Best Years* (on which he had lavished half a million publicity dollars), he held forth for over an hour on the state of the movie industry: "Times have changed but Hollywood hasn't," he declared. "In film after film we have the same old boy-meets-girl, the same old chase, the same tough-guy stories, the same psychological melodramas. . . . Hollywood is facing a challenge. Today it is by the British, tomorrow it may be the French or the Italians or the Russians. To maintain its place, Hollywood must set aside the old formulas. It must find honest stories, stories with something important to say, stories that reflect the disturbing times in which we live."

Smarting at the cool reception afforded his own move upmarket, Zanuck was especially piqued at Goldwyn's central theme: that "Hollywood is not producing enough *significant* pictures." He counterpunched lustily: "The man's a genius when it comes to getting attention for his product. If he doesn't have any significant pictures to release, if he's putting out some little musical comedy or other, he will issue a statement that it's Hollywood's job to brighten the lives of the people and not worry them about serious issues. And then, when he has a significant picture to release and he knows it is going to be praised for its significance—something like *The Best Years of Our Lives*–he will wait until just a day before it comes out and issue a statement saying that Hollywood isn't producing enough significant pictures. My God! It's so obvious! Nobody else would have the nerve to do it! But it doesn't faze Sam. He never bats an eye!"

Feeling that its Oscars were at last secure without further kowtowing to the Actors, Writers and Directors guilds, the Academy ordained that guild members could still join in the nominating process, but final voting would henceforth be restricted to Academy members. "Like the seeds in the Biblical parable," as *Variety* eloquently put it, thousands of ballots had in previous years been "sown on barren ground," making the bulk mailing of voting forms "a waste of time and postage." Studio heads who had never cared whether or not their employees joined the Academy now pressured them to sign up, so they could vote the party line. Membership swiftly doubled; but the exclusion of the guilds brought down the number of Oscar voters from 9,000 to 1,610—a drop of fully 80 percent.

In a moment of demobilization democracy, the Academy had also decided to shift the awards ceremony from the Chinese Theatre to the mammoth, 6,700-seat Shrine Auditorium (where it is still held in most alternate years). The Oscars, it was proclaimed, would no longer be "just an industry celebration"—though the night itself certainly saw some industry one-upmanship. Despite the Academy's express request for black tie, half the audience had not dressed up—largely because they had been pulled in off the street to fill hundreds of empty seats. "That," sniffed an Academy veteran, "is what happens when you let in John Q. Public."

The way the proceedings opened on March 13, 1947, has been recalled in more recent years with some glee. First up on Cedric Gibbons's $10,000 neoclassical set was a montage of past Best Pictures under the title "Parade of Stars"—with narration from Ronald Reagan, newly elected president of the Screen Actors Guild and husband (though not for much longer) of a Best Actress nominee, Jane Wyman. Due to circumstances beyond the production booth's control, the film was shown upside-down and backward, and projected onto the ceiling rather than the screen. "This picture embodies the glories of our past, the memories of our present and the inspiration of our future," intoned an oblivious Reagan, his nose buried too deep in his cue cards to notice.

A meeting of the board of governors the previous evening had voted a series of Special Awards to balance the sweep apparently awaiting *The Best Years of Our Lives,* which did indeed win Best Picture, Actor (Fredric March), Supporting Actor (Harold Russell), Director (William Wyler) and Screenplay (Robert E. Sherwood), as well as Best Score, editing, and the Irving Thalberg Award for Sam Goldwyn. That night, when her husband was unusually late joining her upstairs, Mrs. Goldwyn went back down to find him "sitting on the edge of a couch in the dark living room, his Oscar in one hand, his Thalberg in the other. His head bowed down, he was sobbing."

The first Lifetime Achievement Oscar ever voted* went to the veteran director-producer Ernst Lubitsch, who was known to be seriously ill (and would die only months later). A Special Oscar was also voted to Harold Russell, who had lost both his hands during the war, for "bringing hope and courage to his fellow veterans through his appearance in *The Best Years of Our Lives.*" The board had presumably been nervous that Russell might be beaten to the Supporting Oscar by either Charles Coburn *(The Green Years),* William Demarest *(The Jolson Story),* Claude Rains *(Notorious)* or Clifton Webb *(The Razor's Edge).* When he ended the evening with two Oscars, both for the same performance—a coup that remains unique in Oscar history—Russell's endearing response was to rush backstage and announce his retirement. As he did so, Cary Grant leaned over and whispered: "Where can I get a stick of dynamite?" It took thirty-four years before Russell could be persuaded to appear onscreen again—in *Inside Moves* (1980), Richard Donner's "inoffensive and compassionate" *(Variety)* look at the difficulties faced by handicapped people struggling to hold their own alongside their able-bodied fellow-citizens. In 1992, Russell upset the Academy by auctioning one of his Oscars.

Far the most significant award of 1946 was the Special Oscar

* For a full study of Honorary Awards, see Chapter 11.

voted to Laurence Olivier "for his outstanding achievement as actor, producer and director in bringing *Henry V* to the screen." Filmed at Churchill's suggestion as a wartime morale-booster, *Henry V* was playing to remarkable box office all over the United States, running for almost a year in New York City alone. Many outside the Academy felt it a sufficiently distinctive achievement to have deserved Best Picture over the fairly typical American fare otherwise on offer. Two of the three writing awards had also gone to British talent—Clemence Dane for *Vacation from Marriage,* and Muriel and Sydney Box for *The Seventh Veil*—but *Time* and *Newsweek* were among the nonmovie media who began a sustained protest that the Academy "purposely" shortchanged foreign entries.

The Special Award voted Olivier was quite clearly designed to keep the real Oscars in American hands. Mayer and the other moguls who had seen the phenomenal growth of their accidental brainchild over twenty years, and who now held such sway over the voting process, were quite open in their belief that the awards' prime function was to promote and publicize American products. The Oscars were dependent on the financial support of the studios—the 1947 accounts would show them donating $87,000—and few Hollywood tycoons were prepared to lavish their money on free advertising for rival overseas fare. As *Time* and *Newsweek* smoldered, the Academy's accolade to Olivier drew countermurmurs from the boardrooms of Hollywood that were soon to grow to a critical crescendo. In the words of the *Hollywood Reporter*'s outspoken editor, W. R. ("Billy") Wilkerson, America had helped Europe enough in the war without letting them help themselves to "our Oscars."

The moguls' fears were far from assuaged the following year when British films won eight nominations, including Best Picture and Best Director for David Lean's *Great Expectations.* Also among the Best Actor nominees was the British actor Michael Redgrave, albeit in the U.S.-made *Mourning Becomes Electra.* European opposition was turning Hollywood toward more earnest, even worthy subject matter: the leading films of 1947 were Fox's *Gentleman's Agreement,* a bold portrait of American anti-Semitism directed by Elia Kazan and produced by Darryl Zanuck; and George Cukor's *A Double Life,* in which Ronald Colman played a crazed Othello both onstage and off. Dudley Nichols's version of Eugene O'Neill's *Mourn-*

ing Becomes Electra for RKO Radio was scarcely lightweight entertainment. "It is time," complained the editor of *Variety,* Arthur Unger, "for Hollywood to start making pictures for the public, not the Academy."

Still smarting from the failure of *Wilson* and *The Razor's Edge* with the Academy's voters, Zanuck had steered *Gentleman's Agreement* through the opposition of his (mainly Jewish) peers, who felt there was no need to rock the sociological boat, and was beginning to pick up a string of humanitarian awards. By late November he was able to take the back covers of the trade papers, as was his wont, to announce: "Tomorrow this page will carry the first in a series of reviews of the most widely acclaimed picture in the history of screen achievement."

For *A Double Life,* meanwhile, Universal-International was taking rival space wondering why so "expert" an actor as Ronald Colman had never won an Academy Award. Zanuck hit back by organizing a wave of magazine cover stories for his own Best Actor candidate, Gregory Peck. Though this was each man's third nomination, Colman's first had been as long ago as 1930 (for *Bulldog Drummond* and *Condemned*), while Peck's was his third in a row. Sensing that this might be his last chance, Colman mobilized an armada of friendly Oscar winners to speak up for him in paid advertisements. He had been around, after all, even longer than the Oscars, and he was a universal favorite.

The publicist Henry Rogers was meanwhile looking to make it three in a row for his own distinctive skills at promoting Best Actresses. His chance for a third consecutive home run, he was convinced, came when the producer Fred Brisson asked him to mount a campaign for his wife, Rosalind Russell, on the strength of her powerful performance in *Mourning Becomes Electra.* Although Rogers, as he later confessed, "dozed" his way through much of the film, he was keen to rise to the challenge of campaigning for an actress who was not a regular client. Besides, Brisson was offering "a small bonus if she won a nomination and a big bonus if she won the award."

He placed only one "interesting" obstacle in Rogers's path. "Roz Russell was in the East. The arrangement he had made with us had been done without her knowledge. She would never be available to use for interviews or any other promotional purposes. We would have to conduct our campaign without the cooperation of the principal involved."

Convinced that this made the challenge "even greater," Rogers began by persuading a Las Vegas casino to offer odds on the race, naturally quoting Russell as 6–5 favorite, her nearest rival being Susan Hayward (a bravura alcoholic in *Smash-Up: The Story of a Woman)* at 6–1; Dorothy McGuire *(Gentleman's Agreement)* and Loretta Young *(The Farmer's Daughter)* were quoted at 8–1, with Rogers's own client Joan Crawford *(Possessed)* the outsider at 12–1. When the story "broke big" in the national press, Russell was immediately established as the favorite in the voters' minds.

While planting newspaper profiles to remind Hollywood of Russell's career, implying an Oscar was overdue, Rogers then organized Roz Russell fan clubs all over the West Coast. He got a Beverly Hills PTA to dub her "Actress of the Year" and a USC fraternity to name her "The Outstanding Actress of the Twentieth Century." Just as Hollywood's expectations had been cunningly raised, "unexpected help" came from more "legitimate sources" in the shape of the National Board of Review and the New York Film Critics, both of whom handed Russell their awards. So confident was he of that Oscar bonus that Rogers told his wife to spend $5,000 furnishing their new home. Come the morning of the awards—by which time Brisson had let his wife in on the secret—Rogers delivered a copy of Russell's acceptance speech to her home. Both he and Brisson had booked "victory tables" at Mocambo, a Sunset Strip nightclub.

That night *Gentleman's Agreement* dismissed the British challenge with its expected sweep of Best Picture, Director and Supporting Actress (Celeste Holm), and Colman duly picked up Best Actor for *A Double Life.* But the shock of the evening—still remembered as one of the great Oscar upsets of the period—came when Rosalind Russell stood up as Olivia de Havilland opened the Best Actress envelope. Instead of heading up to the stage to pick up her statuette, she had to stay standing and lead the applause for Loretta Young.

Rogers remembers seeing Rosalind Russell's beads break, and scatter all over the floor, as his own wife (another Roz) mysteriously ran from the auditorium. He didn't find her until the show was over. "I went to the ladies' room," she explained. "I threw up. How are we ever going to pay for our living room?"

Loretta Young had been in town twenty years, and was a universally popular winner. Rogers "learned humility" that night; but he also learned that people don't necessarily vote the way they tell pollsters they intend to. Young's, he later admitted, was the better performance; and Russell's picture had bored the Academy as much as it had bored him. But there was another hidden factor beyond even his control. RKO Radio's head of production, Dore Schary, had proved unwilling to finance the required promotion for any aspect of *Mourning Becomes Electra* because it predated his arrival at the studios, and wasn't one of his own productions. He it was who had brought *Farmer's Daughter* with him to RKO from Selznick's studios, after Ingrid Bergman had turned down the lead. Young had meanwhile been going through the necessary motions for the society columns, notably on a flying visit to war-torn London, in the midst of the Oscar voting period, for the film's royal premiere.

Backstage, Henry Rogers ruefully showed Russell an early edition of the Los Angeles *Times* proclaiming Roz Russell Wins Oscar. But there was a greater irony to be borne. Russell herself, as well as Bergman and de Havilland, had turned down the Cinderella-like role in *Farmer's Daughter* that eventually won the Oscar for Loretta Young. Next day Young was saying all the right things to the press, but with unfounded optimism. "Don't say poor Roz," she said, "because she will go on to win an Academy Award and then some." In fact Roz did not: this was the third of four Russell nominations, all of them unsuccessful, the fourth and last being for *Auntie Mame* in 1958. " 'Always a bridesmaid, never a bride,' she used to say," according to her widower, Fred Brisson. "Glad as I was about it," said Russell herself, "the honor put me under heavy pressure. It means too much to the studios to have their people win; I still can't think about the tension surrounding those races without breaking into a sweat."

It was "so cruel," thought Loretta Young, "for the polls to come out and say she was going to win." *Variety*'s eve-of-Oscar poll was criticized for taking the edge off the evening. The magazine's survey of the voting intentions of two hundred Academy members had predicted an easy win for Rosalind Russell (and for Edmund Gwenn and Ronald Colman), placing Loretta Young in fourth place. "I hope that will discourage them from taking polls next year," said Young in sympathy for Russell. (It did not. *Variety*'s unofficial poll continued for another ten years, for all the Academy's furious efforts to put a stop to it.)

In the face of the moguls' increasing xenophobia, the Academy's actor-president, Jean Hersholt, was concerned to acknowledge the good work coming out of Europe. After awarding a Special Oscar to Italy's Vittorio de Sica, for proving with *Shoeshine* "that the creative spirit can triumph over adversity," he now floated the idea of a Foreign Film Oscar. "An international award, if properly planned and carefully administered, would promote a closer relationship between American film craftsmen and those of other countries."

It was not a notion that went down well with Louis B. Mayer and his chums. Nor did the sight of 19-year-old Jean Simmons picking up four British Oscars in a row, when Rank's *Great Expectations* and *Black Narcissus* swept the Cinematography and Art Direction awards for black-and-white and color respectively. Up and down like a yo-yo, the pulchritudinous Simmons was much admired on all sides, especially by Cecil B. de Mille, who promptly offered her a part in his forthcoming epic *Samson and Delilah*. But she was obliged to turn the great man down. She had just been hired by Olivier, she explained, to play Ophelia to his screen Hamlet.

How all occasions did inform against Hollywood! Within a year, the Prince of Denmark would have much the same impact upon the Oscars as de Mille's Samson on that expensive Egyptian temple.

Ostracized by Hollywood because of her private life, Ingrid Bergman was welcomed back in 1954 to her second Oscar, for Anastasia. She would win a third, twenty years later, for Murder on the Orient Express.

Marlon Brando, 1954's Best Actor at his fourth successive nomination, in On the Waterfront represented the Method school of acting.

Laurence Olivier's Hamlet (1948) was the first non-American film to win Best Picture, much to the resentment of the studio bosses.

Charlton Heston became the luckiest chariot driver in Oscar history as Ben-Hur's all-time record sweep in 1959—11 awards from 12 nominations—wins him the Best Actor award.

7

1948–1959

Television to the Rescue

It looks to us as if the Academy Awards is going to fold.

—Columbia Studios, 1949

"I sure hate to vote for a Britisher, but what can you do? He deserves it."

This, according to *Variety,* was how most Academy members gritted their teeth before voting Laurence Olivier the Best Actor of 1948 for his screen version of Shakespeare's *Hamlet.* The black-and-white British film also won awards for Art Direction and Costume Design.

But a sigh of relief went around the auditorium when Best Director bypassed Olivier in favor of John Huston—who had also steered his father, Walter, to Best Supporting Actor in *The Treasure of the Sierra Madre,* for a performance described by *Theatre Arts* as "the finest ever given on the American screen." The tension in the air was acknowledged by the show's host, Robert Montgomery, when Huston *fils* also won the writing award: "Don't worry, William Shakespeare wasn't nominated."

Montgomery spoke too soon. When the evening ended with

Olivier's *Hamlet* winning Best Picture—the first foreign film ever to do so—the Academy Awards were plunged into another potentially terminal crisis. J. Arthur Rank, the film's British producer and distributor, hadn't even gone in for soliciting votes with the now habitual advertising binge. In voting for Olivier's masterpiece, members of the Academy had put their respect for British talent above their own self-interest.

Nineteen forty-eight had already dealt the "Big Five" studios—MGM, Fox, Warners, Paramount and RKO—a severe financial body blow. That May the Supreme Court had ruled that their ownership of both the studios and the chains of movie theaters that screened their product was a violation of antitrust laws. The theaters, which were responsible for half the studios' profits, would have to be sold off.

Now reliant solely on movie-production profits, and instructed by their East Coast financial controllers to make urgent economies, the studios promptly withdrew their sponsorship from the Academy Awards. A joint statement argued that the step was not a commercial one. "In fact it is in the interest of less commercialization. Remember: the companies, as companies, were never members of the Academy. . . . The companies should not be in a position where they can be accused of subsidizing an artistic and cultural force."

The immediate upshot was that the ceremony was transferred from the 6,700-seat Shrine Auditorium to the Academy's 950-seat screening theater, causing a mass protest from paying members who would be denied admission. "The bottom has fallen out of the motion picture industry generally and Hollywood in particular," wrote the *Hollywood Reporter*. "Playing poverty with the conduct of this year's Academy Awards is a particularly bad thing." *Time* magazine, which denounced the studios' statement as "pious," summed up with one of its pithiest headlines: LITTLE ORPHAN OSCAR.

The Academy's embattled actor-president, Jean Hersholt, opened the proceedings with a tirade against the tightfisted money men who had brought the Academy and its awards ceremony so low. "There have been voices in the industry raised against the Academy," he said. "These voices always say the same thing: 'We don't want the Academy's standards foisted upon us. We want to make commercial pictures unhampered by considerations of artistic excellence.' "

Without the Academy and its awards, he went on, Hollywood would not be making pictures "with the variety, the distinction and the courage of the nominees." He proceeded to tell the national radio audience of the studios' financial withdrawal, adding that they were out to "wreck" the Academy.

It was not widely known that Hersholt had tried to resign when the studios withdrew their sponsorship, but had been persuaded by his fellow governors to stay—to avoid a total collapse of the Academy—until after the ceremony. Now, at the earliest opportunity, he followed through his threat by announcing that the writer-producer Charles Brackett would be taking over the presidency immediately after the show.

So it was against a somewhat somber background that Robert Montgomery introduced a procession of ingenue starlets to present the awards—an Academy innovation designed to win back the studios' support. It fell to 17-year-old Elizabeth Taylor, under contract to MGM, to open the envelope revealing the winner of the year's only new award—for Costume Design. "The basis for the Academy Award," thought the legendary Edith Head, one of that first year's nominees, should not be "how beautiful the costumes are but how much they contribute to the picture, how integral a part they are of telling the story." On that basis, Head was certain she would be taking home the award:

"There was no doubt in my mind that I would win that Oscar," wrote Head in her memoirs. "I deserved it—for longevity if nothing else. I had been doing motion pictures before the Oscar even existed. And besides, my picture had the best costumes of any nominated picture." The "serious competition" to Head's designs for Paramount's *The Emperor Waltz* was RKO's *Joan of Arc,* designed by Madame Karinska and Dorothy Jeakins. To Head, "there was no way Ingrid Bergman's sackcloths and suits of armor could win over my Viennese finery."

But win they did, leaving Head "in shock . . . I do not remember the rest of the evening." She had the consolation of winning the following year, for Paramount's *The Heiress*—the first of eight Costume Design awards she would win over the next twenty-five years, out of thirty-five nominations, making her second only to Walt Disney as the Oscar's most honored individual. As John Huston noted,

"They say about Edith that getting the Oscar is written into her contract."

Taylor's second Costume Design envelope, for achievement in a black-and-white film, named Olivier's friend and colleague Roger Furse for *Hamlet,* starting the anxious buzz that would rise to a crescendo at the Best Picture award. If the Academy was going to use the awards to promote foreign pictures, there was no way studio sponsorship would be wooed back.

Especially aggrieved was Walter Wanger, who had watched his huge investment in Bergman's *Joan of Arc* transformed into an $8.7 million disaster.* The governors barely appeased Wanger with an Honorary Oscar. He had hoped at least for the Thalberg Award; but it went to Jerry Wald for *Key Largo* and *Johnny Belinda,* which was to make a star out of Jane Wyman.

Wyman's virtuoso performance as a deaf-mute rape victim won her Best Actress over Bergman, Olivia de Havilland *(The Snake Pit),* Irene Dunne *(I Remember Mama)* and Barbara Stanwyck *(Sorry, Wrong Number).* As Olivia de Havilland again blamed her failure on her sister—Joan Fontaine had mounted a determined media campaign for her showy, self-produced role in *Letter from an Unknown Woman*—Wyman was a popular winner. She had lost a baby before filming began, and her husband, Ronald Reagan, before it finished. Though the first actress to win an Oscar for a nonspeaking role, Wyman confirmed a lasting trend begun with the very first Best Actress award to Janet Gaynor for *Sunrise:* that the Academy electorate is especially partial to women as victims, especially those who are victims of male infidelity or even violence.

It fell to Ethel Barrymore to present Best Picture, which she did with singularly ill grace, having publicly adjudged that Olivier's *Hamlet* was inferior to her brother John's. Olivier's friend Douglas Fairbanks, Jr., who picked up the Oscar for him, attempted to stem the rising anti-British feeling by reminding the audience that the

* The failure of *Joan of Arc* began a sustained downhill run for the former Academy president. First, the film forced him into bankruptcy. Two years later, convinced that his wife, Joan Bennett, was being unfaithful, Wanger shot her agent, Jennings Lang, in a Beverly Hills parking lot. After serving a jail sentence, he never managed to revive his career. Following a couple of B-movie successes, including the cult picture *Invasion of the Body Snatchers,* Wanger's ultimate nemesis was Elizabeth Taylor's *Cleopatra* (1963), which ran so heavily over budget that he was finally replaced as producer by Darryl F. Zanuck.

Briton had at least won his Hollywood spurs. "I'm sure that Larry, who lived and worked among us for so many years . . ."

But the theater was already emptying.

Given the almost exclusively Jewish origins of the American film industry, xenophobia may be a harsh word to use about their immediate heirs. But that was the way the Oscars had hitherto been seen from Britain. Throughout the 1930s mild-mannered U.K. filmmakers had accused their American cousins of "insularity"—of failing, in other words, to support their product. The first decade of the Academy Awards had seen only two British films win nominations—Alexander Korda's *The Private Life of Henry VIII,* in which Charles Laughton had become the first Briton in a British film to win Best Actor, and Anthony Asquith's *Pygmalion,* which had won nominations for Leslie Howard and Wendy Hiller, and that best screenplay Oscar for an "amused" George Bernard Shaw.

Britain could have shared Shaw's sense of irony, had not the Academy's original rules decreed that "no national or Academy distinctions are to be considered." Voters, in other words, were supposed to show no bias toward Academy members or fellow Americans. After proving as much, by Louis Mayer's lights, by giving the first acting awards to a German and a non-Academy member, the decade had ended with Hollywood again boasting of "objectivity" when both major 1939 acting awards had gone to Britons, Robert Donat and Vivien Leigh—albeit in American-made pictures. "Would the Brits themselves have been as generous? I doubt it," wrote Louella Parsons, before the war had brought a temporary lull in cinematic hostilities.

Olivier might not have won his 1945 Honorary Oscar for *Henry V,* let alone Best Picture and Best Actor for *Hamlet,* had he not spent the late 1930s becoming a respected member of the Hollywood community with Leigh, an Oscar winner before him, and notching two nominations for *Wuthering Heights* and *Rebecca.* But the Academy's recognition of *Henry V* had enraged the studio bosses—one of whom declared the 1946 nominations, which also included Lean's *Brief Encounter* and Pascal's *Caesar and Cleopatra,* "an act of treason." That none of them won was beside the point.

"A certain amount of bias influences Hollywood's Oscar

awards," J. Arthur Rank, Britain's leading producer, declared when the following year saw Lean's *Great Expectations* lose to Kazan's *Gentleman's Agreement.* That year had seen 12,000 British cinema bookings of U.S. films, exactly twice the traffic the other way. Rank testily expressed the hope of "parity before long." The United States may have helped Britain win the war, replied one Hollywood producer, but it should not now help them win "America's" Oscars.

Now, in 1948, came the turning point, when Olivier's investment came good and the Academy braved the wrath of its employers by voting his *Hamlet* the first non-American film ever to win Best Picture, with Best Actor and Costume Design thrown in. Said a diplomatic Olivier, too busy in London's West End to turn up: "It's incredibly generous of Hollywood to confer their honors upon the British film industry."

Hollywood didn't entirely see it that way. The outspoken *Hollywood Reporter*'s Billy Wilkerson climbed onto his soapbox: "From any way you look at it, Hamlet was NOT the best picture of the year. Have we a bunch of goofs among our Academy voters who, like many of the New York critics, kid themselves into believing that Britain is capable of making better pictures than Hollywood?" In the *Saturday Evening Post,* one Academy governor finally ran out of patience. The British victory, to Emmet Lavery, meant that "Oscar" had finally grown up: "At twenty-one, he has shown that he is free to vote as he pleases."

In an attempt to defuse the transatlantic tension, the Academy's outgoing president, Jean Hersholt, himself handed over all eight British-won Oscars to J. Arthur Rank at a special luncheon at the Beverly Hills Hotel a fortnight after the ceremony. "These statuettes are visible evidence," said Hersholt, "of Hollywood's open-minded attitude toward the film industries of other countries." Rank was equally gracious in reply: "In these days when we are so beset with misinformation about one another, and with the misunderstandings which have resulted, these eight Oscars are a particularly significant demonstration of the true sportsmanship of the Academy membership."

The studios' withdrawal of financial support had been kept quiet until after the 1948 ceremony, for fear of a complete collapse. So when Hersholt's last act in office was to reveal it, amid the furor over

Olivier's triumph, he appeared to be saying that the moguls had pulled out *because* of the British success. This caused even more dissent and backbiting. The studios, after all, were the main financial beneficiaries of the awards; it was already common practice to display the Oscar symbol in movie advertisements and promotional material. Yet, as one L.A. columnist put it, "They won't support the Awards—the very persons who profit most from them!" At this three smaller studios—Columbia, Universal-International and Republic—also withdrew their support, bringing the Oscars to the lowest point in their history. "For the last few years, we never thought the Academy handled the awards presentations in the right manner," said a statement from Columbia. "It looks to us as if the Academy Awards is going to fold."

The following year saw little improvement in the studios' dire financial straits. But the "East Coast"—Hollywood's perennially withering term for the money men—finally gave in to unashamed persuasion that the Academy Awards had become the motion picture industry's most cost-effective method of self-advertisement. Crucial to their decision was a Dow Jones study published in *Fortune* magazine, which offered the first statistical proof of the financial benefits of winning the Oscar for Best Picture. The article showed that the winners in 1946–47, *The Best Years of Our Lives* and *Gentleman's Agreement,* had virtually dried up at the box office by the time of the awards—but had earned two million *extra* dollars because of the award.

Such figures made the Oscars an excellent investment. The studios' agreement to restore their subsidy—on a strictly year-by-year basis—meant that the ceremony could now be moved to the Pantages Theatre in the heart of Hollywood itself, at the junction of Hollywood and Vine. At least they could reclaim some glamour.

To reinforce the Oscar's cachet, the Academy's board of governors also announced with due pomp and circumstance that statuettes would henceforth be individually numbered (starting, for some reason, at 500, even though more than five hundred had already been presented). It was a decision symbolic of a zany year, in which the usual interstudio rivalry continued amid every sign that they might any minute reunite to pull the plug. The one thing certain to endanger the Oscars' subsidy was to send any more major awards overseas; as the Academy's financial insecurity continued for the next four years, history records that all the honors went to very different but distinctly American products.

Nineteen forty-nine saw a clutch of patriotic war films do box-office battle, with MGM's *Battleground* and Republic's *Sands of Iwo Jima* lined up against Zanuck's *Twelve O'Clock High* in an attempt to win war veterans back to the cinemas. All were beaten to Best Picture by Columbia's *All the King's Men*—Robert Rossen's parable of political corruption, based on the life of Louisiana Senator Huey Long—which gave Broderick Crawford the role of his career. How had Rossen wrung from Crawford the demonic energy he put into the part of Willie Stark, which saw him beat Kirk Douglas, Gregory Peck, Richard Todd and John Wayne to Best Actor? By insisting, according to Oscar-night rumor, that he base his portrayal on Columbia's boss, Harry Cohn.

With Olivia de Havilland leading the Best Actress race for *The Heiress,* Sam Goldwyn decided to unleash an open letter in the trade press:

> It has been my good fortune to have produced many motion pictures which the public has established among its all-time favorites —such as *Wuthering Heights, The Secret Life of Walter Mitty, The Bishop's Wife, Pride of the Yankees* and, of course, *The Best Years of Our Lives.*
>
> Now I have made *My Foolish Heart.* I am genuinely convinced that the public will add *My Foolish Heart* to the roster of the finest of Goldwyn productions.

Goldwyn was quite as concerned to irritate de Havilland's director, his ex-employee William Wyler, as to promote the Oscar chances of his protégée Susan Hayward in *Foolish Heart.* But de Havilland duly carried off her second Best Actress statuette, leaving Hayward to wait another decade for success at her fifth nomination.

Still television posed a daunting commercial threat to the motion-picture industry, and still the financial security of the Academy Awards was far from certain. But the restoration of postwar glamour at least appeased the perennially gloomy Wilkerson. "Hollywood," he wrote, "last night returned to fundamental showmanship . . . and forcefully served notice to the prophets of gloom of its resurgence as the undisputed entertainment medium for the great masses of the world."

Nineteen fifty, nonetheless, was one of Hollywood's worst years ever at the box office. To compete with television, the Hollywood moguls were desperately coming up with ever bigger and better screens: 3-D, CinemaScope, VistaVision, even Smell-O-Vision. And the next few uncertain years in the Oscars' history were marked by a certain schizophrenia in the results. The midcentury saw a period of strong ensemble acting in movies that either won Best Picture and missed out on the acting awards, or vice versa.

All About Eve's fourteen nominations in 1950 still survives as an all-time record, though it won only six awards. That the film should win Joseph L. Mankiewicz Best Director, Best Screenplay and Best Picture made it all the stranger that the only male among its five nominated stars, George Sanders, should be the solitary winner. The only picture ever to see two actresses nominated in both the Leading and Supporting Role categories, *All About Eve* won Oscars for none of them. Studios have ever since seen it as the classic example of vote-splitting, assuming that Bette Davis and Anne Baxter let through Judy Holliday in *Born Yesterday,* and that Celeste Holm and Thelma Ritter handed the Supporting award to Josephine Hull in *Harvey*.

The following year it was Humphrey Bogart's sentimental win for *The African Queen* that prevented Marlon Brando joining Vivien Leigh, Karl Malden and Kim Hunter in a clean sweep of the acting awards for Elia Kazan's *A Streetcar Named Desire.* But George Stevens *(A Place in the Sun)* beat Kazan to Best Director, and both were beaten to Best Picture by *An American in Paris*—which also won the Thalberg Award for its producer, Arthur Freed, and an Honorary Oscar for its choreographer and star Gene Kelly. It was "unbelievable," raged *The New York Times*'s Bosley Crowther, that the Academy membership contained "so many people so insensitive to the excellence of motion-picture art that they would vote for a frivolous musical picture over a powerful and pregnant tragedy."

Again, in fact, it was campaigning that had swung the key categories, Bogart having hired his own publicity agent for the voting period, and MGM having outspent its rivals in promoting its expensive ballet. Artistic arguments proved as short-lived as usual, however, as the Academy's financial problems returned with a vengeance.

With television still eroding their profits, the studios had spent the year canceling projects, trimming budgets and laying off personnel. They waited until just a week before the 1952 awards show before dropping their latest bombshell, with a joint announcement from Columbia, Warner Bros., Universal-International and Republic that they were again withdrawing their financial support from the Academy Awards. "It is ridiculous," stormed the Academy's president, Charles Brackett, "that we should have to face this uncertainty regarding support within this industry year after year."

Within hours RCA was in touch with an offer of $100,000 for the rights to televise the show on its network, NBC. They would even arrange facilities in New York for nominees who couldn't make it to the West Coast. After long resisting the advances of its enemy, the movie industry was finally forced to succumb to television's blandishments.

Brackett had no option. Without RCA, he would have had to cancel the show and preside over the death of the twenty-five-year-old awards that had so lucratively satisfied the industry's appetite for self-publicity and product promotion. As it was, he was launching the Oscars on a new era that would prove the making of them. Within another twenty-five years, television would have converted the Oscars into a giant annual self-advertisement for the movie industry, paid for by the customers.

"Television?" quipped Bob Hope. "That's where old movies go when they die." An Oscar pariah since his defection to the enemy medium, the show's once perennial host was back aboard now that the rival camps had joined forces. Outside in the unseasonal California rain, helping Hope cover the arrivals, was a damp Ronald Reagan. Hosting the New York end of the hookup was the former Academy president Conrad Nagel.

For the Oscars' television debut, there was an unfortunate combination of first-night nerves and absentee winners. Alfred Newman (father of Randy, himself now a five-time nominee), the year's winner of Best Score for *With a Song in My Heart,* was so nervous that he walked offstage without his Oscar.* John Wayne accepted for the

* The year 1952 marked Newman's fifth of nine Oscars out of a total of forty-three nominations stretching from 1937 *(The Hurricane)* to 1970 *(Airport)*—plus two, both unsuccessful, for Best Song. This makes him by far the composer most honored by the Academy. See Appendix C, section E1.

absent John Ford, for whom *The Quiet Man* won a fourth Best Director award—an achievement unmatched by any other director before or since.

Richard Burton was the favorite for Best Supporting Actor, at his first nomination, for *My Cousin Rachel.* But the surprise winner was another absentee, Anthony Quinn, for *Viva Zapata!* For Burton, it was the beginning of a long and slippery slope to becoming the joint holder of the most dubious Oscar record of them all: seven nominations and no wins.

Even defeated nominees Joan Crawford and Bette Davis could not complain about the Best Actress award—a universally popular win for the veteran stage star Shirley Booth in her film debut, a screen transfer of her Broadway success in *Come Back, Little Sheba.* But the shock of the evening was a Best Picture win for Cecil B. de Mille's *The Greatest Show on Earth;* for the second consecutive year, the supreme prize had gone to an undistinguished movie that had won no acting nominations and had little but box-office success to recommend it for a supposedly artistic award. It was not because the show overran, and NBC pulled the plug on the first televised Oscar show before de Mille had added the Thalberg Award to his haul, that audiences were left wondering why. The explanation lay in a grim offstage drama that had been dragging along for five years, and now tainted the Oscars for the first time.

Oscar Winner Spills to HUAC Today was the (inaccurate) headline in the New York *Daily News* heralding Larry Parks's appearance before the House Un-American Activities Committee in 1951. Parks had in fact been one of 1946's unsuccessful Best Actor nominees for the title role in *The Jolson Story.* One of the many movie people who had flirted with the Communist Party in the 1930s, Parks had now been faced with the dread dilemma of naming names to the committee, thus becoming a Hollywood pariah, or refusing to do so, and facing suspension by every studio in town. When he chose the former option, he arrived back in Hollywood to the infamous headline Jolson Sings Again.

The shameful saga of the Hollywood blacklist had begun in 1947, when ten members of the movie industry had refused to testify before the committee in Washington. Held to be in contempt of Congress, fined $1,000 and jailed for a year, the "Hollywood Ten" became a symbol of the Communist witch-hunt that proceeded to dog the film industry, as it did the rest of American life, into the early 1950s. The Ten, most of them writers, were denied work for years after their release from jail. Others who had agreed to testify, and thus to name names, included the director Elia Kazan, the writer Budd Schulberg and the actors Lee J. Cobb and Sterling Hayden; they worked on, in an atmosphere polluted by resentment, suspicion and fear.

The saga was scarce begun when two of the original Ten, the director Edward Dmytryk and the writer Adrian Scott, had stood a chance of challenging Kazan's *Gentleman's Agreement* in the 1947 Oscars. Their film *Crossfire,* which combined the victimization of homosexuals with its own exposure of anti-Semitism, was a surprise commercial success. Both were nominated for Academy Awards, and the film for Best Picture, but this proved merely a sympathy vote from anonymous supporters; any chances of a win evaporated as soon as they refused to testify, leaving an undistinguished field clear for Kazan to beat David Lean's *Great Expectations.* Ever since, the Academy had watched the unfolding saga of the blacklist from a nervous distance, but the paranoia spreading around town had otherwise steered mercifully clear of the awards.

HUAC's return to Hollywood in 1951 then intensified the crisis. More than a thousand actors, writers and directors found themselves hounded out of work, even out of the country, as the film community allowed itself to be panicked into craven submission. While some chose to denounce friends to save their own careers, others were mystified to find themselves denied work—their names having appeared in a crude publication called *Red Channels,* the studios' dubious and unofficial source for "undesirable" employees (and still available for inspection in the Academy's Margaret Herrick Library). Only a sterling few, among them John Huston and Humphrey Bogart, found the courage to take a public stand against the committee and all its works.

Another writer named at this time was Carl Foreman, who was summoned to Washington—where he took the Fifth Amendment—during the filming of his script for *High Noon.* Knowing he would be blacklisted as soon as the film was finished, Foreman arrived back on the set "frightened but inspired"; he proceeded to write in a number of scenes mirroring the witch-hunt, and attacking America's (and Hollywood's) reluctance to stand up to HUAC's bullying tactics. "Much that was in the script seemed comparable to what was happening," he said. Friends had dropped him; people would turn away when they saw him in the street.

> My associates were afraid for themselves—I don't blame them —and tried to get me off the film, unsuccessfully. They went to Gary Cooper and he refused [to go along with them]. Fred Zinnemann, too, was very staunch and very loyal, and so was our backer, Bruce Church.
>
> There are scenes in the film that are taken from life. The scene in the church is a distillation of meetings I had with partners, associates and lawyers. And there's the scene with the man who offers to help and comes back with his gun and asks, "Where are the others?" Cooper says, "There are no others."

"I became the Cooper character," said Foreman. *High Noon*'s producer, Stanley Kramer, joined Cooper and Zinnemann in approving what Foreman was up to. Once the news leaked around town, however, John Wayne and Hedda Hopper were among the first to launch public attacks on Foreman, Hopper urging that "he never be hired here again." Fearing for his production company, Kramer publicly dissociated himself from his writer, causing a rift between the two men that would last into the 1980s.

But Cooper promptly telephoned his support, telling Foreman to feel free to make it public. When he did so with professional help from Henry Rogers, Hopper began labeling Rogers a "Commie bastard." Soon Rogers was receiving an orchestrated spate of angry, threatening phone calls from Wayne, Ginger Rogers, Ward Bond and others—all members, along with Hopper, of a 1,000-member right-wing group calling itself The Motion Picture Alliance for the Preservation of American Ideals.

Gary Cooper was on vacation, fishing in Montana with his friend Ernest Hemingway, when a cable arrived from Warner Bros. invoking an ancient "morals clause" and threatening to break his contract. There followed further threats from L. B. Mayer and Walter Wanger: Cooper would never get another decent part if he continued to support Foreman. When Cooper called Foreman with the news, the writer sympathized. "I know," he said before Cooper could speak. "Nobody can hold up against this . . . not even you."

Cooper was finally forced to admit defeat. "But he was the only big one who tried," said Foreman. "The only one." The writer emigrated to England (whence he would later revive his career with *The Bridge on the River Kwai). High Noon,* meanwhile, did well enough at the box office to garner seven Oscar nominations, including Best Picture, though it was still regarded as dangerously political. The Academy's dilemma was solved with the arrival of a huge commercial hit for Paramount, *The Greatest Show on Earth;* taking $12 million in its first year, it was the biggest box-office movie for twenty years. With a sigh of relief the Academy voted Paramount's circus epic Best picture; but even Senator Joe McCarthy and all his works could not prevent Gary Cooper proving one of the most popular winners of the Best Actor award in Oscar history.

Though Cooper was not there—John Wayne, of all people, picked up the award for him—the first televised Oscar show was a small-screen milestone, drawing the largest audience in the history of the medium. Amid generally favorable reviews, *Variety* gave its all-important thumbs-up: 1ST MAJOR PIX-TV WEDDING BIG CLICK.

But television was still threatening movie attendance figures. Darryl Zanuck believed the answer to the small screen was to make the big screen even bigger; hence the advent of CinemaScope, which he launched in 1953 with his biblical epic, *The Robe,* earning Richard Burton his first doomed nomination in the Leading Role category. Nominated for the third consecutive year was Marlon Brando, whose Mark Antony was billed as the "sex appeal" in Joseph L. Mankiewicz's production of Shakespeare's *Julius Caesar,* also featuring John Gielgud, James Mason, Greer Garson and Deborah Kerr. "Highlight of the film is the thesping," enthused *Variety* after a willfully stagy opening in a legitimate Broadway theater. When the Bard came to L.A., MGM's touch of class was to ban the sale of popcorn.

Sex also came to Pearl Harbor in the upmarket picture of the year, *From Here to Eternity.* Columbia's Harry Cohn had liked the idea of Joan Crawford romping in the surf with Burt Lancaster, as had his director Fred Zinnemann; La Crawford loved the role of the adulterous Karen Holmes, and negotiated a five-star contract, but then decided she didn't like the costumes. "Fuck her," said Cohn, and handed the part to the hitherto virginal Deborah Kerr, who now had two plum roles going for her in the 1953 acting stakes. Equally steamy films vying for honors were *Mogambo,* which saw Clark Gable and Ava Gardner entwined in the African jungle, and Otto Preminger's willfully daring *The Moon Is Blue,* which became the year's biggest box-office film solely by virtue of earning a Production Code ban for its use of the outlawed words "virgin" and "mistress."

With the fresh face of Audrey Hepburn fluttering her eyelashes at Gregory Peck in *Roman Holiday,* the only old-style hit of the year was *Shane,* a stately family Western which earned its producer-director George Stevens the year's Irving Thalberg Award. *Shane* won nominations for Best Picture, Best Director and two for Supporting Actor (Jack Palance and the film's juvenile, Brandon de Wilde).

But there was nothing for the star for whom the film is remembered, Alan Ladd, whose only role in Oscar history is as a classic victim of the studio system. For years a contract artist at Paramount, Ladd had turned in Oscar-caliber performances in such previous movies as *The Blue Dahlia,* and was undoubtedly the strongest screen presence in *Shane. Variety,* for instance, thought that his performance took on "dimensions not heretofore noticeable in his screen work."

But Ladd had since committed the cardinal sin of quitting Paramount to go freelance. Any actor who went off the payroll was ruthlessly cold-shouldered by his former studio, and naturally denied any of the fringe benefits such as the help of the publicity department with an Oscar campaign. Though his wife, Sue Carol, was herself a publicist and attempted to mount a grass-roots campaign, Ladd failed to win even a nomination—though his performance was far stronger than at least two of that year's nominees. His former studio, Paramount, instead threw all its weight behind one of its contract stars, William Holden, who duly won Best Actor for Billy Wilder's *Stalag 17.*

Shane had won Ladd that year's *Photoplay* Gold Medal, the combined result of a magazine ballot and an "extensive" Gallup poll —an honor he shared that year with Marilyn Monroe (for *Gentlemen Prefer Blondes* and *How to Marry a Millionaire).* Overlooked by the New York critics, and cold-shouldered by the Academy, he took it philosophically; to Ladd, it was "a familiar story: approval from his public, thumbs-down from his fellow actors and New York critics. He really didn't have a prayer, through no fault of his own or his performance in *Shane*. Studio politics, it was felt, prevailed in the Oscar sweepstakes." While de Wilde and Palance canceled each other out in the voting, two more of *Shane*'s stars, Van Heflin and Jean Arthur, also failed to win nominations; like Ladd, they were no longer under contract to Paramount, whose Oscar filly of the year became Audrey Hepburn. *Shane* and *Roman Holiday* split the vote for the other top prizes, adding to the existing strength for the year's overwhelming winner.

From Here to Eternity carried off Best Picture, Best Director for Zinnemann and six other awards, equaling *Gone With the Wind*'s record of eight Oscars for thirteen nominations. The Supporting Actor award revitalized the flagging screen career of Frank Sinatra, who had fought for the role abandoned by Eli Wallach—the tragic Private Maggio, who is beaten to death by Ernest Borgnine. Before this stroke of luck, Sinatra had scarcely been able to get a job in Hollywood; now he proceeded to make six films in two years, even winning himself a Leading Role nomination for *The Man with the Golden Arm* (1955).

While the Screenplay award went to Daniel Taradash for *From Here to Eternity, Roman Holiday* won the Oscar for Best Motion Picture Story for an English writer called Ian McLellan Hunter, whose name would one day return to haunt the Academy. But Paramount's zeal for William Holden at Alan Ladd's expense also cost *Eternity*'s Burt Lancaster and Montgomery Clift likely Oscars, not to mention Brando and Burton. And *Eternity*'s Deborah Kerr, despite the advantage of two showcase roles, was beaten to Best Actress not by Mrs. Sinatra (Ava Gardner) but by Paramount's Audrey Hepburn, the first in a string of ingenue arrivals who would typify the mid-fifties.

Hepburn had been discovered by the French novelist Colette, who suggested her for the title role in a stage production of her novel *Gigi*. It was Hepburn's Broadway success in *Gigi* that had led Paramount to cast her opposite Gregory Peck in the lead of William Wyler's *Roman Holiday;* as an incognito princess who falls for an American journalist, she joined the select ranks of those to win an Oscar in their first major film.

On a similar rising curve was Grace Kelly, who had made her presence felt opposite Cary Cooper in *High Noon* and had now won a Supporting nomination in her third film, *Mogambo.* The following year Kelly starred in no fewer than four pictures, all of them hits: MGM's *Green Fire,* two Hitchcocks (*Dial M for Murder* and *Rear Window*) and *The Country Girl,* in which she was to win Best Actress as the long-suffering wife of an alcoholic Bing Crosby. By agreeing to deglamorize herself in spectacles and drab housedresses, the future Princess Grace followed an Oscar-winning trend started by Olivia de Havilland in *The Heiress* (1949), which would also help win an award for Liz Taylor in *Who's Afraid of Virginia Woolf?* (1966) and nominations for actresses from Bette Davis in *Now, Voyager* (1942) to Lynn Redgrave in *Georgy Girl* (1966) and Jessica Lange in *Music Box* (1989).

Following the ratings success of the first two televised Oscar shows, the Academy now had the bright idea of trying a live telecast of the nominations. Jack Webb, star of NBC TV's *Dragnet,* was the curious choice to host an outside broadcast scattered around sundry Hollywood nightclubs, where a sprinkling of potential nominees seemed prepared to make exhibitions of themselves.

Most surprisingly of all, perhaps, a meek and mild Humphrey Bogart graciously greeted viewers from his regular table at Romanoff's, which he shared with the editor of *Photoplay.* Donna Reed and Sheilah Graham were at Ciro's, and Louella Parsons and Irene Dunne at the Coconut Grove, while Greer Garson played hostess at the "Club NBC"—a mock nightclub created in the studio. Bogart and Dan O'Herlihy were the only Best Actor nominees on hand, while Judy Garland hugging Jane Wyman at "Club NBC" was the only potential Best Actress. The Supporting nominees, as usual, were visible in greater numbers. Easy meat for the critics to pillory, the show drew stunning ratings.

Paramount had launched a trade-paper blitz for *Country Girl,* but Kelly was up against the popular Garland in *A Star Is Born*—a judicious mix of show biz, alcohol/drugs and female suffering that has proved popular with Oscar voters from Janet Gaynor's win in the Awards' first year to Meryl Streep's nominated performance in *Postcards from the Edge* (1990; other examples abound, from Diana Ross in *Lady Sings the Blues* to Bette Midler in *The Rose* and Jessica

Lange in *Frances*). Despite rave reviews, *A Star Is Born* did not do well at the box office; luckily for Grace Kelly, Warner Bros. did not mount an Oscar campaign—not even a single advertisement.

Behind it all lay Garland's uncomfortable local history. Driven out of MGM four years before, thanks to her battles with booze and pills, she had then won many admirers by clawing her way back to work. But the expense of *A Star Is Born* had torpedoed her new deal with Warner Bros., and Jack Warner himself did not like the film. So the studio discreetly let it be known that they were not backing Garland for Best Actress. Hedda Hopper, a veteran at prizing voting figures out of the electorate, always said that the 1954 Garland-Kelly race for Best Actress was the closest short of a tie, and that Kelly won by a mere seven votes. "You know where those seven votes were, don't you?" asked Hopper. "They belonged to those bastards in the front office at MGM."

In an age of Oscar respect for big box office, the other studios ran scared behind the year's two biggest grossers, Columbia's *The Caine Mutiny* and Paramount's *White Christmas.* The contrast was as great between two of the year's other Oscar favorites: MGM's *Seven Brides for Seven Brothers* (which had President Eisenhower enthusing: "If you haven't seen it, you should") and Sam Spiegel's production of Budd Schulberg's novel *On the Waterfront.*

Arthur Miller turned down Elia Kazan's invitation to write the screenplay because of Kazan's testimony to HUAC; Brando decided that his admiration for Kazan's directing skills overcame his distaste for a "songbird." Filmed on location in Sinatra's hometown of Hoboken, New Jersey, at a cost of only $800,000, *On the Waterfront* deservedly made hay with Oscar records. In a rare breakthrough for an independent, it was only the fourth film to amass five acting nominations, and only the second to boast three nominees in the same category (*Mutiny on the Bounty* was the first). Rod Steiger, Lee J. Cobb and Karl Malden inevitably split the vote, handing the Supporting Actor award to Edmond O'Brien in *The Barefoot Contessa.* But Brando's fourth consecutive Best Actor nomination—a male record that still stands—won him the Leading Role award over Bogart (*The Caine Mutiny*), Bing Crosby (*The Country Girl*), Dan O'Herlihy (*The Adventures of Robinson Crusoe*) and James Mason (*A Star Is Born,* the first of his three unsuccessful nominations). In a cunningly successful ploy, Spiegel had also listed his leading lady, Eva Marie Saint, as a Supporting Actress to steer her clear of the Judy Garland–Grace Kelly contest.

Bette Davis, who was presenting the Best Actor award, was "thrilled" that Brando won it: "He and I had much in common. He too had made many enemies. He too is a perfectionist." Like the three films before it with five acting nominations (*Mrs. Miniver, All About Eve* and *From Here to Eternity), On the Waterfront* went on to win Best Picture, thus tying the all-time Oscar record champions *Gone With the Wind* and *From Here to Eternity* with eight awards, from twelve nominations to their thirteen.

The year's most conspicuous loser was Garland, who had given birth to Joey Luft two days before the awards. To ensure a higher turnout of nominees, the show's director, Jean Negulesco, had had the bright idea of inviting all the nominees to double as presenters. In Garland's case, he stationed NBC cameramen in her hospital room in case she won. Once William Holden had pronounced Grace Kelly the winner, Garland's husband Sid Luft told her: "Fuck the Academy Awards, baby, you've got yours in the incubator." There followed "an insane, unreal moment," in the words of Garland's biographer, Anne Edwards, as the TV crew silently dismantled their equipment and left without a word. "She was a loser and alone. It was after ten o'clock and all the hospital lights were switched off. Judy was still propped up, still made up for the television cameras, when the night nurse came in with the sleeping pills."

Among the subsequent telegrams was one from Groucho Marx: "This is the biggest robbery since Brink's." Garland didn't make another movie for six years. Garland's costar and conominee, James Mason, was "really sick" to think of her "prinking herself up in that hospital expecting that any minute the red eye of the CBS camera would light up and make her Queen of the May." Mason took an altogether more sanguine attitude. He had accepted his invitation to attend "without a flicker of hesitation," although he in fact had no intention at all of going to either the rehearsals or the show itself. "The Oscar show is always a little better when things go wrong, so I had no need to feel guilty about letting them down." Lauren Bacall, who was in on his secret, told him he was "a cad—and she was right, of course." Mason was a great defender of the show as a television spectacle; he just didn't wish to be involved. He was fond of citing a remark by Dyan Cannon about the attitude of her ex-husband, Cary Grant, about Oscar night. "She said that he was so emotionally involved that he jumped up and down on the bed abusing the nominees he feared might win. Now that is the proper spirit."

The year's most conspicuous winner, meanwhile, was Brando, the sometime rebel who had pioneered the "torn T-shirt" school of acting, and who now donned black tie and consented to present Best Director. Chastened by his three previous nominations, Brando apparently didn't like losing; suddenly he seemed content to play things Hollywood's way. According to Sidney Skolsky, he chewed gum throughout the evening, stopping only when Bette Davis walked onstage to present Best Actor. When she read out his name, Brando took the gum out, shook hands with Bing Crosby, and accepted with: "I can't remember what I was going to say for the life of me. I don't think ever in my life that so many people were so directly responsible for my being so very, very happy." He even gagged with Hope for the cameras, producing one of the most celebrated photographs in Oscar annals (see p. 52). There were no signs, as yet, of any inclination to refuse Academy Awards.

Fifties schizophrenia climaxed with the 1955 awards, the last to honor a small-scale black-and-white drama before big-screen Technicolor epics swept the rest of the decade. Paddy Chayefsky's *Marty* was the first "crossover" feature film to be made from a television play—to the embattled Hollywood of the mid-fifties, a wonderfully cheap source of fresh material and talent. In the title role, as a lovesick Bronx butcher (played in the TV version by Rod Steiger), Ernest Borgnine won the usual Oscar points for acting out of character; invariably cast as a villainous thug, he had last been seen beating Frank Sinatra to a pulp in *From Here to Eternity*.

Rumor had it that the film's producers, Burt Lancaster and Harold Hecht, had expected to be able to claim a useful tax write-off from the money *Marty* was sure to lose; they were certainly as astonished as everyone else when it became the first American film ever to win at Cannes. When the New York Film Critics' Best Picture award followed, they wound up setting another Oscar precedent by spending more promoting the film's Oscar chances ($400,000) than it had cost to make ($340,000). In 1959, perhaps because of its barbed approach to middle-class values, *Marty* became the first American film since World War II to be shown in the Soviet Union.

Borgnine's win came at the expense of Hollywood's hottest new discovery, James Dean, and the man billed in his own Oscar advertisements as "the hottest thing in show business," Frank Sinatra. Class also told in the Best Actress race, where David Selznick was still engaged in a desperate attempt to win a second Oscar for his wife, Jennifer Jones, twelve years after her first. With Susan Hayward equally desperate to win at her fourth nomination, and Katharine Hepburn apparently indifferent to her sixth, Anna Magnani slipped through the middle in the screenplay written for her by Tennessee Williams, *The Rose Tattoo,* in which *Variety* found her "spellbinding" as a southern signora tormented by her dead husband's infidelity. Jack Lemmon's first Academy Award, for a supporting role opposite Fonda and Cagney in *Mister Roberts,* completed a rich roster in a strong acting year.

With the arrival of Oldsmobile as the show's TV sponsor, Chrysler banned their own national front man, Bob Hope, from taking part. Though Jerry Lewis was deemed a highly successful replacement, the Oscar telecast was blighted by the profusion of deadly dull Oldsmobile ads. The Academy might well have accepted an offer from Liz Taylor's latest beau, Mike Todd, to sponsor the show instead. But it arrived too late, after the TV rights had been renewed. Just as well, perhaps; if Todd had sponsored the 1956 awards show, his next project, *Around the World in 80 Days,* would most likely have been adjudged ineligible.

The nominees for the 1956 writing awards were an interesting bunch, ranging from the French philosopher Jean-Paul Sartre (*The Proud and the Beautiful*) to two gentlemen called Elwood Ullman and Edward Berends, credited in the Best Motion Picture Story category with the screenplay of *High Society.*

When someone protested that *High Society* was not an original motion picture story, but a musical remake of *The Philadelphia Story,* closer investigation revealed that Ullman and Berends hadn't written it at all; they were the authors of a Bowery Boys movie made that same year and also called *High Society.* The Academy fooled no one, and only compounded the confusion, with an announcement that the nomination had in fact been intended to honor the Bowery Boys movie. "The biggest boo-boo in Academy nomination history" was how *Variety* saw it. But the board of governors was spared further blushes when a cable from the two authors graciously withdrew their names from contention. Ullman and Berends nevertheless won themselves a footnote in Oscar history, as their names still appear in the Academy's original register of nominees, with the cryptic addendum: "Withdrawn from final ballot."

"Writer ineligible for nomination under Academy bylaws" was the even more cryptic rider attached to the unnamed author of *Friendly Persuasion,* nominated that year for Best Adapted Screenplay. The name the Academy could not bring itself to print was, in fact, Michael Wilson, who had already won an Oscar in 1951 for the screenplay of *A Place in the Sun.* Later that year, when Wilson's name appeared in *Red Channels,* the Hollywood Film Producers Association had issued a ruling that no blacklisted writer was to receive any screen credit, even for work done in the past, and Wilson's name had duly been excised from release prints of the film.

The following year, 1952, Wilson had taken the Fifth Amendment before the House Un-American Activities Committee, thus cementing his position on the blacklist, and posing the Academy an almighty problem when his name came up four years later as the author of the original-draft adaptation, from Jessamyn West's pacifist Civil War novel, of the screenplay for *Friendly Persuasion.* Though his work on the film long predated the blacklist, Wilson's name was again removed from the credits. This did not prevent the Writers Guild from handing him its own 1956 award for Best Written American Drama. The guild's guest speaker that night was Groucho Marx, who had his own observations on the matter. "Take, for example, *The Ten Commandments.* Original Story by Moses. The producers were forced to keep Moses' name off the credits because they found out he had once crossed the Red Sea."

To the Academy, Wilson's healthy prospects of winning an Oscar were no joke. When he received enough votes to be a nominee, they entered into secret negotiations with the film's producers, finally reaching the dubious compromise that the nomination could go forward—without the writer's name. When the list was published, the curious wording naturally prompted a formal inquiry on Wilson's behalf from the Writers Guild, which in turn forced an embarrassing admission from the Academy. A week before the nominations were published, in the wake of the guild's award to Michael Wilson, the board of governors had passed a new bylaw rendering anyone who had ever been a member of the Communist Party, or refused to talk to a congressional committee, ineligible to receive an Academy Award. This, it should be remembered, came at a time when the Communist witch-hunt was elsewhere fading fast in the wake of the Senate's vote of censure on McCarthy, who had also been stripped of his committee powers.

The Academy's craven "loyalty oath" read in full:

> Any person who, before any duly constituted Federal legislative committee or body, shall have admitted that he is a member of the Communist Party (and has not since publicly renounced the party) or who shall have refused to answer whether or not he is, or was, a member of the Communist Party, or shall have refused to respond to a subpoena to appear before such a committee or body, shall be ineligible for an Academy Award so long as he persists in such a refusal.

To the Academy's horror, the uncomfortable publicity sparked a movement among Oscar voters to steer the award Wilson's way. But a few quiet directives from the studio bosses were enough to divert it to the writers of *Around the World in 80 Days,* themselves involved in a tangled authorship dispute.

As if the Wilson saga were not enough, the 1956 writing awards held another unpleasant surprise, rich in irony, for the Academy. When Deborah Kerr opened the envelope and announced the winner of the Oscar for Best Motion Picture Story to be Robert Rich, writer of a modest bullfighting saga entitled *The Brave One,* there was utter confusion. No one seemed to know Mr. Rich, who was not on hand to pick up his Oscar. It was collected on his behalf by Jesse Lasky, Jr., vice-president of the Writers Guild, which had received a last-minute message that Rich was at his wife's bedside for the birth of their first child. His "good friend," Lasky told the Oscar audience, was "attending the result of another creative effort."

But the press smelled a rat. Next morning, a trawl of California maternity wards discovered no one of that name. Besieged with inquiries, the Writers Guild was obliged to confess that there was no Robert Rich on its books, and that it knew nothing about the man, who was "as much a mystery to us as he is to everybody else." The film's producer, Frank King, told *The New York Times* that Rich was a brilliant young writer whom he had met in Germany a few years back, while on military service. But he had no idea of Rich's current whereabouts. The Oscar was returned to the Academy, where it would lie unclaimed for twenty years.

The Academy, to its subsequent embarrassment, had been conned. Robert Rich was a nom de plume used by the blacklisted screen writer Dalton Trumbo, one of the original "Hollywood Ten," compelled since his emergence from jail to work under a succession of false names. Since 1953, he had also acted as "a kind of central clearing-house for black market work." Now, with his unexpected Oscar, it occurred to Trumbo that he might be able to convert his commercial success into a political assault on the blacklist. So he began a deliberate campaign "to augment and manipulate the industry's considerable commercial interest in Robert Rich, making it appear as if there were a thriving black market all over Hollywood responsible for virtually every important film of the last five years."

Once one of Hollywood's busiest writers, following his Oscar-nominated script for *Kitty Foyle* in 1940, Trumbo now "bided his time as he calculated the effects of the systematic campaign of gossip, innuendo and whispers" that he was orchestrating. Not until 1959 did he reveal on a Los Angeles TV show that he was indeed Robert Rich, author of *The Brave One.* The following year, thanks to the courage of Kirk Douglas in using his real name on *Spartacus* * and Otto Preminger in using it on *Exodus,* Trumbo finally reemerged after ten years behind various noms-de-plume to write such scripts as *Lonely Are the Brave, The Sandpiper, The Fixer* and *Papillon.*

But it was not until 1976, twenty years after Robert Rich fooled Hollywood, that the Academy's president, Walter Mirisch, visited Trumbo on his deathbed to present him with his Oscar for *The Brave One* (see photo p. 480). By then it was also widely known—though he himself always gallantly denied it—that the Oscar accepted for *Roman Holiday* in 1953 by the English writer Ian McLellan Hunter also belonged, in truth, to Trumbo.

Before his own death in 1991, Hunter confirmed that Dalton

* Kirk Douglas's role in ending the blacklist earned him a Special Award at the 1991 awards ceremony of the Screen Writers Guild.

Trumbo was fresh out of jail and unemployable when he wrote the "charming" story that would become Audrey Hepburn's Oscar-winning vehicle. Hunter agreed to "front" for Trumbo, sold the story to Paramount for $40,000, and himself coauthored the screenplay for William Wyler. Ironically, Hunter was nominated for both the Story and Screenplay Oscars—at the time, separate awards. While his own work lost out to Daniel Taradash, Trumbo's won Hunter his only Oscar. Embarrassed about it for the rest of his life—"Nobody likes to take credit for something he didn't do"—the Englishman took the Oscar home, "tossed it in the attic of my New York townhouse," and stayed mum. Much more important, however, he had promptly passed on the $40,000 to Trumbo, who could not have survived the blacklist years without it. To a man who once described the Oscar season as "the intellectual rutting season . . . a thoroughly awful and debasing time," the missing statuettes probably did not cost Trumbo too much sleep.

The writing awards continued to make waves for the rest of the fifties, reflecting the tangled legacy of the blacklist. In 1957 Sam Spiegel picked up the Adapted Screenplay award on behalf of the absent Pierre Boulle, nominated as the author of *The Bridge on the River Kwai.* Accepting a similar prize at the recent British Academy Awards, Boulle had already caused consternation by denying that he could take any credit for the screenplay. He had merely written the novel on which it was based.

Spiegel, the film's producer, had hastily tried to contain the potential Oscar damage by explaining that Boulle was being unduly modest; what the Frenchman really meant was that he had enjoyed the assistance of the film's director, David Lean, and Spiegel himself in the rewrites during filming. Throughout Hollywood, however, it was well known that the rights to Boulle's novel had long belonged to Carl Foreman, who had taken them off with him to his post-*High Noon* exile in England. Rumor had it that Foreman and Michael Wilson had between them written the screenplay and been obliged to hide behind the name of Boulle.

"It was all Sam's idea," explained an "exasperated" David Lean years later. He had told Spiegel that he thought the writing credit should be shared between Wilson and himself, in that order. "So what did Sam go and do? 'Screenplay by Pierre Boulle.' He did not write a single word of the script, I can assure you. He barely spoke a word of English." On Oscar night, after picking up his own award for direction, Lean faced a grilling from the press about who deserved the screenplay credit. "You tell *me* that," he said, "and you've answered the sixty-four-million-dollar question." This did not please the listening Spiegel, who proceeded to engage Lean in a public "duel" with their statuettes.

The mystery was not publicly resolved until 1976, when the two writers had long been rehabilitated back to Hollywood, and Carl Foreman presented Michael Wilson with the Screen Writers Guild lifetime achievement award. "Say," he joked, "maybe Pierre Boulle might now send us our Oscar, and we can work out a custody arrangement?" Boulle, it was revealed, had never written a word of English in his life. Nine years later, in March 1985, the Academy finally made amends in a private ceremony, at which the widows of Carl Foreman and Michael Wilson picked up the Oscars due their late husbands for almost thirty years.

Astonishingly, the Academy's blacklist rule was still in force in 1958, when Harold J. Smith and one Nathan E. Douglas were nominated for the screenplay of *The Defiant Ones,* which paired Tony Curtis and Sidney Poitier in an enlightened exploration of racial attitudes. An anonymous call to the Academy revealed that Nathan E. Douglas was in fact a pseudonym for Ned Young, another writer blacklisted since pleading the Fifth before HUAC. The Academy duly ruled that not even the pseudonym could appear on the ballot. It was fine, meanwhile, for the name of his coauthor, the untainted Harold J. Smith, to go forward without him.

"A lot of people are unhappy about this," one Academy governor leaked anonymously to *Variety.* "The climate has changed. . . . People realize how absurd this rule is." With the film a strong favorite to win the Oscar, the Academy heard terrifying rumors that Ned Young would come forward to claim his prize, revealing to the world the Awards' continuing flirtation with the blacklist.

In January 1959 senior Academy officials met Young and Smith for lunch to try to talk compromise: Young would be allowed to receive his Oscar if he would undertake not to embarrass the Academy on national television. It was as well that he hesitated to agree, for the lunch ended with the Academy at last scrapping its notorious rule instead. An official announcement on January 12, 1959, revoked the bylaw with the explanation that "experience has proven [it] to be unworkable and impractical to administer and enforce."

But subsequent Oscar history still failed, despite it all, to do justice to Ned Young. When he did indeed win the 1958 Oscar, his name was still in the lists as Nathan E. Douglas—and remains so to this day. The Academy refused to change it without a sworn affidavit from the film's producers that Douglas was indeed Young—a demand so absurdly demeaning that nobody ever bothered to act on it. At the time, the final word on the whole shoddy episode was left to *The Defiant Ones'* director, Stanley Kramer, who had just been beaten as Best Director by *Gigi*'s Vincente Minnelli. As his writers went onstage to pick up their Oscars, the man who had disowned Carl Foreman seven years before was at last able to say, "Well, at least we beat the blacklist."

Against this murky background the major Oscar honors had been going to a string of mammoth epics. After the early fifties' recognition of small-scale monochrome dramas, the spate of brash Technicolor panoramas reflected the movies' continuing need to offer bigger and better fare than television. Of the five candidates for the 1956 Best Picture award, *Around the World in 80 Days, The Ten Commandments* and *Giant* all weighed in at three hours or more, *The King and I* and *Friendly Persuasion* at more than two.

By handing the prize to Mike Todd's *Around the World,* the Academy was really choosing one mammoth advertising binge over another. Paramount's campaign for *The Ten Commandments*—Hollywood's biggest grosser since *Gone With the Wind*–featured a ten-page booklet bound like a Bible and stitched into the trade papers, complete with a tribute to the film from God's representative on earth, Cardinal Spellman of New York. For *Around the World*'s composer, Victor Young, there was the consolation that the film's popularity finally won him his first Oscar for Best Score, at his nineteenth nomination. But the continuing reverberations of the 1948 row over Olivier's *Hamlet* were felt in another Best Picture/Director split, with *Giant*'s George Stevens winning the day over *Around the World*'s British director, Michael Anderson.

The 1950s, unsurprisingly, were proving Britain's worst Oscar decade (and have since remained so). Its first five years had seen only Carol Reed's *The Third Man* winning an award for Cinematography and Charles Crichton's *The Lavender Hill Mob* one for writing. Two other British films had vied for Best Screenplay, *The Cruel Sea* and *The Ladykillers,* but neither had won. By 1956, Anderson too regarded himself as a victim of professional isolationism.

The following year, however, even Hollywood could not snub David Lean's *Bridge on the River Kwai.* The first Briton to win Best Director, Lean's Oscar was one of seven from eight nominations, including Best Picture. The Best Actor award went to Alec Guinness, who learned the news in England from his driver, who had heard it on the radio: "You've won what they call an Oscar, sir." They were en route to the set of *The Horse's Mouth,* which would the following year earn Guinness a writing nomination—making him the only winner to pull off that particular double.

Guinnness's win marked a return to sanity after the absurd *King and I* sweep had seen Yul Brynner named Best Actor of 1956 over Olivier's *Richard III,* Kirk Douglas's van Gogh in *Lust for Life,* and James Dean and Rock Hudson in *Giant.* Rooting for a posthumous Oscar for Dean, who had died in a car crash four days after completing the film, Hedda Hopper said that "a shaved head is a strange reason for giving someone an Oscar." And Dean's costar Elizabeth Taylor, though by now desperate to win her first Oscar nomination, was outraged at the Academy's apparent reluctance to make even a posthumous Honorary Award to Dean. "I won't go to the Awards," she said. "I won't honor any group of people who refuse to bestow the recognition due Jimmy—an Oscar for one of the brightest talents ever to come into our industry."

But 1956 was another of those subpar years in which the Best Picture winner received no acting nominations. And its place in the Awards' history, aside from the upheavals in the writing department, would always belong to Ingrid Bergman—voted Best Actress at her fifth nomination, and absolved at last of the supposed moral impropriety that had seen her exiled from Hollywood for most of the decade.

In 1949 Bergman had been ostracized by the motion picture establishment after she had left her husband and daughter to move to Italy with the director Roberto Rossellini, whom she later married.

Anne Baxter (LEFT), Bette Davis and George Sanders—but not, alas, Marilyn Monroe—all won nominations in Joseph L. Mankiewicz's *All About Eve* (1950), whose 14 nominations remain a record to this day.

Such conduct was, for the times, too stark a contrast with the consistently virginal roles Selznick insisted she play onscreen. In the more relaxed moral climate of the fifties Hollywood had begun to feel guilty about its treatment of Bergman, who was finally brought back by Fox's Buddy Adler (who received the Thalberg Award for his pains) to play *Anastasia.* By voting Bergman Best Actress, the film community was expiating its own guilt.

Onstage in Paris that night, Bergman had asked Cary Grant to accept for her. "I seldom went to the ceremony unless I had been nominated, and even then reluctantly," mused Grant, rather grandly. "But I turned up that night so that no other person could get up and say 'Dear Ingrid, we forgive you.' All that crap." She was in the bathtub of her Paris hotel room when he got through with the news.

Bergman's second win, twelve years after her first, made poor Deborah Kerr look Oscar-jinxed; even Twentieth Century Fox's lavish campaign for *The King and I* could not halt Kerr's progress toward sharing the Academy Awards' female wooden spoon with Thelma Ritter: six nominations and not a single win.

Fox's promotion of Kerr had been a deliberate snub to the year's most conspicuous nonnominee, Marilyn Monroe, whose tragicomic performance in *Bus Stop* had widely been deemed worthy of Oscar consideration. Not merely had Monroe, for once, dazzled the critics; the set had buzzed—genuinely, this time—with word of her qualities. Monroe's director, Josh Logan, had leaked a steady stream of praise for her professionalism, and it was all over town that the actress had thrown out her wardrobe and herself gone rooting around used-clothing stores in the seedier parts of Los Angeles. Fox's decision to throw its weight behind *The King and I* was cruelly effective punishment for Monroe's past misbehavior; once the word went out, it was inevitable that the studio's block vote would steer the nomination Kerr's way. Monroe, according to Sheilah Graham, was "bitterly disappointed. . . . The two things she most wanted during that era—an Oscar and a baby—were just to escape her grasp. To her, it meant that they felt she wasn't good enough."

Jack Lemmon's win for *Mister Roberts* had prompted another undignified rush toward the Supporting category, despite more protests that it had never been designed for leading players on the lookout for yet more ways to win awards. Once the Academy had refused a request from the Screen Actors Guild for a rule change, banning leading players from applying, Mickey Rooney, Don Murray and Robert Stack all downgraded their status (in *The Bold and the Brave, Bus Stop* and *Written on the Wind,* respectively) to go for the lesser Oscar. For once the voters' response showed they had a sense of humor; Anthony Quinn could not believe his luck on winning a second Supporting award—making his Oscar record a rare two out of two—for a mere nine minutes onscreen as Gauguin to Kirk Douglas's van Gogh. This remains the shortest Oscar-winning performance on record.

The awards ceremony of 1956 would prove to be the last one attended by Louis B. Mayer, the man who had started the whole bonanza. By the time the next Oscar show rolled around, he and another movie giant, Columbia's Harry Cohn, would both be dead. Mayer had already lost control of his beloved MGM, and the Academy had long ceased to be his personal fiefdom. But his death seemed an appropriate moment for major change.

The awards committee had already been tinkering with some lesser rules; in 1956, for instance, the foreign-language film category became competitive rather than honorary. Thanks to the financial inflow from television, moreover, the Academy had itself sponsored the last couple of awards shows—ridding the screen of those tedious

Oldsmobile ads. In 1957, however, scared by its brush with disaster in the writing categories, it voted for revolutionary change.

Who would rid them of those turbulent writers? The Academy found the means in its own constitution. In the wake of the Michael Wilson and Robert Rich affairs, it summarily dismissed all the Hollywood guilds from the voting process, returning it to Academy members only for the first time since the membership crisis of 1936. No longer in danger of imminent collapse, fueled only by the worldwide success of its awards show, the Academy was finally hugging its "afterthought" back to its own bosom. To highlight the exclusivity of the new arrangements, it also inaugurated the postshow ritual of the Governors Ball, to be held in the Bali Room of the Beverly Hills Hotel.

The electorate for the thirtieth Academy Awards was thus reduced from some 15,000 voters to an elite 1,800. One immediate result was that, for the first time in Oscar history, the nominees for Best Picture and Best Director matched exactly.

The 250 members of the acting branch, taking over from the 13,000 who had voted the previous year, gave pride of place to the cast of Twentieth Century Fox's *Peyton Place* with five nominations —none of which would win. Its four nominated supporting players (Arthur Kennedy, Russ Tamblyn, Hope Lange and Diane Varsi) lost out to Red Buttons and Miyoshi Umeki in Warners' *Sayonara,* a steamy James Michener tale of interracial sex that saw Marlon Brando notch his fifth Leading Role nomination of the decade. Even then, according to his publicists, Brando was threatening to turn down the Oscar "to protest Hollywood's treatment of minorities." Luckily for them—they had threatened to disown him if he carried out his threat—Alec Guinness ensured that the issue did not arise.

The surprise Best Actress was 27-year-old Joanne Woodward, for her remarkable triple portrait of a split personality in *The Three Faces of Eve.* It looked as if the career of the new Mrs. Paul Newman might eclipse that of her husband (who would take almost another thirty years to win an Oscar of his own). But she did not endear herself to the Academy with some tart comments before the ceremony when asked about her prospects of winning—"If I had an infinite amount of respect for the people who I think gave the greatest performance, then it would matter"—or at the ceremony, when she accepted the award in a plain day dress she had herself run up on her sewing machine. "Joanne Woodward has set Hollywood glamour back twenty-five years," droned Joan Crawford—the very star, ironically enough, after whom Woodward's parents had named her. With becoming modesty, Woodward herself explained that she had thought Liz Taylor was going to win for *Raintree County*.

She had good reason. In the great tradition of Joe Kennedy and Gloria Swanson, William Randolph Hearst and Marion Davies, David Selznick and Jennifer Jones, the reigning Best Picture producer Mike Todd had thought he could fix the award for his new wife. On their return to Hollywood from an extended European tour, Todd bought acres of space in the trade papers and glad-handed his way around the production party circuit on Liz's behalf. Sensing it might all be in vain, so strong were the other candidates, he pushed her back to work for Pandro Berman in *Cat on a Hot Tin Roof.* "It's a great script and it will be a great picture," Todd told Liz. "You oughta win the Oscar for *Raintree* but just in case you don't, you'll win for sure with Maggie the Cat."

He was never to find out. Todd died in a plane crash four days before the 1958 awards ceremony, which his widow was too distraught to attend. Cynics pointed out that the ballot had already closed, or a sympathy vote might well have proved Woodward right by scooping the award for Liz. Ironically enough, it would be a sympathy vote of a different order that would soon win Taylor the first of her two Oscars. In the meantime, it was all the Academy could do to prevent her building a nine-foot, two-ton marble replica of the Oscar statuette at the head of Todd's Chicago grave. In vain did Mike Todd, Jr., protest at such vulgarity; it took the threat of a lawsuit from the Academy, which jealously guards the copyright of its treasured symbol, to impose some taste.

Bad taste was also the order of the day on the Oscar stage, where Rock Hudson teamed up with Mae West for a risque rendering of "Baby, It's Cold Outside." At its end, before a long and passionate kiss, Hudson offered her a cigarette with the words "King-sized," to which West famously replied: "It's not the men in your life, it's the life in your men." Black-market copies of the duet are still changing hands more than thirty years later.

Among the other actresses beaten by Woodward (apart from the hapless Deborah Kerr, foiled again in her fourth attempt) was *Peyton Place*'s Lana Turner—like Taylor a sometime glamour girl now taken seriously as an actress for the first time. Turner wasn't about to share her place in the Academy sun with her then boyfriend, Johnny Stompanato, a shady underworld figure who had been her beau for the best part of a year. LANA RETURNS WITH MOB FIGURE had been the L.A. headline when they arrived back from London together for the Oscar ceremony. Stompanato assumed that he would be escorting Turner to the Pantages, but she had other ideas.

"I certainly wasn't going to appear among the leading lights of the industry with John on my arm," said Lana, who instead took along her mother and 14-year-old daughter, Cheryl. "Despite all his threats and pleadings, I wouldn't budge an inch." Enraged that she would not be taking him, Stompanato insisted that she skip the Governors Ball and come straight home to his arms. When she got back late, via the Governors Ball at the Beverly Hilton Hotel, he went berserk, telling her she would never cut him out of anything again. "And he roughed me up for the first time in front of my daughter Cheryl."

A week later, on April 4, 1958, there was another big fight, causing Cheryl to rush to her mother's aid. There ensued a disputed scene in which Turner's daughter stabbed Stompanato to death with a butcher's knife. It was an accident, Cheryl argued at her trial; Johnny had pulled the kitchen door open so abruptly that she had crashed into him with the knife she was carrying in self-defense. Cheryl was acquitted of murder; but her mother couldn't bring herself to attend the Oscars again for five years.

Billy Wilder, who gave all the credit for *Witness for the Prosecution* to its author, Agatha Christie, was one of the year's better losers—along with his stars, the husband-and-wife team of Charles Laughton and Elsa Lanchester. Laughton, ironically enough, had been David Lean's first choice for the role in *Bridge on the River Kwai* in which Alec Guinness beat him to Best Actor. One of the few actors who always remained genuinely indifferent to the Academy and all its works, Laughton openly campaigned for his compatriot rival: "I never understood the part until I saw Guinness play it."

Another disappointed director at the 1957 awards was Sidney

Lumet, who had made a distinguished debut with *Twelve Angry Men.* But the Academy stayed stuck in its fifties schizophrenia, nominating committed social dramas while handing its major awards to grand extravaganzas. Nineteen fifty-eight was so much a "social conscience" year that Rosalind Russell's *Auntie Mame* looked quite out of place amid a clutch of films campaigning about such issues as race and capital punishment, with Best Actor going to a sexual pervert (David Niven in *Separate Tables*) and Best Actress to a vagrant prostitute executed in the gas chamber (Susan Hayward in *I Want to Live!,* based on the true case of Barbara Graham). It was perhaps with a sigh of relief that the electorate gave its highest honors to a musical, *Gigi,* with a record tally of nine wins for nine nominations. None of them, significantly, was for acting—though the Academy tossed an Honorary Award Maurice Chevalier's way, thirty years after his only nomination. Thirty years later, having finally been named Best Actor at his seventh nomination, Paul Newman was able to look back at this, his first, and say: "Nah. That was too early."

In his beset-selling autobiography, *The Moon's a Balloon,* Niven offered the definitive glimpse of Oscar hypocrisy at a party in honor of Ingrid Bergman the night before the 1958 Awards: "Everyone at the party seemed to have voted for me; they didn't say so in so many words, they were content to signal the fact across the room by making a cross in the air and pointing to their own chests and winking knowingly. I was greatly encouraged until I caught the eye of Rosalind Russell, a nominee for Best Actress for whom I had not voted—and found myself winking and pointing and drawing crosses in the empty air."

Niven had other reasons for not expecting to win. On the very day the Oscar ballot papers went out, an article in the *Hollywood Reporter* by Jim O'Neill, film critic of the *Washington Daily News,* quoted a leading Hollywood producer as saying that he would not be voting for Niven, because the actor had slavishly copied Eric Portman's stage performance—having "seen it forty times" and "haunted Portman's dressing room" to the point where he had to be "bodily thrown out of the theatre." After protests from Niven—and confirmation from Portman that the story was wholly untrue—O'Neill printed an apology and gave Niven the name of the producer in question. When the actor confronted him, the producer confessed he had been told the story by the publicist of one of his rival nominees.

Hayward's win at her fifth nomination, helped by a Walter Wanger campaign that quoted even the French philosopher Albert Camus, came at the expense of two veteran Oscar losers: Roz Russell, on the last of her four unsuccessful nominations, and Deborah Kerr *(Separate Tables),* on the fifth of her six. Both had always conducted themselves with a dignity uncharacteristic of the Hollywood gold rush. In 1955 Russell had turned down Cohn's offer of a Supporting Actress campaign for her schoolmarm in Josh Logan's *Picnic,* arguing that she had been a star for years and had no intention of giving up now "simply in hopes of winning an Oscar." Now she again refused to campaign for *Auntie Mame,* a part she had played on Broadway, and loved enough to buy the rights for herself: "I think Academy members vote only for what they see on the screen."

Niven, by contrast, had spent $1,500 of his own money on trade advertisements. But the ad of the year was for Stanley Kramer's *The Defiant Ones,* the Academy's latest blacklist headache. It literally handcuffed together Sidney Poitier and Tony Curtis, as escaped convicts in an eloquent plea for racial tolerance. The advertisement's central image—two hands, one white, one black, rising in handcuffs out of a river—earned the ultimate accolade of parody when Hayward and her director, Robert Wise, ran a picture of themselves standing in the middle of a river, handcuffed to each other.

The backstage drama of the year was provided by Liz Taylor, sharing the honors with Paul Newman, Burl Ives* and Judith Anderson for Richard Brooks's film of Tennessee Williams's *Cat on a Hot Tin Roof.* Widowed just as filming began (the MGM publicity machine portrayed her as acting with "unusual intensity"), Liz promptly undid all her sympathetic publicity by running off with Debbie Reynolds's husband, Eddie Fisher, who had been best man at her wedding to the late Mike Todd. The extent of the damage became clear when the University of California canceled a lecture invitation after receiving "angry letters from housewives all over the United

* Burl Ives's Oscar as Best Supporting Actor that year was the result of a classic deal between two mutually self-interested studios. MGM listed Ives as a Leading Player in *Cat on a Hot Tin Roof,* deliberately to boost his chances of a supporting win for United Artist's *The Big Country.* Both studios would benefit as much as the actor.

States"; and the National Association of Theater Owners withdrew the title of Actress of the Year, saying: "The movie industry is at the mercy of public opinion, and to award Miss Taylor the honor at a time like this is simply out of the question." One highlight of the 1958 awards ceremony was the sniggering throughout the audience when Eddie Fisher performed one of the year's nominated songs, "To Love and Be Loved" (from *Some Came Running).*

In the eyes of the Deep South, however, neither Taylor nor Kerr was a match in infamy for Ingrid Bergman, who returned to Hollywood two years after winning Best Actress to present the 1958 Best Picture award to *Gigi.* Still feeling guilty about ostracizing her, the Academy gave Bergman a standing ovation, moving the *Atlanta Chronicle* to editorialize: "The honor accorded Ingrid Bergman at the Academy Awards ceremony and the thunderous ovation she received from spectators at the Pantages proved at least one point, insofar as we are concerned. Our ideas of moral values and those of the folks in Hollywood are widely separated."

So it was perhaps as well that the show's producer, Jerry Wald, had had the temerity to send all participants a memorandum banning the display of cleavage. "That was one of the major criticisms we received last year, that the necklines were too low. Most of the complaints came from the Middle West." Wald positioned a wardrobe mistress backstage "with enough lace to make a mummy."

Unappeased, Atlanta's city fathers proceeded to ban one of 1959's Best Picture nominees, Britain's *Room at the Top,* while the Kansas state authorities considered *Some Like It Hot* too hot for the locals ("it contains material regarded as too disturbing for Kansans"). The decade ended on a definitively schizophrenic note, with these spicy romps vying for honors with Audrey Hepburn in *The Nun's Story* and Shelley Winters in *The Diary of Anne Frank.* As if this were not enough, Doris Day won her first and only Best Actress nomination for the innocent mummery of *Pillow Talk* against Kate Hepburn and Liz Taylor in another steamy piece by Tennessee Williams out of Gore Vidal, *Suddenly, Last Summer.*

Nineteen fifty-nine was indeed the year of sex and religion. Never to win an Oscar, despite two nominations twenty years apart, Otto Preminger was still making a fortune simply by defying the Hollywood Production Code and the Breen Office that administered it. Despite fine performances from James Stewart, George C. Scott and newcomer Lee Remick, a ban in Chicago was the best possible publicity for Preminger's latest, *Anatomy of a Murder,* which would more accurately have been entitled *Anatomy of a Rape.* Middle America was still not ready to see such subjects explored, in however enlightened a spirit, on the screen.

The only place *Ben-Hur* was banned was the United Arab Emirates, because it was "a film about Jews." For MGM, *Ben-Hur* was a desperate attempt to stay afloat, a $15 million go-for-broke gamble at remaking its great 1926 silent hit in a style to suit the times. Inspired by the financial success of another biblical epic, the late Cecil B. de Mille's *Ten Commandments,* the studio stole his Moses, Charlton Heston, and got feverishly to work. The pressure saw the film's producer, Sam Zimbalist, drop dead during its six months on location in Rome; the picture went through five writers. William Wyler called it "Hollywood's first intimate spectacle," and friendly critics pointed out that only forty-five minutes of its three and a half hours were spent on special effects. But it was the famous chariot race that soon proved the crowd-pleaser; filmed over two months at a cost of a million dollars, it amounted to the most expensive eleven minutes moviegoers had ever seen.

Ben-Hur grossed $37 million domestically and $80 million worldwide, breaking box-office records everywhere. As well as spending $3 million on promotion, MGM perfected the fine art of manipulating the sliding-scale system of voting for nominations. "The men with the keys to the executive washroom," as Peter H. Brown put it, "played the system as if it were a fine violin." Studio insiders were drilled in voting first for the in-house candidate (in this case Charlton Heston) and then listing four no-hopers as choices two through five (in 1959, for instance, Rock Hudson for *Pillow Talk* or Troy Donahue for *A Summer Place*). That way, Heston got five votes instead of one; not merely did it clinch him a nomination, but it ensured there was no heavyweight opposition in the final round of voting.

Even so, Charlton Heston's appearance on the nominations list moved Hollywood to a communal double-take. Universally regarded as the actor of the year was Jack Lemmon in *Some Like It Hot,* but his cause was fatally damaged by his film's absence from the Best

Picture nominees—surely one of the grossest oversights in the Awards' history. Preminger's campaigning courtroom drama and Britain's slice of "angry young man" realism were worthy nominees; but could *Ben-Hur, The Diary of Anne Frank* and *The Nun's Story* really compete with Billy Wilder's classic comedy? Studio manipulation of the voting system was at its worst in 1959, which even saw Doris Day win that unlikely Best Actress nomination for *Pillow Talk*.

Ben-Hur led the field with twelve nominations. Next came *Anatomy of a Murder* with six—but none for its director, Preminger, probably because this perennial outsider had just had the temerity to announce that his next film, *Exodus,* would be scripted by Dalton Trumbo—under his real name. Perhaps Stanley Kramer had spoken too soon about the "death" of the blacklist. When *Exodus* opened there were protests and pickets all over the country. It was Trumbo's first screen credit in fifteen years. To Preminger, "he had paid his debt to society when he served his prison term. Now he had the right again to make a living in his chosen profession like any other citizen."

One of the few categories spared a *Ben-Hur* candidate was Best Actress, regarded as too close to call between three Oscar veterans. Now that she had married Eddie Fisher, Liz Taylor's performance in *Suddenly, Last Summer* saw her back in favor with Oscar voters, alongside both Hepburns: Liz's costar Katharine and *The Nun's Story*'s Audrey. The votes split between them handed victory to a newcomer, Simone Signoret, the brooding seductress of *Room at the Top*'s Laurence Harvey. The French star had helped her cause by arriving in Hollywood on the arm of her husband, Yves Montand, who was filming the star-studded *Let's Make Love* with Marilyn Monroe.

Conspicuous left-wing activists in France, both Montand and Signoret had previously been excluded from the United States under an immigration law forbidding "Communists and subversives"; a special waiver on this occasion was granted for a six-month period. Of the frequent trade-paper ads on her behalf during the Oscar campaign, Signoret said: "It's not my money, I assure you. . . . What can it mean? It is as sensible as if I write a letter to myself and say: 'Dear Simone, you have given a great performance.' What I have done in *Room at the Top* is finished. Publicity will not make it better."

The ABC network took over the telecast (which it has retained ever since), and another year's self-sponsorship by the Academy enabled Bob Hope to return as sole master of ceremonies. Under the presidency of Ronald Reagan, the Screen Actors Guild had gone on strike shortly before the awards over a TV residuals dispute, moving Hope to open the proceedings: "I never thought I'd live to see the day when Ronald Reagan was the only actor working." His reward was to become the third recipient of the Jean Hersholt Humanitarian Award, founded in 1956 in memory of the late Academy president.*

Would the expected *Ben-Hur* sweep see Charlton Heston strike gold? When George C. Scott lost Best Supporting Actor to *Ben-Hur*'s Hugh Griffith—storing up trouble for the Academy in the years ahead—it began to look ominously like it. The film had carried Special Effects, Sound, Editing, Art Direction, Cinematography, Score and Best Director by the time Susan Hayward entered to crown 1959's Best Actor in a Leading Role. Writing in his diary at five AM the next morning, Heston recalled: "Just before Susan read it off, something popped into my head. 'I'm going to get it.' And I did. I kissed my wife and walked to the stage dripping wet, except for a pepper-dry mouth: classic stagefright. I'll never forget that moment, or the night.

"Backstage, posing for photographs with Willy [Wyler], I said, 'I guess this is old hat to you.'

" 'Chuck,' he said, 'It never gets old hat.' "

As the evening ended with Gary Cooper handing the Best Picture award to Sam Zimbalist's widow, *Ben-Hur* had won eleven Oscars from its twelve nominations, losing the Screenplay category only because of a credits dispute among its authors. It is a record that still stands, and is unlikely ever to be broken now that the studios' stranglehold over the voting system has been loosed.

Or to put it another way: if the Oscars are to be taken as an objective measure of artistic excellence, the Academy would have us believe that *Ben-Hur* is the best film ever made.

* This was the fourth of five Academy honors awarded to Hope over the years, from a silver plaque in 1940 "in recognition of his unselfish services to the motion picture industry" via an honorary Oscar in 1952 to the Academy's Gold Medal for "unique and distinguished service to our industry and the Academy" in 1965. (See Chapter 11 on Honorary Awards.)

Elizabeth Taylor's near-fatal illness in 1960 brought Hollywood's forgiveness for running off with Debbie Reynolds's husband, Eddie Fisher: Taylor was handed the Best Actress award for Butterfield 8.

The ultimate victim of the "Oscar curse," Gig Young won Best Supporting Actor in 1969 for They Shoot Horses, Don't They? Nine years later, after failing to win the leading roles he coveted, he killed himself.

8

1960–1969

Politics and Sentiment

> The Academy Awards is all politics and sentiment and nothing to do with merit.
>
> —TRUMAN CAPOTE

It took John Wayne fourteen years to realize his patriotic dream of directing a film of the Alamo, starring himself as Davy Crockett. "These are perilous times," Hollywood's "Duke" told Louella Parsons. To Wayne, the Alamo's suicidal defense of Texas independence 125 years before now served as a rebuke to lapsed American standards. "The eyes of the world are upon us. We must sell America to countries threatened with Communist domination."

The Alamo was designed to remind Americans of "the struggle our ancestors made for the precious freedom which we now enjoy," declared Wayne, after spending $1.5 million rebuilding the 1836 fort and filling it with stars to suit all cinematic tastes. Frankie Avalon (Smitty), Richard Boone (Sam Houston) and Richard Widmark (James Bowie) were lined up alongside Hollywood's latest British discovery, Laurence Harvey, as the dashing Colonel Travis. With Wayne's oldest son as assistant producer, the film even had parts for his second son, Patrick, and his four-year-old daughter Aissa.

Shuffled around a series of unenthusiastic studios, and bankrolled largely by like-minded Texas oilmen, Wayne's $12 million pet project wound up costing him more than $3 million of his own money—and left him, at the age of 53, emotionally and physically spent, and close to bankruptcy. Everything he owned—hotels, cotton plantations, oil wells, uranium mines, ice cream plants, a South American sugar factory and sundry real estate—was mortgaged to the hilt.

No wonder the Duke's ulcer had also returned with a vengeance. For the eighty days on location in remote Bracketville, Texas, four thousand extras had been recruited to enact the attacking Mexican hordes. The film's accounts further revealed the rental or purchase, plus stabling and feeding, of 1,500 horses. Wayne, by his own account, had gone through a "living hell" making the picture. "I've got everything I own in it. I borrowed from banks and friends. Take a look at one scene and you'll never be able to count the thousands of people." When the critics were derisive, and the word-of-mouth lukewarm, *The Alamo*'s bitter and desperate director mounted the most hysterical, ill-judged Oscar campaign in the history of the Academy Awards.

He had been desperate since the July 4 weekend of 1960, when he spent $200,000 on a three-page color foldout in *Life* magazine mysteriously proclaiming THERE WERE NO GHOSTWRITERS AT THE ALAMO. It was a cryptic reference few understood, making an obscure connection between the party conventions then nominating presidential candidates and his belief that American values weren't what they used to be. Wayne's Neanderthal political instincts had been inflamed by the heavy-duty Oscar opposition his pet project was facing.

Nineteen sixty was the year of *The Apartment* and *Elmer Gantry*, of Hitchcock's *Psycho* and Douglas's *Spartacus*, of *Inherit the Wind* and *Exodus*, of Laurence Olivier in his greatest role, *The Entertainer*—all, in their very different ways, cinematic achievements far more distinctive than Wayne's overblown, three-hour epic. In March, returning from a European publicity campaign for *The Alamo*, which had climaxed in an audience with the Pope, the Duke found that even foreign films like *Never on Sunday* were hotter items of Oscar gossip. Confronted by a *Variety* reporter at the Los Angeles airport, he went straight onto the offensive. "This is not the first time *The Alamo* has been the underdog," thundered its producer. "We need defenders today just as they did one hundred twenty-five years ago this month."

Weary of almost a year (and more than a million dollars worth) of remorseless *Alamo* hype, reporters merely mocked the Duke's crusty braggadocio. So Wayne hired Russell Birdwell, the Hollywood "superpublicist" who two decades before had drummed up national hysteria over David O. Selznick's *Gone With the Wind*. He gave Birdwell another quarter of a million and a completely free hand. The results went beyond anything even Hollywood had seen before.

First up was a press release running to a dizzy 183 pages—in the words of one recipient, "dripping with sugary adjectives," and depicting Wayne as "the George Washington of films, storming the celluloid heights for God and country." Across Hollywood Boulevard, Birdwell strung a banner carrying a testimonial (dating from the location) from Wayne's old friend John Ford: THIS IS THE MOST IMPORTANT MOTION PICTURE EVER MADE. IT IS TIMELESS. IT WILL RUN FOREVER. There followed an ad campaign of a scale as breathtaking as its claims and as epic as the movie.

After forty-three consecutive days of hyperbolic boasts, in both *Daily Variety* and the *Hollywood Reporter, The Alamo* campaign climaxed with a crudely drawn, giant tombstone anticipating the death of Hollywood—and implying, as some observers read it, that God himself was canvassing Oscar votes for *The Alamo*.

HOLLYWOOD

BORN 1907 AD—DIED 3000 AD

When the motion picture industry's epitaph is written—what will it say?

Will another civilization, coming upon the ruins, find something of worth: a spool of film spelling out a great dream? Or a sequence that merely featured a sex measurement or an innuendo that "got by" the censors?

Will there be left behind, for the ages to come, an enduring screen literature that played a vital role in the Twentieth Century?

Or do you care?

The sincere and the dedicated do care.

This includes every man and woman who contributed to the making of *The Alamo*.

They believe that the motion picture is the greatest force for good or evil the communications sphere has ever known.

The sincere and dedicated throughout the industry have used it for good.

They know that inexorable evolution will someday, perhaps by 3000 AD, replace the present-day magic of celluloid in a manner not yet born in the ivory towers of those devoted to the science of obsolescence.

But an obituary will come, an epitaph will be written.

What will it say—or do you care?

Next came an ad documenting the number of paychecks paid out to American citizens during the making of *The Alamo*—proudly dubbed "the most expensive picture ever made on American soil." From Paris, Wayne's sometime friend Darryl F. Zanuck accused him of "vulgar solicitation of votes," asking a press conference: "What right has he got to write, direct and produce a motion picture? Look at poor old Duke Wayne—he's never going to see a nickel . . ."

On location in Africa for Howard Hawks's *Hatari!* (which lent some irony to his denouncing Zanuck as an "expatriate" producer), Wayne hit back bitterly by cable: "It is my hope that expatriate American producers shed no crocodile tears over poor old Duke Wayne, who thus far in a thirty-year career has brought over $300 million into producers' tills and plans not only to keep on doing this for producers, but is doing a little bit for himself out of the change. . . . I'm mighty proud that my production company made *The Alamo*. Please inform Mr. Zanuck that as far as poor old Duke Wayne and his picture—which was made, by the way, in the United States—are concerned, it has made just under $2 million in three months in thirteen theaters in America . . . and will end up being one of the highest grossers of all time."*

Wayne's dubious taste in linking his patriotism to the 1960

* It didn't, of course. In its first year of domestic distribution, *The Alamo* earned $8 million—a handsome enough gross in those days, but disastrous for a $12 million film. Now as then, Hollywood's criterion of a successful movie is one that makes at least three times its cost. To complete the film, Wayne had to sell his own stake in it to United Artists. He never recovered his personal investment.

political campaign had already turned many mere cinemagoers against his film before they had even seen it. Now his rampant nationalism was turning off Hollywood, too. The *Alamo* campaign had developed a distinctly bullying tone.

Variants on such themes as WHAT WILL OSCAR SAY TO THE WORLD THIS YEAR?, screaming from paid spreads in the trade press, amounted to moral blackmail. To vote for any other movie, Wayne was implying, would be downright unpatriotic. Bosley Crowther of *The New York Times* was undeterred, attacking the film as "just another beleaguered blockhouse Western." But Brendan Gill of *The New Yorker* met Wayne's cavalry charge head on: "Not like *The Alamo*? What am I—some sort of un-American nut or something? For here is a telling of one of the great American stories, and if I accuse John Wayne . . . of having turned a splendid chapter of our past into sentimental and preposterous flapdoodle, I'm apt to be accused in turn of deliberately downgrading Davy Crockett, Jim Bowie and all the other brave men who died in that heroic fiasco."

More important to the Oscar electorate, it was also too much for Dick Williams, the influential entertainment editor of the Los Angeles *Mirror*. Williams had originally reviewed the film kindly, but now he worried out loud about "one of the most persistent pressure campaigns since I started covering the Oscar show thirteen years ago."

> The implication is unmistakable. Oscar voters are being appealed to on a patriotic basis. The impression is left that one's proud sense of Americanism may be suspected if one does not vote for *The Alamo*. This is grossly unfair. Obviously, one can be the most ardent of American patriots and still think *The Alamo* a mediocre movie.

Williams concluded that Academy officials were "deeply concerned," though not as yet saying so publicly. "Wayne obviously takes his own advertisements seriously. I wonder how many other Academy voters will also?"

Wayne counterattacked with renewed vigor. In an open letter to the L.A. *Times* he complained that he was "sickened" by his "belittling" at the hands of the critics. Birdwell followed up by buying some personal trade-press attacks on Williams, in tandem with a new

Alamo series stressing: "It's up to Oscar," or "Oscar will make up his own mind."

On February 27, 1961, he did. The evening papers announced that *The Alamo* had been nominated for six Academy Awards, including Best Picture, with citations for Dmitri Tiomkin's music and William Clothier's cinematography.

Although there was no acting or directing nomination for Wayne, his publicity offensive on the film's behalf had worked. *The Alamo*'s name was up there contending for the top laurels of 1960 with *The Apartment, Elmer Gantry, Sons and Lovers* and *The Sundowners.* Among the films squeezed out of the Best Picture category that year were *Psycho, Never on Sunday, Inherit the Wind, Spartacus* and *Exodus* (despite an anti-*Alamo* campaign by its producers urging voters to "judge the picture, not the ads").

But *The Alamo* saga was not over yet. Its only acting nomination was in the Supporting category, for Chill Wills, a veteran character actor hired by Wayne to provide some light relief as "The Beekeeper." Suspecting that this might be his only career opportunity to strike gold, and rated third in the Oscar betting behind *Spartacus*'s Peter Ustinov and *Exodus*'s Sal Mineo, Wills was not content to leave his chances to Birdwell. He hired his own publicity agent in the shape of W. S. ("Bow-Wow") Wojciechowicz—a former husband of Sheilah Graham—and mounted a personal campaign which surpassed even Wayne's for both audacity and vulgarity. In the words of *The New York Times*'s Hollywood correspondent, Gladwyn Hill, Chill's "propaganda campaign . . . outbirded Mr. Birdwell's." To Wayne's biographer, Maurice Zolotow, it was "a horrifying display of vanity and bad taste. [Wills] almost seemed to be mooching for votes."

First came a mailshot to all Academy voters quoting a Hedda Hopper plug for his performance. As soon as her own copy arrived, Hopper leaped back into print: "On March 2, I wrote in this column that I hoped Chill Wills would get the Oscar. Now I learn that Chill has sent out letters using my name in an attempt to influence Academy voters to vote for him—and because of this he's just lost my vote." This panicked Wills into a public apology: "Although my representative may have gone too far, it is possible that Miss Hopper has also."

"Bow-Wow" didn't know where too far was. There followed ads

listing all the Oscar winners for whom Chill Wills had voted during his career. Then came a full page of testimonials from prominent Texans; then an advertisement listing every Academy member by name, hundreds of them, alongside a chummy picture of Chill, captioned: "Win, lose or draw, you're still my cousins, and I love you all." One of those listed, Groucho Marx, chose to reply with a paid ad of his own: "Dear Mr. Wills, I am delighted to be your cousin, but I'm still voting for Sal Mineo."

This goaded Bow-Wow, like Birdwell, into enlisting divine support. On the page opposite Groucho's jibe, he plastered a photo of a buckskinned Wills over a group portrait of the entire *Alamo* cast, with the message: "We of *The Alamo* cast are praying—harder than the real Texans prayed for their lives at the Alamo—for Chill Wills to win the Oscar. . . . Cousin Chill's acting was great. Your *Alamo* cousins."

Variety had had enough, and rejected the ad; but the *Hollywood Reporter* published it. The trouble was that neither Wills nor Bow-Wow had actually consulted their *Alamo* cousins before taking their names in vain. That day's meeting between Wayne and Birdwell was funereal. The entire movie community had now turned against their film; the popular slogan now doing the Hollywood rounds was "Forget *The Alamo*," a cruel parody of the film's motto, "Remember the Alamo." He and Wayne, said Birdwell, felt "as if someone had taken a bucket of fecal matter and thrown it over a beautiful red rose." It was more than time to distance themselves from Chill Wills. The next day, March 27, saw Chill's numero uno cousin, Duke Wayne himself, buy space for a magisterial riposte in the very next issues of both *Variety* and the *Hollywood Reporter*:

> I wish to state that the Chill Wills ad published in the *Hollywood Reporter*, of which we had no advance knowledge . . . makes an untrue and reprehensible claim. No one in the Batjac organization [Wayne's production company] or in the Russell Birdwell office has been a party to his trade paper advertising.
>
> I refrain from using stronger language because I am sure his intentions were not as bad as his taste.

This was enough to dish Chill's chances, but had the entire episode done in *The Alamo*? It looked like it, as the columnists declared open season on Wayne and all his works, with the *Los Angeles Times*'s Joe Hyams suggesting that "the battle raging around *The Alamo* threatens to make the original scrap look like a skirmish. . . . For John Wayne to impugn Mr. Wills's taste is tantamount to Jayne Mansfield criticizing Sabrina for too much exposure." Billy Wilder, too, was enjoying himself, as he rightly sensed that all this was swinging the Oscar voting his and *The Apartment*'s way; after collecting the Directors Guild award, Wilder joked with the audience to "Keep praying, cousins! We hope Oscar will say the right thing this year."

A chastened Bow-Wow finally attempted a desperate salvage operation with a signed personal announcement of his own—apologizing, like his client, for his excess of zeal. At $250 a page in those days, the trades were making a mint out of the *Alamo* cousins and their domestic strife:

> Chill Wills was in no way responsible for the *Alamo* ad which appeared in the *Reporter* Friday. Chill Wills did not know anything whatsoever about this ad and when he saw it he was madder than John Wayne and Russell Birdwell put together. I informed John Wayne and Russell Birdwell after the ad appeared that I was fully responsible.

By then, of course, it was too late. After *Spartacus*'s Peter Ustinov had been declared a worthy winner of the 1960 Oscar for Best Supporting Actor, Wills told Hopper's rival Sheilah Graham what he now thought of his publicist: "I always had a very reputable name in this town. One day I'll get even with that so-and-so if it's the last thing I do."

The *Alamo* acrimony destroyed the Oscar chances of its cinematographer, William Clothier, who was beaten by *Spartacus*'s Russell Metty; and its composer, Dmitri Tiomkin, who lost both Best Score and Best Song, to *Exodus*'s Ernest Gold and *Never on Sunday*'s Manos Hadjidakis respectively. Wayne and his *Alamo* wound up winning just one impersonal Oscar—for Sound—while Billy Wilder became only the second man (after *All About Eve*'s Mankiewicz) to win three for one film: as producer, director and writer of *The Apartment*, voted Best Picture of 1960, with five Oscars from ten nominations. Its star, Jack Lemmon, was an unlucky loser to Burt Lancaster's *Elmer Gantry;* but all eyes were much more firmly fixed on what promised to be an unusually open race for Best Actress.

Or *had* so promised—until the news came from the London Clinic, just as the voting period began, that Elizabeth Taylor was "gravely" ill. LIZ DYING screamed the front pages of the Los Angeles tabloids on the same day that Academy members were receiving their ballot papers. It was to prove the best-timed illness in Oscar history.

All bets were suddenly off as MGM launched a massive ad campaign, Liz was hastily forgiven for stealing Debbie Reynolds's husband, and all the other nominees joined forces to sing her praises. Even Debbie Reynolds said she would be voting for her—as did poor Deborah Kerr *(The Sundowners),* who had hoped to avoid becoming the most unsuccessful Best Actress nominee in Oscar annals, with a record of six nominations and no wins. "The Oscar should go to Elizabeth," said Kerr (who had herself recently changed husbands), "not because of her grave illness, but because her performance in *Butterfield 8* is superb. She deserves the prize as Best Actress. She has been in the running many times and perhaps this will be the lucky time." It did MGM's P.R. effort no harm, of course, that Taylor's role in the film climaxed in her sudden, unnecessary death.

Taylor's illness was harder on Melina Mercouri, enjoying her first (and only) nomination for *Never on Sunday,* than on Greer Garson at her sixth (twenty years after her first) as Eleanor Roosevelt in *Sunrise at Campobello*. The young Shirley MacLaine *(The Apartment)* canceled her plans to return from location in Japan for the ceremony—then, somewhat incongruously, called Taylor to ask her to accept for her if she won.

Liz, by now, seemed to have made a dramatic recovery from her mystery illness. Voting had almost closed by the time Taylor fans had unraveled the contradictory diagnoses crossing the Atlantic with each news bulletin. What had started in her Dorchester suite as "flu" —putting an expensive halt to work on *Cleopatra*—had quickly worsened via an abscessed tooth to a virus, pneumonia or meningitis, depending which newspaper you read. It was certainly true that 29-year-old Taylor experienced breathing difficulties and turned blue; given fifteen minutes to live, she underwent an emergency tracheotomy. Her condition was then described as "grave." For four days and nights, as she hovered between life and death, Eddie Fisher kept watch at her bedside. Taylor herself later said that she had died "at least four times." Then began a "miracle" recovery, subsequently attributed to the arrival of her mother, Sara, with a team of Christian Scientists.

By Oscar night, Liz had safely arrived for her recuperation in Santa Monica—in whose Civic Auditorium this year's ceremonies were to be held, as they would be throughout the 1960s, after ten years at the RKO Pantages. She and Fisher had been met at Los Angeles Airport by her former husband, Michael Wilding, who relieved them of his seven-year-old son, Chris. As they drove away, Wilding recalled, Chris "sat in the back seat and began giving a little speech, holding a Coke bottle up in front of him. Then he pretended to cry. 'What are you up to?' I asked. Chris said, 'I'm Mummy collecting her Oscar and I have to look like I'm crying.' "

The rules of the Academy Awards forbid posthumous Oscar nominations. The only nominated actor to die between the nominations and the awards ceremony—Peter Finch in 1976—was to wind up winning Best Actor for *Network*. In 1981, when he was known to be seriously ill, Henry Fonda was voted Best Actor for *On Golden Pond*; astonishingly, Fonda had only one previous (and unsuccessful) nomination, for *The Grapes of Wrath* in 1940. His daughter (and costar) Jane picked up the Oscar for him, and he died five months later.

But Liz Taylor in 1960 remains the only example of someone voted an Oscar because the electorate thought she was at death's door—and then recovering in time to pick it up. To be fair, it was Taylor's fourth consecutive nomination* in the Leading Role category, and she might well have won for either *Cat on a Hot Tin Roof* (1958) or *Suddenly, Last Summer* (1959).

"Play Gloria [Wandrous], and you'll get the Academy Award!" had been one of the lines used by Pandro S. Berman to bully Taylor into reluctantly taking a role she hadn't much liked. But there were very few, Taylor included, who thought that she deserved it. Peter H. Brown speaks for the critical consensus with his view that in 1960

* A feat she shares with Marlon Brando (1951–54), Jennifer Jones (1943–46), Al Pacino (1972–75) and Thelma Ritter (1950–53). Only Bette Davis (1938–42) and Greer Garson (1941-45) have achieved five. See Appendix C, section B6.

"Liz was the sole nominee who obviously did *not* deserve the Oscar." Many believe she merited the award even less than some of that year's unlucky nonnominees: Jean Simmons in *Elmer Gantry*, for instance, or Wendy Hiller in *Sons and Lovers*. Taylor herself has since conceded that she won "because, I'm afraid, I had come within a breath of dying. . . . I was filled with profound gratitude at being considered by the industry an actress and not a movie star. But I knew my performance had not deserved it, that it was a sympathy award." Said a rueful Shirley MacLaine of her own second unsuccessful nomination: "I lost to a tracheotomy." Few expected MacLaine to have to wait another twenty-three years to win.

Her ankle still bandaged from intravenous feeding, Taylor was helped to the podium by Fisher to receive her Oscar from Yul Brynner. "I don't really know how to express my gratitude," she said. "All I can say is thank you." Six months later she charged Twentieth Century Fox a *second* million dollars to restart production of *Cleopatra* in Rome. Ever since Taylor has told all comers how much she hated herself in *Butterfield 8*; when she saw an early print in a projection room, she threw her shoes at the screen, and has never since watched the film through.

Ironically enough, as it transpired, an Honorary Oscar was presented that same night to "the kind of American who's loved in all four corners of the earth"—Gary Cooper, who was too ill to accept it in person. Picking it up on Cooper's behalf, his close friend James Stewart began to weep during his speech, leaving the audience wondering just how ill "Coop" really was. He died less than a month later.

"Thank goodness our Oscars came back to America!" exulted Louella Parsons in her column next day. It was almost a decade since so many major Oscars had been won by native-born Americans, and Hollywood was still hurting. Television might have made the Academy Awards show financially secure, but it was still posing a major threat at the box office. And Parsons's celebrations were to prove premature: 1961 saw Best Actor and Actress go to an Austrian and an Italian, while an all-American musical won virtually everything else. There would then follow another sustained British invasion.

The Mirisch brothers, owners of the film rights to Leonard

Bernstein's *West Side Story*, originally wanted to cast Elvis Presley as Tony, gang leader of the Jets, with three other rock stars of the moment—Fabian, Frankie Avalon and Paul Anka—as his costars. It took the director Jerome Robbins, who had "conceived, directed and choreographed" the musical on Broadway, to talk them out of it; in return for which, the brothers hired Robert Wise to keep Robbins's own artistic zeal in check. Ten weeks were enough for Wise to see Robbins off the set, retaining his assistants to help him wrap the movie. Perhaps by way of sympathy, the Academy handed Robbins an Honorary Oscar "for his brilliant achievements in the art of choreography on film" on top of the directing award he shared with Wise—who, as producer, also carried off the Best Picture award.

West Side Story's ten wins from eleven nominations—Adapted Screenplay was the only category in which it lost out—remains second only to *Ben-Hur*'s eleven-for-twelve in 1959, a clutch of Oscars unmatched to this day. The year 1961 was one of records and precedents, as Robbins and Wise became the first duo to share Best Director, and Sophia Loren the first player to win a Leading Role Oscar for a foreign-language performance, for her subtitled Italian-speaking role in *Two Women*. "You see, I am not just a sexy pot," declared Loren, who had the opportunist Joseph E. Levine to thank for her unlikely transformation from sex siren to award-winning actress. Having bought the foreign rights to *La Ciociara* for "peanuts," Levine traded shamelessly on Loren's name by booking the picture, subtitles and all, into the kind of theaters normally showing Doris Day—and mopped up.

The Swiss actor Maximilian Schell took Best Actor for his stage-to-screen role as the Nazi defense lawyer in *Judgment at Nuremberg*. But "Oscar is a funny brute," as the film historian David Shipman puts it. Schell's was "one of the few Oscar victories unanimously anticipated, and much approved of afterwards . . . but apart from those character actors for whom the Oscar could be only a temporary fillip (Victor McLaglen, Paul Lukas, Broderick Crawford, Ernest Borgnine, F. Murray Ábraham), none has got so little out of it." Schell himself later said: "I had to restart after that. I couldn't go up. I had to go down in order to scale the mountain again."

This was also the year that George C. Scott, two years after losing the Supporting Oscar to *Ben-Hur*'s Hugh Griffith, tried to withdraw his name after it was announced among the five supporting nominees for his performance in *The Hustler*. Handing the Academy Award what *The New York Times* called "a slap in its gold-plated face," Scott declared that "I take the position that actors shouldn't be forced to out-advertise and out-stab each other." Reigning Best Actor Burt Lancaster hit back: "His attitude really doesn't make any sense. He's under no pressure to take any ads. All he has to do is *not* take any ads." Denied his wish to withdraw, on the grounds that it was his performance rather than his person which had been nominated, Scott lost for the second time to another freak "sweep" beneficiary: George Chakiris of *West Side Story*, who was to surpass even Schell in subsequent obscurity.

But Academy insiders were relieved that, in Chakiris and Rita Moreno, the Supporting categories had at least been won by talented young players in genuinely supporting roles. Not since *Around the World in 80 Days* had a film been crammed with as many starry cameos as *Judgment at Nuremberg*, which had now renewed controversy about the Supporting categories by winning nominations for Judy Garland and Montgomery Clift, who already had four Leading Role nominations between them. For stars to be competing in the Supporting category, wrote Louella Parsons, was like "a bank president reducing himself to the title of bookkeeper in order to get a coffee break." The category had never been intended for front-rank stars to maneuver their way toward Academy Awards; it was designed to honor the more talented of second-rank players.

Clift thus did himself double damage with a shameless advertising campaign, stressing his depressed, far from healthy appearance. The clear implication, at the fourth time of asking, was that this was your last chance to vote Monty Clift an Oscar. He had apparently been "very upset" about failing to win for *From Here to Eternity*. "What do I have to do to prove I can act?" he had demanded of *The New York Times*'s movie critic, Howard Thompson, over drinks at P. J. Clarke's. A friend described him at the time as "in despair"; now eight years on, the unseemliness of Clift's Oscar campaign may well have cost him the award.

This was but one of a number of signs that the Oscars were beginning to lose their way. The TV cameras, for instance, showed plenty of empty seats during the 1961 awards. For the first time in memory, a majority of the acting nominees hadn't bothered to show. It was partly that the alternative parties all over town were now more fun to go to than the Oscar show itself. And it was partly the unwillingness of the mighty to risk public humiliation.

Sophia Loren, for instance, at first announced that the honor would naturally bring her flying from Rome. Then she changed her mind: "I decided that I could not bear the ordeal of sitting in plain view of millions of viewers while my fate was being judged. If I lost, I might faint from disappointment; if I won, I would also very likely faint with joy. Instead of spreading my fainting all over the world, I decided it was better that I faint at home."

Having flown over from Europe, Audrey Hepburn *(Breakfast at Tiffany's)* allowed a sore throat to detain her in her hotel room. Judy Garland stayed at the bedside of her son Joey, who had an earache. Liz Taylor, filming *Cleopatra* in Rome, could not be tempted back by the honor of presenting Best Actor—the traditional privilege of the previous year's Best Actress—now that the charms of her latest leading man, Richard Burton, had so publicly replaced the short-lived Eddie Fisher's.

In the same city, Sophia Loren was asleep when Cary Grant telephoned the news of her unique victory. Though "rather giddy," Loren did not faint, after all; instead she mounted a passionate defense of the Oscar: "I know that some actors have deprecated the value and purpose of the Academy Award, but I'm certainly not one of them. As far as I am concerned, if you are a professional actor who has pride in his work, then the judgment of your peers should be important to you. I treasure each and every reward I have ever received." Loren's Oscar was subsequently stolen from her Villa Marino by thieves who apparently thought it was solid gold. "I sent the Academy sixty dollars and they mailed me a replacement."

The year's biggest box-office earner, *The Guns of Navarone*, had won three nominations but no awards. *The Hustler*, despite four acting nominations plus slots in the Best Director and Best Picture categories, had won only for Cinematography. Had *West Side Story* been an aberration? It looked as if the honors were beginning to drift abroad again.

To make things worse, the Academy's board of governors placed itself under widespread suspicion by voting an Honorary Oscar, the Irving Thalberg Award, to *Judgment at Nuremberg*'s Stanley Kramer. Kramer's film had won eleven nominations; he himself was in the running for Best Director and (as sole producer) Best Picture statuettes. Would he still have won the Thalberg if his film had enjoyed a sweep? It seemed harder than ever to believe that the board, for all their ritual protestations, did not know what was inside those envelopes.

As Sidney Skolsky pointed out, the 1961 Oscars had defected not merely to Austria and Italy, but to Broadway. Only by suspicious-looking practice had Hollywood managed to honor its own. "Oscar today," he wrote, "stands ironically as a symbol of Hollywood's lost supremacy rather than of its present glory."

From Hollywood's point of view, things were to get worse before they got better.

Throughout the 1960s Britain competed in Hollywood on equal terms. Four of the next seven years would see British films win both Best Picture and Best Director: David Lean's *Lawrence of Arabia*, Tony Richardson's *Tom Jones*, Fred Zinnemann's *A Man for All Seasons* and Carol Reed's *Oliver!* A parade of British films such as *Darling, Alfie* and *The Lion in Winter* all won Best Picture nominations, while the decade would end with another Briton, John Schlesinger, voted Best Director—though for an American film, *Midnight Cowboy*. British actors would do even better.

Only Lean's *Bridge on the River Kwai* had struck Oscar gold for Britain in the fifteen years since the success of Olivier's *Hamlet* had so convulsed the system. Now the same director was back, working on an even bigger canvas, compensating for refusals from Marlon Brando and Albert Finney by casting a devastating newcomer in the title role of *Lawrence of Arabia*. Peter O'Toole's record-breaking quest for an Oscar* began as a loser to Gregory Peck, a highly popular victor for his courageous small-town lawyer in the Universal

* With seven nominations (all as Best Actor in a Leading Role) and no wins, O'Toole holds the record for the most nominated actor never to win an Oscar. It is a distinction he shares with Richard Burton, who died Oscarless despite six nominations as Best Actor and one as Supporting Actor. As of the 1990 awards, however, one distinguished American was fast catching the two Britons: Al Pacino, whose failure to win Best Supporting Actor for *Dick Tracy* marked his sixth unsuccessful Oscar nomination.

film of Harper Lee's Pulitzer Prize-winning novel, *To Kill a Mockingbird.* "I'm not falsely modest about it," says Peck to this day. "I think I was good in that picture." The part of Atticus Finch was like "putting on an old suit of clothes—just comfortable." Before beginning work, Peck went to Alabama to meet the real Atticus, Lee's elderly father Amasa, who died during the filming. So moved was she by Peck's portrayal of her father that Lee then presented the actor with Amasa's pocket watch, which he had fingered as a prop during forty years of courtroom speeches. Now Peck himself stroked the watch as he waited for Sophia Loren to open the Best Actor envelope.

Ed Begley was a surprise winner of Supporting honors, over *Lawrence of Arabia*'s Omar Sharif, for Tennessee Williams's *Sweet Bird of Youth*. With both female awards going to the same film—to Anne Bancroft and sixteen-year-old Patty Duke in the Helen Keller biopic, *The Miracle Worker*—1962 marked the last year for a while of "worthy" winners in the acting categories. With the significant exception of Sidney Poitier the following year, and *Who's Afraid of Virginia Woolf* in 1966, the mid-sixties would largely see the Academy surrender to music and spectacle.

"This limey is deeply touched and greatly honored," said David Lean, picking up his second Best Director award, as *Lawrence of Arabia*'s seven wins (from ten nominations) shut out a number of torrid American dramas from Sidney Lumet's *Long Day's Journey into Night* to the sentimental favorite—Bette Davis "versus" Joan Crawford in *Whatever Happened to Baby Jane?*

TNT POTENTIAL SEEN IN PAIRING OF BETTE DAVIS AND JOAN CRAWFORD had been *The New York Times*'s reaction to the casting of the two veterans in a Robert Aldrich drama about two reclusive ex-movie sirens. "I wouldn't give you a dime for those two washed-up old bitches," was Jack Warner's (though he later agreed to distribute the film). The world was amazed when La Crawford accepted second billing to Davis, explaining sweetly to Hedda Hopper: "Bette comes first. She plays the title role." And no one believed the press releases denying rumors of a violent feud on the set, especially in view of what happened when the 1962 Best Actress nominations were announced.

Horrified that Davis should have been nominated—and she not—Crawford wrote congratulation notes to all four other nominees, adding that she would be delighted to pick up their Oscar for them if they could not attend the ceremony. Then she started a campaign among her friends on both coasts in favor of Bancroft, stranded on Broadway in a production of Brecht's *Mother Courage*. Bancroft had wanted her *Miracle Worker* costar, Patty Duke, to accept for her if she won; but when the Academy vetoed this, on the grounds that Duke was herself a nominee, she gratefully turned to the celebrated actress who was showing her such unexpected support and kindness: Joan Crawford.

Bancroft and Davis, the favorite, were both up against a Katharine Hepburn evidently desperate, for once, to win. Even Dwight Macdonald, who confessed himself in *Esquire* no great Hepburn fan ("She struck me usually as mannered, to say the least"), thought she had emerged as "a superb tragedienne" in *Long Day's Journey*. It brought Hepburn her ninth nomination—only one of which, almost thirty years before, had proved successful. Now the perpetually unavailable East Coast ice maiden was suddenly telephoning all the columnists, moving Sheilah Graham to observe that "Hepburn, almost as much of a recluse as Garbo, is actually almost as accessible as Zsa Zsa Gabor. She'd love to win."

So, she made it clear, would Davis. "I *want* that Oscar," she told *Variety*'s Army Archerd. "I *have* to be the first to win three!" And she felt confident: "I was positive I would get it, and so was everyone in town."

Come the big night, Crawford held permanent party in her backstage dressing room—with winners, losers and presenters alike invited to join her for canapés and drinks served from coolers bearing the logo of Pepsi-Cola (of which her late husband, Alfred Steele, had been chairman of the board). When the time came for the Best Actress award, she and Davis hovered in the wings three feet apart, both chain smoking. As Maximilian Schell read out the nominees, Davis handed her purse to her friend Olivia de Havilland. When he announced the winner to be Anne Bancroft, Davis "almost dropped dead. I was paralyzed with shock," she said. Crawford placed a hand on her shoulder, muttered, "Excuse me," and pushed past onto the stage as if she herself were the winner.

"Her behavior," to Davis, was "despicable." More than twenty years later, in May 1986, she was still fuming about the episode on

Johnny Carson's *Tonight* show, complaining that this was one Oscar of which she had been "really robbed."

"The widow Steele was there to receive the prize," Davis told Carson. "She carried the Oscar around for a year selling Pepsi-Cola. . . . A year later—*one year later*—she threw a party onstage at the theater where *Mother Courage* was still playing, and finally presented Miss Bancroft with her Oscar." As persistently as Bette Davis told this story, however, Crawford as strenuously denied it, finally sending the writer Shaun Considine a newspaper clipping purporting to show her handing over the Oscar to Anne Bancroft one week after the awards show. Bancroft finally settled the matter by confirming to Considine that Crawford was right. "She brought the award to me, sometime shortly after the awards, while *Mother Courage* was still playing on Broadway."

Thanks perhaps to a subsequent legal threat from Crawford, Davis's memoirs suggest that the "two old broads . . . got along famously" during the filming of *Whatever Happened to Baby Jane*. The film was such a success that Davis felt obliged to drive home her employability in a trade-paper advertisement considered a misjudgment by her friends:

> Mother of three—10, 11 and 15. Divorcee. American. Thirty years experience as an actress in motion pictures. Mobile still and more affable than rumor would have it. Wants steady employment in Hollywood (has had Broadway). BETTE DAVIS, c/o Martin Baum, GAC. References upon request.

A newspaper strike in New York, depriving Academy voters of their usual guidance from the New York critics' awards, proved a mixed blessing when the 1962 Oscar nominations were announced. Unusually close scrutiny by *The New York Times* concluded that "vote-swapping of outrageous proportions" was indicated by the Best Picture nominations. How come two major studio blockbusters had made it to the Best Picture category without winning a single nomination in the acting, directing or writing departments? Twentieth Century Fox's *The Longest Day* and MGM's *Mutiny on the Bounty*, argued the *Times*'s Murray Schumach, must have been beneficiaries of behind-the-scenes horse-trading by the studio moguls who still controlled huge block votes.

"The undercover politics of Oscar campaigning, combined with lavish advertising," wrote Schumach, "make it almost impossible for any movie to be nominated for best film in the future unless it is distributed by the major companies." Newly restored to the head of production's office at Fox, Darryl Zanuck indignantly defended his $10 million baby, *The Longest Day*, while *Bounty*'s producer, Aaron Rosenberg, frankly admitted himself "pleasantly surprised" at the nomination that gave his $20 million disappointment a much-needed shot in the arm.

The same sort of muscle power won unlikely Best Picture nominations the following year for MGM's Cinerama epic, *How the West Was Won*, and Fox's notorious *Cleopatra*—at its last estimate, $44 million, the most expensive picture made to that time. With neither director winning a nomination, *The New York Times* was again on the rampage: "If either Metro or Fox spends a great deal of money on a movie, the members of the Academy may feel an obligation to reward those studios." Elia Kazan's *America, America*, despite dark memories of his conduct during the blacklist, was the year's only "home-grown" Best Picture candidate with a nominated director.

Fox missed a trick by listing the entire cast of *Cleopatra* as Leading Players, thus carelessly depriving Roddy McDowall of a realistic shot at the Supporting Oscar. In vain did the studio plead with the Academy; it was too late, they were told, the ballots were already at the printers. The episode did persuade the Academy to change the rules, as of the following year, so that voters could decide the appropriate categories for themselves. But the only consolation Fox could afford McDowall was a public apology, in the shape of an open letter printed in the trade papers:

> We feel it is important that the industry realize that your electric performance as Octavian in *Cleopatra*, which was unanimously singled out by the critics as one of the best supporting actor performances by an actor this year, is not eligible for an Academy Award nomination in that category . . . due to a regrettable error on the part of 20th Century Fox.

As Britain's *Tom Jones* began stealing all the pre-Oscar awards, its dashing young star, Albert Finney, capitalized on his success with a Broadway run in *Luther*—written and directed by the same team of John Osborne and Tony Richardson. Facing the threat of another British sweep, Hollywood was desperate for an American product to rally behind. As *Tom Jones* was attacked for its moral laxity, however, the "home-grown" alternatives were scarcely more wholesome.

Paul Newman had turned in a stunning performance in *Hud*: "How he rejoices in the mastery of his craft! Luckily, it's a joy without a trace of self-satisfaction, and therefore harmless," wrote *The New Yorker*. "The Academy might as well give him an Oscar right now and get it over with." But the film was not going to win any moral leadership awards. As the Oscar season approached, the perfect alternative suddenly emerged from nowhere in *Lilies of the Field*, the unlikely-sounding saga of some German nuns who build a chapel in New Mexico with the help of an itinerant black workman named Homer Smith. A low-budget film shot in just fourteen days, it offered a showcase part to Sidney Poitier, five years after his nomination for *The Defiant Ones*. Even Paul Newman said: "I'd like to see Sidney Poitier get it. I'd be proud to win for a role I really had to reach for."

Poitier's inevitable nomination for *Lilies* did not carry the usually indispensable bonus of a nomination for his director, Ralph Nelson. But this was the year that a group of Hollywood notables, including Gregory Peck, Judy Garland, Blake Edwards and Martin Ritt (nominated director of *Hud*), had joined Charlton Heston in the summer's civil rights march on Washington. The film might not have been the perfect vehicle—it overflowed, according to *Newsweek*, with "enough brotherhood, piety and honest labor to make even the kindest spectator retch"—but the timing was immaculate. "If ever there was a year when the Negro should be honored," enthused Skolsky, "it is this year for obvious reasons. It would pour soothing oil on troubled waters."

This was the point that began to trouble Poitier himself, as the trade-press ads and the political pressure piled up. Dorothy Dandridge (*Carmen Jones*, 1954) and Poitier himself were then the only black actors ever to have won Leading Role nominations, matched by Ethel Waters (*Pinky*, 1949) and Juanita Moore (*Imitation of Life*, 1959) in the Supporting category. The only two blacks to have won Oscars, Hattie McDaniel in *Gone With the Wind* (Supporting Actress, 1939) and James Baskett (Honorary Award, 1947, for his "heart-warming characterization of Uncle Remus"), had scarcely represented the aspirations of the NAACP.

Thinking he had no chance of victory, Poitier decided to attend "primarily because I felt it would be good for black people to see themselves competing for the top honor, especially since we as a people had not been that close to an Academy Award for some time." Also, he confessed, he thought "it might be a good career move to be present."

But Poitier did not enjoy himself. He later recalled the night with the vivid assistance of the present tense: "I am absolutely beside myself with nervousness. I begin making promises to myself in my mind. I say: 'I can understand that this is an important moment and I have to be here and in fact I want to be here for what it means to us as a people, but I'm never going to put myself through this shit no more—never again under no circumstances am I going to come here again and put myself through this.' "

At the time, even victory seemed to carry little symbolic significance for him: "I do hope there will be some residual benefits for other Negro actors, but I don't fool myself into thinking the effect will be vast." Backstage, after winning an award considered mighty important by black Americans, Poitier told the assembled press corps how "uneasy" he had felt in his early moviegoing days about seeing Negro actors onscreen. "There was the Negro devoid of any dignity: good maids who laughed too loudly, good butlers afraid of ghosts." He wanted to make "motion pictures about the dignity, nobility, the magnificence of human life."

So what did the Leading Role award do for Sidney Poitier? "The only real change in my career," he said, "was in the attitude of newsmen. They started to quiz me on civil rights and the Negro question incessantly. Ever since I won the Oscar, that's what they've been interested in. Period." He had cause to review this statement in March 1992, when the American Film Institute made him the twentieth recipient of its lifetime achievement award. "I speak for two generations of black actors," said Oscar nominee Morgan Freeman, "when I thank you, Mr. Poitier, for sticking to your dream, for in so doing you've set fire to mine." To *Boyz N the Hood*'s John Singleton, who had recently become the first black director ever to win an Academy Award nomination (and, at 23, the youngest directing nominee ever), Poitier was "a pioneer who changed the way African-Americans are regarded on the screen." Columbia Pictures and the Sony Corporation were so moved that they renamed the studio's Louis B. Mayer Building after Poitier.

Albert Finney and Paul Newman had been the front-runners, as the only Best Actor nominees whose directors were also nominated. But the perennially aloof Newman made no attempt to capitalize on *Hud*'s terrific reviews. And Finney, the only one of all five nominees to enjoy the benefit of Best Director and Picture nominations, resisted United Artists' attempts to bring him to campaign in Hollywood; he chose instead to drop out of *Luther* and disappear indefinitely to the South Seas. Finney may thus have assisted Poitier to beat him to Best Actor, but the dreaded British "sweep" for *Tom Jones* otherwise proved irresistible. The film won four of its ten nominations to *Cleopatra*'s four-for-nine; but *Cleopatra*'s honors were for Cinematography and Art Direction, Costumes and Special Effects, whereas *Tom Jones* carried such major categories as Best Screenplay for Osborne, and Best Director and Picture for Richardson.

Tom Jones was only the third film in Oscar history to boast three acting nominations in the same category, though Diane Cilento, Dame Edith Evans and Joyce Redman between them split the vote in favor of their fellow Briton, Dame Margaret Rutherford, in Burton and Taylor's post-*Cleopatra* audience-grabber, *The VIPs*. As many as nine of the year's twenty acting nominees were British; Rutherford was the only British winner, though Patricia Neal, named Best Actress for *Hud*, was regarded as an "honorary Brit" since she had married the English writer Roald Dahl and settled in the U.K. Given Neal's fine performance, it was highly unfair that her victory was widely attributed to a "sympathy vote" for the unusual degree of personal tragedy that had dogged her life.

"I wonder why we hate ourselves?" complained Hedda Hopper of the British uprising. "I'm not going to be narrow enough to claim these fellows can't act. They've had plenty of practice. The weather is so foul on that tight little isle of theirs that, to get in out of the rain, they all gather in theaters and practice *Hamlet* on each other."

The following year would bring Hedda even worse news. For the first and only time in Oscar history, not one acting award stayed in the United States. Ten of the acting nominations went to Britain, one to Italy (Sophia Loren in *Marriage Italian Style*) and one to France: Lila Kedrova, who won Supporting Actress for her first English-language role, in *Zorba the Greek*. An eccentric male Supporting race saw Peter Ustinov pick up his second Oscar (for *Topkapi*). Alongside his two Emmys, for playing Socrates and Dr. Johnson, respectively, the two Oscars standing on Ustinov's desk looked like "two emasculated gentlemen . . . made for a fine mixed-double match with two emasculated ladies." When he subsequently won a third Emmy as an aged Long Island delicatessen-owner, "we had an umpire as well."

Peter Sellers's constant tirades against Hollywood and all its works supposedly cost him an Oscar for his mercurial performance in *Dr. Strangelove*. "If he'd kept his mouth shut," one leading Academician told Sellers's biographer, Peter Evans, "it was in the bag. The man tripped up the actor." As it was, Rex Harrison surprised no one by winning Best Actor for *My Fair Lady*.

The real interest lay in the Best Actress contest. Nineteen sixty-four's unusual saga, which was to have a domino effect on the following year's results, began with Jack Warner's refusal to cast Rex Harrison's stage partner, Julie Andrews, opposite him in the film. "No one in the sticks has ever heard of her," said Warner of Andrews, who had played the part onstage for three and a half years and was regarded as the definitive Eliza Dolittle—until the film appeared, complete with a wholly beguiling performance by his alternative choice, Audrey Hepburn.

Outrage at Warner's snub to Andrews was then matched only by more outrage at the Academy's failure to nominate Hepburn—apparently because her singing voice had been dubbed by Marni Nixon (who had also sung for Natalie Wood in *West Side Story*). Producer Mervyn LeRoy professed himself "very disappointed. . . . I find it very mean of Hollywood not to have nominated this great actress." *My Fair Lady* had been nominated in every major category except Best Actress, where the voters had managed to display a fine sense of irony.

Had she lost the part to anyone but Hepburn, said Andrews, she would have been "blazing mad. Of course I wanted to play it. Who wouldn't have wanted to play Eliza? But in a way it's a good thing having to play a different role. People at least will know I can do something else." That something else was Disney's *Mary Poppins*, which now enabled the Academy to apologize for Jack Warner's behavior by nominating her anyway. With resistible opposition from two previous winners, Anne Bancroft (in *The Pumpkin Eater*) and Sophia Loren (*Marriage Italian Style*), and two longshots, Debbie Reynolds (*The Unsinkable Molly Brown*) and Kim Stanley (*Séance on a Wet Afternoon*), it began to look like Andrews might win Best Actress as a consolation prize for not appearing in *My Fair Lady*, the year's front-runner for Best Picture. Also going for her was *Mary Poppins*'s tally of thirteen nominations to *My Fair Lady*'s twelve, not to mention the film's phenomenal box-office performance.

The week before the nominations, Pat Neal suffered a stroke so severe that it would obviously be impossible for her to perform the reigning Best Actress's ritual task of handing out the Best Actor award. Amid the Andrews-Hepburn acrimony, some Academy genius had the bright idea of inviting Hepburn to take Neal's place—thus asking her, by the look of things, to watch the original Eliza crowned Best Actress. Many a Hollywood grande dame would have had trouble with the idea; but the ever gracious Hepburn accepted, thus showing that she held no grudge over not being nominated, and was prepared to watch Andrews pick up the Oscar that many were saying should have been hers. In a situation fraught with political complexity, Hepburn's gesture was seen in Hollywood as sportsmanship of a heroic order.

Joseph Losey's *The Servant*, Tennessee Williams's *The Night of the Iguana* and The Beatles's *A Hard Day's Night* were among the films overlooked as *Dr. Strangelove, Zorba the Greek* and *Becket* joined the two big musicals as Best Picture nominees. Though *Becket* matched *My Fair Lady* with twelve nominations, including another one each for those perennial losers O'Toole and Burton, it collected only a screenplay award—thus sharing with *Johnny Belinda* (1948) the ignominious record for all-time lowest Oscar success rate.* While *Zorba* collected three and Stanley Kubrick's *Dr. Strangelove* none, *Mary Poppins* went on to win five Oscars, including Best Actress for Julie Andrews, and *My Fair Lady* eight, including

* This dubious distinction was later to be rivaled by *The Turning Point* (1977) and *The Color Purple* (1985), which each won eleven nominations but no Oscars at all.

All smiles on the set, but all-out war behind the scenes as Bette Davis beat her co-star Joan Crawford to a 1962 Best Actress nomination for Whatever Happened to Baby Jane?

Who's Afraid of Virginia Woolf? broke new ground in 1966 when the entire cast—Liz Taylor, Richard Burton, George Segal and Sandy Dennis—was nominated for Oscars (as well as the film's director Mike Nichols and writer producer Ernest Lehman). Only Taylor and Dennis won.

Katharine Hepburn won her second Oscar, 34 years after her first, for Guess Who's Coming to Dinner, the last film she made with Spencer Tracy. She was called "the first person to win because her co-star died."

Sidney Poitier (LEFT), who won an Oscar for Lilies of the Field in 1963, remains the only black actor who has won the Best Actor award. "I don't fool myself into thinking the effect will be vast," he said at the time, but Poitier has since proved an inspirational figure to African-American performers.

Best Actor (Harrison), Director (George Cukor) and Picture. Cukor, on his first success in five nominations over more than thirty years, said, "It is good for the soul, if not very pleasant, to sit there with your nomination and be turned down in front of a hundred million people. But when you do get it, it is a glory. Mine seemed to be an inordinately long time coming, but when I got it, it meant more to me than any other award I ever received."

When Rex Harrison received his Oscar from Hepburn, he tactfully offered thanks and "deep love" to "well, *two* fair ladies." And when Sidney Poitier duly named Mary Poppins Best Actress, the screen Eliza stood up to applaud her stage counterpart. On winning a Golden Globe six weeks before, Andrews had saucily thanked Jack Warner (who was sitting in the front row) "for making it all possible." On Oscar night, she thanked the entire country: "You Americans are famous for your hospitality, but this is ridiculous!"

But Andrews was soon to find the Academy Award a mixed blessing, cementing a saccharine typecasting that would take her years to escape. With *The Sound of Music* breaking all known box-office records, outdoing even *Gone With the Wind* as the biggest grosser then known, she was subsequently indulged to the tune of $14 million in *Star!*, a lavish portrait of Gertrude Lawrence which again proved the Oscar magic fallible. *Thoroughly Modern Millie* had fared little better. Having ended the sixties as the most popular star in her native Britain, and the fourth biggest draw in the United States, she began a desperate search for a break-out role. *Poppins* and *The Sound of Music* had forever fixed the screen image of an actress bedded by James Garner in *The Americanization of Emily* and Paul Newman in Hitchcock's *Torn Curtain*, but now unable even to swear onscreen.

Andrews thought *Star!* failed "because the public wasn't happy seeing me in drunken scenes." Then the public failed to accept her as a spy in *Darling Lili.* "I was a victim of typecasting. I can't knock *The Sound of Music* and *Mary Poppins*, because they gave an awful lot of pleasure to so many people. But that kind of exposure puts you in danger. I won an Oscar for *Mary Poppins* and then went into the most successful musical up to that time. Now I can see that I was too quickly bracketed in one category. And I couldn't escape." *The Julie Andrews Hour*, a syndicated British TV show, did badly enough to be canceled by Lord Grade after one series; and an eight-week, $250,000-a-week contract in Las Vegas was wound up after just one. *Mary Poppins* had left Julie Andrews in the professional wilderness.

After a series of seventies flops, it fell to her husband, Blake Edwards, to go to work on Andrews's screen image with a couple of vehicles that amounted to electric shlock therapy. After both she and Dudley Moore had benefited (though each strangely cast) from the commercial success of Bo Derek's *10*, Edwards had his wife bare her breasts in *S.O.B.* and turn transvestite in *Victor/Victoria.* Though she was nominated for an Oscar in the latter (1982), it failed at the box office, and led only to *Duet for One*—a Konchalovsky picture so dire that Edwards was rumored to be buying up all the prints. "What I'd like one day," said Andrews, forlornly, "is to be someone who is fascinating—a person you want to look at or see no matter what they're doing." As yet, for all her undoubted screen skills, neither her Oscar-mummified Disney sweetness nor her artistically erratic husband has much helped her toward this goal.

Audrey Hepburn, meanwhile, had not merely won herself a legion of new friends; she had inadvertently won the following year's Leading Role Oscar for another British actress. Julie Andrews would undoubtedly have won for her role in 1965's Best Picture, *The Sound of Music*—still one of the most successful films ever made—had it not been for her eccentric win the previous year as *Mary Poppins.* The beneficiary turned out to be Julie Christie, who squeaked to victory past three other Hollywood outsiders, the British Samantha Eggar *(The Collector),* the French Simone Signoret *(Ship of Fools)* and the only American nominee: a 22-year-old newcomer named Elizabeth Hartman, plucked from obscurity to play a blind girl in MGM's *A Patch of Blue.* It was Christie's unusual good fortune, apart from the sidelining of Julie Andrews, to have a leading role in two of the Best Picture nominees: David Lean's *Doctor Zhivago* as well as John Schlesinger's *Darling*, for which she was nominated.

Though flown in from London as a presenter, Christie caused trouble by defying the Academy's official ban on miniskirts—sneaking hers past the Oscar costume chief, Edith Head, even as she went onstage. "This is the most wonderful thing on earth," she stammered, and fled home to headlines like OCAR FOR JULIE, predicting that the award would earn her a million dollars a year for ten years. In fact the next decade held little beyond three entertainments with her lover Warren Beatty—*McCabe and Mrs. Miller, Shampoo* and *Heaven Can Wait*—with the honorable exception of Nicholas Roeg's *Don't Look Now* with Donald Sutherland. By the 1980s Christie's political and personal preoccupations witnessed an almost complete disappearance from mainstream films, with *Heat and Dust* a rare and tantalizing reminder of the talent now deployed in occasional if worthy art-house obscurities.

The 1965 awards were the first to be televised in color. "Just think," said Bob Hope, "you can actually see the losers turn green." In fact, it turned out to be a year of unusually dignified runners-up. Julie Andrews congratulated her compatriot Julie Christie with the observation that winning two years in a row would have been "difficult to live up to." She had been spared "the Luise Rainer jinx."

Like Christie, Rod Steiger had the bonus of a malevolent cameo in *Doctor Zhivago* to contrast with his holocaust survivor in Sidney Lumet's *The Pawnbroker*. But Steiger was equally philosophical when his bravura performance lost out to an eccentric Academy vote for Lee Marvin in *Cat Ballou*. It was eleven years since he had been one of three supporting actors nominated for *On The Waterfront;* merely winning nominations, said Steiger, was in itself "an enormous help in getting directors to listen to me when I feel a scene isn't going right." It simply was not the right year, he acknowledged, for an independent production like *The Pawnbroker*. "When *The Sound of Music* gets an Academy Award, you *know* it's Hollywood's year. The previous year had seen England take the major honors, so Hollywood had to say, 'Wait a minute. This is America. This must be America's year.' " *The Sound of Music* and *Doctor Zhivago* tied with five wins each out of ten nominations, though it was the blockbuster musical that carried off the major honors, including Best Director (Robert Wise) and Best Picture.

Hedda Hopper's death two months before the 1965 ceremonies spared her from seeing her beloved Oscars continuing the export trend she so hated. This was the year in which U.S. actors had to defy the odds to win—as indeed they did, to some raised European eyebrows. The year's three American winners (Lee Marvin, Martin Balsam and Shelley Winters) emerged from only seven Americans among the twenty nominees. Laurence Olivier's film of his stage *Othello* had won nominations for all four of its principals: Olivier in the title role, Frank Finlay (Iago), Maggie Smith (Desdemona) and Joyce Redman (Emilia). Two more Britons, Ian Bannen *(The Flight of the Phoenix)* and Tom Courtenay *(Doctor Zhivago),* were among the nominees for Supporting Actor; and Richard Burton's steely performance in the first John le Carré film, *The Spy Who Came in from the Cold*, was enough to obliterate the memory of *The Sandpiper*, the latest dire vehicle for the Burton-Taylor juggernaut.

Of the three nominated directors whose films were also Best Picture nominees, the lone American won: Robert Wise seeing off a double British challenge from Lean and Schlesinger. But both writing awards went to the U.K.: to Robert Bolt for *Doctor Zhivago* and Frederic Raphael for *Darling*.

Three winners from seven nominees out of twenty: a curious statistic, which was precisely repeated the following year. Nineteen sixty-six saw *The Sound of Music*'s triumphant writer-producer, Ernest Lehman, make a sharp change of direction with the acerbic Edward Albee drama *Who's Afraid of Virginia Woolf?*. He it was who persuaded Jack Warner not to listen to the pleas of Bette Davis, still desperate to be the first actor to win a third Oscar, that she and Henry Fonda should be cast as the warring George and Martha. No, Lehman had hit on a smarter idea: who better to play 1960's most celebrated fictional couple than the decade's most celebrated real-life couple? *Virginia Woolf*, in which the young George Segal and Sandy Dennis were cast opposite Burton and Taylor in top form, became the first film in history whose entire cast was nominated for Academy Awards.

Joining Burton was another distinguished Shakespearean from the British stage, Paul Scofield, the natural choice to repeat his stage success in Fred Zinnemann's film of Robert Bolt's fine play about Sir Thomas More, *A Man for All Seasons.* Flying the Union Jack alongside them was a jaunty cockney in his first starring role: Michael Caine as *Alfie*. The two nominated Americans were again made to seem outsiders: Steve McQueen in *The Sand Pebbles*, and Alan Arkin in *The Russians Are Coming, the Russians Are Coming.*

The Best Actress category rubbed salt in transatlantic wounds. With Fontaine and de Havilland twenty-five years before, Hollywood had so far managed to produce only one pair of sisters nominated for Best Actress in the same year. Now an English theatrical dynasty, the Redgraves, hit back, with sisters Vanessa and Lynn winning nominations for *Morgan* and *Georgy Girl*. Alongside France's Anouk Aimée and Poland's Ida Kaminska, that left British-born Liz Taylor as America's only Best Actress nominee. In the Supporting categories, Walter Matthau *(The Fortune Cookie)* had to beat two Brits, James Mason *(Georgy Girl)* and Robert Shaw *(A Man for All Seasons),* not to mention the Japanese-born Mako *(The Sand Pebbles).* To win Supporting Actress, Sandy Dennis also had to beat two Britons, Wendy Hiller in *A Man for All Seasons* and Vivien Merchant in *Alfie.*

Walter Matthau was the only winner present. The show's producer, Joe Pasternak, was understandably angry at the indifference of the other nominees, a majority of whom could not be bothered to turn up. From France Liz Taylor offered the rather feeble excuse that Burton, who was afraid of flying, had dreamed that she had crashed and begged her not to leave him. "Leaving Richard alone in Paris," sympathized Bob Hope, "is rather like leaving Jackie Gleason locked in a deli." When her husband, for the fifth time, failed to convert a nomination into an Oscar, Taylor flew into a rage. The fact that she had joined Luise Rainer, Olivia de Havilland, Vivien Leigh and Ingrid Bergman in collecting her second Academy Award—and after the same number of nominations as Burton—only made matters worse. "It's nice to win," she said, "but the edge is certainly taken off because Richard didn't. He was the best actor of the year."

Burton's biographer, Melvyn Bragg, agreed. The moody Welshman could be forgiven "a certain ruefulness" over this of all his seven defeats. The sequence under the tree, where he tells the story of the underage boy ordering a drink in a bar, was done in a single take. "Mike Nichols was overwhelmed. He deserved an Oscar for that sequence alone." But Burton, though admired as an actor, was "not entirely popular out on the West Coast. He had made it clear from his early days that he rather disdained their beloved medium, and even though he had now changed, it was too late and they were not listening. He had offended producers by his independence, and the list of ladies enjoyed or rejected made up a fifth column of wives or mistresses of the Hollywood mafia who had a thing or two to say about, or a score or two to settle with, Mr. Burton. He was never their man."

In retrospect, Burton also appears to have been an early victim of the now modish Oscar requirement for cinematic "political correctness." While *A Man for All Seasons* was a prime example of those lavishly produced, high-minded historical epics that have always appealed to the Academy, *Who's Afraid of Virginia Woolf?* was uncomfortably foulmouthed and booze-ridden; and the work of its author, Edward Albee, was too subversive for Hollywood's comfort. Subsequent political casualties among potential winners range from Warren Beatty's *Reds* to Oliver Stone's *Born on the Fourth of July* and *JFK*. Like his friend O'Toole, Burton seemed to have perfected the habit of turning in the right work in the wrong film at the wrong time.

Sandy Dennis won Supporting Actress, though Walter Matthau beat out *Virgina Woolf*'s George Segal. As for the Redgrave sisters: Vanessa was already showing signs of ideological indifference to the entire business, while 23-year-old Lynn took a leaf out of an increasingly familiar loser's album: "It really was an enormous relief to hear them call Liz Taylor's name. At my age, while it was an honor to be nominated, the burden of winning would have been too much."

"It's outrageous!" squawked Truman Capote. "It simply proves that [the Academy Awards] is all politics and sentiment and nothing to do with merit."

Capote's beef was that Richard Brooks's film of his book *In Cold Blood* was nominated for four 1967 Oscars, including Best Director, but was not up for Best Picture. Among the films to have squeezed it out was Fox's absurd attempt to woo families to another Rex Harrison musical, *Doctor Dolittle*. "Anything allowing a *Dolittle* to happen," fumed Capote, "is so rooked up it doesn't mean anything."

The reason *Dolittle* had "happened" was that Fox had laid on the Oscar campaign of the year. Once it became clear that neither children nor parents rated the sight of Harrison singing tuneless songs to imaginary animals, the word came down that the publicity department was to pull out all the stops on the film's behalf. The film already having cost $16 million—and, as Harrison later wrote in his memoirs, sharing with *Cleopatra* the distinction of having dealt "a near-fatal body-blow to Twentieth Century Fox's finances" —money was not much of an object. One Fox internal memo (from *Dolittle*'s producer, Arthur Jacobs, to Jack Hirschberg of the studio publicity office) read:

> As a result of meetings today between [West Coast head of publicity] Perry Lieber and myself, the following has been decided regarding the Academy Award campaign for *Doctor Dolittle.*
>
> 1. We will screen at eight o'clock each night for the following members of the Academy: art directors and costume designers, cinematographers, film editors, music. Each screening will be preceded by champagne or cocktails and a buffet dinner in the Studio commissary. We may also arrange to provide soft drinks at the theater during the intermission.
>
> 2. There will be a meeting Tuesday afternoon of the department heads in [head of production] Stan Hough's office, which Perry and I will attend. At this meeting Perry will discuss pertinent matters with the department heads and inform them that *Doctor Dolittle* is the Studio's prime target for Academy Award consideration.

A second memo the following day spelled out further details for targeting "writers, directors and other branches who ballot at a later date." After breaking down the membership figures branch by branch, Jacobs continued: "This totals, according to my faulty logarithms, 1,350. Multiply it by two and we will need 2,700 seats" (at the Studio Theater, which was to be booked "every night between January 22 and February 6"). "In addition, we plan several screenings for various guilds and unions who give their own awards—notably the Editors, Writers and Directors. These screenings will absorb some of the people who will also be Academy voters, but those Academy members who miss their Guild screenings can come to ours at the Studio. So we are covered at least two ways."

Fox's "dishonest reaction to a bad picture" was thoroughly exposed by the writer John Gregory Dunne, who was given inside track for what the studio stupidly thought would be a reverential portrait. The final product, *The Studio*, instead contains a damning day-by-day chronology of *Doctor Dolittle* from the first day of shooting to the stage of the Academy Awards, via every trick Fox's publicity department could come up with. So ruthless was the writer's exposé of the cynical tricks of their trade that some Hollywood publicists still measure their careers in terms of "Before Dunne" and "After Dunne."

The studio's Academy Award "exploitation campaign for *Doctor Dolittle*," as he concluded, was "highly successful." Despite mediocre reviews and lukewarm box-office returns, the picture garnered nine Academy nominations, including one for Best Picture; on the night it won just two Oscars: Best Song ("Talk to the Animals"—to cries of "Oh no!" around the auditorium) and Best Special Visual Effects, of which Rex Reed wrote: "For the 'best explosions, fires, earthquakes or hurricanes,' Natalie Wood gave the Special Visual Effects award to *Doctor Dolittle*, a film with no explosions, fires, earthquakes or hurricanes."

The competition had got tougher than ever that year, as the Academy halved the prizes available for visual achievement—Cinematography, Art Direction, Costume Design—by doing away with the black-and-white categories. It was a sign of the times again dictated by television. Now that TV was in color, and therefore reluctant to buy black-and-white movies, four out of five films were being made in color. Subsequent Oscar history would leave 1960's *The Apartment* with the distinction of being the last black-and-white film to win Best Picture.

The Dirty Dozen, the biggest box-office film of 1967, failed to win any major Oscar nominations for MGM, its producer-director Robert Aldrich or its roll call of major stars. High on the huge financial success of *My Fair Lady* and *The Sound of Music*, Warners and Fox were leading a studio rush to mass-manufacture giant musicals; Warners cast two nonsinging stars of the moment, Vanessa Redgrave and Richard Harris, in a screen version of *Camelot* (again at the expense of Julie Andrews), while Fox tried to capitalize on Rex Harrison's musical Oscar by inserting him uncomfortably in *Dolittle*. Both were to prove financial disasters; but Fox was also developing a host of musicals in urgent need of exclamation marks, including *Star!* and *Hello, Dolly!*, while Universal picked up their discard, Carol Channing, to team her with Julie Andrews again in *Thoroughly Modern Millie*.

After their dominance of the mid-sixties, the studio bosses would have been stunned to know that only one more musical, and an exclamatory British one at that—*Oliver!*, the following year—would ever win Best Picture.

Some studios believed the future to lie in ever more violent movies, such as *The Dirty Dozen* and *Bonnie and Clyde.* But 1967 saw a spate of films exploring racial tension. There were some real clunkers, such as Otto Preminger's *Hurry Sundown* ("an awful glop of neo-Uncle Tomism"—Bosley Crowther), but there was also *In the Heat of the Night.* In a small southern town, a black cop from Philadelphia arrives to assist the bigoted local sheriff in a murder hunt. "A very nice film and a very good film and, yes, I think it's good to see a black man and a white man working together," said Rod Steiger, who played the sheriff, "but it's not going to take the tension out of New York City; it's not going to stop the riots in Chicago." Maybe not; but many agreed with its Canadian director, Norman Jewison, that the film was a powerfully effective "statement about our time."

For Sidney Poitier, who played a powerfully charged duet with Steiger, it was his third substantial hit of the year. After *To Sir with Love*, a British drama pitting a Jamaican teacher against the tough schoolchildren of London's East End, Poitier also played the black suitor of a middle-class white daughter in *Guess Who's Coming to Dinner.* The anxious parents were played by Katharine Hepburn and Spencer Tracy in their ninth and last film together. Tracy died fifteen days after shooting was completed—leaving 58-year-old Hepburn, ironically enough, in the midst of a professional renaissance. By the time the film appeared, she had already completed her next, *The Lion in Winter,* and was preparing to return to Broadway in her first musical, *Coco.*

Directed by Stanley Kramer, *Guess Who's Coming to Dinner* proved the second-highest grossing film of the year behind *The Graduate*, the second film to be directed by Mike Nichols. The latter introduced the decade's most unlikely romantic lead in a 30-year-old Method actor, Dustin Hoffman, whom Nichols had spotted off-Broadway in a play called *Journey of the Fifth Horse;* the New York *Daily News* described him as "resembling both Sonny and Cher." As Benjamin Braddock, Hoffman was "wrenchingly simple and vividly intelligent," wrote *Newsweek.* "He wears the world like a new pair of shoes." His love scenes with Anne Bancroft, as the wife of his father's law partner, were "as funny as anything ever committed to film."

Although he had appeared earlier that year in a justly neglected film called *The Tiger Makes Out,* Hoffman thus joined the 10 percent or so of Best Actor nominees to have won nominations for their first major film performance (after, in his case, a long and unspectacular apprenticeship on the stage). Others in this category include Paul Muni (*The Valiant,* 1928–29), Montgomery Clift (*The Search*, 1948), Anthony Franciosa (*A Hatful of Rain*, 1957) and Alan Arkin (*The Russians Are Coming, the Russians Are Coming,* 1966).

The Graduate made enough money to turn Joseph E. Levine's Embassy Pictures into a major Hollywood player. "There's no way to describe it," said Levine of the film's box office. It was "like an explosion, a dam bursting." The young Hoffman (who soon spent his $17,000 salary for the film, and signed on for $55-a-week unemployment benefit) declared himself "depressed" by the first of his six Best Actor nominations. If he'd had a vote, he said, it would have gone to Rod Steiger.

Time magazine's pick for movie of the year, *Bonnie and Clyde,* clocked up ten Oscar nominations, sharing the lead with *Guess Who's Coming to Dinner. The Graduate* and *In the Heat of the Night* scored seven each. All four were nominated for Best Picture, along with *Dolittle.* Enter Capote and his outrage, as more deserving films such as *In Cold Blood, Cool Hand Luke, Two for the Road* and *Barefoot in the Park* made way for Fox's expensive turkey.

The Academy's new president, Gregory Peck, tried to inject some young blood into the proceedings by inviting new young stars such as Hoffman, Ross and Streisand to come on the show as presenters. The race in each of the major categories was regarded as more open than usual. But four days before the ceremony came the assassination in Memphis of Dr. Martin Luther King, Jr. At least five stars scheduled to appear—Louis Armstrong, Sidney Poitier, Sammy Davis, Jr., Diahann Carroll and Rod Steiger—said they would not take part if the show was held before Dr. King's funeral. Explaining why he had asked "President Peck" to postpone the show, Sammy Davis told Johnny Carson: "I certainly think any black man should not appear. I find it morally incongruous to sing 'Talk to the Animals' while the man who could have made a better world for my children is lying in state."

The Oscars had never stopped for anything—not even World War II. At Peck's urging, however, the board of governors agreed to postpone this, the fortieth annual ceremony, by two days; the Oscars would be held the day after King's funeral, but the Governors Ball would be canceled. Peck introduced the show by pointing out that two of the Best Picture nominees concerned racial tensions: "We must unite in compassion if we are to survive."

It was unusual, as Patty Duke pointed out on presenting the Supporting Actor award, that "there isn't an English name on the list." The winner was *Cool Hand Luke*'s George Kennedy, who had spent $5,000 of his own money on trade advertising, so fearful had he been that the box-office success of *Camelot* and *Bonnie and Clyde* would see him miss his chance. It proved a good investment. To an unhappy Rex Reed, it was "the first upset in an evening filled with weird and totally unexpected developments." To Kennedy, it was a turning point: "My salary was multiplied by ten the minute I won. But the happiest part was that I didn't have to play only villains anymore." He remains one of the few character actors who has sustained an upwardly mobile career on the strength of a Best Supporting Oscar.

After Best Director went to Mike Nichols for *The Graduate*, Joseph E. Levine was seen adjusting his tie as Julie Andrews opened the Best Picture envelope. But the surprise winner was *In the Heat of the Night*—making this only the sixth time in the twenty postwar years* that the director of the Best Picture did not also win Best Director. To this day the two awards go so closely hand-in-hand that the director of any Best Picture winner feels slighted if he does not win Best Director into the bargain. Twenty years later, friends and colleagues are still outraged that Jewison missed out that year—and has never since won an Oscar, despite nominations for *Fiddler on the Roof* (1971) and *Moonstruck* (1987). To this day, it is hard to find anyone to contradict the theory that Jewison missed out in 1967 because he was a Canadian, and Hollywood directors did not want successful foreigners muscling into an already crowded market.

* The others, since John Ford *(The Grapes of Wrath)* beat out Alfred Hitchcock *(Rebecca)* in 1940, were John Huston *(The Treasure of the Sierra Madre)* over Laurence Olivier *(Hamlet)*, 1948; Joseph L. Mankiewicz *(A Letter to Three Wives)* over Robert Rossen *(All the King's Men)*, 1949; George Stevens *(A Place in the Sun)* over Vincente Minnelli *(An American in Paris)*, 1951; John Ford *(The Quiet Man)* over Cecil B. de Mille *(The Greatest Show on Earth)*, 1952; and George Stevens again *(Giant)* over Michael Anderson *(Around the World in 80 Days)*, 1956. See Appendix C, section C5.

The year's Best Supporting Actress, Estelle Parsons of *Bonnie and Clyde,* admitted to disappointment that her film won only two Oscars out of its ten nominations. It was the beginning of the Oscars' love-hate relationship with Warren Beatty, still simmering almost a quarter of a century later, when his disappointing *Dick Tracy* received the Academy's thumbs down, and again the following year, when *The Silence of the Lambs* shattered his high hopes for *Bugsy.* In the intervening twenty-plus years Beatty had managed to win one Oscar—for directing rather than acting, despite multiple nominations for such films as *Heaven Can Wait* and *Reds.*

In 1967, his costar Faye Dunaway was the victim of the Beatty jinx when the Academy seemed to surprise even itself by voting as Best Actress neither of the front-runners, Dunaway or England's venerable Dame Edith Evans *(The Whisperers),* but the indomitable Katharine Hepburn. Even Sidney Poitier did a double-take when he opened the envelope to find inside the name of his costar, winning her second Oscar thirty-four years after her first. She wasn't there, of course. Telephoned in France by George Cukor, who picked up the award for her, she said of her recently deceased costar and long-time lover: "I suspect my award was really given to the two of us." *Guess Who's Coming to Dinner* was Tracy's seventy-fourth film, and his ninth and last with Hepburn; visibly ill during filming, he had died just fifteen days after it was finished. She was, as one reporter drily summed up, "the first person to win because her costar died."

Hepburn cabled the Academy her thanks: "I'm enormously touched. It is gratifying to find someone else voted for me apart from myself." And she sent another, more private message to its president, Gregory Peck: "It was delightful, a total surprise. I am enormously touched because I feel I have received a great affectionate hug from my fellow workers, and for a variety of reasons, not the least of which being Spencer. . . . [Bill] Rose wrote about a normal, middle-aged, unspectacular, unglamorous creature doing the best she can to do the decent thing in a difficult situation. In other words she was a good wife. Our most unsung and important heroine. I'm glad she's coming back in style. I modeled her after my mother. Thanks again. They don't usually give these things out to the old girls, you know."

Rex Reed had been miserable all evening. Since George Kennedy and *Dolittle*'s Visual Effects, he had been even more astonished to see Art Direction and Set Direction won by *Camelot.* "Pretty amazing for a movie in which you never knew what season it was supposed to be except when they sprayed detergent across the scene for snow. Also pretty amazing is the fact that the same film got the Costume award, when *Bonnie and Clyde,* which only started a fashion revolution, got nothing."

By the end of the evening, Reed had made a vow never to attend the Oscars again. "It was all about over at 3 AM, when model Donyale Luna did the Hokey Poker Broadway in a filthy-looking two-piece nude fishnet bikini as Dame Edith Evans threw down her menu, stuck her fingers in her ears to drown out the noise, marched grandly toward the elevator—fed up with Oscar and his kingdom—and went home for a bowl of cornflakes. I don't blame her. Now I've met Oscar myself in person, and if I ever see him again it'll be on television."

"I find it unbelievable. I find it overwhelming," said Rod Steiger on winning the Best Actor award, thirteen years after he had first been nominated for *On the Waterfront.* Graciously, he also thanked "Mr. Sidney Poitier for the pleasure of his friendship, which gave me the knowledge and understanding of prejudice to enhance my performance." Steiger concluded with the fashionable rallying-cry "We shall overcome," little knowing that he too was about to become a victim of the celebrated "Oscar curse."

Few winners apart from Olivier—and, later, such actors as Hoffman and De Niro—enjoyed such unqualified respect from their peers. Steiger was "an actor's actor." With his fee immediately hiked to $750,000 a film, he squared up with relish to such mighty roles as Mussolini, Lucky Luciano and Napoleon. Within a decade, however, by the time he impersonated W. C. Fields in a lackluster biopic, he had lost not merely the favor of the critics. He had also lost his marriage, his health (undergoing open-heart surgery) and any sustained shape to his career. "I was scared to death, and couldn't work," he testified. "To get out of bed and brush my teeth was a big accomplishment."

Unlike such contemporaries as Lee Marvin, who used his Oscar to parlay high fees in forgettable films, Steiger employed his newfound studio clout to embark on daring, often experimental movies such as *The Illustrated Man* (in which he was tattooed from head to toe) and *The Sergeant*, a bold exploration of Army homosexuality. Reeling from minor acting masterpieces like *No Way to Treat a Lady* to bizarre miscalculations like *Happy Birthday, Wanda June,* Steiger finally admitted: "I felt like a ballplayer who had hit a home run in an empty ball park." The title role in *W. C. Fields and Me* was the catalyst for physical and emotional collapse, from which he barely recovered throughout the 1980s, relapsing instead into made-for-TV material—a tragic waste of a rare screen talent.

But Steiger was always a complex, inward-looking character, perhaps out to satisfy himself more than his audiences. "If you've given a performance that you believe is good," he has said, "there's nothing the matter with taking pride in the recognition an Academy Award symbolizes. I didn't kiss anybody's ass to get it. But its main value is that it protects an actor's position and power. It helps him in the tactical maneuvers that cannot be avoided if he wants to keep his self-respect."

Among the sixties casualties sharing Steiger's limited enthusiasm for the Oscar was Rita Moreno, Best Supporting Actress of 1961. The problem afflicting Moreno, like so many other Oscar winners, was typecasting. "After the Oscar I was convinced producers would come pounding on my door with all sorts of exciting parts." Instead, she was offered nothing but a constant stream of "gypsy fortune tellers, Mexican spitfires, Spanish spitfires, Puerto Ricans—all those 'Yankee peeg, you steel me people's money' parts."

In Moreno's case—and it is not the only one—an Oscar even proved the prelude to a suicide attempt. Also "wearied" by a nine-year relationship with Marlon Brando, she emptied a pill bottle beside her bed. Doctors at the hospital found no reflexes; and it was then, she says, that she decided to live. "Right there, floating between life and death, Rosita finally let Rita be born."

It proved lucky for Moreno that she found it "so demeaning" to be offered the same role so repeatedly. "I could have made a bundle . . . but I knew I had to get out of town." Moreno diversified her career, even developing a Las Vegas stage act, and didn't return to the movie screen for almost ten years, until "the right part" (in *The Night of the Following Day*) came along in 1969. Finally, she too settled for the stable income of a regular TV appearance with James Garner in *The Rockford Files;* and in time she became the only performer (before Barbra Streisand) to add a Grammy (1972), a Tony (1975) and an Emmy (1979) to her Oscar. "The [Oscar] can quickly be turned into a downer by people who try to cash in on it as a promissory note," she now concludes. "That's the curse."

Steiger's successor as 1968 Best Actor turned out to be another, all-time classic victim of the Oscar blues, Cliff Robertson. Before winning his Academy Award for *Charly,* Robertson's finest hour had been as President Kennedy's choice to play his youthful self in *PT 109*, a dim account of Kennedy's wartime heroism. Never before had he even been invited to attend the Oscar show. After winning, he fared little better.

Robertson's freak award combined two perennially dubious Oscar themes: the points-for-effort syndrome, along with a giant advertising campaign. Having starred in two TV plays that had been stolen from under him as successful movies, *The Hustler* and *Days of Wine and Roses*, he bought the rights to a third, *The Two Worlds of Charlie Gordon*, and struggled for years to raise the money to film it. Like Tony Curtis, disappointed not to be nominated that year for playing *The Boston Strangler*, Robertson was intent on a change of screen image.

Based on a novel called *Flowers for Algernon, Charly* told the story of a mentally retarded man who becomes a genius after an operation, and then regresses. A combination of good personal reviews and excellent box office led Robertson to mount one of the most sustained Oscar campaigns in memory, leading *Time* magazine to conclude that his victory was "based more on publicity than performance." Ads on his behalf began as early as October, and culminated in a giant double foldout inserted in *Daily Variety*. Its contents: eighty-three favorable reviews of Robertson from a spectrum of journals. While competitors like Alan Bates and Alan Arkin "may have been content to rest on their performances," said *Time*, "Robertson knew better."

Three years later, in his own defense, Robertson was to be heard making a dubious distinction between advertisements purchased by a studio and personal appeals paid for by an actor. Still smarting over that very piece in *Time,* and claiming he had not spent "one penny" of his own money on advertising, he fumed: "I went to the Philippines to make that piece of junk *(Too Late the Hero)* before the nominations were announced, and I didn't get back until a month after I had won the Oscar. . . . The word from my journalist friends was that that *Time* writer was sure the odds-on favorite, Peter O'Toole, would win. So he was caught with his journalistic pants down. To this day I'm upset because he could have checked and found out that I hadn't purchased any ads."

Alan Bates heard the news of his nomination at the Bristol Old Vic, just before going out to play Otway's *Venice Preserv'd* to an audience of nine people. Campaigning—or, indeed, attending the Hollywood ceremony—did not cross his mind. In England, such local traditions remained shrouded in mystery.

Little good did Cliff Robertson's Oscar do him. The actor bobbed between feeble B-movies and TV miniseries until his inadvertent role in the David Begelman scandal at Columbia in 1977* made him something of a Hollywood pariah. It may have been Cliff Robertson's name that Begelman had forged on the $10,000 check at the heart of the affair, but industry insiders could not forgive him for blowing the whistle. Though both he and Begelman were eventually forgiven (and even, briefly, reunited in an MGM project), Robertson was eventually to be found beached in a TV soap, *Falcon Crest*—alongside another one-time Oscar winner, Jane Wyman, by then as well known for her offscreen role as the first Mrs. Ronald Reagan.

Nineteen sixty-eight saw Gregory Peck, reelected the Academy's president, still desperate to revitalize the awards. Already Peck had led a membership drive among the younger members of the Hollywood community in an attempt to offset the voting influence of older, retired members, and to inject a dash of glamour. Now, to spruce up the show itself he hired the Broadway choreographer Gower Champion, and abandoned the Santa Monica Civic Auditorium after a decade in favor of the Dorothy Chandler Pavilion at downtown Los Angeles's Music Center. Even more drastic, Champion dispensed with the services of Bob Hope in favor of a dozen "Friends of Oscar" as emcees—ranging from Frank Sinatra and Ingrid Bergman to Jane Fonda and Sidney Poitier.

Peck also mounted another attendance drive among the twenty acting nominees, fifteen of whom promised to come. Among the doubtful, ironically, was the man most desperate to be there: Cliff Robertson, anxious to see a return on his campaign investment.

*The full story is told in fascinating detail in David McClintick's superb book *Indecent Exposure*.

Even a personal plea from President Peck, however, failed to move Robertson's director, Robert Aldrich, who was flatly refusing to let his star leave the Philippines location of *Too Late the Hero.* Among the other no-shows, of course, would be the perennial absentee Katharine Hepburn, even though fate would find her in Los Angeles on that night. As Eleanor of Acquitaine bickering with Peter O'Toole's Henry II in *The Lion in Winter*, Hepburn had earned a record eleventh nomination, beating Bette Davis's ten—but no, she told Peck, even he could not persuade her to be in the audience (and thus in television close-up) if she lost again.

She didn't, of course, becoming the first actress to win three Oscars and only the third performer to win successive awards—the last being her favorite leading man, the late Spencer Tracy, thirty years before. But this time Hepburn was obliged to share it with a newcomer, Barbra Streisand, in the only tie since Fredric March and Wallace Beery in 1932.

The two actresses had faced tough competition. Patricia Neal, not entirely recovered from her 1965 stroke, had been obliged to turn down the plum role of Mrs. Robinson in *The Graduate,* and then to watch its surprise success with mixed feelings; determined not to let another such chance slip, she had made a triumphant return opposite Best Supporting Actor Jack Albertson in *The Subject Was Roses.* And Joanne Woodward, after a decade in the doldrums, had revived her flagging career with a subtle performance as a small-town schoolmarm, under the directorship of her husband, Paul Newman, in *Rachel, Rachel.*

Angered by the Academy's failure to vote Newman a nomination for his directorial debut—even though they had both carried off the New York critics' awards and *Rachel, Rachel* was among the Best Picture nominees—Woodward at first refused to attend the ceremony. Though it was Newman who persuaded her to relent, he chimed in with a sour note of his own: "There must be something wrong with a group that hands out awards and then has to send telegrams saying 'Please come.' It should be fun to go—not agony. There's something barbaric about it."

The rank outsider in the race was Vanessa Redgrave, beneficiary of an unusual piece of campaigning by Universal. With no major Oscar contender that year, the studio rushed out Karel Reisz's *Isa-*

dora, starring Redgrave as the doomed danseuse Isadora Duncan. Already unpopular for her political views, Redgrave now managed to offend Hollywood yet further with the "very happy" announcement that she was pregnant by—though not married to—her *Camelot* costar Franco Nero. Concerned about the effect on the older, staider members of the community who made up the awards electorate, Universal took out a trade ad that in effect apologized for Redgrave's self-conduct: "The Academy Awards are not a popularity contest. Members should vote based on what they themselves have seen on the screen, not on what they've heard or read about a performance. We urge you not to vote until you've seen *Isadora*."

For her movie debut as Fanny Brice in *Funny Girl,* the role she had played on Broadway for two years, Streisand was an unusually strong runner; not only had Columbia lined up behind her, but also Fox and Paramount, to whom she was contracted for forthcoming films. But there was some Academy resentment that the singer had been admitted to voting membership before she had even made her first film. Gregory Peck was again obliged to soothe fevered brows: "When an actress has played a great role on the stage, and is coming into films for what will obviously be an important career, it is ridiculous to make her wait two or three years for membership."

Before she went out to open the Best Actress envelope, Ingrid Bergman was enigmatically told by the Price Waterhouse team to "read *everything* inside it." The accountants insisted that the result was "a precise tie" after numerous recounts. This led to complaints that, had Streisand not been made a member of the Academy, and presumably voted for herself, she would not have won. Streisand accepted her Oscar in an outfit subsequently notorious as a pair of "see-through, bell-bottom pajamas" described by Edith Head as "shocking!"

Redgrave apart, 1968 was another good year for Britain. Two Englishmen even set a painful precedent when the winner of the Directors Guild award, *The Lion in Winter*'s Anthony Harvey, failed for the first time in its history to carry off the Oscar for Best Director —beaten by his compatriot Carol Reed, for *Oliver!*, a musical based on Dickens's *Oliver Twist,* which was also the year's surprise choice as Best Picture. "This is the first time we English have tried to compete with Hollywood in the musical department," said Reed.

American audiences were particularly taken with 15-year-old Jack Wild's Artful Dodger.

But the failure of Peck's attempts to rejuvenate the Academy's voting membership was evident in the omission from the Best Picture nominees of the year's cult film among youth audiences—not Zeffirelli's *Romeo and Juliet,* which was unashamedly aimed at the teenage market and squeaked a nomination, but Stanley Kubrick's *2001: A Space Odyssey.* When Kubrick's spectacular collaboration with Arthur C. Clarke had opened in Los Angeles, Charles Champlin had written: "Some of next year's Academy Awards are already bespoken." Also overlooked that year were Roman Polanski's *Rosemary's Baby,* Luis Buñuel's *Belle de Jour* and the most successful of Sergio Leone's "spaghetti Westerns," *The Good, the Bad and the Ugly.*

Never the Academy's favorite genre, Westerns fared no better at the 1969 awards, despite one last stand comprising *True Grit, The Wild Bunch* and one of the few big box-office Westerns of the modern era, *Butch Cassidy and the Sundance Kid.* Neither of *Butch Cassidy*'s stars, Paul Newman and Robert Redford, was nominated, which was perhaps just as well, for the year's other memborable double act, Dustin Hoffman and Jon Voight, joined those perennial losers Burton and O'Toole in watching Hollywood offer a sentimental reward to one of its legends.

John Wayne's voluble right-wing views had made him lasting enemies in Hollywood's politically liberal circles. He had undergone "a profound crisis of the soul" after *The Alamo* had both humiliated and almost bankrupted him. But nine years later, as Rooster Cogburn in *True Grit,* he became the fourth actor—and, most probably, the last—to win Best Actor for playing a cowboy. In four decades of the Oscars only Lee Marvin in *Cat Ballou* and Gary Cooper in *High Noon* had matched Warner Baxter's aberrant win at the second awards as the Cisco Kid. After a celluloid lifetime on horseback, Wayne's only previous acting nomination had been for a war film, *The Sands of Iwo Jima.* But Hollywood sentiment will always favor a local man who has made a very public recovery from apparently terminal cancer. "Wow!" went "Duke" Wayne as Barbra Streisand handed him the Oscar he had never thought to see. "If I'd known, I'd have put on that eyepatch thirty-five years earlier."

If *True Grit* was too soft-edged to earn a Best Picture nomination, other Westerns in a vintage year were too violent. Sam Peckinpah's *The Wild Bunch* and Sergio Leone's *Once Upon a Time in the West* were joined out in the cold by such contemporary contenders as *They Shoot Horses, Don't They?*, *Alice's Restaurant*, *Easy Rider* and *Bob & Carol & Ted & Alice*. How on earth, in such company, did Universal stage-manage a Best Picture nomination for its dreary historical costume drama, *Anne of the Thousand Days*?

Simple: by serving filet mignon and champagne at a series of special Academy showings—set up in panic over the film's dismal box office—and then writing thank-you letters to the elderly swells who snoozed through this woman's-magazine look at Henry VIII's brief marriage to Anne Boleyn. Scores of freeloaders proved venal enough to "vote the card" for what John Simon called "the quintessential work of art for people who haven't the foggiest notion of what art is all about." Astonishingly, it led the Oscar field with ten nominations, including Richard Burton's sixth shot at Oscar gold—but won only for costume design.

Liz Taylor had agreed to present the Best Picture award in the hope that her first Oscar appearance in a decade would at last swing things her husband's way. All she could do, however, was mourn his sixth defeat as she presented the year's top award to an East Coast picture with a Western-sounding title, directed by an Englishman. Following the introduction of a new ratings system, John Schlesinger's *Midnight Cowboy* was the first X film to be nominated for Best Picture, and remains the only one ever to have won.

At the end of a mixed decade for musicals, it was in vain that the producers of Fox's *Hello, Dolly!* had reminded voters in trade-paper ads that theirs was "the only film nominated for a Best Picture Oscar with a G-rating for entire family entertainment, and the only Best Picture nominee made in Hollywood by Hollywood craftsmen." They did, however, have the consolation that it was the most successful musical of the year, losing only $3 million of its $20 million budget, while Universal's *Sweet Charity,* Paramount's *Paint Your Wagon* and MGM's bizarre musical version of *Goodbye, Mr. Chips* (for which a singing Peter O'Toole won his latest vain nomination) all cost their studios dearly. Eleven years since *Gigi,* producers were still dazzled by the mid-sixties success of *Mary Poppins, My Fair*

Lady and *The Sound of Music*. But *Oliver!* would prove the last musical to win Best Picture for sixteen years (if *Amadeus* can be defined as a musical). After *Fiddler on the Roof* and *Cabaret* won nominations but not Best Picture in the early 1970s, the only musicals to be nominated were those with an unusually strong storyline, such as *All That Jazz* and *Coal Miner's Daughter*.

There were others, winners and losers, with complaints about the 1969 awards. Henry Fonda, as yet nominated only once in his thirty-year career, seemed pleased that neither his son Peter nor his daughter Jane had converted their nominations into acting awards: "How in the hell would you like to have been in this business as long as I have, and then have one of your kids win an Oscar before you did?" Maggie Smith, the surprise Best Actress (for *The Prime of Miss Jean Brodie*) over Jane Fonda and Liza Minnelli, later observed that she was never again offered a leading role by Hollywood—although her occasional, patrician forays into film would win her another Oscar, in a supporting role, nine years later.

And Richard Burton, at the time, was morose about his latest wasted trip to the Oscar show. "I suppose," he mused, "that thirty years from now Peter O'Toole and I will still be appearing on talk shows plugging for our first Oscar." John Wayne, according to Melvyn Bragg, "at least had the grace to bash down Burton's door and thrust the statuette into his hands and say, 'You should have this, not me.' Burton was touched." (Touched enough, apparently, to stay up getting drunk with Wayne all night; they were staying in adjacent bungalows at the Beverly Hills Hotel.)

Newsday, a Long Island newspaper, was high on the first Academy nomination for the newcomer who had benefited from Rip Torn's last-minute withdrawal from *Easy Rider*. "If Jack Nicholson doesn't win this year's Best Supporting Actor Oscar," its film critic had enthused, "there's no meaning to the awards at all." After being voted Best Supporting Actor by both the New York Film Critics and the National Society of Film Critics, young Nicholson jauntily declared: "If I get an Oscar, I won't feel like I've stolen anything."

In the same category, however, *Life* magazine was more impressed by Gig Young's world-weary master of ceremonies in Sydney Pollack's *They Shoot Horses, Don't They?*: "If he doesn't get an Academy Award for his portrayal of human devastation, there's no justice." Though justice prevailed, Young's victory was to prove decidedly Pyrrhic.

Born Byron Barr, Gig Young had taken his screen name from an early role supporting Barbara Stanwyck in Warners' *The Gay Sisters.* Nominated for a Supporting Oscar in 1951 for *Come Fill the Cup* (and again seven years later for *Teacher's Pet*), he prophetically told Louella Parsons: "So many people who have been nominated for an Oscar have bad luck afterwards." With a contract at MGM, Young told Louella, he could see nothing but good luck on the horizon. For a man who had started out as a handsome dramatic lead, then wound up the eternal stooge to the likes of Doris Day, James Cagney and Clark Gable, Marty Baum's offer of the dance-marathon "barker" in *They Shoot Horses* came as "a lifeline for a drowning man, a last chance to show [my] talent as a serious actor." Baum's fellow producers took a lot of persuading; only through knowing Young for years as his agent was Baum able to win him the role.

To Young, the Academy Award thus symbolized a hard-earned breakthrough and, with luck, a new impetus to his flagging career. "What he was aching for, as he walked up to collect his Oscar," said his fourth wife, Elaine, "was a role in his own movie—one they could finally call a Gig Young movie." But it failed to materialize. All the award had done was to cement his qualities as one of life's supporting players, the eternal backup man. "For Gig," said Elaine, "the Oscar was literally the kiss of death, the end of the line."

Over the next eight years Young made just four pictures, all in forgettable supporting roles. The fall of 1978 saw him touring Canada, hoping for a Broadway comeback in a play poignantly entitled *Nobody Loves an Albatross.* On October 19, just three weeks after marrying his fifth wife at the age of 64, the 1969 Oscar winner shot her dead and then turned his .38 snub-nosed revolver on himself—the ultimate victim, by any measure, of the Oscar curse.

Manhattan police found Young's Oscar beside the bodies in the den of his apartment. A month later, publication of his $200,000 will revealed that he had left to Mr. and Mrs. Martin Baum "the Oscar that I won because of Martin's help."

"The vicissitudes of being hot and cold in this profession are very hard on a man," said Marty Baum at Young's memorial service. "Gig knew real pain."

In 1975 Miloš Forman's <u>One Flew Over the Cuckoo's Nest</u> became only the second film in Oscar history to take all five top awards, including Best Actor for an exultant Jack Nicholson.

Among the 1972 nominees were Laurence Olivier and Michael Caine, whose mano-a-mano acting contest in Joseph Mankiewicz's <u>Sleuth</u> saw it become the second film in Oscar history to win nominations for the entire cast.

Both the Academy and NBC Television strongly denied rumors that the streaker who interrupted David Niven during the 1973 Oscar show was a deliberate ploy to boost flagging TV ratings.

9

1970–1980

Scott, Brando and the Art of Rejection

No one should have a chance to see so much desire, so much need for a prize, and so much pain when not given it.
—GLENDA JACKSON,
Best Actress,
1970 and 1973

"At forty-three," thought *Variety*, "Oscar looked tired." The 1970 Best Picture nominations suggested an industry in a state of flux, if not downright confusion. Any group who could bracket five such disparate films as *M*A*S*H, Patton, Love Story, Five Easy Pieces* and *Airport* had to have lost its way. Perhaps, in retrospect, the Oscars needed the electric shock treatment they were about to receive from George C. Scott.

At the beginning of the 1970s, despite attempts to woo them, it was fashionable among rising young Hollywood actors to deride the Academy and all its works. By the end of the decade, these same outsiders would be the stars presenting and accepting Oscars as if their careers depended on it. The late seventies would see such unlikely figures as Jane Fonda, Meryl Streep and Dustin Hoffman steadying a ship still reeling from the broadsides of two older heavyweights, Scott and Marlon Brando.

Though not unexpected, Scott's torpedo first hit Hollywood in the shape of a wire service story from Spain, where he was playing a gangster on the run in MGM's *The Last Run* under the directorship of John Huston (soon to be handed over to Richard Fleischer after a falling out with Scott). After news of his nomination for *Patton* reached the actor, back came an announcement that if he won the Oscar, he would refuse to accept it. "Gentlemen," he cabled the Academy:

> Although I have received no official notification, elements of the international press have informed me that I have recently been nominated for an Academy Award. Once again I respectfully request that you withdraw my name from the list of nominees. My position on this matter has been generally well known for some ten years.
>
> Please understand that my request is in no way intended to denigrate my colleagues who saw fit to nominate me nor is it intended to insult or hurt the many talented people with whom and for whom I worked on *Patton.*
>
> Furthermore, peculiar as it may seem, I mean no offense to the Academy. I simply do not wish to be involved. I will not attend the awards ceremony nor will any legitimate respresentative of mine attend.

The Academy's initial, rather petulant response was to withhold its usual telegram of congratulations.

To some, the only redeeming feature of Scott's conduct was that he had held his fire until the nominations had closed. To others, this was proof positive that his expressed wish to withdraw his nomination was merely a publicity stunt designed to secure him the award. Far from being a high-principled East Coast idealist, argued the Hollywood loyalists, Scott was just a bad loser; he bore the

Academy and its awards a grudge because of his two bad experiences as a Best Supporting Actor nominee in 1959 and 1961 (See Chapter 3, pages 60–65).

By the time he appeared on the cover of *Time* magazine (to whom he raged that the awards ceremony was "a bloody bore"), Scott had distinguished support. The Spanish director Luis Buñuel was appalled that his *Tristana* had been nominated for the Best Foreign Film award. "Nothing would disgust me more morally than winning an Oscar," Buñuel told *Variety*. "Nothing in the world would make me go accept it. I wouldn't have it in my home."

The problem did not arise, as Buñuel's outburst was to steer the Oscar Italy's way (to Elio Petri, for his *Investigation of a Citizen Above Suspicion)*. Of Scott, however, Bunuel added. "Even in refusing [the Oscar], one isn't free from its corrupting influence. Look at what happened to him when he said he wouldn't accept it. It was worth a *Time* cover."

In a year of "now" movies, even *Patton* had been subtitled *Salute to a Rebel* in an attempt to woo the youth audience. It opened with its title sequence, preferring to hook the viewer with a six-minute speech from its protagonist in front of the biggest American flag in even Hollywood's history. "You do not die for your country, you make the other poor dumb bastard die for his" was one of many memorable lines from an original screenplay by Francis Ford Coppola, a 32-year-old UCLA film school graduate for whom it would win his first Oscar—shared with a man he never met, Edmund H. North, who had "restructured" his work. The title role, before Scott accepted it, had been passed around among Lee Marvin, Rod Steiger, Burt Lancaster and Robert Mitchum, all of whom had pulled out.

Little Big Man and *Beyond the Valley of the Dolls* were among the films overlooked as Ken Russell's *Women in Love* won nominations for its director and its star, Glenda Jackson, but not for its producers. *Love Story* made the ballot by virtue of its huge commercial success—right up there with *Gone With the Wind* and *The Sound of Music*—and the fact that its female lead, Ali MacGraw, was married to the head of Paramount, Robert Evans. To counteract the hip products of his rivals, Evans had hired a soap opera star, *Peyton Place*'s Ryan O'Neal, to star opposite his wife in a good old-fashioned weepie. Evans's clout around town was in itself enough to win MacGraw a Leading Role nomination.

Hippest of the hip movies that year were *M*A*S*H,* Robert Altman's stylish black comedy about a mobile army hospital in Korea, pairing Elliot Gould and Donald Sutherland as figures anarchic enough to win a cult following, and Bob Rafelson's *Five Easy Pieces,* an elliptical study of alienation that gave Jack Nicholson his first major chance to act—and in turn won him his first Academy nomination in a major category. "I'm voting for myself," said Nicholson, "though I don't expect to win. George C. Scott already has it sewn up, whether he likes it or not." His costar, Karen Black, was also nominated, while Rafelson was elbowed out of the directors' race by Federico Fellini (for *Satyricon).*

Dustin Hoffman, like many through the years, seemed even more annoyed not to have been nominated for *Little Big Man* than by his two previous failures to convert nominations into wins. After losing in 1967 *(The Graduate)* to Rod Steiger and in 1969 *(Midnight Cowboy)* to John Wayne, he now told *Variety*'s Army Archerd he was feeling snubbed. "Sure, I'd like to win an Academy Award. I realize that intellectually it doesn't really mean very much. But it is a means to more power, which in turn enables you to be choosy about your scripts. And it makes you more money—which you can put away toward the day when you won't be in such demand."

Also left in the cold for once was David Lean, thought to have slipped up with his Irish epic, *Ryan's Daughter,* denounced by the English press as "an all-star six-million-quid bore" *(The Sun)* and "too bad even to be funny" *(The Times)*. According to Pauline Kael, however, it was the kind of film "that wins people Academy Awards because the acting is so *conspicuous*." MGM laid on a trade-paper blitz, but *Ryan's Daughter* won only two acting nominations—for John Mills and Sarah Miles, for whom it had been written by her husband, Robert Bolt, already a double Oscar winner for *Doctor Zhivago* and *A Man for All Seasons.*

Always suckers for box-office bucks, the Academy instead voted ten nominations, including Best Picture, to the biggest grosser in Universal's history: *Airport,* a $10 million disaster movie based on an Arthur Hailey blockbuster. Even Burt Lancaster, who had taken a role in the film after turning down *Patton,* was offended: "I don't know why it was nominated. It's the biggest piece of junk ever made." The only Oscar it won was a Best Supporting Actress award for the popular veteran Helen Hayes, thanks largely to an energetic campaign on her behalf by the film's producer, Ross Hunter—even though another *Airport* actress, Maureen Stapleton, had been nominated in the same category.

Hayes was one of numerous nominees that year who did not bother to attend the show. Just as well, in the view of the *The New York Times*'s Vincent Canby: "Helen Hayes's being absent spared her —and us—one of those worthy, embarrassing standing ovations for a performance that was, let's face it, just a teentsy-weentsy bit terrible." When *M*A*S*H* won Best Screenplay for Ring Lardner, Jr., twenty-eight years after his last win, for *Woman of the Year,* the writer exulted: "At last a pattern has been established in my life. See you all again in 1999."

Scott's seminal protest took place against one of the most chaotic Oscar backdrops in years. With the winds of change blowing through Hollywood, the days were at last gone when studio bosses could manipulate the Oscars their way. Now the winners were much more likely to have hired publicists to promote their performance all over town. Private screenings, parties, lobbying telephone calls, stylish gifts: the Oscar electorate has always been highly biddable. Hence *Time*'s weary judgment that the 1970 nominations included "the usual number of mind-boggling mediocrities." Even the music category was jinxed again: when Best Song Score went to the Beatles for *Let It Be,* none of the group was present, as it had disbanded the previous year.

When Bette Davis, her screen idol, handed Glenda Jackson the New York critics' award for *Women in Love,* Davis remarked that she felt "a little like Margo Channing," the aging star of *All About Eve,* "handing over her trophy to her young rival." Jackson's subsequent victory at the Academy Awards, in an "art-house" British film, was probably helped by the fact that she was appearing on public television's *Masterpiece Theatre* as Elizabeth I throughout the voting period. The perennial American respect for such stately British products seems to have overcome any resentment at a spikiness in Jackson worthy of George C. Scott. Hollywood, she told one interviewer between the nominations and the awards, was "a machine run by people who are serving an idea which no longer exists, never did exist and which, in any case, is a lie." Even the distributors of *Women in Love,* United Artists, did not expect her to win, refusing to come up with an air ticket for Jackson after she had complained from England that she couldn't afford to fly over for the Awards.

For the future socialist politician, nevertheless, this was to prove the beginning of a seventies run worthy of Greer Garson or Davis herself thirty years before. Promptly dubbed "the intellectual's Raquel Welch," Jackson would be nominated again the following year for *Sunday, Bloody Sunday*; she would win again in 1973, for *A Touch of Class*; and two years later she would receive a rare "classic" nomination, her fourth in six years, as Ibsen's *Hedda* (Gabler).

Jackson expressed herself "surprised" at how pleased she was to win. The six weeks between the nomination and awards night, she said, were "like being pregnant with a child that, for all your labor pains, someone else may have." Today a Labour member of the British Parliament, at least temporarily retired from acting, she has since delivered a more withering verdict on the Academy Awards: "I felt disgusted, as though I was watching a public hanging. No one should have a chance to see so much desire, so much need for a prize, and so much pain when not given [it]." Her compatriot Maggie Smith, by contrast, on hand as the previous year's Best Actress, praised the Oscar as "the one symbol of achievement in the entertainments field that's recognized around the world."

These two Britons' somewhat unlikely sequence of success—four wins in three years, after Katharine Hepburn's two in a row—underlined the lack of good roles for young Hollywood actresses that was beginning to characterize the early seventies. The studios were after cheap, antiestablishment products aimed at the 18–30 age group. As Pauline Kael put it, "Many of the best recent American movies leave you feeling there's nothing to do but get stoned and die." *Easy Rider* had started something.

Jackson's award was picked up for her by a leading member of Hollywood's British community, Juliet Mills, who also had the pleasure of seeing her father win Best Supporting Actor for his deaf-mute village idiot in *Ryan's Daughter*. That morning, Sir John Mills had heard a Los Angeles TV critic sum up his performance in seven words: "too much makeup and on too long"; by the evening he shared with Jane Wyman (1948) the rare achievement of winning an Oscar without saying a word.

But 1970 would always be remembered for the moment Goldie Hawn opened the envelope and screamed "Oh my God! The winner is George C. Scott!" Scott himself, having announced that he would be "watching the hockey game," was asleep at home, where his sons awoke him to accept a mock substitute: a statue of Abraham Lincoln engraved with the words "God A'mighty, free, free at last." It fell to Scott's producer, Frank McCarthy, to pick up the statuette—only to return it to the Academy, in whose vaults it languishes to this day.

"Mr. Scott's repudiation of the award, well beforehand," wrote Hollis Alpert, "struck me as singularly ungracious at a time when not only is his industry in distress, but most of his fellow actors are unemployed. The well-known fact of the matter is that the Academy Awards show is a promotion. Mr. Scott has made himself available for interviews on his movies—also a form of promotion, which translates into financial benefit. Why approve of one form and cry foul at the other?"

At the time, Frank McCarthy was shrewd enough to offer the Academy praise for its "brave" choice—a sentiment that soon found many an echo. In the ensuing debate a future president, Karl Malden, showed his political savvy by declaring that it added "some prestige to the organization," while a past president, Gregory Peck, reckoned that the Academy was now "only two or three years behind the critics." It was Peck, above all others, who had tried to rejuvenate the organization and its image by encouraging the younger Hollywood stars to join. "But it's impossible," he sighed, "to reach them. People like Dennis Hopper and Peter Fonda belong to the Academy, but they won't get involved."

These two would fail to get involved in much of anything during the rest of the seventies, but the decade would see their peers joining in the annual Oscar bonanza with all the vigor of Hollywood insiders. As if to cheer Peck up, Fonda's sister, "Hanoi Jane," certainly got involved in the awards the following year, beating four British actresses to the supreme prize and breaking all the unwritten rules to do so.

The Academy was still shuddering from the Scott snub, and universally bad reviews for 1970's Oscar telecast. Now there was the prospect of another political embarrassment, in the shape of an acceptance speech from Jane Fonda. Hired as the show's new producer, Howard W. Koch found himself in much the same position as Frank Capra back in 1936. Even a star as ambitious as Barbra Streisand was reluctant to be seen presenting Best Picture (an honor she chose to accept twenty years later); some of the older perennials, meanwhile, were boycotting the show in protest at the nomination of Stanley Kubrick's *A Clockwork Orange.* To prevent total collapse, Koch desperately needed a D. W. Griffith-type rabbit to pull out of the Academy's hat—and he found one in the shape of another lifelong Oscar outcast, Charles Chaplin.

At 82, Chaplin had agreed to return to the United States from his exile in Switzerland to accept an award from the Film Society of Lincoln Center in New York. Having failed to attend the first Oscar ceremony in 1929, when he was voted an Honorary Award, he now accepted the Academy's invitation to travel on to Hollywood and receive a second one. The Academy's proud announcement prompted a spate of newspaper backbiting about Chaplin's left-wing leanings, his neutral nonparticipation in World War II, and his failure to pay U.S. taxes. But Koch was undeterred; Chaplin would be so much the centerpiece of this year's ceremony that all actresses were asked to wear black, white or silver, in nostalgic tribute to the movies' monochrome era.

Chaplin and Jane Fonda: this was a meeting of two movie worlds made in the Academy's dreams—if only Fonda could be persuaded to skip the politics. Several state legislatures had already called for a boycott of Jane Fonda movies because of her antiwar activism. She had been reluctant to take the role of the hooker in Alan J. Pakula's *Klute* so soon after shedding her *Barbarella* screen image, but the film had nevertheless proved a huge critical and commercial success. Disappointed not to win two years before for *They Shoot Horses, Don't They?,* which she had seen as "an indictment of American values . . . a forceful condemnation of the capitalist system," Fonda had high hopes this time around. Only her outspokenness appeared to stand between her and victory over four British actresses: Glenda Jackson again, Vanessa Redgrave, Julie Christie and Janet Suzman.

Suzman, better known for her distinguished stage career in England, owed her nomination to a reverse application of the usual trade advertising syndrome: take out huge spreads, that is, to compensate for the lack of (rather than take advantage of) commercial success and pre-Oscar awards. Sam Spiegel launched a major trade campaign for his indigestible epic *Nicholas and Alexandra,* the first film since *Patton* from the reigning Best Director, Franklin J. Schaffner. Suzman, a ubiquitous interviewee, grew ever more candid as her daily grind wore on: "The film is altogether too long. What a gargantuan monster to condense into three hours!"

Christie was back opposite her beau, Warren Beatty, in a cultish Robert Altman Western, *McCabe and Mrs. Miller,* while Redgrave was now playing *Mary, Queen of Scots* to a Jackson reprise as Elizabeth I. In John Schlesinger's *Sunday, Bloody Sunday,* Jackson was simultaneously able to show her versatility as the only girl in an eternal triangle completed by Peter Finch and Murray Head. Small wonder, perhaps, that Fonda overcame the usually fatal handicap of *Klute*'s failure to win nominations for Best Picture or Best Director. As a hooker pursued by a homicidal maniac, she joined the long line of actresses to win Oscars as women of easy virtue.

"I took *Klute,*" said Fonda, "because in it I expose a great deal of the oppression of women in this country—the system which makes women sell themselves for possessions." On Awards night, however, chastened by a plea from her deeply conservative father, she said nothing to rock the Academy boat. Her peers proved duly grateful; Hollywood officially forgave Hanoi Jane her trespasses, clearing the way for her to win a second Oscar seven years later. Before *Klute,* her career had begun to flag, not least because of the unpopularity of her views; after this Oscar, she was offered more than forty major film roles in three years.

An equally dignified male winner was Gene Hackman, whose gracious acceptance speech for *The French Connection* formed a sharp contrast with the Best Actors immediately before and after him. One of the first stars to be candid about his paydays, Hackman had already testified that his previous Oscar nomination (for *Bonnie and Clyde*) had seen his fee rise to six figures; now he would see it leap from $200,000 to $500,000. Although the seventh actor offered the role by *The French Connection*'s wunderkind director, William Friedkin, Hackman had won the Oscar against some tough opposition: Peter Finch, Walter Matthau and Topol *(Fiddler on the Roof)*.

The fifth Best Actor nominee was the only absent one, despite promises from his colleagues on *The Hospital* to have him there "dead or alive": a still Oscar-shy George C. Scott, whom the Academy prided itself on nominating despite his high-handedness toward it the previous year.

Compared with the embarrassments of 1970, everything was going the Academy's way. Even the Nixon administration helped it to a noncontroversial evening by refusing a visa to Fonda's friend and fellow Best Actress nominee, Vanessa Redgrave (who would more than make up for it six years later). Thanks to the fine ensemble acting in Peter Bogdanovich's *The Last Picture Show,* even the Supporting awards went for once to genuinely supporting players, Ben Johnson and Cloris Leachman. Chaplin's appearance provided what the Academy's current president, Karl Malden, calls "the most emotional moment in the history of the Oscars"—and that's sure saying something.

In the relief that Chaplin made it through the show, and that the winners had all displayed the industry's shiniest public face, Hollywood even managed to sublimate a pretty dismal movie year. *The French Connection* won Best Picture over *A Clockwork Orange, Fiddler on the Roof, The Last Picture Show* and *Nicholas and Alexandra.* But the public still seemed to prefer a number of films the Academy did not consider worthy of awards: Kubrick's *A Clockwork Orange,* Sam Peckinpah's *Straw Dogs* and Ken Russell's *The Boy Friend.*

If the Academy thought it had exorcised the ghost of George C. Scott, it was reckoning without Hollywood's supreme maverick, Marlon Brando. After a decade and more in the doldrums—it was fifteen years since his last nomination—Brando had signed for a mere $50,000 plus "points" to play the Mafia don Vito Corleone in Francis Ford Coppola's film of Mario Puzo's novel *The Godfather.*

Paramount had wanted Burt Lancaster, Orson Welles, George C. Scott or Edward G. Robinson for the role; Coppola himself had wanted Olivier or Brando. The studio had been impressed by the actor's unwonted humility in stuffing his cheeks with tissue paper and submitting to a screen test. His judgment, both artistic and financial, had not of course deserted him. *The Godfather* was to surpass *Gone With the Wind* as Hollywood's all-time record moneymaker.

The year 1973 was also when the Oscars' all-time champion, Katharine Hepburn, made her only appearance at the awards ceremony, to present an Honorary Oscar to her friend Lawrence Weingarten.

Louise Fletcher, 1975's Best Actress (<u>One Flew Over the Cuckoo's Nest</u>) started a trend by accepting her Oscar in sign language.

James Whitmore's 1975 nomination for <u>Give 'em Hell, Harry,</u> his one-man show about Harry Truman, made this the third film whose entire cast had been nominated.

Thinking Brando a racing certainty for Best Actor, the studio was shaken by the verdict of the New York critics. Unable to choose between the array of strong performances in *The Godfather,* they had opted out and handed their award to Olivier for *Sleuth,* a charming black comedy in which the great man went *mano a mano* with Michael Caine. In the run-up to the Oscar nominations, Paramount issued instructions that Brando be regarded as the *only* leading actor in *The Godfather,* with Al Pacino, Robert Duvall and James Caan listed strictly as supporting players. *The Godfather,* as a result, won three Supporting Actor nominations—only the fourth film in Oscar history to do so.

Sleuth equaled another record when Olivier and Caine were both listed among the runners for Best Actor; it was the second time that a film's entire cast had won nominations. Brando was up against Peter O'Toole as an aristocratic British fetishist in Peter Barnes's *The Ruling Class,* offset by his equally eccentric Don Quixote in *Man of La Mancha.* The fifth contender was Paul Winfield in *Sounder,* Martin Ritt's portrait of southern blacks during the 1930s depression. With Best Actress nominations for his costar Cicely Tyson and for Diana Ross (in *Lady Sings the Blues*), another Oscar record was set as black performers won three of the ten Leading Role nominations for the first time. "I've got two words to say about the Oscars," trilled Liza Minnelli. "Diana Ross."

Upon learning about the local tradition of trade-paper advertising, Ross's Svengali, Berry Gordy, Jr., outdid all precedents, buying whole-page photographs of Ross day after day: Diana, as Billie Holiday, looking her worst, shooting up, going through cold turkey in a padded cell, sitting on a toilet seat wearing nothing but a bra. Said Walter Burrell, a black show-biz journalist, "I'm a member of the Academy, and I was personally offended. I was insulted not only by the ads, but by the expensive gifts Berry bought for the voters and by the lavish dinners he hosted for them." Gordy was so confident that Ross would win the award that he publicly christened her new poodle "Oscar."

The local consensus, however, was that his advertising campaign cost her the award. "Berry was literally trying to buy the award," said Burrell. "The saddest part about it is that Diana might have won if Berry hadn't been so greedy and obvious." In the end, ironically enough, it was Liza Minnelli who beat both Ross and Tyson to the award, for *Cabaret,* thus becoming the first Oscar winner whose parents, too, had both received Academy Awards (see Appendix C, section G). Escorted by her father, the director Vincente, Minnelli made a point of thanking the audience for rewarding her as herself, not as Judy Garland's daughter. "It was a hard thing for her to say," commented Liza's biographer, Michael Freedland. Garland was a two-time Oscar loser; the nearest she had come to winning an acting Oscar was accepting a fictitious one in *A Star Is Born.* "Judy would have behaved herself, but would she have quite enjoyed seeing Liza standing on the podium, accepting her little gold statuette? Probably not."

But the 1972 celebrations were again to turn sour. The first sign of impending doom for the Academy had come when Brando turned down the Golden Globe and the Reuters News Agency World Film Favorite awards with a magisterial statement:

> There is a singular lack of honor in this country today, what with the government's change of its citizens into objects of use, its imperialistic and warlike intrusion into other countries and the killing of not only their inhabitants but also indirectly of our own people, its treatment of the Indians and the blacks, the assault on the press, the rape of the ideals which were the foundation of this country. I respectfully ask you to understand that to accept an honor, however well-intentioned, is to subtract from the meager amount left. Therefore, to simplify things, I hereby decline any nomination and deny anyone representing me.

The Godfather, nonetheless, went into the Oscar show with eleven nominations to *Cabaret*'s ten. But it had won no awards at all, and *Cabaret* six, by the time an astonished silence greeted the news that Bob Fosse had beaten Coppola to Best Director, making it 7–0. Could Brando's apparent intention to reject an Oscar have taken its toll? Even *Cabaret*'s Joel Grey had warded off *The Godfather*'s triple challenge in the Supporting Actor stakes.

Immediately after Best Director came the Writing awards, which saw Adapted Screenplay go jointly to Coppola and Puzo. It was *The Godfather*'s first win of the night. "I was beginning to think I wasn't going to get up here at all," muttered Coppola. Then came the moment for Best Actor.

During Coppola's onstage ordeal, an even tenser drama had been developing backstage. For all his formal protestations, Brando had at the last-minute anointed a representative of a somewhat unusual order. When she had arrived at his assigned seats in the Dorothy Chandler Pavilion, waving the nominee's tickets at perplexed security personnel, a nervous messenger had come round the back to inform Howard Koch that a Native American had shown up as Brando's proxy. "I quickly called a powwow offstage," Koch recalled. "We considered everything. We even considered arresting her on the grounds that seats are nontransferable."

The producer decided instead to "learn the worst now." As Julie Andrews and George Stevens were presenting Bob Fosse with his unexpected Best Director statuette, Koch was out in the audience, desperately negotiating with Sacheen Littlefeather, whom he found regaled in white buckskin and leather thong headdress. "You can't read that," he told her, indicating the thick sheaf of paper on her lap.

"If Marlon should win," she replied coolly, "I'm going to read it."

"If you try that," said Koch, "I'll cut you off the air."

"Okay, okay," she replied. "I won't read it *all.*"

After Liv Ullmann and Roger Moore had opened the envelope, the roars from the Dorothy Chandler audience at Brando's comeback victory died into awkward silence as this tiny figure in all her Indian finery came calmly up to the podium, brushed aside the Oscar proffered by Roger Moore, and began to speak extempore:

> Hello. My name is Sacheen Littlefeather. I'm Apache, and I am president of the National Native American Affirmative Image Committee. I'm representing Marlon Brando this evening, and he has asked me to tell you in a very long speech—which I cannot share with you presently, because of time, but I will be glad to share with the press afterwards—that he very regretfully cannot accept this very generous award. And the reasons for this are the treatment of American Indians today by the film industry. . . ."

At this point there was some distinctly unhappy murmuring among the audience, causing the speaker to say "Excuse me. . . ."

This prompted some catcalls before she proceeded with her protest —"and on television in movie reruns and also with the recent happenings at Wounded Knee."

But the lady clearly had a sense of her audience. "I beg at this time" she concluded, "that I have not intruded upon this evening and that we will, in the future, in our hearts and our understanding meet with love and generosity. Thank you on behalf of Marlon Brando."

As Littlefeather walked off to deliver her protest in full to the media, the Dorothy Chandler Pavilion sat in a silent state of collective shock. For Littlefeather, it was the beginning of a sustained nightmare in which she was exposed as a phony—an actress masquerading as an Apache. For the Academy, it was again time to take stock.

Its new president, the screenwriter Daniel Taradash, called an emergency board meeting to discuss the use of the Academy Awards as an international soapbox: "I don't know what we can do about it, but we have to look at the use of the Oscar lectern as a platform." The meeting ended inconsequentially. Although the Academy's senior echelons were scandalized by Brando's behavior, there were others prepared to defend him. In a curious way, his choice of this occasion for a major public protest was a backhanded compliment to the prestige of the Academy and its awards.

"At least," in the view of one moderate, "he showed no overt disrespect. There was no nakedness or foul language. In her way, his emissary conducted herself with great dignity." Howard Koch himself summed up the impossibility of legislating against spontaneity: "You might as well cancel the Oscars if you're going to muzzle the winners. We'll have to bank on the good faith of most Oscar winners." But John Wayne, for once, seemed to speak for the Hollywood consensus when he said he thought it "sad" that Brando had funked his own protest: "If he had something to say, he should have appeared that night and stated his views instead of taking some little unknown girl and dressing her up in an Indian outfit."

In fact, Brando had directly addressed the reasons for his absence in the lengthy speech he had written for Littlefeather, but which she had been unable to deliver in full. Among its powerful sentiments were: "When they laid down their arms, we murdered them. We lied to them. We cheated them out of their lands. We starved them into signing fraudulent agreements that we called treaties which we never kept. We turned them into beggars on a continent that gave life for as long as life can remember. . . . If we are not our brother's keeper, at least let us not be his executioner." Toward the end, Brando said: "I would have been here tonight to speak to you directly, but I felt that perhaps I could be of better use if I went to Wounded Knee to help forestall in whatever way I can the establishment of a peace which would be as dishonorable as long as the rivers shall run and the grass shall grow."

What, beyond sheer perversity, had been Brando's underlying motive? As a founder and heavy financial backer of the new and militant American Indian Movement, the strength of his feelings was undeniably authentic. But Brando's biographer, Richard Schickel, divined a pervasive sense that George C. Scott's motives two years before had been more professional and thus "purer." Scott had taken his stand because he did not believe in competition between artists. "No such logical connection between belief and action could be attributed to Brando, with the result that his protest was not taken as seriously as Scott's." A search began for deeper motives.

At the time, the standard Hollywood wisdom held that Brando was getting back at everyone who had ignored or patronized or rejected him over the years. But there was more to it, in Schickel's view, than that. "Having proved, if not beyond doubt, then to his own satisfaction, that his mature skills were the equal of his youthful ones, he was, in effect, announcing his retirement as, shall we say, 'a contender' "—if not as an occasionally working actor.

Another Brando biographer, David Downing, came to a slightly different conclusion: "Perhaps Brando, thinking back to his first run of success, decided that he didn't want a second round as a 'hot' Hollywood 'property,' didn't want to be a 'film star' again. To accept the Oscar might seem like a legitimization of Hollywood's version of his career, an acceptance of the terms which the film capital used to measure success in life. Everyone was talking about the great comeback, as if all his political work in the sixties had been a way of marking time between hit movies. This was not how Brando saw things; it never had been."

Either way, with *Last Tango in Paris* already in the can, Brando stayed away from movies for three years after winning his Oscar—a period that coincided with the height of his dedication to the American Indian Movement. And, as with Scott, the Academy's membership again displayed a commendable lack of hard feelings by voting Brando another nomination the following year, for his outrageous striptease in Bernardo Bertolucci's *Last Tango.*

In an unusually strong acting year, Robert Redford won the only acting nomination of his career, opposite Paul Newman in *The Sting*—not, as it was publicized, a rematch by popular demand of *Butch Cassidy and the Sundance Kid,* but a part he inherited from Jack Nicholson, who had instead decided to take on Billy "Bad Ass" Buddusky in *The Last Detail.* After failing to win at his third nomination—his chances not improved by the film's high quotient of "Naval" language—Nicholson proved a sore loser. "Not getting our own Academy Award hurt real bad," he told the Chicago *Tribune.* "I did it in that movie, that was my best role. How often does one like that come along, one that fits you?" The fourth nominee was Al Pacino for *Serpico*—the second of the six unsuccessful nominations that by 1990 had seen Pacino join the list of Oscar outcasts.

A TV clairvoyant had predicted that Jack Lemmon would win the Leading Role Oscar of 1973, not least because he had been King of Thailand in a previous life. By voting Lemmon the Best Actor in *Save the Tiger,* however, the Academy was restating one of its weirder unwritten rules: if you like an actor whose gifts are primarily comic, give him the Oscar for a straight dramatic role. Overlooked for *The Apartment* and *Some Like It Hot*—each among the grosser injustices of Oscar history—Lemmon had for the first time donned the mantle of moral campaigner that would later resurface in such movies as *Missing* and *The China Syndrome* (both of which would also win him nominations). In the nervous post-Brando climate, this sometimes outspoken actor confined himself to saying: "In recent years there has been a great deal of criticism about this award, and probably a great deal of that criticism is very justified. But I'd just like to say that I think it's one hell of an honor and I am thrilled."

The rows had started long before the 1973 show began, when the Academy proudly announced that the multiple Olympic swimming champion Mark Spitz would be presenting one of the major awards. There was immediate uproar. Thanks to a deal with a superagent, Norman Brokaw of William Morris, Spitz was already promoting everything from milk to razor blades, and had become a national laughingstock after a very wooden appearance on a television soap opera. There were plans, nevertheless, for a TV and film career "when the right vehicle comes along." An appearance on the Oscar telecast, figured Brokaw, was the perfect way to turn his client into "a male Esther Williams."

Even Hollywood, however, occasionally draws the line. The Oscars were accustomed to offbeat presenters, from Mickey Mouse to Miss Piggy, but they at least had something to do with the motion picture industry. The purpose of the Academy Awards was to hype films and actors, not celebrities intent on becoming movie stars. Within twenty-four hours, Spitz was obliged to withdraw, which he did with a portentous statement: "The honor of being a presenter should be reserved for people who have contributed to the motion-picture industry." ("Ah," wisecracked Peter Brown, "if only it were!")

Scott and Brando, meanwhile, had left a tangled legacy. The Oscar had become "a political or a business gesture," said Joanne Woodward, nominated for *Summer Wishes, Winter Dreams.* "People tell you it adds five million dollars to a movie's gross, and I believe it, but that's not what the Oscar is for." If Woodward was angered by the Academy's latest failure to nominate her husband, she and Newman had the satisfaction of seeing *The Sting* win Best Picture—adding, according to its producers, more like *thirty* million to its box office.

As the first female producer ever to pick up an Oscar for Best Picture, Julia Phillips was the toast of the town that April night in 1974; seventeen years later, she was the butt of many an Oscar-night joke, as the author of an indiscreet Hollywood memoir entitled *You'll Never Eat Lunch in This Town Again,* which enjoyed fleeting notoriety by chronicling her own decline (and that of pretty much everyone else in the business) into drug-taking and decadence. All that day Phillips had been steadying herself for the evening ahead on "the perfect chemical combination": a diet pill, cocaine, two joints, three Valium and a glass and a half of wine. "You'll never know what a trip it is," she said when her big moment came, "for a nice Jewish girl from Great Neck to win an Academy Award and meet Elizabeth Taylor all in the same night." The rest was silence, as Phillips was "enfolded into Liz's very famous cleavage . . . for somewhere between five and thirty seconds."

The Sting's narrow victory over *The Exorcist*—both films had won ten nominations—also saw George Roy Hill beat William Friedkin to Best Director. Although *The Exorcist*'s prime mover, William Peter Blatty, won for Adapted Screenplay, he was moved to an extreme case of sour grapes. "The Academy should fold its tent and go back to baking apple strudel or whatever they can do well," he whined. "*The Exorcist* is head and shoulders the finest film made this year or in several years."

Blatty said that he had sensed a backlash when the Writers and Directors guilds both failed to honor *The Exorcist,* although the writers had given the film a standing ovation at their screening. He openly blamed the veteran director George Cukor, who had led an anti-*Exorcist* drive among the older members of the community, offended by its gruesome subject matter. According to Blatty, Cukor had persuaded senior members of the Academy "to eliminate the Special Effects award, which our film would certainly have won. I think the film is touching a nerve and sometimes that nerve is very raw. If Mr. Cukor was disturbed, he has a narrow view of what constitutes outrage or obscenity." Cukor did not permit himself to be drawn into a reply.

Blatty had other reasons to regret the postnomination period. Already planning *Exorcist II*—the original having broken the magic $100 million barrier—Warner Bros. had mounted a costly campaign to win a nomination for their hot 14-year-old property, Linda Blair. When they succeeded in doing so, largely on the strength of the uncannily scary voice with which she had represented the devil, a protest went up from the 1949 Oscar-winning actress Mercedes McCambridge. "That's not Linda Blair's voice," she told the journalist Charles Higham, "it's mine." All hell broke loose.

Apart from a Broadway stint in *Who's Afraid of Virginia Woolf?*, said McCambridge, dubbing the devil in *The Exorcist* was "the hardest work I have ever done . . . I mean sheer physical work!"

> One of the hardest sequences was the invention of the sound for the bilious green vomit that spewed in projectile surges from the

> child's mouth. . . . When I felt I was ready to go for a take, I would load my mouth with [rotten] apple sections, munching them to a not-quite-mealy consistency; and then, from a paper cup, I would add, in my distended mouth, two eggs—yolk and gluey stuff. At the instant before the pea soup and cornflakes erupted on the screen, I would swallow the glob I'd been holding, down to mid-gullet, flex my diaphragm muscles, and gag it up onto the nest of microphones. . . . I had to do it many times before it was absolutely right. It made me so dizzy and weak that I would have to lie down for an hour between throw-ups, and then I'd go back and have another go at it.

Sterling work. But Warner Bros. and Friedkin had thereafter reneged on their promise to give McCambridge a credit in both the picture and its advertising. Until the row broke, they had even denied rumors of her involvement. As the actress gave ever more graphic details of her sufferings on Blair's part, the Academy was forced to call in legal advisers. The dubbing of Marni Nixon's voice had famously denied nominations to Natalie Wood in *West Side Story* and Audrey Hepburn in *My Fair Lady*. Could an actress be nominated for a performance where her voice was *part*-dubbed? Could another actress, come to that, win a nomination purely for voicing? It was decided to let Linda Blair's nomination stand—but her chances of winning were doomed from that moment. And when *The Exorcist* won the Oscar for Special Effects, Mercedes McCambridge argued, with some justice, that her soundtrack work had "played a large part." As the film's box office burgeoned, she took her revenge on "that louse Friedkin" by blocking release of a soundtrack album.

Even fans took to protesting the 1973 nominations. One Woody Allen aficionado paid to make his own public protest in *Variety*: "Congratulations to the Academy for turning its back on talent and artistry once again by ignoring Woody Allen and his superb film *Sleeper* in the Academy Award nominations. Charlie Chaplin and the Marx Brothers never got any Oscars for their performances either. Doesn't anyone out there like to laugh?" Jack Lemmon's win proved his point—comedy never fares well at the Oscars—but the Academy later denied that it was this advertisement that stung them into organizing an honorary award for Groucho Marx. Woody Allen, moreover, would soon be winning his share of Oscars, despite a more sustained display of indifference toward the Academy than either Scott or Brando.

For the Academy, 1973 was just one of those years. Even one of the *winners* was unhappy—the only Best Actress nominee not to turn up, Glenda Jackson, who watched herself win her second Oscar in four years from the privacy of a New York hotel room. "I was working—but I doubt that I would have been there even if I hadn't been. Watching it in my hotel suite, I kept telling myself that I ought to turn it off and go to bed. I felt disgusted with myself." On winning her second Oscar, her only immediate comment was: "Now my mum has a proper set of bookends." Upon reflection, she said of the whole Oscar circus:

> It's really a three-day wonder, you know, and it doesn't make all the difference people think. It's nice the day you hear the news, and it's nice on the day they actually give you the statuette, and maybe twenty-four hours after that. It doesn't really stretch much further than that. And it doesn't mean that every film script is automatically sent to you. You don't get the pick of the cream. The cream is a very small proportion of any work that is circulating at any given time. I get dreadful scripts sent to me most of the time, and the good ones —now as before—are very rare indeed.

Jackson has also taken the familiar, timeless stand that acting contests are absurd. But for those involved, who take them with deadly seriousness, the 1973 Supporting awards proved cause for more discontent when they went to two "amateurs." John Houseman, Orson Welles's colleague back in the days of the *Mercury Theatre of the Air,* was head of New York's Juilliard School when he was drafted as a last-minute replacement for a sick Edward G. Robinson as the crusty old college professor in *The Paper Chase.* For Houseman, at 71, the Oscar was to prove the beginning of a lucrative Indian summer as an actor, even rivaling Welles in the gravel-voiced TV-commercial department.

Tatum O'Neal's performance opposite her father Ryan in *Paper Moon* was meanwhile said to have been "manufactured" by Peter Bogdanovich. It was revealed that the director had gone to as many as fifty takes of some of her scenes in order to achieve the "natural" performance for which young Tatum was hailed. At 10 years and 148 days—four years younger than her rival nominee, Linda Blair—she remains the youngest person ever to have won a competitive Oscar, and seems to have decided to quit while ahead. After finishing her schooling, Tatum eventually abandoned an acting career for marriage to a tennis champ, John McEnroe.

Seeking another escape from its woes, the Academy did not rest content with persuading Katharine Hepburn to make her only live appearance on an Oscar show, to present the Irving Thalberg Award to her friend Lawrence Weingarten. They also went for a Chaplin-style deus ex machina in the shape of the dying Susan Hayward, so sick that she had to be propped up by Charlton Heston while presenting the Best Actress award to the absent Glenda Jackson. The 1958 Best Actress looked so pale a shadow of the great beauty she had once been that the Academy's gimmick backfired on it. Many of the audience felt ashamed to watch; even in Hollywood, it seems, stage-managed poignancy can curdle to pathos of an unacceptable order.

No wonder one of the year's multiple hosts, John Huston, went out of his way to defend the Oscars—awards, he insisted, "which are not bought and paid for. Christ knows, the ones you gave me weren't." Huston further departed from his script to set about that year's numerous dissenting voices: "They are afraid to appear unsophisticated, as if knocking [the Oscars] is the thing to do." But the Academy just could not win. All its efforts to restore dignity to the occasion came to naught at the ceremony's climactic moment.

David Niven was in the midst of introducing Elizabeth Taylor, presenter of the Best Picture award, when a burst of laughter from the audience made him turn around—to confront a naked man dashing across the stage, complete with a peace sign. "Just think," said Niven, after the streaker had been bundled away, "the only laugh that man will get in his life is by stripping off and showing his shortcomings."

A good line from a witty man—Liz Taylor fell back on the old standby, "That's a tough act to follow"—Niven's joke was just *too* good for some conspiracy theorists, who began to wonder if the streaker had been preplanned. Had a fake press pass really been enough to get him past the backstage security? And why had he subsequently been clothed and paraded backstage before the media, to make the most of any publicity going? How come neither the Academy nor NBC, whose cameras had reveled in the interruption, had decided not to press charges? Jack Haley, Jr., the show's producer, strenuously denied any intent on his or the Academy's part, but *Variety* remained unconvinced, and waxed indignant: "The incident was a most unfortunate lapse on the part of the Academy people responsible for the show, for they destroyed in a few seconds a forty-six-year history—often characterized by pomposity but nevertheless marked by propriety." Other papers next day praised 33-year-old Robert Opal* for brightening up an otherwise dull telecast.

Dustin Hoffman seemed determined to ensure that the 1974 Oscars would be anything but dull. "The Academy Awards are obscene, dirty and no better than a beauty contest," he said in a CBS-TV interview with the critic David Sheehan on the eve of the awards—which he would be not attending, despite his third Best Actor nomination for *Lenny*. The Oscars, he said, were "ugly and grotesque"; in 1968, when the Awards had been postponed because of the assassination of Dr. King, Bob Hope was "making jokes about the postponement and never said a word about Martin Luther King.† That's what I found ugly and grotesque. After that, I said I didn't want to come any more. It was as simple as that."

Unmoved by the compliant lead Jane Fonda had given his generation, Hoffman handed his tickets to his parents and left town. By the end of the decade, he would be taking a very different line; in the meantime, it fell to Frank Sinatra to embarrass the elder Hoffmans by rebuking their son in front of the watching millions.

Sinatra was one of four "old school," almost "ratpack" hosts—the others being Bob Hope, Sammy Davis, Jr., and Shirley MacLaine—drafted by the Academy that year in the hope of a scandal-free evening. But another political controversy lay in store—exacerbated, in fact, by the differing political views of these supposedly "safe" emcees.

This year the trouble came from a wholly unexpected quarter.

* His network exposure enabled Opal to begin a career as a stand-up comedian, appearing on *The Mike Douglas Show* and even being hired by the producer and publicist Allan Carr to streak again at a party for Rudolf Nureyev. When he streaked in front of the Los Angeles City Council, however, he was found guilty of public lewdness and placed on probation. Five years later, in 1979, Opal was found murdered in his San Francisco sex shop.

† This was untrue. Hope, whose script had been toned down for the occasion, revealed among other respectful references to Dr. King that they had once met on an airplane. The civil rights leader had complimented Hope on his hosting of the Academy Awards show: "We enjoy watching it every year."

It was early in the proceedings that one of the minor Academy Awards, for Best Documentary Feature, went to a study of the Vietnam War called *Hearts and Minds.* Hearts in the Dorothy Chandler sank when one of its producers, Peter Davis, accepted by saying, "It's ironic to get a prize for a war movie while the suffering in Vietnam continues." But they hadn't heard anything yet. Davis went on to hope that his children would grow up in "a better atmosphere and a better country" before the coproducer, Bert Schneider, echoed his colleague's sense of irony—this time, that Vietnam was on the point of liberation. He then proceeded to read a wire from the Vietcong delegation at the peace talks then under way in Paris: "Please transmit to all our friends in America our recognition of all they have done on behalf of peace and for the application of the Paris accords on Vietnam. These actions serve the legitimate interests of the American people and the Vietnamese people. Greetings of friendship to all American people."

Backstage, as the show blithely moved on to an Honorary Oscar for Jean Renoir, Bob Hope had producer Howard Koch "pinned to the wall," demanding he broadcast a disclaimer. Shirley MacLaine, standing nearby just before making her big entrance, overheard and screamed at Koch: "Don't you dare!" Everything went swimmingly through the Music, Costume and Art Direction awards, past Sinatra's wrist slap to Hoffman, to the point where Sinatra reappeared to read an impromptu statement issued on behalf of the Academy. He and Hope had in fact cobbled it together on the back of an envelope, seeking only Koch's approval to read it.

The statement said simply: "We are not responsible for any political references made on the program, and we are sorry they had to take place this evening." As the hall responded with a mixture of boos and bravos, Sinatra walked offstage to a roasting from MacLaine. Both were due onstage to join in the closing number, "That's Entertainment." Back in the wings, as the curtain came down on the forty-seventh Oscars, the sentiments were not so buddy-buddy. Bob Hope denounced Schneider's speech as a "cheap shot," and John Wayne was almost apoplectic: that Schneider guy was "a pain in the ass and outa line and against the rules of the Academy." As the phones rang off their hooks, one of the presenters, Brenda Vaccaro, was reminding Howard Koch in no uncertain terms that the Academy had not interrupted the show to apologize for the streaker or

Marlon Brando's Indian surrogate. From Francis Ford Coppola came the not unreasonable point that the film was "not a musical comedy. . . . In voting for that picture the Academy was sanctioning its message, which was in the spirit of Mr. Schneider's remarks."

Coppola was virtually alone in defending Schneider, but he could afford to be expansive. To his anguish, his old nemesis Bob Fosse was again nominated against him, this time for *Lenny*; but 1974 proved Coppola's year. Not merely did *The Godfather II* become the first and only sequel in Oscar history to capture the Best Picture award; it won six of its eleven nominations—including, this time around, Best Director for Coppola himself. In a busy year, he had written the scripts of three successful films: *Godfather II, The Great Gatsby* and *The Conversation* (which he also directed). Unusually, as a result, the Best Director was also a nominee in two writing categories, though he won neither. When his father Carmine also scooped the Best Score award for *Godfather II,* they became the first father-and-son team to win since Walter and John Huston in 1948.

On his first and only Oscar nomination, for a straight dramatic role in *The Towering Inferno,* the local favorite Fred Astaire found himself up against three supporting actors from *Godfather II.* (Of the fifth, one critic wrote: "The steady barrage of ads promoting Jeff Bridges's performance in *Thunderbolt and Lightfoot* is the only possible explanation for his nomination.") No problem, predicted the pundits; sentiment would surely carry the day for Fred, one of the most popular figures in the community.

Though awarded an Honorary Oscar as long ago as 1949, because it was thought he was planning retirement (see Chapter 11), Astaire apparently "did not think much" of seeing all his collaborators and costars win Oscars, from Hermes Pan and Ginger Rogers to Joan Fontaine and Joan Crawford, while he himself missed out. Evidently, for once, in an unsentimental mood, the Academy crushed the aging legend by handing the award to *Godfather II*'s Robert De Niro, at his first nomination—even though the only words he had spoken in English were "I'll make him an offer he can't refuse." As impressed by De Niro's Italian, perhaps, as by his powerful screen presence, the voters thus bracketed him with Sophia Loren as the only performers in Oscar history to win an acting award for a subtitled, foreign-language role (see Appendix C, section G).

With De Niro in Italy on location for *1900*, his award was picked up by Coppola, who glowed: "I'm happy one of my boys made it." De Niro's unabashed screen references to Brando's performance in the original *Godfather* drew praise from the man himself: "He is the most talented actor working today. I doubt if he knows how good he is." He also earned a touching tribute from an equally venerable figure, Lee Strasberg, whose movie debut as the dying mobster Hyman Roth had earned him a nomination in the same category. The "father" of the Method school said he would "probably" have liked to win the Oscar, but had no regrets: "Bobby deserves it."

In a year of big-budget, all-star movies like *Murder on the Orient Express* and *The Towering Inferno,* the other obvious Oscar candidate was Roman Polanski's *Chinatown,* which matched *Godfather II* with ten nominations (to *Lenny*'s seven) and moved the New York *Daily News* to the rash prediction that the Best Actor award was a foregone conclusion: "Not since Ray Milland guzzled his way to an Oscar in *Lost Weekend* has an actor been such a sure bet as Jack Nicholson." The paper went on to quote "one well-known beauty" as saying: "If only half the actresses with whom he's had affairs vote for him, he'll win by their ballots alone."

Much more interest centered around the female categories, where the favorite for Best Actress was one of the victims of the previous year's *Exorcist* controversy, Ellen Burstyn, who had herself hired Martin Scorsese to direct her in *Alice Doesn't Live Here Anymore.* Burstyn had wanted, she said, a relatively inexperienced director, "someone who'd be hungry"—but she also wanted a director who would make Robert Getchell's script "from a woman's point of view about women's real-life problems." That Burstyn did not hire a female director itself says something about the lack of good movie opportunities for women throughout the seventies.

Best Supporting Actress went to Ingrid Bergman for *Murder on the Orient Express,* a verdict with which the almost *too* rehabilitated actress herself, still expiating Hollywood's communal guilt, openly disagreed from the Oscar stage. Sure that the award would go to Valentina Cortese for Truffaut's *Day for Night,* Bergman had attended the ceremony "primarily for another reason," to accept an Honorary Award on behalf of Jean Renoir. When her name emerged from the envelope for the third time in thirty years, she was self-evidently unprepared. "It's always nice to get an Oscar," she began, "[but] in the past Oscar has shown he is forgetful and has the wrong timing. Last year, when *Day for Night* won [Best Foreign Film],* Valentina Cortese gave the most beautiful performance . . ." The camera caught Cortese on her feet, blowing kisses at Bergman, who walked across the stage toward her and pleaded: "Please forgive me, Valentina. I didn't mean to . . ."

Charles Champlin of the *Los Angeles Times,* who over the years had seen everything, grew excited enough to call Bergman's gesture "the high point of the Oscar decade." Others weren't so sure. Cortese, for her part, was naturally delighted by Bergman's public praise—they were copiously photographed together at dinner afterward—but only later did Bergman realize how the other three nominees (Madeline Kahn, Diane Ladd and Talia Shire) must have felt about going unmentioned. "I acted, as usual, too impulsively," Bergman later confessed. "It would have been better if I'd kept my mouth shut."

For Best Actress, Burstyn was up against a mixed enough bunch to prove her point about the female doldrums: Diahann Carroll in *Claudine,* Faye Dunaway in *Chinatown,* Valerie Perrine in *Lenny* and Gena Rowlands in *A Woman Under the Influence.* "There are so few decent roles for women these days," said Burstyn yet again—this time, like Bergman, with inadvertent rudeness to the other nominees—"that if you work, you get nominated." It was enough to persuade her to exercise her contractual right to take a night off, if nominated for an Oscar, from her Broadway role in *Same Time Next Year.* Then, at the last minute, she changed her mind: "I won't win. I never do."

Thus it was that the only Best Actress nominee not present on the big night was the winner, Ellen Burstyn. The same had been true of De Niro and his rivals for Supporting Actor, all of whom were present while the victor stayed home in New York. The winner of the Best Actor award, by contrast, was the only nominee present: Art Carney for *Harry and Tonto* (in which Ellen Burstyn had played his daughter).

Originally written by Paul Mazursky for James Cagney, the role had been grabbed by Carney after refusals from Cagney, Sinatra and

* See footnote on p. 305.

Olivier. A classic case of a character actor winning the Leading Role award for the part of his lifetime—other examples abound, from McLaglen and Ferrer to Duvall and F. Murray Abraham—the popular Carney punched the air on hearing his name announced, and received a standing ovation from the crowd who had adjudged him a better actor than Albert Finney, Al Pacino, Jack Nicholson and Dustin Hoffman. It was perhaps as well that the others were absent. Nicholson, who had fancied his chances for *Chinatown,* shrugged off his fourth loss in four nominations: "Maybe next year I'll be the sentimental favorite."

And so he was. Nineteen seventy-five saw Nicholson, at his fifth attempt, crowned Best Actor for his remarkable simulation of mental illness in Miloš Forman's *One Flew Over the Cuckoo's Nest.* Following the lead of his predecessor, Art Carney, Nicholson's acceptance speech ended with thanks, "last but not least," to his agent—"who ten years ago advised me I had no business being an actor."

After thirteen years trying to film the play in which he had flopped on Broadway, Kirk Douglas had finally given up and handed it on to his son Michael—famous, at that time, only as a TV cop. Douglas Junior had then managed to raise his $3 million budget independently—but only by using Nicholson's name and giving him one-third of the $3 million. As for the dread Nurse Ratched: so hateful was the character that Anne Bancroft, Colleen Dewhurst, Jane Fonda, Angela Lansbury, Geraldine Page and, for all her protests, Ellen Burstyn were among the many who had turned it down. Taking a look at Altman's *Thieves Like Us,* to see if Shelley Duvall could be right for another part in the film, Forman chanced upon Louise Fletcher.

Jack Nicholson confessed that he had begun to wonder if he would ever win an Oscar. But talk of his four unsuccessful nominations irritated him. "After you've been chosen one of the five best actors of the year—and there are only about forty thousand—then people come up to you and ask how it felt to lose. One doesn't *lose* an Academy Award." While conceding that the Oscars are "a promotional device," he has always talked them up—especially after winning another. "My Oscars have had a very positive effect on me. I've tried to reciprocate by spending about sixteen of the most uncomfortable hours of my life attending the ceremonies. I don't like the idea of going, but I've gone out of a sense of fair play."

Cuckoo's Nest swept the top five awards—Best Picture, Director, Adapted Screenplay, Actor and Actress—the only picture to do so since *It Happened One Night* forty-one years before. Ken Kesey, author of the novel on which it was based, skipped Oscar night for a poker game, claiming that Michael Douglas had failed to honor verbal agreements about the screenplay: "I'd like to have subpoenas in some of those award envelopes." Of all the film's Oscar winners, only Miloš Forman even mentioned Kesey's name in his acceptance speech. "They blew it, they just blew their big chance," said Kesey next morning. "Any one of them could have thanked me for writing the book and won all the arguments. But they blew their big chance to be in the big times, the big league. . . . It was like pumps trying to say they're more important than the well and the water. Last night, it was pumps giving pumps awards for being good pumps."

United Artists, confident that it would win Best Picture, had arranged to reopen *Cuckoo's Nest* next day in one thousand theaters throughout the U.S., Canada and the U.K. Post-Oscar alone, the film added more than $50 million to its worldwide box office—plus $25 million more, as time went on, for video sales. Dwarfed by its success at the awards were such other big pictures of 1975 as Warren Beatty's *Shampoo,* Robert Altman's *Nashville,* Sidney Lumet's *Dog Day Afternoon*—and the most successful film ever made, surpassing *Gone With the Wind, The Sound of Music* and *The Godfather*: Steven Spielberg's *Jaws.* The Oscars' long mistreatment of Spielberg began right here, as he underwent the humiliation of seeing his work nominated for Best Picture, but not Best Director—doubly galling in view of his public statement that *Jaws* was "a director's movie."

Foolishly—he would learn better soon enough—Hollywood's latest wunderkind had permitted cameras into his home to film him watching the televised nominations. Captured for posterity, therefore, was the moment Spielberg buried his face in his hands and yelled, "I can't believe it. They went for Fellini instead of me."* For the first time, but by no means the last, he talked plaintively of a

* Under a convoluted Academy rule, candidates for Best Foreign Film are allowed to become candidates in other categories the following year. In 1974, for instance, Fellini's *Amarcord* had won Best Foreign Film; in 1975 Fellini was a Best Director nominee for the same film.

"backlash": "The same people who had raved about *Jaws* began to doubt its artistic merit as soon as it began to bring in so much money."

Musicals were attempting a comeback with Barbra Streisand's Fanny Brice metamorphosing from *Funny Girl* into *Funny Lady,* and Ken Russell co-opting everyone from Elton John and Jack Nicholson to Tina Turner and Ann-Margret into his version of The Who's rock opera, *Tommy.* Both enjoyed modest success, and a smattering of nominations, while Stanley Kubrick's stolid *Barry Lyndon* was up for Best Picture and Director without managing any acting nominations.

So dominant was *Cuckoo's Nest* that the Academy allowed itself a sentimental aberration, launching the octogenarian George Burns on a twilight acting career with a Supporting Role Oscar for *The Sunshine Boys*—a part he had inherited because of the death of Jack Benny. In other categories, voters seemed to have had difficulty thinking of names to fill out the ballot. Joining Nicholson and Pacino, Walter Matthau and Maximilian Schell on the Best Actor list, for instance, was one James Whitmore—whose performance was barely known beyond viewers of the Z cable channel in Los Angeles, which had been repeatedly showing a filmed version of his one-man show about Harry Truman, *Give 'em Hell, Harry,* throughout the voting period. Voters who never left their homes, or indeed their beds, thus gave Whitmore the distinction of being in the third film whose entire cast—himself—had been nominated for an Academy Award.

Supporting Actress, much more significantly, went to Lee Grant of *Shampoo*, marking the high point in the career of the only actress to make a comeback from the blacklist. An Oscar nominee at 24 (in 1951, for *Detective Story*), Grant's only crime was to refuse to testify against her husband, the blacklisted Arnold Manoff. She did not work in Hollywood for twelve years, fighting to clear her name until she won a formal letter of apology from the congressional leadership. There followed a sustained burst of high-quality work in such films as *In the Heat of the Night, The Landlord, Plaza Suite* and finally *Shampoo.* Grant would win another nomination the following year, in *Voyage of the Damned.*

Grant and Fletcher were among the actresses in 1975 not complaining about the paucity of female roles, as *Variety* pointed out that not one of the performances nominated for Best Actress had appeared in a Hollywood production made in the United States. Having secured her own Oscar the previous year, Ellen Burstyn now went on television to urge Academy members to boycott this year's Best Actress award in protest at the shortage of good roles for women. Not surprisingly, she soon received a piqued message from Louise Fletcher. Burstyn told Fletcher she hadn't seen *Cuckoo's Nest* because she felt it would be "too painful an experience"; Fletcher pointedly told Burstyn that it might have been "nicer" to have made her comments in the year she herself had been nominated.

From the stage, Fletcher created a hallowed Oscar moment by accepting her award in sign language, by way of tribute to her deaf parents: "I want to thank you for teaching me to have a dream. You are seeing my dream come true." Devotees of Oscar trivia were also delighted to see a brother and sister, Warren Beatty and Shirley MacLaine, both nominated in unwonted categories—he as writer of *Shampoo,* she as documentary maker. (Both lost.) More trouble was looming, however, in the music department.

For years the Music awards had been a source of grief to the Academy, as the list of embarrassing omissions and inadequate winners grew to laughingstock proportions. The trouble, it seemed, was that the music branch had always been allowed to set its own separate rules; the nominating process, as a result, had become the exclusive preserve of a select executive committee of only some fifteen members, whose choices were always open to accusation of bias and abuse.

The 1975 nominations caused more uproar than ever. Fans of *Mahogany,* a Joan Crawford–style vehicle for Diana Ross, were already charging racism when the singer did not receive an acting nomination. When the film's title song ("Do You Know Where You're Going To?") was not among the preliminary nominations announced by the committee, they became dyspeptic. The Academy's music branch, thundered the *Hollywood Reporter,* was "run like a restricted private club, with the primary objective being to exclude any 'undesirables' from its roster." Robert Altman, too, could not believe that only one of the many original songs from *Nashville* had made the preliminary list; he accused the musicians of "typical Academy cliquishness."

Stung into action, the music branch voted to throw out the

preliminary nominations (chosen that year by a committee of seventeen) and start again. This time, all 207 members of the Academy's music branch would choose the nominees—the system employed by every other major branch of the Academy. Second time around, the *Mahogany* theme did indeed make the short list, though Altman had to rest content with the renomination of just the one *Nashville* song, Keith Carradine's "I'm Easy." He had the ultimate consolation that it beat the *Mahogany* theme to the Oscar for Original Song—the other musical awards that year going to *Jaws* (John Williams) and *Barry Lyndon* (Leonard Rosenman, beating both *Tommy* and *Funny Lady*).

Although all the major winners were present, for once, and the big night went off uneventfully by the standards of the seventies, producer Howard Koch was again unhappy about the high index of absentees among the other nominees and star presenters. This was partly due to rival attractions such as the annual party hosted by the agent Irving "Swifty" Lazar, who refused Koch's plea that he cancel it in the Academy's best interests. But Koch singled out one particular no-show for a public reprimand: "It seems to me that someone who gets three million dollars from a picture owes it to the industry that's making him rich to participate in the Academy Awards—especially if he's a nominee." Whom did he have in mind? The New York columnist Earl Wilson reckoned that it had to be one of the Best Actor nominees, Al Pacino, whom he found spending Oscar night "in jeans, without a tie, in a Greenwich Village restaurant. He had no TV set." Pacino insisted that his performance in a workshop production at the Public Theater was a more important date.

And what about the publicity value of the Awards, even if you don't win? "Fame," pronounced Pacino, "is a perversion of the natural human instinct for attention."

The winner of the 1976 Academy Award for Best Actor in a Leading Role wasn't present, either, for the rather more conventional reason that he was dead.

In a very competitive year—their classy film was up against *All the President's Men, Taxi Driver,* Sylvester Stallone's *Rocky* and Hal Ashby's *Bound for Glory*—MGM decided to promote *Network* for a sweep of the acting awards, running William Holden for Best Actor,

Faye Dunaway for Best Actress, and Peter Finch for the Supporting award. "No way!" protested Finch. "Howard Beale was *not* a supporting role."

Finch's half-mad newscaster in Paddy Chayefsky's satire of television politics had struck a chord throughout America; everywhere people were hanging out of their windows yelling his catchphrase: "I'm mad as hell and I'm not going to take it anymore." Despite its inadequate photography, and close-to-the-bone politics, the film was an unexpected box-office smash—and Finch very much its star. The lesser Oscar categories, he insisted, could be left to *Network*'s fine supporting actors: Robert Duvall, Ned Beatty and Beatrice Straight.

Finch had lost his one previous nomination, for *Sunday, Bloody Sunday* in 1971, and remained publicly equivocal about the Oscars: "I hate the politics of the whole thing, but the nomination is a big help. I'm not even sure that winning is that important, but a nomination lets people know you're there." But his publicist, Michael Maslansky, told a different story: "Peter wanted to win that Oscar. It was an obsession with him." Between August and January, Finch had done three hundred interviews with foreign and domestic media. On January 14 he arrived at the Beverly Hills Hotel to do yet another, for ABC's *Good Morning, America,* and dropped dead in the lobby of a heart attack.

With the ballot forms already dispatched, and the voting process under way, it was too late to invoke the Academy's rule against posthumous nominations. When Finch's name duly joined Holden's on the official returns—alongside Stallone for *Rocky,* De Niro for *Taxi Driver* and Giancarlo Giannini for *Seven Beauties*—it did not please the new producer of the Oscar show, William Friedkin, himself an Oscar-winning director for *The French Connection.*

The four cohosts Friedkin had chosen—Jane Fonda, Richard Pryor, Warren Beatty, Ellen Burstyn—read to one Los Angeles paper like a "gesture of defiance." Not merely was there no Bob Hope; Friedkin could scarcely have chosen four more antiestablishment figures to kick-start the Academy Awards toward their fiftieth anniversary. He had even invited Lillian Hellman, author of a recent study of the blacklist era, to present an award—and arranged for a private jet to pick her up from her East Coast home on Martha's Vineyard. If this were to be the first Oscar telecast of a new era, weeping widows were the last thing Friedkin needed. Already he had vetoed an Academy plan for Loretta Young to pay tribute to her recently deceased friend Rosalind Russell. Now he had a quiet word with Paddy Chayefsky, asking him to accept on Finch's behalf.

Come the big moment, Chayefsky ratted on their agreement. No stranger to controversial moments in Oscar history, Liv Ullman too had a prerehearsed speech written by an Academy scriptwriter: "One measure of an actor may be his willingness not to conceal himself . . . but to show himself in all his humanity, and to expose both the light and darker sides of his nature . . . openly and truly. The nominees for an actor in a leading role are. . . ." When she proceeded to pluck Finch's name from the envelope, Chayefsky duly took to the stage, only to say: "For some obscure reason, I'm up here accepting an award for Peter Finch. There's no reason for me to be here. There's only one person who should be up here, and that's the person Finch wanted to accept his award. Are you in the house, Eletha?"

Mrs. Finch came onstage bearing flowers, and made the most gracious speech, concluding: "Before Peter died, he said to me, 'Darling, if I win I want to say thank you to my fellow actors who have given me encouragement over the years, and Paddy Chayefsky and Barry Kross [Finch's agent]. . . . Most of all, thanks to you, darling, for sending the vibes the right way, and thanks to the members of the Academy.' "

Afterward, unsentimental to the last, Friedkin was furious. At the Governors Ball he buttonholed Chayefsky and *Network*'s producer, Howard Gottfried, and accused them of lying to him. Gradually it emerged that Chayefsky had not merely warned Finch's widow of his intentions; he had written her speech and helped her rehearse it. "I figure this is what movies are all about—'This is Mrs. Norman Maine' . . ." Said Gottfried: "We decided we could not conceive of allowing this kind of injustice to take place. She was the proper recipient."

The *Network* table had plenty to celebrate, with wins for Faye Dunaway as Best Actress, Beatrice Straight as Supporting Actress, and Chayefsky for Screenplay. Not among the winners was the veteran composer Bernard Herrmann, who had also died that year after an astonishing career stretching from *Citizen Kane* via the famous "shower music" for Hitchcock's *Psycho* to two posthumous nominations that year—both in the Original Score category, for *Taxi Driver* and *Obsession.* The winner was Jerry Goldsmith for *The Omen.* The year's Oscar trivia collectible also came in the music category, when 1968's joint Best Actress, Barbra Streisand, pulled off a unique double by winning a second Oscar for cowriting the song "Evergreen" with Paul Williams.

Network's Oscar campaign had been a catch-up operation, so lavish was the earlier publicity accorded *Rocky* and *All the President's Men.* Redford, Hoffman and Stallone had between them hogged every available magazine cover through most of the summer and fall, leaving movie fans to find their own way to the year's other worthy offerings. Also in among the nominations were performances in Martin Scorsese's *Taxi Driver,* Ingmar Bergman's *Face to Face* and John Schlesinger's *Marathon Man* (which won Laurence Olivier his first nomination in the Supporting category, and his ninth in all, equaling Spencer Tracy's male record). For the Italian film *Seven Beauties,* Lina Wertmuller became the first (and still the only) woman ever to be nominated for Best Director.

Before the awards, United Artists and MGM had agreed to rerelease *Network* and *Rocky* as a double bill in nine hundred theaters—an enterprise that earned them $20 million in eight weeks. Each film had garnered ten nominations—a statistic that in itself saw *Rocky* launching one of the less likely Hollywood success stories of recent years.

After attracting no attention in a clutch of supporting roles, Sylvester Stallone had taken the advice of his mother, an astrologist, who assured him that success would come to him as a writer. Stallone proceeded to write the script for *Rocky* in three days, basing it on the 1975 title fight between Muhammad Ali and Chuck Wepner. "I'm astounded by people who take eighteen years to write something," he crowed to *The New York Times*. "That's how long it took that guy to write *Madame Bovary.* And was that ever on the best-seller list? No. It was a lousy book and it made a lousy movie."

In the light of all its dismal sequels, it is frequently forgotten that moviegoers regarded the orginal *Rocky* as an "art-house"-type movie that made good. At the time, it reminded cineastes of the 1930s brand of all-American optimism known as "Capra-corn."

Frank Capra himself was quoted as saying of *Rocky*: "I think it's the best picture in the last ten years. It's got my vote for the Oscars all the way down the line."

Looking back on the 1976 awards, the Oscar-winning writer William Goldman recalls being convinced that *All the President's Men* would win Best Picture. It had received great reviews; it had done good business; most important, it was a significant picture: "No less acute [an] observer of American politics than Governor Reagan of California said he thought the movie eventually cost Gerald Ford the presidency against Jimmy Carter, because the film's release in April of 1976 and its long run flushed to the surface again all the realities of Watergate that the Republicans had tried so hard to bury. We are talking then about a movie that may be one of the few that just might have changed the entire course of American history."

So why did *Rocky* win? "Impossible to say," but it may have been a combination of "spectacular" (as opposed to "good") business, and "the most basic Hollywood dream—dreams can come true." Goldman compared Stallone's "phenomenal emergence from obscurity" with that of a Lana Turner sitting on the right drug-store stool; he could not have won had he already been displaying the public arrogance which has since become his hallmark. Today, Goldman's vote would, of course, go to *Taxi Driver,* perceived at the time as too violent.

Stallone won the Directors Guild award, but nothing from the New York critics, who gave Best Picture to *All the President's Men* and Best Actor to *Taxi Driver*'s De Niro. Come the Oscars, Stallone's dreams remained dreams; with nominations as both actor and writer, he won neither, and has received no Oscar attention since—while making a pile of money in a chain of dire box-office blockbusters. In 1976, none of that mattered, as the Oscar audience cheered Stallone through a mock fight with the year's deus ex machina, Muhammad Ali. "We won the big one," said Sly, predicting that *Rocky* would be "remembered, I think, much more than any other film, ten to fifteen years from now."

The most enduring film of 1976 would, in fact, prove to be Martin Scorsese's *Taxi Driver,* which won nothing. Even Stallone and the Oscar electorate, however, would be obliged to remember it in 1981—for all the wrong reasons.

. . .

The fiftieth Academy Awards show produced a slice of everything that characterized the Oscars' fifth decade: overt snubs both to and from the Academy, more political turmoil, and a freak Oscar that caused the winner little but grief. Nineteen seventy-seven, in short, was the year Woody Allen took all the major honors in absentia, thus missing the barnstorming politics of Vanessa Redgrave and the continuing humiliation of Steven Spielberg. Outside the Dorothy Chandler Pavilion, Herbert Ross's attempts to film the arrival of Michael Caine and Maggie Smith for a segment of *California Suite* were somewhat complicated by the anti-Redgrave protesters; inside the pre-Oscar favorite and box-office champ of the year, George Lucas's *Star Wars,* was to find itself left out in the cold.

Allen's neurotic love story *Annie Hall* saw him become the first man nominated for Best Actor, Director and Screenplay since Orson Welles in 1941. Both were born mavericks, both professional Hollywood outsiders. But Allen, unlike Welles, would win two out of three, plus Best Picture—despite the fact that he would not let United Artists use his name in Oscar advertising, and made it quite clear that he would not be turning up for the awards show. *Variety* best summed up the reasons behind the industry's homage to its least likely new superstar: "In a decade largely devoted to male buddy-buddy films, brutal rape fantasies and impersonal special effects extravaganzas, Allen has almost single-handedly kept alive the idea of heterosexual romance in American films."

Annie Hall had done itself no Oscar favors by being so unremittingly rude about Los Angeles—the city whose sole cultural advantage, according to Allen, was being able to turn right on red. "I still feel guilty when I turn right on red," said his cowriter, Marshall Brickman, when picking up their statuettes. But the film also won Diane Keaton Best Actress; in a (for once) strong year for actresses, she had the useful contrast of a much darker, bar-hopping role as the murder victim in *Looking for Mr. Goodbar*. Unlike Allen, she was there to accept, wearing the "Annie Hall look" that held the nation in thrall, and becoming one of the few winners in Oscar history to remember the names of all her fellow nominees.

When Allen's name emerged from the Best Director envelope, there was not even a proxy to pick it up, so presenters King Vidor and Cicely Tyson simply walked off with it. Allen himself, of course, spent Oscar night at Michael's Pub in Manhattan, playing his clarinet with the New Orleans Marching and Funeral Band, as he does every Monday night. "I couldn't let down the guys," he told the Academy. Michael's Pub has remained his favorite place on Oscar night ever since—through twelve more nominations in fourteen years, if only one more win.

The one award that passed Allen by, Best Actor in a Leading Role, seemed destined at last for Richard Burton, nominated for the seventh time for recreating his stage role as the psychiatrist in Peter Shaffer's *Equus.* After a three-year absence from movies, Burton now had two back-to-back: *Equus* and *The Exorcist II.* Both were commercial disasters, but the good reviews he earned for *Equus* were the kind of material on which an Oscar campaign could be built. As United Artists put it on Z Channel—ever since James Whitmore, the cable channel had played a crucial role—Burton proved tireless on the talk-show circuit. The Hollywood grapevine began to talk of his "touching desire to win." In interview after interview, the actor apologized profusely for "past overindulgence in good whiskey and bad movies."

Although Burton and Taylor had divorced (again), and he had since remarried, Elizabeth Taylor could not be persuaded to take part in the Oscars' fiftieth anniversary show. This was "Richard's big night," and she didn't want to detract from it. Only Allen and the *Annie Hall* sweep seemed to stand between Burton and his Holy Grail; he would surely have little problem seeing off John Travolta *(Saturday Night Fever)* and Marcello Mastroianni *(A Special Day).*

But he had reckoned without *Bogart Slept Here,* a new Neil Simon comedy directed by Mike Nichols. When Robert De Niro quit the set after two weeks, Simon could only explain: "Bob is a very intense actor. He doesn't play joy well." De Niro, explained Nichols, "was just not coming across as funny." Simon rewrote the script; Herbert Ross replaced Nichols; the title was changed to *The Goodbye Girl,* and the central part went to Richard Dreyfuss—opposite Simon's then wife, Marsha Mason, whose 10-year-old daughter, Quinn Cummings, also got a part (and indeed a Supporting nomination).

If Burton was handicapped by *Equus*'s failure to win either its director or its producers nominations, Dreyfuss was mightily assisted by the simultaneous release of *Close Encounters of the Third Kind*

—the latest Spielberg epic to start breaking box-office records. Dreyfuss's director, Herbert Ross, had also been nominated for a different film: the soggy backstage ballet drama *The Turning Point,* a big enough commercial failure for Fox to mount a desperate Oscar campaign. With both of Ross's films nominated for Best Picture, his star was outshone only by that of Woody Allen.

Close Encounters, Spielberg's first film since *Jaws,* put its director through the opposite of his first ordeal: this time his work was nominated for Direction, but not for Best Picture. "In *Jaws,*" said Dreyfuss, cunningly reminding voters that they overlooked him that year, "the shark was the star of the film. In *Close Encounters,* the film is the star of the film." It had become Columbia's most profitable movie ever, prompting speculation that the Academy was punishing not Spielberg but the studio, by now deeply embroiled in the Begelman scandal that so dogged the career of 1968's Best Actor, Cliff Robertson.

At his seventh and last nomination, Burton fell victim to a combination of Hollywood politics and the Oscars' curious reward system. In any other year, a seventh nomination would have wracked the Academy with guilt over failing to honor a film actor of such distinction. In this one, the combination of the Spielberg snub, the Columbia scandal, the Ross double-whammy and Dreyfuss's versatility steered the votes the younger man's way—crowning Richard Dreyfuss, at 29, the youngest man ever to be named Best Actor.

Burton would die six years later, before the Academy could even compensate him with an Honorary Oscar; but victory was to prove somewhat Pyrrhic for Dreyfuss. The story of his subsequent decline, reversed only by a sustained comeback a decade later, points to another victim of the Oscar curse.

"I achieved exactly what I wanted to achieve far too soon," was Dreyfuss's own verdict in 1991. Since his first big part, in *American Graffiti* in 1973, he had very successfully linked his fortunes with Spielberg's before his freak win for *The Goodbye Girl.* "Post-Oscar pickiness," spiced with a dash of arrogance, led to a clutch of mediocre films before a downward, drug-assisted spiral, highlighted by a last-minute flounce off the set of *All That Jazz.* In 1982 Dreyfuss wrapped his Mercedes around a tree and was charged with possession of drugs. "I was struck down," he said, "by Vlad the Impaler."

Sent to a rehabilitation center, he married his nurse and started a new life. "I didn't do any work. I actually thought my career was over." But his new wife thought she had married a movie star. "I have too much pride to be kicked out of show business," he told her. "I will walk out under my own power." Having once assumed he would again become a regular working actor, "I didn't know whether I could handle this—the relegation, the degradation of Richard Dreyfuss."

A dinner with Jeffrey Katzenberg, the new head of Disney, led to the breakthrough Dreyfuss sought. Offered the part of the down-and-out in *Down and Out in Beverly Hills,* and suddenly seeing himself typecast as a bagman, Dreyfuss suggested Nick Nolte for the role and himself for the suaver part of Bette Midler's husband—"a pairing," in the words of Iain Johnstone of the (London) *Sunday Times,* "which magically remade his name." There followed a steady stream of high-visibility work: *Tin Men* with Danny de Vito, *Nuts* with Barbra Streisand and *Always,* back with Spielberg. Ever desperate to show off his versatility, Dreyfuss then stepped into Sean Connery's doublet-and-hose as the Player King in Tom Stoppard's *Rosencrantz and Guildenstern Are Dead,* which saw his final rehabilitation—mentioned alongside Anthony Hopkins, on Awards Night 1991, among the very earliest contenders for the Oscars to be presented a year later.

The champagne flowed in buckets at the Oscars' fiftieth birthday bash, as everyone fumed about Vanessa Redgrave over their lobster, crab and caviar. Though Jane Fonda had missed out on Best Actress, *Julia* had won both Supporting categories—for Jason Robards (his second successive Oscar) and for Redgrave, whose conduct had confirmed the Academy's worst fears (see Chapter 3, pages 70–72). Howard Koch, Redgrave later revealed, had urged her to say only "Thank you" if she won the Oscar. He also told her that the Academy had laid on plainclothes security backstage and in the auditorium, and police sharpshooters on the roof. "I told Howard that I must reserve the right to say whatever I thought was right and necessary."

Not anticipating victory, "because of the press campaign against me," Redgrave was surprised to be seated next to the aisle. Concluding that she might win, after all, she began to gather her thoughts. "I thought of the Palestinians in the camps and the hospitals; and the socialist and communist Jews who were the first to be

Nominated in 1977 for writing, directing, and starring in Annie Hall, Woody Allen equalled Orson Welles's treble for Citizen Kane. Though his movie won Best Picture (and his girlfriend Diane Keaton won Best Actress), Allen chose to stay home in New York, playing his clarinet at Michael's Pub.

sent to the concentration camps. I thought of Lillian Hellman, categorized as a 'premature anti-fascist' by the FBI and blacklisted in the 1950s. I thought of all the American artists and workers in the film, TV and theatre industries who were persecuted because they were trade unionists, or communists, or Jews, or all three." Her thoughts were interrupted only by the arrival of John Travolta with the envelope.

The anti-Redgrave demonstrations outside the hall and her out spokenness inside it combined to distract attention from the snub Woody Allen delivered the Academy. In New York next morning, Allen proved typically indifferent to his Hollywood laurels; he had got home from Michael's Pub, he said, and gone to bed without checking the results. A year later he would say: "I know it sounds horrible, but winning the Oscar didn't mean anything to me. I have no regard for that kind of ceremony. I just don't think they know what they're doing. When you see who wins these things—or doesn't win them—you can see how meaningless this Oscar thing is."

As if to prove his point, the awards were by then deep into their seminal struggle between *The Deer Hunter* and *Coming Home,* two Vietnam War films that would have won Oscars without any hype (also see Chapter 3, pages 73–77). But Universal wasn't taking any chances with *The Deer Hunter.*

Impressed by the marketing of *Grease,* a teenage musical turned into a blockbuster by hyperbolic promotion, they hired the man responsible, Alan Carr, previously known only as the manager of chanteuse Ann-Margret, to hype their somewhat different product.

The Deer Hunter was an unconventional, somber, three-hour sermon on a subject which the American public wanted to forget, and which had never proved big box office. As Carr himself said, when approached by Universal, "I knew I wouldn't like it. It's about two things I don't care about: Vietnam and poor people." It was directed by "this guy Cimino, who I remember directing Ann-Margret in Canada Dry ads five years ago. Three hours of Pittsburgh steelworkers. I'm not going to like it."

Carr had been sitting by his pool drinking champagne, celebrating *Grease*'s arrival at the $100 million threshold, when the call came from *The Deer Hunter*'s producer, Barry Spikings. After his usual lunch at Ma Maison, he arrived half an hour late at the *Deer Hunter* screening, his mind on a fundraising dinner he was hosting at his home that night for Governor Jerry Brown. "By the middle of the movie," he swears, "I was crying so hard I had to go to the men's room to put cold water on my face. . . . I'm truly emotionally undone." That night he had to apologize to Governor Brown: "I have been affected by this film so deeply that I cannot speak."

At a meeting next day, Universal presented Carr with their master plan for this rather unwieldy product. How about reversing the normal process? If a slew of Oscars normally guarantees commercial success for a film already on general release, could they also do so for a picture *about* to go on release? If so, how could they be won?

Carr relished the challenge: "I sensed right away this was an event movie." The secret, he suggested, was to arrange a series of select out-of-town openings, to build up discriminating word-of-mouth, before an invitation-only screening in Beverly Hills which would have even Academy members fighting for tickets. "L.A. is jaded and spoiled by the movies. At previews in Westwood, they cheer for Telly Savalas chasing an airplane."

New York was mildly surprised to find itself selected for a one-week, reserved-seat opening deliberately aimed at the New York critics' awards. "The picture would die if we opened it cold," explained Buddy Young, Universal's vice-president in charge of advertising, publicity and promotion. "It must have awards to give it the stature it needs to be successful." It was the first time any film had organized a special New York opening aimed at the local critics' awards. Young was aware, he confessed to *The New York Times,* that the tactic could prove counterproductive if the New York critics felt they were being steamrolled. "We are taking that chance because *The Deer Hunter* needs awards and the credentials of reviews. If we open in New York, we will get reviewed in *Time, Newsweek* and the other national magazines. Good reviews will help the film to be taken seriously by the Academy." There was also to be an "intense screening program" in which *The Deer Hunter* was shown privately to opinion-makers—"publishers, editors, disc jockeys, anyone who attends parties and is likely to talk about the film," as Young put it. Added Carr: "I knew it would be the Christmas cocktail party subject in New York. Everybody would be asking if you saw it, were you one of the five hundred people who saw one of the eight shows? They said I shouldn't give a film to New York and take it away. I said that's how you treat New York."

He was right. "Just when it seemed time to announce that the American cinema had died as an art form," wrote David Denby of *New York* magazine, "*The Deer Hunter* arrives to restore a little hope." The New York Critics Circle duly named the film its Best Picture of the year, adding Best Supporting Actor for Christopher Walken. Carr had liftoff.

Once he had sent all Academy members a lavish package containing the favorable East Coast reviews, the West Coast preview became one of the hottest tickets in years. He persuaded Universal, unprecedentedly, to restrict admission to Academy members only. "It was pandemonium. People were calling—Nureyev, Betty Bacall—asking for house seats, but there were no house seats. We were saving the film for the Academy." A full-time staffer assigned to tracking how many Academy voters had shown their membership cards to obtain admission calculated that an astonishing 2,400 of the 2,700 L.A.-based members saw *The Deer Hunter* in Westwood during the voting period. The studio then spent an additional $250,000 on a print advertising campaign aimed at the industry only—locking up, for instance, the centerfold of all the trade papers. Promoting the film to the moviegoing public was the last thing on their minds.

Carr's final masterstroke was to arrange a "blue-chip" screening for an audience of just two—Steven Spielberg and Vincente Minnelli, between them representing both extremes of the Directors Guild, whose own awards were just a week away. Again, it worked. Word-of-mouth among directors young and old won Michael Cimino the DGA award, steering him toward a certain win on Oscar night. Best Picture, too, was now in the bag for Universal. "The making of the campaign for *The Deer Hunter,*" wrote the *Los Angeles Times,* "is a case study of what happens when a major studio incorporates a run for the Oscar into its overall marketing strategy for a commercially shaky film." Six months before, *Deer Hunter* had been "both a box-office long shot and an Oscar dark horse." But Carr's campaign seemed to have "pinpointed timing and strategies of exposure." He was backed by the highest levels at Universal, who obviously counted on the Oscar to help them with "a very tough marketing job."

Carr's real success was to have drowned out public opinion. By Oscar night, when the votes were safely in the bank vault, demonstrators outside the Dorothy Chandler Pavilion were denouncing *Deer Hunter* as pro-war and anti-vet, hailing Hal Ashby's *Coming Home* as a more accurate, sympathetic portrayal of the truth. It was too late to change the Academy's mind about Best Picture and Director, though the major acting awards went to *Coming Home*'s Jane Fonda and Jon Voight (over *Deer Hunter*'s Robert De Niro) while the Supporting category saw *Deer Hunter*'s Christopher Walken beat out *Coming Home*'s Bruce Dern.

Invited to present the award for Best Director, an almost magisterial Francis Ford Coppola seized the moment to deliver an uncannily accurate homily on the future: "I can see a communications revolution that's about movies and art and music and digital electronics and satellites but, above all, human talent—and it's going to make the masters of the cinema, from whom we've inherited the business, believe things that they would have thought impossible." Opening the envelope to find Michael Cimino's name inside, he swallowed his sense of irony that a fellow Italian-American's film about Vietnam had made such a mark even before the release of his own *Apocalypse Now.* Coppola nevertheless hugged Cimino, calling him *paisan,* and looking "like the patriarch of the 1970s."

Jane Fonda had played the versatility card, with roles in *Comes a Horseman* and *California Suite*—the film that provided the trivia collectors with another unexpected bonus. By winning her second Oscar, giving her one in each acting category, Fonda's old Oscar rival, Maggie Smith, joined a select group comprising only Ingrid Bergman, Helen Hayes and Jack Lemmon.* Dame Maggie (as she has since become) also earned herself an unlikely niche in the annals as the only person to win an Oscar by playing an Oscar loser.

The summer hits of 1978 were markedly less earnest than the films that dominated the year's end. The big money-makers were *Grease*, a Chevy Chase–Goldie Hawn frolic called *Foul Play*, and National Lampoon's *Animal House*. John Belushi made the cover of *Newsweek* when Lampoon's film grossed an amazing $74 million domestically; but there was no Supporting nomination for him, as expected, and he moodily turned down an invitation to attend the awards as a presenter. The only comedy to make an impact on that year's awards was *Heaven Can Wait*, Warren Beatty's remake of 1941's *Here Comes Mr. Jordan*.

"It doesn't represent moviemaking—it's pifflemaking," wrote Pauline Kael of *Heaven Can Wait*. "Warren Beatty moves through it looking fleecy and dazed, murmuring his lines in a dissociated, muffled manner." Yet Beatty repeated Robert Montgomery's Best Actor nomination, adding more for Best Picture, Direction (with Buck Henry) and Writing (with Elaine May)—becoming the first man since Orson Welles to secure all four major nominations at once. But he proceeded to lose them all—a cruel reminder that he was more admired than liked, and admired more for his talent in the boudoir than the cinema.

Beatty's big sister, Shirley MacLaine, tried to cheer him up when she went onstage to present the Best Actress award: "I want to take this opportunity to say how proud I am of my little brother, my dear, sweet, talented brother. Just imagine what you could accomplish if you tried celibacy!" Sitting out front with Diane Keaton, the umpteenth conquest he had escorted to the Oscar show, Beatty shot back a noticeably frosty look.

Adding Keaton's name to a catalogue worthy of Don Giovanni —including herself, Natalie Wood, Julie Christie and countless oth-

* This exclusive club has since been joined by Meryl Streep and Jack Nicholson, who has expressed his ambition to go on to an unprecedented triple with Best Director. His 1990 attempt with *The Two Jakes* proved overly optimistic.

ers—Leslie Caron afterward mused that "Warren has an interesting psychology. He has always fallen in love with girls who have just won or been nominated for an Academy Award." The ultimate proof of Caron's point came in 1991–92, when Beatty fell in love with the girl he would finally marry, Annette Bening, when they costarred in *Bugsy* after her nomination for *The Grifters*.

The rest of that year's Oscar losers were a frankly gloomy bunch: Woody Allen on divorce in *Interiors*; Ingmar Bergman on mothers and daughters in *Autumn Sonata*; and *Midnight Express,* a grim account of drug-running in Turkey, which saw David Puttnam to his first nomination as a producer, and won the Screenplay award for a young writer named Oliver Stone. Cunning tactics by one publicist won an unlikely nomination for Gary Busey in the title role of *The Buddy Holly Story,* while another probably lost Best Actress for Jill Clayburgh (who had won Cannes in *An Unmarried Woman*). "The difference between winning and losing is around fifty votes," declared Clayburgh's campaign manager, who promptly blew at least that many by pulling her off the *Tonight* show. "They couldn't tell us who the host was going to be, and Jill could have been on with a *juggler*."

Z Channel reached its zenith that year, with *Coming Home, California Suite, Heaven Can Wait, Interiors* and *An Unmarried Woman* all receiving repeated airings for stay-at-home voters. So did the music branch, which had failed the previous year to nominate the Bee Gees' number-one hits from *Saturday Night Fever,* moving Robert Stigwood to complain that they were "a bunch of retired violinists who probably still play seventy-eights on their Victrolas." Now the show's producer, Jack Haley, Jr., suggested redeeming themselves with a little gentle self-parody: a medley of famous songs overlooked by the Oscars under the title "Oscar's Only Human." When the plan was protested, Haley and his new host, Johnny Carson, threatened to quit; eventually the medley went ahead, performed by Steve Lawrence and Sammy Davis, but only three of its thirty songs were from the last twenty years: "Stayin' Alive," "New York, New York" and Davis's big personal number, "Candy Man."

The climax of the evening was a dose of pure Hollywood as an emaciated John Wayne, who would die of cancer two months later, took to the stage to present Best Picture. Even an equally sick Laurence Olivier, on hand to receive a second Honorary Award, managed to rise for the standing ovation. "That's just about the only medicine a fella'd ever really need," said the "Duke," before meekly presenting the supreme award to an anti-Vietnam War film of which he could scarcely have approved. *The Deer Hunter*'s moment of glory was somewhat dimmed by Wayne's, as he continued: "Believe me when I tell you I'm mighty pleased that I can amble down here tonight. Oscar and I have something in common. Oscar first came to the Hollywood scene in 1928. So did I. We're both a little weatherbeaten, but we're still here and plan to be around for a whole lot longer."

The Deer Hunter's final claim to fame was that it saw the first nomination (in the Supporting category) of Meryl Streep, who would soon be heading toward Oscar records herself. "My dress had sweat marks under the arm," she told reporters after losing to Maggie Smith, "and I was glad I didn't have to get up to get the Oscar." As of the 1990 awards, Streep had notched up nine nominations and two wins in just twelve years. At the same age—forty—the Oscars' all-time champion Katharine Hepburn had earned only four of her final, as yet unmatched tally of twelve. So Streep seems well on track to break every record in the Oscars' book.

Her first win came in 1979, for *Kramer vs. Kramer,* which added $25 million to its box office take by winning Best Picture for Stanley Jaffe, Best Director for Robert Benton and Best Actor for Dustin Hoffman, the Oscar rebel-turned-cherub. "Beautifully said" was Johnny Carson's verdict on Hoffman's acceptance speech (page 59), which publicly shared his award with the "artistic family" of actors who, unlike him, spend most of their lives out of work.

In the run-up to the Oscars, when he and Streep had swept most of the lesser awards, Hoffman had astonished seasoned observers by cooperating with the studio's publicity department to an unprecedented degree. He had even posed meekly for twenty minutes of photographs at the New York opening—with his parents, with his eight-year-old costar Justin Henry, even with Justin's parents. He had attended a retrospective of his work in Dallas, toured the campus circuit lecturing on the film, and graced an American Film Institute screening in Williamsburg, Pennsylvania—not too far from Harrisburg, Pennsylvania, where a nuclear accident at the Three Mile Island plant took place just two weeks after the opening of *The China Syndrome,* Michael Douglas's chilling prediction of just such a disaster.

Douglas's movie even contained a line to the effect that a nuclear accident "could render an area the size of Pennsylvania uninhabitable." The coincidence, said Douglas, was "incredible. . . . I can't put it together. It's disturbingly ironic." Suddenly a heavyweight drama which had quickly begun to sink, as expected, at the box office was doing booming business, even causing Columbia stock to rise sharply. But both the studio and Douglas, as actor-producer, were careful not to give the impression of exploiting the accident for commercial gain. "We're all very wary of capitalizing in any sense on the tragedy," Douglas told *The New York Times.* With the imminent Oscars clearly in mind, he added: "We will do anything to stay clean."

He imposed a publicity blackout and himself canceled a scheduled appearance on the *Tonight* show with Johnny Carson. Douglas also instructed Jack Lemmon, whom he had considered a shoo-in for Best Actor before Hoffman started winning the pre-Oscar awards, to pull out of a CBS news special on the accident. Such restraint, of course, proved too much for their costar Jane Fonda, who called a press conference with her husband, Tom Hayden, to demand that President Carter dismiss his energy secretary, James Schlesinger.

Hoffman duly collected the Oscar, at the expense of Lemmon, Roy Scheider *(All That Jazz)*, Al Pacino (his fifth vain nomination, for *. . . And Justice for All)*—and above all Peter Sellers, unlucky to lose fifteen years before for his multiple contribution to Kubrick's *Dr. Strangelove,* and now given the part of his life as Chance, the half-witted gardener who becomes president of the United States in Jerzy Kosinski's *Being There.* "Never mind," said the maverick British actor, who was to die that summer, aged 54. "I still think it's my clincher. I'll settle for it as my monument any time."

Streep's win came in the Supporting category, where she beat her own costar Jane Alexander. She had not been the producers' first choice for the part, nor had her first meeting with Hoffman been entirely happy: "He came up to me and said 'I'm Dustin—burp—Hoffman' and he put his hand on my breast. I thought, what a creep." Though disappointed not to have been considered a Leading Role candidate, Streep had logged simultaneous appearances in Woody Allen's *Manhattan* and Alan Alda's *The Seduction of Joe Tynan,* which left little hope for Alexander and the other contenders—Barbara Barrie, Candice Bergen and Mariel Hemingway.

It was sometime after Streep left the stage with her first statuette that a shriek was heard from a stall in the ladies' room at the Dorothy Chandler Pavilion: "Hey, someone left an Oscar in here!" The moment has gone down in history as the most high-handed treatment, this side of rejection, ever accorded Tinseltown's supreme prize. "Oh, my God," said Streep at the time. "How could I have done that? It shows how nervous I really am."

Jane Fonda, strange to relate, turned down the title role in *Norma Rae*, Martin Ritt's sinewy portrait of a southern labor union organizer. So had Jill Clayburgh, Marsha Mason and Diane Keaton. Even more surprising, however, was Ritt's alternative choice: one of television's eternal children, the sometime Gidget and Flying Nun. Sally Field proved her own best satirist, putting herself down before anyone else could: "Who in America would have wanted to pay to see anything like me in the movies? I was a continual put-down, a national joke, a running gag."

But Martin Ritt thought Field "sexy, funny, photogenic, zany, bouncy and tough," with the potential to become another Carole Lombard. "I know a superior player even when they're playing on an inferior team. . . . There's something indomitable about that little girl. I knew I had to have that quality in Norma Rae, a woman who had to lift herself up by her bootstraps. She had to be a really tough nut. Sally is that. Something about her makes me feel she's a champion."

When the script of *Norma Rae* arrived, Field still needed some sort of morale boost to have the nerve to take it on. Just that was provided by her live-in lover Burt Reynolds, who read it and intoned: "May I have the envelope, please? The winner is Sally Field for *Norma Rae*."

After telling the story to his biographer, A. E. Hotchner, Reynolds added a candid confession: "I've never told anyone this, because I'm really ashamed of it. But after I'd read *Norma Rae,* I did everything I could to stop Sally from doing that picture. I criticized everything, trying to discourage her, lying about what I really thought, because I knew that the Academy Award was hers. She was nominated, of course, but I didn't accompany her to the awards ceremony. I sat alone that night, like a wounded Citizen

Kane, visualizing her dancing with Dustin Hoffman at the Academy ball."

Before the show, Field tried to show her new maturity with a surprising outburst: "I think [the Oscars] are exploitative, over-commercialized, frequently offensive and should not be televised." She ended, however, somewhat lamely: "Sure, I'll be there. If I said I wasn't coming, they'd still go on with the show." Just as well; if Reynolds was all too aware that he was not himself quite the right cut for the Academy Awards—he was again passed over that year, for *Starting Over*—he had displayed powers of Oscar prophecy. At her first nomination, which would prove by no means her last, Field was voted Best Actress over Jill Clayburgh, Jane Fonda and Marsha Mason—all of whom had turned down the part of Norma Rae. Field had agreed to do the film for the bargain-basement price of $150,000—which certainly helped Ritt to persuade Twentieth Century Fox to take a risk on her.

The fifth nominee was Bette Midler, who had chosen a Janis Joplin–style role in *The Rose* for her movie debut after turning down parts in films from *Nashville* and *The Fortune* to *Foul Play* and *Rocky*. Massive Fox hype had been enough to win their dynamic new star an Oscar nomination, despite a dismal film that was never going to win any awards. Even the Music Oscars went elsewhere. But the power of the Academy Awards was awesomely demonstrated when Midler clips alone proved enough to propel the six-month-old film into the top ten box-office list and send the soundtrack album to the top of the *Billboard* chart.

Similarly, the commercial power of a Visual Effects nomination—now an annual stunt by studios out to save lame gizmo pics—has rarely been more clearly demonstrated. Paramount's expensive turkey *Star Trek* and Disney's *The Black Hole* were both saved from utter financial disaster by the simple expedient of slapping "Oscar nominee" on the marquee. *Alien* beat them both; but nobody notices who wins for Special Effects—now, above all, the category in which even a loser's tag can prove priceless at the box office.

For Field and Reynolds, the distaff Oscar also proved the beginning of the end of their relationship. "We saw each other after that, but we were never the same," confessed Reynolds. "I had become obsessed with the notion that two stars could not coexist in the same galaxy—which is, of course, nonsense." Since being passed over for *Deliverance* in 1972, the same year he posed nude for *Cosmopolitan*, Reynolds had suffered something of a complex about the Academy Awards. He may have been America's number-one box-office star, and never out of the top ten since 1973, but Field had now gained the high ground on him.

The Oscars can have that effect on couples. Just as Taylor and Burton's marriage began to fade after *Virginia Woolf,* Maggie Smith left Robert Stephens behind after *California Suite,* and Barbra Streisand's debut Oscar for *Funny Girl* proved too much for Elliott Gould, so *Norma Rae* did in Field and Reynolds. She later confirmed as much to *Ladies' Home Journal*: "Burt really thinks I went out after that Oscar because he thinks the award is so important. I don't. To me the work is the important thing." It always remained unclear whether Field was more upset over the Academy's failure to nominate Reynolds for *Starting Over* or the other man in her life, Martin Ritt, for *Norma Rae.*

With Ritt unfairly excluded, Francis Ford Coppola faced up again to his Oscar nemesis, Bob Fosse, as *Apocalypse Now* jousted with *All That Jazz* for both Best Director and Best Picture. In Coppola's film Martin Sheen had taken over from Steve McQueen and Harvey Keitel a role rejected by Redford, Nicholson, Hackman, Pacino and Caan; for six hard months in the jungle, Sheen was rewarded with a heart attack but no Oscar nomination. In Fosse's film, Roy Scheider took over from the sinking Richard Dreyfuss, only to receive his second nomination and his second defeat. Despite starting the awards on a par with *Kramer vs. Kramer*'s nine nominations, Coppola and Fosse carried off only a handful of the Technical awards.

As Douglas had feared, *The China Syndrome* proved too political to win anything, moving the official Soviet news agency to voice a rare Oscar complaint. Though clearly "the best film of the year," said Tass, it was "too close to the truth, which is unacceptable to the Hollywood canon." But the sourest note of the year was struck by the veteran character actor Melvyn Douglas, who was not there to pick up his second Supporting Oscar—sixteen years after *Hud*—for *Being There.* "The whole thing is absurd," said 78-year-old Douglas. "Me competing with an eight-year-old!"

Eight-year-old Justin Henry, the source of Douglas's wrath, had earned himself a Supporting nomination for the composure with which he had performed as young Kramer, the object of the tug-of-love between Hoffman and Streep. It had been the sight of Justin dissolving into tears, upon failing to win a Golden Globe, that had moved Hoffman to denounce all awards as "silly . . . they hurt a lot when you don't win." When Justin failed to win the Oscar, too, Hoffman began his own acceptance speech with another consoling reference: "If he loses again, we'll have to give him a lifetime achievement award." One of those child stars who has not converted juvenile success into stardom, Justin Henry has the consolation that at 8 years and 352 days he made Oscar history by becoming the youngest Academy Award nominee ever, in any category—a record that still stands.

The following year, by coincidence, would see the youngest winner in that category: Timothy Hutton, 20 years and 227 days old when he picked up the Supporting Oscar for his screen debut in a film directed by a man who seemed to have given up on the acting awards. Though one of the biggest box-office stars of his day, Robert Redford had never come close to winning an acting Oscar; his lone nomination, for *The Sting* in 1973, lost out to Jack Lemmon. It was feeling "reduced," he said, by becoming "a glamour figure of cartoon proportions," that had decided Redford to turn director for Alvin Sargent's study of a traumatized American family, *Ordinary People*. "Never a very expressive actor," wrote Kenneth Turan in *New West*, Redford the director revealed "a depth of feeling he couldn't manage in front of the camera." And it gained Redford his revenge on the acting branch. For *Ordinary People,* which also won Best Picture and Best Screenplay, he became only the third man (and the first actor) to win Best Director on his debut.*

"I just didn't think I was going to see this," said Redford as he collected his Oscar, "but I'm no less grateful." Having already been "thrilled and shocked" to win the Directors Guild Award—"This is a heavyweight crowd. I am honored"—he made a decision there and then to part-quit while ahead. He has since been extremely choosy

* The others were Delbert Mann (*Marty,* 1955) and Jerome Robbins (*West Side Story*, 1961), later to be joined by James L. Brooks (*Terms of Endearment*, 1983) and Kevin Costner (*Dances with Wolves,* 1990). For a full list (including all those nominated on their debut), see appendix C, section C4, page 616.

about his roles, which have ranged from the strangely successful *Out of Africa* to the disastrous *Havana,* both with Sydney Pollack—and concentrated on building his annual Sundance Festival into a respected film institution. As with Beatty, Newman and other of Hollywood's more independent-minded leading men, Redford has also been rumored to nurture political ambitions.

One of Redford's more unlikely achievements as a director of *Ordinary People* was to bring out the "dark side" of Mary Tyler Moore—hitherto a light comedy actress with a range strictly limited to television sitcoms, now a Best Actress nominee alongside Sissy Spacek, Ellen Burstyn, Goldie Hawn and Gena Rowlands. All the major players in *Ordinary People* were nominated except Donald Sutherland, widely regarded as having given the finest performance of a patchy career under Redford's direction. Never Oscar-nominated, not even for *M*A*S*H* in 1970, Sutherland said on breakfast TV that he was not surprised. "I know that community, and I didn't expect a nomination."

He might have compromised himself by standing at Jane Fonda's shoulder during her war protests; but perhaps more to the point, especially now that "Hanoi Jane" had been forgiven her sins, was Sutherland's Canadian birth. In 1988, on its fiftieth anniversary, the National Film Board of Canada would deservedly be given an Honorary Oscar in recognition of its "dedicated commitment to originating artistic, creative and technological activity and excellence in every area of filmmaking." Such Canadian-born filmmakers as Sutherland and Norman Jewison otherwise testify, however, to the Academy's apparent meanness to its cousins from across the border.

But even when his career began to look less lustrous than that of his son Kiefer—suitor of Hollywood's hottest star, Julia Roberts, until she left him standing at the altar in 1991—Donald Sutherland has never been a man to show hard feelings. Back in 1981, despite the cold shoulder from his peers, he generously agreed to step in as a presenter for Neil Diamond, who could not rearrange a concert date when a last-minute crisis obliged the Academy to postpone the awards show by a night.

For Oscar Night 1981 was providing the Academy with an unexpected and brutal reminder of one of the great films of the 1970s that it had signally failed to honor.

The 1981 Oscar ceremony was postponed for 24 hours after President Reagan was shot by a deranged movie fan (BELOW) for love of Jodie Foster (LEFT, CENTER), Robert DeNiro's co-star in Martin Scorsese's Taxi Driver.

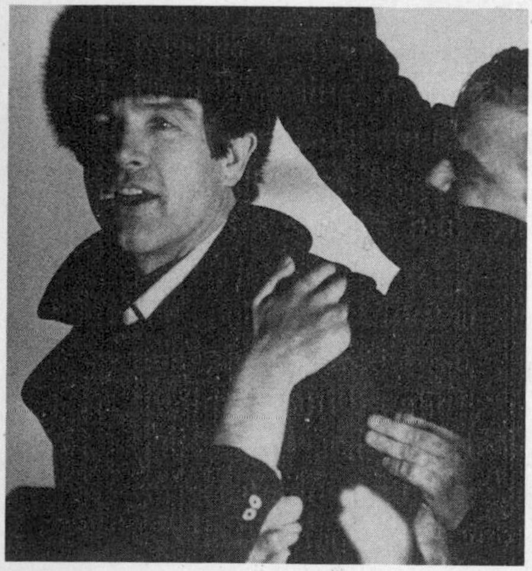

After Heaven Can Wait (1978), Reds (1981) saw Warren Beatty (LEFT) become the only man twice to win multiple nominations as producer, director, actor, and co-writer. Though it won him the direction award, Beatty's Reds otherwise lost out to the surprise British hit, Chariots of Fire.

Katharine Hepburn won a record fourth Oscar, and Henry Fonda his first, in 1981's On Golden Pond, which also won a Supporting nomination for two-time Best Actress Jane Fonda.

10

1981–1987

History vs. Popcorn

The tendency is for important films to win over popcorn entertainment. . . . History is more weighty than popcorn.

—Steven Spielberg

On March 30, 1981, outside the Hilton Hotel in Washington, D.C., a deranged movie fan chose the afternoon of the Academy Awards to reenact a scene from an Oscar movie—by shooting the president of the United States, himself a former film star, in the lovesick hope of impressing an Oscar nominee.

The pervasive power of the Oscars has never been so grimly demonstrated. The would-be assassin modeled himself and his behavior on the role that five years before had won a Best Actor nomination for Robert De Niro (the favorite, by chance, to win the same award that very night). And another recent Oscar movie turned out to have figured in his preparations.

It was early afternoon in Washington, midmorning on the West Coast, when President Reagan was shot in the chest by John W.

Hinckley, Jr. After some indecision, the Academy announced that the awards ceremony would be postponed for twenty-four hours. At Hinckley's home, meanwhile, police discovered a letter written that morning, and addressed to Jodie Foster: "By sacrificing my freedom, and possibly my life, I hope to change your mind about me. This letter is being written an hour before I leave for the Hilton Hotel."

Seventeen at the time, and a student at Yale, Foster had been just twelve when she won a Supporting nomination as the drugged-out teenage hooker in Martin Scorsese's *Taxi Driver.* In the title role De Niro played a Vietnam veteran sickened by the squalor of New York street life; unrequited love drives him to attempt a political killing, before wreaking an orgy of bloody revenge on Foster's corrupters. Scorsese's film, too dark for the taste of the 1976 Academy electorate, has been aptly described as "unlovely but brilliant."

Its writer, Paul Schrader, had modeled his story on the diaries of Arthur Bremer, the obsessive psychopath who shadowed and finally gunned down Governor George Wallace of Alabama in 1972. The Secret Service subsequently developed a psychological profile called "The Bremer Type"—a phrase first used on the screen in Altman's *Nashville,* yet another film that climaxes in a political assassination attempt. It was in Nashville that Hinckley had been arrested six months earlier, while trying to board a flight with three handguns in his possession. Asked later why the arrest had been reported only to the FBI, not to the Secret Service, the airport police said it had "not occurred" to them to link the incident with the presence in Nashville that day of the then president, Jimmy Carter.

De Niro confessed himself "deeply disturbed," and couldn't work for six months after winning the 1980 Oscar for *Raging Bull.* The incident had an even more profound effect on Foster, who spent three years treading water before taking on a sequence of increasingly mature performances, climaxing in the 1988 and 1991 Best Actress awards. "A great change came over me, or so I am told," she wrote in a 1982 article for *Esquire* entitled "Why Me?"

> I started perceiving death in the most mundane but distressing events. Being photographed felt like being shot; it still does. I thought everyone was looking at me in crowds; perhaps they were. Every sick letter I received I made sure to read, to laugh at, to read again. People were punishing me because I was there.

At Reagan's own request, the show began as scheduled with an introduction he had taped a week before, designed to stress to the movie community that one of their own—no Oscar winner, but a former president of the Screen Actors Guild—had made it all the way to the White House. From behind his desk in the Oval Office, the new president began: "It's surely no state secret that Nancy and I share your interest in the results of this year's balloting." Johnny Carson returned to the podium with a crack about Ronald Reagan's demand for cuts in aid to the humanities: "It's Reagan's strongest attack on the arts since he signed with Warner Brothers." Then he and the audience sobered up with a get-well message to the president, said to be watching from his hospital bed.

De Niro, who had put on sixty pounds to play the prizefighter Jake La Motta in his declining years, attended the Awards show for the first time. In the somber atmosphere, this professional outsider wound up giving a caricature of an Oscar acceptance speech, thanking everyone from La Motta (who was in the audience) to his parents "for having me, and my grandmothers and grandfathers for having them, and everyone else involved with the film, and anyone that this award means anything to, and the rest of the world. . . . I love everyone."

Among the absentees was Roman Polanski, who had won his second Direction nomination for *Tess,* but would have faced an even worse fate than losing to Robert Redford if he had returned to see how his film's six nominations fared. On the eighth anniversary of his wife Sharon Tate's murder by the Charles Manson "family," Polanski had been thrown in jail for having sex with a 13-year-old girl; released pending trial, he had skipped the country: "Since the judge seemed determined to prevent me from ever again living and working in the United States, and since it was clear that I had served my forty-two days in Chino for nothing, an obvious question arose: What had I to gain by staying? The answer appeared to be: Nothing."

In Europe, Polanski had spent the first year of his exile filming Thomas Hardy's *Tess of the D'Urbervilles,* which had won warm approval back in the United States, despite the director's moral and legal record. When his nomination was announced, the L.A. district attorney envisaged a very different kind of Oscar arrivals ceremony: "If Polanski returns to Los Angeles or anywhere in the country, we would have him arrested to go before a judge to face sentencing."

Ten years later Polanski still remains in exile from Hollywood, though he resurfaced in 1991 as chairman of the jury at the Cannes Film Festival.

Two movies about grotesques led the 1980 field with eight nominations each: Scorsese's *Raging Bull* and David Lynch's *The Elephant Man* (in which American audiences first registered Anthony Hopkins). There were seven for *Coal Miner's Daughter,* the English director Michael Apted's biopic of the country singer Loretta Lynn, who was in the audience to see her alter ego, Sissy Spacek, win Best Actress over *Ordinary People*'s Mary Tyler Moore and the actress recently voted America's number-one female star, Goldie Hawn, in *Private Benjamin.* After thanking Loretta Lynn, "the woman who gave me all that hair," Spacek told the press: "Just to be nominated makes me feel like a real actress. I used to watch the Oscars growing up, so all this is like a dream come true, like living out a fantasy."

Among the other crumbs left by Redford's sweep, Mary Steenburgen beat the oldest ever Oscar nominee, 82-year-old Eva Le Gallienne, to Best Supporting Actress for *Melvin and Howard,* Jonathan Demme's beguiling fantasy about the last days of Howard Hughes. Trivialists also noted Peter O'Toole's sixth nomination, for *The Stunt Man,* and Jack Lemmon's seventh, a feat then achieved by only seven actors before him—Katharine Hepburn, Bette Davis, Greer Garson, Laurence Olivier, Spencer Tracy, Richard Burton and Marlon Brando.

But the 1981 awards saw a new and still unmatched record. It was a strong acting year for women, with Sally Field *(Absence of Malice),* Sissy Spacek *(Raggedy Man),* Candice Bergen *(Rich and Famous)* and Faye Dunaway *(Mommie Dearest)* all excluded as the nominations went to Diane Keaton for *Reds,* Marsha Mason for *Only When I Laugh,* Susan Sarandon for *Atlantic City,* Meryl Streep for *The French Lieutenant's Woman* and the absent (as always) Katharine Hepburn. At her twelfth nomination,* all in the Leading Role category, Hepburn won an unparalleled fourth Best Actress

* The current (1992) standings in the nominations league table for actors are: Katharine Hepburn (12, all Leading Role, including four wins); Bette Davis (10, all Leading Role, two wins); Laurence Olivier (10 nominations, one win and two Honorary Oscars); Jack Nicholson (9, two wins); Spencer Tracy (9, two wins); Meryl Streep (9, two wins); Marlon Brando (8, two wins); Jack Lemmon (8, two wins); and Geraldine Page (8, one win). On 7 nominations are Ingrid Bergman (three wins); Jane Fonda (two wins); Greer Garson (one win); Paul Newman (one win and one Honorary Award); and Richard Burton and Peter O'Toole, both with no wins. See Appendix C, section B1.

award for *On Golden Pond,* the film which finally realized Jane Fonda's dream of acting with her father.

Henry Fonda's failure to win an Oscar in forty-six years of distinguished film performances had become a sick joke in Hollywood, belying the conventional wisdom that the Academy Awards may make the odd mistake, but sooner or later the system would honor its own for consistently good work. Fonda had been nominated only once—in 1940, for *The Grapes of Wrath*—despite almost half a century of Oscar-level performances in such films as *Jezebel, Young Mr. Lincoln, The Oxbow Incident, My Darling Clementine, Mister Roberts, War and Peace, Twelve Angry Men, Advise and Consent* and *Once Upon a Time in the West.* Even Fonda's B-list was consistently impressive: *Jesse James, Drums Along the Mohawk, Chad Hannah, The Male Animal, The Big Street, The Fugitive, The Wrong Man.*

Two years before, in Billy Wilder's film *Fedora,* Fonda had himself shown a sense of humor about it all by agreeing to play a cameo role as the president of the Academy, handing a long overdue Oscar to an aging, Sunset Boulevard–style star making one final comeback. The following year, as if responding to the reminder, the Academy had invited the frail, 75-year-old actor to accept an Honorary Award "in recognition of his brilliant accomplishments and enduring contribution to the art of motion pictures." With polite understatement, Fonda remarked that this moment "had to be the climax" of his half-century in the business.

But the Academy had reckoned without his daughter, who had already taken matters into her own hands. It was entirely to right the Academy's wrongs and win her ailing father the Oscar she thought he deserved that Jane Fonda had formed her own production company and bought the rights to Ernest Thompson's sentimental stage play about an elderly professor's last summer with his wife and daughter. Despite an almost suffocating schmaltz factor—the film's catchline was "Growing up isn't easy, at any age"—the moviegoing public's affection for Fonda senior gave it a surprise box-office bonanza, and it became the highest-grossing movie of 1981 as it broke the $100 million barrier.

"Moments of truth survive some cloying contrivance," wrote the magazine *Sight and Sound.* "Mark Rydell directs on bended knee." Out of six nominations, *On Golden Pond* won Adapted Screenplay for Thompson, and Leading Role awards for Fonda and Hepburn.

Following *It Happened One Night, One Flew Over the Cuckoo's Nest, Network* and *Coming Home, On Golden Pond* became the fifth film in Oscar history to win both Best Actor and Best Actress—a feat that would not be achieved again for a decade.

Henry Fonda was too ill to attend the ceremony. Jane, the sometime militant who had worn the same outfit to the 1977 and 1978 awards, sparkled in a golden Valentino gown as she took four minutes to accept his statuette for him. Theirs was known to have been a combustible relationship, but this was its redemption.

"Oh, Dad," sobbed Jane directly into the camera, "I'm so happy and proud for you." Both were in tears—he in bed at home, and she on national television—as she turned back to the Oscar audience to say: "My father didn't really believe that this was going to happen. But he told me a while back that if it did, he wanted his wife, Shirlee, to accept the award for him. But Shirlee wanted to be with him tonight, as is her way, and so I'm here. . . . I know that he's watching right now and I know that he's very, very honored and very happy and surprised—and I bet when he heard it just now he said, 'Hey, ain't I lucky,' as though luck had anything to do with it." After a good deal more in the same vein, Jane turned back to the camera with a final message: "Dad, me and all the grandchildren are coming over with this right away!"

Back at the Fonda residence, the subsequent celebrations were recorded for posterity. As Jane handed over the statuette, Henry admitted that he was not totally surprised. "It was in the wind," he whispered, swathed in blankets up to his white beard. "It was very, very touching," recalled Jane's then husband, Tom Hayden. "He was so overwhelmed when Jane handed the Oscar to him, he couldn't say a word. He was just sitting there in a state of bemused shock with the Oscar in his lap." Eventually, for the cameras, Fonda declared it "one of the high points of my life." And Jane seemed entirely genuine when she too said, some time later, "It was, I think, the happiest night of my life."

Four months later Henry Fonda died at the age of 77. His widow Shirlee told *Time* that anticipation of the possible Oscar had been "another way of not letting him fade away. When he won, I flew into his arms. He held me tight and I saw the tears in his eyes, and they told me he was overwhelmed with a profound sense of happiness.

'Hell, if I hadn't won,' he told me, 'I wouldn't have been able to walk with my head up any more.' "

Fonda's sentimental victory cost Burt Lancaster an almost certain second Oscar for his brooding presence in *Atlantic City,* Louis Malle's elegiac study of small-time New Jersey crooks. Twenty years after winning for *Elmer Gantry,* Lancaster had found a place in the awards' history as the dream costar for those in search of an Oscar. Stars who won awards opposite him include Shirley Booth in *Come Back, Little Sheba* (1952), Frank Sinatra and Donna Reed in *From Here to Eternity* (1953), Anna Magnani in *The Rose Tattoo* (1955), and David Niven and Wendy Hiller in *Separate Tables* (1958, which Lancaster also produced). Barbara Stanwyck was nominated opposite Lancaster in *Sorry, Wrong Number* (1948); Katharine Hepburn won her seventh Oscar nomination as his belle in *The Rainmaker* (1956), and Thelma Ritter her sixth as his mother in *Birdman of Alcatraz* (1962). Although he is now reduced to lager commercials, Lancaster's own four Oscar nominations spanned almost thirty years, from *Here to Eternity* in 1953 to *Atlantic City* in 1981.

Lancaster had dominated the acting prizes in the home stretch to the awards, while *Atlantic City* shared the rest of the honors with Paramount's other class act of the year, Warren Beatty's *Reds.* Paramount also had Steven Spielberg's latest blockbuster, *Raiders of the Lost Ark,* which this time won him both the top nominations. More than compensating for the failure of his last film, *1941, Raiders* finally wound up fourth on the list of all-time money-makers, behind *Star Wars, Jaws* and *The Empire Strikes Back*—all of them films by either George Lucas or Steven Spielberg or both.

Could this at last be Spielberg's year? The favorite for Best Director was Warren Beatty—who, like Robert Redford, seemed to have given up hope of winning an acting award. But Beatty had spent eighteen months filming and editing *Reds,* a panoramic biopic starring himself as the American Communist John Reed, with Jack Nicholson as Eugene O'Neill, Diane Keaton as Reed's wife and Maureen Stapleton as Emma Goldman. Nicholson in particular was praised by *Newsweek*'s David Ansen for his "best work in years," but received an even more lasting tribute—"the greatest compliment I ever got"—in a letter from Oona O'Neill Chaplin, estranged daughter of the playwright since her marriage at 17 to Charlie Chaplin. "After a lifetime of acquired indifference, the inevitable finally happened. Thanks to you, dear Jack, I fell in love with my father."

Time magazine went overboard about *Reds:* "A big, smart movie, vastly ambitious and entertaining, it combines the majestic sweep of *Lawrence of Arabia* and *Dr. Zhivago* with the rueful comedy and historical fatalism of *Citizen Kane."* Most other critics were less enthusiastic, notably Pauline Kael in *The New Yorker:* "It's because of the way *Reds* wavers and searches for what it's trying to say that it needs this length." But Diane Keaton seemed to steal the film from Beatty; as David Thomson wrote in *Film Comment,* "Beatty is not the easiest actor to play with: he can be chilly and hidden on screen —not so much out of vanity as caution. Some actresses have wilted in his presence, but Keaton assaults him, reads him the riot act, mauls him until the actor-producer-director rediscovers his own charm." *Rolling Stone* agreed that "Keaton convinces us, as she never has before, that she can play a woman of backbone."

By the time the picture opened, Beatty was either too tired or too temperamental—reports varied—to set out on the promotional trail, much less to mount an Oscar campaign. Cover stories set up in magazines from *Newsweek* to *The New York Times* were canceled. Though the film won lavish praise, one industry observer thought that Beatty "may have committed the biggest *faux pas* in the last fifty years of filmmaking" by opting to play the prima donna, making himself unavailable for publicity. To another, it took "high perversity: only a shell-shocked showman declines to promote the biggest picture he has ever made."

Such talk is infectious, and may have contributed to one of the great Oscar surprises of the modern era as *Reds*'s results failed to live up to the promise of its nominations. "The Academy has been a little reticent to give [Warren] his due," said Beatty's buddy Nicholson. "They think he's a little too pretty and cute." Beatty again received four nominations in his own right—for acting, writing, directing and producing—just as he had three years before with his last film, *Heaven Can Wait.* And his picture won twelve nominations in all, to ten for *On Golden Pond;* Paramount looked set for a big payday with three Best Picture candidates—*Reds, Raiders* and *Atlantic City*—with thirty-three nominations among them.

The first award boded well for Beatty, as *Reds*'s Maureen Stapleton beat *Golden Pond*'s Jane Fonda to the Supporting Actress award (raising a laugh by thanking "everyone I ever met in my entire life"). But *Reds* missed out on Art Direction, which went to *Raiders of the Lost Ark,* before Vincent Price came out to present this year's innovation: an Oscar for Makeup, introduced after a row the previous year over the Academy's refusal to create one for John Hurt's remarkable appearance as *The Elephant Man* (and won by the team from *An American Werewolf in London*). Roger Moore presented the Irving Thalberg Award to Albert "Cubby" Broccoli, only begetter of the James Bond films, which had never been deemed worthy of major Oscar recognition.

Then came the Original Score award, presented by one mononym to another as Liberace handed the Oscar to Vangelis for his synthesized theme from the British film which had crept up on the 1981 Oscars, *Chariots of Fire.* An unlikely movie scenario—the spiritual journeys of a Jew and a Scotsman running for Britain in the 1924 Olympics—had struck an emotional, quasireligious chord with American audiences, making David Puttnam's low-budget period piece the highest-grossing import in the history of American cinema. Acted and directed by unknowns, *Chariots of Fire* had won seven last-minute Oscar nominations after opening the New York Film Festival.

For once, Costume Design was a pivotal award. Both Beatty and Puttnam believed it the key to their respective fortunes. As Morgan Fairchild announced that the winner was Milena Canonero, for *Chariots of Fire,* Puttnam looked over to see Beatty with his head in his hands. "What the heck were our costumes, after all? A few shorts and singlets," Puttnam said later. "I knew from that moment that things looked good for *Chariots.* It was the end for Beatty and *Reds.*"

Next up was Visual Effects, for which neither was eligible. Before handing *Raiders* its second Oscar, Dan Aykroyd broke a promise he had made to Howard Koch. The producer had begged Aykroyd not to pay public tribute to John Belushi, due to have been his copresenter, who had died of a drug overdose three weeks before in a poolside bungalow at the Chateau Marmont Hotel. "I wouldn't be part of a tribute to Belushi," Koch had confided to a friend. "I couldn't face myself if I were." But Aykroyd proved a more loyal friend, telling the watching millions that Belushi "would have loved" handing out this award, being "something of a special effect himself."

Reds evened the score at two apiece with the Cinematography award, for which *Chariots of Fire* had not been nominated. But Beatty and Puttnam then had to sweat their way through an honorary Oscar for Barbara Stanwyck, and some show-hogging by Bette Midler. "Don't you hate it when presenters use this moment for their own personal aggrandizement?" asked Midler, who proceeded to "rise to the occasion" by pushing up her breasts during a long, self-aggrandizing routine while presenting the Best Song award to the four composers of the theme from *Arthur.* This humdrum comedy —for which the Academy, at its most indulgent, had given a Best Actor nomination to Dudley Moore—then proceeded to win the Supporting Actor award for 78-year-old Sir John Gielgud. Nominated only once before (for *Becket* in 1964), largely because of an undisguised distaste for acting in films, Gielgud was majestically absent from the ceremony. If only by beating *Reds*'s Jack Nicholson, however, he had kept the Union Jack flying.

Jack Lemmon and Walter Matthau then swung things back Beatty's way by naming him Best Director, his first Oscar in ten nominations over fifteen years. After mawkish tributes to Keaton and Nicholson, Beatty paid a heady tribute to the capitalists who had financed his Communist epic:

> I want to name Mr. Barry Diller, who runs Paramount . . . and Mr. Charles Bluhdorn, who runs Gulf & Western and God knows what else, and I want to say to you gentlemen that no matter how much we may have wanted to strangle each other from time to time, I think that your decision, taken in the great capitalistic tower of Gulf & Western, to finance a three-and-a-half-hour romance which attempts to reveal for the first time just something of the beginnings of American socialism and American communism, reflects credit not only upon you; I think it reflects credit upon Hollywood and the movie business wherever that is, and I think it reflects more particular credit upon [the] freedom of expression that we have in American society, and the lack of censorship we have from the government or the people who put up the money.

Spielberg again licked his wounds, along with Louis Malle and Mark Rydell, and Puttnam began to doubt his intuition. Hugh Hudson, director of *Chariots of Fire,* may have been a first-time nominee; but only twice in the last quarter of a century had Best Director and Best Picture been won by different films.*

Beatty's euphoria was short-lived. He was also up for the next award, Original Screenplay, along with his British (ironically enough) collaborator, Trevor Griffiths. But it went to another British actor-writer, Colin Welland, who had responded to Puttnam's request for "another *Man for All Seasons*—someone who didn't behave in an expedient manner" by coming up with *Chariots of Fire.* "You may have started something," exulted Welland. "The British are coming!"

Reds and *Chariots* had won three Oscars each. As the supreme prize drew near, Beatty and Puttnam had to grind their teeth through three more Oscars for *On Golden Pond.* The entire audience, in fact, gnashed its teeth as the Adapted Screenplay award prompted Ernest Thompson to promise: "If you would all see me later I would love to suck face with you all." (*The New York Times*'s Janet Maslin wrote of this moment that Thompson "exemplified everything that can be wrong with Oscar and its winners.") There followed the coronation of Katharine Hepburn and Henry Fonda, at the expense of Beatty and Diane Keaton.

Loretta Young delivered an agonizingly long homily on cinematic taste before opening the Best Picture envelope and announcing David Puttnam's name. This "out-of-left-field" victory provoked, in one description, "an avalanche of obscenities to be uttered throughout Hollywood." Not unaware of the community's tendency toward insularity, Puttnam diplomatically called the Academy "the most generous people on God's earth," and thanked the whole of America for going "in droves" to his "Cinderella picture." Highly conscious of the slight done his director, Hugh Hudson, Puttnam called him onstage to take a bow.

Reds had gone 3-for-12, *Chariots of Fire* 4-for-7. Made for a paltry $6 million, *Chariots* had been turned down by every major Hollywood studio; only after its injection of Oscars did it become the most successful foreign film in U.S. box-office history. On the night,

*In 1967 Norman Jewison, director of the Best Picture *(In the Heat of the Night),* lost to Mike Nichols *(The Graduate),* and in 1972 Francis Ford Coppola *(The Godfather)* lost to Bob Fosse *(Cabaret).* Other victims of such coups include Alfred Hitchcock *(Rebecca),* Laurence Olivier *(Hamlet),* Vincente Minnelli *(An American in Paris)* and Cecil B. de Mille *(The Greatest Show on Earth).* For a complete list, see Appendix C, section C6.

Beatty displayed a very English stiff upper lip: "I think we were treated very nicely." Much more American-competitive was Puttnam, still fuming about the Best Director award. "Hugh [Hudson] is without doubt a better director than Warren is, or ever will be," he told the columnist Marilyn Beck. "And so are Steven Spielberg and Louis Malle." Beatty's Oscar, he went on, was merely "the Academy's acknowledgment that a gorgeous actor, a pretty boy, could raise $50 million to make that picture . . . that lumbering picture." (*Reds* proved another commercial failure for Beatty, grossing only $21 million—half what it cost to make.)

When he woke up next morning in the Beverly Hills Hotel, David Puttnam wondered if he had dreamed the whole thing. "I opened one eye and looked toward the TV set. There, sitting on it, was the Oscar. So it was true!" But his dream was in danger of turning into a nightmare. Before the decade was out, Hollywood would have its revenge on Puttnam—by hiring him as the head of Columbia Studios, then firing him after barely a year. At the time, the movie world's feelings about another British hijack of the Oscars were reflected in a headline in the New York *Daily News:* HOLLYWOOD FUMING OVER WIN BY CHARIOTS OF FIRE. The paper quoted an unidentified "top Academy official" as saying: "I'm afraid this could be the beginning of a trend we saw in the 1960s. Twenty years ago, we started a love affair with the English that lasted about ten years. Their actors and actresses could do no wrong. We have extremely talented people here in America and I don't want to see them get short shrift."

The sixties, Britain's decade *mirabilis* at the Oscars, had in fact testified more to the depressed state of the U.S. film industry, desperately struggling to compete with television. The same problem had reached the U.K. in the seventies, when Britain's only Oscar hopes were carried (in vain) by just three pictures. Though made in England, Stanley Kubrick's *A Clockwork Orange* and *Barry Lyndon* were both American-financed, and neither won. The same was true of Puttnam's *Midnight Express,* directed by Alan Parker and Britain's third Best Film nominee of the decade.

"The British are coming," Colin Welland's celebrated 1981 rallying cry, was now to signal only a brief resurgence. The success of *Chariots of Fire* came thirteen years after *Oliver!* had been the last

British film to win Best Picture; but the momentum would continue only one more year. In 1982 Richard Attenborough's worthy biopic *Gandhi* broke all British Oscar records with eleven nominations and eight wins, including Best Picture, Director and Actor. But Hollywood suddenly seemed weary of "handing out foreign aid," as the Oscar emcee Bob Hope put it. For Britain, the rest of the eighties would be a story of honorable mentions—multiple nominations, but no major awards, for Peter Yates's *The Dresser,* David Lean's *A Passage to India,* John Boorman's *Home and Glory* and two more Puttnam-Goldcrest enterprises, *The Killing Fields* and *The Mission.*

The decade would end on a surreal note, with a Screenplay nomination of Monty Python zaniness for John Cleese's *A Fish Called Wanda.* It seemed somehow appropriate that an American actor, *Wanda*'s Kevin Kline, broke all precedents by winning a Supporting Oscar for his work in an American-financed but very British film—even having the temerity to edge out Sir Alec Guinness in *Little Dorrit.*

The British Academy (BAFTA) itself gave Hollywood a lesson in xenophobia that year by handing Cleese its Best Actor award, ignoring the fact that he had passed up British finance for MGM clout. Even Cleese himself, with a willfully absurd acceptance speech—by satellite, ironically enough, from Hollywood—showed that he could see how warped the award was. It was Sarah Miles, Oscar-nominated for *Ryan's Daughter* back in 1970, who had given the definitive verdict on the BAFTA Awards: "The American Oscar is the only award that carries any weight. Ours is just a lot of shit."

Gandhi's victorious loincloth looked positively conventional beside the contributions of other costume designers to the 1982 Academy awards. Dustin Hoffman, the apparent front-runner for Best Actor, was only one of four cross-dressers amid a heavyweight crop of nominees.

In *Tootsie,* Hoffman was wonderfully convincing as an out-of-work actor who dons drag to win a job in a TV soap opera. In *Victor/Victoria* Julie Andrews was less so as a girl who pretends to be a female impersonator, with even more predictable consequences for her love life. Written and directed by Andrews's husband, Blake Edwards, the film also won Robert Preston a Supporting nomination, in a transvestite role several light years removed from *The Music Man.*

John Lithgow was at it, too, as the transsexual former football pro Roberta Muldoon in George Roy Hill's film of the John Irving best seller, *The World According to Garp.* Lithgow's chances of an Academy Award were sniffed well in advance by an enterprising journalist named Jerry Lazar, who persuaded the actor to cooperate in recording the agonies and ecstasies of a long-drawn-out Oscar race. Chunks from Lithgow's diary were printed in the June 1983 issue of *California* magazine. They are a stark illustration of the hold of the Oscars over the most modest, literate and otherwise sanguine of actors.

On the very day they met, three months before the Awards show, Lithgow confessed to Lazar: "I think about the Oscars constantly. I want to put it out of my mind, but people won't let me. Even [his wife] Mary's friends say corny stuff to me like 'See you at the Dorothy Chandler!' " Even more than an Oscar, however, Lithgow wanted a job. It was January 4, and he had worked "only thirteen days since June 28."

When his name failed to appear among the Golden Globe nominations, Lithgow wrote in his diary: "This is all to the good, more evidence that I will definitely *not* be nominated for an Oscar. Why waste more time thinking about it?" Typical self-delusion: within days, he had broken a self-imposed vow by hiring a publicist, Neil Konigsberg of PMK, one of Hollywood's leading public relations agencies. It was also one of the most expensive: Lithgow was forced to take out a $10,000 bank loan—half for a deposit on a new car, half for PMK's up-front payment.

From the start, Konigsberg's slogan was, "There's life after the Oscars." He was intent less on a traditional Academy Award campaign than a "career publicity plan" to keep his client from riding the grueling Oscar roller coaster. But Warner Bros. was proving little help. They had already written *Garp* out of their Oscar plans when Lithgow won the New York Film Critics Award. It was all Konigsberg could do to persuade the ungrateful studio to part with $500 toward his client's coast-to-coast air fare.

By mid-February, as the Oscar nominations approached, Lithgow was firmly installed on that roller coaster, despite forgoing a second car to pay Konigsberg's monthly fees. One day he was ranting to Lazar: "I'm in the lead. I stole the fucking show!" The next he was wandering moodily around New York, still swinging between self-deception and candor: "Who has time to think about the Oscars? At the moment I feel like a good infusion. A little glory fix to pull me out of a rotten mood. I begin to see the awards as brightly colored decals that we stick onto our drab and humdrum lives."

Things began to look up when his name appeared among the Oscar nominees. Now Warners recanted, buying five center spreads in *Variety* and the *Hollywood Reporter* to promote Lithgow and his costar Glenn Close, also a Supporting nominee. The advertisements cost the studio $52,000—two thousand more than they had paid Lithgow for the film. He came last in a *People* magazine poll, which correctly forecast that Louis Gosset, Jr., in *An Officer and a Gentleman,* would become the first black actor to win an Oscar since Sidney Poitier twenty years before. Still voters kept wishing Lithgow luck, but few seemed to have seen his performance. He got another job, opposite Kevin Bacon in *Footloose,* but at prenomination rates. Convinced that he would lose, Lithgow grew acutely depressed. Then a local TV show offered him a free $1,000 tuxedo for the big night, if he would allow the fitting to be filmed for a promotional video. "I feel," he told Lazar, "like my whoredom has reached its apotheosis."

Lithgow's wife, Mary, a UCLA professor, was also suffering. "His glories are of the moment. My career is on a different schedule," she told Lazar. "All this publicity John's gotten—I love it, I think it's just great, but it's distracted me so that I resent it sometimes. I'd like to just go back and do my work. I'm used to being around people who care about me, and ask what I have to talk about. Ever since the nomination, I've felt, 'Give me my John back!' "

He was back after Oscar night, a sadder and a wiser man. Unsure about the use of a publicist—"I was bombarded by reporters with no particular concern for me or my career"—Lithgow had finally got his life back in perspective. "An Oscar nomination is a splendid thing. It fills you up with helium; you feel that your life has been elevated forever. And then something very real happens to you. In my case, close friends lost their baby four days after the nomination. Dealing with the split between the way the nomination makes you feel your life *should* be, and the fact that your life remains the same, can get you awfully depressed."

At least he got a free tux out of it. And more. The next year

Lithgow was nominated again, for *Terms of Endearment,* and this time he knew how to handle it. Although he lost again, two successive nominations had catapulted him into the league of those actors who are "hot, hot—whether or not you win." His salary took "quantum jumps" with subsequent post-*Garp* roles, from *Terms of Endearment* to *Buckaroo Bonzai* to *The Manhattan Project.* "This is all connected with the Oscar nominations—we may as well be honest about it. I was paid $50,000 for *Garp,* and now I make half a million. It may not be much compared to Robert Redford, but I consider myself well paid. That's a *lot* of money."

Lithgow's ordeal was a mere sideshow to the *Gandhi* hype that saw Richard Attenborough taking to the high road—linking hands with the peace movement, hobnobbing with Andrew Young and Coretta King, visiting UNICEF and the National Council of Churches, even winning the Martin Luther King Peace Prize. It became a triumphal procession, overshadowing the most commercially successful film ever made, Steven Spielberg's *E.T.* East and West were typically divided as the New York Film Critics chose *Gandhi* and *Tootsie*'s director Sydney Pollack, while their Los Angeles counterparts gave Best Film and Director to Spielberg. The pre-Oscar acting awards were monopolized by the two eventual Academy Award winners, Ben Kingsley and Meryl Streep.

A heavily pregnant Streep dropped her acceptance speech, which was retrieved for her by a gallant Sylvester Stallone, but this time there were no reports of the Best Actress leaving her Oscar in the ladies' room. Streep's Polish-accent performance in Alan Pakula's film of William Styron's *Sophie's Choice* had won her the Leading Role award just three years after her Supporting Oscar for *Kramer vs. Kramer.* Only five performers before her had managed wins in both acting categories: Helen Hayes, Jack Lemmon, Ingrid Bergman, Maggie Smith and Robert De Niro (to be joined in 1983 by Jack Nicholson). "Oh boy," gushed Streep, "no matter how much you try to imagine what this is like, it's just so incredibly thrilling right down to your toes."

Later, she almost seemed to regret it. "Privacy is very hard to come by these days," she told one of several interviewers allowed to invade it as she appeared on the covers of *Life, Time, Newsweek, Rolling Stone* and *The New York Times* magazine. "You think it was easy for me when *Life* magazine proclaimed me 'America's Best Actress'? My friends wouldn't speak to me for weeks. Excessive hype like that is very destructive. There is no such thing as 'best' in my field, and proclaiming otherwise makes newspaper wraps for tomorrow's fish." Asked by reporters how she had celebrated her second Oscar, she confessed to a spending spree on a washer, dryer and Cuisinart—"handy to have with a baby in the house."

Before *Gandhi,* Ben Kingsley was a respected rank-and-file member of Britain's Royal Shakespeare Company. In winning Best Actor for his film debut, he beat four Oscar intimates with twenty-six nominations among them: Jack Lemmon (for *Missing,* his eighth nomination), Peter O'Toole (*My Favorite Year,* his seventh), Paul Newman (*The Verdict,* his sixth) and Dustin Hoffman (*Tootsie,* his fifth). For a while it seemed that he would join the long line of flash-in-the-pan Best Actors never heard of again; nine years later, however, Kingsley secured another nomination, this time in the Supporting category, for *Bugsy.*

O'Toole's seventh defeat, all in the Leading Role category, was a distinction so extreme that the bravura Irishman seemed almost to relish it; the first of his fellow Celt Richard Burton's seven defeats had been, after all, in the mere Supporting stakes. As for the Academy's continuing failure to honor Paul Newman, one outraged fan took matters into his own hands with a paid advertisement in *Daily Variety:*

> To the members of the Academy: I would surely like you to see *The Verdict* once more and tell me what Paul Newman has to do to win an Academy Award. . . .
>
> Supervisor Ed Jones
> Ventura County

For his own part, Newman waxed reflective over his sixth unsuccessful nomination: "To say that I'm not interested would be hypocritical. . . . I'm not competitive as an actor or a director, but by the same token I'm enough of a pragmatist to realize that the Academy Awards are good for the industry, they're good for a film. If you worked as hard as I did on this film, and with as much affection, you will naturally want the largest number of people to see it. So I would say that it's very comforting to be recognized by your peers." When he arrived back on the set of *Harry and Son,* after taking the day off to attend the Oscars, Newman was applauded by cast, crew and spectators. As Peter W. Kaplan reported in *Life* magazine, "Newman's skin got redder than usual, and his white teeth got wider, and his blues pointed straight at the ground."

As Dustin Hoffman's girlfriend in *Tootsie,* and as Frances Farmer, the doomed thirties movie star, 33-year-old Jessica Lange has displayed a versatility few would have expected from her decorative debut in *King Kong*'s palm in the 1976 Dino de Laurentiis remake of the 1933 classic. "I have never seen someone," observed her former lover Bob Fosse, "go from so cold to so hot." Lange's reward was a feat achieved only twice before, by Fay Bainter in 1938 and Teresa Wright in 1942: two nominations, as both Leading Role and Supporting Actress. Escorted by her brother George, to deflect publicity from her recent transfer of affection from Mikhail Baryshnikov to Sam Shepard, she won an almost inevitable victory (like both Bainter and Wright) in the lesser category. Apart from her *Frances* costar Kim Stanley, Glenn Close in *Garp,* and Lesley Ann Warren in *Victor/Victoria,* Lange's main victim was a none too pleased Teri Garr, also up for *her* supporting role in *Tootsie.*

Between them, the studios had spent nearly $2 million trying to win nominations. Paramount's vice-president for worldwide marketing, Gordon Weaver, insisted that such huge spending was reserved "only for those films which deserve the acclaim. Otherwise this whole thing becomes a joke, and the Academy is no joke." His words soon came back to haunt him when the studio ran full-page advertisements for the 3-D merits of *Friday the 13th Part 3.* Universal had mailed all Academy members a glossy twelve-page booklet about *Missing,* which by voting time had been missing from the cinema circuit for six months. But nothing could slow the progress of the year's three juggernauts, as *Gandhi* won eleven nominations, *Tootsie* ten, and *E.T.* nine. *Das Boot,* a German World War II submarine drama, set a new record for foreign-language films with six, including Best Director (though it failed to win any).

Gandhi's 8-for-11 British landslide, including a Best Picture-Director double for Attenborough, began according to the Puttnam theory, with that telling early win for Costume Design. Direction and

Screenplay, Cinematography, Editing and Sound—in all these departments it beat *E.T.,* which won only Original Score, Visual Effects and Sound Effects Editing. "We were almost precluded from any awards," said Spielberg, "because people feel we've already been amply rewarded. . . . The tendency is for important films to win over popcorn entertainment. History is more weighty than popcorn."

Even the movie community had overdosed on *E.T.*'s ubiquitous dolls and other spin-off merchandise—the ruination of indulgent parents the world over. And amid all his success, Spielberg had suffered a serious misfortune. The previous July, during his production of a movie version of TV's *The Twilight Zone,* the actor Vic Morrow and two small children had died in a helicopter accident. Spielberg had been nowhere near the location at the time—though he was executive producer, this particular segment was being directed by John Landis—but *Film Comment* magazine felt moved to wonder "whether Academy members will see the tragedy as an all-but-inevitable by-product of young directors who'll try anything for effect." Voting for *Gandhi,* by contrast, could make an Academy member feel "noble."

Vincent Canby was among those on Spielberg's side. "*E.T.* and *Tootsie* are films," wrote the veteran *New York Times* critic. "*Gandhi* is a laboriously illustrated textbook." Canby was seconded by his colleague Janet Maslin: "The Oscar seemed to have been confused with the Nobel Peace Prize." Someday, she forecast, "the sweep that brought *Gandhi* eight Academy Awards may be known as one of the great injustices in the annals of Oscardom." To many, *E.T.* deserved to be accorded the status of such other childhood classics as J. M. Barrie's *Peter Pan* (itself to be colonized by Spielberg in his 1991 version, *Hook*).

In the *Village Voice,* Andrew Sarris too was feeling sour: "Make no mistake about it, the Oscar ceremony is now intentionally designed to inflict as much pain and suffering as possible on both its participants and its viewers." The 1982 ceremony had certainly inflicted unexpected pain upon the Polish filmmaker Zbigniew Rybcyznski. After winning the Oscar for Best Animated Short Subject, he had left the hall for a well-deserved cigarette. On attempting to reenter, he was refused readmission by a zealous security guard, wary of an unfamiliar face with sneakers beneath his tux. In vain did the

Pole repeatedly plead, "I have Oscar." After kicking the guard in sheer frustration, he was arrested and thrown in jail—whence he asked for the help of the only Hollywood lawyer he had heard of, Marvin Mitchelson. "First bring me an interpreter," said Mitchelson, "and then tell me how to pronounce his name." The charges were eventually dropped; but a rueful Rybcyznski left Hollywood, Oscar in hand, complaining that "success and defeat appear quite intertwined."

From the Academy's point of view, the 1980s were proving much plainer sailing than the turbulent seventies. The early years of the decade were mercifully free from the protests of a Scott or a Brando, the tub-thumping of a Redgrave or a pre-*Klute* Fonda. The Oscars seemed to have regained their sense of fun, and with it a little healthy irreverence. Since the decline of the studio system, the awards were no longer manipulated by the whims of Hollywood moguls and potentates; at last the voters were free to follow their inclinations rather than the studio line. The studios still campaigned, of course, but trade-paper advertising and exclusive previews increasingly looked like just another branch of their usual movie promotion. The Academy Awards, as a result, were often headed in unexpected directions.

If the Oscars stood for anything, it was good old-fashioned "feel-good" Hollywood values—dictated by the high average age of the electorate, perhaps, but widely shared in an era of special effects and gizmo movies. *Terms of Endearment,* for instance, was welcomed by the New York *Daily News* as "at long last . . . a juicy, utterly captivating movie that not only features wonderfully human characters, but actually dares to deal with the joys and frustrations of maintaining a mother-and-daughter relationship at a time when the average Hollywood movie is concerned mostly with overwrought computers." It took an upmarket journal like *Sight and Sound* to speak for the anti-Oscar aesthetes: "A crassly constructed slice of anti-feminism that contrives to rub liberal amounts of soap into the viewer's eyes."

With bravura performances from Shirley MacLaine and Jack Nicholson, James L. Brooks's overgrown soap opera was the kind of movie the Oscars dream of. The Academy was not yet ready for a picture as sophisticated as Martin Scorsese's *The King of Comedy,* in which Robert De Niro and Jerry Lewis were both enthralling as an aspiring stand-up comedian and the talk-show host he holds to ransom for a spot on his show. But neither, it could be argued, was the moviegoing public. *Terms of Endearment* was a huge box-office hit, *The King of Comedy* a puzzling flop. Brooks's film won eleven nominations and five Oscars, including Best Picture, Director, Actress and Supporting Actor; *The King of Comedy* won none. The one will be shown forever on TV; the other will grow in popularity as an undervalued cult classic. Such was, is and always will be the way of the Academy Awards.

MacLaine had been rehearsing her acceptance speech for a quarter of a century, since the first of her five Leading Role nominations back in 1958. "I'm gonna cry," she began, "because this show has been as long as my career. I have wondered for twenty-six years what this would feel like." She was not, said MacLaine, going to thank "everybody I've ever met in my entire life," then proceeded to do pretty much that, confiding that being in bed with Jack Nicholson was "middle-aged joy." God was asked to bless "the potential that we all have for making anything possible if we think we deserve it," before Shirley started to leave, paused, and turned back to add: "I deserve this!"

As Garrett Breedlove, overweight ex-astronaut, Nicholson's second Oscar defied those critics who described this as his "comeback" role: "I ain't been away, guys! And I've been after *this* one for a while." As Best Supporting Actor, Nicholson became the seventh actor in Oscar history—behind Helen Hayes, Jack Lemmon, Ingrid Bergman, Maggie Smith, Robert De Niro and Meryl Streep—to have won in both categories. "I think you've got to have nutty goals in life," he exulted. "I'd like to win more Oscars than Walt Disney, and I'd like to win them in every category." In which vein he sauntered up to the podium without removing his shades, raised a fist and accepted with a brief speech all his own: "All you rock people down at the Roxy and up in the Rockies, rock on!"

The year's other top honor went to a fine American actor with the good sense to step out of character when graduating from supporting to leading roles. Vincent Canby called him "one of the most resourceful, technically proficient, most remarkable actors in America today . . . he may well be the best we have, the American Olivier."

Nominated three times before, for very different roles in *The Godfather, Apocalypse Now* and *The Great Santini,* Robert Duvall claimed his almost inevitable due as an ex-alcoholic country-and-western singer in *Tender Mercies.* When his new country friends were refused admission to the Governors Ball, the Best Actor abandoned the event for a down-home party at Johnny Cash's house.

All five of the 1983 Best Actor nominees, in fact, played drunks, and the other four were British. Although Duvall had refused to campaign before the nominations, he suddenly began giving interviews when they were announced: dealing with "the Limey syndrome," the American Olivier complained that "the attitude with a lot of people in Hollywood is that what they do in England is somehow better than what we do here." Michael Caine—present, for once, because he thought he was going to win for *Educating Rita*—said he wanted the Oscar so that "I'd get more scripts without other actors' coffee stains on them." Tom Conti wanted it to hike his asking price, which he did anyway—from $100,000 to $1 million per movie after his nomination for an American film, *Reuben, Reuben. The Dresser*'s Albert Finney and Tom Courtenay remained above the fray—Finney by absenting himself, as usual, from the proceedings.

Robert De Niro's weight gain for *Raging Bull* seemed to have inspired several of the 1983 acting nominees. Michael Caine had put on thirty-five pounds to play the drunken professor who educates Rita; but it was Nicholson, like De Niro before him, who turned his middle-age spread to Oscar advantage. Mariel Hemingway also gained weight, if of a different kind, to play a murdered Playboy bunny; for *Star 80,* Bob Fosse's version of the Dorothy Stratten story, Hemingway took Method acting to extremes by having her breasts enlarged, then displaying them across ten pages of *Playboy.* It proved as effective a way of winning an Oscar nomination as Meryl Streep's weight-loss diet for *Silkwood.*

As a male Chinese photographer in *The Year of Living Dangerously,* Linda Hunt became the first actor to win an Oscar by playing a member of the opposite sex. But cross-dressing, for all its growing Oscar tradition, failed to work for Barbra Streisand. She had struggled for fifteen years to get *Yentl* on the screen—the kind of personal crusade which amounts to another hallowed way of winning Oscars, most recently demonstrated by Attenborough's twenty-year quest to make *Gandhi.* MGM-UA spent some $200,000 in trade paper advertisements, and Streisand herself did some low-key campaigning, especially aimed at the Jewish and female sectors of the film industry. "If I fail," she told one interviewer, "not only would the film fail, I would set back the cause of women." She was further helped by generally good reviews. In a line eagerly repeated in the "For Your Consideration" ads, Gary Arnold of *The Washington Post* declared that "it would constitute a Hollywood scandal if Barbra Streisand were denied an Oscar nomination for her direction of *Yentl.*"

She was, and it did. Guests arriving for the 1983 Academy Awards were greeted at the Chandler Pavilion by a poster proclaiming AN OSCAR FOR "YENTL"—THE LOST CAUSE, with an angry subhead: BEST DIRECTOR NOMINEES—1927 TO PRESENT: MEN 273, WOMEN 1. The protest was mounted by a group calling itself PEP (Principles, Equality and Professionalism in Film), one of whose pickets proclaimed: "We're not avid Barbra Streisand fans by any means, but the way the Academy has treated her is really the spark that lit the flame. Even though her movie represents a significant accomplishment, the Academy doesn't want to admit that a woman is solely responsible for it."

MGM-UA was proclaiming Streisand some kind of Renaissance woman for her feat in producing, cowriting, directing and starring in *Yentl,* the tale of a young Polish Jewess who dresses as a boy to get on in the world. Although she won the Golden Globe (for Direction, losing Best Actress to Julie Walters), Streisand failed to win even a nomination from the Directors Guild, which only intensified her fans' rage when *Yentl* was nominated for five Oscars—none of them for her.

"Barbra was *stunned,*" said a friend. "It was like someone hit her on the head with a bag of bricks. . . . She was inconsolable. She couldn't eat or drink. She didn't know whether to cry or be angry. Everyone around her was furious."

Amid accusations of sexism on all sides, Shelley Winters demanded a recount: "I haven't talked to anybody who didn't vote for her." It diminished her own nomination for *Terms of Endearment,* said Shirley MacLaine: "I am very saddened." Columnist Marilyn Beck thought Streisand had "every reason to be bitter and bewildered by what amounts to a flagrant slap in the face from the show business community." Redford and Beatty had both won Best Director on their debuts (in Beatty's case, solo debut); "Why not Streisand?" asked another Academy member. "Barbra is a woman—not allowed into this elect society." Streisand's own explanation oozed bitterness: "In Hollywood, a woman can be an actress, a singer, a dancer—but don't let her be too much more."

So why was Hollywood gunning for Barbra? *Yentl,* wrote Charles Champlin, "is, with all else, a sensational job of preplanning and editing . . . it carries an almost palpable aura of being a labor by all hands." Perhaps inadvertently, this enigmatic comment from the *Los Angeles Times*'s influential entertainment editor had helped to swell dark rumors from London, where Steven Spielberg, George Lucas and Sydney Pollack had all been spied entering Streisand's editing studios during breaks in their own work. Had they been helping her "fix" her picture?

More to the point, she had had a public falling-out with Isaac Bashevis Singer, Yentl's creator, who declared himself thoroughly unimpressed: "My Yentl wanted to study the Torah—she didn't want to be a singer." Even before seeing the film, Singer had declared: "First I'll see the killing; then I'll perform the autopsy." Now, interviewing himself in *The New York Times,* the writer carped: "I must say that Miss Streisand was exceedingly kind to herself [as a director]. The result is that Miss Streisand is always present, while Yentl is absent. . . . The whole splashy production has nothing but commercial value."

The first to leap to Streisand's defense was the unlikely figure of Mrs. Walter Matthau, who called Singer "a mean-spirited, ungenerous and cranky man." In the *Los Angeles Times,* Streisand herself mounted a strident defense against both slurs. Of Singer she said simply: "If a writer doesn't want his work changed, he shouldn't sell it." And of the rumors from London: "I hate tooting my own horn but after Steven [Spielberg] saw *Yentl,* he said, 'I wish I could tell you how to fix your picture, but I can't. It's terrific. It's the best film I have seen since *Citizen Kane.*' "

That did it. Streisand had taken two sacred names in vain, and awkwardly reminded the Academy of its slights to both Spielberg and Orson Welles. It was a combination of superstar arrogance and adverse publicity that did her in, it seems, quite as much as her gender.

The only Academy Awards won by *Yentl* were for Music, to Michel Legrand and Marilyn and Alan Bergman. Streisand did not attend the show—nor, she let it be known, even watch the telecast. It was not the last time she would have to face such a humiliation.

By 1985 Irving "Swifty" Lazar's Oscar-night party was proving more popular than the Awards show itself. As he moved it from the Bistro to Spago, where it is held to this day, Lazar was asked about its appeal. "It's a religious experience," he replied, as his guests mused that maybe the original Oscar show was like this: just a party, no press allowed, even Oscar winners turned away if their names are not on Swifty's exclusive list. As the show's TV ratings dipped yet further (Appendix C, page 622), some bright spark suggested getting the septuagenarian superagent to organize it—as well as the Governors Ball, the Academy Governors' own thinly attended party.

The Academy's middle-aged, middle-brow electorate was looking less in touch than ever with the cinemagoing public. Criticized by movie buffs for honoring schmaltz and pap, they were also losing the interest of the paying customers, who spent 1984 flocking to *Beverly Hills Cop, Ghostbusters* and other comedy blockbusters that would not get so much as a sniff of an Academy Award. "Can't Oscar laugh?" asked *People* magazine of the year's five Best Picture nominees, which had all done mediocre box office. Gone were the days, it seemed, when the Academy took flak for honoring box-office hits like *The Greatest Show on Earth* and *Ben-Hur*.

To make matters worse, Vanessa Redgrave was again looming on Oscar's horizon. Was the trouble-free decade to reach a premature end? Redgrave had experienced problems getting back into the United States to film Merchant-Ivory's latest adaptation of a classic novel, Henry James's *The Bostonians;* had it not been for a movie fan in the immigration department, who had liked Ismail Merchant's *The Europeans,* she might never have played the part which was to win her a fifth Oscar nomination. The sometime rebel was the only Best Actress candidate to attend the nominees' lunch that year, panicking Academy officials into fearing another hijack of their show. But fate intervened. Five days before the ceremony she received the news of the death of her father Sir Michael, a nominee back in 1947 for *Mourning Becomes Electra.* Vanessa and Dame Peggy Ashcroft, herself a first-time nominee, immediately flew home for the funeral.

Ashcroft's citation came for *A Passage to India,* David Lean's first film for fourteen years. The director had "lost heart," he confessed, after all the criticism of *Ryan's Daughter.* Filming the E. M. Forster novel had been a pet project since 1958, when the author had refused him the rights; now that they were available, Lean sank some of his own money into a project that had difficulty finding backers. No one, said the studios, would want to see a film about an elderly woman. Peggy Ashcroft, too, had her doubts. "Even the experience of India seemed to me almost more than I could perhaps take at my age. When I was asked to do it, I said, 'Mr Lean, I am 76,' and he said, 'So am I.' So that shamed me [into doing it]."

Though Columbia's advertising campaign touted Ashcroft for Best Actress in a Leading Role, the Academy's voters for once exercised their right to think otherwise. The leading roles were surely those played by the Australian actress Judy Davis and the Indian Victor Banerjee, whose exploits in a remote mountain cave form the pivotal moment in Forster's story. Ashcroft, in fact, would probably have won in either category, so impressed were the voters by the qualities brought to the screen by another distinguished British Shakespearean.

In the male Supporting category, by contrast, John Malkovich for once had no Brits to contend with. No living ones, anyway. As Malkovich tastelessly put it, "I'm up against two Orientals, one of them an amateur, a black guy and a dead man." Another distinguished British classical actor, Sir Ralph Richardson, once nominated for *The Heiress* back in 1949, had died before the release of his cameo in Hugh Hudson's *Greystoke: The Legend of Tarzan;* at the age of 82 years and 96 days, this won Olivier's lifelong friend and Old Vic colleague the posthumous distinction of becoming the oldest Oscar nominee ever—a record that still stands. The "black guy" was Adolph Caesar, the only acting nominee from *A Soldier's Story,* another powerful racial movie from Norman Jewison—which again saw the Canadian missing from the Direction lists despite a Best Picture nomination. "Years ago it would have bothered me," said Jewison. "If you take the Oscar too seriously, you're in trouble. But if you take it as a game, it's wonderful."

Of the two nominees of Asian descent, the professional was a karate pro-turned-actor, Noriyuki ("Pat") Morita, in the astonish-

John Lithgow (LEFT), who co-starred with Glenn Close and Robin Williams in The World According to Garp, kept a revealing diary of life as an Oscar nominee.

William Hurt's surprise 1985 Oscar as a homosexual drug addict opposite Raul Julia in Kiss of the Spider Woman was seen as a breakthrough for the acting awards, honoring a Brazilian "art-house" movie over mainstream Hollywood products.

One of a series of elderly stars wheeled on to boost the TV ratings, a frail Bette Davis proved an embarrassment at the 1986 ceremony.

Though Whoopi Goldberg (LEFT) was one of three actresses to win nominations in The Color Purple, the Academy yet again snubbed its director, Steven Spielberg. Despite the consolation of an honorary award that same year, 1986, Spielberg has yet to win a competitive Oscar.

ingly successful *The Karate Kid.* It was the other—the "amateur"—who would emerge as one of the Oscars' unlikeliest ever winners.

Dr. Haing S. Ngor, an expatriate Cambodian gynecologist, was living and working in California as a supervisor in the Indo-Chinese employment program when a Los Angeles casting agent saw his picture among a group of wedding guests in a local paper and brought it to the attention of David Puttnam. Puttnam was working with Roland Joffé on development of *The Killing Fields,* based on a *New York Times* article in which the Pulitzer Prize-winning journalist Sydney Schanberg detailed his long search for his Cambodian interpreter, Dith Pran. Puttnam and Joffé had auditioned more than three hundred Cambodians without finding their Pran; on meeting Haing Ngor, they discovered the authentic passion they were looking for. While most of Dith Pran's family had made it safely to the United States, nearly all of Ngor's had died of starvation. Like Pran, Ngor had escaped into Thailand; but his mother, father, four brothers and his fiancée had all perished.

Killing Fields saw Puttnam back in the Best Picture frame, with Joffe nominated for his feature-film debut, and Ngor in the Supporting category—where he wound up carrying off one of the most unlikely Oscars ever. Backstage, the Cambodian attacked the film for not being realistic enough. Reporters listened "in stunned silence," according to *TV Guide,* as Ngor described "in gruesome detail" how he'd been tortured by the Khmer Rouge guerrillas.

To Charles Kipps, features editor of *Variety,* Ngor's victory "played out as one of the most dramatic in Academy Award history. The small and slightly built Haing Ngor, who had been so mired in desperation just a year before, looked overwhelmed as he hugged his statuette. . . . The underdog—courtesy of the American dream—could indeed come up a winner." But the Hollywood columnist James Bacon spoke for an astonished consensus when he wrote: "For the life of me, I can never understand why they give Oscars to non-actors who, in all probability, will never work again."*

Struck down with flu since her return to London, Peggy Ash-

* Ngor was the fifth actor of Asian origin to be nominated for an Oscar, and the second to win, following Miyoshi Umeki's Supporting Actress award for *Sayonara* in 1957. The other nominees were Sessue Hayakawa (*Bridge on the River Kwai,* also 1957), Mako (*The Sand Pebbles,* 1966) and Morita (*The Karate Kid,* 1984).

croft had wanted her costar Victor Banerjee to pick up her Oscar, "to thank India for inspiring Forster and Lean." For Banerjee, the moment was to have been some consolation for his lack of a nomination, after winning at the National Board of Review. Instead, to his astonishment, Angela Lansbury leaped to the stage burbling about "this incredibly happy, joyous moment" and the "consummate artistry, delicacy and beauty" of her "dear friend." Ashcroft subsequently received an "abject" apology from Gregory Peck on behalf of the Academy. But her win was little consolation, either, for David Lean, who lost all three of his nominations—for Director, Adapted Screenplay and Editing. "It never gets easier," he said afterward. "You worry and wonder and keep telling yourself you haven't got a chance of winning—but it still hurts when you lose."

Ashcroft's demotion to the Supporting category left the Best Actress race wide open for her costar Judy Davis, Vanessa Redgrave and three previous Oscar winners—Sally Field, Jessica Lange and Sissy Spacek. Field's win for *Norma Rae* five years before seemed to have done little for her career, which had staggered through such turkeys as *Beyond the Poseidon Adventure, Back Roads* and *Kiss Me Goodbye*—until Robert Benton saved her the lead in another soap opera aimed at moviegoers' heartstrings, *Places in the Heart*. Had Sally really shed her television "bubblehead" image? Replied a gallant Benton: "If she hadn't been so good at Gidget and the Flying Nun, do you think anyone would remember her in those roles?" It was Field's chance to match only Helen Hayes, Vivien Leigh and Luise Rainer by winning Best Actress twice in two nominations.

When her name emerged from the envelope again, Field uttered a heartfelt and subsequently celebrated cry. "I haven't had an orthodox career," she began, "and I wanted more than anything to have your respect. The first time I didn't feel it." This time around she did. "I can't deny the fact that you like me. Right now you really *like* me!" she sobbed in disbelief, to a gust of sympathetic laughter from the audience. "It was a beautiful moment," gushed Gene Siskel, "one of the most open, honest admissions of the nervousness that every performer has."

More than a year later, when Field's confessional "You like me" had passed securely into Oscar folklore, she told Lawrence Grobel in a *Playboy* interview that she was glad she had been so openly emotional. "I remember sitting and watching the Academy Awards as a kid; it was a big event . . . and part of the joy was that you got to see these people talking to their peers about a business that's tough, that's competitive, that's mean, that's grueling and that's delightful. And they cried or laughed or fell down. When I won my first one, I was so contained, I never allowed myself to feel it. . . . I felt I denied myself that moment."

By the climax of the show, and the Best Picture award, *The Killing Fields* was trailing three-to-seven to *Amadeus,* the Mozart biopic that won Miloš Forman his second award as Best Director. At the end of a mixed night for British fortunes, the supreme prize was to be presented by a frail, 77-year-old Laurence Olivier, recently recovered from serious illness. Steven Spielberg—shut out again for *Indiana Jones and the Temple of Doom*—patted Puttnam encouragingly on the back during Olivier's standing ovation, which he ended by intoning with his too familiar mock-modesty: "Dear ladies and gentlemen, I hope I don't let the evening down too badly."

Forgetting to read the nominees' names from the back of the envelope, where they were listed in alphabetical order, Olivier then proceeded to announce, with a tremendous theatrical flourish, the first name he saw. "The winner is *Amadeus!*" There was an awkward pause before Saul Zaentz, producer of the apparent winner, shook hands with Puttnam and every other potential Best Film winner en route to the stage, where he took the envelope from Olivier, read out all the names, and checked the result inside before picking up his Oscar. "It was a tricky moment, which Saul handled extremely well," Puttnam could laugh years later. "I guess Olivier was lucky that the winner's name began with an A."

Amadeus thus became the seventh film in the Awards' history to win eight Oscars (for eleven nominations)—joining *Gone with the Wind, From Here to Eternity, On the Waterfront, My Fair Lady, Caberet* and *Gandhi* behind only *Gigi, West Side Story* and *Ben-Hur.* But was it a musical? Mozartians shudder at the very word, but *Amadeus* is so listed in the Academy's official archives. Its multiple triumph—Best Picture, Best Director and Best Adapted Screenplay for the British playwright Peter Shaffer—did not extend to Best Score, which went to *A Passage to India*'s Maurice Jarre, who declared himself "lucky that Mozart wasn't eligible." The year's other music awards went to Prince and Stevie Wonder, who accepted "in the name of Nelson Mandela."

The *Amadeus* sweep did, however, win the Leading Role Oscar for F. Murray Abraham, a New York stage actor hitherto best known for his brief TV role in a Fruit of the Loom underwear commercial. Abraham's memorable performance as Salieri, the rival court composer driven mad by jealousy of Mozart, prevailed over Albert Finney's second consecutive nomination (again as a drunk), and his fourth over twenty years, in John Huston's *Under the Volcano*. Finney had won his nomination without the benefit of a single campaigning advertisement, whereas a record Warner Bros. splurge for Clint Eastwood in *Tightrope* failed to deliver the goods. *The Killing Fields*'s Sam Waterston, waxed philosophical: "The Oscar," he said, "has never been part of my daydream." Also disappointed were Tom Hulce, Mozart to Abraham's Salieri, and Jeff Bridges, who could thank a huge Columbia campaign for his unlikely nomination as an earthbound alien in *Starman*.

Looking back five years later, Abraham was still endearingly wide-eyed. "As for the general speculation about an Oscar jinx," he said, "what hogwash. The Oscar is the single most important event of my career. I have dined with kings, shared equal billing with my idols, lectured at Harvard and Columbia, and am professor of theater at the City University in Brooklyn. I am privileged to have taken part in the greatest international gathering of artists in the world. If this is a jinx, I'll take two."

The year's real loser was Steve Martin, winner of the New York Film Critics award for *All of Me,* but conspicuously absent from the Oscar lists, another victim of the Academy's perennial hauteur toward comedy and comedians. The omission began to look like a distinction when Martin learned that the only other two actors to be so snubbed—honored by New York but ignored by the Academy—were two British theatrical knights, Richardson and Gielgud. Though visibly wounded, the wild-and-crazy guy proved big enough to agree to attend as a presenter.

Defeated by Peggy Ashcroft in 1984, Geraldine Page became the only woman alongside Burton and O'Toole in the select ranks of those with no win from seven nominations. The following year she was nominated again, as the crotchety old lady going home to die in

Horton Foote's screen version of his play, *The Trip to Bountiful.* Could she make it a record 0-for-8?

"I'd love to be a champion for the most nominations without ever winning," said Page. She was out of luck. As F. Murray Abraham opened the Best Actress envelope and swooned, "Oh, I consider this woman the greatest actress in the English language," Anne Bancroft, Whoopi Goldberg, Jessica Lange and Meryl Streep all wondered for the tiniest moment if he might have meant them. But no, the winner was the lady who had kicked off her shoes, and was now having trouble finding them beneath her seat. Page was long overdue an award; in a career of just twenty-five films, her record of nominations placed her with Jack Lemmon and Jack Nicholson on a plateau since joined by Marlon Brando. All her fellow nominees, for once, stood to join in her ovation.

If there was a just inevitability about Page's award, there was none about 1985's Best Actor: William Hurt, as a gay window dresser sharing a South American jail cell with a Marxist political prisoner (Raul Julia) in Hector Babenco's *Kiss of the Spider Woman.* In the year of *Rambo* and a spate of teenage sci-fi comedies, the Academy excelled itself in honoring a fine performance in an unabashed art-house movie that had been unable to find a major distributor. "Hurt's mesmerizing performance is no stunt," wrote *Time.* "Risking foolishness, he achieves a heartbreaking metamorphosis." Apart from Jack Nicholson in *Prizzi's Honor,* the opposition was unusually weak: Harrison Ford in *Witness,* James Garner in *Murphy's Romance* and Jon Voight in *Runaway Train.* But there had been a time when the Academy would have voted for Stallone's *Rambo* over what one studio executive called "an anarchist project." Hurt's win was "a watershed," commented David Puttnam. "The acting awards would never be quite the same again. At last they had really grown up."

"My honor is my work, there is none greater," said Hurt. "I'm very proud to be an actor. But there are so many people who do good work, who are as good as I am who are not up here." If he didn't believe in awards for actors, why hadn't he turned it down? "Because I'm not a politician. . . . I won an honor. I'm glad to accept."

Hurt later revealed that he had not originally intended to go to the Awards. Then someone had put him straight. " 'If people are going to honor you,' he told me, 'how dare you not accept that?' "

. . .

The Academy stalwart who had changed Hurt's mind was none other than Steven Spielberg, despite the fact that he himself was that year receiving the latest in a procession of Academy snubs unprecedented in Oscar history. After producing the year's most profitable film, *Back to the Future,* Spielberg had "dived in deeper" by directing his first mature drama, chronicling the growth of a southern family during the first half of this century. "The biggest risk for me," he said before its premiere, "is doing a movie about people for the first time in my career." The early returns were more than promising. "It should be against the law," said NBC's Gene Shalit next morning, "not to see *The Color Purple."*

Not all reviewers were quite so enthusiastic, and there were the inevitable protests about stereotyping from sundry black-rights groups. But Spielberg garnered his share of critical esteem, and again showed the magical touch at the box office. Said the *New York Post:* "The only thing left for Spielberg to do is decide which tux to wear as he picks up his Oscar." When the nominations were announced, *The Color Purple* was among the Best Picture nominees, alongside John Huston's *Prizzi's Honor,* Sydney Pollack's *Out of Africa,* Peter Weir's *Witness* and Hector Babenco's *Kiss of the Spider Woman.*

Huston, Pollack, Weir and Babenco were all duly nominated for Best Director. The fifth slot—incredibly—went not to Steven Spielberg, but to one of his heroes, Akira Kurosawa, for *Ran.* OMISSION IMPOSSIBLE gasped the *New York Post.*

AFRICA, PURPLE 11, SPIELBERG 0 echoed the Los Angeles *Herald-Examiner,* highlighting the extraordinary fact that *The Color Purple* had won eleven nominations—including three for its actors—but nothing for its director. To put the scale of the snub in its true perspective: in fifty-eight years of the Academy Awards, only thirty-two other films had won eleven or more Oscar nominations—and thirty-one of their directors had been nominated. The only previous exception was Sam Wood, omitted for *The Pride of the Yankees* in 1942, when there were ten Best Picture nominees to five Best Director slots. "If a movie has eleven nominations," as the *Herald-Examiner* put it, "someone has to be responsible." Spielberg, according to another headline, had been SNUBBED BY JEALOUS COLLEAGUES.

The crestfallen director was said to be vacationing on a yacht "in undisclosed waters" when a Warner Bros. ad appeared in the trade press expressing "sincere appreciation" to the Academy for the film's eleven nominations, but continuing: "At the same time, the company is shocked and dismayed that the movie's primary creative force—Steven Spielberg—was not recognized."

Had Spielberg masterminded the statement? Warners denied it. But the *Hollywood Reporter*'s Martin Grove attacked the "archaic" voting procedures of the directors branch, and demanded the formation of a blue-ribbon panel to investigate any organized effort to dissuade voters from nominating Spielberg. The Academy's new president, Robert Wise, rejected the idea, insisting that the voters had followed their "artistic and creative feelings." It emerged that Sidney Lumet had been campaigning for Kurosawa, after the director's nonappearance at the Tokyo Film Festival had irritated his fellow countrymen into refusing to submit *Ran* as the Japanese entry for Best Foreign Film. But the directors branch soon began to rue their choice of Spielberg as sacrificial lamb.

Whoopie Goldberg—chosen by Spielberg to make her debut in *The Color Purple,* for which she had won a Best Actress nomination—knew just what she thought of the directors branch. Throwing tact (and all chances of an Oscar) to the winds, she denounced them as "a small bunch of people with small minds who chose to ignore the obvious." If she and Oprah Winfrey had both won Oscar nominations on their acting debuts, did it not say something for the qualities of their director? John Huston sounded almost indecently gleeful as he told Army Archerd: "Spielberg has had so much success, he can afford to miss a beat." Thanks to Spielberg's absence from the lists, Huston had emerged as the front-runner for Best Director. As he had won in 1948 while directing his father, could he repeat it nearly forty years later when directing his daughter?

It fell to the 8,000-member Directors Guild to right the wrong done Spielberg by its elite of some 230 in the Academy's directors branch. At its annual dinner, the Guild presented Spielberg with Best Director, its highest award, to which the most commercially successful director in the seventy-year history of the movies replied: "I am floored by this. I never won anything before." Acknowledging the boldness of the Guild's gesture, Spielberg went on: "If some of you are making a statement, thank God, and I love you for it." To the press he added: "Anyone's feelings would have been hurt, but with all the support I've received from people in the last few weeks, I've begun to feel like Jimmy Stewart in *It's a Wonderful Life.*"

By the time Spielberg said he would be attending the Awards, snub or no snub, even the Academy was beginning to feel guilty. The show's producer, Stanley Donen, invited him to present the Best Actor award, which Spielberg declined with dignity: "I felt that under the current circumstances, my presence as a presenter might diminish the importance of the actual award." Then Donen rubbed salt in the Academy's wounds by including three Spielberg films in a compilation of the Oscars' all-time favorite losers: *Seven Brides for Seven Brothers, Treasure of the Sierra Madre* and *Tootsie*—plus *Jaws, Raiders of the Lost Ark,* and *E.T.*

Two of *The Color Purple*'s supporting actresses, Winfrey and Margaret Avery, joined Goldberg among the acting nominees; the film had been nominated for Adapted Screenplay, Cinematography, Art Direction, Song, Score, Costume Design and Makeup as well as Best Picture; and it won nothing. Spielberg had gone 0-for-11. Of the thirty-two other films to have achieved eleven nominations, only a film as weak as *The Turning Point* had previously been so utterly humiliated. Only twice in the previous forty years had the Directors Guild's winner failed to go on to the Best Picture Oscar.

Out of Africa had received as much criticism as *The Color Purple* for its "National Geographic" approach to moviemaking—and indeed to Oscar campaigning, when both films were commended to voters by way of glossy booklets containing color photographs of their stars on location. Sydney Pollack, said some, had managed no better than Spielberg with his actors: Robert Redford again failed to win a nomination; Meryl Streep's latest accent, Scandinavian, won her a nomination but no more; only Klaus Maria Brandauer had been worthy of an Oscar—but not worthy enough to overcome a sentimental vote for 77-year-old Don Ameche in *Cocoon,* his first nomination in a fifty-year career.

Yet it was Sydney Pollack and *Out of Africa* who carried off the two top awards, leaving Spielberg to ruminate: "When I'm sixty, Hollywood will forgive me. I don't know for what, but they'll forgive me." The Spielberg furor came to be seen as the Oscars' biggest scandal since Bette Davis was overlooked for *Of Human Bondage* in 1934. "Anyone who says that envy didn't affect Spielberg's chances would be crazy," said Peter Bogdanovich, "but don't look for any changes in the near future. They won't be forthcoming."

One of Spielberg's actresses, Margaret Avery, had evoked memories of Chill Wills a quarter of a century before, with one of the tackiest pieces of Oscar campaigning in memory. Knowing, perhaps, that she had been lucky to be in the film in the first place—she had once worked in a TV ad with Spielberg, who called her only after Tina Turner pulled out—she decided to push her luck yet further. On the last day of voting, there appeared in the trade papers one of the creepiest messages in the history of a decidedly creepy business.

> Dear God,
>
> My name is Margaret Avery. I knows dat I been blessed by Alice Walker, Steven Spielberg and Quincy Jones, who gave me the part of "Shug" Avery in *The Color Purple.* Now I is up for one of the nominations fo' Best Supporting Actress alongst with some fine, talented ladies that I is proud to be in the company of. Well, God, I guess the time has come fo' the Academy's voters to decide whether I is one of the Best Supporting Actresses this year or not! Either way, thank you, Lord, for the opportunity.
>
> Your little daughter,
> Margaret Avery

God smiled on Margaret Avery—she got her nomination—if not on her director. The ad, Avery admitted, had cost her a kitchen stove she had wanted for ten years. She might have done better to buy the stove. The Oscar went to the actress who had won all but one of the pre-Oscar awards, Anjelica Huston, directed by her father in *Prizzi's Honor.* Though John Huston was beaten as Best Director by Pollack, he had earned the unique distinction of directing both his father and his daughter to Academy Awards. And though Nicholson had lost to Hurt, he seemed more than consoled by victory for Anjelica, his longtime lover: "That's all we wanted out of the night. Just wanted one for Toots . . ." *Prizzi's Honor,* he added, "dropped a lot of dead weight off Anjelica's psyche." From the stage Anjelica paid tribute to her father, then said: God, I've got to win another, because then it will be really real, really serious." Despite a 1990 Best Actress nomination for *The Grifters,* it is a double she has yet to achieve.

Other films did find help in the heavens that year. After *Witness* won Harrison Ford his first nomination, its producer admitted: "We got terrific help from the airlines. At least 150 Academy members told me they saw it on an airplane." James Garner's nomination as Sally Field's leading man in *Murphy's Romance* was a complete surprise, put down to the man's sheer popularity around town. Equally surprising, but more easily explained, were the nominations accorded Eric Roberts and Jon Voight in a Golan-Globus chase movie called *Runaway Train.* By spending almost $500,000 promoting their mediocre product, the producers broke all previous Oscar advertising records. A seven-page spread hailed the film's opening; there were thirty trade-paper ads during the voting season; and Golan boasted of spending more than $30,000 arranging special screenings for Academy members—including, in more than thirty cases, taking the picture to their homes. "I called every person in the Academy," crowed Menahem Golan, "and said if they couldn't get out of the house, I would show it to them there."

The Academy was even hyping itself in 1985. Given a steady slide in the Oscar's TV ratings throughout the decade, it bought a sixteen-page "Viewers Guide to the Oscars" in newspapers all over the country, and replaced Johnny Carson with Robin Williams. Although Cher tried to help, celebrating her nonnomination (for *The Mask*) with the most outrageous outfit the Oscars had ever seen—part punk queen, part high sexual priestess, complete with tribal headdress—her naked navel was lost on Middle America, and the show's TV ratings dipped to an all-time low.

The highest-grossing film of 1986 was *Top Gun,* in which the Academy saw nothing of Oscar merit beyond the work of its technicians. Hollywood's top money-makers were increasingly eschewing the Academy Awards—with the frequent exception of Visual Effects, which helped countless gizmo movies to claim Oscar status on the cinema marquees. The major awards, as a result, were tending to go to high-quality films and performers, often made outside the Hollywood system. This was true of all the leading contenders of 1986: Oliver Stone's *Platoon* and Merchant-Ivory's *A Room with a View* (eight nominations each), David Puttnam's *The Mission* and Woody

Allen's *Hannah and Her Sisters* (seven each). They would never satisfy art-house moviegoers, who preferred their films in black-and-white, usually with subtitles, but the Oscars were otherwise in danger of getting a good name.

There were, of course, exceptions. Big box office had always clouded the Academy's judgment, but only up to a point. Now even a film like *Aliens* could see an actress like Sigourney Weaver achieve a Best Actress nomination—the first ever to go to a woman in an all-action role. And even the art-house circuit was happy to see the Academy, in its most eccentric mood, nominating the maverick director David Lynch for his highly personal film *Blue Velvet,* which helped a rehabilitated Dennis Hopper back into the acting lists (with a simultaneous performance in *Hoosiers*) nearly twenty years after *Easy Rider.*

But still they could make provocative mistakes. This year's slighted director—it was becoming a habit—happened to be a woman, Randa Haines, whose *Children of a Lesser God* won five major nominations including Best Picture, while she was nudged out of the Director stakes by Lynch. The snub seemed all the greater when Haines's deaf-and-dumb star, Marlee Matlin, beat Jane Fonda (as a drunk in *The Morning After*), Sissy Spacek *(Crimes of the Heart),* Kathleen Turner *(Peggy Sue Got Married)* and Sigourney Weaver *(Aliens)* as Best Actress, thus perforce sharing with Jane Wyman and Sir John Mills the distinction of winning an acting Oscar without saying a word. With Shirley Booth (*Come Back, Little Sheba,* 1952), Julie Andrews (*Mary Poppins,* 1964) and Barbra Streisand (*Funny Girl,* 1968), Matlin became only the fourth actress to win the Leading Role Oscar on her screen debut (see appendix C, section B5).

With habitual subtlety, the Academy also chose Matlin to present the award for Best Sound. It was not a great acting year—none of the other Best Actress nominees were in Best Picture candidates—but Matlin's saccharine award was among the ultimate examples of the Academy's ancient penchant for rewarding onscreen suffering. And the fact that she had moved in with her costar William Hurt—the reigning Best Actor, who won his second successive nomination opposite her—did Matlin no harm in the publicity stakes. It even fell to Hurt to announce from the stage to his girlfriend (in sign language, of course) that she had won.

The man to beat in the male category was Britain's Bob Hoskins, who had won every previous award from Cannes to the Golden Globe for his gangland chauffeur in Neil Jordan's *Mona Lisa.* It was, after all, twenty years since the Academy had exported a Best Actor statuette in the arms of Paul Scofield, since when only the late Peter Finch and the *Gandhi* sweep's Ben Kingsley had defied the patriotic odds. Again only one of the nominees, William Hurt, was in a Best Picture candidate. But it was Hoskins's bad luck to come up against the seventh Leading Role nomination accorded one of the Oscars' all-time losers, Paul Newman, who for once had the unexpected bonus of a commercial hit. Thanks to the presence of Tom Cruise, Newman's recreation of the role of Fast Eddie Felson in Martin Scorsese's *The Color of Money* was vastly more successful than *The Hustler,* to which it was a sequel, and for which he had won his second nomination a quarter of a century before.

As *People* magazine enthused: "Paul Newman makes everything he's learned in three decades of screen acting pay off in this forceful follow-up to his 1961 role. . . . An Oscar nomination and win would stick it smartly to the Academy for sending him prematurely out to pasture last year with one of those honorary gold-watch awards." Newman vetoed any attempt at an Oscar campaign by his publicist, Warren Cowan, and flatly announced that he was "too busy" to attend the awards show. It seemed quite like old times when the only absentee among the Best Actor nominees turned out to be the winner, making the Academy look doubly foolish for presenting him with a Lifetime Achievement Award the previous year."Paul gave a performance that was controlled yet emotional," said his director, Scorsese. "His Oscar was no consolation prize."

"When you look down the pike and see that your work is finite," Newman himself told a television interviewer, "these awards mean more than when you're a kid." Presented privately with his statuette a month later, at a party at Cowan's home, Newman seemed embarrassed. Loretta Young confided that she asked him, "Was it too little, too late?" and Newman simply nodded his head: "It's like chasing a beautiful woman for eighty years. Finally she relents and you say, 'I'm terribly sorry. I'm tired.' "

The Best Supporting Actor wasn't there, either. Having attended in 1983, because he thought he was going to win Best Actor for *Educating Rita,* Michael Caine had decided that his performance in *Hannah and Her Sisters* stood no chance against two nominees from the Oscar film of the year, *Platoon.* Even Dennis Hopper, believed Caine, had a better chance to beat Tom Berenger and Willem Dafoe than Caine or his fellow countryman Denholm Elliott *(A Room with a View).* Caine was thus on location in the Bahamas when his name emerged from the envelope at its fourth attempt in twenty years—two decades during which two British knights and one Cambodian gynecologist had been the only non-Americans to steal this particular statuette.

The most prolific of actors, Caine had had the benefit of three other starring roles that year, including a cockney double-act with Hoskins in *Mona Lisa.* At the time, he was "delighted, naturally." But within a few years Caine, like many other Supporting Role winners, was telling friends: "It was only the Supporting award, after all. Me, I'm after the big one." And there were other Britons putting down significant markers in 1986. *A Room with a View* and *My Beautiful Laundrette* gave Oscar voters their first sight of Daniel Day-Lewis; while *The Mission* showed Jeremy Irons holding his own against Robert De Niro.

Though *The Mission* was proving the last $23 million nail in the coffin of Goldcrest, the British production company that had ridden high since *Chariots of Fire* and *Gandhi,* it was managing to book David Puttnam's now regular ticket to the Oscars. The first British picture in thirteen years to win the Palme d'Or at Cannes, written by double-Oscar-winner Robert Bolt and directed by *The Killing Fields*'s Roland Joffé, it won no honors for Irons, De Niro or even Ray MacAnally, one of those fine character actors for whom the Supporting category might have been invented. Critics and audiences alike found its esoteric story line, a colonial dispute among clerics in the eighteenth-century South American jungle, almost incomprehensible. Even the Goldcrest executive Jake Eberts admitted: "I've seen it a dozen times and I still don't understand it."

The Mission owed its Best Picture and Director nominations to a six-figure campaign from Warner Bros. Michael Caine, who by now had been living in Hollywood for some years, had also helped his chances by leading the first promotion tour ever accorded the cast of a Woody Allen film. It was, of course, *Hamlet* without the Prince, as Allen spurned all Orion's entreaties to go along. He even worked for a rival camp by declaring David Lynch's *Blue Velvet* the best film of the year—yes, better even than his own *Hannah and Her Sisters,* which had surprised him at the box office. "If you make a popular movie," mused Woody, "you start to think where have I failed? I must be doing something that's unchallenging, or reinforcing the prejudices of the middle class, or being simplistic or sentimental."

Oliver Stone would not have agreed. While Woody, as always, was playing his clarinet at Michael's Pub, Stone was receiving what he clearly thought his due: Best Director and Best Picture for his Vietnam War epic *Platoon,* the first of a planned trilogy of films based on his own combat experience. A Yale dropout who had served fourteen months with the 25th Infantry Division, Stone had written the first draft of *Platoon* before David Puttnam had hired him to adapt *Midnight Express* back in 1978. But no studio proved willing to support a project so remorselessly negative.

He was at last rescued by the independent Hemdale, even though they had lost thousands with Stone's *Salvador,* a less ambitious study of El Salvador's civil war (which many still think the better of the two films). "We felt we couldn't do any worse than we did with *Salvador,*" said Hemdale's John Daly, after Stone had teamed up with the producer Arnold Kopelson. Orion's *Platoon* hype, and *Salvador*'s early release on video, both helped James Woods to a well-deserved Best Actor nomination for *Salvador,* even though he had passed on a return to the jungle for *Platoon.*

Come the writing nominations, Stone found himself in the unusual position of competing against himself—not permitted in the other major categories—with Original Screenplay citations for both *Salvador* and *Platoon.* Still he lost out—to, of all people, Woody Allen.

This was grim news too for Paul Hogan, Australia's Bruce Willis, whose offbeat comedy, *Crocodile Dundee,* had been the year's second-biggest grosser, and had won him too a Screenplay nomination. "I realize I'm not exactly the odds-on favorite," Hogan had warned, "but I've traveled 13,000 miles to be here for this. I've come from the other side of the planet. And if they read out someone else's name instead of mine, it's not going to be pretty."

It was deeply ironic that the same Academy to have trembled at a visit from Hanoi Jane Fonda, and to have waved the flag in the face of other Vietnam protesters, now felt able to use *Platoon* to reassure the world that it was, broadly speaking, antiwar. Stone's success at the 1986 Oscars typified a ten-year time warp between protest and respectability in matters from race and mental illness to sex and warfare. By the end of the decade there would be protesters picketing the Awards for shrinking from nominating the first of the AIDS movies that will no doubt be winning Oscars during the nineties.

Eight years on from *The Deer Hunter,* Oliver Stone used the Oscar rostrum less as a soapbox than a pulpit: "What you're saying is that for the first time you really understood what happened over there . . . and that it should never, ever in our lifetime happen again." He was echoed by Kopelson: "If, perhaps, *Platoon* could influence people in this and other countries in the world to hesitate before they engage in war, to demand facts and ask questions before the bombs, then we, not just those of us that made *Platoon,* but the entire motion picture industry, will have succeeded beyond our wildest imagination."

Had the Academy declared itself opposed to the Vietnam War or to war in general? The voters seemed as confused as both director and producer. Either way, the message failed to reach the White House, which managed to end its *next* war, in the Gulf, just in time to stifle protests at the 1991 awards ceremony.

However much Hollywood had changed, as independent producers and agents seized the power once held by the studios, the Oscars could never resist wallowing in nostalgia. Had Paul Newman been present, he would have received his statuette from one of those frail, elderly local legends so beloved of the show's changing parade of producers. At 78, Bette Davis looked ghostly enough to evoke memories of Mary Pickford, and managed to make as much of a mess as Laurence Olivier of the ritual reading of nominees' names. Afterward, she longed for bygone days: "The Academy Awards have completely changed . . . we had them in beautiful hotel rooms and we had no time limit on our speeches. There is an impersonality to this now via television."

The following year, on the Oscars' sixtieth anniversary, nostalgia ran rampant. In an attempt to mount a parade of actors from each of the fifty-nine Best Pictures to date, Samuel Goldwyn, Jr., wound up with more of an action replay than he bargained for, when those feuding sisters Joan Fontaine and Olivia de Havilland found themselves booked into adjacent rooms at the Four Seasons Hotel. Fontaine moved floors.

To accommodate the larger-than-usual crowd, the show moved out of the Dorothy Chandler Pavilion after eighteen years and back to the Shrine Auditorium—scene of the backstage rows between Fontaine and de Havilland in 1946. By now the area surrounding the Shrine had become less than savory, and the management was obliged to spend $160,000 on an eight-foot perimeter fence to reassure Bel Air that it was safe to venture downtown en masse. The only danger, warned the Academy, was limo gridlock. Maps were printed in that morning's newspapers with an exhortation to leave home early: "Traffic will be heavy—allow extra travel time."

The hotshots really should have listened. Stars from de Havilland to Streep drew excited gasps from passersby as they were forced to abandon their limos and dash in all their finery past gas stations and taco stands to reach the Shrine on time. Even eight-months-pregnant Glenn Close was seen climbing over fenders for six blocks in (vain) pursuit of the Best Actress award. Among those caught up in the traffic was the mayor of Los Angeles himself, Tom Bradley, who angrily demanded an inquiry the next morning. Still squabbling with her sister, Fontaine despaired of her limo and wailed: "It's the last Oscar show for me. From now on, they can muck it up by themselves." One of the few to make it on time, and parade her décolletage around the arrivals area for the cameras in solitary splendor, was one of the year's unlikeliest nominees, Sally Kirkland.

Kirkland had been the beneficiary of what is generally agreed among Hollywood publicists to have been one of the most effective Oscar campaigns of all time. Although she had been in Hollywood for twenty years, landing small parts in such movies as *The Sting* and *The Way They Were,* Kirkland was still better known as the first actress to appear completely naked onstage, in a dim distant show called *Sweet Eros*—and again baring all, this time astride a pig, on the cover of *Screw* magazine. In a low-budget movie called *Anna,* however, she had finally won a leading role worthy of her extrovert talents. Though few had seen her portrayal of a Czech-born stage actress betrayed by a young admirer (rather in the manner of *All About Eve*), Kirkland believed she had turned in a performance worthy of Oscar nomination. And she was prepared to spend plenty of her own money to get it.

So she hired one of Hollywood's leading publicists, Dale Olson, and told him she was prepared to do anything, anytime, anywhere. While Olson fixed her a tireless interview schedule, he also laid on parties and screenings of *Anna* at his home for the entire movie community. Print and broadcasting media were invited, so that famous stars could sing Kirkland's praises for publication while thanking their host for another of his legendary shindigs. Kirkland meanwhile arranged personal meetings with every member of the Hollywood Foreign Press Association, who vote the Golden Globes, and wrote personal letters to every member of the Academy. Friends such as Shelley Winters meanwhile canvassed votes for her in hundreds of personal phone calls.

Holly Hunter, who was mopping up most of the pre-Oscar awards for *Broadcast News,* now found herself sharing the Los Angeles Critics award with Kirkland, who also clocked up a Golden Globe. Olson promptly laid on a last-gasp evening of congratulations, at which *Entertainment Tonight*'s cameras caught such luminaries as Robert De Niro toasting Kirkland's claim to be "the Eleonora Duse of the twentieth century".

And so it came to pass that Sally Kirkland's name appeared alongside those of Hunter, Close, Streep and Cher in the 1987 stakes for Best Actress. The nomination alone was enough to win her a spate of scripts in the mail, a special "Spotlight" profile in the *Hollywood Reporter,* a three-page spread in *People* magazine and countless invitations to be a presenter in the day-by-day awards ceremonies of pre-Oscar week. That Cher proved the Oscar winner for *Moonstruck* was really beside the point—though Olson claims to this day that the result was "a pretty close call."

By winning (or buying) herself an Oscar nomination, Sally Kirkland had put her name on that Treasure Island map which hangs in the minds of all Hollywood producers and casting directors. The actress has rarely been out of work since, for fees of which she could only dream before *Anna,* though she still displays a somewhat self-destructive penchant for flashy roles in movies way beneath Oscar consideration. But Kirkland remains a fixture of the Oscar arrivals scene, flaunting herself before the cameras with an endearing lack of inhibition; and the system suggests that she requires only the right part to be back in the frame for an even better return on that 1987 investment. A conspicuous cameo in Oliver Stone's high-profile 1991 nominee, *JFK,* will not have hindered the process.

Moonstruck was Cher's third movie of the year, following *Suspect* and *The Witches of Eastwick,* making hers another of those "versatility" Oscars available even to willfully outrageous ex-singers. She had also been doing her stuff for the Academy, stepping in at the last minute when Glenn Close dropped out of a New York salute to Johnny Mercer. The lure of the Oscars had ensured, it appeared, that another professional outsider had now been Academy-trained. "I don't think this means I am somebody," she said by way of acceptance, "but I guess I'm on my way." Her most heartfelt thanks went to her fellow nominee "Mary Louise Streep . . . I feel so unbelievable that I did my first movie with her and now I was nominated with her." The sometime partner of Sonny Bono, mayor of Palm Springs, appeared to have forgotten that before making *Silkwood* with Streep four years before, she had also filmed *Good Times* (1967), *Chastity* (1969) and *Come Back to the Five & Dime, Jimmy Dean, Jimmy Dean* (1982).

Ironweed won Jack Nicholson an unprecedented *sixth* Best Actor award from the New York Film Critics, and his ninth Oscar nomination (to Streep's seventh), placing him in a tie for fourth with Spencer Tracy in the all-time Oscar league table, behind only Hepburn, Davis and Olivier—quite an achievement for an actor still barely fifty. Neither he nor Streep won, and *Ironweed* looked like being the last film they would make together. Word from the set was that Streep had become "disillusioned" with Nicholson, finding him "rather weird." Not merely did she no longer wish to dine with him or accept his flow of lavish gifts; she no longer wished to work with him, either, which put an end to plans to reunite them in a romantic comedy being custom-written by Michael Christofer.

William Hurt scored his third successive nomination for *Broadcast News,* the latest Best Picture nominee from *Terms of Endearment*'s James L. Brooks, who had used his experience as a producer of *The Mary Tyler Moore Show* to explore the internal politics of television. Robin Williams began his long haul from TV comedian to screen actor with his first Best Actor nomination, for *Good Morning, Vietnam*; and Marcello Mastroianni clocked up his third unsuccessful nomination twenty-five years after his first.

But the runaway winner of the 1987 Best Actor award was Michael Douglas, as everyone's favorite corporate raider, Gordon Gekko, in Oliver Stone's *Wall Street.* For Douglas, already the proud owner of a Best Picture statuette for *One Flew Over the Cuckoo's Nest,* divine providence had struck twice. Just as the Three Mile Island accident had helped *The China Syndrome* in 1979, so the stock market crash of October 1987 came just two months before *Wall Street*'s release. In a tribute to his father—another of the Oscarless, first nominated as long ago as 1949 but only twice since—Douglas touchingly dedicated his Oscar to Kirk, "for helping a son step out of a shadow. I'll be eternally grateful to you, Dad."

Like Cher, Douglas owed his award at least in part to another film—*Fatal Attraction,* Adrian Lyne's blockbuster study of the perils of marital infidelity. It had also won Leading and Supporting Role nominations for Glenn Close and Anne Archer as Douglas's crazed mistress and wronged wife. Both lost out to actresses from *Moonstruck,* Cher and Olympia Dukakis, underlining the injustice again done the director Norman Jewison, passed over for Best Director for the third time in twenty years. Cousin of the Democratic presidential contender, Dukakis held her Oscar aloft and cried, "Come on, Michael, let's go!" in front of a billion people. Although he subsequently lost the election, her career has since flourished; once rejected by Otto Preminger as "unphotogenic," Dukakis has testified that "Winning the Oscar made me a player, a name to be considered. . . . People think of an Oscar as the culmination of your life, payment for so many sacrifices. To me, it's less about reward than evolution."

The year's most successful film, *Beverly Hills Cop II,* was again absent from the Oscar skirmishing, as eventually proved true of the three films subjected to the most feisty Oscar campaigns: Richard Attenborough's *Cry Freedom,* Faye Dunaway's *Barfly* and Barbra Streisand's *Nuts.* Following her humiliation over *Yentl,* Streisand was this time accused of overdoing her publicity, for all Warner Bros.'s protests that they were "very careful not to overhype, or overcampaign." Campaigning of any kind was a rarity for *The Untouchables*'s Sean Connery, who locked up the Supporting award—making it two in a row for Britain—by hiring a press agent, gritting his teeth and setting out on the fearsome interview trail. The fees commanded by the original James Bond, known to Hollywood studios as a fearsome litigant, subsequently went through the stratosphere.

It was a year of further humiliation for Steve Martin, again denied even a nomination for *Roxanne,* despite winning two pre-Oscar awards; and for the hapless Steven Spielberg, whose *Empire of the Sun* won six nominations, all in the technical categories.

In the schadenfreude department, Spielberg at least had the consolation that, for the first and only time in Oscar history, not one of the five Best Director nominees was American. Britain's Adrian Lyne had inherited *Fatal Attraction*—on the strength of his one hit, *Flashdance*—only after two more of that year's nominees had passed it up. Brian De Palma had deemed the script too similar to Clint Eastwood's *Play Misty for Me,* and slunk off to direct *The Untouchables.* Lyne's compatriot John Boorman had also rejected *Fatal Attraction* in favor of a memoir of his wartime childhood in Britain, *Hope and Glory,* for which his financing came from no fewer than nineteen countries (including Germany, but not Britain). If Boorman's evocative but highly personal film seemed an unlikely nominee, Oliver Stone and James L. Brooks were highly put out to find themselves bumped by the Swedish director Lasse Hallström for what Jack Nicholson told *Rolling Stone* was his favorite film of the year, *My Life as a Dog.* Brooks's only reward was a Screenplay nomination.

But they were all whistling in the wind. Since the days of the studio system, it had become a rare phenomenon for one major film to sweep most of the nominations and awards. The freak 1980s exception turned out to be Bernardo Bertolucci's *The Last Emperor,* a sprawling biopic of China's last imperial ruler—"a man," according to the film's publicity, "kidnapped by history." The Italian director's British-produced epic won all nine Oscars for which it was nominated, including Best Picture and Director. Just like *Gigi,* the only previous film to have won nine-for-nine three decades before, *The Last Emperor* received not one single acting nomination—not even a Supporting nod for poor Peter O'Toole, who might surely have benefited at last from its extraordinary sweep. Whatever this strange statistic may say about its director, Bertolucci's epic became the most honored movie since 1961—and the third most garlanded film in Oscar history, behind only *Ben-Hur* and *West Side Story.*

Chosen for the signal honor of presenting Best Picture, the (as yet) un-Oscared figure of Eddie Murphy, hottest box-office star of the moment, chose to make some waves. He wasn't going to accept the invitation, said Murphy, until his agent had said he must—his reason being that "black people don't win Oscars—except about once every twenty years." He warned the assembled glitterati that "black people will not ride the caboose of society . . . we will not bring up the rear anymore."

An unlikely candidate to pick up the Redgrave baton of Oscar controversy, Murphy gave way to a suaver Bertolucci, who said that as an Italian, as a European, the Academy Awards had always seemed to him like "a distant ceremony, something fascinating, very remote. Something I really didn't belong to." Then *The Last Emperor* got nine nominations and everything immediately changed. "I became immediately a kind of Oscar victim. I started to learn the rules of the game and to check the odds, to start with the colitis. . . . I want to do a Chinese kowtow to the Academy because this is one of the strongest emotions of my life and I can't hide it." If New York was the Big Apple, concluded Bertolucci, "then tonight Hollywood is the Big Nipple."

Not one of *The Last Emperor*'s nine Oscar winners had mentioned the name of David Puttnam, the man who had brought the film to Columbia, but who was watching the awards show in Toronto, where he was now an unpaid lecturer at the Canadian Center for Advanced Film Studies. Asked how he felt about it, Puttnam diplomatically said: "Those who made the film deserve all the credit." Asked why he gave Puttnam no public credit for his role, producer Jeremy Thomas snapped: "I don't understand the question." When it was spelled out for him that Puttnam was the head of Columbia, Thomas said merely: "This is not an award for David Puttnam. He didn't produce the picture. I did."

Despite a strike by Hollywood writers, which had forced Sam Goldwyn, Jr., to hire presenters capable of witty ad-libbing—Chevy Chase, for one, as host—the viewing figures were up again, the highest in four years. To go yet bigger and better, the Academy hired a new producer for the 1988 awards: Allan Carr, the man who had given the world *Grease* and that dubious 1978 campaign for *The Deer Hunter*.

As he prepared to fly in a million tulips from Holland, Carr's chosen theme was "Couples, Costars, Companions, Compadres." The show, he decided, was all about its presenters. Michael Caine and Sean Connery were only too happy to team up, but would Dennis Quaid and Susan Sarandon? No. Okay, then, Dennis Quaid and Michelle Pfeiffer. Bob Hope and Lucille Ball? Sure. Paul Newman and Joanne Woodward? Not coming. Raquel Welch and *anyone?* Maybe. Loretta Young? Only if she could present Best Picture—on her own. As his giant planning board became an index of Hollywood egos, the stars of Carr's bonding program turned out to be Kurt Russell and Goldie Hawn. Yes: to present Best Director, Kurt would even propose marriage to Goldie in front of a billion people.

Blissfully indifferent to all this were Dustin Hoffman and the team from Barry Levinson's *Rain Man,* set for a classic sweep with the irresistible Oscar formula of a big box-office, buddy-buddy road movie about mental illness, pairing the respected Hoffman with the adored Tom Cruise. Hoffman's opposition was virtually nonexistent: apart from his one serious challenger, Gene Hackman in *Mississippi Burning,* the voters had cleared his path to a second Best Actor award in six nominations by naming a clutch of no-hopers: Tom Hanks in *Big,* Edward James Olmos in *Stand and Deliver* and Max von Sydow in the subtitled *Pelle the Conqueror.* Only Hoffman and Hackman, moreover, were in Best Picture nominees.

To *Dangerous Liaisons'* Glenn Close, her fifth nomination must have seemed sweeter than maneuvering her swollen belly around all those fenders in vain the previous year. Only one opponent, first-time nominee Melanie Griffith, was also in a Best Picture candidate —but it was an unashamed comedy, *Working Girl.* Apart from the statutory Meryl Streep—this time with an Australian accent, in *A Cry in the Dark*—seniority alone would surely see Close home against Sigourney Weaver as the murdered anthropologist, Diane Fossey, in *Gorillas in the Mist,* and Jodie Foster as a rape victim in *The Accused.* But Close had come up against the Academy in its occasional heart-goes-out mode. Just as they preferred Hoffman's autistic savant to Hackman's sixties liberal cop, so they preferred Foster's contemporary American victim over Close's antique French femme fatale.

As Close moved into the unenviable 0-for-5 category, Foster set out on a sustained rise up the Hollywood power ladder. After three halfhearted post-Hinckley years in and out of the movies, she had also been gang-raped on her return, in Tony Richardson's film of John Irving's best-seller *The Hotel New Hampshire.* Foster's choices of roles, she liked to think, were "courageous"; the strength of *The Accused* lay in depicting a rape "many men would have said she asked for."

"Cruelty might be very human and it might be very cultural," she said in her acceptance speech, "but it is *not* acceptable." At 26, the diminutive Foster was a very different figure from that teenage hooker in *Taxi Driver.* An increasingly versatile actress, soon to show the true extent of her range as an FBI agent pursuing serial killers in *The Silence of the Lambs,* she was already planning her directorial debut. A devout feminist, and target of homosexual pressure groups in search of symbolic celebrities, Foster seems likely to have the Academy honoring powerful women's themes during the 1990s. "For too long women have been portrayed as the second sex. I want to make a movie about that, about my generation and sexuality. It's about time people had frank movies where sexuality is treated really honestly, where women are sexual people instead of constantly being on some nonsexual pedestal." The Academy's geriatric electorate can only hold its collective breath.

At the end of the 1980s, however, they found *The Accused* heap strong medicine—too strong to nominate for Best Picture. But even the combination of racial, feminist and marital themes that they did honor stood no chance against autism. For several weeks ahead of time a tide of Hollywood opinion, helped along by a $500,000 campaign from United Artists, had crowned Barry Levinson and *Rain Man* for the two top prizes, carrying Original Screenplay in its slipstream.

But maverick directors and their themes did seem to be becoming increasingly respectable—more so, perhaps, than they would have liked. Just as David Lynch had elbowed Randa Haines out of the 1986 Director stakes, so Martin Scorsese *(The Last Temptation of Christ)* and Charles Crichton *(A Fish Called Wanda)* now nudged aside *The Accidental Tourist*'s Lawrence Kasdan and *Dangerous Liaisons*' Stephen Frears (whose British compatriot Christopher Hampton did win Adapted Screenplay).

Comedies and comic performances had also received noticeably more respect from the Academy in recent years—winning nominations if no Oscars for Kathleen Turner in *Peggy Sue Got Married,* Robin Williams in *Good Morning, Vietnam* and Hanks in *Big.* It was thus typically eccentric of the Academy to reward a fine dramatic actor, Kevin Kline, for his outrageous caricature in *A Fish Called Wanda,* while Geena Davis could thank the outstanding Best Picture nominee, *Accidental Tourist,* for her equally eccentric success against strong opposition: Joan Cusack in *Working Girl,* Frances McDormand in *Mississippi Burning,* Michelle Pfeiffer in *Dangerous Liaisons* and Sigourney Weaver again, this time in *Working Girl.* The unfortunate Miss Weaver that night became the first actress in Oscar history to be voted simultaneous nominations in both categories, but win neither.

Who was looking good for the 1989 Oscars? A year ahead of time, the *Los Angeles Times*'s Jack Mathews put his head on the block with a few predictions. Best Actor would be between Paul Newman in *Blaze,* Marlon Brando in *A Dry White Season,* Al Pacino in *Sea of Love,* Colin Firth in *Valmont* and Jack Nicholson in *Batman* or *The Two Jakes:* also in with a shout were Robert De Niro, Richard Dreyfuss, Tom Cruise, Jack Lemmon, William Hurt and Robert Duvall. Glenn Close would at last win her overdue Best Actress award in either *Immediate Family* or *The White Crow,* despite strong opposition from Meryl Streep in *She-Devil,* Jane Fonda in *Stanley & Iris,* Shirley MacLaine and Sally Field in *Steel Magnolias,* and Bette Midler in yet another remake of *Stella Dallas;* other runners could be Jessica Lange, Barbara Hershey, Susan Sarandon, Emily Lloyd and Holly Hunter.

Best Picture would range Woody Allen's *Crimes and Misdemeanors* against Roland Joffé's *Fat Man and Little Boy,* Miloš Forman's *Valmont,* Norman Jewison's *In Country,* Lawrence Kasdan's *I Love You to Death* and Jack Nicholson's long-awaited sequel to *Chinatown, The Two Jakes.* But let all of them beware. Warren Beatty's *Dick Tracy* was heading for a sweep.

"Predicting next year's nominees," bragged Mathews, "is not the strain it seems." But the eventual winners, in the best traditions of Oscar caprice, would include none of the above.

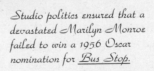

Studio politics ensured that a devastated Marilyn Monroe failed to win a 1956 Oscar nomination for Bus Stop.

11

Whoops, We Forgot You

When they sign you up for one of those special awards, you know it's time to cash it in.

—JOAN CRAWFORD

On the eve of the 1992 Academy Awards ceremony, during a pre-Oscar bash at a Beverly Hills restaurant, Billy Wilder was overheard to remark: "If you win, by the end of May it's not such a big deal. If you lose, it's not such a big deal either." That's all very well if you've won six Academy Awards in twenty-one nominations over forty-five years, not to mention an Irving Thalberg Award to keep them company. But there are many other distinguished and talented filmmakers to whom the absence of an Oscar from their mantel is all too big a deal.

The roll call of the Oscar-less (or "The Unawarded," as some members of this exclusive club call themselves) is curiously long and distinguished. The Academy Awards may not be everyone's measure of cinematic excellence; but in their six and a half decades they have somehow managed to honor most of the big movie names of the century. The omissions thus become all the more glaring. How come Alfred Hitchcock, Charlie Chaplin, Greta Garbo, Cary Grant, Fred

Astaire, Richard Burton never won an Oscar? How did the movie world pass over such of its own as Kirk Douglas, Mickey Rooney, Maurice Chevalier, Barbara Stanwyck, Robert Mitchum? Why were Errol Flynn, the Marx Brothers, Edward G. Robinson never even nominated?

Other anomalies abound, in a field where artistic merit is far from being the sole criterion for success. Two contemporary box-office titans, Warren Beatty and Robert Redford, have both won awards for direction but not for their acting. Some might say this is shrewd judgment on the Academy's part. If so, what made it hand out its highest acting award to Victor McLaglen, Yul Brynner, Julie Andrews, Art Carney, Charlton Heston?

Aware of the potential pitfalls from Year One, even the infant Academy was shrewd enough to lay on a fail-safe mechanism in the shape of Honorary Oscars, sometimes dressed up as Lifetime Achievement Awards—otherwise known as the "Whoops, sorry, we forgot you" syndrome, even the Deathbed or Intensive Care Awards. Officially, the Academy's board of governors votes Honorary Awards "for exceptionally distinguished service in the making of motion pictures or for outstanding service to the Academy"; the rules also stipulate that they "are not limited to the awards year" and "shall not be voted posthumously." Unofficially, they are usually a grim sign that the obituary writers are booting up their word processors.

Sally Field acknowledged as much when presenting one in 1985. Honorary Oscars, said the reigning Best Actress, are usually given to "individuals whose careers are behind them or who are contemplating retirement. . . . Well, tonight's recipient is hardly ready to retire. In fact, at this very moment, he's working on a film set in Chicago."

Paul Newman said he found the timing of his award "very strange." He was especially grateful that it did not come "wrapped as a gift certificate from Forest Lawn." One of the Academy's all-time losers, Newman had been nominated for Best Actor six times—from *Cat on a Hot Tin Roof* in 1958 to *The Verdict* in 1982—and lost to a decidedly mixed bunch of sentimental or freak winners: David Niven, Maximilian Schell, Sidney Poitier, Rod Steiger, Henry Fonda, Ben Kingsley. According to his lawyer and friend Irving I. Axelrad, Newman had to be dissuaded from refusing the Academy's honor: "He said they'd always treated him as second, and now they were acting as though he were old and through." But Newman thought better of it: "You don't kick people in the butt who are trying to be nice to you."

The Academy seemed to sniff an especial poignancy in the fact that Newman's wife, Joanne Woodward, had won her own statuette as long ago as 1957. Newman's, said the official citation, was bestowed "in recognition of his many memorable and compelling screen performances and for his personal integrity and dedication to his craft." His way of marking the occasion was to quote Spencer Tracy, who had once "been accosted by a young man who said, 'I'm going to be an actor.' To which Tracy replied, 'That's terrific. Just don't let 'em catch you at it."

Having declined to accept in person, Newman seemed at pains to emphasize—via satellite from Chicago—that he was neither ill nor close to retirement. "My best work is down the pike in front of me." With a fine sense of irony, the Oscar gods proved him right the following year, when that same film he was making in Chicago won him the Best Actor award in his own right, at his seventh attempt. As Fast Eddie Felson in *The Color of Money,* Newman had recreated the role that had won him his second unsuccessful nomination in 1961. He was pleased, he said, "to have evened the score with my wife," and the Academy looked rather foolish.

Honorary Awards had played a useful role since the very first Oscar night, when the fledgling Academy garlanded the film it had banned from competition, *The Jazz Singer,* and a Hollywood giant whom his peers were too small-minded to honor, Charles Chaplin. The first time an Honorary Oscar amounted to a farewell present was in 1946, when the five-time loser Ernst Lubitsch, though only 54, was known to be seriously ill. The German-born producer-director of *The Patriot, The Love Parade* and the original *Heaven Can Wait* was given a scroll to mark "his distinguished contributions to the art of the motion picture." He died six months later.

Three years on, in 1949, there was a flurry of rumors that Fred Astaire—who had never, at the time, received a single nomination —was planning to retire. An Honorary Oscar was hurriedly organized to mark Astaire's "unique artistry and contributions to the technique of musical pictures." The rumors, of course, proved unfounded; and Astaire went on to win a Supporting Actor nomination twenty-five years later for *The Towering Inferno.* He lost to Robert De Niro.

Throughout the fifties the Academy continued to use the Honorary Oscars as poignant farewells to movie giants the Academy Awards had passed by. In 1952 it was Harold Lloyd, "master comedian and good citizen," in 1956 Eddie Cantor "for distinguished service to the film industry," in 1959 Buster Keaton "for his unique talents which brought immortal comedies to the screen," in 1960 Stan Laurel "for his creative pioneering in the field of cinema comedy." None of them had ever been so much as nominated.

Greta Garbo had been, three times: for *Anna Christie* and *Romance* in 1929–30, *Camille* in 1937 and *Ninotchka* in 1939. Each time, according to Frances Marion, she "merely shrugged her shoulders"; on losing to Luise Rainer, she "again shrugged her shoulders with indifference. An Oscar meant nothing to her." But Hollywood had never warmed to Garbo any more than she to Hollywood, and the Oscar electorate had preferred Norma Shearer, Luise Rainer and Vivien Leigh. By 1954 Garbo had not made a film for thirteen years, but the Academy's memory was jogged by a rare profile of the reclusive siren in *Life* magazine. To tick her name off the list of its most embarrassing oversights, the governors voted her an Honorary Oscar "for her unforgettable screen performances." Garbo did not, of course, turn up to accept it, but a chapter of movie folklore had been closed.

Lillian Gish received one belated nomination in 1946, when she lost the Supporting Actress award to Anne Baxter in *The Razor's Edge.* But Gish's citation was as much recognition of her successful transition from the era of silent film to the talkies, and indeed of her whole career, as of her specific performance in *Duel in the Sun.* The Academy has always adored gutsy comebacks, as in the case of Gloria Swanson in *Sunset Boulevard,* and an Honorary Oscar seemed long overdue in 1970, when Gish was rewarded for her "superlative artistry and for distinguished contribution to the progress of motion pictures." Had it not been for this award, it seems likely that Oscar schmaltz would have seen her a certain nominee—and winner—in 1987, when at the age of 90 she teamed up with Bette Davis for *The Whales of August.*

The voters had missed a trick in 1965, when Edward G. Robinson's poker player opposite Steve McQueen in *The Cincinnati Kid* might well have deprived Lee Marvin or Martin Balsam of an acting Oscar. Although a major star since the 1930s, and an actor of more versatility and range than he is given credit for, Robinson was never even nominated by the Academy in a fifty-year career that saw him grow from the definitive thirties gangster into a huge variety of sleuths, villains and other heavies. A brush with the House Un-American Activities Committee was partly responsible; though his name was cleared, Robinson's appearance before the committee was itself enough to see his career dip through most of the fifties and sixties. He had made his last screen appearance, opposite Charlton Heston in the science-fiction film *Soylent Green,* almost a decade before news of his mortal illness stung the Academy into organizing an Honorary Oscar in 1972. It marked his "greatness as a player, a patron of the arts and a dedicated citizen . . . in sum, a Renaissance man." Alas, Robinson died before he could receive it.

However worthy the recipient, even Honorary Awards are rarely voted without some discreet lobbying by family, friends or just fans of an aging, overlooked candidate. In 1973 it was Groucho Marx's companion Erin Fleming who successfully mobilized the governors, as Groucho himself acknowledged from the stage. Accepting an award citing his "brilliant creativity" and "the unequaled achievements of the Marx Brothers in the art of motion picture comedy," he said sadly: "I wish Harpo and Chico were here to share this great honor. And I wish Margaret Dumont were here too. She was a great straight woman, even though she never got any of my jokes. I'd like to thank Erin Fleming, who makes my life worth living and who understands all of my jokes."

An Honorary Oscar can also provide revenge, as it did in 1978 for the veteran director King Vidor, cheated of the very first Direction award by the Machiavellian Louis B. Mayer, and unsuccessfully nominated four more times in the subsequent thirty years. Twenty-two years after his last nomination in 1956, when his *War and Peace* lost to George Stevens's *Giant,* the 85-year-old director was at last rewarded "for his incomparable achievements as a cinematic creator and innovator." Receiving his Oscar from Audrey Hepburn, Vidor joked that it should offer inspiration to any other old-timers "who didn't make it the first twenty-five years."

Even before the curious case of Paul Newman, Honorary Oscars could come back to embarrass the Academy. In 1980 it made good its neglect of a frail and elderly Henry Fonda—nominated only once, forty years before, for *The Grapes of Wrath*—by laying on Robert Redford to present a special award to "the consummate actor, in recognition of his brilliant accomplishments and enduring contribution to the art of motion pictures." When word first spread that he might be dying, 75-year-old Fonda had been positively showered with lifetime achievement awards, the Oscar being merely the last in a chain stretching from the American Film Institute to the Golden Globes. With a fine anticipation of the Newman syndrome, however, Fonda proved the very next year that he was still quite capable of winning an Oscar in his own right, when he shared the top honors with Katharine Hepburn for *On Golden Pond*.

In 1981 it was the turn of 74-year-old Barbara Stanwyck, by then better known to younger audiences as a television star, to be compensated for four unsuccessful Best Actress nominations stretching from *Stella Dallas* in 1937 to *Sorry, Wrong Number* in 1948. In 1977, presenting an Oscar with William Holden, Stanwyck had been ambushed by an unrehearsed tribute. "Thirty-nine years ago this month," said Holden, "Barbara and I were working together in a film called *Golden Boy*. And it wasn't going well. I was going to be replaced. But due to this lovely human being, and her interest and understanding, and her professional integrity and her encouragement, and above all her generosity, I'm here tonight." Four years later, receiving the award from John Travolta for her "superlative creativity and unique contribution to the art of screen acting," Stanwyck repaid her recently deceased friend with an equally emotional tribute: "A few years ago I stood on this stage with William Holden as a presenter. I loved him very much, and I miss him. Bill always wished that I would get an Oscar. And so tonight, my golden boy, you've got your wish."

Some Honorary Awards are offered simply to make amends. In 1937, in memory of Hollywood's prematurely dead "Boy Wonder," the Irving Thalberg Memorial Award was established to honor the producer or director with "the most consistent high level of production achievement." It has been used, as have other Honorary Awards, to apologize for apparent aberrations on the part of the voters. It has been used as excess baggage for those already weighed down with statuettes and trophies. It has also been used to mollify filmmakers of undoubted distinction who simply slipped through the net.

Legend has it that Alfred Hitchcock's first nomination in 1940 made him a nervous wreck. He could not bring himself to attend the awards show, preferring to stay home in Beverly Hills, pacing up and down while wondering whether to listen in on the radio. "Okay, turn it on," he told his wife. "No, turn it off again." Mrs. Hitchcock's patience finally ran out. "Don't take it so seriously," she complained. "Remember that this is the group who gave an Oscar to Luise Rainer. Twice!"

Hitchcock's laughter dispelled his Oscar nerves for good. Just as well, for he was to fare badly with the electorate throughout his long and masterly career. Though one of the Academy's most conspicuous omissions, "Hitch" set little store by the annual hoopla, which saw him win five vain nominations—for *Rebecca* (1940), *Lifeboat* (1944), *Spellbound* (1945), *Rear Window* (1954) and *Psycho* (1960). He was beaten by John Ford (*The Grapes of Wrath*), Leo McCarey (*Going My Way*), Billy Wilder (*The Lost Weekend*), Elia Kazan (*On the Waterfront*), and Billy Wilder again (*The Apartment*).

Finally, in 1967, when *Torn Curtain* failed to win even a nomination, Hitchcock was offered the Academy's consolation prize of an Irving Thalberg Award. As he reached the stage, the audience settled back in expectation of the kind of vintage Hitchcock speech—witty, offbeat—which they knew so well from his TV series and after-dinner speeches. This promised to be one of those big "set-piece" moments so beloved of the Oscar show's producers.

"Thank you very much," was all Hitchcock chose to say, without expression, before walking off. "Some thought this brevity bespoke a quiet, lightly veiled contempt," wrote his biographer, Donald Spoto. "They were probably correct."

Among directors, for years, Hitchcock's absence from the Oscar scoreboard was regarded as the grossest oversight on the part of the Academy's fallible voters. But the past two decades have seen that distinction pass to the man who began his movie career by hiding out on Hitchcock's sets at Universal, and has since become the most commercially successful filmmaker of all time.

Steven Spielberg's films have among them won more than fifty

Oscar nominations, and almost twenty awards—but not one for their progenitor, who has lived through a series of bizarre and painful humiliations.

In 1975, *Jaws* won a nomination for Best Picture but not for Best Director; in 1977, with *Close Encounters of the Third Kind,* it was the other way around. In 1981, *Raiders of the Lost Ark* was the first Spielberg film to be nominated for both the top awards, but won neither; the same proved true of *E.T.* the following year, beaten by *Gandhi.* In 1984 *Indiana Jones and the Temple of Doom* won just two nominations, for Score and Visual Effects; and the following year came the biggest scandal yet, when *The Color Purple* won eleven nominations including Best Picture—but still no Director slot for Spielberg, although he had won the Directors Guild award. Another huge box-office success, *The Color Purple* joined *The Turning Point* as the only two films in Oscar history to win none of the eleven categories in which they were nominated.

What was it about Spielberg? His young arrogance? His huge wealth? His alleged inability to direct adult actors in mature dramas? To judge by *The Color Purple*'s three acting nominations, the Academy had overruled the last of these three objections. Arrogance had not prevented Oliver Stone from winning a slew of Oscars for films that could scarcely be called subtle; and wealth beyond the dreams of ordinary mortals had proved no handicap to the vast majority of Oscar winners. "He's too successful. He's too young. His genius is too great. They'll never give him the gold," said Clint Eastwood of Spielberg after the 1985 snub. Professional and fiscal jealousy do seem to have barred Spielberg's way, for all his good behavior around town, his support of the Academy and his stalwart work for Hollywood charities. Tinseltown's wunderkind was evidently being punished for producing the biggest box-office film of the year, *Back to the Future*—which failed to win its sole Oscar nomination, for Original Screenplay.

The following year, in 1986, Spielberg too was offered the Thalberg Award, which he accepted with good grace. On the podium, he joked that he was "resisting like crazy" the temptation to use Sally Field's famously arch line: "You like me, you really like me." Afterward, however, he waxed diplomatic: "I don't look upon this award as amends for anything that some people think I deserved a year ago." Pointing out that the award was a bust of Irving Thalberg, not an Oscar statuette, he made it clear that he was still laying down a defiant marker for future years.

That year Spielberg had produced the feature-length cartoon *An American Tail,* which also lost its only nomination (for Best Song, "Somewhere Out There"). Still the voters continued to rub salt in his wounds. In 1987 his *Empire of the Sun* was voted six nominations, all of them in the minor categories, and won none; in 1988 his production company's *Who Framed Roger Rabbit?* brought home yet more money and yet more technical awards. The third of his Indiana Jones trilogy, *The Last Crusade,* lost both its 1989 nominations, for Score and Sound, while *Back to the Future II* lost Visual Effects. In 1990 the Academy was wholly unimpressed by his latest attempt to prove his directing maturity, *Always,* and in 1991 by his latest overt assault on the box office, *Hook.* Again Spielberg proved a gracious enough loser to attend the Awards—this time, to present the Thalberg Award to his close friend and collaborator George Lucas, another immensely successful filmmaker whom the Academy had otherwise failed to honor.

But Spielberg will haunt the Oscars for many a year yet—living proof of the Academy's collective capacity for gracelessness, for honoring sentimental favorites at the expense of those few moviemakers capable of combining cinematic quality with the Midas touch. *E.T.,* an imaginative classic on a par with J. M. Barrie's *Peter Pan,* may be his only unequivocally Oscar-deserving product; and it was unlucky to come up against Attenborough's *Gandhi,* one of those worthily dull panoramas that announces its own importance so grandly that the Academy's electorate cannot fail to hear, duly installing it in their own dubious pantheon of high cinematic art.

Spielberg's ostracism from the Oscar arena has much in common with that of Cecil B. de Mille, the prototype Hollywood showman, who made himself unpopular enough to be denied a single nomination. His fellow Academicians even proved capable of nominating five other directors in 1952, when de Mille's *The Greatest Show on Earth* won Best Picture. The Academy leaped in with a consolation Thalberg Award—on top of the Special Award de Mille had already received three years before, after a long string of Spielberg-like snubs. Choosing their words, for once, with extreme care, the governors had given de Mille an Honorary Oscar to mark "thirty-seven years of brilliant showmanship" as a "distinguished motion picture pioneer."

Other maverick directors with passionate public followings, from America's Robert Altman to Britain's Ken Russell, have also inhabited an atmosphere too rarefied to win Academy Awards, despite having guided a number of actors into the winners' enclosure. Elsewhere in that atmosphere live and work a number of foreign directors who have inspired their Hollywood brethren toward filmmaking's Holy Grail, but have never themselves made the compromises required to win an Oscar. They may secure the occasional nomination, but that is merely to add class to the lists; the voters are never going to hand a legitimate Oscar to a Renoir, a Kurosawa, a Bergman. So the Academy has had to step in, lending itself a welcome artistic gloss in the process.

In 1945 Jean Renoir's sole Hollywood nomination as Best Director, for *The Southerner,* lost to Billy Wilder's *The Lost Weekend;* in 1974 he accepted an Honorary Oscar from Ingrid Bergman, hailed as "a genius who, with grace, responsibility and enviable devotion through silent film, sound film, feature, documentary and television, has won the world's admiration." Akira Kurosawa also received just one unsuccessful nomination—for *Ran,* in 1985, when the Best Director was Sydney Pollack for *Out of Africa.* The man he bumped out of the list that year, Steven Spielberg, proudly joined with George Lucas in 1989 to hand Kurosawa an Honorary Oscar for "accomplishments that have inspired, delighted, enriched and entertained audiences and influenced filmmakers throughout the world."

Two years later Audrey Hepburn traveled back to Hollywood to preside over the award of an Honorary Oscar to the Indian director Satyajit Ray, for his "rare mastery of the art of motion pictures and for his profound humanitarian outlook, which has had an indelible influence on filmmakers and audiences throughout the world." Too ill to attend, the director thanked Hollywood in a taped message from his Calcutta hospital bed. "I am very happy receiving Oscar. It is the highest award in the film world," he said, concluding poignantly, "I have nothing more to expect." Ray died three weeks later.

The tradition of honoring upmarket overseas directors, highly unlikely to win any Oscars from a commercially minded electorate, dates back to 1970. When the governors of the Academy voted him the Irving Thalberg Award, Ingmar Bergman was not sufficiently impressed to fly over to collect it. Picking it up for him, his private and professional partner, Liv Ullman, told the audience that Bergman was "sitting on his little island in the Baltic writing a new script." The director apparently believed that "he shows his respect and his gratefulness by staying home and finishing his script." The script turned out to be *Cries and Whispers,* which would win him a hopeless Best Director nomination in 1973, as did *Face to Face* in 1976 and *Fanny and Alexander* in 1983.

The Thalberg honors those who might not otherwise have made it—such as Mervyn LeRoy, nominated as a producer in 1939 for *The Wizard of Oz* and as a director in 1942 for *Random Harvest,* and finally handed the coveted bust in 1975. But the 1942 Thalberg went to *Random Harvest*'s producer, Sidney Franklin, who also won Best Picture that year for his other nominee, *Mrs. Miniver.* Spreading the goodies around like this can make the governors look guilty of overkill.

One dubious use of the Thalberg is to add to the already weighty laurels of producer-directors in years when their latest product has not quite made the grade. Nineteen fifty-three, for instance, was one of the few years George Stevens did not come good, when *From Here to Eternity* robbed his *Shane* of both Best Picture and Director. Although he had already won Best Director in 1951 for *A Place in the Sun,* and would win again in 1956 for *Giant,* Stevens was handed the 1953 Irving Thalberg as interim congratulations for *Shane.* It might have been better used to encourage one of the many filmmakers with empty trophy cabinets, rather than a man with two Oscars from eleven nominations—six as a producer and five as a director. Howard Hawks, for instance, received only one nomination throughout a fifty-year career: for *Sergeant York,* which won Gary Cooper the 1941 Best Actor award. Yet Hawks was never awarded the Thalberg, and had to wait until 1974 for an Honorary Oscar as "a master American filmmaker whose creative efforts hold a distinguished place in world cinema."

The Thalberg's record is extremely patchy. Jerry Wald, an unsuccessful Best Picture nominee for *Mildred Pierce, Johnny Belinda, Peyton Place* and *Sons and Lovers,* received it as compensation in

1948, the year *Johnny Belinda* lost to Olivier's *Hamlet* and the Oscars went into a xenophobic tailspin. In 1951 it was given to Arthur Freed, who anyway won the Best Picture Oscar that year for *An American in Paris,* and another in 1958 for *Gigi* (as well as an Honorary Award nine years later, for producing six Oscar telecasts). By 1963, the year it was his turn for the Thalberg, Sam Spiegel had already clocked up three Best Picture Oscars for *On the Waterfront, Bridge on the River Kwai* and *Lawrence of Arabia;* whereas Lawrence Weingarten had lost out twice in a forty-year career, for *Libeled Lady* (1936) and *Cat on a Hot Tin Roof* (1958), by the time Katharine Hepburn made her only Oscar appearance to hand him the Thalberg in 1973.

Pandro S. Berman deserved it. After six misses over twenty years, the producer of *The Gay Divorcée, Alice Adams, Top Hat, Stage Door, Father of the Bride* and *Ivanhoe* was finally given the Thalberg over forty years after his first nomination and a quarter of a century since his last.

Ray Stark had lost twice, for *Funny Girl* and *The Goodbye Girl,* when he accepted the Thalberg's solace in 1979. Eight years later David Puttnam told Charles Kipps, the features editor of *Variety:* "Ray Stark would kill for an Oscar. He'd do anything. If you told him he could buy one for ten million dollars, he'd be there with a check so fast, you wouldn't believe it. Why don't you ask him?" So Kipps did. Stark just smiled and cited his Thalberg, plus the "dozens and dozens of Oscar nominations and many Academy Awards in so many different categories" won by his films over the years.

No way were Albert ("Cubby") Broccoli's James Bond films going to win any Oscars beyond the technical categories, so he was persuaded to stop counting his money long enough to accept the Thalberg in 1981.

Walter Mirisch had already won his fair share, as producer of such Best Pictures as *The Apartment, West Side Story* and *In the Heat of the Night,* by the time he was given the Thalberg after his presidency of the Academy in 1977. Five years later he added the Jean Hersholt Humanitarian Award—a complete set of competitive and Honorary Oscars that remains unparalleled.

Compare Mirisch's record with that of his colleague Norman Jewison, with whom he had coproduced a 1966 Best Picture nominee, *The Russians Are Coming, the Russians Are Coming*—and who had been passed over as Best Director the following year for *In the Heat of the Night* even as it won Mirisch his third Best Picture Oscar. Both the Academy's voters and the board of governors alike have doggedly refused to hand the Canadian-born Jewison any return on five further nominations, as producer-director of *Fiddler on the Roof* (1971), producer of *A Soldier's Story* (1984) and producer-director of *Moonstruck* (1987). Jewison has even produced, directed and written box-office hits deemed unworthy of major Academy Awards, such as *The Thomas Crown Affair* (1968), *Jesus Christ Superstar* (1973) and *. . . And Justice for All* (1979). He has won Oscars for Mirisch and Rod Steiger, Cher and Olympia Dukakis, and nominations for Topol and Al Pacino, Leonard Frey and Vincent Gardenia, but somehow Jewison cannot seem to win anything for himself.

William Wyler, Robert Wise and Billy Wilder are also names that have appeared in the Oscar lists ad infinitum, with thirteen Oscars among them out of forty-two nominations. *Mrs. Miniver, The Best Years of Our Lives* and *Ben-Hur* won Wyler three Academy Awards out of twelve nominations as director and three nominations as producer; *West Side Story* and *The Sound of Music* won Wise four statuettes out of three nominations as director and three as producer; *The Lost Weekend, Sunset Boulevard* and *The Apartment* won Wilder six Oscars out of eight nominations as director, twelve as writer and one as producer. Yet all three were further honored with the Thalberg—Wyler in 1965, when he lost Best Director for *The Collector;* Wise in 1966, when he lost Best Picture for *The Sand Pebbles;* and Wilder in 1987, when he seemed due yet another Lifetime Achievement Award.

The first winner of the Irving Thalberg Award, Darryl F. Zanuck in 1937, was given two more in 1944 and 1950 to place alongside the three Best Picture Oscars he won in thirteen nominations. The first two were consolation prizes for losing with *In Old Chicago* and *Wilson;* the third was perhaps to adjust his balance as he carried home the Best Picture statuette for *All About Eve.*

Zanuck would have won another in 1949, had he not argued that the Thalberg was too important to be left to a mere plurality of the governors' votes. The winner should receive a two-thirds majority, he argued, or the award should not be made. The board adopted his suggestion, and it later emerged that Zanuck himself had been that year's leading candidate—falling one vote short of the requisite two-thirds. Nineteen forty-nine, the year his *Twelve O'Clock High* lost Best Picture to Robert Rossen's *All the King's Men,* thus became one of the twenty-four occasions in its fifty-five-year history that the Irving Thalberg Award has not been presented.*

Hal B. Wallis won the Thalberg twice, in 1938 and 1943. The first time around all three of his Best Picture nominees—*The Adventures of Robin Hood, Four Daughters* and *Jezebel*—had lost to Frank Capra's *You Can't Take It with You.* The next time, like Zanuck, Wallis also won Best Picture with *Casablanca* (as well as losing with a second runner, *Watch on the Rhine*). In 1939 David O. Selznick was given the Thalberg to add to the record eight Oscars won by *Gone with the Wind.* In 1941 it went to Walt Disney, who must have been pushed to find space for it alongside the record thirty-two Academy Awards he won in all—including his third Honorary Oscar that very same year.

Nineteen forty-six was the year Samuel Goldwyn won his first Best Picture award, at the seventh attempt, for *The Best Years of Our Lives.* It was also the year he was voted the Irving Thalberg. The following year Goldwyn was again a loser, for *The Bishop's Wife,* the last film for which he would ever be nominated. The next decade would see his fortunes slide; by the end of it, however, there was yet another free award on offer from the Academy.

In 1956, on the death of its sometime president, the actor Jean Hersholt, the Academy founded an award in his name to reward humanitarian work by film folk. Sam Goldwyn was its second recipient, in 1957. Though also sometimes abused, merely heaping yet more honors on those already groaning with them, the Hersholt Award has joined the Thalberg as a useful way of recognizing others whom the Oscars have passed by. In 1985, for instance, it went to 81-year-old Charles "Buddy" Rogers, the only man still alive who had attended the very first Oscar dinner in 1929, and who had indeed performed sterling service to such groups as the Boy Scouts of Amer-

* In 1990 the Thalberg Award went to Zanuck's son Richard (jointly with his partner David Brown), a year after he had won the Best Picture Oscar, at his third nomination, for *Driving Miss Daisy.*

ica and the Navy League. Rogers was "a regular fixture on skid row every Christmas," joked Bob Hope as he handed it over. The happy recipient, Mary Pickford's widower, said he would take it home and put it "proudly beside Mary's two Oscars."

Rogers's mention of Pickford's name served as a reminder of the Academy's less seemly use of Honorary Awards. There are times when it seems shameful to parade elderly former stars, their screen beauty long since faded, to squeeze some tawdry sentiment into an already oversentimental occasion. Such was the general consensus in 1990, when 85-year-old Myrna Loy was seen by satellite in her New York home, barely able to speak as she accepted an Honorary Oscar "in recognition of her extraordinary qualities both on screen and off, with appreciation for a lifetime's worth of indelible performances." This dubious tradition dates back to 1935, when a desperate Frank Capra sought to defeat the boycott threatened by the guilds —and thus to save the awards themselves from terminal collapse— by turning the occasion into a testimonial dinner to D. W. Griffith, whose movie proposals had long been shunned by Hollywood.

Ever since Capra dragged Griffith "out of cold storage," as Peter H. Brown put it, "one of Oscar's three rings has been reserved for fading or dying stars." Rarely was there a more excruciating Oscar sight than that of the skeletal, 83-year-old Mary Pickford, barely able to hold the Honorary Oscar handed over in 1976 by the Academy's president, Walter Mirisch. Pickford had won the second Best Actress award in 1928–29, for *Coquette*. But she remained one of the most popular stars in Hollywood's history (as well as one of its most astute financial operators), and the Oscar show's flagging TV ratings required another Griffith-style deus ex machina. Officially given "in recognition of her unique contribution to the film industry and the development of film as an artistic medium," the award really bespoke the Academy at its most desperate. Rogers, her husband, had vetoed a live appearance at the show because "the sheer excitement might prove too much for her"; but the indomitable Pickford lived on for another three years.

From Susan Hayward to Bette Davis, the elderly or dying stars wheeled on to provoke standing ovations and better ratings could make even Hollywood blush. A long series of apparently terminal illnesses could not keep Laurence Olivier away in 1984, when he matched Davis for geriatric ineptitude in stumbling over the nominees' names or forgetting them altogether. Already, with Davis, the holder of ten nominations—second only to Katharine Hepburn's twelve—Olivier was one of the select few to have received more than one Honorary Award, on top of his Best Actor award in 1948 for his *Hamlet,* the first non-American film ever to win Best Picture, for which he remains the only actor ever to direct himself to an Oscar. Two years before, in 1946, Olivier had been voted an Honorary Oscar to mark "his outstanding achievement as actor, producer and director in bringing *Henry V* to the screen"—and, in the process, to compensate for the patriotic voting that had preferred Fredric March as Best Actor and *The Best Years of Our Lives* as Best Film.

In 1978 Olivier happened to be passing through California while his son Richard was interviewing for a place at UCLA. He was already nominated as Best Actor for *The Boys from Brazil*—he would lose to Jon Voight in *Coming Home*—but the Academy seized the moment to present a Lifetime Achievement Award to a man already drowning in honors. It was enough to make a willing guest out of a perennial no-show; despite nine more nominations, the last time Olivier had attended was in 1939, when he had been up for *Wuthering Heights* and his wife-to-be, Vivien Leigh, had won for *Gone with the Wind.* Never the most circumspect of speakers, Olivier evidently intended to make up for lost time.

He was introduced by Cary Grant as the man who "represents the ultimate in acting." For two men who had met perhaps twice in their lives, Grant and Olivier had suddenly become a mutual appreciation society par excellence. "Those of us who have had the joy of knowing him since he came to Hollywood," Grant went on, "warmly and fondly, yet respectfully, call him Larry." Bearded for his forthcoming, lucrative cameo as Zeus in the absurd *Clash of the Titans,* Lord Olivier of Brighton proceeded to accept a second Honorary Oscar for "the full body of his work, for the unique achievements of his entire career and his lifetime of contribution to the art of film." Throwing away his cue cards—to the alarm of his retinue, who had seen and heard it all before—Olivier began:

> Oh, dear friends, am I supposed to speak after that? Cary, my dear old friend for many a year—from the earliest years of either of

Academy president Frank Capra (LEFT) saved the Oscars from extinction in 1935 by turning the awards ceremony into a tribute to "the father of the movies," D. W. Griffith (CENTER).

Richard Burton and Peter O'Toole—the Oscars' all-time losers, each without a single win from seven nominations—both won Best Actor nominations for *Becket* in 1964.

After winning no Oscars in five nominations, Alfred Hitchcock grudgingly accepted the Irving Thalberg award in 1967.

In 1971 the Academy made amends with an honorary award to Charlie Chaplin, another movie giant never to win a competitive Oscar.

> us working in this country—thank you for that beautiful citation and the trouble you have taken to make it and for all the warm generosities in it. Mr. President and governors of the Academy, committee members, fellows, my very noble and approved good masters,* my colleagues, my friends, my fellow students. In the great wealth, the great firmament of your nation's generosities, this particular choice may perhaps be found by future generations as a trifle eccentric, but the mere fact of it—the prodigal, pure, human kindness of it—must be seen as a beautiful star in the firmament which shines upon me at this moment, dazzling me a little, but filling me with warmth and the extraordinary elation, the euphoria that happens to so many of us at the first breath of the majestic glow of a new tomorrow. From the top of this moment, in the solace, in the kindly emotion that is charging my soul and my heart at this moment, I thank you for this great gift which lends me such a very splendid part in this, your glorious occasion. Thank you.

At the end of this incantation, the television cameras caught a wide-eyed, ecstatic Jon Voight half out of his seat, his hands high in the air, exclaiming, "Oh, wow!" Backstage, bumping into one of the show's writers, Buz Kohan, Olivier exclaimed: "God, I mucked that up. I had no idea what I was saying but I didn't want to stop." In next day's *New York Times,* John J. O'Connor reported that "Olivier lapsed into a curiously rambling, slightly sticky, extended metaphor about stars and firmaments."

Himself the recipient of an Honorary Oscar in 1969, it was Cary Grant whom the Academy chose again six years later, in 1984, to present an Honorary Award to James Stewart "for his fifty years of memorable performances," and for "his high ideals both on and off the screen." Nominated for Best Actor five times between 1939 and 1959, and the winner in 1940 for *The Philadelphia Story,* Stewart was 76 years old and had not appeared in a movie for six years. Reports of his imminent demise proved premature, but this ever popular figure indulged in some folksy reminiscence about the good old days of Frank Capra and the other directors who had "so generously and brilliantly guided me through the no-man's-land of my own intentions" before thanking "the audience—all you wonderful

* Shakespeare, *Othello,* Act I, Scene 3, line 77.

folks out there who have been so kind to me over the years. You've given me a wonderful life."

Many another Hollywood giant was deemed worthy of an extra Oscar to carry to the film world's pearly gates along with those they already possessed. In 1958, on hearing that he had been involved in a potentially fatal car crash, the Academy's governors hurriedly voted the Thalberg Award to Jack L. Warner; the old rogue lived another twenty years, but he never gave it back. In 1960, however, no one questioned their judgment in voting a spare Oscar to Gary Cooper. Nominated five times between 1936 and 1952, and voted Best Actor for *Sergeant York* (1941) and *High Noon* (1952), Cooper was still popular enough to be worth another statuette "for his many memorable screen performances and the international recognition he, as an individual, has gained for the motion picture industry."

In 1983 the Academy made another popular choice by honoring a giant of the silent era, and thus Oscar-less almost by definition. Ninety-one-year-old Hal Roach was best remembered for his pre-Oscar alliances with Harold Lloyd, Our Gang, and Laurel and Hardy; but he was enough of a survivor to have produced Lewis Milestone's fine 1939 film of John Steinbeck's novel, *Of Mice and Men,* and to have seen war service as an Army filmmaker before defecting, in its infancy, to television. In March 1992, at the age of 100, Roach was back in the Oscar-night audience to receive a standing ovation from his affectionate colleagues. He died six months later.

As in Roach's case, it is yet another hidden purpose of the Honorary Award to reward those who are never going to get an Oscar by any other means. "That master of fun, discoverer of stars, sympathetic, kindly, understanding comic genius," Mack Sennett, had already squeaked one in that 1932 recount; this did not stop him being honored in 1937 for his "lasting contribution to the comedy technique of the screen." But the same year saw the then governors stray to the outer reaches of show business by presenting an oh-so-cutesy, specially made wooden Oscar to the ventriloquist Edgar Bergen, in official recognition of "his outstanding comedy creation, Charlie McCarthy." In 1938 Shirley Temple was on parade to present Walt Disney with one Oscar and seven miniature ones "for *Snow White and the Seven Dwarfs,* recognized as a significant screen innovation which has charmed millions and pioneered a great new entertainment field for the motion picture cartoon." It was Disney's second Honorary Award, following one in 1932 "for the creation of Mickey Mouse."

In 1941, after Disney's *Fantasia* had become his first box-office flop, the Academy again compensated for both its voters' and the moviegoing public's inadequacies with special certificates to Disney and the entire *Fantasia* team, including the RCA company, for "their outstanding contribution to the advancement of the use of sound in motion pictures through the production of *Fantasia.*" The conductor Leopold Stokowski also received one for his "unique achievement in the creation of a new form of visualized music in . . . *Fantasia,* thereby widening the scope of the motion picture as entertainment and as an art form."

The following year Charles Boyer, a popular figure unlikely ever to convert his handful of Oscar nominations into a win, was voted an ingenious Honorary Award "for his progressive cultural achievement in establishing the French Research Foundation in Los Angeles as a source of reference for the Hollywood motion picture industry." In 1954 it was the turn of Danny Kaye, never Oscar-nominated, "for his unique talents, his service to the Academy, the motion picture industry, and the American people." Kaye later joined his friend Olivier as the recipient of a second Honorary Oscar—a well-deserved Jean Hersholt Humanitarian Award, in 1981.

Some Honorary Oscars have provoked controversy by appearing to rebuke the voters for making wrong choices. In 1958, for instance, *Gigi* won all nine of the categories for which it was up, including Best Screenplay, Director and Picture. Yet there had been not even a nomination for Maurice Chevalier, almost thirty years since he had been nominated at the third Academy Awards dinner in 1930, for *The Love Parade* and *The Big Pond.* After he had won the New York Film Critics award, MGM had more or less promised Chevalier an Oscar for *Gigi.* When the studio's might failed to win him even a nomination—there were murmurs, supposedly, about the Frenchman's dubious war record—it leaned heavily on the Academy's governors to deliver. Citing his "contribution to the world of entertainment for more than half a century," the board brazenly denied that there was any connection between this Honorary Oscar and Chevalier's absence from that year's electoral lists. The guy just happened to be in town. But it went down in some Oscar notebooks as a dangerous precedent.

Cary Grant, for instance, was precisely the kind of actor the voters were apt to overlook. A prototype Hollywood figure, immensely popular with audiences, Grant's gift for light comedy made him appear to lack the *gravitas* required for an award that takes itself so seriously. Though cited by many colleagues, from Olivier down, as the consummate screen actor, Grant was never even nominated for any of the great comic roles that showed (or perhaps concealed) his true skills: *The Awful Truth, Bringing Up Baby, His Girl Friday.* He was even passed over for a fine dramatic performance in Hitchcock's *North by Northwest.* Nominated only twice, for performances against type in *Penny Serenade* and *None But the Lonely Heart,* Grant spent twenty-five years as the quintessential Oscar refugee before the Academy set matters to rights in 1969.

His string of failures had upset Grant more than Hollywood realized. His conspicuous omission among *The Philadelphia Story*'s slate of 1940 nominees had apparently "deepened his inveterate sense of being an outsider . . . confirming his suspicions about the film community, convincing him that he was right to remain slightly apart and aloof from it." His subsequent failure to win nominations for his best work seemed to have wounded him even more than his failure to convert his two nominations into awards.

Now, for his "unique mastery of the art of screen acting," Grant was voted an Honorary Oscar "with the respect and affection of his colleagues." He was almost obliged to turn it down, thanks to a paternity suit that had turned him unusually publicity-shy. But it was three years since he had announced his official retirement, and he was unlikely to get another chance. "Thanks," he told the audience. "You're applauding my stamina." He paid tribute to all the great directors he had worked with: Hawks, Hitchcock, McCarey, Stevens, Cukor, Donen. "You know, I've never been a joiner or a member of any particular social set, but I've been privileged to be a part of Hollywood's most glorious era."

In 1972 it was the Jean Hersholt Award that came to the rescue of Rosalind Russell, another victim of the system who was not going to win an Academy honor any other way. After three unsuccessful nominations in the forties, and a last vain attempt with *Auntie Mame* in 1958, Russell had indeed become one of Hollywood's most vigorous charity workers, and fully deserved any humanitarian award going. If not quite a Lifetime Achievement Award, it was the next best thing.

Given changing styles of Oscar manipulation, decade by decade, Russell could claim to be one of the many deprived of a legitimate award by a system prone to anomalies. Not unaware of this, the Academy has frequently used Honorary Oscars as a fail-safe mechanism to right the wrongs inflicted by a fickle electorate. In 1942, for instance, after rendering his film ineligible with a last-minute change of deadline, an Academy in patriotic mood handed Noel Coward a special certificate "for his outstanding production achievement in *In Which We Serve.*" This did not stop the film being renominated the following year, when it lost to *Casablanca.*

Whenever the governors have either sensed or feared that an injustice might be done, Honorary Oscars have been standing ready. Olivier's *Henry V* is a classic case in point, proving (against the Academy's own code) that nomination is not in itself enough for an achievement as "outstanding" as Olivier's. "One of the greatest foreign films," said the citation, at a time when it was unthinkable for a non-American film to win Best Picture. "No play of classic theater was ever translated to celluloid with such faithful, flawless art." Olivier himself would soon rewrite all the ground rules, when his next Shakespeare film needed no special favors to carry the day, and to throw the Oscars into turmoil.

Picking winners regardless of the envelopes can, of course, go wrong—as it did that same year, when the Academy wanted to be sure that Harold Russell was rewarded for his courage in making a movie despite the loss of both his hands in the war. Fearing that he might not win Best Supporting Actor, for which he was nominated in *The Best Years of Our Lives,* the governors awarded Russell an Honorary Oscar "for bringing hope and courage to his fellow veterans." Within the hour he took the Oscar as well—thus winning two for the same performance, a feat that remains unique.

Did the governors occasionally peek inside those envelopes? It was a controversy that raged throughout the Oscars' middle years, although moments like this appeared to suggest not. In 1961, however, they seemed to have an uncanny way of knowing that the director Stanley Kramer, an unsuccessful nominee in 1958 for *The*

Defiant Ones, would again prove unlucky as his *Judgment at Nuremberg* squared up to the Oscar might of *West Side Story.* "Among his colleagues," as *The New York Times* discreetly put it, "Kramer the director has never quite achieved the status of Kramer the producer." That year's Irving Thalberg looked distinctly like a runner-up award, and may well have deprived Kramer of winning at his only other nomination, in 1967, for *Guess Who's Coming to Dinner.*

The presentation of Honorary Awards to compensate for voting vagaries has always been a hazardous business. It started in 1948, with the Academy's official regrets that its former president, Walter Wanger, had lost so much money on his latest vehicle for Ingrid Bergman. As Olivier's *Hamlet* carried off Best Film, an Honorary Oscar lauded Wanger's "distinguished service to the industry in adding to its moral stature in the world community by his production of the picture *Joan of Arc.*"

Three years later it seemed fairer that Gene Kelly, an unsuccessful nominee for *Anchors Aweigh* in 1945, should receive some recognition for the success of *An American in Paris;* as Arthur Freed lifted the Best Picture Oscar on the strength of Kelly's work, the dancer himself received an Honorary Oscar "in appreciation of his versatility as an actor, singer, director and dancer, and specifically for his brilliant achievements in the art of choreography on film." But this, too, soon proved another gambit which could go wrong. To compensate, again, for the lack of a choreography Oscar, the Academy voted an Honorary Award to Jerome Robbins "for his brilliant achievements in the art of choreography on film" in 1961—the year that he anyway won a Best Director statuette for *West Side Story.*

While overgarlanding some, the Academy has also proved capable of admitting that it has underrewarded others. In 1970, almost thirty years after their predecessors had humiliated him over *Citizen Kane,* the governors tried to make good the damage they had done Orson Welles's career with an Honorary Oscar "for superlative artistry and versatility in the creation of motion pictures." Not entirely forgiving, but unused to such institutionalized respect from his peers, Welles decided not to accept in person. In a taped message, he told his supposedly adoring public: "I hope they understand it means much more to me because it doesn't come from them, much less the critics."

John Huston, who picked up Welles's award for him, mused

that "although he was being paid this tribute, none of the studios was offering him a picture to direct." Huston thought Hollywood was "afraid" of Welles. "People who haven't his stamina, his force or his talent . . . standing close to him, their own inadequacies show up all too clearly. They're afraid of being overwhelmed by him."

Mickey Rooney was another species of movie thoroughbred whose only reward from the Academy had been one of the patronizing miniature statuettes it had once handed out to child stars.* By 1982, at the age of 62, Rooney was deemed worthy of an Honorary Oscar "in recognition of his sixty years of versatility in a variety of memorable film performances." An unsuccessful four-time nominee over four decades—the first for *Babes in Arms* in 1939 and the most recent for *The Black Stallion* in 1979—Rooney reminded his audience that at 19 he had been "the world's number one star. When I was forty, nobody wanted me. I couldn't get a job." Then came *Sugar Babies,* which resurrected his career. Understandably, perhaps, Rooney continued with a litany of the other awards he had recently won, so that this Oscar didn't look too much like an act of charity. The solemnity was cleverly punctured with a laugh at the end: "I'd love to kiss even Louis B. Mayer."

But the cruelest Oscar hard-luck story paled beside that of the composer Alex North, who had recorded no fewer than fourteen unsuccessful nominations for a series of memorable movie scores over thirty-five years, not to mention one for Best Song.† The Academy was goaded into action in 1985, when a lack of entries of sufficient quality caused the abandonment of the Music Score (Adaptation) category, thus ruling out of contention North's score

* The miniature Oscars were invented in 1934, at the suggestion of Fredric March, as a way of involving Shirley Temple in the Awards show. Judy Garland, Deanna Durbin and the 19-year-old Rooney followed in 1939, the year he lost for *Babes in Arms.* Other recipients were Margaret O'Brien (1944), Peggy Ann Garner (1945), Claude Jarman, Jr. (1946), Ivan Jandl (1948), Bobby Driscoll (1949), Jon Whiteley and Vincent Winter (1954). The notion was revived for *Polyanna*'s Hayley Mills in 1960; since then child stars such as *Kramer vs. Kramer*'s 8-year-old Justin Henry have competed on equal terms in the main categories. One of them, Tatum O'Neal (*Paper Moon,* 1973), even managed to win at the ripe old age of 10.

† North's unsuccessful nominations were for *Death of a Salesman* and *A Streetcar Named Desire* (both 1951), *Viva Zapata!* (1952), *The Rose Tatoo* (1955), *The Rainmaker* (1956), *Spartacus* (1960), *Cleopatra* (1963), *The Agony and the Ecstasy* (1965), *Who's Afraid of Virginia Woolf?* (1966), *The Shoes of the Fisherman* (1968), *Shanks* (1974), *Bite the Bullet* (1975), *Dragonslayer* (1981) and *Under the Volcano* (1984). In 1955 his eponymous title music for the film *Unchained Melody* (written with Hy Zaret), which subsequently became a contemporary classic, lost to Sammy Fain and Paul Francis Webster's "Love Is a Many-Splendored Thing," from the movie of the same name.

for *Prizzi's Honor.* Possibly the best-deserved Honorary Oscar of all time was handed over by Quincy Jones in recognition of North's "brilliant artistry in the creation of memorable music for a host of distinguished motion pictures."

A far cry from the copiously neglected are those figures whom the Academy has already honored, but cannot resist garlanding again. Often, like those with one foot in Forest Lawn, they add a touch of class to a TV show always in need of extra ratings appeal. Sometimes, they merely symbolize the closed world of Hollywood, at which the paying public must feel privileged to play voyeur—as in the case, for instance, of the 1970 Jean Hersholt Award to Frank Sinatra, who had won his acting Oscar in 1953 and been a frequent participant ever since. "To Mr. and Mrs. John Doe," crooned Sinatra, holding out his Oscar toward the television audience, "I want you to reach out and get your share." The cameras cut to his daughter, Nancy, in tears.

Sir Alec Guinness, 1957's Best Actor, looked suitably surprised more than two decades later to be handed the unexpected bonus of an Honorary Oscar "for advancing the art of screen acting through a host of memorable and distinguished performances." Having most recently advanced the art by taking gross points in *Star Wars,* Guinness confessed to feeling "fraudulent" about accepting; but he was "grabbing this" (from a well-behaved Dustin Hoffman) "while the going's good."

No Thalberg has seemed more otiose than that handed in 1987 to Billy Wilder, already the possessor of six Oscars from twenty-one nominations. Wilder began an overlong acceptance speech by thanking "all the millions of fans I have all over the world," then sent a get-well message to his collaborator I. A. L. Diamond, who was to die ten days later. A touch more class was added in 1990 by Sophia Loren, voted an Honorary Oscar as "one of the genuine treasures of world cinema who, in a career rich with memorable performances, has added permanent luster to our art form." Thirty years after she had become the only woman to win Best Actress for a foreign-language performance, a magnificent-looking Loren managed to upstage a host of actresses thirty years younger.

If such awards come out of left field, the Academy is not above more overt use of the Oscar to look after its own. It seemed perfectly acceptable, back in 1948, to honor a titan of the industry whose time had come and gone. As a producer, Adolph Zukor had been a losing nominee in the first year of the Academy Awards, for *The Way of All Flesh;* twenty years later he was hailed as "a man who has been called the father of the feature film in America, for his services to the industry over a period of forty years." It was a dozen years since Zukor had lost control of Paramount, and he was 76 years old. But how were the Academy's governors to know that he would live to be 103?

There was rather more muttering in 1950, when an Honorary Oscar was voted to a man with a cupboardful, Louis B. Mayer, the founding father of the Academy—and thus, albeit inadvertently, of the Academy Awards. Having manipulated them to his own benefit all those years, and made many enemies in the process, Mayer received a rather bald citation simply "for distinguished service to the motion picture industry." As in the case of Zukor, however, the timing of the award seemed more to do with the fact that he was in the throes of losing control of his beloved MGM.

Another way to win an Oscar—besides, that is, inventing them —is to serve as president of the Academy, which has been quick to honor its outgoing leaders. Examples include Douglas Fairbanks, Sr. (1939), Walter Wanger (a special plaque, 1945), Jean Hersholt (1949), Charles Brackett (1957) and Gregory Peck (the Hersholt Award, 1967, in addition to his 1962 Best Actor award). Long-serving Academy personnel have also received a legion of special awards.

Even an actor with as remarkable a career as Ralph Bellamy, nominated in 1937 and rediscovered in the 1980s, owed his 1986 Honorary Oscar less to his one hundred films than to his curriculum vitae within the industry: president of Actors Equity for twelve years, founder-member of the Screen Actors Guild and long-serving governor of the Academy. Other industry figures to be so honored, often for shrewdly political reasons, have included the Chinese Theatre's Sid Grauman (1948, for "raising the standard of exhibition of motion pictures"), the censor Joseph Breen (1953, for "his conscientious, open-minded and dignified management of the Motion Picture Production Code") and the "enlightened" labor leader Charles S. Boren (1972, "architect of [the industry's] policy of nondiscrimination").

The Academy has handed out awards to Army personnel (Colonel Nathan Levinson, 1940, for his Army training films) and the producers of the Oscar telecasts (Arthur Freed, 1967). It has honored the creators of Woody Woodpecker (Walter Lantz, 1978) and Uncle Remus (James Baskett, 1947). In 1966 it gave its supreme prize to a stuntman, Yakima Canutt—precursor of the movement in the early 1990s to introduce an annual Oscar for stuntmen into the regular categories.

In 1936 the Academy gave a corporate Oscar to the March of Time "for having revolutionized the newsreel." Ever since, other institutions have occasionally found Oscars coming their way, from the Department of Film at New York's Museum of Modern Art to the National Endowment for the Arts and the National Film Board of Canada. Since 1953, when Twentieth Century Fox was awarded an Honorary Oscar for the invention of CinemaScope, technical achievements have also been rewarded. Companies such as Bell & Howell, the Bausch & Lomb Optical Company and Eastman Kodak have found Honorary Oscars glamorizing their workaday lives. In 1981 the Academy institutionalized an annual award for such craftsmanship with the introduction of an Oscar in memory of Gordon E. Sawyer for "technical contributions that have brought credit to the motion picture industry."

Among the other Oscars few get to hear about are those for technical expertise beyond the existing categories. Before the introduction of a Makeup award, as a result of the Academy's embarrassment over *The Elephant Man,* special Oscars were handed in 1964 to William Tuttle for *7 Faces of Dr. Lao,* and in 1968 to John Chambers for *Planet of the Apes.* The lack of a choreography Oscar, which saw those all but redundant Oscars going to Gene Kelly and Jerome Robbins, led to a Special Award in 1968 to Onna White for *Oliver!* Choreography was a vital element in Carol Reed's British film becoming only the sixth musical since the war—and the last to date—to win Best Picture.

But the best way to win an Oscar, without ever having received a single nomination in a long screen career, is quite simply to be Bob Hope—whose loyalty to the Academy and its awards over five decades has paid off with an unmatched degree of sycophancy from his employers. Hope has received no fewer than five Honorary Awards: a silver plaque in 1940 "in recognition of his unselfish services to the motion picture industry"; life membership in 1944 "for his many services to the Academy"; an Oscar in 1952 "for his contribution to the laughter of the world, his service to the motion picture industry, and his devotion to the American premise"; the Jean Hersholt Humanitarian Award in 1959; and the Academy's Gold Medal in 1965 for his "unique and distinguished service to our industry and the Academy."

If some Oscars, therefore, are more honorary than others, there are occasional figures who cut across all the politics behind them. The supreme example is Charlie Chaplin, who was handed an emergency Oscar at the first awards in 1928 for his "versatility and genius in writing, acting [in], directing and producing *The Circus*"—and a second in 1971, after a lifetime in exile, "for the incalculable effect he has had in making motion pictures the art form of this century."

If it was Hollywood's whims that deprived a giant like Chaplin of a competitive Oscar, they also spared the Academy's blushes by voting *virtually* Honorary Oscars to such figures as John Wayne, whose Best Actor victory in 1969 was tantamount to a community long-service award. Had the voters not given way to sentiment—telling the world that Wayne gave a better performance in *True Grit* than Richard Burton in *Anne of the Thousand Days,* Peter O'Toole in *Goodbye, Mr. Chips,* or Dustin Hoffman and Jon Voight in *Midnight Cowboy*—the governors would surely have felt obliged to vote Wayne an Honorary Oscar before his death ten years later. Numerous other legitimate Oscars have come perilously close to this category, as do those awarded as compensation for missing out in the past—thus creating the long list of otherwise deserving cases who won their Oscar for the wrong performance.

Wayne's coronation may have shut out Burton and O'Toole, the Oscars' joint all-time losers, but a win for either of them in that particular year would also have been a sentimental injustice.* The first example of a consolation or "holdover" award came as early as

* O'Toole should have been a first-time victor. His *Lawrence of Arabia* in 1962 was a classic candidate for the ranks of irresistible debut winners; but he was unlucky to come up against an overdue Gregory Peck in *To Kill a Mockingbird.* O'Toole's other defeats came at the hands of Rex Harrison, Cliff Robertson, John Wayne, Marlon Brando, Robert De Niro and Ben Kingsley. Burton deserved to win at his fifth nomination in 1966 and to create an Oscar precedent by sharing the top honors with his wife, Elizabeth Taylor, for *Who's Afraid of Virginia Woolf?* But he was obliged to concede graciously to a compatriot, Paul Scofield, in one of those freak victories by a screen debutant rarely seen since. The other actors deemed better than Burton were Anthony Quinn, William Holden, Rex Harrison, Lee Marvin, John Wayne and Richard Dreyfuss.

1935, the Oscars' eighth year, when even the winner, Bette Davis, said that Katharine Hepburn should have won for *Alice Adams.* Davis's win in *Dangerous* was public atonement for the injustice done her the previous year in *Of Human Bondage.*

Robert Donat's win in 1939, for his version of *Goodbye, Mr. Chips,* was also a clear apology for his loss the previous year—in a better performance in *The Citadel*—to Spencer Tracy in *Boys Town.* This kind of tactical voting has always created laughable chain reactions, adding insult to other actors' injuries. By consoling Donat, the voters failed to give the 1939 award to what was clearly the year's best performance, by James Stewart in *Mr. Smith Goes to Washington.* The following year, therefore, they felt obliged to vote for Stewart in *The Philadelphia Story,* thus shutting out Chaplin in *The Great Dictator,* not to mention Henry Fonda in *The Grapes of Wrath,* who was himself forced to remain unconsoled until his Honorary Oscar forty years later.

While the Honorary Oscars have been used to make amends, some actors not quite up to them have proved luckier than others. Julie Andrews won an Oscar for *Mary Poppins* because she had not been cast in *My Fair Lady.* Actresses, more than actors, tend to create a momentum that makes victory at their umpteenth nomination a virtual inevitability: cases of Best Actresses winning for the wrong performance abound, from Susan Hayward to Ellen Burstyn and Faye Dunaway. But they are not complaining. Even though the Honorary Oscars have been used to sweep up many deserving cases, many of them wronged by historical accidents, there still remains a striking list of major film performers absent from the Academy's roll of honor. The hard-luck stories of the stars only add, of course, to the Oscars' magic. But the Academy's claim to honor performers of real distinction must stand alongside a gallery of those to have missed out—as yet, in some cases—on Hollywood's Holy Grail.

A Special Award should really have been created for the likes of Burton and O'Toole. A popular winner would have been that great supporting actress Thelma Ritter, who received six nominations in twelve years, from *All About Eve* in 1950 to *Birdman of Alcatraz* in 1962, and somehow managed to lose them all. Deborah Kerr also won none of her six nominations, between *Edward, My Son* in 1949 and *The Sundowners* in 1960—not even her Anna opposite Yul Brynner's victorious King of Siam in *The King and I.* The most conspicuous omission among contemporary male stars is Al Pacino, who in 1990 joined Ritter on six unsuccessful nominations over eighteen years—four Leading Roles sandwiched between two supporting nominations, from *The Godfather* in 1972 to *Dick Tracy* in 1990. After the 1990 awards, Glenn Close ranked as the most consistent recent female loser, with nothing to show for five nominations in eight years, from *The World According to Garp* in 1982 to *Reversal of Fortune* in 1990, for which her costar Jeremy Irons won Best Actor.

Upon her death in 1992 Marlene Dietrich joined the ranks of movie legends not to have been rewarded with any kind of Oscar, Honorary or otherwise. Nominated in 1930–31 for *Morocco,* Dietrich's problem seems to have been that she was about as popular in Hollywood as Garbo, the MGM star to whom she was supposed to be Paramount's answer. Defiantly anti-Nazi in the 1930s, she became an American citizen at about the same time that her movie career went into decline, but largely hid herself away from the world.

Other great movie names not even given consolation prizes by 1992 included several evergreen Hollywood figures of the kind the community tends to honor sooner or later. Kirk Douglas, for instance, is a three-time nominee unlucky to be beaten in 1956 by Yul Brynner, and rash enough to hand over to his son Michael the production rights to *One Flew Over the Cuckoo's Nest.* "I would like to win an Oscar because it is an award given by your peers," he muttered in 1984. "The Oscars have been more fair than most other awards . . . how they could not give it to me was a bit of stupidity." After winning his own for *Wall Street* in 1988, Michael Douglas said of his father: "He was nominated three times and by the luck of the draw never selected. And luck is what it really is. I hope I was clear that I share this with him."

A certain woodenness has not hampered other big box-office names, past or present; so it seems somewhat unfair that Robert Mitchum, nominated in 1945 for *The Story of G.I. Joe,* is now seen more in TV miniseries than at the Oscar show. Tony Curtis, nominated in 1958 for *The Defiant Ones,* and another victim of the Academy's absurd disdain for *Some Like It Hot,* was unlucky not to be recognized for stepping out of character as *The Boston Strangler* in 1968. It seems amazing that such names as Lauren Bacall and Glenn

Ford have hung around all these years without winning the Academy's blessing. But perhaps the most surprising name still to be Oscar-free is that of Douglas Fairbanks, Jr., son of the Academy's first president.

Lists of the overlooked are bound, of course, to be highly personal. Setting aside those whose time has yet to come, however, a selection of eligible names who have never won so much as a nomination would be headed by Alan Alda, Catherine Deneuve, Mia Farrow, Christopher Plummer, Martin Sheen, Donald Sutherland and Eli Wallach.

But any roll of honor of the Oscar-less should give priority to those with no chance to make amends. Defeated nominees who remain surprising omissions, and died without even an Honorary Oscar, include Montgomery Clift (nominated 1948, 1951, 1953, 1961), John Garfield (1938, 1947), Leslie Howard (1932–33, 1938), Steve McQueen (1966), James Mason (1954, 1966, 1982), Merle Oberon (1935), William Powell (1934, 1936, 1947), Peter Sellers (1964, 1979) and Irene Dunne (1930–31, 1936, 1937, 1939, 1948). Unlucky supporting actors included Charles Bickford (1943, 1947, 1948), Claude Rains (1939, 1943, 1944, 1946) and Sydney Greenstreet (1941).

The roll call of other great Hollywood names who died without any Academy recognition, whether competitive or honorary, includes (in alphabetical order) such stars as:

Dana Andrews, Edward Arnold, Lucille Ball, Tallulah Bankhead, John Barrymore, Constance Bennett, Lon Chaney, Joseph Cotten, Dolores del Rio, Colleen Dewhurst, W. C. Fields, Errol Flynn, John Gilbert, Betty Grable, Sir Cedric Hardwicke, Jean Harlow, Rita Hayworth, Al Jolson, Boris Karloff, Alan Ladd, Veronica Lake, Gertrude Lawrence, Peter Lorre, Ida Lupino, Fred MacMurray, Joel McCrea, Herbert Marshall, Marilyn Monroe, Zero Mostel, Pat O'Brien, Dick Powell, Tyrone Power, George Raft, Paul Robeson, Will Rogers, Ann Sheridan, Robert Taylor, Mae West . . . and no doubt many more, according to taste.

As yet, anyway, the governors have even failed to vote an Honorary Academy Award to a former cohost of the Oscar show who also served as a president of the Screen Actors Guild, and has since returned from a temporary sojourn on the East Coast to dwell in their midst again: Ronald Reagan.

Britain's traditionally strong showing in the acting awards continued in 1990 with a Best Actor Oscar for Jeremy Irons, as Claus von Bulow in Barbet Schroeder's Reversal of Fortune.

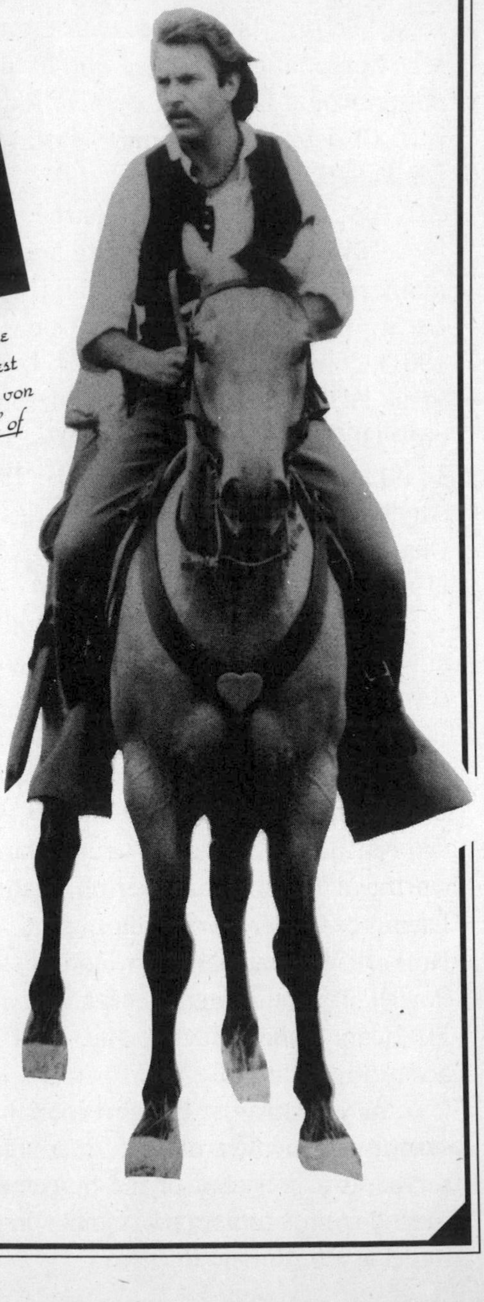

Among Dances With Wolves's twelve 1990 nominations were three for Kevin Costner as actor, director, and producer—a treble previously achieved only by Orson Welles and Warren Beatty. As well as winning Best Picture, Costner joined the select few to win an Oscar for his directorial debut.

12

Who's Afraid of Dancing with Wolves?

Whether Hollywood likes it or not, the voter casts his ballot emotionally, not critically.

—Henry Rogers

How were the campus radicals of the 1960s faring at thirtysomething? *The Big Chill,* one of the cult movies of 1983, set out to provide some modish answers. "We were great then," they concluded, "and we're shit now." Its screenplay written by a former social worker, its soundtrack embellished by vintage sixties hits, the film baptized an ensemble of movie talent, most of which has since continued to rise: William Hurt, Kevin Kline, Jeff Goldblum and Tom Berenger, Glenn Close, Mary Kay Place, Meg Tilly and Jobeth Williams. "The feel-good movie of the year," enthused *Time* magazine. "The eight star actors deserve one big Oscar."

They won none. But there was another, even less fortunate kindred spirit, whose performance wound up on the cutting-room floor. As the tragically dead friend at whose funeral the college alumni regather, he had filmed a number of flashbacks with which the director, Lawrence Kasdan, eventually decided to dispense. Appearing merely as a corpse, his fleeting appearance not even meriting a credit, was one Kevin Costner—whose celluloid revenge would be swift and absolute. After a number of solid if unexceptional performances—most notably as Eliot Ness opposite Oscar-winning Sean Connery in Brian De Palma's *The Untouchables*—Costner set out to show that he was more than merely a competent jobbing actor. Within him lurked the makings of movie greatness.

In the early spring of 1991, still reeling from his son's conviction for manslaughter, Marlon Brando had nothing public to say about Costner's *Dances with Wolves,* one of 1990's most talked-about movies. Yet it seemed to be just the film Brando had called for in 1973, when he sent Sacheen Littlefeather onstage to reject his Oscar for *The Godfather* and protest Hollywood's treatment of the American Indian. Almost two decades later, Costner's glossy epic had at last made Brando's scenario flesh, painting "the white man," especially the U.S. Army, as the villain of a historical piece in which the Sioux are a civilized, peace-loving people with a legitimate prior claim to the land from which they were ruthlessly evicted. "I had never known a people so eager to laugh, so devoted to family, so dedicated to each other," mused Costner's Union soldier, Lieutenant Dunbar, who of course goes native. "The only word that sprang to mind was harmony."

When Costner had first touted his audacious project around town in 1988, the only word that sprang to studio minds was no. Despite the popularity of the 1970s "spaghetti" strain, the Western had long been written off as a movie genre even before its final Oscar flicker with *Butch Cassidy and the Sundance Kid* in 1969. If Arthur Penn's *Little Big Man* troubled its ghost the following year, Michael Cimino's *Heaven's Gate* finally laid it to rest in 1980: a $44 million disaster that discredited cowboy-and-Indian films for all time. Apart from the bratpack appeal of *Young Guns I* and *II, Heaven's Gate* looked like the end of the line for a genre which had spawned seven thousand movies in seventy-five years.

Another ten years, and another directorial stranger strode into town with yet another dream. "Genres," he said, "are not dead as long as they are treated with sophistication." Kevin Costner, so rumor had it, was looking to make his own Western—despite the failure of Kasdan's *Silverado,* in which he himself had again figured, to arrest the Western's death throes five years before. But that was not all. For an actor with just six leading roles behind him, out of fourteen films in nine years, Costner's plans were unusually ambitious. When the full details got around, local wags soon rechristened his project "Kevin's Gate."

Costner's mid-1860s Western was going to be three hours long. It would feature Native American actors speaking large chunks of dialogue in the Sioux tribe's authentic Lakota language—complete with subtitles, traditional box-office poison. The film would boast no stars beside Costner himself, who would also be producing and directing, both for the first time—and insisting on control of the final cut. Not since Orson Welles's *Citizen Kane* fifty years before had an actor's directorial debut sounded quite so audacious.

Costner was planning on a truly epic scale: an $18 million budget involving 130 shooting days in sixteen scattered South Dakota locations, with a cast of 48 speaking roles and a crew of 150 swelling to personnel of more than 500 including extras. The film's centerpiece was to be a stampede of 3,500 buffalo, a species now virtually extinct in the American west. Its polemical theme—the wrongs done the Native Americans by the boorish, uncomprehending white man—would be played out against the majestic panorama of America's oldest frontier, in the tender cinematographic hands of Dean Semler. *Dances with Wolves,* according to Costner's sales pitch, would be "about confusion and the desire to communicate, out of which comes friendship—which I think is a really good lesson, almost globally."

By November 1988, Costner declared that he was glad to have been turned down by six Hollywood studios. It would give him the freedoms he needed, he decided, and gamely got on with his acting career. On location for *Revenge* in Cuernavaca, Mexico, he received a visit from an enterprising British distributor, Guy East of Majestic, who was intrigued by the grapevine gossip about his plans. East knew a thing or two about Oscars, having been head of Goldcrest's sales team while the company won nineteen of them; from the stage of the 1990 awards, while collecting the Best Picture Oscar with her husband, Lili Zanuck had thanked Majestic for its role in making *Driving Miss Daisy* possible. Over dinner that Mexican evening, on the whitewashed wall of a local cafe, Costner treated East to a slide show of the locations he had already scouted for *Dances with Wolves,* matching them to his storyboard, and explaining his intentions in meticulous detail. The following day, he even donned his cavalry uniform and mounted a horse to show his potential investor from Britain how his Dunbar would look. East was sufficiently impressed to guarantee half the $18 million; Costner, prepared to defer his own salary if necessary, was on his way.

Though cunningly attuned to its times, Costner's theme was not really as original as his marketing team was to make out. The white man's mistreatment of the American Indian had first been explored as long ago as a 1927 silent, *Spoilers of the West*. The most notable break with movie cliché came in 1950 with Delmer Daves's *Broken Arrow,* in which James Stewart played an 1870s ex-soldier who befriends a fierce Apache chief and falls for an Apache maiden. For once, celluloid Indians were no longer the stock villains of cinema tradition—primitive savages barring the westering progress of civilization, whooping their way down a scalp-laden warpath; they were a noble people worthy of white respect, with their own codes of honor and decency. Now it was the white man's turn to play the baddie: boorish, unscrupulous and distinctly forked of tongue.

Daves's seminal Western sired a trail of movies offering the Indian more sympathetic portrayal, and musing to mixed effect upon the burden of white guilt. Its immediate heirs were Anthony Mann's *Devil's Doorway* (1950), Robert Aldrich's *Apache* (1954), John Ford's *Cheyenne Autumn* (1964) and Abraham Polonsky's *Tell Them Willie Boy Is Here* (1969). The 1970s saw debunking Westerns of wildly varying quality: *Soldier Blue, Doc, Little Big Man* and *Buffalo Bill and the Indians* all reexamined Western myths in the context of the sixties and the Vietnam War, while *A Man Called Horse* anticipated Costner by employing huge tracts of Indian dialogue (but without subtitles).

Altman's *McCabe and Mrs. Miller,* Penn's *Missouri Breaks,* Peckinpah's *The Wild Bunch* and *Pat Garrett and Billy the Kid* were all forlorn elegies to a vanished West, as mythical as any movie scenario. More recently, and more realistically, a Native American Producers Consortium had helped midwife such Indian-made films as Jonathan Wacks's *Powwow Highway* (1989). More than forty such projects, involving stars from Redford and De Niro to Daniel Day-Lewis and Lou Diamond Phillips, were slated for production by the time Costner's epic opened to huge acclaim. Its producer-director-star was confident enough to tell the *Los Angeles Times:* "It's a dumb first movie. Full of kids, animals, first-time actors speaking in a foreign language. A period piece on top of that. My friends are afraid I'm going to be eaten up. . . . But I don't care what Hollywood thinks. And you can underline that."

Cunningly, Costner's version of the genre made its pitch through contemporary concerns. "I've always wanted to see the frontier," says Costner's Dunbar, "before it's gone." This was "hindsight talking, not history," in the view of one London critic, Geoff Brown. Dunbar later salutes the Sioux's pride in fighting for food and family rather than warring over "some dark political objective"; once again Costner's screenwriter, Michael Blake, was putting a late twentieth century "spin" on events.

Perhaps it should come as no surprise that Costner's degree from California State University, Fullerton, was in marketing. Orion, the U.S. distributor with which he finally joined forces, followed his lead in downplaying the film's doom-laden Western angle, emphasizing instead its ecological vibrations, promoting it as a grand-scale, life-affirming epic with magnificent panoramic photography and an almost documentarylike portrayal of Native American life. Witness the evidence of a Native American academic, Patricia Nelson Limerick, associate professor of history at the University of Colorado:

> With gifts not found in the average Western American historian, Kevin Costner has been a valuable messenger, carrying a vital lesson on conquest to a wide audience. . . . Virtually every scene in *Dances with Wolves* reawakens us to the power of nature in the West. This is the most photogenic of the nation's regions; its mountains, deserts and plains virtually audition for the camera. Too often used to sell cigarettes and silly adventure tales, that visual power could be enlisted on behalf of stories that genuinely help us understand, and live responsibly, in the West.

The ploy worked: by the time 1990's Academy Awards ballots went out, Costner's $18 million "folly" had broken the magic $100 million box-office barrier. With its success reinforced by a lavish trade-advertising campaign, and a 144-page glossy booklet about its genesis mailed to all Academy members, *Dances with Wolves* picked up twelve Oscar nominations—including Best Picture, Director and Actor for Costner himself, a treble previously achieved only by Orson Welles (*Citizen Kane,* 1941), Woody Allen (*Annie Hall,* 1977) and Warren Beatty (*Heaven Can Wait,* 1978, and *Reds,* 1981).

The rapidity of Costner's rise up the Hollywood power ladder was approached only by that of a somewhat gawky, skinny young Georgian, whose overlarge mouth could flash a multimillion dollar smile.

In April 1990, on a cold and windy night in Wilmington, North Carolina, a 23-year-old actress making only her seventh feature film suddenly turned prima donna.

On the umpteenth take of a scene that required her to be wet, bedraggled and all but naked, Julia Roberts decided that enough was enough. If she was to carry on working in these bone-chilling conditions, she announced, she required some solidarity from the crew. She would not continue unless they too agreed to take off most of their clothes.

The moment has gone down in recent Hollywood folklore as the first sign of Roberts's metamorphosis into a true movie star. Her bemused director, Joseph Ruben, veteran of such productions as *The Stepfather* and *True Believer,* was amazed to hear himself telling his crew to take their trousers off. Roberts called it "bonding." The crew called it crazy, and many of them walked off the set—leaving Ruben, minus most of his technical team, in danger of losing his authority as well as his pants.

The director later conceded that he should have told Roberts to shut up and get on with it. "But I was at a low ebb, and Julia was so cold, and having such a hard time, and somehow her request did not seem so unreasonable. . . . With the benefit of hindsight, I think it was *very* unreasonable."

There was another reason Ruben felt obliged to bow to his young leading lady's every whim. When shooting had begun on *Sleeping with the Enemy,* Julia Roberts had been a talented but still rising actress, dependent largely on her toothy grin, not too proud to take over a role rejected by Kim Basinger. Despite a recent Oscar nomination, as a supporting player in *Steel Magnolias,* Roberts had yet to make her personal mark at the box office. Apart from some critical attention as a waitress in the cult hit *Mystic Pizza,* her other appearances to date (*Blood Red,* 1986; *Baja Oklahoma* and *Satisfaction,* 1988) had been entirely forgettable.

During her first few weeks on this new film, however, a remarkable phenomenon began to take shape all over America. A low-budget movie she had recently made with Richard Gere, of which even its studio had minimal expectations, began to take off like no small-scale comedy before it—defying every apparent Hollywood truth of the hour. The film was yet another *Pygmalion* rehash, coupling an apparent has-been with an unknown. Gere's once zooming career had long been on the slide; Disney executives doubted that even he could save the film from becoming yet another "straight-to-video special."

Within weeks word-of-mouth success had seen *Pretty Woman* soar through the $100 million barrier and had transformed Julia Roberts into the first major new movie star of the 1990s. Soon the girl who had arrived on location in Wilmington as an unknown needed armed guards outside her hotel room. When her presence alone ensured disproportionate success for her next film, *Flatliners* —a so-so thriller costarring her then boyfriend, Kiefer Sutherland —Roberts became more than merely another overnight superstar. She was suddenly one of the few women in recent movie history whom the public would pay to go and see. Soon the girl who made *Pretty Woman* for barely half a million dollars was set to command ten times as much per film—more than the 1980s' unrivaled female superstar, Meryl Streep.

Asked why Hollywood's men earn so much more than they do, even the most feminist of female stars will shrug and say: "They bring in more money." The male superleague (Tom Cruise, Jack Nicholson, Harrison Ford, Michael Douglas and Kevin Costner upmarket, Mel Gibson, Bruce Willis, Stallone and Schwarzenegger further down) can command a minimum $10 million per film; even Barbra Streisand, the highest-paid female star, can barely stretch to $5 million, while Streep averages a mere three. "Men's salaries are preposterous," Streep has complained on frequent occasions. "If actresses had parity, you couldn't make a movie. Men pay men more. Period." Now Roberts, sixteen years younger than Streep, had become the unlikely one to reverse the trend.

Herself a 1990 Oscar candidate for *Postcards from the Edge,* her ninth nomination in thirteen years, Streep scornfully cites Screen Actors Guild figures that show women are down to twenty-nine percent of roles in feature films, compared with one-third three years before. "Isn't that sorta stunning? That means that seventy-one percent of all roles are male. If the Martians landed and did nothing but go to the movies this year, they would come to the fair conclusion that the chief occupation of women on earth is hooking."

A more direct way to secure an acting Oscar—or at least a nomination—is to write a personal letter to every member of the Academy's acting branch, wherever in the world they may live, politely drawing their attention to your work. It takes some chutzpah, but Diane Ladd has that to spare.

Typed on pink paper, embellished by a hand-inscribed *Harmony–Peace–Love,* Ladd's letter began with a dissertation on the exercise of free will at a time when Planet Earth was confronted by so many dilemmas. The way that actors reflect life, she went on, should be judged by their work rather than any hype surrounding it; on that basis she hoped to receive a Supporting nomination for her performance in *Wild at Heart*.

It had been sixteen years since her last "worthy" role, in Scorsese's *Alice Doesn't Live Here Any More* (which had won Ladd her only previous nomination). All that time she had waited for a part like Marietta. When it finally came along, she made a pledge to bare her emotions and put them "out there" with "total vulnerability."

Some studios, Ladd continued, were waging very expensive campaigns on behalf of their potential nominees. As hers was an independent film, she had no such support system. Her only hope, therefore, was that her performance in the film for which David Lynch had won the Palme d'Or at Cannes would speak for itself. But this couldn't happen unless people saw it. Details followed of three special screenings during the nominating period, at the Beverly Hills offices of the Samuel Goldwyn Company.

Concluding "in Light with Love," Ladd made it clear that her own credit cards had paid for the three advertisements in the trade press seeking Oscar "consideration" for her performance. But, as she put it, "everyone doesn't read the trades." So she was sending this letter to invite its recipient and a guest to judge for themselves. She was not—repeat not—soliciting votes, but politely asking her colleagues to view her work. For so doing, she thanked them with all her heart.

Six weeks later, the 1990 nominees for Best Supporting Actress turned out to be Annette Bening, Lorraine Bracco, Whoopi Goldberg, Mary McDonnell . . . and Diane Ladd.

The most popular film on both sides of the Atlantic in 1990 was *Ghost,* a modest little special-effects drama defying the seasoned Hollywood wisdom that films about the afterlife don't pay. Only the ninth film in movie history to pass the $200 million mark at the domestic box office alone,* *Ghost* was also one of nine films that year—all of them American-made—to gross more than $100 million in the U.S. market. It is a potent fact of contemporary movie life that to pass this magic figure—increasingly, the measure of true commercial success—a film requires a significant percentage of moviegoers to pay to see it more than once.

Early in 1991, however, all nine of these movies, even *Ghost,* were swiftly overtaken by a surprise Christmas hit, *Home Alone;* made for just $18 million, it grossed $126 million in its first six weeks, and had reached $275 million after thirty, making a seven-figure star out of 10-year-old Macauley Culkin. With a 47 percent rise in its fifth week, Christmas week, *Home Alone* seemed to be proving several points: that it was, as originally intended, a vacation comedy aimed at children; that box-office success is becoming ever less predictable; and that modest-budget comedies and dramas—"small" films, in Hollywood-speak—appeared in the early nineties to be usurping the recent success patterns of the megabucks epics. As Frank Capra said all those years ago: "The only rule in filmmaking is that there are no rules, and the only prediction is that all predictions are by guess and by God until the film plays in theaters."

Only three of 1990's nine $100 million grossers answered to the standard definition of conventional megabuck movies, costing at least half their nine-figure gross, with their attendant hype eating

* The others were *Ghostbusters, The Empire Strikes Back, Beverly Hills Cop, Raiders of the Lost Ark, Batman, Return of the Jedi, Star Wars* and *E.T.* (still the movies' all-time box-office champion with $360 million in North America alone). None of these blockbusters won Academy Awards for anything but Music, Special Effects, Sound or Editing.

well into the other half: *Die Hard 2, Dick Tracy* and *Back to the Future Part III.* Two of them were sequels to previous successes, the latest and lamest of Hollywood trends. The other six were low-budget, "small" comedies or dramas, like *Ghost* and *Pretty Woman.*

Throughout 1990, before the major Oscar aspirants were released, the Academy grapevine had throbbed with excitement about a whole clutch of pictures based on best-selling books. The first out was the only unqualified disaster: Brian De Palma's overambitious, $45 million attempt to film Tom Wolfe's *The Bonfire of the Vanities,* with Tom Hanks and Bruce Willis disastrously miscast opposite Melanie Griffith. Billed as a surefire Oscar contender when it went into production, *Bonfire* fared so badly with both critics and audiences that it was quite forgotten by the time of the Oscar nominations. "Not a bonfire, but a pilot light of the inanities," wrote *The Washington Post.* "No one cast in this movie ever stood a chance; they all go down with the ship," added *Newsweek*'s David Ansen, echoing other criticism that De Palma had broadened Wolfe's robust satire into gross, cartoonlike comedy. "A misfire of a thousand inanities," declared ABC's Joel Siegel. "This is a failure of epic proportions. You've got to be a genius to make a movie this bad." Even New York's former mayor Ed Koch, himself caricatured in the film, sniffed: "*Bonfire* is worth seeing if you liked *Dick Tracy* and *Batman.*"

The surprise success of the paperback pack was Barbet Schroeder's version of *Reversal of Fortune,* Alan Dershowitz's account of his courtroom battles on behalf of Claus von Bulow. Two rather more predictable hits were Mike Nichols's film of Carrie Fisher's *Postcards from the Edge,* with Meryl Streep, Shirley MacLaine, Richard Dreyfuss and Gene Hackman; and Penny Marshall's version of Oliver Sacks's *Awakenings,* with Robin Williams as Dr. Sacks and Robert De Niro as one of the "living dead" encephalitic patients whom he treated with the supposed miracle drug L-dopa. The fifth contender was *Goodfellas,* Martin Scorsese's dark vision of the memoirs of the Mafia turncoat Henry Hill, played by Ray Liotta amid a superb cast led by De Niro and Joe Pesci.

These were among the few of the record thirty-one Christmas releases to avoid a critical drubbing. The end-of-year blitz of movies in search of Oscar nominations saw a number of big names brought low, with scathing receptions for Bernardo Bertolucci's *The Shelter-*

ing Sky, Robert Redford in Sydney Pollack's *Havana,* Sylvester Stallone's *Rocky V* and Clint Eastwood in *The Rookie.* Nineteen-ninety had already seen such would-be summer blockbusters as *Robocop 2* and Tom Cruise's *Days of Thunder* trounced at the box office by the much-lower-budgeted *Ghost* and *Pretty Woman.*

Home Alone's success was especially embarrassing for Warner Bros., which had let its option on the film lapse when its producer, John Hughes, asked for a $2.5 million budget increase; as Twentieth Century Fox took over the project, Warners instead plowed $45 million into *Bonfire of the Vanities.* Paramount too was having its problems. With a week to go to the Oscar eligibility deadline, Francis Ford Coppola was still tinkering with his long-awaited *The Godfather Part III,* and the studio was already seven months into a $7 million promotional campaign designed to recoup at least some of its $65 million investment.

Coppola had been filming in Rome when the studio first launched its saturation advertising campaign. Making-of-the-movie specials were readied for cable television, which would be rescreening the first two *Godfathers* to coincide with the third's release. Italian restaurants around the country were made offers they couldn't refuse to recreate the film's banquet scene, on which a prepackaged feature was also distributed to the cookery editors of national newspaper chains. Coppola's daughter Sofia, controversially cast in the pivotal role of Michael Corleone's daughter, Mary, was meanwhile featured in fashion spreads and chic advertisements for the Gap clothing chain.

Most lurid of all, *The Godfather* saga received several shameless plugs in Paramount's other big Christmas release, *Almost an Angel.* When it, too, fell victim to the critical rout—spelling the end of the Hollywood line for "Crocodile" Dundee himself, Paul Hogan—Paramount executives could only wait, hope and throw more money at the problem in the shape of saturation trade ads. There was some consolation in a $16 million gross for *Godfather Part III* in Christmas week alone—matching that of the new Schwarzenegger romp, *Kindergarten Cop*—but worrying signs of a tailspin in the New Year.

The hype alone was enough to secure *Godfather III* a Best Picture nomination alongside *Goodfellas, Awakenings* and the inevitable *Dances with Wolves.* Also commended to Academy members by a flashy, embossed family album, the third act in the *Godfather* saga had opened to muted reviews, which descended to cruel mockery at Coppola's casting of his daughter in the role originally intended for Winona Ryder. The fifth nominee was a shock to supporters of *Reversal of Fortune* and *Postcards from the Edge.* By nominating *Ghost,* the Academy was dancing to the music of cash registers. For all the respect due the $215 million it had taken through the nominations, *Ghost* could count itself lucky; this was an honorable mention, with scant chance of ultimate victory.

For once, Academy members were letting their personal enthusiasms overcome their gullibility. MGM, for instance, had spent $500,000 on 45 pages of trade-paper ads touting Sean Connery and Michelle Pfeiffer in John le Carré's *The Russia House,* without a single nomination for their pains. Disney had taken 46 pages for *Green Card* (which registered two nominations but no wins) and *Pretty Woman* (a surprise, but unsuccessful, nomination for Julia Roberts). In the case of *Dances with Wolves,* a mere 27 pages were enough to help secure a stunning twelve nominations.

Though its triumph in this first round of voting gave *Dances with Wolves* huge muscle power in the second, all the other nominated films (with the possible exception of *Ghost*) were also broadly respected—placing more emphasis than ever on their box-office takes. By mid-February 1991, at the time of its nomination, *Dances with Wolves* had grossed $117 million—more than three times its nearest rivals, *Awakenings* and *Goodfellas,* which could each boast only $42 million. At a mere $11 million, *Reversal of Fortune* could scarcely have hoped for a Best Picture nomination; indeed it seemed lucky to boast two first-time nominees: Schroeder for Best Director and Jeremy Irons as Best Actor.

As he amassed funds for his TriBeCa Studio in New York, the usually picky Robert De Niro was beginning to look like a prodigal workaholic. With *Guilty by Suspicion, Backdraft* and a remake of *Cape Fear* on the horizon, his 1990 versatility wound up accounting for one of *Awakenings*' three nominations rather than *Goodfellas*' six. While Martin Scorsese earned his third shot at Best Director, however, there was no mention for *Awakenings*' Penny Marshall (sister of Garry Marshall, director of *Pretty Woman*). She and *Ghost*'s Jerry Zucker had been bumped by Schroeder and the British director

Stephen Frears. Overlooked for the Oscar-nominated *My Beautiful Laundrette* and *Dangerous Liaisons,* Frears had now made an immensely stylish first movie about America, *The Grifters.*

Marshall's omission provoked such a feminist furor that even the trade press, slavishly following an angry studio handout, lamented her failure to become "the first woman to be nominated for Best Director"—quite forgetting Lina Wertmuller, nominated for *Seven Beauties* in 1976. For angry activists, recalling the Academy's omission of Randa Haines for *Children of a Lesser God* in 1986, this was the second time in five years that a woman had directed a Best Picture nominee, only to be snubbed herself. A brave few even dared to invoke the insults dealt Barbra Streisand's *Yentl* in 1983; but they were looking forward to next year, bucked by word of mouth about Streisand's *Prince of Tides.*

Godfather III's nomination saw Paramount capitalize, despite that New Year slide at the box office, by opening it on seven hundred extra screens nationwide. Thanks in itself to Joanne Woodward's Best Actress nomination, James Ivory's *Mr. & Mrs. Bridge* expanded from thirty-five to two hundred screens; even *The Nasty Girl,* a foreign-language nominee from Germany, jumped from nine to twenty-five. Despite the odds against their winning anything, the producers of *The Grifters* and *The Field* also stepped up distribution while the going was good. The AIDS drama *Longtime Companion* had already ended its run; now, thanks to a Supporting nomination for Bruce Davison, it was rereleased.

Nineteen-ninety was proving the year of the videocassette. For small-budget independent films with much less theater exposure than the studio blockbusters, it is the only way to force their product on the voters' attention. Orion Classics won *Cyrano de Bergerac*'s five nominations that way, while Miramax also won five after mailing out copies of *The Grifters* and *Mr. & Mrs. Bridge.* Avenue Films did the same for *The Field,* in the hope of winning acting recognition for Richard Harris and John Hurt; though seen in only thirty cinemas nationwide, it arrived in video form in the homes of 1,300 voting members of the Academy's acting branch.

Less successful were Ion Pictures, a small independent company whose video mailshot for an otherwise unheard-of Danny Aiello film, *The Closer,* ended with a none too subtle reminder that "now is the time to return your ballot," pleading for "consideration" for Aiello and the film's director, writers and composers. If some producers are less inhibited than others, it is because even in the lesser categories a nomination alone can mean big box office. Few think it seemly to concentrate as much effort on converting anything but a Best Picture nomination into a win; among the 1990 exceptions were the producers of *Metropolitan,* who waited until after gaining a screenplay nomination to start sending out cassettes—accompanied, as an in-joke for the film's aficionados, by teabags.

Among disappointed contenders already out of the running was Shirley MacLaine, whose bravura turn in *Postcards from the Edge* seemed made-for-Oscar show-biz material. But MacLaine and her studio had campaigned for a Supporting nomination, against the advice of her publicist, Dale Olson—the man who had won a nomination for Sally Kirkland, and one of Hollywood's shrewdest Oscar-watchers. The female Supporting category was unusually competitive in 1990, while Best Actress seemed wide open. "Shirley didn't even get a nomination, and would probably have lost anyway," said Olson. "Had she gone for Best Actress, I'm convinced she would have gone on to win." As it was, MacLaine's shelves would have to wait a while longer for that second bookend.

Though it had won none of the previous Best Picture awards, Las Vegas and London bookies both made *Awakenings* second favorite to the odds-on *Dances with Wolves,* which had taken the Golden Globe (Drama) and National Board of Review. The last picture to win twelve Oscar nominations, Warren Beatty's *Reds* in 1981, had been almost totally eclipsed at the awards by the British film *Chariots of Fire;* now the 1990 opposition was proving feisty, with the Los Angeles, New York and National Society of Film Critics all preferring *Goodfellas.* But the writing was on the wall for Scorsese's latest masterpiece in the April issue of *American Film.*

Of eighty U.S. film critics participating in the magazine's second annual poll, a healthy majority of forty-five voted Scorsese Director of the Year for *Goodfellas.* "In a year that had many first-rate directors on the job—Francis Coppola, Bernardo Bertolucci, Stephen Frears, David Lynch, Robert Altman, Tim Burton and Woody Allen—Scorsese was working closest to the top of his form," wrote

Peter Travers of *Rolling Stone.* (He made no mention of Costner, who polled only twelve votes for Best Director.) *Goodfellas* won the poll's Best Picture category, but ominously drew less support than its director. "Scorsese is obviously the ultimate director," explained Joan Bunke of the Des Moines *Register.* "But I'm unwilling to go on record saying that such a violent and foul-mouthed film is the best of the year." *American Film* noticed that *Goodfellas'* admirers tended to be the "urban scribes . . . which may account in part for its domination of awards from the big-city critics."

Hollywood was in the grip of what the trades inelegantly called an "antiviolence backlash," which seemed to single out for defeat everyone and everything associated with *Goodfellas, Godfather III* and *The Grifters,* including the Best Actress favorite, Anjelica Huston. The pre-Oscar buzz suggested that even Kathy Bates—otherwise favored for the style with which she had broken James Caan's ankles in Rob Reiner's film of Stephen King's *Misery*—might also fall victim to this new wave of Hollywood prudery, clearing the way for Joanne Woodward to win a second Oscar thirty-three years after her first. Also in danger, according to the grapevine, was Joe Pesci's otherwise certain Supporting Oscar for *Goodfellas.* Could Hollywood really give an award to an actor seen stuffing himself with pizza while a man lay dying in the trunk of his car?

Only two of the Best Actor nominees, Costner and De Niro, were American. But there was no mention of Australia, for all Mel Gibson's hopes of refining his screen image as a moodily middlebrow *Hamlet* for Franco Zeffirelli. Glenn Close's chances of success at her fifth nomination lay in a double whammy as two distinctly ill-fated women, Mel Gibson's mother and Jeremy Irons's wife; but it was Irons's remarkable impersonation of Claus von Bulow, admired for its ramrod back and mid-European accent, which proved the capstone of another good year for Britain.

Thanks to their continuing liberality with videocassettes, and the lingering goodwill toward *My Left Foot,* the same Irish team of Noel Pearson and Jim Sheridan also managed to win a Best Actor nomination for Richard Harris—twenty-seven years after his only previous mention, for *This Sporting Life,* had lost to Sidney Poitier. "If *Sporting Life* was my *Hamlet,* then this is my *Lear,*" said Harris. Made for $10 million—paltry by Hollywood standards, but five times as much as *My Left Foot—The Field* had yet to reach one million dollars at the U.S. box office, and won no other nominations.

The fifth candidate for Best Actor was the most unlikely Hollywood sex symbol since "Crocodile" Dundee: 42-year-old Gérard Dépardieu, an unkempt, overweight, clumsy-featured Frenchman who had risen from an orphanage in the Paris slums to become one of his country's leading stage and screen actors—but had yet to make an international name. *Cyrano de Bergerac* had already won Jose Ferrer an Oscar in 1950; now, as well as offering the chance of an unusual double* to Dépardieu, who managed to bring to the role a dazzling blend of bravado and vulnerability, it was far and away the front-running nominee for Best Foreign Film.

Costner's box-office takings in the previous eight years—the aggregate gross of all the films in which he had starred since 1982—had reached almost $400 million, compared with $281 million for De Niro, $38 million for both Irons and Dépardieu, and less than a million for Harris. Irons had won the Golden Globe (Drama), the Los Angeles and National Film Critics; De Niro had won the New York Film Critics and the National Board of Review (in a tie with his *Awakenings* costar, Robin Williams); Costner, Dépardieu and Harris had won nothing.

With Costner favored for Best Picture and Director, and thus ruled out of the acting stakes on overload as much as on merit, Dépardieu was emerging as a dark horse worth an investment. As the final round of voting began, the Frenchman seemed likely to become the first man ever to win the Leading Role Oscar in a subtitled, foreign-language film—a feat achieved to date only by Sophia Loren, thirty years before, in *Two Women.* It was his further good fortune to be highly visible during the voting period in a completely contrasting role, both contemporary and romantic, as a would-be U.S. immigrant opposite Andie MacDowell in *Green Card,* which won its director, Peter Weir, a screenplay nomination. Weir's stylish com-

* Cyrano is one of fourteen movie roles to have won separate Oscar nominations in the hands of different actors, from Arthur Chipping in *Goodbye, Mr Chips* (Robert Donat, 1939; Peter O'Toole, 1969) to Norman Maine/Ernest Gubbins in *A Star Is Born* (Fredric March, 1937; James Mason, 1954). While actors have won separate nominations for reprises of the same role (Paul Newman, for instance, as Fast Eddie Felson in *The Hustler,* 1961, and *The Color of Money,* 1986, or Peter O'Toole as King Henry II in *Becket,* 1964, and *The Lion in Winter,* 1968), the only role in movie history to have won Oscars for two different actors is the Godfather himself, Vito Corleone (Marlon Brando, 1972; Robert De Niro, 1974). For a complete list, see Appendix C, section B7.

edy was full of awkward reminders for the Academy: that it had overlooked MacDowell for *sex, lies and videotape,* not to mention Weir himself for *Dead Poets Society.* Dépardieu appeared to have everything going for him.

Disaster struck when he gave an interview to *Time* magazine, printed during the final round of voting, in which he was quoted as saying that from the age of nine he had been involved in regular bouts of gang rape. It was a natural part of life, the article implied, in the hardened demimonde to which fate had consigned the young Dépardieu after he had run away from home. During the ensuing uproar, protests about misquotation and misunderstanding came from the higher reaches of the French government itself. The minister of culture, Jack Lang, and *Cyrano*'s director, Jean-Paul Rappeneau, promptly started legal proceedings (but later allowed the matter to drop).

The truth of the matter seems likely to remain forever sunk beneath a mid-Atlantic confusion of tongues. While Dépardieu may well have been exaggerating for the sake of effect, there were suggestions that the French word *assister,* meaning to "attend" or "witness," had been mistranslated as "participate." There also seems to have been some confusion between *voler,* to steal, and *violer,* to rape. In any case, as Simon Hoggart pointed out in the (London) *Observer, violer* can mean "something hardly stronger than 'rough sex.' "

Hoggart was concerned to make a rather British point: that the episode demonstrated "the worst side of prescriptive American liberalism: the belief that nobody can be deemed acceptable in any way unless, throughout the whole of their lives, they have adhered rigidly to this year's tenets of American liberalism." But for Dépardieu, the consequences of this semantic morass were rather more damaging. There can be little doubt that it cost him a spectacular Academy Award, and thus the chance to realize his ambition to become a major American star. It also led to the most surprising result of the 1990 awards, when a Swiss film called *Journey of Hope,* not even released in the United States,* beat the superb *Cyrano de Bergerac* as Best Foreign Language Film.

* Section Fourteen of the Academy Awards rulebook, covering the Best Foreign Language Film Award, restricts the category to "feature-length motion pictures produced with basically non-English dialogue track, first released between November 1 and October 31 [of the relevant year], and first publicly shown in the commercial theater." Dialogue track must be "predomi-

That was not enough for the National Organization for Women, who mounted a concerted campaign against Dépardieu, telling film insurance companies that "women might consider him a danger on the set." Tammy Bruce, president of NOW's 4,000-member Los Angeles chapter, told the *Los Angeles Times:* "We will not let up. We will make things as miserable for him as possible. We want him to feel the repercussions of his actions and his attitude." As the Awards approached, NOW lobbied the State Department to refuse Dépardieu admission to the country because of the "many self-incriminating remarks he has made."

Filming in Africa, the actor was forced into a last-minute decision to stay away from Hollywood in the pre-award period—a time when most first-time Oscar contenders, especially non-Americans, eagerly capitalize on their newfound celebrity with a heavy schedule of public and private glad-handing. Suddenly the favorite, Irons also chose to stay away, rather in the manner of an aloof presidential front-runner—though he was cunning enough to show another side to his character by guest-hosting NBC's *Saturday Night Live* on the eve of the ceremony. De Niro, as always, sulked in his New York tent. Costner's publicity had been all-pervasive; the correct tactical position for him was now to descend at the last minute, a deus ex machina arriving for his coronation in at least two, maybe three of the major categories. This left the field clear for Richard Harris, the reformed hell-raiser who now resembled a wild-eyed, white-maned King Lear, to attend every pre-Oscar event going. Which is saying something.

The week before the Academy Awards sees Hollywood host a long-running orgy of lesser awards shows, at which the lesser Oscar nominees hand out enough prizes to start a museum. By this stage those already bestowed by the New York and Los Angeles film critics, the National Board of Review, the National Society of Film Critics and Hollywood's Foreign Press Association (the Golden Globes) have wielded their due influence upon the Academy's 4,830 voters. Now,

---

nantly in a language of the country of origin"; though candidates must have English subtitles, they "need not have been released in the United States." Entries are submitted by the cinematic authorities of the countries themselves, who are restricted to one candidate per year.

just before the ballots close, the Directors Guild, the Writers Guild, the Publicists Guild, the Independent Film-Makers and countless other groups down to film editors and sound recordists hand out their own trophies in lavish Beverly Hills ceremonies.

A sweep of all these pre-Oscar awards will add to a front-runner's momentum, but their results can sometimes be intriguingly different. Rarely does the winner of the Directors Guild award fail to win the Oscar for Direction, largely because the 286-strong membership of the Academy's directors branch are much the same people as those who can be bothered to vote in either contest. Having scooped Best Director at the Golden Globes, Costner now entered the home stretch by picking up the same award from the Directors Guild—one of only a handful of contenders to have won at his first attempt.

On Tuesday he failed, as do most of each year's potential winners, to attend a reception held for all Oscar nominees at the Beverly Hilton Hotel. The primary purpose of the Nominees' Lunch, a tradition started by the Academy in 1982, is a pep talk from the producer, urging winners to keep their acceptance speeches short. They will see a warning light, they are warned, gradually turning from red to green as they think of people to thank. After forty-five seconds, even in midsentence, they will be summarily cut off by the orchestra. "Be prepared, be singular, be brief and be fair," producer Gil Cates told lunch guests. "Don't be foolish on the show. You've been nominated by your peers because of your outstanding work in film, not because of your political beliefs. . . ."

"Just remember, if you thank a long list of people, four will be very happy but ninety-nine million will be bored and go to the refrigerator."

Next day, Wednesday, saw the Writers Guild awards dinner, also at the Beverly Hilton. *Dances with Wolves'* Michael Blake picked up the award for Best Screenplay Based on Material from Another Medium, while Best Original Screenplay went to Barry Levinson for *Avalon* (who would lose on Oscar night to *Ghost*'s Bruce Joel Rubin).

By Friday there was a bewildering array of functions to choose from. Richard Harris, Andy Garcia, Whoopi Goldberg, Diane Ladd, Bruce Davison and the other nominees doing the rounds were back at the Beverly Hilton for the Publicists Guild luncheon, at which they handed out awards for the best promotional campaigns. (To

Davison, the "relentless" pace of Oscar fever was "like being caught up in a Fellini movie.") Walter Matthau presented the guild's Lifetime Achievement Award to Howard W. Koch—an Oscar nominee fifty years before as coauthor of *Sergeant York,* a winner in 1943 for *Casablanca.*

That evening thirteen hundred guests headed for the Century Plaza, where the annual Moving Picture Ball in aid of the American Cinematheque took the form of a salute to Martin Scorsese, hosted by Robert De Niro. Tributes were paid by De Niro, Harvey Keitel, Barbara Hershey, Ray Liotta, Jodie Foster, Peter Gabriel, Sam Arkoff, Irwin Winkler and many more. But the elaborate trophy presented to Scorsese was to prove his only prize of the week.

Down the road at L'Orangerie, the second annual pre-Oscar bash was already being hailed as a "tradition." Its proud boast is to be the only Hollywood function all week at which no speeches are made, no awards handed out and no honorees feted. Harris, Ladd and Davison were again on hand, mingling with luminaries from Maximilian Schell to Roger Moore, JoBeth Williams and Jackie Collins. "I'm feeling exhaustion, fear, enjoyment, hysteria, fun, catatonia, all in major doses," said Davison. "But Richard Dreyfuss told me to enjoy the ride." Also enjoying the ride, he said, was Richard Harris: "I'm sixty years old. I know how to deal with it. I'm not expecting too much."

Both were back on parade the following lunchtime, when the Independent Spirit Awards were hosted by Buck Henry at the Beverly Hills Hotel. Started ten years before by the Independent Feature Project (West), to honor movies made and distributed independently, the "Indies" are now resembling a parody of themselves. What began as an informal lunch in a now defunct restaurant on La Cienega Boulevard has grown into a very grand affair, attended by the crème de la Hollywood crème, with tributes and acceptance speeches longer and more lavish than the Academy gush they were designed to offset. On parade for the first time all week was Hollywood's number-one power broker, Michael Ovitz of the Creative Artists Agency (CAA), who represented every single one of the 1990 Best Actor and Director nominees. At the Ovitz table, also making his first outing of the week, was the man of the moment: Kevin Costner. Keynote speaker at the event, Costner grandly told his independent colleagues: "Only hard work makes a great movie."

The Independents gave their Best Picture award to *The Grifters,* whose Anjelica Huston also took Best Actress. But it was the dramatic comedy *To Sleep with Anger* that dominated the show; the chronicle of a black family in south-central Los Angeles won both top awards for its writer-director Charles Burnett, Best Actor for Danny Glover and Supporting Actress for Sheryl Lee Ralph, who drew a standing ovation for a tub-thumping complaint about Hollywood's treatment of black actors. By the end of the five-hour ceremony, Bruce Davison finally had something to show for his very long week: a Supporting Actor award.

Out in the men's room, Richard Harris said he had just about had enough of awards shows; he would be slipping out as soon as he had handed over whatever award he was presenting today. No, he would not be attending the sound recordists' shindig on Sunday. It was enough of a blessing to have missed the traditional Directors Symposium for Foreign Film nominees, held that morning at the Academy. He was "a million-to-one shot" for Monday night's Oscars, and could not wait for the whole shebang to be over.

None of the 1990 Oscar nominees—nor indeed anyone who had ever been anywhere near the Academy Awards—was in evidence at Sunday lunchtime in the Hollywood Roosevelt Hotel, scene of the first Academy Awards dinner back in 1929. Sixty-three years on, the Roosevelt was now hosting the eleventh annual "Razzies"—the Golden Raspberry Awards, handed out on Oscar eve to honor the *worst* achievements in film that year. Previous recipients include Sylvester Stallone (sundry *Rambo*s and *Rocky*s) and Liza Minnelli (*Arthur 2*), Bill Cosby (*Leonard Part 6*) and Madonna (*Shanghai Surprise*). Worst Pictures of the Eighties included *Mommie Dearest, Inchon, Bolero, Howard the Duck* and *Cocktail.* Worst Career Achievements awards, the Razzies' highest honor, have gone to Ronald Reagan ("retired movie star," 1981); Irwin Allen ("the master of disaster," 1983), Linda Blair ("Scream Queen," 1985) and Bruce, the rubber shark from *Jaws, Jaws 2, Jaws 3-D* and *Jaws the Revenge* (1987).

The Worst Actor of 1990 turned out to be Andrew Dice Clay (*The Adventures of Ford Fairlane*) in a convincing win over Stallone (*Rocky V*), Prince (*Graffiti Bridge*), Mickey Rourke (*Wild Orchids*) and George C. Scott (*Exorcist III*). Worst Actress went for a record third time to Bo Derek (*Ghosts Can't Do It*) over Melanie Griffith

(*The Bonfire of the Vanities*), Bette Midler (*Stella*), Molly Ringwald (*Betsy's Wedding*) and Talia Shire (*Rocky V*). The Supporting awards were won by Donald Trump in *Ghosts Can't Do It* and poor Sofia Coppola in *Godfather III.* Worst Picture of 1990 was a tie between *The Adventures of Ford Fairlane* and *Ghosts Can't Do It,* beating out *Bonfire of the Vanities, Rocky V* and *Graffiti Bridge.* Not one of the winners, alas, could make it.

The 1990 Academy Awards took place in the aftermath of the Gulf War, which had cast a nervous shadow over preparations. As much as the threat of terrorism, the Academy was worried that presenters or winners might use the occasion to revive the seventies penchant for political protest: many of the younger members of the Hollywood community were publicly against the war. Though spared that particular threat, there was no relaxation of the precautions against a terrorist attack. Any broadcast out of the United States to a billion people in ninety-nine countries, crammed with the world's most recognizable celebrities, had to be a prime target.

The main victims were the two thousand fans headed for the bleachers, now a constituent element of Oscar night's arrivals sequence. For the first time in memory, they were not allowed to pitch camp in the temporary grandstands during the weekend before the show; police protection was instead accorded the early arrivals as they slept out on two blocks of sidewalk in one of Los Angeles' less salubrious areas. Because of contractual difficulties, the ceremony for the 1990 Oscars had returned to the Shrine Auditorium from the Dorothy Chandler Pavilion. It was a less attractive venue for the stars, who were nervous about venturing so deep into downtown combat zones, but a better one for the organizers, who could seat 6,000 people rather than 3,700. Black-market tickets, even so, were changing hands for $1,000 and up.

The extra security entailed instructions to stars and fans alike to "Get there early, expect delays, and don't carry—or wear—anything metallic." From his command center at the Shrine, chief of security Jerry Moon said: "There does exist a calm at the moment. But it could heat up. You never know." Spectators and superstars both had to submit to precautions similar to those at international airports, passing through a metal-detector arch in a discreetly screened-off tent, where all hand luggage was also searched. For the first time, no cameras or binoculars were allowed.

The security, agreed Gil Cates, was "cumbersome," but it would make the stars "more comfortable" at "the mother of all awards shows." His chosen theme this year was "One Hundred Years of the Movies," marking the centenary of George Eastman's invention of celluloid film in 1891. The biggest name scheduled to appear, causing the most excited anticipation among the crowd, was neither a presenter nor a nominee, but a singer: Madonna, who arrived on the arm of Michael Jackson, and would be performing one of the Best Song nominees, Stephen Sondheim's "Sooner or Later (I'll Always Get My Man)," which she had herself sung in Warren Beatty's *Dick Tracy.* Harry Connick, Jr., was also slated to sing "Promise Me You'll Remember" from *Godfather III,* and Jon Bon Jovi his own composition, "Blaze of Glory," from *Young Guns II.* But a very pregnant Meryl Streep was obliged to hand over to Reba McEntire for "I'm Checkin' Out," the song Streep had belted out with such panache at the end of her nominated performance in *Postcards from the Edge.*

The talk of the town that week was the abrupt departure of Paramount's chairman, Frank Mancuso, and his $45 million lawsuit against the company. This gave Billy Crystal, who took to the stage on horseback as host for the second year running, the chance to open the show with a topical joke designed to defuse any postwar tension: "We're thankful that no Americans are fighting anywhere in the world tonight—except at Paramount." Backstage in the press tents, five hundred print and broadcast reporters from all over the world were installed in prized seats applied for by five thousand. Each was equipped with radio headphones to follow the show—also visible on closed-circuit TV—while simultaneously interviewing the winners fed through to them straight from the stage. First up was Whoopi Goldberg.

Annette Bening would have been the critics' choice for 1990's Best Supporting Actress. A San Francisco and Broadway stage actress, nominated for a Tony in Tina Howe's *Coastal Disturbances,* Bening had moved into films as the Marquise in Milos Forman's ill-fated *Valmont,* and had stolen a scene from Meryl Streep in *Postcards from the Edge,* before making her very stylish mark as the lubricious Myra Langtry in *The Grifters.* Set to appear as De Niro's ex-wife in *Guilty by Suspicion,* Irwin Winkler's blacklist movie, as Harrison Ford's wife in *Regarding Henry,* and (until her pregnancy by Warren Beatty forced her to withdraw) as Catwoman in Tim Burton's *Batman II,* she was already marked out as a major star for the nineties.

Only a *Dances with Wolves* sweep could have won for 37-year-old Mary McDonnell, another stage actress picked by Costner as his love interest—the only white, to predictable controversy, amid the otherwise ethnic casting. Other nominees were *Goodfellas'* Lorraine Bracco and a hopeful Diane Ladd. But it was the phenomenal commercial box-office success of *Ghost* that saw Whoopi Goldberg become the first black actress to win an Oscar in more than fifty years. As the film's ditzy medium—a role in which one critic described her as "less irritating than usual"—Goldberg had also become the first black actress in Oscar history to have won two nominations. As she had been reminding people all week at pre-Oscar functions, "I'm carrying a lot of people with me on this one." Now, from the hands of another black Oscar-winner, Denzel Washington, Goldberg had her revenge for the 1985 *Color Purple* fiasco.

"I come from New York," she told her peers in the Shrine. "When I was a little kid, I lived in the projects. You're the people I watched, the people I wanted to be. I'm proud to be an actor." The six weeks since the nominations, she said backstage with relief, had been "a long time to keep cheerful." Goldberg became only the fifth black player to win an Academy Award in its sixty-three-year history, during which twenty-two black artists had received twenty-six acting nominations—ten for Leading Roles, sixteen for Supporting. The previous winners were Hattie McDaniel, Sidney Poitier, Louis Gosset, Jr., and Denzel Washington;* the only black actor to have received

* In chronological order, with winners in capital letters, the nominees were: HATTIE McDANIEL (*Gone with the Wind,* 1939); Ethel Waters (*Pinky,* 1949); Dorothy Dandridge (*Carmen Jones,* 1954); Sidney Poitier (*The Defiant Ones,* 1958); Juanita Moore (*Imitation of Life,* 1959); SIDNEY POITIER (*Lilies of the Field,* 1963); Beah Richards (*Guess Who's Coming to Dinner,* 1967); Rupert Crosse (*The Reivers,* 1969); James Earl Jones (*The Great White Hope,* 1970); Diana Ross (*Lady Sings the Blues,* 1972); Cicely Tyson (*Sounder,* 1972); Paul Winfield (*Sounder,* 1972); Diahann Carroll (*Claudine,* 1974); Howard Rollins, Jr. (*Ragtime,* 1981); LOUIS GOSSETT, JR. (*An Officer and a Gentleman,* 1982); Alfre Woodard (*Cross Creek,* 1983); Adolph Caesar (*A Soldier's Story,* 1984); Margaret Avery, Whoopi Goldberg, Oprah Winfrey (*The Color Purple,* 1985); Dexter Gordon (*Round Midnight,* 1986); Morgan Freeman (*Street Smart,* 1987); Denzel Washington (*Cry Freedom,* 1987); Morgan Freeman (*Driving Miss Daisy,* 1989); DENZEL WASHINGTON (*Glory,* 1989); WHOOPI GOLDBERG (*Ghost,* 1990).

an Honorary Oscar was James Baskett, honored in 1947 as "friend and story-teller to the children of the world" for his portrayal of Uncle Remus in Walt Disney's *Song of the South.*

After the Sound award had notched up *Dances with Wolves'* first win, and Makeup had gone to the team from *Dick Tracy, My Left Foot*'s Brenda Fricker arrived onstage to present the award for Best Supporting Actor. Last year's Supporting Actress had wandered through the entire arrivals area, where TV crews grab at stars like kids in a candy store, totally unrecognized—a discomfiting sign of the Oscar's transient glories. Bruce Davison's previous wins had made *Longtime Companion* supporters hopeful; *Dances with Wolves'* Kicking Bird, Graham Greene, was many people's favorite to pick up the first Native American Oscar; but the dashing new star Andy Garcia seemed a longshot alongside his costar Al Pacino's sixth nomination—not for shouldering the lead in the third *Godfather,* but for a whacky cameo in *Dick Tracy.* Would Pacino, overlooked for both previous *Godfathers, Serpico, Dog Day Afternoon* and . . . *And Justice for All,* finally win one of those awards given to the right leading actor for the wrong supporting role?

No: the winner was Joe Pesci, who had cunningly counterbalanced his dark role in *Goodfellas* by spending the voting period raising laughs on several thousand other screens as one of *Home Alone*'s long-suffering burglars and as the kinetic accountant in *Lethal Weapon 2.* Just as Vito Corleone was the only role in Oscar history to have won awards for two different actors, so Pesci's mobster belied the Oscar rule that Bad Guys Don't Win—received Hollywood wisdom ever since two of the screen's toughest tough guys, Jimmy Cagney and Humphrey Bogart, each won his only award in pussycat roles, in *Yankee Doodle Dandy* and *The African Queen.* Wholly unconcerned with such details, Pesci left the stage with just five words: "It's my privilege. Thank you."

Though universally deemed a worthy winner, the diminutive Pesci had more reason than most to figure himself "lucky." Backstage he recalled how he had given up acting in the early seventies and opened an Italian restaurant. One day in 1979 the restaurant took a booking from Robert De Niro, who remembered its manager from the only film he had made, a gangster movie called *Death Collector.* De Niro brought Martin Scorsese to dinner, and both tried to persuade Pesci to return to films as Jake La Motta's brother Joey in *Raging Bull.* "I told them I didn't want to go back into acting unless I got a part that could prove I'm good. Joey was not a great role, but it was a good one. I took it." Now he was one of the busiest actors in the business.

Academicians seized the chance of the Short Film awards to head for the rest rooms, outside which Julia Roberts was to be found in a passionate embrace with Kiefer Sutherland. Given recent gossip that the scale of her success had strained their relationship, the Shrine was audibly abuzz with the news as *Cyrano de Bergerac* picked up the Costume award, depriving *Dances with Wolves* of its fourth shot at an Oscar and Zeffirelli's *Hamlet* of its first. Arnold Schwarzenegger's *Total Recall* picked up Visual Effects—not difficult, since it was the only nominee—before Costner's fortunes began to rise again. Mary McDonnell, Graham Greene and the wardrobe department may have missed out, but *Dances with Wolves* now scooped Original Score for John Barry and Editing for Neil Travis. Could this be the beginning of the expected "Kevalanche" for Costner? No, Richard Gere and Susan Sarandon handed the Art and Set Direction awards to *Dick Tracy*'s Richard Sylbert and Rick Simpson.

There was a brief flurry of excitement as one guest (who turned out to be a gay rights activist, David Lacaillade) leaped to his feet shouting, "AIDS action! 102,000 dead!" Then it was back to the rest rooms during the Documentary awards, to check on Julia and Kiefer while *The Hunt for Red October* picked up Sound Effects, giving it the chance to plaster "Oscar winner" across theater marquees.

Costner's momentum began to revive as Cinematography went to Dean Semler and Adapted Screenplay to Michael Blake, who brought a Lakota interpreter onstage for a mawkish vote of thanks. *Dances with Wolves* had scored five-for-nine as the major Oscars approached. Madonna had just won Sondheim his first Oscar, and *Dick Tracy* its third, as Daniel Day-Lewis entered to announce the Best Actress of 1990. As predicted by the pundits, a vote split between Anjelica Huston and Joanne Woodward had handed the crown to a stunned Kathy Bates. For Julia Roberts, there would be many more chances; for Meryl Streep, there had already been quite enough.

Another stage actress as yet scarcely noticed on film, 42-year-old Bates was one of the all-time unlikely winners—the beneficiary of a most unusual Oscar syndrome. Many voters confessed that they had barely heard of her before *Misery,* which they had taken in purely out of interest in their old comrade James Caan. Two decades after his Oscar nomination as Sonny Corleone, since which a once promising career had slid slowly downhill, could Jimmy still hack it? That was the brutal question in the minds of those who went to see Caan and came away stunned by the powers of Bates.

In a very emotional acceptance speech, Bates thanked her mother, "watching at home," and her late father "who I hope is watching somewhere." In all other ways she was far from being the stereotypic Hollywood leading lady. "All of us practice our Academy Award speech in the shower, but it seemed like something that would never happen to me," she said later. "My whole life has changed because Rob Reiner had the opportunity to take a chance on somebody. If he had needed permission from studio people, he wouldn't have been able to use me. I remember asking him, 'Who else has to decide this?' And he said, 'Nobody. It's my company.' "

Bates's age and looks had combined to lose her the chance to film a number of roles she had created onstage—one of which, *Frankie and Johnny (in the Clair de Lune),* went to Michelle Pfeiffer even though Terence McNally had originally written it for Bates. "It boggles the mind," she said. "I thought it was wonderful to see a love story about people over forty, ordinary people who were trying to connect. We haven't seen it before, and I don't think we are going to see it with this movie." But Bates blamed the system, not Pfeiffer. "I imagine Michelle gets grief because she's so gorgeous. She doesn't get a chance to play roles that are really meaty. If I were her, I would have gone after this too." Now Bates was set to offer further proof of her own worth in Hector Babenco's *At Play in the Field of the Lord,* based on Peter Matthiessen's novel, and Athol Fugard's *The Road to Mecca.* Future projects also included *Fried Green Tomatoes at the Whistle Stop Café* with Jessica Tandy.

Costner's face remained expressionless as Tandy opened the Best Actor envelope to reveal the name of Jeremy Irons. The Briton's win was not as unexpected as it might have been six weeks before, when Dépardieu had been riding high. De Niro's tour de force in *Awakenings,* which climaxed in an astonishing descent back into mental illness, came too hard on the heels of Day-Lewis's simulation of cerebral palsy; however much Method there may have been in both men's madness, voters were all too aware of the pitfalls involved in a third consecutive mental illness Oscar. Costner's cup was about to run over quite enough for most tastes. Very few voters beyond the acting branch, which had nominated him, had seen Richard Harris's film. So Irons it was.

As he acknowledged in his acceptance speech, Irons was winning as much for a previous performance as for his uncanny impersonation of Claus von Bulow. He had been unlucky not to have been nominated in 1988, when he won the New York critics' award for the Canadian film *Dead Ringers,* in which he played twins, two very different gynecologists who gradually swap characters and finally take each other's lives. As he thanked its director, David Cronenberg, from the stage, apparently irrelevantly, Irons directly addressed his fellow actors: "Some of you will understand why." Paul Newman had been among those to have written to him commiserating at missing out that year. "I have no doubt," said Irons later, "that if it wasn't for *Dead Ringers* I wouldn't have received this Oscar. It was a reward for both parts." *

Irons's career amounted to a master class in Oscar and anti-Oscar roles. Ten years before, Karel Reisz had cast him in *The French Lieutenant's Woman* because "he was prepared to be unsympathetic—very pinched, dry and savage—which I considered really courageous, because most young actors are so image-conscious." Regardless of any actor's merits, the Academy was never going to nominate an unsympathetic Englishman who abandons his fiancée for a sultry vamp—even if she was played by Meryl Streep, who of course did win a nomination (her first in a leading role). After finding fame on television in *Brideshead Revisited,* Irons proceeded to be far more eclectic than most of his contemporaries about film work. A Polish building worker in Jerzy Skolimowski's *Moonlighting;* the title role in Volker Schlöndorff's film of Proust's *Swann in Love;* then, anxious

* Irons's Oscar for *Reversal of Fortune* (which was down to only twenty-two theaters at the time of the awards) was subsequently reckoned to have boosted its $11 million gross to $16 million—a puny total, but a decent percentage increase. With three unsuccessful nominations, including De Niro's, *Awakenings* meanwhile added $12 million to its pre-Oscar $40 million. But *Goodfellas*' six nominations, despite Joe Pesci's win, added only $5 million to the picture's gross, raising it from $41 million to $46 million.

to cast off his too familiar languor, he braved the treacherous waters of the low-budget British comedy, with his son Sam and his father-in-law Cyril Cusack, in Roald Dahl's *Danny, the Champion of the World.* As one British critic put it: "This is not the filmography of one anxious for glory."

The last thing Irons did before mounting the stage was to lean into the front row and kiss Madonna, whose husband he had just declined to play in the forthcoming screen version of Andrew Lloyd Webber's *Evita.* "At a moment like that," he later explained, "you feel like kissing the whole world." As the second consecutive Briton to win Best Actor—again, moreover, in a biopic—Irons could count himself lucky. If inadvertently, he seemed to have damaged the prospects next year for Anthony Hopkins—already being talked about as a possible contender for a 1991 Oscar, as the serial killer Hannibal Lecter in Jonathan Demme's cultish *Silence of the Lambs.* An Oscar presenter that night, with his costar Jodie Foster, Hopkins had been lionized around town all week.

But the man of the moment at the 1990 Academy Awards was Kevin Costner, whose name now came out of the envelopes opened by Tom Cruise for Best Director and by Barbra Streisand for Best Picture. "It's very easy for people to trivialize what we do," declared Costner, an Oscar in each hand. "They say, 'If it's such a big deal, how come nobody remembers who won the Oscar last year?' But I've got a real flash for you. I will never forget what happened here tonight. My family will never forget. And my Native American brothers and sisters across the country will never forget."

In Oscar terms, *Dances with Wolves'* seven awards made it the only Western ever to win more than four awards, and the first to win Best Picture since *Cimarron* at the fourth Academy Awards banquet sixty years before. In cinematic terms, the Academy Awards heaped upon it said as much about the current climate of Hollywood—and indeed postwar America—as about artistic merit. *Dances with Wolves* was the "politically correct" film of the year. For all its treacly sentimentality—never a disadvantage with the Oscar electorate—the film possessed what the *Los Angeles Times* was pleased to call "a sweeping, epic heart," and enough conventional action to keep the audience awake throughout its three long hours on the screen. But its main Oscar asset was its moral dimension, its unapologetic attempt to set the record straight about America's past. The "real message to filmmakers," according to the *L.A. Times,* was: "Make more spiritually uplifting movies."

At one point during the 3-hour, 27-minute awards show, local hero Ronald Reagan appeared on tape to say that Westerns were his favorite kind of movie—"because they are simple tales of good against evil." As Reagan would have wished, however much critics and movie fans the world over might demur, the Academy had voted for the simple, uplifting virtue of Costner's Western over the complex, downbeat evil of Scorsese's *Goodfellas.* Which one of the two films reflected the real values of contemporary America, rather than the phony American dreams peddled by Hollywood for eighty years, was not a matter for relevant discussion.

Out on the Sioux reservation at Pine Ridge, South Dakota, home to most of Costner's Native American friends, a heavy discussion was well under way. They may have enjoyed Kevin's triumph from a distance, as they had enjoyed brief excitement (and welcome income) as extras in *Dances with Wolves,* but their plight did not otherwise seem to have changed very much since the 1860s of his life-affirming film. Now, thanks to their newfound celebrity, a legion of journalists arrived to report, in one typical example, that "alcoholism is rife. A quarter of babies are born with delirium tremens and are likely to suffer learning disabilities because their mothers have drinking problems."

Could Costner's film improve those statistics? Post-Oscar visitors painted a very grim picture of life in Pine Ridge. A child was twice as likely to die there, in the midst of the American heartland, as in Bulgaria, Cuba or Costa Rica. The incidence of diabetes was five times as high as America's national average, and the suicide rate double. Eighty-five percent of the adult population was unemployed (compared with national figures of 35 percent for Indians and 6 percent of all Americans). According to Congressman George Miller, chairman of the House committee responsible for Indian affairs, 45 percent of America's 1.7 million Indians were on the breadline, and only 43 percent managed to graduate from high school.

In the context of *Dances with Wolves'* seven Oscars, not to mention the $200 million it had grossed soon after, the most striking revelation of all was that the Sioux were still fighting to get their land back. The film might educate the outside world about Indian culture, said tribal leaders, but that was not their real problem. Pine Ridge was their home by necessity, not by choice. It was a century since they had been forced off their ancestral lands in the Black Hills, only a hundred miles away, in a land grab recently adjudged illegal by the Supreme Court—which had ordered the federal government to pay the Sioux $300 million in compensation. "We were not thinking of the money," said Wilbur Between Lodges, a former U.S. Marine who was now vice-president of the Pine Ridge Council. "Land is sacred to us, and we will never accept money in exchange for land. It is insulting."

The return of almost two million acres, some of the most beautiful farmland in America, seemed likely to remain a pipe dream. The Sioux would have to continue to eke a living from the near-sterile soil of the badlands. At the least, they hoped, the film might "help other people to help us."

But if *Dances with Wolves* could not help Kevin Costner, what hope was there that it could help the Native American? Within six months of his Oscar triumph, and his coronation as Hollywood's most bankable star, Costner was deep in trouble—for his lamentable attempt at an English accent and an acting display more wooden than ever, as one of two simultaneous Robin Hoods fighting it out more for box-office megabucks than the moral rewards on offer from King Richard the Lionheart. Virtue, as embodied in their respective Maid Marians, did not have time for much of a say before Costner and Patrick Bergin were both brought low by critics and audiences alike. In Hollywood, it seemed, Oscar or no Oscar, there was no escaping the ancient truth that you're only as good as your last film.

Costner sighed, counted his fee, and moved on to his next assignment, as the New Orleans district attorney Jim Garrison in Oliver Stone's latest monument to his beloved sixties, the Hollywood version of John F. Kennedy's assassination. Not too many roles for Pine Ridge in that one. As directors called cut on innumerable Native American projects, their minds were already turning to Hollywood's latest cultural fad, the "eco-movie." Deep in the troubled rain forests, a thousand location scouts stirred.

In 1991 The Silence of the Lambs became only the third film in Oscar history to sweep all five top awards: Best Picture, Best Director (Jonathan Demme), Best Actor (Anthony Hopkins), Best Actress (Jodie Foster), and Best Adapted Screenplay (Ted Tally). Hopkins and Foster were the sixth movie co-stars to carry off both the top acting awards.

13 Silence Is Golden

As much as I love the
Oscar night pageantry,
it's a silly bingo game.
—JODIE FOSTER,
Best Actress, 1988
and 1991

When Columbia Pictures removes the free crackers from its office pantry, you know that recession has reached even Hollywood. Or when the owner of a car rental company is *rebuked* by a studio executive for offering stretch limos at sedan prices: "He said he didn't want his stars to be seen leaving in such a big car." Or when trade-paper advertisements in the run-up to the Oscar nominations are down by 33 percent. The 64th Academy Awards, to be presented on March 30, 1992, were billed in advance as "The Austerity Oscars."

To some extent, naturally, all this was a display of political correctness, Hollywood-style. "It is L.A. recession chic," said the public relations director of the Bel Air Hotel, "not to be seen in a fur coat going to a caviar and champagne do." But party organizers, florists and caterers all reported business down by 25 percent. "Our clients don't want to look ostentatious and read next day how insensitive they were to the economic crisis," said the caterer to MCA-

Universal and Time Warner. So those engraved party invitations costing $100 in themselves were this year replaced by flimsy five-dollar bits of cardboard.

If they arrived at all. With party bookings drastically down from last year, some chefs were even preparing three- instead of four-course meals. There was talk of the usual champagne and caviar giving way to beer and sausages—served off the ultimate indignity, paper plates. How could it have come to this?

The studio moguls were said to have spent Christmas 1991 weeping into their swimming pools. Was Tinseltown losing its way again? For the first time in fifteen years, American cinemas had sold fewer than a billion tickets. While admissions had declined by 6.4 percent, the budget of the average film had risen 10 percent to $27 million. To make matters worse, the audience was deserting during a recession, when people traditionally escape their problems by going to the movies. This year, Americans did not appear to have rated the country's 27,000 cinemas high among their places of solace. As video rentals topped $4 billion for the first time, it was clear that Hollywood's product was becoming increasingly resistible. More and more people were prepared to wait longer to pay less to see it at home.

In the summer of 1991, West Coast studios spent $2 billion to make $2 billion—"not a very reassuring statistic," in the words of one industry analyst. There had followed a spate of reluctant belt-tightening by all. MGM-Pathe anyway spent the year in turmoil, thanks to its flirtation with Giancarlo Paretti, the Italian waiter-turned-financier who saw the year out in an Italian jail. But even high fliers like Carolco, makers of the *Rambo* films, started laying off staff and canceling projects; the year's top grosser, *Terminator 2: Judgment Day,* could not stop the company finishing the year $171 million in debt. No fewer than fifteen independent filmmaking companies filed for bankruptcy in 1991.

They weren't the only ones. There was no starker symbol of Hollywood's apparent crisis than Orion, the distributors of last year's Academy Award winner for Best Picture (who would wind up winning this year's as well). An apparently triumphant decade championing such other independent, and Oscar-winning, products as *Amadeus* and *Platoon* was ending in tears. Orion was already in bankruptcy protection, despite a post-Oscar bonus of $70 million (out of a $177 million total domestic gross) from *Dances with Wolves,* and an apparently huge windfall from *The Silence of the Lambs.*

If a disastrous venture into television had proved Orion's ultimate undoing, this late burst of hit movies came too late to save the day. By the time *The Silence of the Lambs* began coining big bucks, Orion had been forced into a last-ditch deal with Columbia, handing over the foreign and video rights to its next fifty films for $175 million. The company could only watch with chagrin as *The Addams Family* also came good, taking $67 million in its first three weeks; distribution rights had been sold off in advance to Paramount for just $20 million.

Ten days before Christmas, Orion was forced to file for protection under Chapter 11 of the Federal Bankruptcy Code. The company's debt was estimated at $510 million, with further liabilities of at least $175 million. Among its creditors were such big hitters as Kevin Costner (whose TIG production company was owed $3 million) and Jonathan Demme, director of *The Silence of the Lambs* (owed $364,000). Projects Orion was forced to postpone or sell off included Woody Allen's *Shadows and Fog,* Michelle Pfeiffer's *Love Fields* and the projected third installment of *Robocop.*

There was little schadenfreude in other boardrooms; there but for the grace of Schwarzenegger could go any of them. Even in Hollywood, however, everything is relative. Global earnings may have fallen as much as 6.4 percent, but they still constituted a gross take of $4.6 billion. Four 1991 films had exceeded the $100 million mark: *Terminator 2* at $204 million, *Robin Hood, Prince of Thieves* ($165 million), *The Silence of the Lambs* ($130 million) and *City Slickers* ($123 million). *Sleeping with the Enemy* had clipped $100 million on the presence of Julia Roberts alone. From the industry's point of view, the profligacy that had followed the huge commercial success of *Batman* reached a dead end with the comparative failure of its direct descendant, *Dick Tracy* (a film that had cost $46 million to make and $54 million to promote).

The studios had grown complacent during the good times, said *Variety* analyst A. D. Murphy, "greenlighting too many iffy products," producing a year with more than its share of dud movies. Even Jack Valenti, the perennially bullish president of the Motion Picture Association, admitted there were lessons to be learned. "This adversity may be the best thing that has happened to us in a long time. We have become flabby. . . . We allowed our kinship with audiences to grow slack. We offered them less than we are capable of, and not as much as they deserve."

Amid the dross, the public seemed also to have tired of the megabucks "event" pictures which had become not just Hollywood's standard fare, but its proudest boast and biggest risk. "There seemed to be more absolutely awful, abysmal, terrible, unwatchable films out this year than any year in recent memory," complained Hal Hinson of *The Washington Post.* It was, to one London critic, a "vintage year for flops, stinkers and turkeys." Among the expensive disappointments cited were Bruce Willis's $50 million disaster *Hudson Hawk,* Dustin Hoffman in the $45 million failure *Billy Bathgate,* and the Woody Allen-Bette Midler bomb *Scenes from a Mall.*

In Britain (where audience figures meanwhile rose to near record levels), the previous year's American flops bombed again—from *Havana* to *Godfather III* and *Bonfire of the Vanities.* "The surprise," as seen from London, was "not that American cinemas experienced a virtual boycott by many previous patrons, but that almost a thousand million were still willing to risk being bored, patronized or disappointed throughout 1991."

It was time for Hollywood to face some stern home truths. Escapism was still marketable—by way of violent action, unnerving suspense, overt sexuality or stylish comedy—but, in all these genres, an ever more discriminating audience now demanded higher production standards. Acting, direction and writing of top quality were the key to success, in big-budget movies and small. Could Jeffrey Katzenberg, the head of Disney, have been right that "Small is better," in a widely leaked January memo calling for cost cuts? "In the beginning and end," wrote Katzenberg, complaining especially about the money squandered on *Dick Tracy,* "the story is what counts. Everything else depends on that."

On Oscar day 1992, Disney executives confirmed the first redundancies in a 25 percent reduction in staff. The company had already cut its average production budget from $24.5 million to $16.3 million. Far more significantly, 1991 had seen Disney spend $9 million on two box-office stars rather than $55 million on eleven the previous year. Many other studio chiefs also took comfort in showing less indulgence to their spoiled superstars. Some, of course, remained sacrosanct: such bankable figures as Schwarzenegger, Nicholson, Costner, Gibson and Roberts could still command fees as vast as ever. But a few big names whose slips were beginning to show —Robert Redford, for instance, after the failure of his $45 million *Havana,* Bruce Willis after *Hudson Hawk*—agreed to work on new projects for a percentage of the gross, with no upfront fees, thus submitting their reputations to a stern trial in the marketplace.

Most studios still found it hard *completely* to abandon the ritual pursuit of rich pickings from occasional blockbusters. At $100 million, *Terminator 2* had been the costliest film ever made, with Schwarzenegger himself on a fee of $10 million (plus a private jet). But it had already earned more than double that on domestic release alone; swiftly the best-selling video rental title of all time, the film could wind up grossing as much as $500 million worldwide. The year's end, by contrast, brought an ominous warning in the shape of Steven Spielberg's *Hook,* whose poor first week of Christmas business suggested that the Sony Corporation had little chance of grossing the $250 million required even to recover its $80 million investment.

Two hundred and thirty-eight feature-length films were eligible for the 1991 Academy Awards, fifteen more than in 1990. The year's most profitable film had been *Boyz N the Hood,* with a take approaching $60 million for an outlay of just $6.5 million. Next up, with a gross of $130 million from production costs of $19 million, came Jonathan Demme's film of Thomas Harris's novel, *The Silence of the Lambs.*

Demme's dark, satanic film was certainly a huge commercial success of the kind the Academy loves to honor, but was it too bleak to win awards? Not if it were judged by its opposition. If Hopkins's Hannibal Lecter enjoyed taking bites out of his victims, so did Robert De Niro's Max Cady in Martin Scorsese's *Cape Fear.* The 1991 race for Best Actor, in short, lay between a cannibalistic serial killer and a psychotic rapist, a cynically murderous gangster, a football coach screwed up since childhood by male rape, and a university professor so unhinged by his wife's murder that he sets out to find the Holy Grail on Fifth Avenue.

Beside Max Cady, Benjamin "Bugsy" Siegel, Tom Wingo and mad Professor Parry, Hannibal Lecter looked almost lovable.

• • •

At the 1992 awards lunch of the Publicists Guild of America, traditionally held three days before the Oscar ceremony, guild president Henri Bollinger committed a Hollywood-style Freudian slip when introducing his star guest. "Here to present our Showmanship Award, the guild's highest honor," he announced, "is one of this year's Academy Award nominees as Best Actor—Anthony Perkins."

Anthony Hopkins stepped up to the microphone, leaned round it menacingly toward Bollinger, and adopted his most chilling Hannibal Lecter voice. "Where are you having dinner tonight, Henri? I'll be right round . . . wrapped in a shower curtain!"

The publicists roared. Not even a surprise appearance by the reclusive Julia Roberts (whisked in and out to present an award to her *Pretty Woman* director, Garry Marshall) could upstage Hollywood's favorite serial killer. Hollywood publicists, you might think, have pretty much seen it all, met them all. As the lunch broke up, however, a throng of aging publicists-turned-groupies jostled for Hopkins's autograph on the Hannibal Lecter stills they all had ready in their pockets.

There had been similar scenes the year before, when Hopkins had graced the publicists' lunch at the height of *The Silence of the Lambs*' box-office success. As he joined forces with Jodie Foster that last Oscar night, the costars-of-the-moment-turned-copresenters, backstage scuttlebutt had marked him down as a longshot for the 1991 Supporting award.

No film in the history of the Academy Awards had lasted more than a year in the notoriously fickle memories of the Oscar electorate. This one had been released six weeks before the *previous* year's show, and had peaked at the box office a month before Hopkins's compatriot, Jeremy Irons, carried off the 1990 Best Actor award.

The Silence of the Lambs would be out on video and cable TV well before most of the big 1991 Oscar movies had even opened: Warren Beatty's *Bugsy,* for instance, Barbra Streisand's *Prince of Tides,* Oliver Stone's *JFK,* Scorsese's *Cape Fear.* Only the Coen Brothers' *Barton Fink,* which had swept the board at Cannes, had been around remotely as long; like most Cannes successes, it was deemed too arty and eccentric to win much more than a Supporting nomination for a bravura impersonation from Michael Lerner of the Oscars' founding-father, Louis B. Mayer.

Hannibal Lecter seemed to have faded from Academy memories months before the emergence of the year's surprise Oscar contender, Ridley Scott's *Thelma & Louise,* which rode high on a heady blend of box-office clout and high-octane controversy. Or had he? Thanks especially to the dark, dream-invading stillness of Hopkins's performance, *The Silence of the Lambs* just wouldn't go away. By the time the 1991 Oscar nominations were announced in mid-February 1992, few were surprised to see Hannibal the Cannibal in there somewhere. Henri Bollinger's subconscious had a point: more than a year after the film's release, his "Lecterspeak" still being mimicked all over the world, Hopkins appeared to have created a classic movie monster to rival Perkins's Norman Bates in the collective filmgoing consciousness.

If ever there had been a chance for Academy voters to belie their much-mocked short memories, this had been it. But Best Actor in a Leading Role? Wouldn't Hopkins and Orion have been smarter to go for the Supporting category, where the competition looked so much weaker? Would Hollywood *really* show unprecedented self-denial by exporting its Best Actor award to Britain three years in succession?

Barbara Walters seemed to think so. She booked Hopkins as the one nominee among the three superstar guests on her Oscar night movie special, now part of the annual circus, and flew to London to interview him on the Old Vic stage where once he had understudied Laurence Olivier. Industry analysts narrowed their eyes. La Walters was developing a reputation for foresight: the previous year her choice had been Jeremy Irons. How come she hadn't chosen Warren Beatty?

Beatty had finally become a father, and even married the child's mother (who just happened to be his *Bugsy* costar), right at the height of the voting period—which duly brought his film ten nominations, the year's highest crop. His own two personal mentions, as actor and producer, made his cumulative Oscar track record quite unparalleled.

Thirty years before, when Annette Bening was just three years old, Beatty had attended the Oscars with Natalie Wood, costar of his first film, *Splendor in the Grass.* Over the subsequent quarter of a century, since *Bonnie and Clyde* in 1967, he had produced and starred in five films which had between them won fifty-one Oscar nominations. Already Beatty had twice achieved what only Orson Welles had managed even once before him: simultaneous nominations for producing, directing, writing and acting—in *Heaven Can Wait* (1978) and *Reds* (1981). With the 1992 awards show falling on his fifty-fifth birthday, surely *Bugsy* would see the Oscar electorate compensating for his *Dick Tracy* disappointments of the previous year.

"I go for the enjoyment of seeing the people that I've worked with and know," was all the man himself would say. "With the understanding that it's all slightly masochistic. . . . It's enjoyable in the way that bobbing for apples is enjoyable. You can't take the game too seriously."

Beatty's acting and producing citations for *Bugsy* brought his grand total of personal Oscar nominations to thirteen over twenty-four years: four as producer, two as director (one of them on his debut), four as actor and three as cowriter. Of all these, only one (as director of *Reds*) had proved successful. Though Beatty's history of multiple nominations was unique, approached only by Welles and Woody Allen, he had this time handed over the screenplay to James Tobak and direction to Barry Levinson (also a coproducer). These two were also nominated; and Beatty's casting of Harvey Keitel and Ben Kingsley earned *Bugsy* its place on another Oscar record list as the fourteenth film in history to win two Supporting Actor nominations (Appendix C, section A4). The sheer heft of Beatty's record, plus his poor win rate with the Academy, looked set to ensure that his stylish period piece would sweep the board. And set a record: Best Actor for Beatty would make him the first person in Oscar history to win as both actor and director.

Such was the feeling as voting opened, reinforced by his well-timed marriage, which astonished a community convinced that bachelorhood was a lifetime commitment for Hollywood's cross between Don Giovanni and Dorian Gray. Beatty, for his part, clearly thought he stood an unusually strong chance for glory. Amid an unprecedented rash of personal interviews, in which he waxed lyrical about the joys of fatherhood and monogamy, the normally tongue-tied star even flew to England to answer questions (mostly, as it turned out, about his sex life) in the hallowed debating chamber of Oxford University's Union Society.

Yet how could even Beatty, let alone Hopkins, hope to rival a set of freak Oscar credentials as impressive as those mustered by the new, streamlined nineties-model Nick Nolte?

Though Beatty's Bugsy was the only real-life character among this year's nominee roles, the all-American football coach played by Nolte in Streisand's *Prince of Tides* made a stark contrast to Beatty's murderous gangster and Hopkins's mass-murdering cannibal. Nolte's bravura showing in an unlikely romantic lead opposite his director also enjoyed the classic Oscar bonus of a simultaneous contrasting leading role in another of the year's nominated films, Scorsese's *Cape Fear.* If Hollywood loves anything more than versatility, it's a comeback, and Nolte's return from a decade of drink-stained womanizing was shrewdly touted by his campaign team.

Until the age of 35, Nolte's feet had remained firmly on the stage. Disappointed by his failure to become a pro footballer, he had trashed the cinema and all its works, refusing all celluloid offers until a mid-1970s TV miniseries, *Rich Man, Poor Man,* steered him via the small screen to the big one. For the following fifteen years he had relished playing the Hollywood outsider, the town drunk gleefully pouring scorn on the system. Most tales of Nolte's drunken binges included a bit part for his dead father's artificial leg, which he was in the habit of waving from his convertible as he cruised Sunset Boulevard in his green surgeon's scrubs. On one occasion, having woken up in a Malibu house he could not remember renting, Nolte ordered sixteen tons of rock to be dumped on the lawn—"because I had always wondered what sixteen tons of rock would look like." An understandable point to reach, perhaps, if the best-remembered moment in your career is an underwater wrestle with a ten-foot moray eel (in *The Deep,* 1977).

But Nolte had since progressed to worthier roles, via a pro footballer in Ted Kotcheff's *North Dallas Forty,* a Vietnam vet in Karel Reisz's *Dog Soldiers* and a war photographer in Roger Spottiswoode's *Under Fire* to a bigoted redneck cop in Sidney Lumet's *Q & A* (1990). Fast perfecting a patent line in flawed heroes, he also developed a reputation for role preparation unheard of outside the Method School. Before *Down and Out in Beverly Hills* so bad did he smell, after sleeping rough and failing to wash for a fortnight, that his costar Bette Midler refused to go near him. Martin Scorsese was equally impressed by the amount of time Nolte spent among New

York painters before going Bohemian for *New York Stories.* It was while filming Walter Hill's *48 Hours,* however, that the real Nick Nolte shone through—boldly telling his costar, Eddie Murphy, then Hollywood's hottest box-office property, that he would never do any "really good work" until he stopped demanding salaries "the size of a third world country's gross domestic product."

For Scorsese's *Cape Fear,* the first film in which he had ever been cast as a happily married middle-class family man, Nolte seemed likely to have to do more research than ever. Before abandoning the bottle in 1990, he had himself got through three marriages on his apparently hell-bent spiral of self-destruction. By early 1992, not merely had he reformed, to the point of donning a dinner jacket to meet the Princess of Wales at *Prince of Tides'* London premiere, he had even enlisted as a paid-up member of the establishment. In 1991, as he celebrated his fiftieth birthday, Nolte finally signed on as a member of the Academy. As if to stress that this was not merely to vote for himself, it was also announced that one of the show's fiercest critics would this year be attending for the first time. "I don't work for awards," said Nolte, in a spate of interviews as unwonted as Beatty's. "So whatever happens is fine." Or again: "It's all a matter of perspective. Hell, if you win an Oscar it doesn't mean you're going to be excellent in your next film. And if you don't win, it doesn't make you a failure."

This from the man who had once said that the Academy Awards epitomized "the worst of America"? Nolte couldn't bring himself to sell out entirely. "I have some difficulty with the Oscars," he felt constrained to add. "I don't like it that if a film wins an Oscar, it can make another $20 million. I think that slants things. I don't like the fact that it's a five-hour event. I don't like the aspect of winners and losers. There's no way I can be Dustin Hoffman or De Niro. You can't put us in the same pot."

Nevertheless, he would still be breaking his "no-attendance-on-principle" habit of a lifetime. "I'm too old for that. If this was 1968 or 1969, I'd play that game. But now, I'll be there." In another interview Nolte repeated his long-held view that "Hollywood politics, not talent" determined Oscar winners and losers. "If he wins, he will be amused to have this theory proved wrong," concluded the interviewer. "If he loses, he will be amused to have his theory proved right."

• • •

Six weeks before Oscar night, as the final ballot forms went out, the Las Vegas oddsmakers installed Nick Nolte as the odds-on favorite for the Best Actor award. Beatty was second favorite at 3–1, with Hopkins in midfield at 4–1. "Nick's already won it," one Hollywood publicist told a journalist in early March. There were two rank outsiders: Robert De Niro, Nolte's *Cape Fear* costar (the film deemed too bleak to win awards and the actor already sufficiently laureled); and *The Fisher King*'s Robin Williams, still unable at his third nomination to convince the Oscar electorate that he was more than an overgrown television comic.

At 39, Williams was the youngest of the five nominees, whose average age was a mere decimal point shy of an unusually high 50. He also carried the biggest box-office clout. Films starring the former Oscar host over the previous decade had grossed a huge $591.5 million domestically, compared with $479 million for Nolte, $458.4 million for De Niro, $163.8 million for Beatty and $160.3 million for Hopkins. But *The Fisher King* itself could muster only a $42 million take by the voting period, as against $40 million for *Bugsy,* $68 million for *The Prince of Tides,* $66 million for *JFK* and $118 million for *Beauty and the Beast*—all of which paled beside *The Silence of the Lambs*' $130 million.

Hopkins and Nolte were the only debut nominees; this was Williams's third shot at Best Actor, Beatty's fourth and De Niro's fifth. Only De Niro, a member of the exclusive seven-strong club boasting both Supporting and Leading Role Oscars, had already logged enough awards to rule him out. He and Williams also shared the disadvantage that their films were not among the nominees for Best Picture.

It was, according to *Variety,* "the closest Oscar race for years." Not in recent memory, said the Awards' official historian, Robert Osborne, had an Academy Award race been "less predictable or more riddled with question marks. It's anyone's ball game."

Try telling that to Barbra Streisand. Amazingly, to all but its members, the directors branch of the Academy chose to repeat their *Yentl* snub of eight years before by failing to nominate her as Best Director while her film, *Prince of Tides,* made the list for Best Picture. Streisand had won a nomination from the Directors Guild (whose voting membership overlaps, more than most Academy branches, with its Oscar counterpart); this time around, however, she had been bumped from the Oscar race by a name not on the DGA list: *Boyz N The Hood*'s John Singleton, the first black director ever to win an Oscar nomination, whose debut at 23 also ended the fifty-year reign of Orson Welles as the youngest direction nominee.

The week that Streisand failed to appear among the Oscar nominations was a big week in other ways for directors who happened to be female. Penelope Spheeris's *Wayne's World* became America's number-one grossing picture; Nora Ephron's *This Is My Life* opened in New York to warm reviews; Martha Coolidge's *Rambling Rose* earned two acting nominations, the first for a mother-and-daughter team in Oscar history; and Agnieszka Holland's *Europa, Europa* dominated the Berlin Festival. "A curious week," noted *Variety,* "for women to complain about male bias."

One reason *Prince of Tides* might have been left out, whatever the gender of its director, was concisely put by the (female) critic who complained that it traded in "the pseudo-psychotherapy slop that used to appear in politically correct newspapers under titles like *The Child Inside You.*" No less an authority than *Variety*'s editor, Peter Bart, nevertheless took it upon himself to ask around about the Streisand snub, eliciting predictable female complaints of an "unconscious fear of women"—especially of Streisand herself, "the first woman to wield power in Hollywood."

Jean Firstenberg, director of the American Film Institute, "gloomily" confessed to the opposite view: that when perks, jobs or awards were being handed out, it was still "a distinct advantage" to be a woman. Dawn Steel, former production chief at Columbia, disagreed: "If women look at themselves as victims, we'll be losers." Himself an experienced studio executive, Bart had no time for the chauvinist camp. "Come off it," he cajoled Streisand. Having sat through countless closed-door meetings where arguments had raged about the choice of directors or executives, Bart could not recall "a single instance" where a woman was shot down on the grounds of gender. "Quite the opposite: more often, there was an effort to redress the balance." The blunt evidence from her voting fellow directors was that Streisand had damaged her chances by casting herself as Nick Nolte's love interest and then ordering the camera to linger longingly on the results.

The other candidate for ousting Streisand from the list, ironically, was the director of the feminist film *Thelma & Louise,* Britain's Ridley Scott. The only direction nominee apart from Singleton without a Best Picture nomination, he had apparently made way for Disney's *Beauty and the Beast.* The first animated film ever to be nominated for Best Picture, it also enjoyed the distinction of being the first movie ever to boast three different Best Song nominees.

Beauty and the Beast's nomination appeared to signal Hollywood's short-term solution to its problems: more family fare. When Warners announced that they were planning a new division, Warner Bros. Family Films, Universal, TriStar, Paramount and Columbia were said to be looking to a similar future. Disney was learning from the success of *The Little Mermaid* and *Home Alone,* and the $100 million it expected to earn from the video release, after fifty years, of *Fantasia,* its founding father's one commercial flop. *Fantasia Continued* was already in the pipeline, along with an animated version of *Aladdin.* Disney was also readying two *Bugsy Malone*–style "kiddie" musicals: *Swing Kids,* the story of a band of jazz-playing youngsters in prewar Nazi Germany, and *Newsies,* about an 1895 newsboys' strike against the Hearst and Pulitzer publishing empires.

Other studios were looking to reproduce on the screen the new wave of success enjoyed on both sides of the Atlantic by stage musicals. Among film versions of proven stage hits, Warners was planning to film *Les Misérables,* Columbia Stephen Sondheim's *Into the Woods,* Universal an animated version of Andrew Lloyd Webber's *Cats,* while a screen version of his *Evita* remained delayed only by casting rows worthy of *Gone with the Wind.* TriStar was meanwhile planning to star Bette Midler in a Lotte Lenya biopic.

Public complaints about a lowering of standards were heard only from those with nothing to lose—among them a former president of the Academy, Gregory Peck. Veteran of fifty-five movies, Peck disliked the changing priorities of the film industry and was not afraid to say so. In an outspoken interview with *The Washington Post,* the 1962 Best Actor revealed that his latest work opposite Danny de Vito in *Other People's Money*—a sign-of-the-times, Wall Street–type tale of asset-stripping sharks—was altered after being shown to test audiences. "It absolutely takes the backbone out of everything," stormed Peck. "You get pictures that aren't going to make anybody mad, certainly not challenge anybody's intelligence. . . . They've tried to turn motion picture-making into an industry like making shoes and sausage."

When *Beauty and the Beast*'s name was read out (first, thanks to alphabetical order) at the dawn press conference announcing the Oscar nominations on February 19, the roar from the assembled press corps led *Film Comment* magazine to conclude that the Academy voters had a point: "Nineteen ninety-one was the kind of movie year that deserved to have a cartoon named as Best Picture." On behalf of more discerning cinemagoers, the magazine unfolded a roll call of worthy 1991 names wholly overlooked by the Academy, including Bruce Beresford, Jeff Bridges, Martha Coolidge, Judy Davis, Robert Duvall, Larry Fishburne, Robin Givens, John Goodman, Elliott Gould, Jane Horrocks, Mike Leigh, River Phoenix, Alison Steadman, Peter Weller and Calder Willingham.

Given the Academy's choices, however, the race for Best Director also looked very tight. Would Beatty's *Bugsy* win a second Oscar for *Rain Man*'s Barry Levinson? Or *JFK* three out of three for Oliver Stone (out of ten nominations in all as director-producer-writer), putting him up there with Frank Capra and William Wyler—and a strong chance of catching John Ford, the only man to win four direction Oscars? Or could his work with Hopkins and Foster win the award for Jonathan Demme—whose previous credits included *Melvin and Howard, Something Wild* and *Married to the Mob*—at his first nomination?

A vociferous slice of California hoped not. The fact that the film's serial killer, Buffalo Bill, was portrayed as a transvestite misogynist offended sundry gay rights groups. They also took exception to the suggestion in Stone's *JFK* that the assassination of John Kennedy was a homosexual conspiracy. When word got round about Carolco's $40 million thriller *Basic Instinct,* another blockbuster built around a bisexual chain murderess, they took to the streets in protest. As Michael Douglas and his director Paul Verhoeven began location work in San Francisco, angry opponents threw paint, blew car horns and chanted obscene slogans to disrupt filming.

By depicting lesbian and bisexual women as butch antimale criminals, they argued, the film's script was perpetuating offensive stereotypes. In recent months, U.S. filmmakers had become inclined to listen to angry minority groups: the previous year had seen fights and killings in a number of cinemas, climaxing only the previous week in the death of a Chicago cinemagoer during a protest about *Juice,* a tale of young black murderers in Harlem, New York. Joe Eszterhas, who had been paid $3 million for the script of *Basic Instinct,* met the protesters, decided they had a point, and fell out with his producer, director and star by making some politically correct changes. "Joe Eszterhas is a snivelling hypocrite and I have no use for him," Carolco's chief executive, Peter Hoffman, told *Vanity Fair.* "Now we know this man has no principles," added Michael Douglas.

"Everything's so repressive now," complained Douglas (whose fee for the film was $15 million). "It's like the 'No' generation. You can't do anything, you can't eat anything, you have to abstain." Was he supposed to make movies "with representatives from gay/lesbian organizations, from women's groups, from Arabs, from Jews, from everybody else going through the script telling me everything that I can and cannot do?" Queer Nation, the West Coast group leading the protests, remained unappeased. "Our sexuality is used only when filmmakers want to spice up the plot or make the psychotic killer more *other,*" complained Patt Riese, a lesbian and self-styled Queer National. "We're never shown in a realistic light. Nobody ever gives us an opportunity to show ourselves with norman human qualities."

When *Basic Instinct* opened, gay protesters picketed cinemas wearing T-shirts proclaiming CATHERINE DID IT! in an attempt to sabotage the film's cliffhanger ending. ICE-PICK WIELDING BISEXUAL FAG-DYKE—DO NOT AGITATE read the back of the shirts. "This movie has the largest publicity machine on the planet promoting it, and we're riding that machine," rejoiced Queer Nation.

But many observers felt they had picked the wrong target. The film's fundamental flaw, argued *Time* magazine, was "arrogance: a smug faith in the ability of its own speed, smartness and luxe to wow the yokels. It is its attitude, not its morality, that ultimately undoes *Basic Instinct.*" And dynamic opening business proved *People* magazine right: "The protesters give the film credit for a seriousness it doesn't deserve, and probably assures its mega-boxoffice success." *Basic Instinct* took $15,129,385 at 1,567 screens in its first three days—second only to the hit comedy *Wayne's World.*

With the announcement of the 1992 Oscar nominations, there

were gay protests about the omission of such films as *Paris Is Burning,* a documentary about drag queens in Harlem, and Madonna's *Truth or Dare,* which treated gay and lesbian couples as a normal part of any megastar's social furniture. So Queer Nation decided to disrupt the Academy Awards. A thousand people, they announced, would be mounting a program of civil disobedience outside the Dorothy Chandler Pavilion specifically designed to provoke arrests. Leaflets would be distributed demanding "No awards for homo hatred." Even more alarming to Academy officials was the group's claim that it had infiltrated the Oscar-night audience and staff to mount "vocal public demonstrations."

Two nights before the ceremony, Queer Nation marchers invaded the Directors Guild theater to disrupt the screening of those documentaries that *had* been nominated. Their leader, Michelangelo Signorile, even received mild applause for his ten-minute speech arguing Queer Nation's case. But Academy officials maintained that they were confident of their security arrangements, even though they would be less stringent than last year's extreme post-Gulf War measures.

It was "entirely possible" that the protest groups had infiltrated the organizational staff, said an embattled Gil Cates, producing the show for the third time—"and the last," he said, having won an Emmy for the previous year's. There were three hundred people backstage, plus a hundred singers and dancers. "There's nothing you can do about it," sighed Cates, taking his tenth vitamin C tablet that day. If there was a disruption, security guards would "take out" the offender within twenty to thirty seconds. "If something outrageous happens, we'll cut to a commercial. Okay?"

On Thursday March 26, four days before the 1991 Academy Awards were to be presented, Senator David Boren of Oklahoma and Representative Louis Stokes of Ohio introduced legislation in each house of Congress that would open sealed FBI, CIA, military and other government files relating to the assassination of President Kennedy in 1963. It was a moment of film history, in the view of both *Daily Variety* and the *Hollywood Reporter,* as the initiative was "directly attributed" to Oliver Stone's "conspiracy film," *JFK,* which had opened in Christmas week to a tidal wave of controversy. Said Stone, who had recently met with the politicians, "They deserve an

Oscar for their courage and vision as leaders in the battle to make the American government open and fully accountable."

Frank Mankiewicz, former press secretary to Robert Kennedy, had been helping Stone lobby for government disclosure of files not due to be opened until the year 2029. Now a vice-chairman of the public relations firm Hill & Knowlton, Mankiewicz had laid on Capitol Hill screenings of the film and discreetly steered Stone around the seats of power. The legislation, said the director, was "the first step toward giving Americans a complete and honest look at the most grievous act of this century. . . . It could be the key that unlocks the answers to questions troubling Americans since 1963."

For Stone it came as something of a triumph after several months under heavy fire. "Dallas in Wonderland" and "Dances with Facts" were among the headlines which greeted his film before it had even opened. "In his three-hour lie," declared the columnist George Will, "Stone falsifies so much he may be an intellectual sociopath." Stone replied that he had every right to present alternative theories and shape a myth for the next generation. "The artist's obligation," he declared, "is to his conscience only. If he accepts the concept of social responsibility, it smacks of censorship. Everything I've done, I've done feeling good, and clear in my conscience." *JFK* was the most important film he had ever made. "No matter if the press drives me out of the country and I wind up making movies in England or France, it was worth it."

Stone appeared to be enjoying his latest bout of martyrdom; but America was growing corporately weary of his celluloid seminars on the sixties. By general consensus, this latest provocative essay was a technically accomplished and very powerful piece of filmmaking; by combining genuine archive footage with quasi-archive, documentary-style and narrative material, Stone swept the viewer through three hours of complex argument without once allowing the attention to wander. But that superbly edited conflation was also his problem. Which was truth and which fiction? When did fact end and speculation begin? Given Stone's own confession that he had made a composite character out of a real one, the New Orleans district attorney Jim Garrison, how was a moviegoing generation ignorant of the facts to sift through this welter of loaded, unsourced, revisionist material?

If the strength of Stone's film lay in the questions it raised, its weakness lay in his confusion of answers. The "lone gunman" and "magic bullet" theories, for instance, were usefully discredited. But was America really to believe that J. Edgar Hoover and the FBI, the CIA, the military, the Mafia, the government and even the vice-president, Lyndon B. Johnson, were *all* parties to so outrageous a conspiracy? To hand the picture any major awards, from the Academy's point of view, would be to endorse some of the wildest—and most dangerous—theories ever advanced on film.

JFK seemed a shoo-in for the editing award (which indeed it deservedly won for Joe Hutshing and Pietro Scalia) but little else. The Academy flirted with political trouble merely by handing Stone and his film nominations for Best Picture and Director; a Supporting nomination for Tommy Lee Jones, as the outlandish New Orleans businessman Clay Shaw, was due tribute to a film-stealing performance. The role of Jim Garrison proved a perfect match for Kevin Costner's limited acting talents; but he had been amply rewarded the previous year—when his Robin Hood deservedly won him the 1991 Raspberry Award as the year's Worst Actor.

Martin Scorsese, meanwhile, was widely reckoned to have put both feet wrong with his remake of the 1962 thriller *Cape Fear*. Amid all sorts of references to the British director J. Lee Thompson's original—including roles for its stars, Robert Mitchum and Gregory Peck, and an Elmer Bernstein reworking of Bernard Herrmann's original score—Scorsese also introduced some very nineties ambiguities. Where Gregory Peck's cruelly hounded Bowden was an unimpeachable prosecutor, for instance, Nick Nolte's was a defense counsel who had withheld vital evidence. The film climaxed in an orgy of superbly filmed, utterly mindless violence.

There was nothing here to challenge the sudden shadow of knife on shower curtain in Hitchcock's *Psycho* as still the scariest moment in cinema history. But as one critic asked, reviewing the development of thriller movies since the real world had hardened audiences to violence, from Vietnam via the Falklands to Croatia: "Could any director, from Scorsese to Spielberg, remake the *Psycho* shower scene today without showing us a pile of female flesh oozing blood over the white tiles?"

While as admiring as ever of Scorsese's mastery of his medium, most critics detected an unwonted commercialism in *Cape Fear* that had pushed him beyond acceptable limits. "Have our lives truly become so hollow that this kind of unapologetic bludgeoning of our sensibilities passes for jolly weekend entertainment?" asked Kenneth Turan in the *Los Angeles Times.* "A slasher film by Scorsese is still a slasher film," agreed Dave Kehr of the *Chicago Tribune.* "What's puzzling at this stage in his career," mused *The Washington Post*'s Hal Hinson, "is the way Scorsese could have set his sights so low."

Though *Cape Fear,* to *Sight & Sound,* defied thresholds, "revelling in its own transgressiveness," its climax lurched "towards the ridiculous"; the greatest horror in the film was "the death of imagination brought about by its suffocating reliance on pastiche." When Scorsese loses even the top-drawer critics, there is no way he is going to win over the Academy. Though he secured a nomination for a beguiling newcomer, Juliette Lewis, the man widely considered the finest director at work today failed yet again to make the lists himself. However high-minded, Scorsese is a filmmaker prepared to play Hollywood's game, who would be far from averse to the establishment acceptance conferred by an Oscar; yet he can look back on only three nominations, for *Raging Bull* (1980), *The Last Temptation of Christ* (1988) and *Goodfellas* (1990). The first and last of these, moreover, he lost to middlebrow actors-turned-debut-directors, Robert Redford and Kevin Costner.

But Scorsese's (or indeed Streisand's) ill luck with the Academy was as nothing to its continuing rejection of Steven Spielberg, still an electoral outcast, with only his bust of Irving Thalberg to mark the respect of the Academy's governors. This year, apart from producing Scorsese's *Cape Fear,* Spielberg's confection was *Hook,* an elaborate, $80 million personal fantasy. "I've always wanted to be Peter Pan. It's typecasting," said the 44-year-old director, who had spent his paper budget of $48 million by the time he splurged another $25 million on a scale replica of a seventeenth-century galleon complete with complex special effects. Add distribution and advertising, and the outlay approached the $100 million mark, making *Hook* the second most expensive film in history, after *Terminator 2.* No wonder TriStar's directors were said to look as if they could hear the ticking of an alarm clock within their costly crocodile.

"In all its opulence and frenzy," wrote *Variety,* "*Hook* may be singled out not necessarily on its merits as a movie, but as a metaphor for a time that is no more." Even the star presence of Dustin Hoffman in the title role, with Robin Williams as a confusingly adult Pan and Julia Roberts as a toothy Tinker Bell, could not rescue Spielberg's overcomplex scenario from disappointing both children and their parents alike. "It tends to be easier for a camel to go through the eye of a needle," concluded the *Los Angeles Times,* "than for a $60 million movie to genuinely touch the heart."

Better box office abroad, especially in Britain, offered TriStar its only hope of salvation, underlining another new feature of the 1991 movie scene: that American films now make more than 40 percent of their revenue outside the United States—almost twice as much as a decade ago. For his part, Spielberg ruefully echoed the austerity theme of the hour: "I feel really privileged that I was given a chance to make *Hook* at this critical time in our industry, when everbody is trying to figure out how to tighten their belts." His failure ensured that Americans would have to go on a movie diet: "They'll have to accept low-cal movies for a while."

Comparing Spielberg with Orson Welles, his most obvious precursor in the Hollywood sandbox, one critic concluded that "the master of cinema is exiled because his mastery begins to look like waste, profligacy, indulgence. It is too much what it is." As with so much of his previous work, *Hook* won Spielberg himself nothing in the way of Academy recognition, while his team received the usual nominations for Art Direction, Costume Design, Makeup, Visual Effects and Music. *Terminator 2* seemed an even stronger candidate for Visual Effects, with nominations thrown in for Editing, Cinematography, Makeup, Sound and Sound Effects Editing. Art Direction, Cinematography, Costume Design and Score were also among *Bugsy*'s ten nominations, adding weight to its otherwise manufactured appeal.

So the early stages of the voting period seemed to bode well for the cosmetic charms of *Bugsy,* just as the Beatty-Bening-baby show took to the road. Once voters actually saw the picture, however, the disappointment quotient grew. Wasn't this a somewhat two-dimensional, cardboard-cutout gangster, despite the hype suggesting that Beatty the actor had never showed more range? The public seemed to agree. The picture had taken barely $40 million by the time of the nominations; the weakest of the Best Picture nominees at the box office, *Bugsy* had still grossed only $47.5 million by the time of the awards.

Then the legendary Oscar name of Wilkerson returned to haunt another generation, as W. R. ("Willie") Wilkerson, Jr., son of the founder-editor of the *Hollywood Reporter,* lodged a loud public protest that it was his father—not "Bugsy" Siegel—who had first stood in the Nevada desert and envisioned Las Vegas.

It was when Wilkerson ran out of money, according to his son, that Siegel and his friends at Murder Inc. stepped in. "It was my father's idea, plain and simple," said Wilkerson Jr. It was "infuriating" to see a film like *Bugsy* "roll over history." As to the scene where Beatty's Siegel stands out in the desert hatching the idea of a glittering resort complex, over whose construction he then presides: "Believe me, [Siegel] never saw the Flamingo until he bought into it. He wasn't going to be caught out in the Nevada desert." It was Wilkerson, Sr., who had dreamed in the desert ("not of his own volition . . . he'd suffered a flat tire and was waiting for a tow") and it was he who had thought up the name Flamingo ("all his life he had a love of exotic birds").

The truth was that after hearing about Billy Wilkerson's financial problems, Siegel approached him at Ciro's one evening and offered to bail him out with a million dollars, which "turned out to be syndicate money." Willie, Jr., added the striking footnote that Siegel's girlfriend Virginia Hill (the Annette Bening character) was "nowhere near" Las Vegas at the time; she was in Paris. "Do powerful Hollywood revisionists like Beatty and Stone get a free ride at the expense of history?" he asked. "Should nondocumentary filmmakers be held accountable? When does art become fact? Is a blending of fact and fiction truly good for our diet?"

Wilkerson's claims were lent academic support by Susan Jarvis, director of the Gaming Resource Center of the University of Nevada at Las Vegas, who confirmed that it was indeed his father whose idea it had originally been to turn a barren stretch of desert into a gaming mecca, and who had initially drawn up plans and broken ground for the Flamingo Hotel-Casino. On Oscar night itself, an award-winning TV documentary added to the controversy by accusing Siegel of promoting racial segregation on the Las Vegas strip in the late 1940s.

"It's like telling the story of the Civil War without mentioning slavery," said its producer, William Drummond, of Beatty's *Bugsy.* "It's a grave oversight never to mention that this was a guy who decided he was going to institutionalize segregation in the entertainment industry." Drummond and his film cited the example of Lena Horne, who refused to stay in the rundown shacks of Vegas's shanty town, as Siegel had compelled other black performers to do. "He reluctantly allowed her to stay in a cabana. But the hotel maids were instructed to burn her linen every day."

Where was Beatty's political correctness now? As the *Bugsy* bandwagon stalled, so *The Silence of the Lambs* gathered momentum. Never before had the Academy handed its top honor to so dark a picture. Call it a Gothic thriller, even a horror film: it would be the first in either category to be dubbed the proudest product of Hollywood's year. Nor was the Academy in the habit of honoring serial killers for their beguiling qualities. Witness Bogart and Cagney, two of the toughest of screen tough guys, who had both been obliged to step out of character—as lovable rogue and a song-and-dance man—to pick up their long overdue Oscars.

The recurrent targeting of Jodie Foster led at least one magazine to comment that "it must have been galling when the gay press, denouncing the film as homophobic, singled her out for attack." Amid the furor, *The Silence of the Lambs* brought Foster her third Oscar nomination, three years after she had won Best Actress for *The Accused.*

Demme had originally wanted Michelle Pfeiffer for the role of FBI agent Clarice Starling. When Pfeiffer declared the script "too bleak," Foster openly lobbied for the part. Perhaps the only contemporary female star yet to enjoy a screen romance, she argued that Clarice was "the first authentic female hero" in American film history. Foster had further improved her 1991 Oscar credentials by making her directing debut with the well-received *Little Man Tate,* in which she also starred as the single-parent mother of an unusually gifted child. On set she won herself the nickname of B.L.T.: Bossy Little Thing. "Winning the Oscar," Foster testified, "helped me to get the kind of budget I needed."

Sharing the title roles in *Thelma & Louise* seemed likely to split the Best Actress votes of Geena Davis and Susan Sarandon. This traditional pattern tended to break only when one nominee was self-evidently the senior partner—as, for instance, Dustin Hoffman over Tom Cruise in *Rain Man,* Shirley MacLaine over Debra Winger in *Terms of Endearment,* or even F. Murray Abraham over Tom Hulce in *Amadeus.* Only eighteen winners had emerged from the fifty-one twosomes previously conominated—and only one of them, MacLaine, was in the Best Actress category. This year, Sarandon's edge over Davis looked too slight to alter the statistics. Davis already possessed a Supporting Oscar; and Sarandon enjoyed the bonus of a rich but unrewarded decade of work since her only previous mention, opposite Burt Lancaster in *Atlantic City*—not to mention a highly conspicuous pregnancy at the age of 45. But Foster was looking very tough to beat.

Many voters professed themselves baffled by the nomination of Bette Midler in one of the year's real duds, Mark Rydell's $40 million antiwar musical *For the Boys.* Oscar trivialists meanwhile noted the first mother-and-daughter team to win simultaneous nominations: Laura Dern for Best Actress and Diane Ladd's second consecutive shot at the Supporting award, both in Martha Coolidge's *Rambling Rose.* Dern's was a well-deserved honorable mention; her time would no doubt come. As she recycled last year's campaign letters, however, Ladd must have fancied her chances against Kate Nelligan (*Prince of Tides*) and Mercedes Ruehl (*The Fisher King*). Even at 52, she looked a mere stripling to 82-year-old Jessica Tandy (*Fried Green Tomatoes*) and a veteran beside 18-year-old Juliette Lewis (*Cape Fear*).

Stylistically torn between reserved ("a Maggie Smith/Vanessa Redgrave–type dress") and racy ("to go for the sex while I can still walk up the aisle"), Ladd declared that she wanted a new man in her life: "Oscar's been courting me, flirting with me, pretending to come home to my bed. But I want him to get serious this time. Come on, man, make that commitment! Come live with me now!"

By awards night the major studios were reckoned to have spent more than $7 million promoting their wares for Oscar nominations and awards. The biggest spenders were Columbia and TriStar, both bought by the Sony Corporation in 1991 for $3 billion, and desperate to prove to their new Japanese bosses that their films could both make money *and* win awards. The two company heads, Peter Guber and Mike Medavoy, were reckoned to have spent at least $3 million promoting the Oscar chances of *The Prince of Tides, City Slickers* and *Boyz N the Hood* (Columbia) and *Bugsy, The Fisher King, Hook* and *Terminator 2* (TriStar). Next came Disney, who lavished $1 million-plus on *Beauty and the Beast* and *Rocketeer.* Providentially, Orion had set aside a $350,000 promotional budget for *The Silence of the Lambs* before sliding toward bankruptcy—including $50,000 for a post-Oscar party at Beverly Hills' Rex 11 Ristorante.

As special couriers toured Academy members' homes delivering "Hollywood scuds"—sleek presentation packs containing videos, picture books and soundtrack CDs—*City Slickers*' Jack Palance and *Barton Fink*'s Michael Lerner were among the Supporting hopefuls who hired themselves publicists for the duration of the campaign. "Actors I've never met before have been running up to me with nice things to say," enthused Lerner during Elizabeth Taylor's sixtieth birthday bash at Disneyland. "I've been at it for twenty-four years, but now I'm an overnight success." Lerner was given more chance, what's more, of catching Palance than *Bugsy*'s Harvey Keitel and Ben Kingsley, or *JFK*'s Tommy Lee Jones.

Such are the rewards of trade-paper advertisements at $10,000 a spread, well-publicized screenings of a $10 million movie, and some tireless glad-handing around the party circuit. Ads also appear for hopeless causes, such as TriStar's touting of Arnold Schwarzenegger as Best Actor. This is now a standard part of the Hollywood star-stroking system. It's good for everyone's ego, and it raises visibility or status. Many stars now have expensive Oscar campaigns written as standard clauses into their contracts.

It is a system that leaves the independents still in dire need of their own separate awards show, even when one of them scores a rare breakthrough. In 1991 it was Britain's Mike Leigh, whose *Life Is Sweet* won the National Society of Film Critics award for Best Picture, and Best Actress for his wife, Alison Steadman. With any thought of an Oscar campaign way beyond Leigh's pocket, however, the film made not so much as a ripple with the Academy.

The other pre-Oscar awards had been spread around fairly evenly. The West Coast favored its own, with Beatty's *Bugsy* winning Best Picture from both the Los Angeles Critics and the Foreign Press Association (Golden Globes), who respectively chose Levinson and Stone as Best Director. Both gave Best Actor to Nolte, while splitting

Best Actress between Ruehl and Foster. Then both further confused the Oscar picture by handing other awards to *Beauty and the Beast.* The East Coast also showed tribal loyalty by giving Best Director to the New York–based Demme, Best Picture to *The Silence of the Lambs* and Best Actor and Actress to Hopkins and Foster. "This will show them in La-La land," crowed Demme injudiciously in New York. It was not a remark calculated to win over West Coast voters traditionally reluctant to hand their awards to easterners. By the time Demme also picked up the Directors Guild award, however, he had history on his side: only three times since 1949 has the DGA winner not gone on to take the Academy Award.

As the Independent Spirit awards celebrated *Rambling Rose* and *My Own Private Idaho,* Billy Crystal languished in his hotel room with flu. Would the show host be in shape for the awards by Monday night? Saturday saw him miss rehearsals, unnerving Gil Cates: "He's really sick. I'm worried about him." Cates grew even more worried when "Thing," the disembodied hand from *The Addams Family,* failed to work in rehearsal when required to bring an Oscar envelope onstage. With all 2,600 seats sold, $400 tickets were changing hands on the black market for $1,500. And right down to the wire, the *Los Angeles Times* was declaring that all bets were off. "Not only has no consensus emerged in the Best Picture category," wrote Kenneth Turan, "but opinions are so disparate that whatever candidate does win will doubtless do so by no more than a handful of votes." Perhaps the clearest category to call was Best Actor. "The smart money has to remain with Nolte, who fits the classic winner's profile of a paid-his-dues actor who gives a superior performance in an Academy-type film."

On the night there was no sign of illness in Crystal, fast becoming the latest Oscar institution. Coming onto the stage in a Hannibal Lecter mask, he strode down into the audience to shake a delighted Anthony Hopkins by the hand—the beginning of a third successive deft performance in charge of TV's unwieldiest annual special. But Crystal admitted to being at a low physical ebb; the show came ten days from the end of a demanding stint directing himself as an aging comic in *Mr. Saturday Night.* His debut behind the camera was one reward for carrying 1991's fourth-biggest grosser, the comedy Western *City Slickers.*

Too busy becoming the show's resident host even to dream of

nominations, Crystal had to fall back on satisfaction in the precedent set by his costar, Jack Palance, whose victory at his third Supporting nomination came a record thirty-nine years after his first (for *Sudden Fear;* he was also nominated in 1953 for *Shane*). If Crystal's smile seemed a mite forced, it only confirmed location gossip of a certain tension between the two—reinforced, it seemed, by Palance's bizarre choice of opening line to his acceptance speech: "Billy Crystal? I crap bigger 'n him." When the 72-year-old supergrouch proceeded to set another precedent, by performing some one-handed push-ups on the Oscar stage, he at least handed Crystal his running gag for the evening. "It's nice," said Palance, as laid-back afterward as he had been onstage, "but it would have meant more forty years ago. I would have tried different things in the movie business." And how many one-handed push-ups could he do offstage? "It depends on who's there. Usually 27,643."

Outside, the disruption threatened by Queer Nation had succeeded only in raising the noise level, as a handful of some five hundred protesters were arrested by police careful to wear rubber gloves. The most they achieved was to place suggestive stickers on the groin of a giant gold Oscar, and to shout, "We're gay, so are you," as various stars paraded by, while handing out maps showing the Hollywood homes of supposedly gay members of the movie community. Inside the Dorothy Chandler Pavilion, the majority of nominees and presenters wore the chic red ribbons which had come to signify support for AIDS awareness and research. Academy staff kept a supply in the wings for surprised or forgetful participants anxious to avoid politically incorrect dress.

Mercedes Ruehl had been named Best Supporting Actress, and *Terminator 2* taken the Oscar for Makeup (successfully hand-delivered by *The Addams Family*'s "Thing") before Beatty and Bening could smile at each other as she herself presented *Bugsy* with its first award, for Art Direction. After losing Sound Effects Editing to *Terminator 2, Bugsy* proceeded to add Costume Design, no doubt reminding Beatty of the same moment ten years before, when both he and David Puttnam saw this award signal the surrender of *Reds* to *Chariots of Fire.* Piqued that his new wife had not received a Best Actress nomination, Beatty now had reason to believe there would be ample compensations.

But *Bugsy* was to win nothing more—its two Oscars from ten

nominations making it the third time that a Beatty film, to his visible chagrin, had failed the general rule that the most nominated film is the most rewarded. Stone's *JFK* took Editing and Cinematography (which Robert Richardson was the first American to win for sixteen years, since Haskell Wexler for *Bound for Glory*). *Terminator 2* had won its third Oscar, for Sound, and Callie Khouri secured *Thelma & Louise*'s only award of the evening, as the first woman ever to win a solo Oscar for Original Screenplay, before *The Silence of the Lambs* first made its presence felt with the Adapted Screenplay award for Ted Tally.

There followed another brief moment of Oscar history when a New York architect called Bill Lauch became the first proxy to accept a posthumous Oscar on behalf of an AIDS victim—Howard Ashman, his mate of seven years, who had died at age 40 a year before seeing his partnership with Alan Menken on *Beauty and the Beast* repeat their 1989 Best Song success with *The Little Mermaid.* "Howard," said Menken, "I wish you could have seen the finished product. You would have been so proud."

"All good things come to those who wait," Tally had said, quoting his own script, and now he was proved right with a vengeance. For the rest of the evening—all four major awards—it was a climactic *Silence of the Lambs* procession. When Kathy Bates announced Anthony Hopkins's name as Best Actor, and Michael Douglas handed Best Actress to Jodie Foster, it was clear that a pro-*Silence* sweep had developed during the second half of the voting period.

Before the show, the 1988 Best Actress had said: "As much as I love the Oscar night pageantry, it's a silly bingo game. It's like five names in a hat, and one gets pulled out. If they don't call your name, it's not like you say, 'I wish I did that scene another way.' " That night Jodie Foster became the eleventh actress to be twice named Best Actress, joining Luise Rainer, Bette Davis, Olivia de Havilland, Vivien Leigh, Ingrid Bergman, Elizabeth Taylor, Katharine Hepburn, Glenda Jackson, Jane Fonda and Sally Field. She dedicated her award to "all the women who came before me and who never had the chances I had" and to "all the people in this industry who have respected my choices and not been afraid of the power and dignity that entitled me to."

Nothing was said publicly, but Foster's triumph further exorcised the moment eleven years before, to the day, when John W.

Hinckley, Jr., chose Oscar Night to shoot the President of the United States in a forlorn attempt to impress her.

Hopkins, who had donned his twenty-year-old "lucky" patent leather shoes for the occasion, had persuaded himself that Nick Nolte would win. "I can't believe this," he said onstage, with obviously genuine emotion. "It's really unexpected." Backstage in the press room, he stopped the questions to watch the Best Actress award, then led the cheers for Foster. Now it was her turn to look on as Kevin Costner handed the Oscar for Best Director to Jonathan Demme, whose acceptance speech rivaled Greer Garson's 1942 epic for length and unintelligibility. The grand finale saw Liz Taylor and Paul Newman sweep regally onstage, thirty-four years after starring together in *Cat on a Hot Tin Roof,* to present Best Picture to the producers of *Lambs:* Edward Saxon, Kenneth Utt and Ron Bozman.

For its $350,000 promotional budget Orion had won five major Oscars, all for *The Silence of the Lambs.* For the Sony Corporation's $3 million, Columbia and TriStar had between them won eight, all technical (or "minor") apart from the two Supporting actors. Warner Bros. and Buena Vista had won two awards each, with MGM, Columbia and Miramax on one each. Columbia's *Prince of Tides,* TriStar's *Hook,* Universal's *Backdraft,* Fox's *Barton Fink* and Seven Arts' *Rambling Rose* had all gone home empty-handed. In the audience as the nominated producer of *Prince of Tides,* Barbra Streisand at least had the consolation that, before presenting awards, Liza Minnelli, Jessica Tandy and Shirley MacLaine all made pointed remarks about her nonnomination as its director. Billy Crystal also repeated his *Driving Miss Daisy* joke of 1989 (when the Best Picture's director, Bruce Beresford, wasn't even nominated) by referring to *Prince of Tides* as "the film that apparently directed itself."

To an audience awash with the irony of Orion's plight, Edward Saxon seemed to be speaking for the entire community when he thanked its management for an "unwavering commitment to artistic freedom throughout the years." Jodie Foster, too, spoke of Orion "the way it used to be, and the way it will always be in my heart." But a bankrupt distributor was far from being *The Silence of the Lambs'* only claim to Oscar fame. The first thriller ever to win Best Picture, it was also the first top award winner to have been sold to cable TV and released on video before the awards. Though Orion

Home Video had released 575,000 copies of the video the previous fall—sold out so long ago that it was no longer in the top 50 video chart—the company had shrewdly taken advantage of the film's seven nominations by upping the price as it was readied for rerelease.

The Silence of the Lambs was only the third film in Oscar history to sweep all four top awards—Best Picture, Director, Actor and Actress—after Capra's *It Happened One Night* (1934) and Forman's *One Flew Over the Cuckoo's Nest* (1975). Hopkins and Foster were only the sixth movie couple to win both Leading Role Oscars, and the first for a decade.*

It was ten years since Colin Welland's Cassandra-like cry, "The British are coming!" The subsequent decade had seen the once-proud British film industry wither and die, largely thanks to the total indifference of a government that removed tax incentives while profiting hugely from ticket revenues. But British actors still commanded huge respect in Hollywood, even if they tended to win their awards in American films. The sixteenth Briton to be named Best Actor in the Oscars' sixty-four years (though the first to affect an American accent), Hopkins had set yet another Oscar precedent as the third British Best Actor in succession.

He was not an actor prone to detailed research. "I didn't do any," he admitted backstage. I just showed up, and did it. When you have a good writer, that's half the battle." Upon first reading the script, he sensed that it would "touch the pulse of people." On his second reading, he had clicked into the character of Lecter. "I always learn a part very thoroughly. As I start learning, the character becomes like a photographic plate. The image begins to show itself to me, and from inside my head I begin to see what he looks like. If I can hear the voice and begin to get a bead on how he walks, how he moves, all I have to do is become that image and bring it to the screen."

From the same Welsh town as Richard Burton, whose seven failed nominations he had avenged at his first, Hopkins could claim to share Nolte's track record as a reformed alcoholic and hellraiser.

* The others were Clark Gable and Claudette Colbert in *It Happened One Night* (1934), Jack Nicholson and Louise Fletcher in *One Flew Over the Cuckoo's Nest* (1975), Peter Finch and Faye Dunaway in *Network* (1976), Jon Voight and Jane Fonda in *Coming Home* (1978) and Henry Fonda and Katharine Hepburn in *On Golden Pond* (1981).

Like his mentor Olivier, he had been through an unsuccessful and unhappy period living and working in Hollywood before his return to the English stage proved the springboard for a grander return to the screen.

Dark and malevolent figures had never previously been his forte; he was better remembered, for instance, as the kindly doctor in *The Elephant Man* than the deranged ventriloquist in Joseph E. Levine's *Magic* (1978). He had, it should be said, proved worth an Emmy award as Hitler in American TV's *The Bunker*. But his Hannibal Lecter bucked trends on all sides. Before Hopkins, only Brando as the Godfather, Vito Corleone, had won an Oscar playing a character to whom audiences and Academy voters warmed despite his evil nature.

The Oscar truism that unsympathetic characters usually lose, regardless of the actor's merit, appears to have deprived Brando of the Oscar he deserved in 1951 in *A Streetcar Named Desire*. While the rest of the cast all won (Vivien Leigh, Karl Malden and Kim Hunter), Brando—in a performance now regarded as a screen classic —was snubbed. The Academy voted in character by preferring Humphrey Bogart's likable slob in *The African Queen,* Charlie Allnut, to Brando's callous, sexually violent Stanley Kowalski. The same went for Paul Newman's Hud in 1963, beaten by Sidney Poitier while his costars Patricia Neal and Melvyn Douglas mopped up. The rule does not, however, seem to apply to women; Bette Davis and Louise Fletcher both won Best Actress playing monsters.

"Giving Best Picture to as bloody and noninspirational a film as this," in the view of the *Los Angeles Times*'s film critic, Kenneth Turan, had to be "some kind of first in the Academy's long and curious history." It took the British critic Philip French to remind the alarmists that there were numerous Best Picture precedents for ghoulishness outside the law: in *Gone with the Wind,* for instance, Melanie and Scarlett shoot a menacing soldier and dispose of his body. But there were those who believed that *The Silence of the Lambs*' victory more probably indicated a healthy shift in the nature of the Academy's membership. "A few years ago, that film would be regarded as a slasher film by most of the Academy members," said a studio executive. "Only a younger membership would vote for it for Best Picture."

There were others lobbying for change. In an open letter to the

Academy, Miramax's Weinstein brothers called for sweeping changes to the documentary category. Contending that the very word documentary suggested "a kind of medicine the public don't want to take," and again citing the omission of *Paris Is Burning,* they charged the judges with undue emphasis "on subject matter rather than filmmaking."

More significantly, a group of heavyweight producers were arguing behind the scenes for the annual date of the Oscar ceremony to be moved. The December 31 cutoff resulted in "playtime hysteria" as films courting nominations created a "Christmas scheduling crunch" to remain fresh in the minds of the voters. The existing schedule, argued Terry Semel, president of Warner Bros., diminished excitement for the viewers, and damaged films' commercial chances. "It should all happen sooner. If the year-end is going to be the yardstick for what films qualify, that means we must wait too long for the nominations and too long for the show itself." So should the Oscars be moved to the fall? "That," said one Academy governor, "is the stupidest idea I've ever heard." Agreed another: "If it ain't broke, don't fix it."

In these enlightened times, however, when actresses like to be called actors, shouldn't categories such as Best Actor and Actress be merged? Few thought so, including actresses. "As far as I'm concerned, the more categories the better," said the winner, Jodie Foster. "There are too few exciting roles out there for everyone. So why encourage even less to be honored?" The Best Supporting Actress of 1988, Geena Davis, agreed: "Male and female actresses are judged equally now. Separately and equally. If they were in the same category, and the percentage was anything like it was for directors and editors, it would no longer be equal. Maybe we should add separate categories for women editors and directors instead." But 1990–91 nominee Diane Ladd put a hex on that: "An actor derives his qualifications from his sexual gender; an actress derives her qualifications from her sexual gender; a director's or editor's job is not qualified by his sexual gender." The consensus from the contestants, unsurprisingly, was against anything that might reduce the number of awards; far better, they said, to increase them.

In a meditation entitled "The Paranoia Pageant," the editor of *Variety* nevertheless canvassed opinions on changing the Oscars. "In an ideal world," said one director, "there should be no winners, just five nominees for each category, discussing their work. It would be a sort of colloquy among artists." An Oscar-winning writer agreed: "Not only should we honor our best films, but we should also devise a way to acknowledge our ambitious failures . . . those films that tried to advance the art but didn't quite make it. These are the projects that should be singled out at Oscar time."

Other opinions were less exalted. "Oscar night isn't about art, it's about commerce," said a producer. "The Academy has allowed its show to become too long and self-important." One nominee suggested abandoning the voting process and handing Best Picture to the top-grossing film and Best Actor to the biggest box-office star. "If the public wants down-and-dirty, I say let's give them down-and-dirty." Perhaps, mused an Oscar-winning actor, the show should be moved to Japan, "where all our money comes from. Then we can forget the statuettes. We can just hand out bags stuffed with yen."

The volatile nature of the 1990s, Peter Bart diplomatically concluded, led him personally to believe that the Academy Awards show was one American institution that should be left untouched. "In the end, I suspect everyone would be quite content to see the Oscars remain the same."

At 3 hours 38 minutes the 1992 show was only seven minutes short of the record for the all-time longest Oscar telecast, set on April 9, 1984. ABC Television made $11.5 million selling 21 minutes of advertising at a rate of $550,000 for each 30-second spot. The year's token technical glitch deprived the audience of hearing an impromptu speech from Hal Roach during a standing ovation in honor of his hundredth birthday ("I think that's fitting," ad-libbed Billy Crystal, "because Mr. Roach started his career in silent movies.") The token departures from script came when Richard Gere spoke up on behalf of AIDS victims and when Debra Chasnoff, winner of Best Documentary for *Deadly Deception: General Electric, Nuclear Weapons and Our Environment,* stunned the Hollywood plutocracy with a victory cry of "Boycott GE!" The show ended with a surprise satellite hookup with the shuttle Atlantis, whose crew floated an Oscar statuette in space. Few knew that the segment had been pretaped, just in case.

Steven Spielberg presented the Irving Thalberg Award to his buddy George Lucas, honoring him as "a creative producer whose body of work reflects a consistently high quality of motion picture production." The Thalberg's thirty-first recipient in its fifty-five years, the producer and/or director of the *Star Wars* and *Indiana Jones* trilogies, was also hailed for technical innovations such as his THX sound system. In the words of the Academy governors, Lucas had "carried the producer's role beyond the post-production phase of moviemaking into the theaters. . . . His leadership in encouraging exhibitors to upgrade their sound and projection quality [has been] an incalculable service to the motion picture art."

The Silence of the Lambs was the sixty-fourth of 382 nominated films to be chosen by the Academy as Best Picture, reflecting little more than changing middlebrow tastes over the years; Anthony Hopkins was one of 152 different actors over 64 years to be nominated for Best Actor, reflecting only Hollywood's changing tastes in leading men. Since the first Oscar ceremony in 1929, a total of 676 different actors and actresses had been nominated for the four acting awards—of whom 210 had won one acting Oscar, and a select 28 more than one. Only three artists—Katharine Hepburn, Ingrid Bergman and Walter Brennan—have ever won more than two.

What does the roll call of the victorious tell us about the history of the movies, about the growth and development of the major art form to have emerged from the United States in the twentieth century? Not, in the end, a great deal. The Academy Awards are about Hollywood, which is in turn about power, intrigue, the fickleness of fame, and above all money. The Academy Awards began as part of a high-stakes game orchestrated by the studio bosses to advertise their wares and swell their profits; now they have taken on a curious logic and life of their own, designed primarily to exploit the audience yet further, thus increasing the already disproportionate rewards on offer to those who work in the mainstream of commercial cinema.

The films and performers honored by the Academy tend to be those reflecting the celluloid American dream invented and nurtured by Hollywood. It is thus only logical, perhaps, that the awards bear much the same relationship to artistic standards as does that dream to the everyday lives of most Americans.

If film is an edited version of life, the Oscars are generally given to those who interpret life as Academy members would like to see it—not necessarily as the rest of us, mere moviegoers, would like to see it, and least of all as it is.

After three unsuccessful nominations, Greta Garbo accepted an honorary Oscar in 1954—but sent someone else to collect it.

In 1976, twenty years after "Robert Rich" had won the screenplay award for The Brave One, Academy President Walter Mirisch handed over his Oscar to a dying Dalton Trumbo, who had been forced to use a nom de plume during the dark years of the Hollywood blacklist.

Appendix A: Winners and Losers

Nominees in the Main Categories, 1927–91

[Note: * indicates winner.]

1: BEST PICTURE

1927–28 **Wings* (Paramount), Lucien Hubbard.
The Last Command (Paramount), J. G. Bachmann, with B. P. Schulberg.
Seventh Heaven (Fox), William Fox.
The Way of All Flesh (Paramount), Adolph Zukor and Jesse L. Lasky.

1928–29 **Broadway Melody* (Metro-Goldwyn-Mayer), Harry Rapt.
Alibi (Feature Productions, United Artists), Roland West.
Hollywood Revue (Metro-Goldwyn-Mayer), Harry Rapt.
In Old Arizona (Fox), Winfield Sheehan.
The Patriot (Paramount), Ernst Lubitsch.

1929–30 **All Quiet on the Western Front* (Universal), Carl Laemmle, Jr.
The Big House (Metro-Goldwyn-Mayer), Irving G. Thalberg.
Disraeli (Warner Bros.), Jack L. Warner, with Darryl F. Zanuck.
The Divorcée (Metro-Goldwyn-Mayer), Robert Z. Leonard.
The Love Parade (Paramount), Ernst Lubitsch.

1930–31 *Cimarron* (RKO Radio), William LeBaron.
East Lynne (Fox), Winfield Sheehan.
The Front Page (Caddo, United Artists), Howard Hughes.
Skippy (Paramount), Adolph Zukor.
Trader Horn (Metro-Goldwyn-Mayer), Irving G. Thalberg.

1931–32 *Grand Hotel* (Metro-Goldwyn-Mayer), Irving Thalberg.
Arrowsmith (Goldwyn, United Artists), Samuel Goldwyn.
Bad Girl (Fox), Winfield Sheehan.
The Champ (Metro-Goldwyn-Mayer), King Vidor.
Five Star Final (First National), Hal B. Wallis.
One Hour with You (Paramount), Adolph Zukor.
Smiling Lieutenant (Paramount), Ernst Lubitsch.

1932–33 *Cavalcade* (Fox), Winfield Sheehan.
A Farewell to Arms (Paramount), Adolph Zukor.
Forty-Second Street (Warner Bros.), Darryl F. Zanuck.
I Am a Fugitive from a Chain Gang (Warner Bros.), Hal B. Wallis.
Lady for a Day (Columbia), Frank Capra.
Little Women (RKO Radio), Merian C. Cooper, with Kenneth MacGowan.
The Private Life of Henry VIII (London Films, United Artists; British), Alexander Korda.
She Done Him Wrong (Paramount), William LeBaron.
Smilin' Thru (Metro-Goldwyn-Mayer), Irving Thalberg.
State Fair (Fox), Winfield Sheehan.

1934 *It Happened One Night* (Columbia), Harry Cohn.
The Barretts of Wimpole Street (Metro-Goldwyn-Mayer), Irving Thalberg.
Cleopatra (Paramount), Cecil B. de Mille.
Flirtation Walk (First National), Jack L. Warner and Hal B. Wallis, with Robert Lord.
The Gay Divorcée (RKO Radio), Pandro S. Berman.
Here Comes the Navy (Warner Bros.), Lou Edelman.
The House of Rothschild (Twentieth Century, United Artists), Darryl F. Zanuck, with William Goetz and Raymond Griffith.
Imitation of Life (Universal), John M. Stahl.
One Night of Love (Columbia), Harry Cohn, with Everett Riskin.
The Thin Man (Metro-Goldwyn-Mayer), Hunt Stromberg.
Viva Villa! (Metro-Goldwyn-Mayer), David O. Selznick.
The White Parade (Fox), Jesse L. Lasky.

1935 *Mutiny on the Bounty* (Metro-Goldwyn-Mayer), Irving Thalberg, with Albert Lewin.
Alice Adams (RKO Radio), Pandro S. Berman.
Broadway Melody of 1936 (Metro-Goldwyn-Mayer), John W. Considine, Jr.
Captain Blood (Warner Bros.–Cosmopolitan), Hal B. Wallis, with Harry Joe Brown and Gordon Hollingshead.

David Copperfield (Metro-Goldwyn-Mayer), David O. Selznick.
The Informer (RKO Radio), Cliff Reid.
Les Misérables (Twentieth Century, United Artists), Darryl F. Zanuck.
Lives of a Bengal Lancer (Paramount), Louis D. Lighton.
A Midsummer Night's Dream (Warner Bros.), Henry Blanke.
Naughty Marietta (Metro-Goldwyn-Mayer), Hunt Stromberg.
Ruggles of Red Gap (Paramount), Arthur Hornblow, Jr.
Top Hat (RKO Radio), Pandro S. Berman.

1936 **The Great Ziegfeld* (Metro-Goldwyn-Mayer), Hunt Stromberg.
Anthony Adverse (Warner Bros.), Henry Blanke.
Dodsworth (Goldwyn, United Artists), Samuel Goldwyn, with Merritt Hulbert.
Libeled Lady (Metro-Goldwyn-Mayer), Lawrence Weingarten.
Mr. Deeds Goes to Town (Columbia), Frank Capra.
Romeo and Juliet (Metro-Goldwyn-Mayer), Irving Thalberg.
San Francisco (Metro-Goldwyn-Mayer), John Emerson and Bernard H. Hyman.
The Story of Louis Pasteur (Warner Bros.), Henry Blanke.
A Tale of Two Cities (Metro-Goldwyn-Mayer), David O. Selznick.
Three Smart Girls (Universal), Joseph Pasternak, with Charles Rogers.

1937 **The Life of Emile Zola* (Warner Bros.), Henry Blanke.
The Awful Truth (Columbia), Leo McCarey, with Everett Riskin.
Captains Courageous (Metro-Goldwyn-Mayer), Louis D. Lighton.
Dead End (Goldwyn, United Artists), Samuel Goldwyn, with Merritt Hulbert.
The Good Earth (Metro-Goldwyn-Mayer), Irving Thalberg, with Albert Lewin.
In Old Chicago (Twentieth Century Fox), Darryl F. Zanuck, with Kenneth MacGowan.
Lost Horizon (Columbia), Frank Capra.
One Hundred Men and a Girl (Universal), Charles R. Rogers, with Joe Pasternak.
Stage Door (RKO Radio), Pandro S. Berman.
A Star Is Born (Selznick International, United Artists), David O. Selznick.

1938 **You Can't Take It with You* (Columbia), Frank Capra.
The Adventures of Robin Hood (Warner Bros.), Hal B. Wallis, with Henry Blanke.
Alexander's Ragtime Band (Twentieth Century Fox), Darryl F. Zanuck, with Harry Joe Brown.
Boys Town (Metro-Goldwyn-Mayer), John W. Considine, Jr.
The Citadel (Metro-Goldwyn-Mayer; British), Victor Saville.
Four Daughters (Warner Bros.–First National), Hal B. Wallis, with Henry Blanke.
Grand Illusion (R.A.O., World Pictures; French), Frank Rollmer and Albert Pinkovitch.

	Jezebel (Warner Bros.), Hal B. Wallis, with Henry Blanke.
	Pygmalion (Metro-Goldwyn-Mayer; British), Gabriel Pascal.
	Test Pilot (Metro-Goldwyn-Mayer), Louis D. Lighton.
1939	**Gone With the Wind* (Selznick, Metro-Goldwyn-Mayer), David O. Selznick.
	Dark Victory (Warner Bros.), David Lewis.
	Goodbye, Mr. Chips (Metro-Goldwyn-Mayer; British), Victor Saville.
	Love Affair (RKO Radio), Leo McCarey.
	Mr. Smith Goes to Washington (Columbia), Frank Capra.
	Ninotchka (Metro-Goldwyn-Mayer), Sidney Franklin.
	Of Mice and Men (Roach, United Artists), Lewis Milestone.
	Stagecoach (Wanger, United Artists), Walter Wanger.
	The Wizard of Oz (Metro-Goldwyn-Mayer), Mervyn LeRoy.
	Wuthering Heights (Goldwyn, United Artists), Samuel Goldwyn.
1940	**Rebecca* (Selznick International, United Artists) David O. Selznick.
	All This, and Heaven Too (Warner Bros.), Jack L. Warner and Hal B. Wallis, with David Lewis.
	Foreign Correspondent (Wanger, United Artists), Walter Wanger.
	The Grapes of Wrath (Twentieth Century Fox), Darryl F. Zanuck, with Nunnally Johnson.
	The Great Dictator (Chaplin, United Artists), Charles Chaplin.
	Kitty Foyle (RKO Radio), David Hempstead.
	The Letter (Warner Bros.), Hal B. Wallis.
	The Long Voyage Home (Argosy-Wanger, United Artists), John Ford.
	Our Town (Lesser, United Artists), Sol Lesser.
	The Philadelphia Story (Metro-Goldwyn-Mayer), Joseph L. Mankiewicz.
1941	**How Green Was My Valley* (Twentieth Century Fox), Darryl F. Zanuck.
	Blossoms in the Dust (Metro-Goldwyn-Mayer), Irving Asher.
	Citizen Kane (Mercury, RKO Radio), Orson Welles.
	Here Comes Mr. Jordan (Columbia), Everett Riskin.
	Hold Back the Dawn (Paramount), Arthur Hornblow, Jr.
	The Little Foxes (Goldwyn, RKO Radio), Samuel Goldwyn.
	The Maltese Falcon (Warner Bros.), Hal B. Wallis.
	One Foot in Heaven (Warner Bros.), Hal B. Wallis.
	Sergeant York (Warner Bros.), Jesse L. Lasky and Hal B. Wallis.
	Suspicion (RKO Radio), RKO Radio production.
1942	**Mrs. Miniver* (Metro-Goldwyn-Mayer), Sidney Franklin.
	The Invaders (Ortus, Columbia; British), Michael Powell.
	Kings Row (Warner Bros.), Hal B. Wallis.
	The Magnificent Ambersons (Mercury, RKO Radio), Orson Welles.
	The Pied Piper (Twentieth Century Fox), Nunnally Johnson.
	The Pride of the Yankees (Goldwyn, RKO Radio), Samuel Goldwyn.
	Random Harvest (Metro-Goldwyn-Mayer), Sidney Franklin.
	The Talk of the Town (Columbia), George Stevens.
	Wake Island (Paramount), Joseph Sistrom.

Yankee Doodle Dandy (Warner Bros.), Jack Warner and Hal B. Wallis, with William Cagney.

1943 **Casablanca* (Warner Bros.), Hal B. Wallis.
For Whom the Bell Tolls (Paramount), Sam Wood.
Heaven Can Wait (Twentieth Century Fox), Ernst Lubitsch.
The Human Comedy (Metro-Goldwyn-Mayer), Clarence Brown.
In Which We Serve (Two Cities, United Artists; British), Noel Coward.
Madame Curie (Metro-Goldwyn-Mayer), Sidney Franklin.
The More the Merrier (Columbia), George Stevens.
The Ox-Bow Incident (Twentieth Century Fox), Lamar Trotti.
The Song of Bernadette (Twentieth Century Fox), William Perlberg.
Watch on the Rhine (Warner Bros.), Hal B. Wallis.

1944 **Going My Way* (Paramount), Leo McCarey.
Double Indemnity (Paramount), Joseph Sistrom.
Gaslight (Metro-Goldwyn-Mayer), Arthur Hornblow, Jr.
Since You Went Away (Selznick International, United Artists), David O. Selznick.
Wilson (Twentieth Century Fox), Darryl F. Zanuck.

1945 **The Lost Weekend* (Paramount), Charles Brackett.
Anchors Aweigh (Metro-Goldwyn-Mayer), Joe Pasternak.
The Bells of St. Mary's (Rainbow, RKO Radio), Leo Carey.
Mildred Pierce (Warner Bros.), Jerry Wald.
Spellbound (Selznick International, United Artists), David O. Selznick.

1946 **The Best Years of Our Lives* (Goldwyn, RKO Radio), Samuel Goldwyn.
Henry V (Rank–Two Cities, United Artists; British), Laurence Olivier.
It's a Wonderful Life (Liberty, RKO Radio), Frank Capra.
The Razor's Edge (Twentieth Century Fox), Darryl F. Zanuck.
The Yearling (Metro-Goldwyn-Mayer), Sidney Franklin.

1947 **Gentleman's Agreement* (Twentieth Century Fox), Darryl F. Zanuck.
The Bishop's Wife (Goldwyn, RKO Radio), Samuel Goldwyn.
Crossfire (RKO Radio), Adrian Scott.
Great Expectations (Rank-Cineguild, U-I; British), Ronald Neame.
Miracle on 34th Street (Twentieth Century Fox), William Perlberg.

1948 **Hamlet* (Rank–Two Cities, U-I; British), Laurence Olivier.
Johnny Belinda (Warner Bros.), Jerry Wald.
The Red Shoes (Rank-Archers, Eagle-Lion; British), Michael Powell and Emeric Pressburger.
The Snake Pit (Twentieth Century Fox), Anatole Litvak and Robert Bassler.
The Treasure of the Sierra Madre (Warner Bros.), Henry Blanke.

1949 **All the King's Men* (Rossen, Columbia), Robert Rossen.
Battleground (Metro-Goldwyn-Mayer), Dore Schary.
The Heiress (Paramount), William Wyler.
A Letter to Three Wives (Twentieth Century Fox), Sol C. Siegel.
Twelve O'Clock High (Twentieth Century Fox), Darryl F. Zanuck.

1950 **All About Eve* (Twentieth Century Fox), Darryl F. Zanuck.
Born Yesterday (Columbia), S. Sylvan Simon.
Father of the Bride (Metro-Goldwyn-Mayer), Pandro S. Berman.
King Solomon's Mines (Metro-Goldwyn-Mayer), Sam Zimbalist.
Sunset Boulevard (Paramount), Charles Brackett.

1951 **An American in Paris* (Metro-Goldwyn-Mayer), Arthur Freed.
Decision Before Dawn (Twentieth Century Fox), Anatole Litvak and Frank McCarthy.
A Place in the Sun (Paramount), George Stevens.
Quo Vadis (Metro-Goldwyn-Mayer), Sam Zimbalist.
A Streetcar Named Desire (Feldman, Warner Bros.), Charles K. Feldman.

1952 **The Greatest Show on Earth* (de Mille, Paramount), Cecil B. de Mille.
High Noon (Kramer, United Artists), Stanley Kramer.
Ivanhoe (Metro-Goldwyn-Mayer), Pandro S. Berman.
Moulin Rouge (Romulus, United Artists), John Huston.
The Quiet Man (Argosy, Republic), John Ford and Merian C. Cooper.

1953 **From Here to Eternity* (Columbia), Buddy Adler.
Julius Caesar (Metro-Goldwyn-Mayer), John Houseman.
The Robe (Twentieth Century Fox), Frank Ross.
Roman Holiday (Paramount), William Wyler.
Shane (Paramount), George Stevens.

1954 **On the Waterfront* (Horizon-American, Columbia), Sam Spiegel.
The Caine Mutiny (Kramer, Columbia), Stanley Kramer.
The Country Girl (Perlberg-Seaton, Paramount), William Perlberg.
Seven Brides for Seven Brothers (Metro-Goldwyn-Mayer), Jack Cummings.
Three Coins in the Fountain (Twentieth Century Fox), Sol C. Siegel.

1955 **Marty* (Hecht-Lancaster, United Artists), Harold Hecht.
Love Is a Many Splendored Thing (Twentieth Century Fox), Buddy Adler.
Mister Roberts (Orange, Warner Bros.), Leland Hayward.
Picnic (Columbia), Fred Kohlmar.
The Rose Tattoo (Wallis, Paramount), Hal B. Wallis.

1956 **Around the World in 80 Days* (Todd, United Artists), Michael Todd.
Friendly Persuasion (Allied Artists), William Wyler.
Giant (Warner Bros.), George Stevens and Henry Ginsberg.
The King and I (Twentieth Century Fox), Charles Brackett.
The Ten Commandments (De Mille, Paramount), Cecil B. de Mille.

1957 **The Bridge on the River Kwai* (Horizon, Columbia), Sam Spiegel.
Peyton Place (Wald, Twentieth Century Fox), Jerry Wald.
Sayonara (Goetz, Warner Bros.), William Goetz.
Twelve Angry Men (Orion-Nova, United Artists), Henry Fonda and Reginald Rose.

Witness for the Prosecution (Small-Hornblow, United Artists), Arthur Hornblow, Jr.

1958 **Gigi* (Freed, Metro-Goldwyn-Mayer), Arthur Freed.
Auntie Mame (Warner Bros.), Jack L. Warner.
Cat on a Hot Tin Roof (Avon, Metro-Goldwyn-Mayer), Lawrence Weingarten.
The Defiant Ones (Kramer, United Artists), Stanley Kramer.
Separate Tables (Clifton, United Artists), Harold Hecht.

1959 **Ben-Hur* (Metro-Goldwyn-Mayer), Sam Zimbalist.
Anatomy of a Murder (Preminger, Columbia), Otto Preminger.
The Diary of Anne Frank (Twentieth Century Fox), George Stevens.
The Nun's Story (Warner Bros.), Henry Blanke.
Room at the Top (Romulus, Continental; British), John and James Woolf.

1960 **The Apartment* (Mirisch, United Artists), Billy Wilder.
The Alamo (Batjac, United Artists), John Wayne.
Elmer Gantry (Lancaster-Brooks, United Artists), Burt Lancaster.
Sons and Lovers (Wald, Twentieth Century Fox), Jerry Wald.
The Sundowners (Warner Bros.), Fred Zinnemann.

1961 **West Side Story* (Mirisch, B&P, United Artists), Robert Wise.
Fanny (Mansfield, Warner Bros.), Joshua Logan.
The Guns of Navarone (Foreman, Columbia), Carl Foreman.
The Hustler (Rossen, Twentieth Century Fox), Robert Rossen.
Judgment at Nuremberg (Kramer, United Artists), Stanley Kramer.

1962 **Lawrence of Arabia* (Horizon (GB)-Spiegel-Lean, Columbia), Sam Spiegel.
The Longest Day (Zanuck, Twentieth Century Fox), Darryl F. Zanuck.
The Music Man (Warner Bros.), Morton Da Costa.
Mutiny on the Bounty (Arcola, Metro-Goldwyn-Mayer), Aaron Rosenberg.
To Kill a Mockingbird (U-I, Pakula-Mulligan-Brentwood), Alan J. Pakula.

1963 **Tom Jones* (Woodfall, United Artists–Lopert; British), Tony Richardson.
America, America (Athena, Warner Bros.), Elia Kazan.
Cleopatra (Wanger, Twentieth Century Fox), Walter Wanger.
How the West Was Won (Metro-Goldwyn-Mayer and Cinerama), Bernard Smith.
Lilies of the Field (Rainbow, United Artists), Ralph Nelson.

1964 **My Fair Lady* (Warner Bros.), Jack L. Warner.
Becket (Wallis, Paramount), Hal B. Wallis.
Dr. Strangelove, or: How I Learned to Stop Worrying and Love the Bomb (Hawk, Columbia), Stanley Kubrick.
Mary Poppins (Disney), Walt Disney and Bill Walsh.

Zorba the Greek (Rochley, International Classics), Michael Cacoyannis.

1965 **The Sound of Music* (Argyle, Twentieth Century Fox), Robert Wise.
Darling (Anglo-Amalgamated, Embassy; British), Joseph Janni.
Doctor Zhivago (Sostar, Metro-Goldwyn-Mayer), Carlo Ponti.
Ship of Fools (Columbia), Stanley Kramer.
A Thousand Clowns (Harrell, United Artists), Fred Coe.

1966 **A Man for All Seasons* (Highland, Columbia), Fred Zinnemann.
Alfie (Sheldrake, Paramount; British), Lewis Gilbert.
The Russians Are Coming, the Russians Are Coming (Mirisch, United Artists), Norman Jewison.
The Sand Pebbles (Argyle-Solar, Twentieth Century Fox), Robert Wise.
Who's Afraid of Virginia Woolf? (Chenault, Warner Bros.), Ernest Lehman.

1967 **In the Heat of the Night* (Mirisch, United Artists), Walter Mirisch.
Bonnie and Clyde (Tatira-Hiller, Warner Bros.), Warren Beatty.
Doctor Dolittle (Apjac, Twentieth Century Fox), Arthur P. Jacobs.
The Graduate (Nichols-Turman, Embassy), Lawrence Turman.
Guess Who's Coming to Dinner (Columbia), Stanley Kramer.

1968 **Oliver!* (Romulus, Columbia), John Woolf.
Funny Girl (Rastar, Columbia), Ray Stark.
The Lion in Winter (Haworth, Avco Embassy), Martin Poll.
Rachel, Rachel (Kayos, Warner Bros.–Seven Arts), Paul Newman.
Romeo and Juliet (BHE–Verona–De Laurentiis, Paramount), Anthony Havelock-Allan and John Brabourne.

1969 **Midnight Cowboy* (Hellman-Schlesinger, United Artists), Jerome Hellman.
Anne of the Thousand Days (Wallis, Universal), Hal B. Wallis.
Butch Cassidy and the Sundance Kid, (Hill-Monash, Twentieth Century Fox), John Foreman.
Hello, Dolly! (Chenault, Twentieth Century Fox), Ernest Lehman.
Z (Reggane-ONCIC, Cinema V; Algerian), Jacques Perrin and Hamed Rachedi.

1970 **Patton* (Twentieth Century Fox), Frank McCarthy.
Airport (Hunter, Universal), Ross Hunter.
Five Easy Pieces (BBS, Columbia), Bob Rafelson and Richard Wechsler.
Love Story (Paramount), Howard G. Minsky.
*M*A*S*H* (Aspen, Twentieth Century Fox), Ingo Preminger.

1971 **The French Connection* (D'Antoni-Schine-Moore, Twentieth Century Fox), Philip D'Antoni.
A Clockwork Orange (Hawk, Warner Bros.), Stanley Kubrick.

Fiddler on the Roof (Mirisch-Cartier, United Artists), Norman Jewison.
The Last Picture Show (BBS, Columbia), Stephen J. Friedman.
Nicholas and Alexandra (Horizon, Columbia), Sam Spiegel.

1972 **The Godfather* (Ruddy, Paramount), Albert S. Ruddy.
Cabaret (ABC, Allied Artists), Cy Feuer.
Deliverance (Warner Bros.), John Boorman.
The Emigrants (Svensk, Warner Bros.; Swedish), Bengt Forslund.
Sounder (Radnitz/Mattel, Twentieth Century Fox), Robert B. Radnitz.

1973 **The Sting* (Bill/Phillips-Hill, Zanuck-Brown, Universal), Tony Bill, Michael and Julia Phillips.
American Graffiti (Universal-Lucasfilm-Coppola), Francis Ford Coppola.
Cries and Whispers (Svensk, New World; Swedish), Ingmar Bergman.
The Exorcist (Hoya, Warner Bros.), William Peter Blatty.
A Touch of Class (Brut, Avco Embassy), Melvin Frank.

1974 **The Godfather, Part II* (Coppola, Paramount), Francis Ford Coppola, coproduced by Gray Frederickson and Fred Roos.
Chinatown (Evans, Paramount), Robert Evans.
The Conversation (Directors Co., Paramount), Francis Ford Coppola.
Lenny (Worth, United Artists), Marvin Worth.
The Towering Inferno (Allen, Twentieth Century Fox/Warner Bros.), Irwin Allen.

1975 **One Flew Over the Cuckoo's Nest* (Fantasy, United Artists), Saul Zaentz and Michael Douglas.
Barry Lyndon (Hawk, Warner Bros.), Stanley Kubrick.
Dog Day Afternoon (Warner Bros.), Martin Bregman and Martin Elfand.
Jaws (Zanuck/Brown, Universal), Richard D. Zanuck and David Brown.
Nashville (ABC-Weintraub-Altman, Paramount), Robert Altman.

1976 **Rocky* (Chartoff-Winkler, United Artists), Irwin Winkler and Robert Chartoff.
All the President's Men (Wildwood, Warner Bros.), Walter Coblenz.
Bound for Glory (United Artists), Robert F. Blumofe and Harold Leventhal.
Network (Gottfried/Chayefsky, Metro-Goldwyn-Mayer/United Artists), Howard Gottfried.
Taxi Driver (Bill/Phillips-Scorsese, Columbia), Michael Phillips and Julia Phillips.

1977 **Annie Hall* (Rollins-Joffe, United Artists), Charles H. Joffe.
The Goodbye Girl (Stark, Metro-Goldwyn-Mayer/Warner Bros.) Ray Stark.
Julia (Twentieth Century Fox), Richard Roth.
Star Wars (Lucasfilm, Twentieth Century Fox), Gary Kurtz.

The Turning Point (Twentieth Century Fox), Herbert Ross and Arthur Laurents.

1978 **The Deer Hunter* (EMI/Cimino, Universal), Barry Spikings, Michael Deeley, Michael Cimino and John Peverall.
Coming Home (Hellman, United Artists), Jerome Hellman.
Heaven Can Wait (Dogwood, Paramount), Warren Beatty.
Midnight Express (Casablanca–Filmworks, Columbia), Alan Marshall and David Puttnam.
An Unmarried Woman (Twentieth Century Fox), Paul Mazursky and Tony Ray.

1979 **Kramer vs. Kramer* (Jaffe, Columbia), Stanley R. Jaffe.
All That Jazz (Columbia/Twentieth Century Fox), Robert Alan Aurthur.
Apocalypse Now (Omni Zoetrope, United Artists), Francis Ford Coppola, coproduced by Fred Roos, Gray Frederickson and Tom Sternberg.
Breaking Away (Twentieth Century Fox), Peter Yates.
Norma Rae (Twentieth Century Fox), Tamara Asseyev and Alex Rose.

1980 **Ordinary People* (Wildwood, Paramount), Ronald L. Schwary.
Coal Miner's Daughter (Schwartz, Universal), Bernard Schwartz.
The Elephant Man (Brooksfilms, Paramount), Jonathan Sanger.
Raging Bull (Chartoff-Winkler, United Artists), Irwin Winkler and Robert Chartoff.
Tess (Renn-Burrill, SFP, Columbia), Claude Berri, coproduced by Timothy Burrill.

1981 **Chariots of Fire* (Enigma, Ladd/Warner Bros.), David Puttnam.
Atlantic City (ICC, Paramount), Denis Heroux.
On Golden Pond (ITC/IPC, Universal), Bruce Gilbert.
Raiders of the Lost Ark (Lucasfilm, Paramount), Frank Marshall.
Reds (JRS, Paramount), Warren Beatty.

1982 **Gandhi* (Indo-British, Columbia), Richard Attenborough.
E.T.—The Extra-Terrestrial (Universal), Steven Spielberg and Kathleen Kennedy.
Missing (Universal/Polygram, Universal), Edward Lewis.
Tootsie (Mirage/Punch, Columbia), Sydney Pollack and Dick Richards.
The Verdict (Fox-Zanuck/Brown, Twentieth Century Fox), Richard D. Zanuck and David Brown.

1983 **Terms of Endearment* (Brooks, Paramount), James L. Brooks.
The Big Chill (Carson, Columbia), Michael Schamberg.
The Dresser (Goldcrest/World Films, Columbia), Peter Yates.
The Right Stuff (Chartoff-Winkler/Ladd, Warner Bros.), Irwin Winkler and Robert Chartoff.
Tender Mercies (EMI–Antron Media, Universal/AFD), Philip S. Hobel.

1984 *Amadeus* (Zaentz, Orion), Saul Zaentz.
The Killing Fields (Enigma, Warner Bros.), David Puttnam.
A Passage to India (GW Films, Columbia), John Brabourne and Richard Goodwin.
Places in the Heart (Tri-Star), Arlene Donovan.
A Soldier's Story (Caldix, Columbia), Norman Jewison, Ronald L. Schwary and Patrick Palmer.

1985 *Out of Africa* (Universal), Sydney Pollack.
The Color Purple (Warner Bros.), Steven Spielberg, Kathleen Kennedy, Frank Marshall and Quincy Jones.
Kiss of the Spider Woman (HB/Sugarloaf, Island Alive), David Weisman.
Prizzi's Honor (ABC, Twentieth Century Fox), John Foreman.
Witness (Feldman, Paramount), Edward S. Feldman.

1986 *Platoon* (Hemdale, Orion), Arnold Kopelson.
Children of a Lesser God (Sugarman, Paramount), Burt Sugarman and Patrick Palmer.
Hannah and Her Sisters (Rollins-Joffe, Orion), Robert Greenhut.
The Mission (Warners/Goldcrest/Kingsmere, Warner Bros.), Fernando Ghia and David Puttnam.
A Room with a View (Merchant Ivory, Goldcrest/Cinecom), Ismail Merchant.

1987 *The Last Emperor* (Hemdale, Columbia), Jeremy Thomas.
Broadcast News (Twentieth Century Fox), James L. Brooks.
Fatal Attraction (Jaffe/Lansing, Paramount), Stanley R. Jaffe and Sherry Lansing.
Hope and Glory (Davros, Columbia), John Boorman.
Moonstruck (Palmer-Jewison, Metro-Goldwyn-Mayer), Patrick Palmer and Norman Jewison.

1988 *Rain Main* (Guber-Peters, United Artists), Mark Johnson.
The Accidental Tourist (Warner Bros.), Lawrence Kasdan, Charles Okun and Michael Grillo.
Dangerous Liaisons (Warner Bros.), Norma Heyman and Hank Moonjean.
Mississippi Burning (Zollo, Orion), Frederick Zollo and Robert F. Colesberry.
Working Girl (Twentieth Century Fox), Douglas Wick.

1989 *Driving Miss Daisy* (Zanuck, Warner Bros.), Richard D. Zanuck and Lili Fini Zanuck.
Born on the Fourth of July (Ho-Ixtlan, Universal), A. Kitman Ho and Oliver Stone.
Dead Poets Society (Touchstone/Silver Screen, Buena Vista), Steven Haft, Paul Junger Witt and Tony Thomas.
Field of Dreams (Gordon Co., Universal), Lawrence Gordon and Charles Gordon.
My Left Foot (Ferndale/Granada, Miramax), Noel Pearson.

1990 *Dances with Wolves* (Tig, Orion), Jim Wilson and Kevin Costner.
Awakenings (Columbia Prods., Columbia), Walter F. Parkes and Lawrence Lasker.
Ghost (Howard W. Koch, Paramount), Lisa Weinstein.
The Godfather, Part III (Zoetrope, Paramount), Francis Ford Coppola.
Goodfellas (Warner Bros.), Irwin Winkler.

1991 *The Silence of the Lambs* (Orion, Strong Heart/Demme), Edward Saxon, Kenneth Utt, Ron Bozman.
Beauty and the Beast (Buena Vista, Disney), Don Hahn.
Bugsy (TriStar), Mark Johnson, Barry Levinson, Warren Beatty.
JFK (Warner Bros., Camelot), A. Kitman Ho, Oliver Stone.
The Prince of Tides (Columbia, Barwood/Longfellow), Barbra Streisand, Andrew Karsch.

1992 **Unforgiven* (Warner Bros.), Clint Eastwood
The Crying Game (Miramax), Stephen Woolley
Howards End (Sony Classics), Ismail Merchant
Scent of a Woman (Universal), Martin Brest
A Few Good Men (Columbia), David Brown, Rob Reiner, Andrew Scheinman

2: BEST DIRECTOR

1927–28 *Frank Borzage, *Seventh Heaven*
Herbert Brenon, *Sorrell and Son*
King Vidor, *The Crowd*

Comedy Direction

*Lewis Milestone, *Two Arabian Knights*
Charles Chaplin, *The Circus*
Ted Wilde, *Speedy*

1928–29 *Frank Lloyd, **The Divine Lady, Weary River* and *Drag*
Lionel Barrymore, *Madame X*
Harry Beaumont, *Broadway Melody*
Irving Cummings, *In Old Arizona*
Ernst Lubitsch, *The Patriot*

1929–30 *Lewis Milestone, *All Quiet on the Western Front*
Clarence Brown, *Anna Christie* and *Romance*
Robert Leonard, *The Divorcée*
Ernst Lubitsch, *The Love Parade*
King Vidor, *Hallelujah*

1930–31 *Norman Taurog, *Skippy*
Clarence Brown, *A Free Soul*
Lewis Milestone, *The Front Page*
Wesley Ruggles, *Cimarron*
Josef von Sternberg, *Morocco*

1931–32 *Frank Borzage, *Bad Girl*
King Vidor, *The Champ*
Josef von Sternberg, *Shanghai Express*

1932–33 *Frank Lloyd, *Cavalcade*
Frank Capra, *Lady for a Day*
George Cukor, *Little Women*

1934 *Frank Capra, *It Happened One Night*
Victor Schertzinger, *One Night of Love*
W. S. Van Dyke, *The Thin Man*

1935 *John Ford, *The Informer*
Henry Hathaway, *Lives of a Bengal Lancer*
Frank Lloyd, *Mutiny on the Bounty*

1936 *Frank Capra, *Mr. Deeds Goes to Town*
Gregory LaCava, *My Man Godfrey*
Robert Z. Leonard, *The Great Ziegfeld*
W. S. Van Dyke, *San Francisco*
William Wyler, *Dodsworth*

1937 *Leo McCarey, *The Awful Truth*
William Dieterle, *The Life of Emile Zola*
Sidney Franklin, *The Good Earth*
Gregory LaCava, *Stage Door*
William Wellman, *A Star Is Born*

1938 *Frank Capra, *You Can't Take It with You*
Michael Curtiz, *Angels with Dirty Faces* and *Four Daughters*
Norman Taurog, *Boys Town*
King Vidor, *The Citadel*

1939 *Victor Fleming, *Gone with the Wind*
Frank Capra, *Mr. Smith Goes to Washington*
John Ford, *Stagecoach*
Sam Wood, *Goodbye, Mr. Chips*
William Wyler, *Wuthering Heights*

1940 *John Ford, *The Grapes of Wrath*
George Cukor, *The Philadelphia Story*
Alfred Hitchcock, *Rebecca*
Sam Wood, *Kitty Foyle*
William Wyler, *The Letter*

1941 *John Ford, *How Green Was My Valley*
Alexander Hall, *Here Comes Mr. Jordan*
Howard Hawks, *Sergeant York*
Orson Welles, *Citizen Kane*
William Wyler, *The Little Foxes*

1942 *William Wyler, *Mrs. Miniver*
Michael Curtiz, *Yankee Doodle Dandy*

John Farrow, *Wake Island*
Mervyn LeRoy, *Random Harvest*
Sam Wood, *Kings Row*

1943 *Michael Curtiz, *Casablanca*
Clarence Brown, *The Human Comedy*
Henry King, *The Song of Bernadette*
Ernst Lubitsch, *Heaven Can Wait*
George Stevens, *The More the Merrier*

1944 *Leo McCarey, *Going My Way*
Alfred Hitchcock, *Lifeboat*
Henry King, *Wilson*
Otto Preminger, *Laura*
Billy Wilder, *Double Indemnity*

1945 *Billy Wilder, *The Lost Weekend*
Clarence Brown, *National Velvet*
Alfred Hitchcock, *Spellbound*
Leo McCarey, *The Bells of St. Mary's*
Jean Renoir, *The Southerner*

1946 *William Wyler, *The Best Years of Our Lives*
Clarence Brown, *The Yearling*
Frank Capra, *It's a Wonderful Life*
David Lean, *Brief Encounter*
Robert Siodmak, *The Killers*

1947 *Elia Kazan, *Gentleman's Agreement*
George Cukor, *A Double Life*
Edward Dmytryk, *Crossfire*
Henry Koster, *The Bishop's Wife*
David Lean, *Great Expectations*

1948 *John Huston, *The Treasure of the Sierra Madre*
Anatole Litvak, *The Snake Pit*
Jean Negulesco, *Johnny Belinda*
Laurence Olivier, *Hamlet*
Fred Zinnemann, *The Search*

1949 *Joseph L. Mankiewicz, *A Letter to Three Wives*
Carol Reed, *The Fallen Idol*
Robert Rossen, *All the King's Men*
William A. Wellman, *Battleground*
William Wyler, *The Heiress*

1950 *Joseph L. Mankiewicz, *All About Eve*
George Cukor, *Born Yesterday*
John Huston, *The Asphalt Jungle*
Carol Reed, *The Third Man*
Billy Wilder, *Sunset Boulevard*

1951 *George Stevens, *A Place in the Sun*
John Huston, *The African Queen*
Elia Kazan, *A Streetcar Named Desire*
Vincente Minnelli, *An American in Paris*
William Wyler, *Detective Story*

1952 *John Ford, *The Quiet Man*
Cecil B. de Mille, *The Greatest Show on Earth*
John Huston, *Moulin Rouge*
Joseph L. Mankiewicz, *Five Fingers*
Fred Zinnemann, *High Noon*

1953 *Fred Zinnemann, *From Here to Eternity*
George Stevens, *Shane*
Charles Walters, *Lili*
Billy Wilder, *Stalag 17*
William Wyler, *Roman Holiday*

1954 *Elia Kazan, *On the Waterfront*
Alfred Hitchcock, *Rear Window*
George Seaton, *The Country Girl*
William Wellman, *The High and the Mighty*
Billy Wilder, *Sabrina*

1955 *Delbert Mann, *Marty*
Elia Kazan, *East of Eden*
David Lean, *Summertime*
Joshua Logan, *Picnic*
John Sturges, *Bad Day at Black Rock*

1956 *George Stevens, *Giant*
Michael Anderson, *Around the World in 80 Days*
Walter Lang, *The King and I*
King Vidor, *War and Peace*
William Wyler, *Friendly Persuasion*

1957 *David Lean, *The Bridge on the River Kwai*
Joshua Logan, *Sayonara*
Sidney Lumet, *Twelve Angry Men*
Mark Robson, *Peyton Place*
Billy Wilder, *Witness for the Prosecution*

1958 *Vincente Minnelli, *Gigi*
Richard Brooks, *Cat on a Hot Tin Roof*
Stanley Kramer, *The Defiant Ones*
Mark Robson, *The Inn of the Sixth Happiness*
Robert Wise, *I Want to Live!*

1959 *William Wyler, *Ben-Hur*
Jack Clayton, *Room at the Top*
George Stevens, *The Diary of Anne Frank*

	Billy Wilder, *Some Like It Hot*
	Fred Zinnemann, *The Nun's Story*
1960	*Billy Wilder, *The Apartment*
	Jack Cardiff, *Sons and Lovers*
	Jules Dassin, *Never on Sunday*
	Alfred Hitchcock, *Psycho*
	Fred Zinnemann, *The Sundowners*
1961	*Jerome Robbins and Robert Wise, *West Side Story*
	Federico Fellini, *La Dolce Vita*
	Stanley Kramer, *Judgment at Nuremberg*
	Robert Rossen, *The Hustler*
	J. Lee Thompson, *The Guns of Navarone*
1962	*David Lean, *Lawrence of Arabia*
	Pietro Germi, *Divorce Italian Style*
	Robert Mulligan, *To Kill a Mockingbird*
	Arthur Penn, *The Miracle Worker*
	Frank Perry, *David and Lisa*
1963	*Tony Richardson, *Tom Jones*
	Federico Fellini, *8½*
	Elia Kazan, *America, America*
	Otto Preminger, *The Cardinal*
	Martin Ritt, *Hud*
1964	*George Cukor, *My Fair Lady*
	Michael Cacoyannis, *Zorba the Greek*
	Peter Glenville, *Becket*
	Stanley Kubrick, *Dr. Strangelove or: How I Learned to Stop Worrying and Love the Bomb*
	Robert Stevenson, *Mary Poppins*
1965	*Robert Wise, *The Sound of Music*
	David Lean, *Doctor Zhivago*
	John Schlesinger, *Darling*
	Hiroshi Teshigahara, *Women in the Dunes*
	William Wyler, *The Collector*
1966	*Fred Zinnemann, *A Man for All Seasons*
	Michelangelo Antonioni, *Blow-Up*
	Richard Brooks, *The Professionals*
	Claude LeLouch, *A Man and a Woman*
	Mike Nichols, *Who's Afraid of Virginia Woolf?*
1967	*Mike Nichols, *The Graduate*
	Richard Brooks, *In Cold Blood*
	Norman Jewison, *In the Heat of the Night*
	Stanley Kramer, *Guess Who's Coming to Dinner*
	Arthur Penn, *Bonnie and Clyde*

1968 *Carol Reed, *Oliver!*
Anthony Harvey, *The Lion in Winter*
Stanley Kubrick, *2001: A Space Odyssey*
Gillo Pontecorvo, *The Battle of Algiers*
Franco Zeffirelli, *Romeo and Juliet*

1969 *John Schlesinger, *Midnight Cowboy*
Costa–Gavras, *Z*
George Roy Hill, *Butch Cassidy and the Sundance Kid*
Arthur Penn, *Alice's Restaurant*
Sydney Pollack, *They Shoot Horses, Don't They?*

1970 *Franklin J. Schaffner, *Patton*
Robert Altman, *M*A*S*H*
Federico Fellini, *Satyricon*
Arthur Hiller, *Love Story*
Ken Russell, *Women in Love*

1971 *William Friedkin, *The French Connection*
Peter Bogdanovich, *The Last Picture Show*
Norman Jewison, *Fiddler on the Roof*
Stanley Kubrick, *A Clockwork Orange*
John Schlesinger, *Sunday, Bloody Sunday*

1972 *Bob Fosse, *Cabaret*
John Boorman, *Deliverance*
Francis Ford Coppola, *The Godfather*
Joseph L. Mankiewicz, *Sleuth*
Jan Troell, *The Emigrants*

1973 *George Roy Hill, *The Sting*
Ingmar Bergman, *Cries and Whispers*
Bernardo Bertolucci, *Last Tango in Paris*
William Friedkin, *The Exorcist*
George Lucas, *American Graffiti*

1974 *Francis Ford Coppola, *The Godfather, Part II*
John Cassavetes, *A Woman Under the Influence*
Bob Fosse, *Lenny*
Roman Polanski, *Chinatown*
François Truffaut, *Day for Night*

1975 *Miloš Forman, *One Flew Over the Cuckoo's Nest*
Robert Altman, *Nashville*
Federico Fellini, *Amarcord*
Stanley Kubrick, *Barry Lyndon*
Sidney Lumet, *Dog Day Afternoon*

1976 *John G. Avildsen, *Rocky*
Ingmar Bergman, *Face to Face*
Sidney Lumet, *Network*

	Alan J. Pakula, *All the President's Men* Lina Wertmuller, *Seven Beauties*
1977	*Woody Allen, *Annie Hall* George Lucas, *Star Wars* Herbert Ross, *The Turning Point* Steven Spielberg, *Close Encounters of the Third Kind* Fred Zinnemann, *Julia*
1978	*Michael Cimino, *The Deer Hunter* Woody Allen, *Interiors* Hal Ashby, *Coming Home* Warren Beatty, and Buck Henry, *Heaven Can Wait* Alan Parker, *Midnight Express*
1979	*Robert Benton, *Kramer vs. Kramer* Francis Ford Coppola, *Apocalypse Now* Bob Fosse, *All That Jazz* Edouard Molinaro, *La Cage aux Folles* Peter Yates, *Breaking Away*
1980	*Robert Redford, *Ordinary People* David Lynch, *The Elephant Man* Roman Polanski, *Tess* Richard Rush, *The Stunt Man* Martin Scorsese, *Raging Bull*
1981	*Warren Beatty, *Reds* Hugh Hudson, *Chariots of Fire* Louis Malle, *Atlantic City* Mark Rydell, *On Golden Pond* Steven Spielberg, *Raiders of the Lost Ark*
1982	*Richard Attenborough, *Gandhi* Sidney Lumet, *The Verdict* Sydney Pollack, *Tootsie* Wolfgang Petersen, *Das Boot* Steven Spielberg, *E.T.—The Extra-Terrestrial*
1983	*James L. Brooks, *Terms of Endearment* Bruce Beresford, *Tender Mercies* Ingmar Bergman, *Fanny and Alexander* Mike Nichols, *Silkwood* Peter Yates, *The Dresser*
1984	*Miloš Forman, *Amadeus* Woody Allen, *Broadway Danny Rose* Robert Benton, *Places in the Heart* Roland Joffé, *The Killing Fields* David Lean, *A Passage to India*

1985 *Sydney Pollack, *Out of Africa*
Hector Babenco, *Kiss of the Spider Woman*
John Huston, *Prizzi's Honor*
Akira Kurosawa, *Ran*
Peter Weir, *Witness*

1986 *Oliver Stone, *Platoon*
Woody Allen, *Hannah and Her Sisters*
James Ivory, *A Room with a View*
Roland Joffé, *The Mission*
David Lynch, *Blue Velvet*

1987 *Bernardo Bertolucci, *The Last Emperor*
John Boorman, *Hope and Glory*
Lasse Hallström, *My Life as a Dog*
Norman Jewison, *Moonstruck*
Adrian Lyne, *Fatal Attraction*

1988 *Barry Levinson, *Rain Man*
Charles Crichton, *A Fish Called Wanda*
Mike Nichols, *Working Girl*
Alan Parker, *Mississippi Burning*
Martin Scorsese, *The Last Temptation of Christ*

1989 *Oliver Stone, *Born on the Fourth of July*
Woody Allen, *Crimes and Misdemeanors*
Kenneth Branagh, *Henry V*
Jim Sheridan, *My Left Foot*
Peter Weir, *Dead Poets Society*

1990 *Kevin Costner, *Dances with Wolves*
Francis Ford Coppola, *The Godfather, Part III*
Stephen Frears, *The Grifters*
Martin Scorsese, *Goodfellas*
Barbet Schroeder, *Reversal of Fortune*

1991 *Jonathan Demme, *The Silence of the Lambs*
Barry Levinson, *Bugsy*
Ridley Scott, *Thelma and Louise*
John Singleton, *Boyz N the Hood*
Oliver Stone, *JFK*

1992 *Clint Eastwood, *Unforgiven*
Neil Jordan, *The Crying Game*
James Ivory, *Howards End*
Martin Brest, *Scent of a Woman*
Robert Altman, *The Player*

3: BEST ACTOR IN A LEADING ROLE

1927–28 *Emil Jannings, *The Last Command* and *The Way of All Flesh*
Richard Barthelmess, *The Noose* and *The Patent Leather Kid*
Charles Chaplin, *The Circus*

1928–29 *Warner Baxter, *In Old Arizona*
George Bancroft, *Thunderbolt*
Chester Morris, *Alibi*
Paul Muni, *The Valiant*
Lewis Stone, *The Patriot*

1929–30 *George Arliss, *Disraeli** and *The Green Goddess*
Wallace Beery, *The Big House*
Maurice Chevalier, *The Love Parade* and *The Big Pond*
Ronald Colman, *Bulldog Drummond* and *Condemned*
Lawrence Tibbett, *The Rogue Song*

1930–31 *Lionel Barrymore, *A Free Soul*
Jackie Cooper, *Skippy*
Richard Dix, *Cimarron*
Fredric March, *The Royal Family of Broadway*
Adolphe Menjou, *The Front Page*

1931–32 *Wallace Beery, *The Champ*
*Fredric March, *Dr. Jekyll and Mr. Hyde*
Alfred Lunt, *The Guardsman*

1932–33 *Charles Laughton, *The Private Life of Henry VIII*
Leslie Howard, *Berkeley Square*
Paul Muni, *I Am a Fugitive from a Chain Gang*

1934 *Clark Gable, *It Happened One Night*
Frank Morgan, *Affairs of Cellini*
William Powell, *The Thin Man*

1935 *Victor McLaglen, *The Informer*
Clark Gable, *Mutiny on the Bounty*
Charles Laughton, *Mutiny on the Bounty*
Franchot Tone, *Mutiny on the Bounty*

1936 *Paul Muni, *The Story of Louis Pasteur*
Gary Cooper, *Mr. Deeds Goes to Town*
Walter Huston, *Dodsworth*
William Powell, *My Man Godfrey*
Spencer Tracy, *San Francisco*

1937 *Spencer Tracy, *Captains Courageous*
Charles Boyer, *Conquest*
Fredric March, *A Star Is Born*
Robert Montgomery, *Night Must Fall*
Paul Muni, *The Life of Emile Zola*

1938 *Spencer Tracy, *Boys Town*
Charles Boyer, *Algiers*
James Cagney, *Angels with Dirty Faces*
Robert Donat, *The Citadel*
Leslie Howard, *Pygmalion*

1939 *Robert Donat, *Goodbye, Mr. Chips*
Clark Gable, *Gone With the Wind*
Laurence Olivier, *Wuthering Heights*
Mickey Rooney, *Babes in Arms*
James Stewart, *Mr. Smith Goes to Washington*

1940 *James Stewart, *The Philadelphia Story*
Charles Chaplin, *The Great Dictator*
Henry Fonda, *The Grapes of Wrath*
Raymond Massey, *Abe Lincoln in Illinois*
Laurence Olivier, *Rebecca*

1941 *Gary Cooper, *Sergeant York*
Cary Grant, *Penny Serenade*
Walter Huston, *All That Money Can Buy*
Robert Montgomery, *Here Comes Mr. Jordan*
Orson Welles, *Citizen Kane*

1942 *James Cagney, *Yankee Doodle Dandy*
Ronald Colman, *Random Harvest*
Gary Cooper, *The Pride of the Yankees*
Walter Pidgeon, *Mrs. Miniver*
Monty Woolley, *The Pied Piper*

1943 *Paul Lukas, *Watch on the Rhine*
Humphrey Bogart, *Casablanca*
Gary Cooper, *For Whom the Bell Tolls*
Walter Pidgeon, *Madame Curie*
Mickey Rooney, *The Human Comedy*

1944 *Bing Crosby, *Going My Way*
Charles Boyer, *Gaslight*
Barry Fitzgerald, *Going My Way*
Cary Grant, *None But the Lonely Heart*
Alexander Knox, *Wilson*

1945 *Ray Milland, *The Lost Weekend*
Bing Crosby, *The Bells of St. Mary's*
Gene Kelly, *Anchors Aweigh*
Gregory Peck, *The Keys of the Kingdom*
Cornel Wilde, *A Song to Remember*

1946 *Fredric March, *The Best Years of Our Lives*
Laurence Olivier, *Henry V*
Larry Parks, *The Jolson Story*

	Gregory Peck, *The Yearling*
	James Stewart, *It's a Wonderful Life*
1947	*Ronald Colman, *A Double Life*
	John Garfield, *Body and Soul*
	Gregory Peck, *Gentleman's Agreement*
	William Powell, *Life with Father*
	Michael Redgrave, *Mourning Becomes Electra*
1948	*Laurence Olivier, *Hamlet*
	Lew Ayres, *Johnny Belinda*
	Montgomery Clift, *The Search*
	Dan Dailey, *When My Baby Smiles at Me*
	Clifton Webb, *Sitting Pretty*
1949	*Broderick Crawford, *All the King's Men*
	Kirk Douglas, *Champion*
	Gregory Peck, *Twelve O'Clock High*
	Richard Todd, *The Hasty Heart*
	John Wayne, *Sands of Iwo Jima*
1950	*José Ferrer, *Cyrano de Bergerac*
	Louis Calhern, *The Magnificent Yankee*
	William Holden, *Sunset Boulevard*
	James Stewart, *Harvey*
	Spencer Tracy, *Father of the Bride*
1951	*Humphrey Bogart, *The African Queen*
	Marlon Brando, *A Streetcar Named Desire*
	Montgomery Clift, *A Place in the Sun*
	Arthur Kennedy, *Bright Victory*
	Fredric March, *Death of a Salesman*
1952	*Gary Cooper, *High Noon*
	Marlon Brando, *Viva Zapata!*
	Kirk Douglas, *The Bad and the Beautiful*
	José Ferrer, *Moulin Rouge*
	Alec Guinness, *The Lavender Hill Mob*
1953	*William Holden, *Stalag 17*
	Marlon Brando, *Julius Caesar*
	Richard Burton, *The Robe*
	Montgomery Clift, *From Here to Eternity*
	Burt Lancaster, *From Here to Eternity*
1954	*Marlon Brando, *On the Waterfront*
	Humphrey Bogart, *The Caine Mutiny*
	Bing Crosby, *The Country Girl*
	James Mason, *A Star Is Born*
	Dan O'Herlihy, *Adventures of Robinson Crusoe*
1955	*Ernest Borgnine, *Marty*
	James Cagney, *Love Me or Leave Me*

	James Dean, *East of Eden*
	Frank Sinatra, *The Man with the Golden Arm*
	Spencer Tracy, *Bad Day at Black Rock*
1956	*Yul Brynner, *The King and I*
	James Dean, *Giant*
	Kirk Douglas, *Lust for Life*
	Rock Hudson, *Giant*
	Laurence Olivier, *Richard III*
1957	*Alec Guinness, *The Bridge on the River Kwai*
	Marlon Brando, *Sayonara*
	Anthony Franciosa, *A Hatful of Rain*
	Charles Laughton, *Witness for the Prosecution*
	Anthony Quinn, *Wild Is the Wind*
1958	*David Niven, *Separate Tables*
	Tony Curtis, *The Defiant Ones*
	Paul Newman, *Cat on a Hot Tin Roof*
	Sidney Poitier, *The Defiant Ones*
	Spencer Tracy, *The Old Man and the Sea*
1959	*Charlton Heston, *Ben-Hur*
	Laurence Harvey, *Room at the Top*
	Jack Lemmon, *Some Like It Hot*
	Paul Muni, *The Last Angry Man*
	James Stewart, *Anatomy of a Murder*
1960	*Burt Lancaster, *Elmer Gantry*
	Trevor Howard, *Sons and Lovers*
	Jack Lemmon, *The Apartment*
	Laurence Olivier, *The Entertainer*
	Spencer Tracy, *Inherit the Wind*
1961	*Maximilian Schell, *Judgment at Nuremberg*
	Charles Boyer, *Fanny*
	Paul Newman, *The Hustler*
	Spencer Tracy, *Judgment at Nuremberg*
	Stuart Whitman, *The Mark*
1962	*Gregory Peck, *To Kill a Mockingbird*
	Burt Lancaster, *Birdman of Alcatraz*
	Jack Lemmon, *Days of Wine and Roses*
	Marcello Mastroianni, *Divorce Italian Style*
	Peter O'Toole, *Lawrence of Arabia*
1963	*Sidney Poitier, *Lilies of the Field*
	Albert Finney, *Tom Jones*
	Richard Harris, *This Sporting Life*
	Rex Harrison, *Cleopatra*
	Paul Newman, *Hud*

1964 *Rex Harrison, *My Fair Lady*
Richard Burton, *Becket*
Peter O'Toole, *Becket*
Anthony Quinn, *Zorba the Greek*
Peter Sellers, *Dr. Strangelove or: How I Learned to Stop Worrying and Love the Bomb*

1965 *Lee Marvin, *Cat Ballou*
Richard Burton, *The Spy Who Came in from the Cold*
Laurence Olivier, *Othello*
Rod Steiger, *The Pawnbroker*
Oskar Werner, *Ship of Fools*

1966 *Paul Scofield, *A Man for All Seasons*
Alan Arkin, *The Russians Are Coming, the Russians Are Coming*
Richard Burton, *Who's Afraid of Virginia Woolf?*
Michael Caine, *Alfie*
Steve McQueen, *The Sand Pebbles*

1967 *Rod Steiger, *In the Heat of the Night*
Warren Beatty, *Bonnie and Clyde*
Dustin Hoffman, *The Graduate*
Paul Newman, *Cool Hand Luke*
Spencer Tracy, *Guess Who's Coming to Dinner*

1968 *Cliff Robertson, *Charly*
Alan Arkin, *The Heart Is a Lonely Hunter*
Alan Bates, *The Fixer*
Ron Moody, *Oliver!*
Peter O'Toole, *The Lion in Winter*

1969 *John Wayne, *True Grit*
Richard Burton, *Anne of the Thousand Days*
Dustin Hoffman, *Midnight Cowboy*
Peter O'Toole, *Goodbye, Mr. Chips*
Jon Voight, *Midnight Cowboy*

1970 *George C. Scott, *Patton*
Melvyn Douglas, *I Never Sang for My Father*
James Earl Jones, *The Great White Hope*
Jack Nicholson, *Five Easy Pieces*
Ryan O'Neal, *Love Story*

1971 *Gene Hackman, *The French Connection*
Peter Finch, *Sunday, Bloody Sunday*
Walter Matthau, *Kotch*
George C. Scott, *The Hospital*
Topol, *Fiddler on the Roof*

1972 *Marlon Brando, *The Godfather*
Michael Caine, *Sleuth*

	Laurence Olivier, *Sleuth*
	Peter O'Toole, *The Ruling Class*
	Paul Winfield, *Sounder*
1973	*Jack Lemmon, *Save the Tiger*
	Marlon Brando, *Last Tango in Paris*
	Jack Nicholson, *The Last Detail*
	Al Pacino, *Serpico*
	Robert Redford, *The Sting*
1974	*Art Carney, *Harry and Tonto*
	Albert Finney, *Murder on the Orient Express*
	Dustin Hoffman, *Lenny*
	Jack Nicholson, *Chinatown*
	Al Pacino, *The Godfather, Part II*
1975	*Jack Nicholson, *One Flew Over the Cuckoo's Nest*
	Walter Matthau, *The Sunshine Boys*
	Al Pacino, *Dog Day Afternoon*
	Maximilian Schell, *The Man in the Glass Booth*
	James Whitmore, *Give 'em Hell, Harry!*
1976	*Peter Finch, *Network* [posthumous]
	Robert De Niro, *Taxi Driver*
	Giancarlo Giannini, *Seven Beauties*
	William Holden, *Network*
	Sylvester Stallone, *Rocky*
1977	*Richard Dreyfuss, *The Goodbye Girl*
	Woody Allen, *Annie Hall*
	Richard Burton, *Equus*
	Marcello Mastroianni, *A Special Day*
	John Travolta, *Saturday Night Fever*
1978	*Jon Voight, *Coming Home*
	Warren Beatty, *Heaven Can Wait*
	Gary Busey, *The Buddy Holly Story*
	Robert De Niro, *The Deer Hunter*
	Laurence Olivier, *The Boys from Brazil*
1979	*Dustin Hoffman, *Kramer vs. Kramer*
	Jack Lemmon, *The China Syndrome*
	Al Pacino, *. . . And Justice for All*
	Roy Scheider, *All That Jazz*
	Peter Sellers, *Being There*
1980	*Robert De Niro, *Raging Bull*
	Robert Duvall, *The Great Santini*
	John Hurt, *The Elephant Man*
	Jack Lemmon, *Tribute*
	Peter O'Toole, *The Stunt Man*

1981	*Henry Fonda, *On Golden Pond*
	Warren Beatty, *Reds*
	Burt Lancaster, *Atlantic City*
	Dudley Moore, *Arthur*
	Paul Newman, *Absence of Malice*
1982	*Ben Kingsley, *Gandhi*
	Dustin Hoffman, *Tootsie*
	Jack Lemmon, *Missing*
	Paul Newman, *The Verdict*
	Peter O'Toole, *My Favorite Year*
1983	*Robert Duvall, *Tender Mercies*
	Michael Caine, *Educating Rita*
	Tom Conti, *Reuben, Reuben*
	Tom Courtenay, *The Dresser*
	Albert Finney, *The Dresser*
1984	*F. Murray Abraham, *Amadeus*
	Jeff Bridges, *Starman*
	Albert Finney, *Under the Volcano*
	Tom Hulce, *Amadeus*
	Sam Waterston, *The Killing Fields*
1985	*William Hurt, *Kiss of the Spider Woman*
	Harrison Ford, *Witness*
	James Garner, *Murphy's Romance*
	Jack Nicholson, *Prizzi's Honor*
	Jon Voight, *Runaway Train*
1986	*Paul Newman, *The Color of Money*
	Dexter Gordon, *Round Midnight*
	Bob Hoskins, *Mona Lisa*
	William Hurt, *Children of a Lesser God*
	James Woods, *Salvador*
1987	*Michael Douglas, *Wall Street*
	William Hurt, *Broadcast News*
	Marcello Mastroianni, *Dark Eyes*
	Jack Nicholson, *Ironweed*
	Robin Williams, *Good Morning, Vietnam*
1988	*Dustin Hoffman, *Rain Man*
	Gene Hackman, *Mississippi Burning*
	Tom Hanks, *Big*
	Edward James Olmos, *Stand and Deliver*
	Max von Sydow, *Pelle the Conqueror*
1989	*Daniel Day-Lewis, *My Left Foot*
	Kenneth Branagh, *Henry V*
	Tom Cruise, *Born on the Fourth of July*
	Morgan Freeman, *Driving Miss Daisy*
	Robin Williams, *Dead Poets Society*

1990 *Jeremy Irons, *Reversal of Fortune*
Kevin Costner, *Dances with Wolves*
Robert De Niro, *Awakenings*
Gérard Dépardieu, *Cyrano de Bergerac*
Richard Harris, *The Field*

1991 *Anthony Hopkins, *The Silence of the Lambs*
Warren Beatty, *Bugsy*
Robert De Niro, *Cape Fear*
Nick Nolte, *The Prince of Tides*
Robin Williams, *The Fisher King*

1992 *Al Pacino, *Scent of a Woman*
Robert Downey, Jr., *Chaplin*
Clint Eastwood, *Unforgiven*
Stephen Rea, *The Crying Game*
Denzel Washington, *Malcolm X*

4: BEST ACTRESS IN A LEADING ROLE

1927–28 *Janet Gaynor, *Seventh Heaven, Street Angel* and *Sunrise*
Louise Dresser, *A Ship Comes In*
Gloria Swanson, *Sadie Thompson*

1928–29 *Mary Pickford, *Coquette*
Ruth Chatterton, *Madame X*
Betty Compson, *The Barker*
Jeanne Eagels, *The Letter*
Bessie Love, *Broadway Melody*

1929–30 *Norma Shearer, **The Divorcée* and *Their Own Desire*
Nancy Carroll, *The Devil's Holiday*
Ruth Chatterton, *Sarah and Son*
Greta Garbo, *Anna Christie* and *Romance*
Gloria Swanson, *The Trespasser*

1930–31 *Marie Dressler, *Min and Bill*
Marlene Dietrich, *Morocco*
Irene Dunne, *Cimarron*
Ann Harding, *Holiday*
Norma Shearer, *A Free Soul*

1931–32 *Helen Hayes, *The Sin of Madelon Claudet*
Marie Dressler, *Emma*
Lynn Fontanne, *The Guardsman*

1932–33 *Katharine Hepburn, *Morning Glory*
May Robson, *Lady for a Day*
Diana Wynyard, *Cavalcade*

1934 *Claudette Colbert, *It Happened One Night*
Grace Moore, *One Night of Love*
Norma Shearer, *The Barretts of Wimpole Street*

1935 *Bette Davis, *Dangerous*
Elisabeth Bergner, *Escape Me Never*
Claudette Colbert, *Private Worlds*
Katharine Hepburn, *Alice Adams*
Miriam Hopkins, *Becky Sharp*
Merle Oberon, *The Dark Angel*

1936 *Luise Rainer, *The Great Ziegfeld*
Irene Dunne, *Theodora Goes Wild*
Gladys George, *Valiant Is the Word for Carrie*
Carole Lombard, *My Man Godfrey*
Norma Shearer, *Romeo and Juliet*

1937 *Luise Rainer, *The Good Earth*
Irene Dunne, *The Awful Truth*
Greta Garbo, *Camille*
Janet Gaynor, *A Star Is Born*
Barbara Stanwyck, *Stella Dallas*

1938 *Bette Davis, *Jezebel*
Fay Bainter, *White Banners*
Wendy Hiller, *Pygmalion*
Norma Shearer, *Marie Antoinette*
Margaret Sullavan, *Three Comrades*

1939 *Vivien Leigh, *Gone with the Wind*
Bette Davis, *Dark Victory*
Irene Dunne, *Love Affair*
Greta Garbo, *Ninotchka*
Greer Garson, *Goodbye, Mr. Chips*

1940 *Ginger Rogers, *Kitty Foyle*
Bette Davis, *The Letter*
Joan Fontaine, *Rebecca*
Katharine Hepburn, *The Philadelphia Story*
Martha Scott, *Our Town*

1941 *Joan Fontaine, *Suspicion*
Bette Davis, *The Little Foxes*
Olivia de Havilland, *Hold Back the Dawn*
Greer Garson, *Blossoms in the Dust*
Barbara Stanwyck, *Ball of Fire*

1942 *Greer Garson, *Mrs. Miniver*
Bette Davis, *Now, Voyager*
Katharine Hepburn, *Woman of the Year*
Rosalind Russell, *My Sister Eileen*
Teresa Wright, *The Pride of the Yankees*

1943 *Jennifer Jones, *The Song of Bernadette*
Jean Arthur, *The More the Merrier*
Ingrid Bergman, *For Whom the Bell Tolls*

	Joan Fontaine, *The Constant Nymph*
	Greer Garson, *Madame Curie*
1944	*Ingrid Bergman, *Gaslight*
	Claudette Colbert, *Since You Went Away*
	Bette Davis, *Mr. Skeffington*
	Greer Garson, *Mrs. Parkington*
	Barbara Stanwyck, *Double Indemnity*
1945	*Joan Crawford, *Mildred Pierce*
	Ingrid Bergman, *The Bells of St. Mary's*
	Greer Garson, *The Valley of Decision*
	Jennifer Jones, *Love Letters*
	Gene Tierney, *Leave Her to Heaven*
1946	*Olivia de Havilland, *To Each His Own*
	Celia Johnson, *Brief Encounter*
	Jennifer Jones, *Duel in the Sun*
	Rosalind Russell, *Sister Kenny*
	Jane Wyman, *The Yearling*
1947	*Loretta Young, *The Farmer's Daughter*
	Joan Crawford, *Possessed*
	Susan Hayward, *Smash Up—The Story of a Woman*
	Dorothy McGuire, *Gentleman's Agreement*
	Rosalind Russell, *Mourning Becomes Electra*
1948	*Jane Wyman, *Johnny Belinda*
	Ingrid Bergman, *Joan of Arc*
	Olivia de Havilland, *The Snake Pit*
	Irene Dunne, *I Remember Mama*
	Barbara Stanwyck, *Sorry, Wrong Number*
1949	*Olivia de Havilland, *The Heiress*
	Jeanne Crain, *Pinky*
	Susan Hayward, *My Foolish Heart*
	Deborah Kerr, *Edward, My Son*
	Loretta Young, *Come to the Stable*
1950	*Judy Holliday, *Born Yesterday*
	Anne Baxter, *All About Eve*
	Bette Davis, *All About Eve*
	Eleanor Parker, *Caged*
	Gloria Swanson, *Sunset Boulevard*
1951	*Vivien Leigh, *A Streetcar Named Desire*
	Katharine Hepburn, *The African Queen*
	Eleanor Parker, *Detective Story*
	Shelley Winters, *A Place in the Sun*
	Jane Wyman, *The Blue Veil*

1952	*Shirley Booth, *Come Back, Little Sheba* Joan Crawford, *Sudden Fear* Bette Davis, *The Star* Julie Harris, *The Member of the Wedding* Susan Hayward, *With a Song in My Heart*
1953	*Audrey Hepburn, *Roman Holiday* Leslie Caron, *Lili* Ava Gardner, *Mogambo* Deborah Kerr, *From Here to Eternity* Maggie McNamara, *The Moon Is Blue*
1954	*Grace Kelly, *The Country Girl* Dorothy Dandridge, *Carmen Jones* Judy Garland, *A Star Is Born* Audrey Hepburn, *Sabrina* Jane Wyman, *Magnificent Obsession*
1955	*Anna Magnani, *The Rose Tattoo* Susan Hayward, *I'll Cry Tomorrow* Katharine Hepburn, *Summertime* Jennifer Jones, *Love Is a Many Splendored Thing* Eleanor Parker, *Interrupted Melody*
1956	*Ingrid Bergman, *Anastasia* Carroll Baker, *Baby Doll* Katharine Hepburn, *The Rainmaker* Nancy Kelly, *The Bad Seed* Deborah Kerr, *The King and I*
1957	*Joanne Woodward, *The Three Faces of Eve* Deborah Kerr, *Heaven Knows, Mr. Allison* Anna Magnani, *Wild Is the Wind* Elizabeth Taylor, *Raintree County* Lana Turner, *Peyton Place*
1958	*Susan Hayward, *I Want to Live!* Deborah Kerr, *Separate Tables* Shirley MacLaine, *Some Came Running* Rosalind Russell, *Auntie Mame* Elizabeth Taylor, *Cat on a Hot Tin Roof*
1959	*Simone Signoret, *Room at the Top* Doris Day, *Pillow Talk* Audrey Hepburn, *The Nun's Story* Katharine Hepburn, *Suddenly, Last Summer* Elizabeth Taylor, *Suddenly, Last Summer*
1960	*Elizabeth Taylor, *Butterfield 8* Greer Garson, *Sunrise at Campobello* Deborah Kerr, *The Sundowners* Shirley MacLaine, *The Apartment* Melina Mercouri, *Never on Sunday*

1961 *Sophia Loren, *Two Women*
Audrey Hepburn, *Breakfast at Tiffany's*
Piper Laurie, *The Hustler*
Geraldine Page, *Summer and Smoke*
Natalie Wood, *Splendor in the Grass*

1962 *Anne Bancroft, *The Miracle Worker*
Bette Davis, *Whatever Happened to Baby Jane?*
Katharine Hepburn, *Long Day's Journey into Night*
Geraldine Page, *Sweet Bird of Youth*
Lee Remick, *Days of Wine and Roses*

1963 *Patricia Neal, *Hud*
Leslie Caron, *The L-Shaped Room*
Shirley MacLaine, *Irma La Douce*
Rachel Roberts, *This Sporting Life*
Natalie Wood, *Love with the Proper Stranger*

1964 *Julie Andrews, *Mary Poppins*
Anne Bancroft, *The Pumpkin Eater*
Sophia Loren, *Marriage Italian Style*
Debbie Reynolds, *The Unsinkable Molly Brown*
Kim Stanley, *Séance on a Wet Afternoon*

1965 *Julie Christie, *Darling*
Julie Andrews, *The Sound of Music*
Samantha Eggar, *The Collector*
Elizabeth Hartman, *A Patch of Blue*
Simone Signoret, *Ship of Fools*

1966 *Elizabeth Taylor, *Who's Afraid of Virginia Woolf?*
Anouk Aimée, *A Man and a Woman*
Ida Kaminska, *The Shop on Main Street*
Lynn Redgrave, *Georgy Girl*
Vanessa Redgrave, *Morgan!*

1967 *Katharine Hepburn, *Guess Who's Coming to Dinner*
Anne Bancroft, *The Graduate*
Faye Dunaway, *Bonnie and Clyde*
Edith Evans, *The Whisperers*
Audrey Hepburn, *Wait Until Dark*

1968 *Katharine Hepburn, *The Lion in Winter*
*Barbra Streisand, *Funny Girl*
Patricia Neal, *The Subject Was Roses*
Vanessa Redgrave, *Isadora*
Joanne Woodward, *Rachel, Rachel*

1969 *Maggie Smith, *The Prime of Miss Jean Brodie*
Genevieve Bujold, *Anne of the Thousand Days*
Jane Fonda, *They Shoot Horses, Don't They?*
Liza Minnelli, *The Sterile Cuckoo*
Jean Simmons, *The Happy Ending*

1970	*Glenda Jackson, *Women in Love*
	Jane Alexander, *The Great White Hope*
	Ali MacGraw, *Love Story*
	Sarah Miles, *Ryan's Daughter*
	Carrie Snodgress, *Diary of a Mad Housewife*
1971	*Jane Fonda, *Klute*
	Julie Christie, *McCabe and Mrs. Miller*
	Glenda Jackson, *Sunday, Bloody Sunday*
	Vanessa Redgrave, *Mary, Queen of Scots*
	Janet Suzman, *Nicholas and Alexandra*
1972	*Liza Minnelli, *Cabaret*
	Diana Ross, *Lady Sings the Blues*
	Maggie Smith, *Travels with My Aunt*
	Cicely Tyson, *Sounder*
	Liv Ullmann, *The Emigrants*
1973	*Glenda Jackson, *A Touch of Class*
	Ellen Burstyn, *The Exorcist*
	Marsha Mason, *Cinderella Liberty*
	Barbra Streisand, *The Way We Were*
	Joanne Woodward, *Summer Wishes, Winter Dreams*
1974	*Ellen Burstyn, *Alice Doesn't Live Here Anymore*
	Diahann Carroll, *Claudine*
	Faye Dunaway, *Chinatown*
	Valerie Perrine, *Lenny*
	Gena Rowlands, *A Woman Under the Influence*
1975	*Louise Fletcher, *One Flew over the Cuckoo's Nest*
	Isabelle Adjani, *The Story of Adele H*
	Ann-Margret, *Tommy*
	Glenda Jackson, *Hedda*
	Carol Kane, *Hester Street*
1976	*Faye Dunaway, *Network*
	Marie-Christine Barrault, *Cousin, Cousine*
	Talia Shire, *Rocky*
	Sissy Spacek, *Carrie*
	Liv Ullmann, *Face to Face*
1977	*Diane Keaton, *Annie Hall*
	Anne Bancroft, *The Turning Point*
	Jane Fonda, *Julia*
	Shirley MacLaine, *The Turning Point*
	Marsha Mason, *The Goodbye Girl*
1978	*Jane Fonda, *Coming Home*
	Ingrid Bergman, *Autumn Sonata*
	Ellen Burstyn, *Same Time, Next Year*
	Jill Clayburgh, *An Unmarried Woman*
	Geraldine Page, *Interiors*

1979 *Sally Field, *Norma Rae*
Jill Clayburgh, *Starting Over*
Jane Fonda, *The China Syndrome*
Marsha Mason, *Chapter Two*
Bette Midler, *The Rose*

1980 *Sissy Spacek, *Coal Miner's Daughter*
Ellen Burstyn, *Resurrection*
Goldie Hawn, *Private Benjamin*
Mary Tyler Moore, *Ordinary People*
Gena Rowlands, *Gloria*

1981 *Katharine Hepburn, *On Golden Pond*
Diane Keaton, *Reds*
Marsha Mason, *Only When I Laugh*
Susan Sarandon, *Atlantic City*
Meryl Streep, *The French Lieutenant's Woman*

1982 *Meryl Streep, *Sophie's Choice*
Julie Andrews, *Victor/Victoria*
Jessica Lange, *Frances*
Sissy Spacek, *Missing*
Debra Winger, *An Officer and a Gentleman*

1983 *Shirley MacLaine, *Terms of Endearment*
Jane Alexander, *Testament*
Meryl Streep, *Silkwood*
Julie Walters, *Educating Rita*
Debra Winger, *Terms of Endearment*

1984 *Sally Field, *Places in the Heart*
Judy Davis, *A Passage to India*
Jessica Lange, *Country*
Vanessa Redgrave, *The Bostonians*
Sissy Spacek, *The River*

1985 *Geraldine Page, *The Trip to Bountiful*
Anne Bancroft, *Agnes of God*
Whoopi Goldberg, *The Color Purple*
Jessica Lange, *Sweet Dreams*
Meryl Streep, *Out of Africa*

1986 *Marlee Matlin, *Children of a Lesser God*
Jane Fonda, *The Morning After*
Sissy Spacek, *Crimes of the Heart*
Kathleen Turner, *Peggy Sue Got Married*
Sigourney Weaver, *Aliens*

1987 *Cher, *Moonstruck*
Glenn Close, *Fatal Attraction*
Holly Hunter, *Broadcast News*

	Sally Kirkland, *Anna*
	Meryl Streep, *Ironweed*
1988	*Jodie Foster, *The Accused*
	Glenn Close, *Dangerous Liaisons*
	Melanie Griffith, *Working Girl*
	Meryl Streep, *A Cry in the Dark*
	Sigourney Weaver, *Gorillas in the Mist*
1989	*Jessica Tandy, *Driving Miss Daisy*
	Isabelle Adjani, *Camille Claudel*
	Pauline Collins, *Shirley Valentine*
	Jessica Lange, *Music Box*
	Michelle Pfeiffer, *The Fabulous Baker Boys*
1990	*Kathy Bates, *Misery*
	Anjelica Huston, *The Grifters*
	Julia Roberts, *Pretty Woman*
	Meryl Streep, *Postcards from the Edge*
	Joanne Woodward, *Mr. and Mrs. Bridge*
1991	*Jodie Foster, *The Silence of the Lambs*
	Geena Davis, *Thelma & Louise*
	Laura Dern, *Rambling Rose*
	Bette Midler, *For the Boys*
	Susan Sarandon, *Thelma & Louise*
1992	*Emma Thompson, *Howards End*
	Catherine Deneuve, *Indochine*
	Mary McDonnell, *Passion Fish*
	Michelle Pfeiffer, *Love Field*
	Susan Sarandon, *Lorenzo's Oil*

5: BEST ACTOR IN A SUPPORTING ROLE

1936	*Walter Brennan, *Come and Get It*
	Mischa Auer, *My Man Godfrey*
	Stuart Erwin, *Pigskin Parade*
	Basil Rathbone, *Romeo and Juliet*
	Akim Tamiroff, *The General Died at Dawn*
1937	*Joseph Schildkraut, *The Life of Emile Zola*
	Ralph Bellamy, *The Awful Truth*
	Thomas Mitchell, *The Hurricane*
	H. B. Warner, *Lost Horizon*
	Roland Young, *Topper*
1938	*Walter Brennan, *Kentucky*
	John Garfield, *Four Daughters*
	Gene Lockhart, *Algiers*
	Robert Morley, *Marie Antoinette*
	Basil Rathbone, *If I Were King*

1939	*Thomas Mitchell, *Stagecoach* Brian Aherne, *Juarez* Harry Carey, *Mr. Smith Goes to Washington* Brian Donlevy, *Beau Geste* Claude Rains, *Mr. Smith Goes to Washington*
1940	*Walter Brennan, *The Westerner* Albert Bassermann, *Foreign Correspondent* William Gargan, *They Knew What They Wanted* Jack Oakie, *The Great Dictator* James Stephenson, *The Letter*
1941	*Donald Crisp, *How Green Was My Valley* Walter Brennan, *Sergeant York* Charles Coburn, *The Devil and Miss Jones* James Gleason, *Here Comes Mr. Jordan* Sydney Greenstreet, *The Maltese Falcon*
1942	*Van Heflin, *Johnny Eager* William Bendix, *Wake Island* Walter Huston, *Yankee Doodle Dandy* Frank Morgan, *Tortilla Flat* Henry Travers, *Mrs. Miniver*
1943	*Charles Coburn, *The More the Merrier* Charles Bickford, *The Song of Bernadette* J. Carrol Naish, *Sahara* Claude Rains, *Casablanca* Akim Tamiroff, *For Whom the Bell Tolls*
1944	*Barry Fitzgerald, *Going My Way* Hume Cronyn, *The Seventh Cross* Claude Rains, *Mr. Skeffington* Clifton Webb, *Laura* Monty Woolley, *Since You Went Away*
1945	*James Dunn, *A Tree Grows in Brooklyn* Michael Chekhov, *Spellbound* John Dall, *The Corn Is Green* Robert Mitchum, *The Story of G.I. Joe* J. Carrol Naish, *A Medal for Benny*
1946	*Harold Russell, *The Best Years of Our Lives* Charles Coburn, *The Green Years* William Demarest, *The Jolson Story* Claude Rains, *Notorious* Clifton Webb, *The Razor's Edge*
1947	*Edmund Gwenn, *Miracle on 34th Street* Charles Bickford, *The Farmer's Daughter* Thomas Gomez, *Ride the Pink Horse* Robert Ryan, *Crossfire* Richard Widmark, *Kiss of Death*

1948 *Walter Huston, *The Treasure of the Sierra Madre*
Charles Bickford, *Johnny Belinda*
José Ferrer, *Joan of Arc*
Oscar Homolka, *I Remember Mama*
Cecil Kellaway, *The Luck of the Irish*

1949 *Dean Jagger, *Twelve O'Clock High*
John Ireland, *All the King's Men*
Arthur Kennedy, *Champion*
Ralph Richardson, *The Heiress*
James Whitmore, *Battleground*

1950 *George Sanders, *All About Eve*
Jeff Chandler, *Broken Arrow*
Edmund Gwenn, *Mister 880*
Sam Jaffe, *The Asphalt Jungle*
Erich von Stroheim, *Sunset Boulevard*

1951 *Karl Malden, *A Streetcar Named Desire*
Leo Genn, *Quo Vadis*
Kevin McCarthy, *Death of a Salesman*
Peter Ustinov, *Quo Vadis*
Gig Young, *Come Fill the Cup*

1952 *Anthony Quinn, *Viva Zapata!*
Richard Burton, *My Cousin Rachel*
Arthur Hunnicutt, *The Big Sky*
Victor McLaglen, *The Quiet Man*
Jack Palance, *Sudden Fear*

1953 *Frank Sinatra, *From Here to Eternity*
Eddie Albert, *Roman Holiday*
Brandon de Wilde, *Shane*
Jack Palance, *Shane*
Robert Strauss, *Stalag 17*

1954 *Edmond O'Brien, *The Barefoot Contessa*
Lee J. Cobb, *On the Waterfront*
Karl Malden, *On the Waterfront*
Rod Steiger, *On the Waterfront*
Tom Tully, *The Caine Mutiny*

1955 *Jack Lemmon, *Mister Roberts*
Arthur Kennedy, *Trial*
Joe Mantell, *Marty*
Sal Mineo, *Rebel Without a Cause*
Arthur O'Connell, *Picnic*

1956 *Anthony Quinn, *Lust for Life*
Don Murray, *Bus Stop*
Anthony Perkins, *Friendly Persuasion*
Mickey Rooney, *The Bold and the Brave*
Robert Stack, *Written on the Wind*

1957	*Red Buttons, *Sayonara* Vittorio de Sica, *A Farewell to Arms* Sessue Hayakawa, *The Bridge on the River Kwai* Arthur Kennedy, *Peyton Place* Russ Tamblyn, *Peyton Place*
1958	*Burl Ives, *The Big Country* Theodore Bikel, *The Defiant Ones* Lee J. Cobb, *The Brothers Karamazov* Arthur Kennedy, *Some Came Running* Gig Young, *Teacher's Pet*
1959	*Hugh Griffith, *Ben-Hur* Arthur O'Connell, *Anatomy of a Murder* George C. Scott, *Anatomy of a Murder* Robert Vaughn, *The Young Philadelphians* Ed Wynn, *The Diary of Anne Frank*
1960	*Peter Ustinov, *Spartacus* Peter Falk, *Murder, Inc.* Jack Kruschen, *The Apartment* Sal Mineo, *Exodus* Chill Wills, *The Alamo*
1961	*George Chakiris, *West Side Story* Montgomery Clift, *Judgment at Nuremberg* Peter Falk, *Pocketful of Miracles* Jackie Gleason, *The Hustler* George C. Scott, *The Hustler*
1962	*Ed Begley, *Sweet Bird of Youth* Victor Buono, *Whatever Happened to Baby Jane?* Telly Savalas, *Birdman of Alcatraz* Omar Sharif, *Lawrence of Arabia* Terence Stamp, *Billy Budd*
1963	*Melvyn Douglas, *Hud* Nick Adams, *Twilight of Honor* Bobby Darin, *Captain Newman, M.D.* Hugh Griffith, *Tom Jones* John Huston, *The Cardinal*
1964	*Peter Ustinov, *Topkapi* John Gielgud, *Becket* Stanley Holloway, *My Fair Lady* Edmond O'Brien, *Seven Days in May* Lee Tracy, *The Best Man*
1965	*Martin Balsam, *A Thousand Clowns* Ian Bannen, *The Flight of the Phoenix* Tom Courtenay, *Doctor Zhivago* Michael Dunn, *Ship of Fools* Frank Finlay, *Othello*

1966	*Walter Matthau, *The Fortune Cookie* Mako, *The Sand Pebbles* James Mason, *Georgy Girl* George Segal, *Who's Afraid of Virginia Woolf?* Robert Shaw, *A Man for All Seasons*
1967	*George Kennedy, *Cool Hand Luke* John Cassavetes, *The Dirty Dozen* Gene Hackman, *Bonnie and Clyde* Cecil Kellaway, *Guess Who's Coming to Dinner* Michael J. Pollard, *Bonnie and Clyde*
1968	*Jack Albertson, *The Subject Was Roses* Seymour Cassel, *Faces* Daniel Massey, *Star!* Jack Wild, *Oliver!* Gene Wilder, *The Producers*
1969	*Gig Young, *They Shoot Horses, Don't They?* Rupert Crosse, *The Reivers* Elliott Gould, *Bob & Carol & Ted & Alice* Jack Nicholson, *Easy Rider* Anthony Quayle, *Anne of the Thousand Days*
1970	*John Mills, *Ryan's Daughter* Richard Castellano, *Lovers and Other Strangers* Chief Dan George, *Little Big Man* Gene Hackman, *I Never Sang for My Father* John Marley, *Love Story*
1971	*Ben Johnson, *The Last Picture Show* Jeff Bridges, *The Last Picture Show* Leonard Frey, *Fiddler on the Roof* Richard Jaeckel, *Sometimes a Great Notion* Roy Scheider, *The French Connection*
1972	*Joel Grey, *Cabaret* Eddie Albert, *The Heartbreak Kid* James Caan, *The Godfather* Robert Duvall, *The Godfather* Al Pacino, *The Godfather*
1973	*John Houseman, *The Paper Chase* Vincent Gardenia, *Bang the Drum Slowly* Jack Gilford, *Save the Tiger* Jason Miller, *The Exorcist* Randy Quaid, *The Last Detail*
1974	*Robert De Niro, *The Godfather, Part II* Fred Astaire, *The Towering Inferno* Jeff Bridges, *Thunderbolt and Lightfoot* Michael V. Gazzo, *The Godfather, Part II* Lee Strasberg, *The Godfather, Part II*

1975	*George Burns, *The Sunshine Boys*
	Brad Dourif, *One Flew over the Cuckoo's Nest*
	Burgess Meredith, *The Day of the Locust*
	Chris Sarandon, *Dog Day Afternoon*
	Jack Warden, *Shampoo*
1976	*Jason Robards, *All the President's Men*
	Ned Beatty, *Network*
	Burgess Meredith, *Rocky*
	Laurence Olivier, *Marathon Man*
	Burt Young, *Rocky*
1977	*Jason Robards, *Julia*
	Mikhail Baryshnikov, *The Turning Point*
	Peter Firth, *Equus*
	Alec Guinness, *Star Wars*
	Maximilian Schell, *Julia*
1978	*Christopher Walken, *The Deer Hunter*
	Bruce Dern, *Coming Home*
	Richard Farnsworth, *Comes a Horseman*
	John Hurt, *Midnight Express*
	Jack Warden, *Heaven Can Wait*
1979	*Melvyn Douglas, *Being There*
	Robert Duvall, *Apocalypse Now*
	Frederic Forrest, *The Rose*
	Justin Henry, *Kramer vs. Kramer*
	Mickey Rooney, *The Black Stallion*
1980	*Timothy Hutton, *Ordinary People*
	Judd Hirsch, *Ordinary People*
	Michael O'Keefe, *The Great Santini*
	Joe Pesci, *Raging Bull*
	Jason Robards, *Melvin and Howard*
1981	*John Gielgud, *Arthur*
	James Coco, *Only When I Laugh*
	Ian Holm, *Chariots of Fire*
	Jack Nicholson, *Reds*
	Howard E. Rollins, Jr., *Ragtime*
1982	*Louis Gossett, Jr., *An Officer and a Gentleman*
	Charles Durning, *The Best Little Whorehouse in Texas*
	John Lithgow, *The World According to Garp*
	James Mason, *The Verdict*
	Robert Preston, *Victor/Victoria*
1983	*Jack Nicholson, *Terms of Endearment*
	Charles Durning, *To Be or Not to Be*
	John Lithgow, *Terms of Endearment*
	Sam Shepard, *The Right Stuff*
	Rip Torn, *Cross Creek*

1984 *Haing S. Ngor, *The Killing Fields*
Adolph Caesar, *A Soldier's Story*
John Malkovich, *Places in the Heart*
Noriyuki "Pat" Morita, *The Karate Kid*
Ralph Richardson, *Greystoke: The Legend of Tarzan, Lord of the Apes*

1985 *Don Ameche, *Cocoon*
Klaus Maria Brandauer, *Out of Africa*
William Hickey, *Prizzi's Honor*
Robert Loggia, *Jagged Edge*
Eric Roberts, *Runaway Train*

1986 *Michael Caine, *Hannah and Her Sisters*
Tom Berenger, *Platoon*
Willem Dafoe, *Platoon*
Denholm Elliott, *A Room with a View*
Dennis Hopper, *Hoosiers*

1987 *Sean Connery, *The Untouchables*
Albert Brooks, *Broadcast News*
Morgan Freeman, *Street Smart*
Denzel Washington, *Cry Freedom*
Vincent Gardenia, *Moonstruck*

1988 *Kevin Kline, *A Fish Called Wanda*
Alec Guinness, *Little Dorrit*
Martin Landau, *Tucker: The Man and His Dream*
River Phoenix, *Running on Empty*
Dean Stockwell, *Married to the Mob*

1989 *Denzel Washington, *Glory*
Danny Aiello, *Do the Right Thing*
Dan Aykroyd, *Driving Miss Daisy*
Marlon Brando, *A Dry White Season*
Martin Landau, *Crimes and Misdemeanors*

1990 *Joe Pesci, *Goodfellas*
Bruce Davison, *Longtime Companion*
Andy Garcia, *The Godfather, Part III*
Graham Greene, *Dances with Wolves*
Al Pacino, *Dick Tracy*

1991 *Jack Palance, *City Slickers*
Tommy Lee Jones, *JFK*
Harvey Keitel, *Bugsy*
Ben Kingsley, *Bugsy*
Michael Lerner, *Barton Fink*

1992 *Gene Hackman, *Unforgiven*
Jaye Davidson, *The Crying Game*
Jack Nicholson, *A Few Good Men*
Al Pacino, *Glengarry Glen Ross*
David Paymer, *Mr. Saturday Night*

6: BEST ACTRESS IN A SUPPORTING ROLE

1936 *Gale Sondergaard, *Anthony Adverse*
Beulah Bondi, *The Gorgeous Hussy*
Alice Brady, *My Man Godfrey*
Bonita Granvile, *These Three*
Maria Ouspenskaya, *Dodsworth*

1937 *Alice Brady, *In Old Chicago*
Andrea Leeds, *Stage Door*
Anne Shirley, *Stella Dallas*
Claire Trevor, *Dead End*
Dame May Whitty, *Night Must Fall*

1938 *Fay Bainter, *Jezebel*
Beulah Bondi, *Of Human Hearts*
Billie Burke, *Merrily We Live*
Spring Byington, *You Can't Take It with You*
Miliza Korjus, *The Great Waltz*

1939 *Hattie McDaniel, *Gone with the Wind*
Olivia de Havilland, *Gone with the Wind*
Geraldine Fitzgerald, *Wuthering Heights*
Edna May Oliver, *Drums Along the Mohawk*
Maria Ouspenskaya, *Love Affair*

1940 *Jane Darwell, *The Grapes of Wrath*
Judith Anderson, *Rebecca*
Ruth Hussey, *The Philadelphia Story*
Barbara O'Neil, *All This, and Heaven Too*
Marjorie Rambeau, *Primrose Path*

1941 *Mary Astor, *The Great Lie*
Sara Allgood, *How Green Was My Valley*
Patricia Collinge, *The Little Foxes*
Teresa Wright, *The Little Foxes*
Margaret Wycherly, *Sergeant York*

1942 *Teresa Wright, *Mrs. Miniver*
Gladys Cooper, *Now, Voyager*
Agnes Moorehead, *The Magnificent Ambersons*
Susan Peters, *Random Harvest*
Dame May Whitty, *Mrs. Miniver*

1943 *Katina Paxinou, *For Whom the Bell Tolls*
Gladys Cooper, *The Song of Bernadette*
Paulette Goddard, *So Proudly We Hail*
Anne Revere, *The Song of Bernadette*
Lucile Watson, *Watch on the Rhine*

1944 *Ethel Barrymore, *None But the Lonely Heart*
Jennifer Jones, *Since You Went Away*

	Angela Lansbury, *Gaslight*
	Aline MacMahon, *Dragon Seed*
	Agnes Moorehead, *Mrs. Parkington*
1945	*Anne Revere, *National Velvet*
	Eve Arden, *Mildred Pierce*
	Ann Blyth, *Mildred Pierce*
	Angela Lansbury, *The Picture of Dorian Gray*
	Joan Lorring, *The Corn Is Green*
1946	*Anne Baxter, *The Razor's Edge*
	Ethel Barrymore, *The Spiral Staircase*
	Lillian Gish, *Duel in the Sun*
	Flora Robson, *Saratoga Trunk*
	Gale Sondergaard, *Anna and the King of Siam*
1947	*Celeste Holm, *Gentleman's Agreement*
	Ethel Barrymore, *The Paradine Case*
	Gloria Grahame, *Crossfire*
	Marjorie Main, *The Egg and I*
	Anne Revere, *Gentleman's Agreement*
1948	*Claire Trevor, *Key Largo*
	Barbara Bel Geddes, *I Remember Mama*
	Ellen Corby, *I Remember Mama*
	Agnes Moorehead, *Johnny Belinda*
	Jean Simmons, *Hamlet*
1949	*Mercedes McCambridge, *All the King's Men*
	Ethel Barrymore, *Pinky*
	Celeste Holm, *Come to the Stable*
	Elsa Lanchester, *Come to the Stable*
	Ethel Waters, *Pinky*
1950	*Josephine Hull, *Harvey*
	Hope Emerson, *Caged*
	Celeste Holm, *All About Eve*
	Nancy Olson, *Sunset Boulevard*
	Thelma Ritter, *All About Eve*
1951	*Kim Hunter, *A Streetcar Named Desire*
	Joan Blondell, *The Blue Veil*
	Mildred Dunnock, *Death of a Salesman*
	Lee Grant, *Detective Story*
	Thelma Ritter, *The Mating Season*
1952	*Gloria Grahame, *The Bad and the Beautiful*
	Jean Hagen, *Singin' in the Rain*
	Colette Marchand, *Moulin Rouge*
	Terry Moore, *Come Back, Little Sheba*
	Thelma Ritter, *With a Song in My Heart*

1953 *Donna Reed, *From Here to Eternity*
Grace Kelly, *Mogambo*
Geraldine Page, *Hondo*
Marjorie Rambeau, *Torch Song*
Thelma Ritter, *Pickup on South Street*

1954 *Eva Marie Saint, *On the Waterfront*
Nina Foch, *Executive Suite*
Katy Jurado, *Broken Lance*
Jan Sterling, *The High and the Mighty*
Claire Trevor, *The High and the Mighty*

1955 *Jo Van Fleet, *East of Eden*
Betsy Blair, *Marty*
Peggy Lee, *Pete Kelly's Blues*
Marisa Pavan, *The Rose Tattoo*
Natalie Wood, *Rebel Without a Cause*

1956 *Dorothy Malone, *Written on the Wind*
Mildred Dunnock, *Baby Doll*
Eileen Heckart, *The Bad Seed*
Mercedes McCambridge, *Giant*
Patty McCormack, *The Bad Seed*

1957 *Miyoshi Umeki, *Sayonara*
Carolyn Jones, *The Bachelor Party*
Elsa Lanchester, *Witness for the Prosecution*
Hope Lange, *Peyton Place*
Diane Varsi, *Peyton Place*

1958 *Wendy Hiller, *Separate Tables*
Peggy Cass, *Auntie Mame*
Martha Hyer, *Some Came Running*
Maureen Stapleton, *Lonelyhearts*
Cara Williams, *The Defiant Ones*

1959 *Shelley Winters, *The Diary of Anne Frank*
Hermione Baddeley, *Room at the Top*
Susan Kohner, *Imitation of Life*
Juanita Moore, *Imitation of Life*
Thelma Ritter, *Pillow Talk*

1960 *Shirley Jones, *Elmer Gantry*
Glynis Johns, *The Sundowners*
Shirley Knight, *The Dark at the Top of the Stairs*
Janet Leigh, *Psycho*
Mary Ure, *Sons and Lovers*

1961 *Rita Moreno, *West Side Story*
Fay Bainter, *The Children's Hour*
Judy Garland, *Judgment at Nuremberg*

	Lotte Lenya, *The Roman Spring of Mrs. Stone*
	Una Merkel, *Summer and Smoke*
1962	*Patty Duke, *The Miracle Worker*
	Mary Badham, *To Kill a Mockingbird*
	Shirley Knight, *Sweet Bird of Youth*
	Angela Lansbury, *The Manchurian Candidate*
	Thelma Ritter, *Birdman of Alcatraz*
1963	*Margaret Rutherford, *The VIPs*
	Diane Cilento, *Tom Jones*
	Dame Edith Evans, *Tom Jones*
	Joyce Redman, *Tom Jones*
	Lilia Skala, *Lilies of the Field*
1964	*Lila Kedrova, *Zorba the Greek*
	Gladys Cooper, *My Fair Lady*
	Dame Edith Evans, *The Chalk Garden*
	Grayson Hall, *The Night of the Iguana*
	Agnes Moorehead, *Hush . . . Hush, Sweet Charlotte*
1965	*Shelley Winters, *A Patch of Blue*
	Ruth Gordon, *Inside Daisy Clover*
	Joyce Redmen, *Othello*
	Maggie Smith, *Othello*
	Peggy Wood, *The Sound of Music*
1966	*Sandy Dennis, *Who's Afraid of Virginia Woolf?*
	Wendy Hiller, *A Man for All Seasons*
	Jocelyn Lagarde, *Hawaii*
	Vivien Merchant, *Alfie*
	Geraldine Page, *You're a Big Boy Now*
1967	*Estelle Parsons, *Bonnie and Clyde*
	Carol Channing, *Thoroughly Modern Millie*
	Mildred Natwick, *Barefoot in the Park*
	Beah Richards, *Guess Who's Coming to Dinner*
	Katharine Ross, *The Graduate*
1968	*Ruth Gordon, *Rosemary's Baby*
	Lynn Carlin, *Faces*
	Sondra Locke, *The Heart Is a Lonely Hunter*
	Kay Medford, *Funny Girl*
	Estelle Parsons, *Rachel, Rachel*
1969	*Goldie Hawn, *Cactus Flower*
	Catherine Burns, *Last Summer*
	Dyan Cannon, *Bob & Carol & Ted & Alice*
	Sylvia Miles, *Midnight Cowboy*
	Susannah York, *They Shoot Horses, Don't They?*
1970	*Helen Hayes, *Airport*
	Karen Black, *Five Easy Pieces*

Lee Grant, *The Landlord*
Sally Kellerman, *M*A*S*H*
Maureen Stapleton, *Airport*

1971 *Cloris Leachman, *The Last Picture Show*
Ellen Burstyn, *The Last Picture Show*
Barbara Harris, *Who Is Harry Kellerman and Why Is He Saying Those Terrible Things About Me?*
Margaret Leighton, *The Go-Between*
Ann-Margret, *Carnal Knowledge*

1972 *Eileen Heckart, *Butterflies Are Free*
Jeannie Berlin, *The Heartbreak Kid*
Geraldine Page, *Pete 'n' Tillie*
Susan Tyrrell, *Fat City*
Shelley Winters, *The Poseidon Adventure*

1973 *Tatum O'Neal, *Paper Moon*
Linda Blair, *The Exorcist*
Candy Clark, *American Graffiti*
Madeline Kahn, *Paper Moon*
Sylvia Sidney, *Summer Wishes, Winter Dreams*

1974 *Ingrid Bergman, *Murder on the Orient Express*
Valentina Cortese, *Day for Night*
Madeline Kahn, *Blazing Saddles*
Diane Ladd, *Alice Doesn't Live Here Anymore*
Talia Shire, *The Godfather, Part II*

1975 *Lee Grant, *Shampoo*
Ronee Blakley, *Nashville*
Sylvia Miles, *Farewell, My Lovely*
Lily Tomlin, *Nashville*
Brenda Vaccaro, *Once Is Not Enough*

1976 *Beatrice Straight, *Network*
Jane Alexander, *All the President's Men*
Jodie Foster, *Taxi Driver*
Lee Grant, *Voyage of the Damned*
Piper Laurie, *Carrie*

1977 *Vanessa Redgrave, *Julia*
Leslie Browne, *The Turning Point*
Quinn Cummings, *The Goodbye Girl*
Melinda Dillon, *Close Encounters of the Third Kind*
Tuesday Weld, *Looking for Mr. Goodbar*

1978 *Maggie Smith, *California Suite*
Dyan Cannon, *Heaven Can Wait*
Penelope Milford, *Coming Home*
Maureen Stapleton, *Interiors*
Meryl Streep, *The Deer Hunter*

1979 *Meryl Streep, *Kramer vs. Kramer*
Jane Alexander, *Kramer vs. Kramer*
Barbara Barrie, *Breaking Away*
Candice Bergen, *Starting Over*
Mariel Hemingway, *Manhattan*

1980 *Mary Steenburgen, *Melvin and Howard*
Eileen Brennan, *Private Benjamin*
Eva Le Gallienne, *Resurrection*
Cathy Moriarty, *Raging Bull*
Diana Scarwid, *Inside Moves*

1981 *Maureen Stapleton, *Reds*
Melinda Dillon, *Absence of Malice*
Jane Fonda, *On Golden Pond*
Joan Hackett, *Only When I Laugh*
Elizabeth McGovern, *Ragtime*

1982 *Jessica Lange, *Tootsie*
Glenn Close, *The World According to Garp*
Teri Garr, *Tootsie*
Kim Stanley, *Frances*
Lesley Ann Warren, *Victor/Victoria*

1983 *Linda Hunt, *The Year of Living Dangerously*
Cher, *Silkwood*
Glenn Close, *The Big Chill*
Amy Irving, *Yentl*
Alfre Woodard, *Cross Creek*

1984 *Peggy Ashcroft, *A Passage to India*
Glenn Close, *The Natural*
Lindsay Crouse, *Places in the Heart*
Christine Lahti, *Swing Shift*
Geraldine Page, *The Pope of Greenwich Village*

1985 *Anjelica Huston, *Prizzi's Honor*
Margaret Avery, *The Color Purple*
Amy Madigan, *Twice in a Lifetime*
Meg Tilly, *Agnes of God*
Oprah Winfrey, *The Color Purple*

1986 *Dianne Wiest, *Hannah and Her Sisters*
Tess Harper, *Crimes of the Heart*
Piper Laurie, *Children of a Lesser God*
Mary Elizabeth Mastrantonio, *The Color of Money*
Maggie Smith, *A Room with a View*

1987 *Olympia Dukakis, *Moonstruck*
Norma Aleandro, *Gaby—A True Story*
Ann Sothern, *The Whales of August*

Anne Archer, *Fatal Attraction*
Anne Ramsey, *Throw Momma from the Train*

1988 *Geena Davis, *The Accidental Tourist*
Joan Cusack, *Working Girl*
Frances McDormand, *Mississippi Burning*
Michelle Pfeiffer, *Dangerous Liaisons*
Sigourney Weaver, *Working Girl*

1989 *Brenda Fricker, *My Left Foot*
Anjelica Huston, *Enemies, a Love Story*
Lena Olin, *Enemies, a Love Story*
Julia Roberts, *Steel Magnolias*
Dianne Wiest, *Parenthood*

1990 *Whoopi Goldberg, *Ghost*
Annette Bening, *The Grifters*
Lorraine Bracco, *Goodfellas*
Diane Ladd, *Wild at Heart*
Mary McDonnell, *Dances with Wolves*

1991 *Mercedes Ruehl, *The Fisher King*
Diane Ladd, *Rambling Rose*
Juliette Lewis, *Cape Fear*
Kate Nelligan, *The Prince of Tides*
Jessica Tandy, *Fried Green Tomatoes*

1992 *Marisa Tomei, *My Cousin Vinny*
Judy Davis, *Husbands and Wives*
Joan Plowright, *Enchanted April*
Vanessa Redgrave, *Howards End*
Miranda Richardson, *Damage*

The Writing and Music Awards

1: WRITERS

[Note: Given frequent changes of definition in the Writing and Music categories, they are listed here exactly as they appeared in each year.]

1927–28 *Adaptation*

*Benjamin Glazer, *Seventh Heaven*
Alfred Cohn, *The Jazz Singer*
Anthony Coldeway, *Glorious Betsy*

Original Story

*Ben Hecht, *Underworld*
Lajos Biro, *The Last Command*
Rupert Hughes, *The Patent Leather Kid*

Title Writing [not awarded again after this year]

*Joseph Farnham, *Telling the World, The Fair Co-Ed* and *Laugh, Clown, Laugh*
Gerald Duffy, *The Private Life of Helen of Troy*
George Marion, Jr., *Oh Kay!*

1928–29 *Achievement*

*Hans Kraly, *The Patriot*
Tom Barry, *In Old Arizona* and *The Valiant*
Elliott Clawson, *The Leatherneck*
Josephine Lovett, *Our Dancing Daughters*
Bess Meredyth, *Wonder of Women*

1929–30 *Achievement* [not awarded again after this year]

*Frances Marion, *The Big House*
George Abbott, Maxwell Anderson and Dell Andrews, *All Quiet on the Western Front*
Julian Josephson, *Disraeli*
John Meehan, *The Divorcée*
Howard Estabrook, *Street of Chance*

1930–31 *Adaptation*

*Howard Estabrook, *Cimarron*
Horace Jackson, *Holiday*
Francis Faragoh and Robert N. Lee, *Little Caesar*
Joseph Mankiewicz and Sam Mintz, *Skippy*
Seton Miller and Fred Niblo, Jr., *The Criminal Code*

Original Story

*John Monk Saunders, *The Dawn Patrol*
John Bright and Kubec Glasmon, *The Public Enemy*
Rowland Brown, *Doorway to Hell*
Harry D'Abbadie D'Arrast, Douglas Doty and Donald Ogden Stewart, *Laughter*
Lucien Hubbard and Joseph Jackson, *Smart Money*

1931–32 *Adaptation*

*Edwin Burke, *Bad Girl*
Percy Heath and Samuel Hoffenstein, *Dr. Jekyll and Mr. Hyde*
Sidney Howard, *Arrowsmith*

Original Story

*Frances Marion, *The Champ*
Lucien Hubbard, *Star Witness*
Grover Jones and William S. McNutt, *Lady and Gent*
Adela Rogers St. John, *What Price Hollywood?*

1932–33 *Adaptation*

*Victor Heerman and Sarah Y. Mason, *Little Women*
Paul Green and Sonya Levien, *State Fair*
Robert Riskin, *Lady for a Day*

Original Story

*Robert Lord, *One Way Passage*
Charles MacArthur, *Rasputin and the Empress*
Frances Marion, *The Prizefighter and the Lady*

1934 *Adaptation*

*Robert Riskin, *It Happened One Night*
Frances Goodrich and Albert Hackett, *The Thin Man*
Ben Hecht, *Viva Villa!*

Original Story

*Arthur Caesar, *Manhattan Melodrama*
Mauri Grashin, *Hide-Out*
Norman Krasna, *The Richest Girl in the World*

1935 *Original Story*

*Ben Hecht and Charles MacArthur, *The Scoundrel*
Moss Hart, *Broadway Melody of 1936*
Don Hartman and Stephen Avery, *The Gay Deception*

Screenplay

*Dudley Nichols, *The Informer*
Achmed Abdullah, John L. Balderston, Grover Jones, William Slavens McNutt and Waldemar Young, *Lives of a Bengal Lancer*
Jules Furthman, Talbot Jennings and Carey Wilson, *Mutiny on the Bounty*

1936 *Original Story*

*Pierre Collings and Sheridan Gibney, *The Story of Louis Pasteur*
Adele Commandini, *Three Smart Girls*
Norman Krasna, *Fury*
William Anthony McGuire, *The Great Ziegfeld*

Screenplay

*Pierre Collings and Sheridan Gibney, *The Story of Louis Pasteur*
Frances Goodrich and Albert Hackett, *After the Thin Man*
Eric Hatch and Morris Ryskind, *My Man Godfrey*
Sidney Howard, *Dodsworth*
Robert Riskin, *Mr. Deeds Goes to Town*

1937 *Original Story*

*William A. Wellman and Robert Carson, *A Star Is Born*
Niven Busch, *In Old Chicago*

Heinz Herald and Geza Herczeg, *The Life of Emile Zola*
Hans Kraly, *100 Men and a Girl*
Robert Lord, *Black Legion*

Screenplay

*Heinz Herald, Geza Herczeg and Norman Reilly Raine, *The Life of Emile Zola*
Alan Campbell, Robert Carson and Dorothy Parker, *A Star Is Born*
Marc Connolly, John Lee Mahin and Dale Van Every, *Captains Courageous*
Viña Delmar, *The Awful Truth*
Morris Ryskind and Anthony Veiller, *Stage Door*

1938 *Adaptation*

*Ian Dalrymple, Cecil Lewis and W. P. Liscomb, *Pygmalion*

Original Story

*Eleanore Griffin and Dore Schary, *Boys Town*
Irving Berlin, *Alexander's Ragtime Band*
Rowland Brown, *Angels with Dirty Faces*
Marcella Burke and Frederick Kohner, *Mad About Music*
John Howard Lawson, *Blockade*
Frank Wead, *Test Pilot*

Screenplay

*George Bernard Shaw, *Pygmalion*
Lenore Coffee and Julius J. Epstein, *Four Daughters*
Ian Dalrymple, Elizabeth Hill and Frank Wead, *The Citadel*
John Meehan and Dore Schary, *Boys Town*
Robert Riskin, *You Can't Take It with You*

1939 *Original Story*

*Lewis R. Foster, *Mr. Smith Goes to Washington*
Mildred Cram and Leo McCarey, *Love Affair*
Felix Jackson, *Bachelor Mother*
Melchior Lengyel, *Ninotchka*
Lamar Trotti, *Young Mr. Lincoln*

Screenplay

*Sidney Howard, *Gone With the Wind* [posthumous]
Charles Brackett, Walter Reisch and Billy Wilder, *Ninotchka*
Sidney Buchman, *Mr. Smith Goes to Washington*
Ben Hecht and Charles MacArthur, *Wuthering Heights*
Eric Maschwitz, R. C. Sherriff and Claudine West, *Goodbye, Mr. Chips*

1940 *Original Story*

*Benjamin Glazer and John S. Toldy, *Arise, My Love*
Hugo Butler and Dore Schary, *Edison the Man*

Stuart N. Lake, *The Westerner*
Leo McCarey, Bella Spewack and Samuel Spewack, *My Favorite Wife*
Walter Reisch, *Comrade X*

Original Screenplay

*Preston Sturges, *The Great McGinty*
Charles Bennett and Joan Harrison, *Foreign Correspondent*
Norman Burnside, Heinz Herald and John Huston, *Dr. Ehrlich's Magic Bullet*
Charles Chaplin, *The Great Dictator*
Ben Hecht, *Angels over Broadway*

Screenplay

*Donald Ogden Stewart, *The Philadelphia Story*
Nunnally Johnson, *The Grapes of Wrath*
Dudley Nichols, *The Long Voyage Home*
Robert E. Sherwood and Joan Harrison, *Rebecca*
Dalton Trumbo, *Kitty Foyle*

1941 *Original Story*

*Harry Segall, *Here Comes Mr. Jordan*
Richard Connell and Robert Presnell, *Meet John Doe*
Monckton Hoffe, *The Lady Eve*
Thomas Monroe and Billy Wilder, *Ball of Fire*
Gordon Wellesley, *Night Train*

Original Screenplay

*Herman J. Mankiewicz and Orson Welles, *Citizen Kane*
Harry Chandlee, Abem Finkel, John Huston and Howard Koch, *Sergeant York*
Paul Jarrico, *Tom, Dick and Harry*
Norman Krasna, *The Devil and Miss Jones*
Karl Tunberg and Darrell Ware, *Tall, Dark and Handsome*

Screenplay

*Sidney Buchman and Seton I. Miller, *Here Comes Mr. Jordan*
Charles Brackett and Billy Wilder, *Hold Back the Dawn*
Philip Dunne, *How Green Was My Valley*
Lillian Hellman, *The Little Foxes*
John Huston, *The Maltese Falcon*

1942 *Original Story*

*Emeric Pressburger, *The Invaders*
Irving Berlin, *Holiday Inn*
Robert Buckner, *Yankee Doodle Dandy*
Paul Gallico, *The Pride of the Yankees*
Sidney Harmon, *The Talk of the Town*

Original Screenplay

*Michael Kanin and Ring Lardner, Jr., *Woman of the Year*
Frank Butler and Don Hartman, *The Road to Morocco*
W. R. Burnett and Frank Butler, *Wake Island*
George Oppenheimer, *The War Against Mrs. Hadley*
Michael Powell and Emeric Pressburger, *One of Our Aircraft Is Missing*

Screenplay

*George Froeschel, James Hilton, Claudine West and Arthur Wimperis, *Mrs. Miniver*
Rodney Ackland and Emeric Pressburger, *The Invaders*
Sidney Buchman and Irwin Shaw, *The Talk of the Town*
George Froeschel, Claudine West and Arthur Wimperis, *Random Harvest*
Herman J. Mankiewicz and Jo Swerling, *The Pride of the Yankees*

1943 *Original Story*

*William Saroyan, *The Human Comedy*
Steve Fisher, *Destination Tokyo*
Guy Gilpatric, *Action in the North Atlantic*
Gordon McDonnell, *Shadow of a Doubt*
Frank Ross and Robert Russell, *The More the Merrier*

Original Screenplay

*Norman Krasna, *Princess O'Rourke*
Noel Coward, *In Which We Serve*
Lillian Hellman, *The North Star*
Dudley Nichols, *Air Force*
Allan Scott, *So Proudly We Hail*

Screenplay

*Julius J. Epstein, Philip G. Epstein & Howard Koch, *Casablanca*
Richard Flournoy, Lewis R. Foster, Frank Ross and Robert Russell, *The More the Merrier*
Dashiell Hammett, *Watch on the Rhine*
Nunnally Johnson, *Holy Matrimony*
George Seaton, *The Song of Bernadette*

1944 *Original Story*

*Leo McCarey, *Going My Way*
David Boehm and Chandler Sprague, *A Guy Named Joe*
Edward Doherty and Jules Schermer, *The Sullivans*
Alfred Neumann and Joseph Than, *None Shall Escape*
John Steinbeck, *Lifeboat*

Original Screenplay

*Lamar Trotti, *Wilson*
Jerome Cady, *Wing and a Prayer*
Richard Connell and Gladys Lehman, *Two Girls and a Sailor*
Preston Sturges, *Hail the Conquering Hero*
Preston Sturges, *The Miracle of Morgan's Creek*

Screenplay

*Frank Butler and Frank Cavett, *Going My Way*
John L. Balderston, Walter Reisch and John Van Druten, *Gaslight*
Irving Brecher and Fred F. Finkelhoffe, *Meet Me in St. Louis*
Raymond Chandler and Billy Wilder, *Double Indemnity*
Jay Dratler, Samuel Hoffenstein and Betty Reinhardt, *Laura*

1945 *Original Story*

*Charles G. Booth, *The House on 92nd Street*
Alvah Bessie, *Objective, Burma!*
Laszlo Gorog and Thomas Monroe, *The Affairs of Susan*
Ernst Marischka, *A Song to Remember*
John Steinbeck and Jack Wagner, *A Medal for Benny*

Original Screenplay

*Richard Schweizer, *Marie-Louise*
Myles Connolly, *Music for Millions*
Milton Holmes, *Salty O'Rourke*
Harry Kurnitz, *What Next, Corporal Hargrove?*
Philip Yordon, *Dillinger*

Screenplay

*Charles Brackett and Billy Wilder, *The Lost Weekend*
Leopold Atlas, Guy Endore and Philip Stevenson, *The Story of G.I. Joe*
Frank Davis and Tess Slesinger, *A Tree Grows in Brooklyn*
Ranald MacDougall, *Mildred Pierce*
Albert Maltz, *Pride of the Marines*

1946 *Original Story*

*Clemence Dane, *Vacation from Marriage*
Charles Brackett, *To Each His Own*
Jack Patrick, *The Strange Love of Martha Ivers*
Vladimir Pozner, *The Dark Mirror*
Victor Trivas, *The Stranger*

Original Screenplay

*Muriel Box and Sydney Box, *The Seventh Veil*
Raymond Chandler, *The Blue Dahlia*
Ben Hecht, *Notorious*

Norman Panama and Melvin Frank, *The Road to Utopia*
Jacques Prévert, *Children of Paradise*

Screenplay

*Robert E. Sherwood, *The Best Years of Our Lives*
Sergio Amidei and Federico Fellini, *Open City*
Sally Benson and Talbot Jennings, *Anna and the King of Siam*
Anthony Havelock-Allan, David Lean and Ronald Neame, *Brief Encounter*
Anthony Veiller, *The Killers*

1947 *Original Story*

*Valentine Davies, *Miracle on 34th Street*
Georges Chaperot and Rene Wheeler, *A Cage of Nightingales*
Herbert Clyde Lewis and Frederick Stephani, *It Happened on Fifth Avenue*
Eleazar Lipsky, *Kiss of Death*
Dorothy Parker and Frank Cavett, *Smash-Up—The Story of a Woman*

Original Screenplay

*Sidney Sheldon, *The Bachelor and the Bobby-Soxer*
Sergio Amidei, Adolfo Franci, C. G. Viola and Cesare Zavattini, *Shoeshine*
Charles Chaplin, *Monsieur Verdoux*
Ruth Gordon and Garson Kanin, *A Double Life*
Abraham Polonsky, *Body and Soul*

Screenplay

*George Seaton, *Miracle on 34th Street*
Moss Hart, *Gentleman's Agreement*
David Lean, Ronald Neame and Anthony Havelock-Allan, *Great Expectations*
Richard Murphy, *Boomerang!*
John Paxton, *Crossfire*

1948 *Motion Picture Story*

*Richard Schweizer and David Wechsler, *The Search*
Borden Chase, *Red River*
Frances Flaherty and Robert Flaherty, *The Louisiana Story*
Emeric Pressburger, *The Red Shoes*
Malvin Wald, *The Naked City*

Screenplay

*John Huston, *The Treasure of the Sierra Madre*
Charles Brackett, Billy Wilder and Richard L. Breen, *A Foreign Affair*
Frank Partos and Millen Brand, *The Snake Pit*
Richard Schweizer and David Wechsler, *The Search*
Irmgard Von Cube and Allen Vincent, *Johnny Belinda*

1949 *Motion Picture Story*

*Douglas Morrow, *The Stratton Story*
Harry Brown, *Sands of Iwo Jima*
Virginia Kellogg, *White Heat*
Clare Booth Luce, *Come to the Stable*
Shirley W. Smith and Valentine Davies, *It Happens Every Spring*

Screenplay

*Joseph L. Mankiewicz, *A Letter to Three Wives*
Carl Foreman, *Champion*
Graham Greene, *The Fallen Idol*
Robert Rossen, *All the King's Men*
Cesare Zavattini, *The Bicycle Thief*

Story and Screenplay

*Robert Pirosh, *Battleground*
Sidney Buchman, *Jolson Sings Again*
T. E. B. Clarke, *Passport to Pimlico*
Alfred Hayes, Federico Fellini, Sergio Amidei, Marcello Pagliero and Roberto Rossellini, *Paisan*
Helen Levitt, Janice Loeb and Sidney Meyers, *The Quiet One*

1950 *Motion Picture Story*

*Edna Anhalt and Edward Anhalt, *Panic in the Streets*
William Bowers and Andre de Toth, *The Gunfighter*
Giuseppe De Santis and Carlo Lizzani, *Bitter Rice*
Sy Gomberg, *When Willie Comes Marching Home*
Leonard Spigelgass, *Mystery Street*

Screenplay

*Joseph L. Mankiewicz, *All About Eve*
Michael Blankfort, *Broken Arrow*
Frances Goodrich and Albert Hackett, *Father of the Bride*
Ben Maddow and John Huston, *The Asphalt Jungle*
Albert Mannheimer, *Born Yesterday*

Story and Screenplay

*Charles Brackett, Billy Wilder and D. M. Marshman, Jr., *Sunset Boulevard*
Carl Foreman, *The Men*
Ruth Gordon and Garson Kanin, *Adam's Rib*
Virginia Kellogg and Bernard C. Schoenfeld, *Caged*
Joseph L. Mankiewicz and Lesser Samuels, *No Way Out*

1951 *Motion Picture Story*

*Paul Dehn and James Bernard, *Seven Days to Noon*
Budd Boetticher and Ray Nazarro, *The Bullfighter and the Lady*

Alfred Hayes and Stewart Stern, *Teresa*
Oscar Millard, *The Frogmen*
Robert Riskin and Liam O'Brien, *Here Comes the Groom*

Screenplay

*Michael Wilson and Harry Brown, *A Place in the Sun*
James Agee and John Huston, *The African Queen*
Jacques Natanson and Max Ophuls, *La Ronde*
Tennessee Williams, *A Streetcar Named Desire*
Philip Yordan and Robert Wyler, *Detective Story*

Screenplay and Story

*Alan Jay Lerner, *An American in Paris*
Philip Dunne, *David and Bathsheba*
Clarence Greene and Russell Rouse, *The Well*
Robert Pirosh, *Go for Broke!*
Billy Wilder, Lesser Samuels and Walter Newman, *The Big Carnival*

1952 *Motion Picture Story*

*Frederic M. Frank, Theodore St. John and Frank Cavett, *The Greatest Show on Earth*
Edna Anhalt and Edward Anhalt, *The Sniper*
Martin Goldsmith and Jack Leonard, *The Narrow Margin*
Leo McCarey, *My Son John*
Guy Trosper, *The Pride of St. Louis*

Screenplay

*Charles Schnee, *The Bad and the Beautiful*
Carl Foreman, *High Noon*
Roger MacDougall, John Dighton and Alexander MacKendrick, *The Man in the White Suit*
Frank S. Nugent, *The Quiet Man*
Michael Wilson, *Five Fingers*

Story and Screenplay

*T. E. B. Clarke, *The Lavender Hill Mob*
Sydney Boehm, *The Atomic City*
Ruth Gordon and Garson Kanin, *Pat and Mike*
Terence Rattigan, *Breaking the Sound Barrier*
John Steinbeck, *Viva Zapata!*

1953 *Motion Picture Story*

*Ian McLellan Hunter, *Roman Holiday*
Ray Ashley, Morris Engel and Ruth Orkin, *Little Fugitive*
Alec Coppel, *The Captain's Paradise*
Beirne Lay, Jr., *Above and Beyond*
(Fifth nominee, Louis L'Amour, *Hondo,* withdrew).

Screenplay

*Daniel Taradash, *From Here to Eternity*
Eric Ambler, *The Cruel Sea*
Helen Deutsch, *Lili*
A. B. Guthrie, Jr., *Shane*
Ian MacLellan Hunter and John Dighton, *Roman Holiday*

Story and Screenplay

*Charles Brackett, Walter Reisch and Richard Breen, *Titanic*
Betty Comden and Adolph Green, *The Bandwagon*
Millard Kaufman, *Take the High Ground*
Richard Murphy, *The Desert Rats*
Sam Rolfe and Harold Jack Bloom, *The Naked Spur*

1954 *Motion Picture Story*

*Philip Yordan, *Broken Lance*
François Boyer, *Forbidden Games*
Jed Harris and Tom Reed, *Night People*
Ettore Margadonna, *Bread, Love and Dreams*
Lamar Trotti, *There's No Business Like Show Business*

Screenplay

*George Seaton, *The Country Girl*
Albert Hackett, Frances Goodrich and Dorothy Kingsley, *Seven Brides for Seven Brothers*
John Michael Hayes, *Rear Window*
Stanley Roberts, *The Caine Mutiny*
Billy Wilder, Samuel Taylor and Ernest Lehman, *Sabrina*

Story and Screenplay

*Budd Schulberg, *On the Waterfront*
Valentine Davies and Oscar Brodney, *The Glenn Miller Story*
Joseph L. Mankiewicz, *The Barefoot Contessa*
Norman Panama and Melvin Frank, *Knock on Wood*
William Rose, *Genevieve*

1955 *Motion Picture Story*

*Daniel Fuchs, *Love Me or Leave Me*
Joe Connelly and Bob Mosher, *The Private War of Major Benson*
Beirne Lay, Jr., *Strategic Air Command*
Jean Marsan, Henry Troyat, Jacques Perret, Henri Verneuil and Raoul Ploquin, *The Sheep Has Five Legs*
Nicholas Ray, *Rebel Without a Cause*

Screenplay

*Paddy Chayefsky, *Marty*
Richard Brooks, *Blackboard Jungle*

Daniel Fuchs and Isobel Lennart, *Love Me or Leave Me*
Millard Kaufman, *Bad Day at Black Rock*
Paul Osborn, *East of Eden*

Story and Screenplay

*William Ludwig and Sonya Levien, *Interrupted Melody*
Betty Comden and Adolph Green, *It's Always Fair Weather*
Melville Shavelson and Jack Rose, *The Seven Little Foys*
Milton Sperling and Emmet Lavery, *The Court-Martial of Billy Mitchell*
Jacques Tati and Henri Marquet, *Mr. Hulot's Holiday*

1956 *Motion Picture Story*

*Dalton Trumbo [a.k.a. Robert Rich], *The Brave One*
Edward Bernds and Elwood Ullman, *High Society* [withdrawn from final ballot]
Leo Katcher, *The Eddy Duchin Story*
Jean-Paul Sartre, *The Proud and the Beautiful*
Cesare Zavattini, *Umberto D*

Screenplay—Adapted

*James Poe, John Farrow and S. J. Perelman, *Around the World in 80 Days*
Norman Corwin, *Lust for Life*
Fred Guiol and Ivan Moffat, *Giant*
Tennessee Williams, *Baby Doll*
Michael Wilson [ineligible], *Friendly Persuasion*

Screenplay—Original

*Albert Lamorisse, *The Red Balloon*
Federico Fellini and Tullio Pinelli, *La Strada*
Robert Lewin, *The Bold and the Brave*
William Rose, *The Lady Killers*
Andrew L. Stone, *Julie*

1957 [Note: Rules changed as of this year to accommodate two writing awards rather than three]

Screenplay Based on Material from Another Medium

*Pierre Boulle, Michael Wilson and Carl Foreman, *The Bridge on the River Kwai*
John Michael Hayes, *Peyton Place*
John Lee Mahin and John Huston, *Heaven Knows, Mr. Allison*
Paul Osborn, *Sayonara*
Reginald Rose, *Twelve Angry Men*

Story and Screenplay Written Directly for the Screen

*George Wells, *Designing Woman*
Federico Fellini, Ennio Flaiano and Tullio Pinelli (story), Federico

Fellini and Ennio Flaiano (screenplay), *Vitelloni*
Leonard Gershe, *Funny Face*
Barney Slater and Joel Kane (story), Dudley Nichols (screenplay), *The Tin Star*
Ralph Wheelwright (story), R. Wright Campbell, Ivan Goff and Ben Roberts (screenplay), *Man of a Thousand Faces*

1958 *Screenplay Based on Material from Another Medium*

*Alan Jay Lerner, *Gigi*
Richard Brooks and James Poe, *Cat on a Hot Tin Roof*
Nelson Gidding and Don Mankiewicz, *I Want to Live!*
Alec Guinness, *The Horse's Mouth*
Terence Rattigan and John Gay, *Separate Tables*

Story and Screenplay Written Directly for the Screen

*Nathan E. Douglas and Harold Jacob Smith, *The Defiant Ones*
Paddy Chayefsky, *The Goddess*
James Edward Grant (story), William Bowers and James Edward Grant (screenplay), *The Sheepman*
Fay and Michael Kanin, *Teacher's Pet*
Melville Shavelson and Jack Rose, *The Houseboat*

1959 *Screenplay Based on Material from Another Medium*

*Neil Paterson, *Room at the Top*
Robert Anderson, *The Nun's Story*
Wendell Mayes, *Anatomy of a Murder*
Karl Tunberg, *Ben-Hur*
Billy Wilder and I. A. L. Diamond, *Some Like it Hot*

Story and Screenplay Written Directly for the Screen

*Russell Rouse and Clarence Greene (story), Stanley Shapiro and Maurice Richlin (screenplay), *Pillow Talk*
Ingmar Bergman, *Wild Strawberries*
Paul King and Joseph Stone (story), Stanley Shapiro and Maurice Richlin (screenplay), *Operation Petticoat*
Ernest Lehman, *North by Northwest*
François Truffaut and Marcel Moussy, *The 400 Blows*

1960 *Screenplay Based on Material from Another Medium*

*Richard Brooks, *Elmer Gantry*
Nathan E. Douglas and Harold Jacob Smith, *Inherit the Wind*
James Kennaway, *Tunes of Glory*
Gavin Lambert and T. E. B. Clarke, *Sons and Lovers*
Isobel Lennart, *The Sundowners*

Story and Screenplay Written Directly for the Screen

*Billy Wilder and I. A. L. Diamond, *The Apartment*
Jules Dassin, *Never on Sunday*

Marguérite Duras, *Hiroshima, Mon Amour*
Richard Gregson and Michael Craig (story), Bryan Forbes (screenplay), *The Angry Silence*
Norman Panama and Melvin Frank, *The Facts of Life*

1961 *Screenplay Based on Material from Another Medium*

*Abby Mann, *Judgment at Nuremberg*
George Axelrod, *Breakfast at Tiffany's*
Sidney Carroll and Robert Rossen, *The Hustler*
Carl Foreman, *The Guns of Navarone*
Ernest Lehman, *West Side Story*

Story and Screenplay Written Directly for the Screen

*William Inge, *Splendor in the Grass*
Sergio Amidei, Diego Fabbri and Indro Montanelli, *General Della Rovere*
Federico Fellini, Tullio Pinelli, Ennio Flaiano and Brunello Rondi, *La Dolce Vita*
Stanley Shapiro and Paul Henning, *Lover Come Back*
Valentin Yoshov and Grigori Chukhrai, *Ballad of a Soldier*

1962 *Screenplay Based on Material from Another Medium*

*Horton Foote, *To Kill a Mockingbird*
Robert Bolt, *Lawrence of Arabia*
William Gibson, *The Miracle Worker*
Vladimir Nabokov, *Lolita*
Eleanor Perry, *David and Lisa*

Story and Screenplay Written Directly for the Screen

*Ennio de Concini, Alfredo Giannetti and Pietro Germi, *Divorce—Italian Style*
Ingmar Bergman, *Through a Glass Darkly*
Charles Kaufman (story), Charles Kaufman and Wolfgang Reinhardt (screenplay), *Freud*
Alain Robbe-Grillet, *Last Year at Marienbad*
Stanley Shapiro and Nate Monaster, *That Touch of Mink*

1963 *Screenplay Based on Material from Another Medium*

*John Osborne, *Tom Jones*
Serge Bourguignon and Antoine Tudal, *Sundays and Cybèle*
Richard L. Breen, Phoebe and Henry Ephron, *Captain Newman, M.D.*
James Poe, *Lilies of the Field*
Irving Ravetch and Harriet Frank, Jr., *Hud*

Story and Screenplay Written Directly for the Screen

*James R. Webb, *How the West Was Won*
Federico Fellini, Ennio Flaiano, Tullio Pinelli and Brunello Rondi, *8½*

Pasquale Festa Campanile, Massimo Franciosa, Nanni Loy and Vasco Pratolini (story), Carlo Bernari, Pasquale Festa Campanile, Massimo Franciosa and Nanni Loy (screenplay), *The Four Days of Naples*
Elia Kazan, *America, America*
Arnold Schulman, *Love with the Proper Stranger*

1964 *Screenplay Based on Material from Another Medium*

*Edward Anhalt, *Becket*
Michael Cacoyannis, *Zorba the Greek*
Stanley Kubrick, Peter George and Terry Southern, *Dr. Strangelove or: How I Learned to Stop Worrying and Love the Bomb*
Alan Jay Lerner, *My Fair Lady*
Bill Walsh and Don DaGradi, *Mary Poppins*

Story and Screenplay Written Directly for the Screen

*S. H. Barnett (story), Peter Stone and Frank Tarloff (screenplay), *Father Goose*
Age, Scarpelli and Mario Monicelli, *The Organizer*
Orville H. Hampton (story), Raphael Hayes and Orville H. Hampton (screenplay), *One Potato, Two Potato*
Alun Owen, *A Hard Day's Night*
Jean-Paul Rappeneau, Ariane Mnouchkine, Daniel Boulanger and Philippe de Broca, *That Man from Rio*

1965 *Screenplay Based on Material from Another Medium*

*Robert Bolt, *Doctor Zhivago*
Herb Gardner, *A Thousand Clowns*
Abby Mann, *Ship of Fools*
Stanley Mann and John Kohn, *The Collector*
Walter Newman and Frank R. Pierson, *Cat Ballou*

Story and Screenplay Written Directly for the Screen

*Frederic Raphael, *Darling*
Age, Scarpelli, Mario Monicelli, Tonino Guerra, Giorgio Salvioni and Suso Cecchi D'Amico, *Casanova '70*
Franklin Coen and Frank Davis, *The Train*
Jack Davies and Ken Annakin, *Those Magnificent Men in Their Flying Machines*
Jacques Demy, *The Umbrellas of Cherbourg*

1966 *Screenplay Based on Material from Another Medium*

*Robert Bolt, *A Man for All Seasons*
Richard Brooks, *The Professionals*
Ernest Lehman, *Who's Afraid of Virginia Woolf?*
Bill Naughton, *Alfie*
William Rose, *The Russians Are Coming, the Russians Are Coming*

Story and Screenplay Written Directly for the Screen

*Claude Lelouch (story), Pierre Uytterhoeven and Claude Lelouch (screenplay), *A Man and a Woman*
Michelangelo Antonioni (story), Michelangelo Antonioni, Tonino Guerra and Edward Bond (screenplay), *Blow-Up*
Robert Ardrey, *Khartoum*
Clint Johnston and Don Peters, *The Naked Prey*
Billy Wilder and I. A. L. Diamond, *The Fortune Cookie*

1967 *Screenplay Based on Material from Another Medium*

*Stirling Silliphant, *In the Heat of the Night*
Richard Brooks, *In Cold Blood*
Donn Pearce and Frank R. Pierson, *Cool Hand Luke*
Joseph Strick and Fred Haines, *Ulysses*
Calder Willingham and Buck Henry, *The Graduate*

Story and Screenplay Written Directly for the Screen

*William Rose, *Guess Who's Coming to Dinner*
Robert Kaufman (story), and Norman Lear (screenplay), *Divorce American Style*
David Newman and Robert Benton, *Bonnie and Clyde*
Frederic Raphael, *Two for the Road*
Jorge Semprun, *La Guerre Est Finie*

1968 *Screenplay Based on Material from Another Medium*

*James Goldman, *The Lion in Winter*
Vernon Harris, *Oliver!*
Roman Polanski, *Rosemary's Baby*
Neil Simon, *The Odd Couple*
Stewart Stern, *Rachel, Rachel*

Story and Screenplay Written Directly for the Screen

*Mel Brooks, *The Producers*
John Cassavetes, *Faces*
Stanley Kubrick and Arthur C. Clarke, *2001: A Space Odyssey*
Franco Solinas and Gillo Pontecorvo, *The Battle of Algiers*
Ira Wallach and Peter Ustinov, *Hot Millions*

1969 *Screenplay Based on Material from Another Medium*

*Waldo Salt, *Midnight Cowboy*
John Hale and Bridget Boland, with Richard Sokolove (adaptation), *Anne of the Thousand Days*
James Poe and Robert E. Thompson, *They Shoot Horses, Don't They?*
Arnold Schulman, *Goodbye, Columbus*
Jorge Semprun and Costa-Gravas, *Z*

Story and Screenplay Based on Material Not Previously Published or Produced

*William Goldman, *Butch Cassidy and the Sundance Kid*
Nicola Badalucco (story), Nicola Badalucco, Enrico Medioli and Luchino Visconti, *The Damned*
Peter Fonda, Dennis Hopper and Terry Southern, *Easy Rider*
Walon Green and Roy N. Sickner (story), Walon Green and Sam Peckinpah (screenplay), *The Wild Bunch*
Paul Mazursky and Larry Tucker, *Bob & Carol & Ted & Alice*

1970 *Screenplay Based on Material from Another Medium*

*Ring Lardner, Jr., *M*A*S*H*
Robert Anderson, *I Never Sang for My Father*
Larry Kramer, *Women in Love*
George Seaton, *Airport*
Renee Taylor, Joseph Bologna and David Zelag Goodman, *Lovers and Other Strangers*

Story and Screenplay Based on Factual Material or Material Not Previously Published or Produced

*Francis Ford Coppola and Edmund H. North, *Patton*
Bob Rafelson and Adrien Joyce (story), Adrien Joyce (screenplay), *Five Easy Pieces*
Eric Rohmer, *My Night at Maud's*
Erich Segal, *Love Story*
Norman Wexler, *Joe*

1971 *Screenplay Based on Material from Another Medium*

*Ernest Tidyman, *The French Connection*
Bernardo Bertolucci, *The Conformist*
Stanley Kubrick, *A Clockwork Orange*
Larry McMurtry and Peter Bogdanovich, *The Last Picture Show*
Ugo Pirro and Vittorio Bonicelli, *The Garden of the Finzi-Continis*

Story and Screenplay Based on Factual Material or Material Not Previously Published or Produced

*Paddy Chayefsky, *The Hospital*
Penelope Gilliatt, *Sunday, Bloody Sunday*
Andy and Dave Lewis, *Klute*
Elio Petri and Ugo Pirro, *Investigation of a Citizen Above Suspicion*
Herman Raucher, *Summer of '42*

1972 *Screenplay Based on Material from Another Medium*

*Mario Puzo and Francis Ford Coppola, *The Godfather*
Jay Allen, *Cabaret*
Lonne Elder III, *Sounder*
Julius J. Epstein, *Pete 'n' Tillie*
Jan Troell and Bengt Forslund, *The Emigrants*

Story and Screenplay Based on Factual Material or Material Not Previously Published or Produced

*Jeremy Larner, *The Candidate*
Luis Buñuel and Jean-Claude Carrière, *The Discreet Charm of the Bourgeoisie*
Carl Foreman, *Young Winston*
Louis Malle, *Murmur of the Heart*
Terence McCloy, Chris Clark and Suzanne de Passe, *Lady Sings the Blues*

1973 *Screenplay Based on Material from Another Medium*

*William Peter Blatty, *The Exorcist*
James Bridges, *The Paper Chase*
Waldo Salt and Norman Wexler, *Serpico*
Alvin Sargent, *Paper Moon*
Robert Towne, *The Last Detail*

Story and Screenplay Based on Factual Material or Material Not Previously Published or Produced

*David S. Ward, *The Sting*
Ingmar Bergman, *Cries and Whispers*
Melvin Frank and Jack Rose, *A Touch of Class*
George Lucas, Gloria Katz and Willard Huyck, *American Graffiti*
Steve Shagan, *Save the Tiger*

1974 *Original Screenplay*

*Robert Towne, *Chinatown*
Francis Ford Coppola, *The Conversation*
Robert Getchell, *Alice Doesn't Live Here Anymore*
Paul Mazursky and Josh Greenfeld, *Harry and Tonto*
François Truffaut, Jean-Louis Richard and Suzanne Schiffman, *Day for Night*

Screenplay Adapted from Other Material

*Francis Ford Coppola and Mario Puzo, *The Godfather, Part II*
Julian Berry, *Lenny*
Paul Dehn, *Murder on the Orient Express*
Mordecai Richler (screenplay) and Lionel Chetwynd (adaptation), *The Apprenticeship of Duddy Kravitz*
Gene Wilder and Mel Brooks, *Young Frankenstein*

1975 *Original Screenplay*

*Frank Pierson, *Dog Day Afternoon*
Ted Allan, *Lies My Father Told Me*
Federico Fellini and Tonino Guerra, *Amarcord*
Claude LeLouch and Pierre Uytterhoeven, *And Now My Love*
Robert Towne and Warren Beatty, *Shampoo*

Screenplay Adapted from Other Material

*Lawrence Hauben and Bo Goldman, *One Flew Over the Cuckoo's Nest*
John Huston and Gladys Hill, *The Man Who Would Be King*
Stanley Kubrick, *Barry Lyndon*
Ruggero Maccari and Dino Risi, *Scent of a Woman*
Neil Simon, *The Sunshine Boys*

1976 *Screenplay Written Directly for the Screen*

*Paddy Chayefsky, *Network*
Jean-Charles Tacchella (story and screenplay) and Daniele Thompson (adaptation), *Cousin, Cousine*
Walter Bernstein, *The Front*
Sylvester Stallone, *Rocky*
Lina Wertmuller, *Seven Beauties*

Screenplay Based on Material from Another Medium

*William Goldman, *All the President's Men*
Federico Fellini and Bernardino Zapponi, *Fellini's Casanova*
Robert Getchell, *Bound for Glory*
Nicholas Meyer, *The Seven Percent Solution*
Steve Shagan and David Butler, *Voyage of the Damned*

1977 *Screenplay Written Directly for the Screen*

*Woody Allen and Marshall Brickman, *Annie Hall*
Robert Benton, *The Late Show*
Arthur Laurents, *The Turning Point*
George Lucas, *Star Wars*
Neil Simon, *The Goodbye Girl*

Screenplay Based on Material from Another Medium

*Alvin Sargent, *Julia*
Luis Buñuel and Jean-Claude Carrière, *That Obscure Object of Desire*
Larry Gelbart, *Oh, God!*
Gavin Lambert and Lewis John Carlino, *I Never Promised You a Rose Garden*
Peter Shaffer, *Equus*

1978 *Screenplay Written Directly for the Screen*

*Nancy Dowd (story), Waldo Salt and Robert C. Jones (screenplay), *Coming Home*
Woody Allen, *Interiors*
Ingmar Bergman, *Autumn Sonata*
Michael Cimino, Deric Washburn, Louis Garfinkle and Quinn K. Redeker (story), Deric Washburn (screenplay), *The Deer Hunter*
Paul Mazursky, *An Unmarried Woman*

Screenplay Based on Material from Another Medium

*Oliver Stone, *Midnight Express*

Elaine May and Warren Beatty, *Heaven Can Wait*
Walter Newman, *Bloodbrothers*
Neil Simon, *California Suite*
Bernard Slade, *Same Time, Next Year*

1979 *Screenplay Written Directly for the Screen*

*Steve Tesich, *Breaking Away*
Woody Allen and Marshall Brickman, *Manhattan*
Robert Alan Aurthur and Bob Fosse, *All That Jazz*
Valerie Curtin and Barry Levinson, *. . . And Justice for All*
Mike Gray, T. S. Cook and James Bridges, *The China Syndrome*

Screenplay Based on Material from Another Medium

*Robert Benton, *Kramer vs. Kramer*
Allan Burns, *A Little Romance*
John Milius and Francis Ford Coppola, *Apocalypse Now*
Irving Ravetch and Harriet Frank, Jr., *Norma Rae*
Francis Veber, Edouard Molinaro, Marcello Danon and Jean Poiret, *La Cage aux Folles*

1980 *Screenplay Written Directly for the Screen*

*Bo Goldman, *Melvin and Howard*
Christopher Gore, *Fame*
Jean Gruault, *Mon Oncle d'Amérique*
Nancy Meyers, Charles Shyer and Harvey Miller, *Private Benjamin*
W. D. Richter and Arthur Ross (story), W. D. Richter (screenplay), *Brubaker*

Screenplay Based on Material from Another Medium

*Alvin Sargent, *Ordinary People*
Christopher DeVore, Eric Bergren and David Lynch, *The Elephant Man*
Jonathan Hardy, David Stevens and Bruce Beresford, *Breaker Morant*
Lawrence B. Marcus (screenplay) and Richard Rush (adaptation), *The Stunt Man*
Tom Rickman, *Coal Miner's Daughter*

1981 *Screenplay Written Directly for the Screen*

*Colin Welland, *Chariots of Fire*
Warren Beatty and Trevor Griffiths, *Reds*
Steve Gordon, *Arthur*
John Guare, *Atlantic City*
Kurt Luedtke, *Absence of Malice*

Screenplay Based on Material from Another Medium

*Ernest Thompson, *On Golden Pond*
Jay Presson Allen and Sidney Lumet, *Prince of the City*
Harold Pinter, *The French Lieutenant's Woman*

Dennis Potter, *Pennies from Heaven*
Michael Weller, *Ragtime*

1982 *Screenplay Written Directly for the Screen*

*John Briley, *Gandhi*
Larry Gelbart and Murray Schisgal (screenplay), Don McGuire and Larry Gelbart (story), *Tootsie*
Barry Levinson, *Diner*
Melissa Mathison, *E.T.—The Extra-Terrestrial*
Douglas Day Stewart, *An Officer and a Gentleman*

Screenplay Based on Material from Another Medium

*Costa-Gavras and Donald Stewart, *Missing*
Blake Edwards, *Victor/Victoria*
David Mamet, *The Verdict*
Alan J. Pakula, *Sophie's Choice*
Wolfgang Petersen, *Das Boot*

1983 *Screenplay Written Directly for the Screen*

*Horton Foote, *Tender Mercies*
Ingmar Bergman, *Fanny and Alexander*
Nora Ephron and Alice Arlen, *Silkwood*
Lawrence Kasdan and Barbara Benedek, *The Big Chill*
Lawrence Lasker and Walter F. Parkes, *War Games*

Screenplay Based on Material from Another Medium

*James L. Brooks, *Terms of Endearment*
Julius J. Epstein, *Reuben, Reuben*
Ronald Harwood, *The Dresser*
Harold Pinter, *Betrayal*
Willy Russell, *Educating Rita*

1984 *Screenplay Written Directly for the Screen*

*Robert Benton, *Places in the Heart*
Woody Allen, *Broadway Danny Rose*
Lowell Ganz, Babaloo Mandel and Bruce Jay Friedman (screenplay), Bruce J. Friedman (screen story), Brian Grazer (story), *Splash*
Gregory Nava and Anna Thomas, *El Norte*
Daniel Petrie, Jr., (screenplay), Danilo Bach and Daniel Petrie, Jr. (story), *Beverly Hills Cop*

Screenplay Based on Material from Another Medium

*Peter Shaffer, *Amadeus*
Charles Fuller, *A Soldier's Story*
David Lean, *A Passage to India*
Bruce Robinson, *The Killing Fields*
P. H. Vazak and Michael Austin, *Greystoke: The Legend of Tarzan, Lord of the Apes*

1985 *Screenplay Written Directly for the Screen*

*William Kelley, Pamela Wallace and Earl W. Wallace, *Witness*
Woody Allen, *The Purple Rose of Cairo*
Terry Gilliam, Tom Stoppard and Charles McKeown, *Brazil*
Luis Puenzo and Aida Bortnik, *The Official Story*
Robert Zemeckis and Bob Gale, *Back to the Future*

Screenplay Based on Material from Another Medium

*Kurt Luedtke, *Out of Africa*
Richard Condon and Janet Roach, *Prizzi's Honor*
Horton Foote, *The Trip to Bountiful*
Menno Meyjes, *The Color Purple*
Leonard Schrader, *Kiss of the Spider Woman*

1986 *Screenplay Written Directly for the Screen*

*Woody Allen, *Hannah and Her Sisters*
Paul Hogan, Ken Shadie and John Cornell (screenplay), Paul Hogan (story), *"Crocodile" Dundee*
Hanif Kureishi, *My Beautiful Laundrette*
Oliver Stone, *Platoon*
Oliver Stone and Richard Boyle, *Salvador*

Screenplay Based on Material from Another Medium

*Ruth Prawer Jhabvala, *A Room with a View*
Hesper Anderson and Mark Medoff, *Children of a Lesser God*
Raynold Gideon and Bruce A. Evans, *Stand by Me*
Beth Henley, *Crimes of the Heart*
Richard Price, *The Color of Money*

1987 *Screenplay Written Directly for the Screen*

*John Patrick Shanley, *Moonstruck*
Woody Allen, *Radio Days*
John Boorman, *Hope and Glory*
James L. Brooks, *Broadcast News*
Louis Malle, *Au Revoir les Enfants*

Screenplay Based on Material from Another Medium

*Mark Peploe and Bernardo Bertolucci, *The Last Emperor*
James Dearden, *Fatal Attraction*
Lasse Hallström, Reidar Jönsson, Brasse Brannström and Per Berglund, *My Life as a Dog*
Tony Huston, *The Dead*
Stanley Kubrick, Michael Herr and Gustav Hasford, *Full Metal Jacket*

1988 *Screenplay Written Directly for the Screen*

*Ronald Bass and Barry Morrow, *Rain Man*
John Cleese and Charles Crichton, *A Fish Called Wanda*
Naomi Foner, *Running on Empty*

Gary Ross and Anne Spielberg, *Big*
Ron Shelton, *Bull Durham*

Screenplay Based on Material from Another Medium

*Christoper Hampton, *Dangerous Liaisons*
Jean-Claude Carrière and Philip Kaufman, *The Unbearable Lightness of Being*
Christine Edzard, *Little Dorrit*
Frank Galati and Lawrence Kasdan, *The Accidental Tourist*
Anna Hamilton Phelan and Tab Murphy, *Gorillas in the Mist*

1989 *Screenplay Written Directly for the Screen*

*Tom Schulman, *Dead Poets Society*
Woody Allen, *Crimes and Misdemeanors*
Nora Ephron, *When Harry Met Sally . . .*
Spike Lee, *Do the Right Thing*
Steven Soderbergh, *sex, lies, and videotape*

Screenplay Based on Material from Another Medium

*Alfred Uhry, *Driving Miss Daisy*
Phil Alden Robinson, *Field of Dreams*
Jim Sheridan and Shane Connaughton, *My Left Foot*
Roger L. Simon and Paul Mazursky, *Enemies, A Love Story*
Oliver Stone and Ron Kovic, *Born on the Fourth of July*

1990 *Screenplay Written Directly for the Screen*

*Bruce Joel Rubin, *Ghost*
Woody Allen, *Alice*
Barry Levinson, *Avalon*
Whit Stillman, *Metropolitan*
Peter Weir, *Green Card*

Screenplay Based on Material from Another Medium

*Michael Blake, *Dances with Wolves*
Nicholas Kazan, *Reversal of Fortune*
Nicholas Pileggi and Martin Scorsese, *Goodfellas*
Donald E. Westlake, *The Grifters*
Steven Zaillian, *Awakenings*

1991 *Screenplay Written Directly for the Screen*

*Callie Khouri, *Thelma & Louise*
Lawrence Kasdan and Meg Kasdan, *Grand Canyon*
Richard LaGravenese, *The Fisher King*
John Singleton, *Boyz N the Hood*
James Tobak, *Bugsy*

Screenplay Based on Material from Another Medium

*Ted Tally, *The Silence of the Lambs*
Pat Conroy and Becky Johnston, *The Prince of Tides*

Fannie Flagg and Carol Sobieski, *Fried Green Tomatoes*
Agnieszka Holland, *Europa, Europa*
Oliver Stone and Zachary Sklar, *JFK*

1992 *Screenplay Written Directly for the Screen*

*Neil Jordan, *The Crying Game*
Woody Allen, *Husbands and Wives*
George Miller and Nick Enright, *Lorenzo's Oil*
John Sayles, *Passion Fish*
David Webb Peoples, *Unforgiven*

Screenplay Based on Material from Another Medium

*Ruth Prawer Jhabvala, *Howards End*
Peter Barnes, *Enchanted April*
Michael Tolkin, *The Player*
Richard Friedenberg, *A River Runs Through It*
Bo Goldman, *Scent of a Woman*

2A: MUSIC: SCORING AWARDS

[Note: From 1934 through 1937, this was regarded as a Studio Music Department achievement, and the award was given to the department head rather than the composer. Studios are therefore listed for those years only.]

1934 *Louis Silvers (Columbia), *One Night of Love.* Thematic Music by Victor Schertzinger and Gus Kahn.
Max Steiner (RKO Radio), *The Gay Divorcée.* Score by Kenneth Webb and Samuel Hoffenstein.
Max Steiner (RKO Radio), *The Lost Patrol.* Score by Max Steiner.

1935 *Max Steiner (RKO Radio), *The Informer.* Score by Max Steiner.
Nat W. Finston (MGM), *Mutiny on the Bounty.* Score by Herbert Stothart.
Irvin Talbot (Paramount), *Peter Ibbetson.* Score by Ernst Toch.

1936 *Leo Forbstein (Warner Bros.), *Anthony Adverse.* Score by Erich Wolfgang Korngold.
Leo Forbstein (Warner Bros.), *The Charge of the Light Brigade.* Score by Max Steiner.
Boris Morros (Paramount), *The General Died at Dawn.* Score by Werner Janssen.
Nathaniel Shilkret (RKO Radio), *Winterset.* Score by Nathaniel Shilkret.
Max Steiner (Selznick), *The Garden of Allah.* Score by Max Steiner.

1937 *Charles Previn (Universal), *One Hundred Men and a Girl.* Score by uncredited composer.
C. Bakaleinikoff (Grand National), *Something to Sing About.* Score by Victor Schertzinger.

Alberto Colombo (Republic), *Portia on Trial.* Score by Alberto Colombo.
Nat W. Finston (MGM), *Maytime.* Score by Herbert Stothart.
Leo Forbstein (Warner Bros.), *The Life of Emile Zola.* Score by Max Steiner.
Leigh Harline (Disney), *Snow White and the Seven Dwarfs.* Score by Frank Churchill, Leigh Harline and Paul J. Smith.
Marvin Hatley (Hal Roach), *Way Out West.* Score by Marvin Hatley.
Boris Morros (Paramount), *Souls at Sea.* Score by W. Franke Harling and Milan Roder.
Alfred Newman (Goldwyn), *The Hurricane.* Score by Alfred Newman.
Alfred Newman (Selznick), *The Prisoner of Zenda.* Score by Alfred Newman.
Dr. Hugo Riesenfeld (Principal), *Make a Wish.* Score by Dr. Hugo Riesenfeld.
Louis Silvers (Twentieth Century Fox), *In Old Chicago.* Score by uncredited composer.
Morris Stoloff (Columbia), *Lost Horizon.* Score by Dimitri Tiomkin.
Roy Webb (RKO Radio), *Quality Street.* Score by Roy Webb.

[Note: From 1938 onward, the Academy Award was presented to the composer rather than the production studio.]

1938 *Score*

*Alfred Newman, *Alexander's Ragtime Band*
Victor Baravalle, *Carefree*
Cy Feuer, *Storm over Bengal*
Marvin Hatley, *There Goes My Heart*
Boris Morros, *Tropic Holiday*
Alfred Newman, *Goldwyn Follies*
Charles Previn and Frank Skinner, *Mad About Music*
Max Steiner, *Jezebel*
Morris Stoloff and Gregory Stone, *Girls School*
Herbert Stothart, *Sweethearts*
Franz Waxman, *The Young in Heart*

Original Score

*Erich Wolfgang Korngold, *The Adventures of Robin Hood*
Russell Bennett, *Pacific Liner*
Richard Hageman, *If I Were King*
Marvin Hatley, *Blockheads*
Werner Janssen, *Blockade*
Alfred Newman, *The Cowboy and the Lady*
Louis Silvers, *Suez*
Herbert Stothart, *Marie Antoinette*
Franz Waxman, *The Young in Heart*
Victor Young, *Army Girl*
Victor Young, *Breaking the Ice*

1939 *Score*

*Richard Hageman, Frank Harling, John Leipold and Leo Shuken, *Stagecoach*
Phil Boutelje and Arthur Lange, *The Great Victor Herbert*
Aaron Copland, *Of Mice and Men*
Roger Edens and George Stoll, *Babes in Arms*
Lou Forbes, *Intermezzo*
Cy Feuer, *She Married a Cop*
Erich Wolfgang Korngold, *The Private Lives of Elizabeth and Essex*
Alfred Newman, *The Hunchback of Notre Dame*
Alfred Newman, *They Shall Have Music*
Charles Previn, *First Love*
Louis Silvers, *Swanee River*
Dimitri Tiomkin, *Mr. Smith Goes to Washington*
Victor Young, *Way Down South*

Original Score

*Herbert Stothart, *The Wizard of Oz*
Anthony Collins, *Nurse Edith Cavell*
Aaron Copland, *Of Mice and Men*
Lud Gluskin and Lucien Moraweck, *The Man in the Iron Mask*
Werner Janssen, *Eternally Yours*
Alfred Newman, *The Rains Came*
Alfred Newman, *Wuthering Heights*
Max Steiner, *Dark Victory*
Max Steiner, *Gone with the Wind*
Victor Young, *Golden Boy*
Victor Young, *Gulliver's Travels*
Victor Young, *Man of Conquest*

1940 *Score*

*Alfred Newman, *Tin Pan Alley*
Anthony Collins, *Irene*
Aaron Coplan, *Our Town*
Cy Feuer, *Hit Parade of 1941*
Erich Wolfgang Korngold, *The Sea Hawk*
Charles Previn, *Spring Parade*
Artie Shaw, *Second Chorus*
George Stoll and Roger Edens, *Strike Up the Band*
Victor Young, *Arise My Love*

Original Score

*Leigh Harline, Paul J. Smith and Ned Washington, *Pinocchio*
Aaron Copland, *Our Town*
Louis Gruenberg, *The Fight for Life*
Richard Hageman, *The Howards of Virginia*
Richard Hageman, *The Long Voyage Home*
Werner Heymann, *One Million B.C.*

Alfred Newman, *The Mark of Zorro*
Miklos Rozsa, *The Thief of Bagdad*
Frank Skinner, *The House of Seven Gables*
Max Steiner, *The Letter*
Herbert Stothart, *Waterloo Bridge*
Franz Waxman, *Rebecca*
Roy Webb, *My Favorite Wife*
Meredith Willson, *The Great Dictator*
Victor Young, *Arizona*
Victor Young, *The Dark Command*
Victor Young, *North West Mounted Police*

1941 *Scoring of a Dramatic Picture*

*Bernard Herrmann, *All That Money Can Buy*
Cy Feuer and Walter Scharf, *Mercy Island*
Louis Gruenberg, *So Ends Our Night*
Richard Hageman, *This Woman Is Mine*
Bernard Herrmann, *Citizen Kane*
Werner Heymann, *That Uncertain Feeling*
Edward Kay, *King of the Zombies*
Alfred Newman, *Ball of Fire*
Alfred Newman, *How Green Was My Valley*
Miklos Rozsa, *Lydia*
Miklos Rozsa, *Sundown*
Frank Skinner, *Back Street*
Max Steiner, *Sergeant York*
Morris Stoloff and Ernst Toch, *Ladies in Retirement*
Edward Ward, *Cheers for Miss Bishop*
Edward Ward, *Tanks a Million*
Franz Waxman, *Dr. Jekyll and Mr. Hyde*
Franz Waxman, *Suspicion*
Meredith Willson, *The Little Foxes*
Victor Young, *Hold Back the Dawn*

Scoring of a Musical Picture

*Frank Churchill and Oliver Wallace, *Dumbo*
Robert Emmett Dolan, *Birth of the Blues*
Cy Feuer, *Ice Capades*
Emil Newman, *Sun Valley Serenade*
Charles Previn, *Buck Privates*
Heinz Roemheld, *The Strawberry Blonde*
Morris Stoloff, *You'll Never Get Rich*
Herbert Stothart and Bronislau Kaper, *The Chocolate Soldier*
Edward Ward, *All American Co-Ed*

1942 *Scoring of a Dramatic or Comedy Picture*

*Max Steiner, *Now, Voyager*
Frank Churchill and Edward Plumb, *Bambi*

Richard Hageman, *The Shanghai Gesture*
Leigh Harline, *The Pride of the Yankees*
Werner Heymann, *To Be or Not to Be*
Frederick Hollander and Morris Stoloff, *The Talk of the Town*
Edward Kay, *Klondike Fury*
Alfred Newman, *The Black Swan*
Miklos Rozsa, *Jungle Book*
Frank Skinner, *Arabian Nights*
Herbert Stothart, *Random Harvest*
Max Terr, *The Gold Rush*
Dimitri Tiomkin, *The Corsican Brothers*
Roy Webb, *I Married a Witch*
Roy Webb, *Joan of Paris*
Victor Young, *Flying Tigers*
Victor Young, *Silver Queen*
Victor Young, *Take a Letter, Darling*

Scoring of a Musical Picture

*Ray Heindorf and Heinz Roemheld, *Yankee Doodle Dandy*
Robert Emmett Dolan, *Holiday Inn*
Roger Edens and Georgie Stoll, *For Me and My Gal*
Leigh Harline, *You Were Never Lovelier*
Alfred Newman, *My Gal Sal*
Charles Previn and Hans Salter, *It Started with Eve*
Walter Scharf, *Johnny Doughboy*
Edward Ward, *Flying with Music*

1943 *Scoring of a Dramatic or Comedy Picture*

*Alfred Newman, *The Song of Bernadette*
C. Bakaleinikoff and Roy Webb, *The Fallen Sparrow*
Phil Boutelje, *Hi Diddle Diddle*
Gerard Carbonara, *The Kansan*
Aaron Copland, *The North Star*
Hanns Eisler, *Hangmen Also Die*
Louis Gruenberg and Morris Stoloff, *The Commandos Strike at Dawn*
Leigh Harline, *Johnny Come Lately*
Arthur Lange, *Lady of Burlesque*
Edward H. Plumb, Paul J. Smith and Oliver G. Wallace, *Victory Through Air Power*
Hans J. Salter and Frank Skinner, *The Amazing Mrs. Holliday*
Walter Scharf, *In Old Oklahoma*
Max Steiner, *Casablanca*
Herbert Stothart, *Madame Curie*
Dimitri Tiomkin, *The Moon and Sixpence*
Victor Young, *For Whom the Bell Tolls*

Scoring of a Musical Picture

*Ray Heindorf, *This Is the Army*
Robert Emmett Dolan, *Star Spangled Rhythm*
Leigh Harline, *The Sky's the Limit*
Alfred Newman, *Coney Island*
Edward H. Plumb, Paul J. Smith and Charles Wolcott, *Saludos Amigos*
Frederic E. Rich, *Stage Door Canteen*
Walter Scharf, *Hit Parade of 1943*
Morris Stoloff, *Something to Shout About*
Herbert Stothart, *Thousands Cheer*
Edward Ward, *The Phantom of the Opera*

1944 *Scoring of a Dramatic or Comedy Picture*

*Max Steiner, *Since You Went Away*
C. Bakaleinikoff and Hanns Eisler, *None But the Lonely Heart*
Karl Hajos, *Summer Storm*
Franke Harling, *Three Russian Girls*
Arthur Lange, *Casanova Brown*
Michel Michelet, *Voice in the Wind*
Michel Michelet and Edward Paul, *The Hairy Ape*
Alfred Newman, *Wilson*
Edward Paul, *Up in Mabel's Room*
Frederic E. Rich, *Jack London*
David Rose, *The Princess and the Pirate*
Miklos Rozsa, *Double Indemnity*
Miklos Rozsa, *Woman of the Town*
Hans J. Salter, *Christmas Holiday*
Walter Scharf and Roy Webb, *The Fighting Seabees*
Max Steiner, *The Adventures of Mark Twain*
Morris Stoloff and Ernst Toch, *Address Unknown*
Robert Stolz, *It Happened Tomorrow*
Herbert Stothart, *Kismet*
Dimitri Tiomkin, *The Bridge of San Luis Rey*

Scoring of a Musical Picture

*Carmen Dragon and Morris Stoloff, *Cover Girl*
C. Bakaleinikoff, *Higher and Higher*
Robert Emmett Dolan, *Lady in the Dark*
Leo Erdody and Ferdie Grofé, *Minstrel Man*
Louis Forbes and Ray Heindorf, *Up in Arms*
Ray Heindorf, *Hollywood Canteen*
Werner R. Heymann and Kurt Weill, *Knickerbocker Holiday*
Edward Kay, *Lady Let's Dance*
Mahlon Merrick, *Sensations of 1945*
Alfred Newman, *Irish Eyes Are Smiling*
Charles Previn, *Song of the Open Road*
Hans J. Salter, *The Merry Monahans*

Walter Scharf, *Brazil*
Georgie Stoll, *Meet Me in St. Louis*

1945 *Scoring of a Dramatic or Comedy Picture*

*Miklos Rozsa, *Spellbound*
Daniele Amfitheatrof, *Guest Wife*
Louis Applebaum and Ann Ronell, *The Story of G.I. Joe*
Dale Butts and Morton Scott, *Flame of the Barbary Coast*
Robert Emmett Dolan, *The Bells of St. Mary's*
Lou Forbes, *Brewster's Millions*
Hugo Friedhofer and Arthur Lange, *The Woman in the Window*
Karl Hajos, *Man Who Walked Alone*
Werner Janssen, *Captain Kidd*
Werner Janssen, *Guest in the House*
Werner Janssen, *The Southerner*
Edward J. Kay, *G.I. Honeymoon*
Alfred Newman, *The Keys of the Kingdom*
Miklos Rozsa, *The Lost Weekend*
Miklos Rozsa and Morris Stoloff, *A Song to Remember*
Hans J. Salter, *This Love of Ours*
Herbert Stothart, *The Valley of Decision*
Alexander Tansman, *Paris Underground*
Franz Waxman, *Objective, Burma!*
Roy Webb, *Enchanted Cottage*
Victor Young, *Love Letters*

Scoring of a Musical Picture

Georgie Stoll, *Anchors Aweigh*
Robert Emmett Dolan, *Incendiary Blonde*
Lou Forbes and Ray Heindorf, *Wonder Man*
Walter Greene, *Why Girls Leave Home*
Ray Heindorf and Max Steiner, *Rhapsody in Blue*
Charles Henderson and Alfred Newman, *State Fair*
Edward J. Kay, *Sunbonnet Sue*
Jerome Kern and H. J. Salter, *Can't Help Singing*
Arthur Lange, *Belle of the Yukon*
Edward Plumb, Paul J. Smith and Charles Wolcott, *The Three Caballeros*
Morton Scott, *Hitchhike to Happiness*
Marlin Skiles and Morris Stoloff, *Tonight and Every Night*

1946 *Scoring of a Dramatic or Comedy Picture*

*Hugo Friedhofer, *The Best Years of Our Lives*
Bernard Herrmann, *Anna and the King of Siam*
Miklos Rozsa, *The Killers*
William Walton, *Henry V*
Franz Waxman, *Humoresque*

Scoring of a Musical Picture

*Morris Stoloff, *The Jolson Story*
Robert Emmett Dolan, *Blue Skies*
Lennie Hayton, *The Harvey Girls*
Ray Heindorf and Max Steiner, *Night and Day*
Alfred Newman, *Centennial Summer*

1947 *Scoring of a Dramatic or Comedy Picture*

*Miklos Rozsa, *A Double Life*
Hugo Friedhofer, *The Bishop's Wife*
Alfred Newman, *Captain from Castile*
David Raskin, *Forever Amber*
Max Steiner, *Life with Father*

Scoring of a Musical Picture

*Alfred Newman, *Mother Wore Tights*
Daniele Amfitheatrof, Paul J. Smith and Charles Wolcott, *Song of the South*
Robert Emmett Dolan, *Road to Rio*
Johnny Green, *Fiesta*
Ray Heindorf and Max Steiner, *My Wild Irish Rose*

1948 *Scoring of a Dramatic or Comedy Picture*

*Brian Easdale, *The Red Shoes*
Hugo Friedhofer, *Joan of Arc*
Alfred Newman, *The Snake Pit*
Max Steiner, *Johnny Belinda*
William Walton, *Hamlet*

Scoring of a Musical Picture

*Johnny Green and Roger Edens, *Easter Parade*
Lennie Hayton, *The Pirate*
Ray Heindorf, *Romance on the High Seas*
Alfred Newman, *When My Baby Smiles at Me*
Victor Young, *The Emperor Waltz*

1948 *Scoring of a Dramatic or Comedy Picture*

*Aaron Copland, *The Heiress*
Max Steiner, *Beyond the Forest*
Dimitri Tiomkin, *Champion*

Scoring of a Musical Picture

*Roger Edens and Lennie Hayton, *On the Town*
Ray Heindorf, *Look for the Silver Lining*
Morris Stoloff and George Dunning, *Jolson Sings Again*

1950 *Scoring of a Dramatic or Comedy Picture*

*Franz Waxman, *Sunset Boulevard*

George Duning, *No Sad Songs for Me*
Alfred Newman, *All About Eve*
Max Steiner, *The Flame and the Arrow*
Victor Young, *Samson and Delilah*

Scoring of a Musical Picture

*Adolph Deutsch and Roger Edens, *Annie Get Your Gun*
Ray Heindorf, *The West Point Story*
Lionel Newman, *I'll Get By*
André Previn, *Three Little Words*
Oliver Wallace and Paul J. Smith, *Cinderella*

1951 *Scoring of a Dramatic or Comedy Picture*

*Franz Waxman, *A Place in the Sun*
Alfred Newman, *David and Bathsheba*
Alex North, *Death of a Salesman*
Alex North, *A Streetcar Named Desire*
Miklos Rozsa, *Quo Vadis*

Scoring of a Musical Picture

*Johnny Green and Saul Chaplin, *An American in Paris*
Peter Herman Adler and Johnny Green, *The Great Caruso*
Adolph Deutsch and Conrad Salinger, *Show Boat*
Alfred Newman, *On the Riviera*
Oliver Wallace, *Alice in Wonderland*

1952 *Scoring of a Dramatic or Comedy Picture*

*Dimitri Tiomkin, *High Noon*
Herschel Burke Gilbert, *The Thief*
Alex North, *Viva Zapata!*
Miklos Rozsa, *Ivanhoe*
Max Steiner, *Miracle of Our Lady of Fatima*

Scoring of a Musical Picture

*Alfred Newman, *With a Song in My Heart*
Lennie Hayton, *Singin' in the Rain*
Ray Heindorf and Max Steiner, *The Jazz Singer*
Gian-Carlo Menotti, *The Medium*
Walter Scharf, *Hans Christian Andersen*

1953 *Scoring of a Dramatic or Comedy Picture*

*Bronislau Kaper, *Lili*
Louis Forbes, *This is Cinerama*
Hugo Friedhofer, *Above and Beyond*
Miklos Rozsa, *Julius Caesar*
Morris Stoloff and George Duning, *From Here to Eternity*

Scoring of a Musical Picture

*Alfred Newman, *Call Me Madam*
Adolph Deutsch, *The Band Wagon*
Ray Heindorf, *Calamity Jane*
Frederick Hollander and Morris Stoloff, *The 5,000 Fingers of Dr. T.*
André Previn and Saul Chaplin, *Kiss Me Kate*

1954 *Scoring of a Dramatic or Comedy Picture*

*Dimitri Tiomkin, *The High and the Mighty*
Leonard Bernstein, *On the Waterfront*
Muir Mathieson, *Genevieve*
Max Steiner, *The Caine Mutiny*
Franz Waxman, *The Silver Chalice*

Scoring of a Musical Picture

*Adolph Deutsch and Saul Chaplin, *Seven Brides for Seven Brothers*
Herschel Burke Gilbert, *Carmen Jones*
Joseph Gershensen and Henry Mancini, *The Glenn Miller Story*
Ray Heindorf, *A Star Is Born*
Alfred Newman and Lionel Newman, *There's No Business Like Show Business*

1955 *Scoring of a Dramatic or Comedy Picture*

*Alfred Newman, *Love Is a Many Splendored Thing*
Elmer Bernstein, *The Man with the Golden Arm*
George Duning, *Picnic*
Alex North, *The Rose Tattoo*
Max Steiner, *Battle Cry*

Scoring of a Musical Picture

*Robert Russell Bennett, Jay Blackton and Adolph Deutsch, *Oklahoma!*
Jay Blackton and Cyril J. Mockridge, *Guys and Dolls*
Percy Faith and George Stoll, *Love Me or Leave Me*
Alfred Newman, *Daddy Long legs*
André Previn, *It's Always Fair Weather*

1956 *Scoring of a Dramatic or Comedy Picture*

*Victor Young, *Around the World in 80 Days*
Hugo Friedhofer, *Between Heaven and Hell*
Alfred Newman, *Anastasia*
Alex North, *The Rainmaker*
Dimitri Tiomkin, *Giant*

Scoring of a Musical Picture

*Alfred Newman and Ken Darby, *The King and I*
Johnny Green and Saul Chaplin, *High Society*
Lionel Newman, *The Best Things in Life Are Free*
George Stoll and Johnny Green, *Meet Me in Las Vegas*
Morris Stoloff and George Duning, *The Eddy Duchin Story*

1957 [Note: Rules changed this year to one award for Music Scoring instead of separate awards for Drama/Comedy and Musical.]

*Malcolm Arnold, *The Bridge on the River Kwai*
Hugo Friedhofer, *An Affair to Remember*
Hugo Friedhofer, *Boy on a Dolphin*
Johnny Green, *Raintree County*
Paul Smith, *Perri*

1958 [Note: Rules changed back to one award for Drama/Comedy Scoring, one for Musical.]

Scoring of a Dramatic or Comedy Picture

*Dimitri Tiomkin, *The Old Man and the Sea*
Hugo Friedhofer, *The Young Lions*
Jerome Moross, *The Big Country*
David Raksin, *Separate Tables*
Oliver Wallace, *White Wilderness*

Scoring of a Musical Picture

*André Previn, *Gigi*
Yuri Faier and G. Rozhdestvensky, *The Bolshoi Ballet*
Ray Heindorf, *Damn Yankees*
Alfred Newman and Ken Darby, *South Pacific*
Lionel Newman, *Mardi Gras*

1959 *Scoring of a Dramatic or Comedy Picture*

*Miklos Rozsa, *Ben-Hur*
Ernest Gold, *On the Beach*
Frank DeVol, *Pillow Talk*
Alfred Newman, *The Diary of Anne Frank*
Franz Waxman, *The Nun's Story*

Scoring of a Musical Picture

*André Previn and Ken Darby, *Porgy and Bess*
George Bruns, *Sleeping Beauty*
Nelson Riddle and Joseph J. Lilley, *Li'l Abner*
Lionel Newman, *Say One for Me*
Leith Stevens, *The Five Pennies*

1960 *Scoring of a Dramatic or Comedy Picture*

*Ernest Gold, *Exodus*
Elmer Bernstein, *The Magnificent Seven*
Alex North, *Spartacus*
André Previn, *Elmer Gantry*
Dimitri Tiomkin, *The Alamo*

Scoring of a Musical Picture

*Morris Stoloff and Harry Sukman, *Song Without End*

Johnny Green, *Pepe*
Lionel Newman and Earle H. Hagen, *Let's Make Love*
André Previn, *Bells Are Ringing*
Nelson Riddle, *Can-Can*

1961 *Scoring of a Dramatic or Comedy Picture*

*Henry Mancini, *Breakfast at Tiffany's*
Elmer Bernstein, *Summer and Smoke*
Miklos Rozsa, *El Cid*
Morris Stoloff and Harry Sukman, *Fanny*
Dimitri Tiomkin, *The Guns of Navarone*

Scoring of a Musical Picture

*Saul Chaplin, Johnny Green, Sid Ramin and Irwin Kostal, *West Side Story*
George Bruns, *Babes in Toyland*
Duke Ellington, *Paris Blues*
Alfred Newman and Ken Darby, *Flower Drum Song*
Dimitri Shostakovich, *Khovanshchina*

1962 *Music Score—Substantially Original*

*Maurice Jarre, *Lawrence of Arabia*
Elmer Bernstein, *To Kill a Mockingbird*
Jerry Goldsmith, *Freud*
Bronislau Kaper, *Mutiny on the Bounty*
Franz Waxman, *Taras Bulba*

Scoring of Music—Adaptation or Treatment

*Ray Heindorf, *The Music Man*
Leigh Harline, *The Wonderful World of the Brothers Grimm*
Michel Magne, *Gigot*
Frank Perkins, *Gypsy*
George Stoll, *Billy Rose's Jumbo*

1963 *Music Score—Substantially Original*

*John Addison, *Tom Jones*
Ernest Gold, *It's a Mad, Mad, Mad, Mad World*
Alfred Newman and Ken Darby, *How the West Was Won*
Alex North, *Cleopatra*
Dimitri Tiomkin, *55 Days at Peking*

Scoring of Music—Adaptation or Treatment

*André Previn, *Irma La Douce*
George Bruns, *The Sword in the Stone*
John Green, *Bye Bye Birdie*
Maurice Jarre, *Sundays and Cybèle*
Leith Stevens, *A New Kind of Love*

1964 *Music Score—Substantially Original*

*Richard M. Sherman and Robert B. Sherman, *Mary Poppins*
Frank DeVol, *Hush . . . Hush, Sweet Charlotte*
Henry Mancini, *The Pink Panther*
Laurence Rosenthal, *Becket*
Dimitri Tiomkin, *The Fall of the Roman Empire*

Scoring of Music—Adaptation or Treatment

*André Previn, *My Fair Lady*
Robert Armbruster, Leo Arnaud, Jack Elliott, Jack Hayes, Calvin Jackson, and Leo Shuken, *The Unsinkable Molly Brown*
Irwin Kostal, *Mary Poppins*
George Martin, *A Hard Day's Night*
Nelson Riddle, *Robin and the 7 Hoods*

1965 *Music Score—Substantially Original*

*Maurice Jarre, *Doctor Zhivago*
Jerry Goldsmith, *A Patch of Blue*
Michel Legrand and Jacques Demy, *The Umbrellas of Cherbourg*
Alfred Newman, *The Greatest Story Ever Told*
Alex North, *The Agony and the Ecstasy*

Scoring of Music—Adaptation or Treatment

*Irwin Kostal, *The Sound of Music*
Frank DeVol, *Cat Ballou*
Michel Legrand, *The Umbrellas of Cherbourg*
Lionel Newman and Alexander Courage, *The Pleasure Seekers*
Don Walker, *A Thousand Clowns*

1966 *Original Music Score*

*John Barry, *Born Free*
Elmer Bernstein, *Hawaii*
Jerry Goldsmith, *The Sand Pebbles*
Toshiro Mayuzumi, *The Bible*
Alex North, *Who's Afraid of Virginia Woolf?*

Scoring of Music—Adaptation or Treatment

*Ken Thorne, *A Funny Thing Happened on the Way to the Forum*
Luis Enrique Bacalov, *The Gospel According to St. Matthew*
Elmer Bernstein, *Return of the Seven*
Al Ham, *Stop the World—I Want to Get Off*
Harry Sukman, *The Singing Nun*

1967 *Original Music Score*

*Elmer Bernstein, *Thoroughly Modern Millie*
Richard Rodney Bennett, *Far from the Madding Crowd*
Leslie Bricusse, *Doctor Dolittle*

Quincy Jones, *In Cold Blood*
Lalo Schifrin, *Cool Hand Luke*

Scoring of Music—Adaptation or Treatment

*Alfred Newman and Ken Darby, *Camelot*
Frank DeVol, *Guess Who's Coming to Dinner*
Lionel Newman and Alexander Courage, *Doctor Dolittle*
André Previn and Joseph Gershenson, *Thoroughly Modern Millie*
John Williams, *Valley of the Dolls*

1968 *Original Score for a Motion Picture—Not a Musical*

*John Barry, *The Lion in Winter*
Jerry Goldsmith, *Planet of the Apes*
Michel Legrand, *The Thomas Crown Affair*
Alex North, *The Shoes of the Fisherman*
Lalo Schifrin, *The Fox*

Score of a Musical Picture—Original or Adaptation

*John Green, *Oliver!*
Lennie Hayton, *Star!*
Ray Heindorf, *Finian's Rainbow*
Michel Legrand and Jacques Demy, *The Young Girls of Rochefort*
Walter Scharf, *Funny Girl*

1969 *Original Score for a Motion Picture—Not a Musical*

*Burt Bacharach, *Butch Cassidy and the Sundance Kid*
Georges Delerue, *Anne of the Thousand Days*
Jerry Fielding, *The Wild Bunch*
Ernest Gold, *The Secret of Santa Vittoria*
John Williams, *The Reivers*

Score of a Musical Picture—Original or Adaptation

*Lennie Hayton and Lionel Newman, *Hello, Dolly!*
Leslie Bricusse and John Williams, *Goodbye, Mr. Chips*
Cy Coleman, *Sweet Charity*
John Green and Albert Woodbury, *They Shoot Horses, Don't They?*
Nelson Riddle, *Paint Your Wagon*

1970 *Original Score*

*Francis Lai, *Love Story*
Frank Cordell, *Cromwell*
Jerry Goldsmith, *Patton*
Henry Mancini, *Sunflower*
Alfred Newman, *Airport*

Original Song Score

*The Beatles, *Let It Be*
Fred Karlin and Tylwyth Kymry, *The Baby Maker*

Rod McKuen, John Scott Trotter, Bill Melendez and Al Shean (adapted by Vince Guaraldi), *A Boy Named Charlie Brown*
Henry Mancini and Johnny Mercer, *Darling Lili*
Leslie Bricusse (adapted by Ian Fraser and Herbert W. Spencer), *Scrooge*

1971 *Original Dramatic Score*

*Michel Legrand, *Summer of '42*
John Barry, *Mary, Queen of Scots*
Richard Rodney Bennett, *Nicholas and Alexandra*
Jerry Fielding, *Straw Dogs*
Isaac Hayes, *Shaft*

Scoring: Adaptation and Original Song Score

*John Williams, *Fiddler on the Roof*
Leslie Bricusse and Anthony Newley (adapted by Walter Scharf), *Willy Wonka and the Chocolate Factory*
Peter Maxwell Davies and Peter Greenwell, *The Boy Friend*
Richard M. Sherman and Robert B. Sherman (adapted by Irwin Kostal), *Bedknobs and Broomsticks*
Dimitri Tiomkin, *Tchaikovsky*

1972 *Original Dramatic Score*

*Charles Chaplin, Raymond Rasch and Larry Russel, *Limelight*
John Addison, *Sleuth*
Buddy Baker, *Napoleon and Samantha*
John Williams, *Images*
John Williams, *The Poseidon Adventure*

Scoring: Adaptation and Original Song Score

*Ralph Burns, *Cabaret*
Gil Askey, *Lady Sings the Blues*
Laurence Rosenthal, *Man of La Mancha*

1973 *Original Dramatic Score*

*Marvin Hamlisch, *The Way We Were*
John Cameron, *A Touch of Class*
Georges Delerue, *The Day of the Dolphin*
Jerry Goldsmith, *Papillon*
John Williams, *Cinderella Liberty*

Scoring: Original Song Score and/or Adaptation

*Marvin Hamlisch, *The Sting*—adaptation
André Previn, Herbert Spencer and Andrew Lloyd Webber, *Jesus Christ Superstar*
Richard M. Sherman and Robert B. Sherman (adapted by John Williams), *Tom Sawyer*

1974 *Original Dramatic Score*

*Nino Rota and Carmine Coppola, *The Godfather, Part II*
Richard Rodney Bennett, *Murder on the Orient Express*
Jerry Goldsmith, *Chinatown*
Alex North, *Shanks*
John Williams, *The Towering Inferno*

Scoring: Original Song Score and/or Adaptation

*Nelson Riddle, *The Great Gatsby*
Alan Jay Lerner and Frederick Loewe (adapted by Angela Morley and Douglas Gamley), *The Little Prince*
Paul Williams (adapted by Paul Williams and George Aliceson Tipton), *Phantom of the Paradise*

1975 *Original Score*

*John Williams, *Jaws*
Gerald Fried, *Birds Do it, Bees Do It*
Alex North, *Bite the Bullet*
Jack Nitzsche, *One Flew Over the Cuckoo's Nest*
Jerry Goldsmith, *The Wind and the Lion*

Scoring: Original Score and/or Adaptation

*Leonard Rosenman, *Barry Lyndon*
Peter Matz, *Funny Lady*
Peter Townshend, *Tommy*

1976 *Original Score*

*Jerry Goldsmith, *The Omen*
Jerry Fielding, *The Outlaw Josey Wales*
Bernard Herrmann, *Obsession*
Bernard Herrmann, *Taxi Driver*
Lalo Schifrin, *Voyage of the Damned*

Original Song Score and Its Adaptation or Adaptation Score

*Leonard Rosenman, *Bound for Glory*
Paul Williams, *Bugsy Malone*
Roger Kellaway, *A Star Is Born*

1977 *Original Score*

*John Williams, *Star Wars*
Georges Delerue, *Julia*
Marvin Hamlisch, *The Spy Who Loved Me*
Maurice Jarre, *Mohammad—Messenger of God*
John Williams, *Close Encounters of the Third Kind*

Original Song Score and Its Adaptation or Adaptation Score

*Jonathan Tunick, *A Little Night Music*

Al Kasha and Joel Hirschhorn (adapted by Irwin Kostal), *Pete's Dragon*
Richard M. Sherman and Robert B. Sherman (adapted by Angela Morley), *The Slipper and the Rose*

1978 *Original Score*

*Giorgio Moroder, *Midnight Express*
Jerry Goldsmith, *The Boys from Brazil*
Dave Grusin, *Heaven Can Wait*
Ennio Morricone, *Days of Heaven*
John Williams, *Superman*

Original Song Score and Its Adaptation or Adaptation Score

*Joe Renzetti, *The Buddy Holly Story*
Quincy Jones, *The Wiz*
Jerry Wexler, *Pretty Baby*

1979 *Original Score*

*Georges Delerue, *A Little Romance*
Jerry Goldsmith, *Star Trek—The Motion Picture*
Dave Grusin, *The Champ*
Henry Mancini, *10*
Lalo Schifrin, *The Amityville Horror*

Original Song Score and Its Adaptation or Adaptation Score

*Ralph Burns, *All That Jazz*
Patrick Williams, *Breaking Away*
Paul Williams and Kenny Ascher (adapted by Paul Williams), *The Muppet Movie*

1980 *Original Score*

*Michael Gore, *Fame*
John Corigliano, *Altered States*
John Morris, *The Elephant Man*
Philippe Sarde, *Tess*
John Williams, *The Empire Strikes Back*

Original Song Score and Its Adaptation or Adaptation Score

No award given this year due to insufficient eligible films.

1981 *Original Score*

*Vangelis, *Chariots of Fire*
Dave Grusin, *On Golden Pond*
Randy Newman, *Ragtime*
Alex North, *Dragonslayer*
John Williams, *Raiders of the Lost Ark*

Original Song Score and Its Adaptation or Adaptation Score

No award given this year due to insufficient eligible films.

1982 *Original Score*

*John Williams, *E.T.—The Extra-Terrestrial*
Jerry Goldsmith, *Poltergeist*
Marvin Hamlisch, *Sophie's Choice*
Jack Nitzsche, *An Officer and a Gentleman*
Ravi Shankar and George Fenton, *Gandhi*

Original Score and Its Adaptation or Adaptation Score

*Henry Mancini and Leslie Bricusse, *Victor/Victoria*
Ralph Burns, *Annie*
Tom Waits, *One from the Heart*

1983 *Original Score*

*Bill Conti, *The Right Stuff*
Jerry Goldsmith, *Under Fire*
Michael Gore, *Terms of Endearment*
Leonard Rosenman, *Cross Creek*
John Williams, *Return of the Jedi*

Original Song Score or Adaptation Score

*Michel Legrand, Alan and Marilyn Bergman, *Yentl*
Lalo Schifrin, *The Sting II*
Elmer Bernstein, *Trading Places*

1984 *Original Score*

*Maurice Jarre, *A Passage to India*
Randy Newman, *The Natural*
Alex North, *Under the Volcano*
John Williams, *Indiana Jones and the Temple of Doom*
John Williams, *The River*

Original Song Score

*Prince, *Purple Rain*
Kris Kristofferson, *Songwriter*
Jeff Moss, *The Muppets Take Manhattan*

1985 *Original Score*

*John Barry, *Out of Africa*
Bruce Broughton, *Silverado*
Georges Delerue, *Agnes of God*
Maurice Jarre, *Witness*
Quincy Jones, Jeremy Lubbock, Rod Temperton, Caiphus Semenya, Andrae Crouch, Chris Boardman, Jorge Calandrelli, Joel Rosenbaum, Fred Steiner, Jack Hayes, Jerry Hey, and Randy Kerber, *The Color Purple*

1986 *Original Score*

*Herbie Hancock, *Round Midnight*
Jerry Goldsmith, *Hoosiers*
James Horner, *Aliens*
Ennio Morricone, *The Mission*
Leonard Rosenman, *Star Trek IV: The Voyage Home*

1987 *Original Score*

*Ryuichi Sakamoto, David Byrne and Cong Su, *The Last Emperor*
George Fenton and Jonas Gwangwa, *Cry Freedom*
Ennio Morricone, *The Untouchables*
John Williams, *Empire of the Sun*
John Williams, *The Witches of Eastwick*

1988 *Original Score*

*Dave Grusin, *The Milagro Beanfield War*
George Fenton, *Dangerous Liaisons*
Maurice Jarre, *Gorillas in the Mist*
John Williams, *The Accidental Tourist*
Hans Zimmer, *Rain Man*

1989 *Original Score*

*Alan Menken, *The Little Mermaid*
David Grusin, *The Fabulous Baker Boys*
James Horner, *Field of Dreams*
John Williams, *Born on the Fourth of July*
John Williams, *Indiana Jones and the Last Crusade*

1990 *Original Score*

*John Barry, *Dances with Wolves*
David Grusin, *Havana*
Maurice Jarre, *Ghost*
Randy Newman, *Avalon*
John Williams, *Home Alone*

1991 *Original Score*

*Alan Menken, *Beauty and the Beast*
George Fenton, *The Fisher King*
James Newton Howard, *The Prince of Tides*
Ennio Morricone, *Bugsy*
John Williams, *JFK*

1992 *Original Score*

*Alan Menken, *Aladdin*
Joan Barry, *Chaplin*
Jerry Goldsmith, *Basic Instinct*

Mark Isham, *A River Runs Through It*
Richard Robbins, *Howards End*

2B: MUSIC: BEST SONG

[Note: Credit for Music is given first, followed by an ampersand (&) and then the credit for Lyrics. If there is no ampersand, but the word "and" is used, then the individuals involved collaborated on both Music and Lyrics.]

1934 *Con Conrad & Herb Magidson, "The Continental" from *The Gay Divorcée*
Ralph Rainger & Leo Robin, "Love in Bloom" from *She Loves Me Not*
Vincent Youmans & Edward Eliscu and Gus Kahn, "Carioca" from *Flying Down to Rio*

1935 *Harry Warren & Al Dubin, "Lullaby of Broadway" from *Gold Diggers of 1935*
Irving Berlin, "Cheek to Cheek" from *Top Hat*
Jerome Kern & Dorothy Fields and Jimmy McHugh, "Lovely to Look At" from *Roberta*

1936 *Jerome Kern & Dorothy Fields, "The Way You Look Tonight" from *Swing Time*
Louis Alter & Sidney Mitchell, "A Melody from the Sky" from *Trail of the Lonesome Pine*
Walter Donaldson & Harold Adamson, "Did I Remember" from *Suzy*
Arthur Johnston & Johnny Burke, "Pennies from Heaven" from *Pennies from Heaven*
Cole Porter, "I've Got You Under My Skin" from *Born to Dance*
Richard A. Whiting & Walter Bullock, "When Did You Leave Heaven" from *Sing Baby Sing*

1937 *Harry Owens, "Sweet Leilani" from *Waikiki Wedding*
Sammy Fain & Lew Brown, "That Old Feeling" from *Vogues of 1938*
George Gershwin & Ira Gershwin, "They Can't Take That Away from Me" from *Shall We Dance*
Frederick Hollander & Leo Robin, "Whispers in the Dark" from *Artists and Models*
Harry Warren & Al Dubin, "Remember Me" from *Mr. Dodd Takes the Air*

1938 *Ralph Rainger & Leo Robin, "Thanks for the Memory" from *Big Broadcast of 1938*
Irving Berlin, "Change Partners and Dance with Me" from *Carefree*
Irving Berlin, "Now It Can Be Told" from *Alexander's Ragtime Band*
Phil Craig & Arthur Quenzer, "Merrily We Live" from *Merrily We Live*
Johnny Marvin, "Dust" from *Under Western Stars*
Jimmy McHugh & Harold Adamson, "My Own" from *That Certain Age*
Lionel Newman & Arthur Quenzer, "The Cowboy and the Lady" from *The Cowboy and the Lady*

Ben Oakland & Oscar Hammerstein II, "A Mist over the Moon" from *The Lady Objects*
Edward Ward & Chet Forrest and Bob Wright, "Always and Always" from *Mannequin*
Harry Warren & Johnny Mercer, "Jeepers Creepers" from *Going Places*

1939 *Harold Arlen & E. Y. Harburg, "Over the Rainbow" from *The Wizard of Oz*
Irving Berlin, "I Poured My Heart into a Song" from *Second Fiddle*
Buddy de Sylva, "Wishing" from *Love Affair*
Ralph Rainger & Leo Robin, "Faithful Forever" from *Gulliver's Travels*

1940 *Leigh Harline & Ned Washington, "When You Wish upon a Star" from *Pinocchio*
Roger Edens and George Stoll, "Our Love Affair" from *Strike Up the Band*
Chet Forrest & Bob Wright, "It's a Blue World" from *Music in My Heart*
Jimmy McHugh & Johnny Mercer, "I'd Know You Anywhere" from *You'll Find Out*
James Monaco & Johnny Burke, "Only Forever" from *Rhythm on the River*
Artie Shaw & Johnny Mercer, "Love of My Life" from *Second Chorus*
Robert Stolz & Gus Kahn, "Waltzing in the Clouds" from *Spring Parade*
Jule Styne & Walter Bullock, "Who Am I?" from *Hit Parade of 1941*
Harry Warren & Mack Gordon, "Down Argentine Way" from *Down Argentine Way*

1941 *Jerome Kern & Oscar Hammerstein II, "The Last Time I Saw Paris" from *Lady Be Good*
Lou Alter & Frank Loesser, "Dolores" from *Las Vegas Nights*
Harold Arlen & Johnny Mercer, "Blues in the Night" from *Blues in the Night*
Gene Autry and Fred Rose, "Be Honest with Me" from *Ridin' on a Rainbow*
Frank Churchill & Ned Washington, "Baby Mine" from *Dumbo*
Lloyd B. Norlind, "Out of the Silence" from *All American Co-Ed*
Cole Porter, "Since I Kissed My Baby Goodbye" from *You'll Never Get Rich*
Hugh Prince & Don Raye, "Boogie Woogie Bugle Boy of Company B" from *Buck Privates*
Harry Warren & Mack Gordon, "Chattanooga Choo Choo" from *Sun Valley Serenade*

1942 *Irving Berlin, "White Christmas" from *Holiday Inn*
Frank Churchill & Larry Morey, "Love Is a Song" from *Bambi*

Gene de Paul & Don Raye, "Pig Foot Pete" from *Hellzapoppin'*
Jerome Kern & Johnny Mercer, "Dearly Beloved" from *You Were Never Lovelier*
Burton Lane & Ralph Freed, "How About You" from *Babes on Broadway*
Ernesto Lecuona & Kim Gannon, "Always in My Heart" from *Always in My Heart*
Harry Revel & Mort Greene, "There's a Breeze on Lake Louise" from *The Mayor of 44th Street*
Jule Styne & Sammy Cahn, "It Seems I Heard That Song Before" from *Youth on Parade*
Edward Ward & Chet Forrest and Bob Wright, "Pennies for Peppino" from *Flying with Music*
Harry Warren & Mack Gordon, "I've Got a Gal in Kalamazoo" from *Orchestra Wives*

1943 *Harry Warren & Mack Gordon, "You'll Never Know" from *Hello, Frisco, Hello*
Harold Arlen & E. Y. Harburg, "Happiness Is a Thing Called Joe" from *Cabin in the Sky*
Harold Arlen & Johnny Mercer, "Black Magic" from *Star Spangled Rhythm*
Harold Arlen & Johnny Mercer, "My Shining Hour" from *The Sky's the Limit*
Jimmy McHugh & Herb Magidson, "Say a Prayer for the Boys over There" from *Hers to Hold*
James Monaco & Al Dubin, "We Mustn't Say Goodbye" from *Stage Door Canteen*
Cole Porter, "You'd Be So Nice to Come Home To" from *Something to Shout About*
Arthur Schwartz & Frank Loesser, "They're Either Too Young or Too Old" from *Thank Your Lucky Stars*
Jule Styne & Harold Adamson, "Change of Heart" from *Hit Parade of 1943*
Charles Wolcott & Ned Washington, "Saludos Amigos" from *Saludos Amigos*

1944 *James Van Heusen & Johnny Burke, "Swinging on a Star" from *Going My Way*
Harold Arlen & Ted Koehler, "Now I Know" from *Up in Arms*
Ary Barroso & Ned Washington, "Rio de Janeiro" from *Brazil*
Ralph Blane and Hugh Martin, "The Trolley Song" from *Meet Me in St. Louis*
M. K. Jerome & Ted Koehler, "Sweet Dreams Sweetheart" from *Hollywood Canteen*
Walter Kent & Kim Gannon, "Too Much in Love" from *Song of the Open Road*
Jerome Kern & Ira Gershwin, "Long Ago and Far Away" from *Cover Girl*

Jimmy McHugh & Harold Adamson, "I Couldn't Sleep a Wink Last Night" from *Higher and Higher*
James V. Monaco & Mack Gordon, "I'm Making Believe" from *Sweet and Lowdown*
Lew Pollack & Charles Newman, "Silver Shadows and Golden Dreams" from *Lady Let's Dance*
Harry Revel & Paul Webster, "Remember Me to Carolina" from *Minstrel Man*
Jule Styne & Sammy Cahn, "I'll Walk Alone" from *Follow the Boys*

1945 *Richard Rodgers & Oscar Hammerstein II, "It Might as Well Be Spring" from *State Fair*
Harold Arlen & Johnny Mercer, "Accentuate the Positive" from *Here Come the Waves*
Ray Heindorf and M. K. Jerome & Ted Koehler, "Some Sunday Morning" from *San Antonio*
Walter Kent & Kim Gannon, "Endlessly" from *Earl Carroll Vanities*
Jerome Kern & E. Y. Harburg, "More and More" from *Can't Help Singing*
Jay Livingston & Ray Evans, "The Cat and the Canary" from *Why Girls Leave Home*
Ann Ronell, "Linda" from *The Story of G.I. Joe*
David Rose & Leo Robin, "So in Love" from *Wonder Man*
Jule Styne & Sammy Cahn, "Anywhere" from *Tonight and Every Night*
Jule Styne & Sammy Cahn, "I Fall in Love Too Easily" from *Anchors Aweigh*
James Van Heusen & Johnny Burke, "Aren't You Glad You're You" from *The Bells of St. Mary's*
James Van Heusen & Johnny Burke, "Sleighride in July" from *Belle of the Yukon*
Allie Wrubel & Herb Magidson, "I'll Buy That Dream" from *Sing Your Way Home*
Victor Young & Edward Heyman, "Love Letters" from *Love Letters*

1946 *Harry Warren & Johnny Mercer, "On The Atchison, Topeka and Santa Fe" from *The Harvey Girls*
Irving Berlin, "You Keep Coming Back Like a Song" from *Blue Skies*
Hoagy Carmichael & Jack Brooks, "Ole Buttermilk Sky" from *Canyon Passage*
Jerome Kern & Oscar Hammerstein II, "All Through the Day" from *Centennial Summer*
James Monaco & Mack Gordon, "I Can't Begin to Tell You" from *The Dolly Sisters*

1947 *Allie Wrubel & Ray Gilbert, "Zip-A-Dee-Doo-Dah" from *Song of the South*
Ralph Blane, Hugh Martin and Roger Edens, "Pass That Peace Pipe" from *Good News*

Frank Loesser, "I Wish I Didn't Love You So" from *The Perils of Pauline*
Josef Myrow & Mack Gordon, "You Do" from *Mother Wore Tights*
Arthur Schwartz & Leo Robin, "A Girl in Calico" from *The Time, the Place and the Girl*

1948 *Jay Livingston & Ray Evans, "Buttons and Bows" from *The Paleface*
Harold Arlen & Leo Robin, "For Every Man There's a Woman" from *Casbah*
Frederick Hollander & Leo Robin, "This Is the Moment" from *That Lady in Ermine*
Ramey Idriss and George Tibbles, "The Woody Woodpecker Song" from *Wet Blanket Policy*
Jule Styne & Sammy Cahn, "It's Magic" from *Romance on the High Seas*

1949 *Frank Loesser, "Baby, It's Cold Outside" from *Neptune's Daughter*
Eliot Daniel & Larry Morey, "Lavender Blue" from *So Dear to My Heart*
Alfred Newman & Mack Gordon, "Through a Long and Sleepless Night" from *Come to the Stable*
Jule Styne & Sammy Cahn, "It's a Great Feeling" from *It's a Great Feeling*
Victor Young & Ned Washington, "My Foolish Heart" from *My Foolish Heart*

1950 *Ray Evans and Jay Livingston, "Mona Lisa" from *Captain Carey*
Nicholas Brodszky & Sammy Cahn, "Be My Love" from *The Toast of New Orleans*
Mack David, Al Hoffman and Jerry Livingston, "Bibbidy-Bobbidi-Boo" from *Cinderella*
Fred Glickman, Hy Heath and Johnny Lange, "Mule Train" from *Singing Guns*
Josef Myrow & Mack Gordon, "Wilhelmina" from *Wabash Avenue*

1951 *Hoagy Carmichael & Johnny Mercer, "In the Cool, Cool, Cool of the Evening" from *Here Comes the Groom*
Nicholas Brodszky & Sammy Cahn, "Wonder Why" from *Rich, Young and Pretty*
Bert Kalmar, Harry Ruby and Oscar Hammerstein II, "A Kiss to Build a Dream On" from *The Strip*
Burton Lane & Alan Jay Lerner, "Too Late Now" from *Royal Wedding*
Lionel Newman & Eliot Daniel, "Never" from *Golden Girl*

1952 *Dimitri Tiomkin & Ned Washington, "High Noon (Do Not Forsake Me Oh My Darling)" from *High Noon*
Nicholas Brodszky & Sammy Cahn, "Because You're Mine" from *Because You're Mine*
Jack Brooks, "Am I in Love" from *Son of Paleface*
Frank Loesser, "Thumbelina" from *Hans Christian Andersen*

Harry Warren & Leo Robin, "Zing a Little Zong" from *Just for You*

1953 *Sammy Fain & Paul Francis Webster, "Secret Love" from *Calamity Jane*
Nicholas Brodszky & Leo Robin, "My Flaming Heart" from *Small Town Girl*
Herschel Burke Gilbert & Sylvia Fine, "The Moon Is Blue" from *The Moon Is Blue*
Lester Lee & Ned Washington, "Sadie Thompson's Song (Blue Pacific Blues)" from *Miss Sadie Thompson*
Harry Warren & Jack Brooks, "That's Amore" from *The Caddy*

1954 *Jule Styne & Sammy Cahn, "Three Coins in the Fountain" from *Three Coins in the Fountain*
Harold Arlen & Ira Gershwin, "The Man That Got Away" from *A Star Is Born*
Irving Berlin, "Count Your Blessings Instead of Sheep" from *White Christmas*
Jack Lawrence and Richard Myers, "Hold My Hand" from *Susan Slept Here*
Dimitri Tiomkin & Ned Washington, "The High and the Mighty" from *The High and the Mighty*

1955 *Sammy Fain & Paul Francis Webster, "Love Is a Many Splendored Thing" from *Love Is a Many Splendored Thing*
Nicholas Brodszky & Sammy Cahn, "I'll Never Stop Loving You" from *Love Me or Leave Me*
Johnny Mercer, "Something's Gotta Give" from *Daddy Long Legs*
Alex North & Hy Zaret, "Unchained Melody" from *Unchained*
James Van Heusen & Sammy Cahn, "(Love Is) The Tender Trap" from *The Tender Trap*

1956 *Jay Livingston and Ray Evans, "Whatever Will Be, Will Be (Que Será, Será)" from *The Man Who Knew Too Much*
Cole Porter, "True Love" from *High Society*
Leith Stevens & Tom Adair, "Julie" from *Julie*
Dimitri Tiomkin & Paul Francis Webster, "Friendly Persuasion (Thee I Love)" from *Friendly Persuasion*
Victor Young & Sammy Cahn, "Written on the Wind" from *Written on the Wind*

1957 *James Van Heusen & Sammy Cahn, "All the Way" from *The Joker Is Wild*
Ray Evans and Jay Livingston, "Tammy" from *Tammy and the Bachelor*
Sammy Fain & Paul Francis Webster, "April Love" from *April Love*
Dimitri Tiomkin & Ned Washington, "Wild Is the Wind" from *Wild Is the Wind*
Harry Warren & Harold Adamson and Leo McCarey, "An Affair to Remember" from *An Affair to Remember*

1958 *Frederick Loewe & Alan Jay Lerner, "Gigi" from *Gigi*
Sammy Fain & Paul Francis Webster, "A Certain Smile" from *A Certain Smile*
Sammy Fain & Paul Francis Webster, "A Very Precious Love" from *Marjorie Morningstar*
Jay Livingston and Ray Evans, "Almost in Your Arms (Love Song from *Houseboat*)" from *Houseboat*
James Van Heusen & Sammy Cahn, "To Love and Be Loved" from *Some Came Running*

1959 *James Van Heusen & Sammy Cahn, "High Hopes" from *A Hole in the Head*
Sylvia Fine, "The Five Pennies" from *The Five Pennies*
Jerry Livingston & Mack David, "The Hanging Tree" from *The Hanging Tree*
Alfred Newman & Sammy Cahn, "The Best of Everything" from *The Best of Everything*
Dimitri Tiomkin & Ned Washington, "Strange Are the Ways of Love" from *The Young Land*

1960 *Manos Hadjidakis, "Never on Sunday" from *Never on Sunday*
Johnny Mercer, "The Facts of Life" from *The Facts of Life*
André Previn & Dory Langdon, "Faraway Part of Town" from *Pepe*
Dimitri Tiomkin & Paul Francis Webster, "The Green Leaves of Summer" from *The Alamo*
James Van Heusen & Sammy Cahn, "The Second Time Around" from *High Time*

1961 *Henry Mancini & Johnny Mercer, "Moon River" from *Breakfast at Tiffany's*
Henry Mancini & Mack David, "Bachelor in Paradise" from *Bachelor in Paradise*
Miklos Rozsa & Paul Francis Webster, "Love Theme from *El Cid* (The Falcon and the Dove)" from *El Cid*
Dimitri Tiomkin & Ned Washington, "Town Without Pity" from *Town Without Pity*
James Van Heusen & Sammy Cahn, "Pocketful of Miracles" from *Pocketful of Miracles*

1962 *Henry Mancini & Johnny Mercer, "Days of Wine and Roses" from *Days of Wine and Roses*
Elmer Bernstein & Mack David, "Walk on the Wild Side" from *Walk on the Wild Side*
Sammy Fain & Paul Francis Webster, "Tender Is the Night" from *Tender Is the Night*
Bronislau Kaper & Paul Francis Webster, "Love Song from *Mutiny on the Bounty* (Follow Me)" from *Mutiny on the Bounty*
André Previn & Dory Langdon, "Song from *Two for the Seasaw* (Second Chance)" from *Two for the Seasaw*

1963 *James Van Heusen & Sammy Cahn, "Call Me Irresponsible" from *Papa's Delicate Condition*
Ernest Gold & Mack David, "It's a Mad, Mad, Mad, Mad World" from *It's a Mad, Mad, Mad, Mad World*
Henry Mancini & Johnny Mercer, "Charade" from *Charade*
Riz Ortolani and Nino Oliviero & Norman Newell, "More" from *Mondo Cane*
Dimitri Tiomkin & Paul Francis Webster, "So Little Time" from *55 Days at Peking*

1964 *Richard M. Sherman and Robert B. Sherman, "Chim Chim Cher-ee" from *Mary Poppins*
Frank DeVol & Mack David, "Hush . . . Hush, Sweet Charlotte" from *Hush . . . Hush, Sweet Charlotte*
Henry Mancini & Jay Livingston and Ray Evans, "Dear Heart" from *Dear Heart*
James Van Heusen & Sammy Cahn, "My Kind of Town" from *Robin and the 7 Hoods*
James Van Heusen & Sammy Cahn, "Where Love has Gone" from *Where Love Has Gone*

1965 *Johnny Mandel & Paul Francis Webster, "The Shadow of Your Smile" from *The Sandpiper*
Burt Bacharach & Hal David, "What's New Pussycat?" from *What's New Pussycat?*
Michel Legrand & Jacques Demy and Norman Gimbel, "I Will Wait for You" from *The Umbrellas of Cherbourg*
Jerry Livingston & Mack David, "The Ballad of Cat Ballou" from *Cat Ballou*
Henry Mancini & Johnny Mercer, "The Sweetheart Tree" from *The Great Race*

1966 *John Barry & Don Black, "Born Free" from *Born Free*
Burt Bacharach & Hal David, "Alfie" from *Alfie*
Elmer Bernstein & Mack David, "My Wishing Doll" from *Hawaii*
Johnny Mandel & Paul Francis Webster, "A Time for Love" from *An American Dream*
Tom Springfield & Jim Dale, "Georgy Girl" from *Georgy Girl*

1967 *Leslie Bricusse, "Talk to the Animals" from *Doctor Dolittle*
Burt Bacharach & Hal David, "The Look of Love" from *Casino Royale*
Terry Gilkyson, "The Bare Necessities" from *The Jungle Book*
Quincy Jones & Bob Russell, "The Eyes of Love" from *Banning*
James Van Heusen & Sammy Cahn, "Thoroughly Modern Millie" from *Thoroughly Modern Millie*

1968 *Michel Legrand & Alan and Marilyn Bergman, "The Windmills of Your Mind" from *The Thomas Crown Affair*
Quincy Jones & Bob Russell, "For Love of Ivy" from *For Love of Ivy*
Richard M. Sherman and Robert B. Sherman, "Chitty Chitty Bang Bang" from *Chitty Chitty Bang Bang*

Jule Styne & Bob Merrill, "Funny Girl" from *Funny Girl*
Jimmy Van Heusen & Sammy Cahn, "Star!" from *Star!*

1969 *Burt Bacharach & Hal David, "Raindrops Keep Fallin' on My Head" from *Butch Cassidy and the Sundance Kid*
Fred Karlin & Dory Previn, "Come Saturday Morning" from *The Sterile Cuckoo*
Rod McKuen, "Jean" from *The Prime of Miss Jean Brodie*
Elmer Bernstein & Don Black, "True Grit" from *True Grit*
Michel Legrand & Alan and Marilyn Bergman, "What Are You Doing the Rest of Your Life?" from *The Happy Ending*

1970 *Fred Karlin & Robb Royer and James Griffin (a.k.a. Robb Wilson and Arthur James), "For All We Know" from *Lovers and Other Strangers*
Leslie Bricusse, "Thank You Very Much" from *Scrooge*
Michel Legrand & Alan and Marilyn Bergman, "Pieces of Dreams" from *Pieces of Dreams*
Henry Mancini & Johnny Mercer, "Whistling Away the Dark" from *Darling Lili*
Riz Ortolani & Arthur Hamilton, "Till Love Touches Your Life" from *Madron*

1971 *Isaac Hayes, "Theme from *Shaft*" from *Shaft*
Barry DeVorzon and Perry Botkin, Jr., "Bless the Beasts and Children" from *Bless the Beasts and Children*
Marvin Hamlisch & Johnny Mercer, "Life Is What You Make It" from *Kotch*
Henry Mancini & Alan and Marilyn Bergman, "All His Children" from *Sometimes a Great Notion*
Richard M. Sherman and Robert B. Sherman, "The Age of Not Believing" from *Bedknobs and Broomsticks*

1972 *Al Kasha and Joel Hirschhorn, "The Morning After" from *The Poseidon Adventure*
Sammy Fain & Paul Francis Webster, "Strange Are the Ways of Love" from *The Stepmother*
Maurice Jarre & Marilyn and Alan Bergman, "Marmalade, Molasses & Honey" from *The Life and Times of Judge Roy Bean*
Fred Karlin & Marsha Karlin, "Come Follow, Follow Me" from *The Little Ark*
Walter Scharf & Don Black, "Ben" from *Ben*

1973 *Marvin Hamlisch & Alan and Marilyn Bergman, "The Way We Were" from *The Way We Were*
George Barrie & Sammy Cahn, "All That Love Went to Waste" from *A Touch of Class*
George Bruns & Floyd Huddleston, "Love" from *Robin Hood*
Paul and Linda McCartney, "Live and Let Die" from *Live and Let Die*
John Williams & Paul Williams, "Nice to Be Around" from *Cinderella Liberty*

1974 *Al Kasha and Joe Hirschhorn, "We May Never Love Like This Again" from *The Towering Inferno*
Elmer Bernstein & Don Black, "Wherever Love Takes Me" from *Gold*
Euel Box & Betty Box, "Benji's Theme (I Feel Love)" from *Benji*
Frederick Loewe & Alan Jay Lerner, "Little Prince" from *The Little Prince*
John Morris & Mel Brooks, "Blazing Saddles" from *Blazing Saddles*

1975 *Keith Carradine, "I'm Easy" from *Nashville*
George Barrie & Sammy Cahn, "Now That We're in Love" from *Whiffs*
Fred Ebb and John Kander, "How Lucky Can You Get" from *Funny Lady*
Charles Fox & Norman Gimbel, "Richard's Window" from *The Other Side of the Mountain*
Michael Masser & Gerry Goffin, "Theme from *Mahogany* (Do You Know Where You're Going To)" from *Mahogany*

1976 *Barbra Streisand & Paul Williams, "Evergreen (Love Theme from *A Star Is Born*)" from *A Star Is Born*
Bill Conti & Carol Connors and Ayn Robbins, "Gonna Fly Now" from *Rocky*
Sammy Fain & Paul Francis Webster, "A World That Never Was" from *Half a House*
Jerry Goldsmith, "Ave Santani" from *The Omen*
Henry Mancini & Don Black, "Come to Me" from *The Pink Panther Strikes Again*

1977 *Joseph Brooks, "You Light Up My Life" from *You Light Up My Life*
Sammy Fain & Carol Connors and Ayn Robbins, "Someone's Waiting for You" from *The Rescuers*
Marvin Hamlisch & Carole Bayer Sager, "Nobody Does It Better" from *The Spy Who Loved Me*
Al Kasha and Joel Hirschhorn, "Candle on the Water" from *Pete's Dragon*
Richard M. Sherman and Robert B. Sherman, *"The Slipper and the Rose* Waltz (He Danced with Me/She Danced With Me)" from *The Slipper and the Rose*

1978 *Paul Jabara, "Last Dance" from *Thank God It's Friday*
John Farrar, "Hopelessly Devoted to You" from *Grease*
Charles Fox & Norman Gimbel, "Ready to Take a Chance Again" from *Foul Play*
Marvin Hamlisch & Alan and Marilyn Bergman, "The Last Time I Felt Like This" from *Same Time, Next Year*
Richard M. Sherman and Robert B. Sherman, "When You're Loved" from *The Magic of Lassie*

1979 *David Shire & Norman Gimbel, "It Goes Like It Goes" from *Norma Rae*
Marvin Hamlisch & Carole Bayer Sager, "Through the Eyes of Love" from *Ice Castles*

Henry Mancini & Robert Wells, "It's Easy to Say" from *10*
David Shire & Alan and Marilyn Bergman, "I'll Never Say Goodbye" from *The Promise*
Paul Williams and Kenny Ascher, "The Rainbow Connection" from *The Muppet Movie*

1980 *Michael Gore & Dean Pitchford, "Fame" from *Fame*
Michael Gore & Leslie Gore, "Out Here on My Own" from *Fame*
Willie Nelson, "On the Road Again" from *Honeysuckle Rose*
Dolly Parton, "Nine to Five" from *Nine to Five*
Lalo Schifrin & Wilbur Jennings, "People Alone" from *The Competition*

1981 *Burt Bacharach, Carole Bayer Sager, Christopher Cross and Peter Allen, "Arthur's Theme (Best That You Can Do)" from *Arthur*
Bill Conti & Mick Leeson, "For Your Eyes Only" from *For Your Eyes Only*
Randy Newman, "One More Hour" from *Ragtime*
Joe Raposo, "The First Time It Happens" from *The Great Muppet Caper*
Lionel Richie, "Endless Love" from *Endless Love*

1982 *Jack Nitzsche and Buffy Saint-Marie & Will Jennings, "Up Where We Belong" from *An Officer and a Gentleman*
Dave Grusin & Alan and Marilyn Bergman, "It Might Be You" from *Tootsie*
Michel Legrand & Alan and Marilyn Bergman, "How Do You Keep the Music Playing?" from *Best Friends*
Jim Peterik and Frankie Sullivan III, "Eye of the Tiger" from *Rocky III*
John Williams & Alan and Marilyn Bergman, "If We Were in Love" from *Yes, Giorgio*

1983 *Giorgio Moroder & Keith Forsey and Irene Cara, "Flashdance . . . What a Feeling" from *Flashdance*
Michel Legrand & Alan and Marilyn Bergman, "Papa, Can You Hear Me?" from *Yentl*
Michel Legrand & Alan and Marilyn Bergman, "The Way He Makes Me Feel" from *Yentl*
Austin Roberts and Bobby Hart, "Over You" from *Tender Mercies*
Michael Sembello and Dennis Matkosky, "Maniac" from *Flashdance*

1984 *Stevie Wonder, "I Just Called to Say I Love You" from *The Woman in Red*
Phil Collins, "Against All Odds (Take a Look at Me Now)" from *Against All Odds*
Kenny Loggins and Dean Pitchford, "Footloose" from *Footloose*
Ray Parker, Jr., "Ghostbusters" from *Ghostbusters*
Tom Snow and Dean Pitchford, "Let's Hear It for the Boy" from *Footloose*

1985 *Lionel Richie, "Say You, Say Me" from *White Nights*
Stephen Bishop, "Separate Lives" from *White Nights*
Marvin Hamlisch & Edward Kleban, "Surprise, Surprise" from *A Chorus Line*
Chris Hayes and Johnny Colla & Huey Lewis, "The Power of Love" from *Back to the Future*
Quincy Jones and Rod Temperton & Quincy Jones, Rod Temperton and Lionel Richie, "Miss Celie's Blues (Sister)" from *The Color Purple*

1986 *Giorgio Moroder & Tom Whitlock, "Take My Breath Away" from *Top Gun*
Peter Cetera and David Foster & Peter Cetera and Diane Nini, "Glory of Love" from *The Karate Kid, Part II*
James Horner and Barry Mann & Cynthia Weil, "Somewhere Out There" from *An American Tail*
Henry Mancini & Leslie Bricusse, "Life in a Looking Glass" from *That's Life*
Alan Menken & Howard Ashman, "Mean Green Mother from Outer Space" from *Little Shop of Horrors*

1987 *Franke Previte, John DeNicola and Donald Markowitz & Franke Previte, "(I've Had) The Time of My Life" from *Dirty Dancing*
Willy DeVille, "Storybook Love" from *The Princess Bride*
Harold Faltermeyer and Keith Forsey & Harold Faltermeyer, Keith Forsey and Bob Seger, "Shakedown" from *Beverly Hills Cop II*
George Fenton and Jonas Gwanga, "Cry Freedom" from *Cry Freedom*
Albert Hammond and Diane Warren, "Nothing's Gonna Stop Us Now" from *Mannequin*

1988 *Carly Simon, "Let the River Run" from *Working Girl*
Lamont Dozier & Phil Collins, "Two Hearts" from *Buster*
Bob Telson, "Calling You" from *Bagdad Cafe*

1989 *Alan Menken & Howard Ashman, "Under the Sea" from *The Little Mermaid*
Marvin Hamlisch & Alan and Marilyn Bergman, "The Girl Who Used to Be Me" from *Shirley Valentine*
Alan Menken & Howard Ashman, "Kiss the Girl" from *The Little Mermaid*
Randy Newman, "I Love to See You Smile" from *Parenthood*
Tom Snow & Dean Pitchford, "After All" from *Chances Are*

1990 *Stephen Sondheim, "Sooner or Later (I Always Get My Man)" from *Dick Tracy*
Jon Bon Jovi, "Blaze of Glory" from *Young Guns II*
Carmine Coppola & John Bettis, "Promise Me You'll Remember" from *The Godfather, Part III*
Shel Silverstein, "I'm Checkin' Out" from *Postcards from the Edge*
John Williams & Leslie Bricusse, "Somewhere in My Memory" from *Home Alone*

1991 *Alan Menken & Howard Ashman, "Beauty and the Beast" from *Beauty and the Beast*
Michael Kamen & Bryan Adams and Robert John Lange, "(Everything I Do) I Do It For You" from *Robin Hood*
Alan Menken & Howard Ashman, "Be Our Guest" from *Beauty and the Beast*
Alan Menken & Howard Ashman, "Belle" from *Beauty and the Beast*
John Williams & Leslie Bricusse, "When You're Alone" from *Hook*

1992 *Alan Menken & Tim Rice, "A Whole New World" from *Aladdin*
David Foster & Linda Thompson, "I Have Nothing" from *The Bodyguard*
Jud Friedman & Alan Rich, "Run To You" from *The Bodyguard*
Robert Kraft & Arne Glimcher, "Beautiful Maria of My Soul" from *The Mambo Kings*
Alan Menken & Howard Ashman, "Friend Like Me" from *Aladdin*

After just one unsuccessful nomination in his long and distinguished career—for The Grapes of Wrath in 1940—Henry Fonda finally accepted an Honorary Oscar forty years later in 1980. The following year, five months before his death, he was named Best Actor for On Golden Pond.

In 1984, after forgetting to read out the nominees' names, a frail, 77-year-old Laurence Olivier **(LEFT)** *presented the Oscar for Best Picture to the producer of Amadeus, Saul Zaentz.*

Appendix B:

Honorary Oscars

1927–28

Warner Bros. "for producing *The Jazz Singer,* the pioneer outstanding talking picture, which has revolutionized the industry."

Charles Chaplin "for versatility and genius in writing, acting, directing and producing *The Circus.*"

1931–32

Walt Disney "for the creation of Mickey Mouse."

1934

Shirley Temple "in grateful recognition of her outstanding contribution to screen entertainment during the year 1934." [miniature statuette]

1935

D.W. Griffith "for his distinguished creative achievements as director and producer and his invaluable initiative and lasting contributions to the progress of the motion picture arts."

1936

March of Time "for its significance to motion pictures and for having revolutionized one of the most important branches of the industry—the newsreel."

1937
Mack Sennett "for his lasting contribution to the comedy technique of the screen, the basic principles of which are as important today as when they were first put into practice, the Academy presents a Special Award to that master of fun, discoverer of stars, sympathetic, kindly, understanding comic genius—Mack Sennett."

Edgar Bergen "for his outstanding comedy creation, Charlie McCarthy." [wooden statuette]

1938
Deanna Durbin & Mickey Rooney "for their significant contribution in bringing to the screen the spirit and personification of youth, and as juvenile players setting a high standard of ability and achievement." [miniature statuettes]

Walt Disney "for *Snow White and the Seven Dwarfs,* recognized as a significant screen innovation which has charmed millions and pioneered a great new entertainment field for the motion picture cartoon." [one statuette + seven miniature statuettes]

1939
Douglas Fairbanks "Recognizing the unique and outstanding contribution of Douglas Fairbanks, first president of the Academy, to the international development of the motion picture."

Judy Garland "for her outstanding performance as a screen juvenile during the past year." [miniature statuette]

Technicolor Company "for its contributions in successfully bringing three-color feature production to the screen."

1940
Bob Hope "in recognition of his unselfish services to the motion picture industry." [special silver plaque]

Colonel Nathan Levinson "for his outstanding service to the industry and the Army during the past nine years, which has made possible the present efficient mobilization of the motion picture industry facilities for the production of Army training films."

1941
Leopold Stokowski "and his associates for their unique achievement in the creation of a new form of visualized music in Walt Disney's production *Fantasia,* thereby widening the scope of the motion picture as entertainment and as an art form." [certificate]

Walt Disney, William Garity, John N. A. Hawkins and the RCA Manufacturing Company "for their outstanding contribution to the advancement of the use of sound in motion pictures through the production of *Fantasia.*" [certificates]

1942
Charles Boyer "for his progressive cultural achievement in establishing the French Research Foundation in Los Angeles as a source of reference for the Hollywood motion picture industry." [certificate]

Noel Coward "for his outstanding production achievement in *In Which We Serve.*" [certificate]

1944
Bob Hope "for his many services to the Academy, a Life Membership in the Academy of Motion Picture Arts and Sciences. [life membership]

Margaret O'Brien "outstanding child actress of 1944." [miniature statuette]

1945
Walter Wanger "for his six years' service as president of the Academy of Motion Picture Arts and Sciences." [special plaque]

Peggy Ann Garner "outstanding child actress of 1945." [miniature statuette]

1946
Laurence Olivier "for his outstanding achievement as actor, producer and director in bringing *Henry V* to the screen."

Harold Russell "for bringing hope and courage to his fellow veterans through his performance in *The Best Years of Our Lives.*"

Ernst Lubitsch "for his distinguished contributions to the art of the motion picture." [scroll]

Claude Jarman, Jr., "outstanding child actor of 1946." [miniature statuette]

1947
James Baskett "for his able and heart-warming characterization of Uncle Remus, friend and storyteller to the children of the world."

Shoeshine: "The high quality of this motion picture, brought to eloquent life in a country scarred by war, is proof to the world that the creative spirit can triumph over adversity."

Colonel William N. Selig, Albert E. Smith, Thomas Armat and George K. Spoor, "[one of] the small group of pioneers whose belief in a new medium, and whose contributions to its development, blazed the trail along which the motion picture has progressed, in their lifetime, from obscurity to world-wide acclaim."

1948
Ivan Jandl "for the outstanding juvenile performance of 1948 (in *The Search*)." [miniature statuette]

Sid Grauman, "master showman, who raised the standard of exhibition of motion pictures."

Adolph Zukor, "a man who has been called the father of the feature film in America, for his services to the industry over a period of forty years."

Walter Wanger "for distinguished service to the industry in adding to its moral stature in the world community by his production of the picture *Joan of Arc.*"

1949
Bobby Driscoll, "as the outstanding juvenile actor of 1949." [miniature statuette]

Fred Astaire "for his unique artistry and his contributions to the technique of musical pictures."

Cecil B. de Mille, "distinguished motion picture pioneer, for thirty-seven years of brilliant showmanship."

Jean Hersholt "for distinguished service to the motion picture industry."

1950
George Murphy "for his services in interpreting the film industry to the country at large."

Louis B. Mayer "for distinguished service to the motion picture industry."

1951
Gene Kelly "in appreciation of his versatility as an actor, singer, director and dancer, and specifically for his brilliant achievements in the art of choreography on film."

1952
George A. Mitchell "for the design and development of the camera which bears his name and for his continued and dominant presence in the field of cinematography."

Joseph M. Schenck "for long and distinguished service to the motion picture industry."

Merian C. Cooper "for his many innovations and contributions to the art of motion pictures."

Harold Lloyd, "master comedian and good citizen."

Bob Hope "for his contribution to the laughter of the world, his service to the motion picture industry, and his devotion to the American premise."

1953
Pete Smith "for his witty and pungent observations on the American scene in his series of 'Pete Smith Specialties.' "

Twentieth Century Fox Film Corporation "in recognition of their imagination, showmanship and foresight in introducing the revolutionary process known as CinemaScope."

Joseph Breen "for his conscientious, open-minded and dignified management of the Motion Picture Production Code."

Bell and Howell Company "for their pioneering and basic achievements in the advancement of the motion picture industry."

1954
Greta Garbo "for her unforgettable screen performances."

Danny Kaye "for his unique talents, his service to the Academy, the motion picture industry, and the American people."

Jon Whiteley "for his outstanding juvenile performance in *The Little Kidnappers.*" [miniature statuette]

Vince Winter "for his outstanding juvenile performance in *The Little Kidnappers.*" [miniature statuette]

Bausch & Lomb Optical Company "for their contributions to the advancement of the motion picture industry."

Kemp R. Niver "for the development of the Renovare Process which has made possible the restoration of the Library of Congress Paper Film Collection."

1956
Eddie Cantor "for distinguished service to the film industry."

1957
Charles Brackett "for outstanding service to the Academy."

B. B. Kahane "for distinguished service to the motion picture industry."

Gilbert M. ("Bronco Billy") Anderson, "motion picture pioneer, for his contributions to the development of motion pictures as entertainment."

The Society of Motion Picture and Television Engineers "for their contributions to the advancement of the motion picture industry."

1958
Maurice Chevalier "for his contributions to the world of entertainment for more than half a century."

1959
Lee de Forest "for his pioneering inventions which brought sound to the motion picture."

Buster Keaton "for his unique talents which brought immortal comedies to the screen."

1960
Gary Cooper "for his many memorable screen performances and the international recognition he, as an individual, has gained for the motion picture industry."

Stan Laurel "for his creative pioneering in the field of cinema comedy."

Hayley Mills "for *Pollyanna,* the most outstanding juvenile performance during 1960." [miniature statuette]

1961
William L. Hendricks "for his outstanding patriotic service in the conception, writing and production of the Marine Corps film, *A Force in Readiness,* which has brought honor to the Academy and the motion picture industry."

Jerome Robbins "for his brilliant achievements in the art of choreography on film."

Fred L. Metzler "for his dedicated and outstanding service to the Academy of Motion Picture Arts and Sciences."

1964
William Tuttle "for his outstanding makeup achievement for *7 Faces of Dr. Lao.*"

1965
Bob Hope for his "unique and distinguished service to our industry and the Academy." [gold medal]

1966
Y. Frank Freeman "for unusual and outstanding service to the Academy during his thirty years in Hollywood."

Yakima Canutt "for achievement as a stuntman and for developing safety devices to protect stuntmen everywhere."

1967
Arthur Freed "for distinguished service to the Academy and the production of six top-rated Awards telecasts."

1968
John Chambers "for his outstanding makeup achievement for *Planet of the Apes.*"

Onna White "for her outstanding choreography achievement for *Oliver!*"

1969
Cary Grant for his "unique mastery of the art of screen acting with the respect and affection of his colleagues."

1970
Lillian Gish "for superlative artistry and for distinguished contribution to the progress of motion pictures."

Orson Welles "for superlative artistry and versatility in the creation of motion pictures."

1971
Charles Chaplin "for the incalculable effect he has had in making motion pictures the art form of this century."

1972
Charles S. Boren, "leader for thirty-eight years of the industry's enlightened labor relations and architect of its policy of nondiscrimination. With the respect and affection of all who work in films."

Edward G. Robinson, "who achieved greatness as a player, a patron of the arts and a dedicated citizen . . . in sum, a Renaissance man. From his friends in the industry he loves."

1973
Henri Langlois "for his devotion to the art of film, his massive contributions in preserving its past and his unswerving faith in its future."

Groucho Marx "in recognition of his brilliant creativity and for the unequaled achievements of the Marx Brothers in the art of motion picture comedy."

1974
Howard Hawks—"a master American filmmaker whose creative efforts hold a distinguished place in world cinema."

Jean Renoir—"a genius who, with grace, responsibility and enviable devotion through silent film, sound film, feature, documentary and television, has won the world's admiration."

1975
Mary Pickford, "in recognition of her unique contribution to the film industry and the development of film as an artistic medium."

1977
Margaret Booth "for her exceptional contribution to the art of film editing in the motion picture industry."

1978
Walter Lantz (creator of Woody Woodpecker) "for bringing joy and laughter to every part of the world through his unique animated motion pictures."

Laurence Olivier "for the full body of his work, for the unique achievements of his entire career and his lifetime of contribution to the art of film."

King Vidor "for his incomparable achievements as a cinematic creator and innovator."

The Museum of Modern Art, Department of Film "for the contribution it has made to the public's perception of movies as an art form."

1979
Hal Elias "for his dedication and distinguished service to the Academy of Motion Picture Arts and Sciences."

Alec Guinness "for advancing the art of screen acting through a host of memorable and distinguished performances."

1980
Henry Fonda—"the consummate actor, in recognition of his brilliant accomplishments and enduring contribution to the art of motion pictures."

1981
Barbara Stanwyck "for superlative creativity and unique contribution to the art of screen acting."

1982
Mickey Rooney "in recognition of his sixty years of versatility in a variety of memorable film performances."

1983
Hal Roach "in recognition of his unparalleled record of distinguished contributions to the motion picture art form."

1984
James Stewart "for his fifty years of memorable performances, for his high ideals both on and off the screen, with the respect and affection of his colleagues."

National Endowment for the Arts "in recognition of its twentieth anniversary and its dedicated commitment to fostering artistic and creative activity and excellence in every area of the arts."

1985
Paul Newman "in recognition of his many memorable and compelling screen performances and for his personal integrity and dedication to his craft."

Alex North "in recognition of his brilliant artistry in the creation of memorable music for a host of distinguished motion pictures."

1986
Ralph Bellamy "for his unique artistry and his distinguished service to the profession of acting."

1988

National Film Board of Canada "in recognition of its fiftieth anniversary and its dedicated commitment to originating artistic, creative and technological activity and excellence in every area of filmmaking."

Eastman Kodak Company "in recognition of the company's fundamental contributions to the art of motion pictures during the first century of film history."

1989

Akira Kurosawa "for accomplishments that have inspired, delighted, enriched and entertained audiences and influenced filmmakers throughout the world."

1990

Sophia Loren, "one of the genuine treasures of world cinema who, in a career rich with memorable performances, has added permanent luster to our art form."

Myrna Loy "in recognition of her extraordinary qualities both onscreen and off, with appreciation for a lifetime's worth of indelible performances."

1991

Satyajit Ray for his "rare mastery of the art of motion pictures and for his profound humanitarian outlook, which has had an indelible influence on filmmakers and audiences throughout the world."

Irving G. Thalberg Memorial Award (Thalberg bust)

1937 Darryl F. Zanuck
1938 Hal B. Wallis
1939 David O. Selznick
1941 Walt Disney
1942 Sidney Franklin
1943 Hal B. Wallis
1944 Darryl F. Zanuck
1946 Samuel Goldwyn
1948 Jerry Wald
1950 Darryl F. Zanuck
1951 Arthur G. Freed
1952 Cecil B. de Mille
1953 George Stevens
1956 Buddy Adler
1958 Jack L. Warner
1961 Stanley Kramer
1963 Sam Spiegel
1965 William Wyler
1966 Robert Wise
1967 Alfred Hitchcock
1970 Ingmar Bergman
1973 Lawrence Weingarten
1975 Mervyn LeRoy
1976 Pandro S. Berman
1977 Walter Mirisch
1979 Ray Stark
1981 Albert R. Broccoli
1986 Steven Spielberg
1987 Billy Wilder
1990 Richard D. Zanuck and David Brown
1991 George Lucas

Jean Hersholt Humanitarian Award (Oscar statuette)

1956 Y. Frank Freeman
1957 Samuel Goldwyn
1959 Bob Hope
1960 Sol Lesser
1961 George Seaton
1962 Steve Broidy
1965 Edmond L. DePatie
1966 George Bagnall
1967 Gregory Peck
1968 Martha Raye
1969 George Jessel
1970 Frank Sinatra
1972 Rosalind Russell
1973 Lew Wasserman
1974 Arthur B. Krim
1975 Jules C. Stein
1977 Charlton Heston
1978 Leo Jaffe
1979 Robert Benjamin
1981 Danny Kaye
1982 Walter Mirisch
1983 M. J. Frankovich
1984 David L. Wolper
1985 Charles ("Buddy") Rogers
1989 Howard W. Koch

Gordon E. Sawyer Award (Oscar statuette)

[Note: This award is given "for technical contributions that have brought credit to the motion picture industry."]

1981 Joseph B. Walker
1982 John O. Aalberg
1983 Dr. John G. Frayne
1984 Linwood G. Dunn
1987 Fred Hynes
1988 Gordon Henry Cook
1989 Pierre Angenieux
1990 Stefan Kudelski
1991 Ray Harryhausen

Among Walt Disney's record collection of thirty-two Oscars was the specially designed set of seven miniature statuettes presented in 1938 for Snow White and the Seven Dwarfs.

The legendary costume designer Edith Head holds the female record, with eight Oscars from 35 nominations over thirty years.

Appendix C: Oscar Facts and Figures

A: Films
1: *Films That Have Won Most Academy Awards*
2: *Most Nominated Films*
3: *Films Winning Four or More Acting Nominations*
4: *Films with Two or More Players Nominated in Same Category*
5: *Films to Have Won Five or More Academy Awards Without Winning Best Picture*
6: *Best Picture Nominees by Genres*

(a) Biopics
(b) War films
(c) Comedies
(d) Musicals
(e) Action/Adventure
(f) Religious Subjects
(g) Fantasy/Science Fiction/Horror
(h) Mystery/Suspense
(i) Westerns

7: *Foreign-Language Films Nominated for Best Picture*
8: *Foreign-Language Films: Nominations and Wins by Country*

B: Actors
1: *Most Nominated Actors*
2: *Actors to Have Won Most Oscars*

A: Films

1: FILMS THAT HAVE WON MOST ACADEMY AWARDS

11 Oscars
Ben-Hur (MGM, 1959, 12 nominations)

10 Oscars
West Side Story (United Artists, 1961, 11 nominations)

9 Oscars
Gigi (MGM, 1958, 9 nominations)
The Last Emperor (Columbia, 1987, 9)

8 Oscars
Gone with the Wind (MGM, 1939, 13 nominations + 2 special science/technical awards)
From Here to Eternity (Columbia, 1953, 13)
On the Waterfront (Columbia, 1954, 12)
My Fair Lady (Warner Bros., 1964, 12)
Cabaret (Allied Artists, 1972, 10)
Gandhi (Columbia, 1982, 11)
Amadeus (Orion, 1984, 11)

7 Oscars
Going My Way (Paramount, 1944, 10 nominations)
The Best Years of Our Lives (RKO Radio, 1946, 8)
The Bridge on the River Kwai (Columbia, 1957, 8)
Lawrence of Arabia (Columbia, 1962, 10)
Patton, (Twentieth Century Fox, 1970, 10)
The Sting (Universal, 1973, 10)
Out of Africa (Universal, 1985, 11)
Dances with Wolves (Orion, 1990, 12)

6 Oscars
Mrs. Miniver (MGM, 1942, 12 nominations)
All About Eve (Twentieth Century Fox, 1950, 14)
An American in Paris (MGM, 1951, 8)
A Place in the Sun (Paramount, 1951, 9)
A Man for All Seasons (Columbia, 1966, 8)
The Godfather, Part II (Paramount, 1974, 11)
Star Wars (Twentieth Century Fox, 1977, 10 + 1 special award)

5 Oscars
It Happened One Night (Columbia, 1934, 5 nominations)
How Green Was My Valley (Twentieth Century Fox, 1941, 10)
Wilson (Twentieth Century Fox, 1944, 10)
The Bad and the Beautiful (MGM, 1952, 6)
Around the World in 80 Days (United Artists, 1956, 8)
The King and I (Twentieth Century Fox, 1956, 9)
The Apartment (United Artists, 1960, 10)
Mary Poppins (Buena Vista, 1964, 13)
Doctor Zhivago (MGM, 1965, 10)
The Sound of Music (Twentieth Century Fox, 1965, 10)
Who's Afraid of Virginia Woolf? (Warner Bros., 1966, 13)
In the Heat of the Night (United Artists, 1967, 7)
Oliver! (Columbia, 1968, 11 + special award)
The French Connection (Twentieth Century Fox, 1971, 8)
One Flew Over the Cuckoo's Nest (United Artists, 1975, 9)
The Deer Hunter (Universal, 1978, 9)
Kramer vs. Kramer (Columbia, 1979, 9)
Terms of Endearment (Paramount, 1983, 11)
The Silence of the Lambs (Orion, 1991, 7)

2: MOST NOMINATED FILMS

14 Nominations
All About Eve (Twentieth Century Fox, 1950, 6 Oscars)

13 Nominations
Gone with the Wind (MGM, 1939, 8 Oscars + 2 special and scientific/technical awards)
From Here to Eternity (Columbia, 1953, 8 Oscars)

Mary Poppins (Buena Vista, 1964, 5 Oscars)
Who's Afraid of Virginia Woolf? (Warner Bros., 1966, 5 Oscars)

12 Nominations
Mrs. Miniver (MGM, 1942, 6 Oscars)
The Song of Bernadette (Twentieth Century Fox, 1943, 4 Oscars)
Johnny Belinda (Warner Bros., 1948, 1 Oscar)
A Streetcar Named Desire (Warner Bros., 1951, 4 Oscars)
On the Waterfront (Columbia, 1954, 8 Oscars)
Ben-Hur (MGM, 1959, 11 Oscars)
Becket (Paramount, 1964, 1 Oscar)
My Fair Lady (Warner Bros., 1964, 8 Oscars)
Reds (Paramount, 1981, 3 Oscars)
Dances with Wolves (Orion, 1990, 7 Oscars)

11 Nominations
Mr. Smith Goes to Washington, (Columbia, 1939, 1 Oscar)
Rebecca (United Artists, 1940, 2 Oscars)
Sergeant York (Warner Bros., 1941, 2 Oscars)
The Pride of the Yankees (RKO Radio, 1942, 1 Oscar)
Sunset Boulevard (Paramount, 1950, 3 Oscars)
Judgment at Nuremberg (United Artists, 1961, 2 Oscars)
West Side Story (United Artists, 1961, 10 Oscars)
Oliver! (Columbia, 1968, 5 Oscars + 1 honorary award)
Chinatown (Paramount, 1974, 1 Oscar)
The Godfather, Part II (Paramount, 1974, 6 Oscars)
Julia (Twentieth Century Fox, 1977, 3 Oscars)
The Turning Point (Twentieth Century Fox, 1977, 0 Oscars)
Gandhi (Columbia, 1982, 8 Oscars)
Terms of Endearment (Paramount, 1983, 5 Oscars)
Amadeus (Orion, 1984, 8 Oscars)
A Passage to India (Columbia, 1984, 2 Oscars)
The Color Purple (Warner Bros., 1985, 0 Oscars)
Out of Africa (Universal, 1985, 7 Oscars)

10 Nominations
The Life of Emile Zola (Warner Bros., 1937, 3 Oscars)
How Green Was My Valley (Twentieth Century Fox, 1941, 5 Oscars)
Going My Way (Paramount, 1944, 7 Oscars)
Wilson (Twentieth Century Fox, 1944, 5 Oscars)
Roman Holiday (Paramount, 1953, 3 Oscars)
Giant (Warner Bros., 1956, 1 Oscar)
Sayonara (Warner Bros., 1957, 4 Oscars)
The Apartment (United Artists, 1960, 5 Oscars)
Lawrence of Arabia (Columbia, 1962, 7 Oscars)
Tom Jones (United Artists, 1963, 4 Oscars)
Doctor Zhivago (MGM, 1965, 5 Oscars)
The Sound of Music (Twentieth Century Fox, 1965, 5 Oscars)
Bonnie and Clyde (Warner Bros., 1967, 2 Oscars)

Guess Who's Coming to Dinner (Columbia, 1967, 2 Oscars)
Anne of the Thousand Days (Universal, 1969, 1 Oscar)
Airport (Universal, 1970, 1 Oscar)
Patton (Twentieth Century Fox, 1970, 7 Oscars)
Cabaret (Allied Artists, 1972, 8 Oscars)
The Godfather (Paramount, 1972, 3 Oscars)
The Exorcist (Warner Bros., 1973, 2 Oscars)
The Sting (Universal, 1973, 7 Oscars)
Network (MGM/United Artists, 1976, 4 Oscars)
Rocky (United Artists, 1976, 3 Oscars)
Star Wars (Twentieth Century Fox, 1977, 6 Oscars + 1 technical award)
On Golden Pond (Universal, 1981, 3 Oscars)
Tootsie (Columbia, 1982, 1 Oscar)
Bugsy (TriStar, 1991, 2 Oscars)

3: FILMS WINNING FOUR OR MORE ACTING NOMINATIONS

Five	
Mrs. Miniver (1942)	(2 wins)
All About Eve (1950)	(1)
From Here to Eternity (1953)	(2)
On the Waterfront (1954)	(2)
Peyton Place (1957)	(0)
Tom Jones (1963)	(0)
Bonnie and Clyde (1967)	(1)
The Godfather, Part II (1974)	(1)
Network (1976)	(3)
Four	
My Man Godfrey (1963)	(0)
Gone With the Wind (1939)	(2)
For Whom the Bell Tolls (1943)	(1)
The Song of Bernadette (1943)	(1)
Gentleman's Agreement (1947)	(1)
I Remember Mama (1948)	(0)
Johnny Belinda (1948)	(1)
Sunset Boulevard (1950)	(0)
A Streetcar Named Desire (1951)	(3)
The Defiant Ones (1958)	(0)
The Hustler (1961)	(0)
Judgment at Nuremberg (1961)	(1)
Othello (1965)	(0)
Who's Afraid of Virginia Woolf? (1966)	(2)
Guess Who's Coming to Dinner (1967)	(1)
The Last Picture Show (1971)	(2)
The Godfather (1972)	(1)
Rocky (1976)	(0)
Julia (1977)	(2)
The Turning Point (1977)	(0)

Coming Home (1978)	(2)
Kramer vs. Kramer (1979)	(2)
Reds (1981)	(1)
Terms of Endearment (1983)	(2)

4: FILMS WITH TWO OR MORE PLAYERS NOMINATED IN THE SAME CATEGORY

[Note: * indicates winner.]

Three Actors/Actresses in Leading Roles
Mutiny on the Bounty (1935) Clark Gable, Charles Laughton, Franchot Tone

Three Actors/Actresses in Supporting Roles

On the Waterfront (1954)	Lee J. Cobb, Karl Malden, Rod Steiger
Tom Jones (1963)	Diane Cilento, Dame Edith Evans, Joyce Redman
The Godfather (1972)	James Caan, Robert Duvall, Al Pacino
The Godfather, Part II (1974)	Robert De Niro*, Lee Strasberg, Michael Gazzo

Two Nominees in each of Two Separate Categories

All About Eve (1950)	
Anne Baxter, Bette Davis	Leading Role
Celeste Holm, Thelma Ritter	Supp. Role
Peyton Place (1957)	
Arthur Kennedy, Russ Tamblyn	Supp. Role
Hope Lange, Diane Varsi	Supp. Role
The Last Picture Show (1971)	
Ben Johnson*, Jeff Bridges	Supp. Role
Cloris Leachman*, Ellen Burstyn	Supp. Role
Terms of Endearment (1983)	
Shirley MacLaine*, Debra Winger	Leading Role
Jack Nicholson*, John Lithgow	Supp. Role

Two Actors in Leading Roles
Going My Way (1944) Bing Crosby*, Barry Fitzgerald
From Here to Eternity (1953) Montgomery Clift, Burt Lancaster
Giant (1956) James Dean, Rock Hudson
The Defiant Ones (1958) Tony Curtis, Sidney Poitier
Judgment at Nuremberg (1961) Maximilian Schell*, Spencer Tracy
Becket (1964) Richard Burton, Peter O'Toole
Midnight Cowboy (1969) Dustin Hoffman, Jon Voight
Sleuth (1972) Michael Caine, Laurence Olivier
Network (1976) Peter Finch* [posthumous], William Holden
The Dresser (1983) Tom Courtenay, Albert Finney
Amadeus (1984) F. Murray Abraham*, Tom Hulce

Two Actresses in Leading Roles
All About Eve (1950) Anne Baxter, Bette Davis
Suddenly, Last Summer (1959) Katharine Hepburn, Elizabeth Taylor

The Turning Point (1977) Anne Bancroft, Shirley MacLaine
Terms of Endearment (1983) Shirley MacLaine*, Debra Winger
Thelma & Louise (1991) Geena Davis, Susan Sarandon

Two Actors in Supporting Roles
Mr. Smith Goes to Washington (1939) Harry Carey, Claude Rains
Quo Vadis (1951) Leo Genn, Peter Ustinov
Shane (1953) Brandon de Wilde, Jack Palance
Peyton Place (1957) Arthur Kennedy, Russ Tamblyn
Anatomy of a Murder (1959) Arthur O'Connell, George C. Scott
The Hustler (1961) Jackie Gleason, George C. Scott
Bonnie and Clyde (1967) Gene Hackman, Michael J. Pollard
The Last Picture Show (1971) Ben Johnson*, Jeff Bridges
Rocky (1976) Burgess Meredith, Burt Young
Julia (1977) Jason Robards*, Maximilian Schell
Ordinary People (1980) Timothy Hutton*, Judd Hirsch
Terms of Endearment (1983) Jack Nicholson*, John Lithgow
Platoon (1986) Tom Berenger, Willem Dafoe
Bugsy (1991) Harvey Keitel, Ben Kingsley

Two Actresses in Supporting Roles
Gone with the Wind (1939) Hattie McDaniel*, Olivia de Havilland
The Little Foxes (1941) Patricia Collinge, Teresa Wright
Mrs. Miniver (1942) Teresa Wright*, Dame May Whitty
The Song of Bernadette (1943) Gladys Cooper, Anne Revere
Mildred Pierce (1945) Eve Arden, Ann Blyth
Gentleman's Agreement (1947) Celeste Holm*, Anne Revere
I Remember Mama (1948) Barbara Bel Geddes, Ellen Corby
Pinky (1949) Ethel Barrymore, Ethel Waters
Come to the Stable (1949) Celeste Holm, Elsa Lanchester
All About Eve (1950) Celeste Holm, Thelma Ritter
The High and the Mighty (1954) Jan Sterling, Claire Trevor
The Bad Seed (1956) Eileen Heckart, Patty McCormack
Peyton Place (1957) Hope Lange, Diane Varsi
Imitation of Life (1959) Susan Kohner, Juanita Moore
Othello (1965) Joyce Redman, Maggie Smith
Airport (1970) Helen Hayes*, Maureen Stapleton
The Last Picture Show (1971) Cloris Leachman*, Ellen Burstyn
Paper Moon (1973) Tatum O'Neal*, Madeline Kahn
Nashville (1975) Ronee Blakley, Lily Tomlin
Kramer vs. Kramer (1979) Meryl Streep*, Jane Alexander
Tootsie (1982) Jessica Lange*, Teri Garr
The Color Purple (1985) Margaret Avery, Oprah Winfrey
Working Girl (1988) Joan Cusack, Sigourney Weaver
Enemies, A Love Story (1989) Anjelica Huston, Lena Olin

5: FILMS TO HAVE WON FIVE OR MORE ADACEMY AWARDS WITHOUT WINNING BEST PICTURE

8 Oscars
Cabaret (1972)

6 Oscars
A Place in the Sun (1951)
Star Wars (1977)

5 Oscars
Wilson (1944)
The Bad and the Beautiful (1952)
The King and I (1956)
Mary Poppins (1964)
Doctor Zhivago (1965)
Who's Afraid of Virginia Woolf? (1966)

6: BEST PICTURE NOMINEES BY GENRE

[Note: Readers may disagree with some of the following classifications (as indeed does the author, viz. the omission of *Citizen Kane* from Biopics and the inclusion of *The Last Picture Show* under Westerns). Can *Amadeus* really be called a musical? Is *Casablanca* a war film? These lists are based on the Academy's own official definitions. Some pictures naturally appear under more than one heading. (* indicates winner.)]

(a) Biopics *(67 nominees; 11 winners)*

1929–30	*Disraeli*
1932–33	*The Private Life of Henry VIII*
	I Am a Fugitive from a Chain Gang
1934	*The Barretts of Wimpole Street*
	Cleopatra
	The House of Rothschild
	Viva Villa!
1935	*Mutiny on the Bounty**
1936	*The Great Ziegfeld**
	The Story of Louis Pasteur
1938	*Boys Town*
1941	*Sergeant York*
1942	*The Pride of the Yankees*
	Yankee Doodle Dandy
1943	*Madame Curie*
	The Song of Bernadette
1944	*Wilson*
1952	*Moulin Rouge*
1955	*Love Is a Many Splendored Thing*
1956	*The King and I*
	The Ten Commandments
1958	*Auntie Mame*

1959	*The Diary of Anne Frank*
	The Nun's Story
1960	*The Alamo*
1962	*Lawrence of Arabia**
	Mutiny on the Bounty
1963	*America, America*
	Cleopatra
1964	*Becket*
1965	*The Sound of Music**
1966	*A Man for All Seasons**
1967	*Bonnie and Clyde*
1968	*Funny Girl*
	The Lion in Winter
1969	*Anne of the Thousand Days*
	Butch Cassidy and the Sundance kid
1970	*Patton*
1971	*The French Connection**
	Nicholas and Alexandra
1974	*Lenny*
1975	*Dog Day Afternoon*
1976	*All the President's Men*
	Bound for Glory
1977	*Julia*
1978	*Midnight Express*
1979	*All That Jazz*
1980	*Coal Miner's Daughter*
	Raging Bull
	The Elephant Man
1981	*Chariots of Fire**
	Reds
1982	*Gandhi**
	Missing
1983	*The Right Stuff*
1984	*Amadeus**
	The Killing Fields
1985	*Out of Africa**
1986	*The Mission*
1987	*Hope and Glory*
	*The Last Emperor**
1989	*Born on the Fourth of July*
	My Left Foot
1990	*Awakenings*
	Goodfellas
1991	*Bugsy*
	JFK

(b) War Films *(55 nominees; 14 winners)*

1927–28	*Wings**

1929–30	*All Quiet on the Western Front**
1932–33	*A Farewell to Arms*
1934	*Viva Villa!*
1938	*Grand Illusion*
1939	*Gone with the Wind**
1940	*Foreign Correspondent*
	The Great Dictator
1941	*Sergeant York*
1942	*Mrs. Miniver**
	The Invaders
	The Pied Piper
	Wake Island
1943	*Casablanca**
	For Whom the Bell Tolls
	The Human Comedy
	In Which We Serve
	Watch on the Rhine
1944	*Since You Went Away*
1946	*The Best Years of Our Lives**
1949	*Battleground*
1951	*Decision Before Dawn*
1953	*From Here to Eternity**
1954	*The Caine Mutiny*
1955	*Mister Roberts*
1955	*Friendly Persuasion*
1957	*The Bridge on the River Kwai**
	Sayonara
1959	*The Diary of Anne Frank*
	The Nun's Story
1960	*The Alamo*
1961	*The Guns of Navarone*
	Judgment at Nuremberg
1962	*Lawrence of Arabia**
	The Longest Day
1964	*Dr. Strangelove or: How I Learned to Stop Worrying and Love the Bomb*
1965	*The Sound of Music**
	Doctor Zhivago
1966	*The Russians Are Coming, the Russians Are Coming*
	The Sand Pebbles
1970	*M*A*S*H*
	*Patton**
1972	*Cabaret*
1977	*Julia*
1978	*Coming Home*
	*The Deer Hunter**
1979	*Apocalypse Now*
1981	*Reds*
1982	*Missing*

1984	*The Killing Fields*
1986	*Platoon**
	The Mission
1987	*Hope and Glory*
	*The Last Emperor**
1989	*Born on the Fourth of July*

(c) Comedies *(52 nominees; 7 winners)*

1930–31	*The Front Page*
1931–32	*One Hour with You*
1932–33	*Lady for a Day*
	She Done Him Wrong
1934	*It Happened One Night**
	Flirtation Walk
	The Gay Divorcée
	Here Comes the Navy
	The Thin Man
1935	*Ruggles of Red Gap*
	Top Hat
1936	*Libeled Lady*
1937	*The Awful Truth*
1938	*You Can't Take It with You**
1939	*Ninotchka*
1940	*The Philadelphia Story*
1941	*Here Comes Mr. Jordan*
1942	*The Talk of the Town*
1943	*Heaven Can Wait*
	The More the Merrier
1947	*The Bishop's Wife*
	Miracle on 34th Street
1950	*Born Yesterday*
	Father of the Bride
1953	*Roman Holiday*
1955	*Mister Roberts*
1958	*Auntie Mame*
1960	*The Apartment**
1963	*Tom Jones**
1964	*Dr. Strangelove or: How I Learned to Stop Worrying and Love the Bomb*
1965	*A Thousand Clowns*
1966	*Alfie*
	The Russians Are Coming, the Russians Are Coming
1967	*The Graduate*
1970	*M*A*S*H*
1973	*American Graffiti*
	A Touch of Class
1977	*Annie Hall**
	The Goodbye Girl
1978	*Heaven Can Wait*

1979	*Breaking Away*
1982	*Tootsie*
1983	*Terms of Endearment**
1985	*Prizzi's Honor*
1986	*Hannah and Her Sisters*
	A Room with a View
1987	*Broadcast News*
	Hope and Glory
	Moonstruck
1988	*The Accidental Tourist*
	Working Girl
1989	*Driving Miss Daisy**

(d) Musicals *(40 nominees; 10 winners)*

1928–29	*Broadway Melody**
1929–30	*The Love Parade*
1931–32	*One Hour with You*
1932–33	*Forty-Second Street*
1934	*Flirtation Walk*
	The Gay Divorcée
	One Night of Love
1935	*Broadway Melody of 1936*
	Naughty Marietta
	Top Hat
1936	*The Great Ziegfeld**
	Three Smart Girls
1937	*One Hundred Men and a Girl*
1938	*Alexander's Ragtime Band*
1939	*The Wizard of Oz*
1942	*Yankee Doodle Dandy*
1944	*Going My Way**
1945	*Anchors Aweigh*
1948	*The Red Shoes*
1951	*An American in Paris**
1954	*Seven Brides for Seven Brothers*
1956	*The King and I*
1958	*Gigi**
1961	*West Side Story**
	Fanny
1962	*The Music Man*
1964	*My Fair Lady**
	Mary Poppins
1965	*The Sound of Music**
1967	*Doctor Doolittle*
1968	*Oliver!**
	Funny Girl
1969	*Hello, Dolly!*
1971	*Fiddler on the Roof*

1972	*Cabaret*
1975	*Nashville*
1977	*The Turning Point*
1980	*Coal Miner's Daughter*
1984	*Amadeus**
1991	*Beauty and the Beast* (animated)

(e) Action/Adventure *(23 nominees; 3 winners)*

1930–31	*Trader Horn*
1934	*Here Comes the Navy*
	Viva Villa!
1935	*Mutiny on the Bounty**
	Captain Blood
	Lives of a Bengal Lancer
1938	*The Adventures of Robin Hood*
1940	*The Long Voyage Home*
1948	*The Treasure of the Sierra Madre*
1950	*King Solomon's Mines*
1952	*Ivanhoe*
1956	*Around the World in 80 Days**
1961	*The Guns of Navarone*
1962	*Lawrence of Arabia**
	Mutiny on the Bounty
1963	*How the West Was Won*
1970	*Airport*
1972	*Deliverance*
1974	*The Towering Inferno*
1975	*Jaws*
1977	*Star Wars*
1981	*Raiders of the Lost Ark*
1983	*The Right Stuff*

(f) Religious Subjects *(22 nominees; 6 winners)*

1937	*Lost Horizon*
1938	*Boys Town*
1941	*One Foot in Heaven*
1943	*The Song of Bernadette*
1944	*Going My Way**
1945	*The Bells of St. Mary's*
1951	*Quo Vadis*
1953	*The Robe*
1956	*Friendly Persuasion*
	The Ten Commandments
1959	*Ben-Hur**
	The Nun's Story
1960	*Elmer Gantry*
1963	*Lilies of the Field*
1964	*Becket*
1965	*The Sound of Music**

1966	*A Man for All Seasons**
1973	*The Exorcist*
1981	*Chariots of Fire**
1982	*Gandhi**
1985	*Witness*
1986	*The Mission*

(g) Fantasy/Science Fiction/Horror *(21 nominees; 1 winner)*

1937	*Lost Horizon*
1939	*The Wizard of Oz*
1940	*Our Town*
1941	*Here Comes Mr. Jordan*
1943	*Heaven Can Wait*
1946	*It's a Wonderful Life*
1947	*The Bishop's Wife*
	Miracle on 34th Street
1964	*Dr. Strangelove or: How I Learned to Stop Worrying and Love the Bomb*
	Mary Poppins
1967	*Doctor Doolittle*
1971	*A Clockwork Orange*
1973	*The Exorcist*
1975	*Jaws*
1977	*Star Wars*
1978	*Heaven Can Wait*
1981	*Raiders of the Lost Ark*
1982	*E.T.—The Extra-Terrestrial*
1989	*Field of Dreams*
1990	*Ghost*
1991	*The Silence of the Lambs**

(h) Mystery/Suspense *(14 nominees; 2 winners)*

1931–32	*Shanghai Express*
1934	*The Thin Man*
1940	*Rebecca**
	Foreign Correspondent
1941	*The Maltese Falcon*
	Suspicion
1944	*Double Indemnity*
	Gaslight
1945	*Spellbound*
1957	*Witness for the Prosecution*
1967	*In the Heat of the Night**
1974	*Chinatown*
1985	*Witness*
1987	*Fatal Attraction*

(i) Westerns *(12 nominees; 2 winners)*

1930–31	*Cimarron**
1934	*Viva Villa!*

1935	*Ruggles of Red Gap*
1939	*Stagecoach*
1943	*The Ox-Bow Incident*
1952	*High Noon*
1953	*Shane*
1956	*Giant*
1960	*The Alamo*
1963	*How the West Was Won*
1969	*Butch Cassidy and the Sundance Kid*
1971	*The Last Picture Show*
1990	*Dances with Wolves**
1992	*Unforgiven*

7: FOREIGN-LANGUAGE FILMS NOMINATED FOR BEST PICTURE

1938: *Grand Illusion* (France)
1969: *Z* (Algeria) [* won Best Foreign Language Film]
1972: *The Emigrants* (Sweden)
1973: *Cries and Whispers* (Sweden)

8: FOREIGN-LANGUAGE FILMS: NOMINATIONS AND WINS BY COUNTRY

	Nominations	*Wins*
France	27	8 + 3 Special Awards
Italy	24	9 + 3
Spain	14	1
Japan	10	0 + 3
Sweden	10	3
USSR	9	3

2 wins each: Czechoslovakia, Denmark, Switzerland

1 win each: Algeria, Argentina, West Germany, Hungary, Ivory Coast, Netherlands, Spain.

B: Actors

1: MOST NOMINATED ACTORS

(Leading role, supporting role) + (wins in each category)

12 nominations
Katharine Hepburn (All leading role) (4 wins)

10 nominations
Bette Davis (All leading role) (2 wins)
Laurence Olivier (9,1) (1,0) + 1 special award + 1 Honorary Oscar

9 nominations

Jack Nicholson	(6,3)	(1,1)
Meryl Streep	(6,3)	(1,1)
Spencer Tracy	(9,0)	(2)

8 nominations

Marlon Brando	(7,1)	(2,0)
Jack Lemmon	(7,1)	(1,1)
Geraldine Page	(4,4)	(1,0)

7 nominations

Ingrid Bergman	(6,1)	(2,1)
Richard Burton	(6,1)	(0,0)
Jane Fonda	(6,1)	(2,0)
Greer Garson	(7,0)	(1)
Paul Newman	(7,0)	(1) + 1 nomination as a producer + 1 Honorary Oscar
Peter O'Toole	(7,0)	(0)

6 nominations

Robert De Niro	(5,1)	(1,1)
Dustin Hoffman	(6,0)	(2)
Deborah Kerr	(6,0)	(0)
Al Pacino	(5,1)	(0,0)
Thelma Ritter	(0,6)	(0)

5 nominations

Anne Bancroft	(5,0)	(1)
Ellen Burstyn	(4,1)	(1,0)
Glenn Close	(2,3)	(0,0)
Gary Cooper	(5,0)	(2) + 1 Honorary Oscar
Olivia de Havilland	(4,1)	(2,0)
Irene Dunne	(5,0)	(0)
Susan Hayward	(5,0)	(1)
Audrey Hepburn	(5,0)	(1)
Jennifer Jones	(4,1)	(1,0)
Arthur Kennedy	(1,4)	(0,0)
Jessica Lange	(4,1)	(0,1)
Shirley MacLaine	(5,0)	(1)
Fredric March	(5,0)	(2)
Gregory Peck	(5,0)	(1)
Vanessa Redgrave	(4,1)	(0,1)
Norma Shearer	(5,0)	(1)
Maggie Smith	(2,3)	(1,1)
Sissy Spacek	(5,0)	(1)
James Stewart	(5,0)	(1) + 1 Honorary Oscar
Elizabeth Taylor	(5,0)	(2)

2: ACTORS TO HAVE WON MOST OSCARS (* DENOTES WIN AT EVERY NOMINATION)

4 Oscars

Katharine Hepburn (12 nominations)

3 Oscars		
Ingrid Bergman	(7)	
Walter Brennan	(4)	
2 Oscars		
Marlon Brando	(7)	
Gary Cooper	(5) + 1 Honorary Oscar	
Bette Davis	(10)	
Olivia de Havilland	(5)	
Robert De Niro	(5)	
Melvyn Douglas	(3)	
Sally Field	(2)*	
Jane Fonda	(7)	
Jodie Foster	(3)	
Helen Hayes	(2)*	
Dustin Hoffman	(6)	
Glenda Jackson	(4)	
Vivien Leigh	(2)*	
Jack Lemmon	(8)	
Fredric March	(5)	
Jack Nicholson	(8)	
Anthony Quinn	(4)	
Luise Rainer	(2)*	
Jason Robards	(3)	
Maggie Smith	(4)	
Meryl Streep	(6)	
Elizabeth Taylor	(5)	
Spencer Tracy	(9)	
Peter Ustinov	(3 + 1 writing nomination)	
Shelley Winters	(4)	

3: ACTORS TO WIN LEADING OSCARS FOR THEIR ONLY NOMINATION

Best Actor

1927–28	Emil Jannings, *The Last Command* and *The Way of all Flesh*
1928–29	Warner Baxter, *In Old Arizona*
1929–30	George Arliss, *Disraeli* and *The Green Goddess*
1943	Paul Lukas, *Watch on the Rhine*
1945	Ray Milland, *The Lost Weekend*
1949	Broderick Crawford, *All the King's Men*
1955	Ernest Borgnine, *Marty*
1956	Yul Brynner, *The King and I*
1958	David Niven, *Separate Tables*
1959	Charlton Heston, *Ben-Hur*
1965	Lee Marvin, *Cat Ballou*
1966	Paul Scofield, *A Man for All Seasons*
1968	Cliff Robertson, *Charly*
1974	Art Carney, *Harry and Tonto*
1982	Ben Kingsley, *Gandhi*

1984	F. Murray Abraham, *Amadeus*
1987	Michael Douglas, *Wall Street*
1989	Daniel Day-Lewis, *My Left Foot*
1990	Jeremy Irons, *Reversal of Fortune*
1991	Anthony Hopkins, *The Silence of the Lambs*

Best Actress

1928–29	Mary Pickford, *Coquette*
1940	Ginger Rogers, *Kitty Foyle*
1950	Judy Holliday, *Born Yesterday*
1952	Shirley Booth, *Come Back, Little Sheba*
1975	Louise Fletcher, *One Flew Over the Cuckoo's Nest*
1986	Marlee Matlin, *Children of a Lesser God*
1989	Jessica Tandy, *Driving Miss Daisy*
1990	Kathy Bates, *Misery*

4: OLDEST AND YOUNGEST NOMINATED/WINNING ACTORS

	Oldest Nominee	*Oldest Winner*
Leading (M)	Henry Fonda (76 years, 317 days, *On Golden Pond,* 1981)	Henry Fonda
Supporting (M)	Ralph Richardson (d. 82 years, 96 days, *Greystoke,* 1984)	George Burns (80 years, 69 days, *The Sunshine Boys,* 1975
Leading (F)	Jessica Tandy (80 years, 293 days, *Driving Miss Daisy,* 1989)	Jessica Tandy
Supporting (F)	Eva Le Gallienne (82 years, 79 days, *Resurrection,* 1980)	Peggy Ashcroft (77 years, 93 days, *A Passage to India,* 1984)
	Youngest Nominee	*Youngest Winner*
Leading (M)	Jackie Cooper (9 years, 56 days, *Skippy,* 1930–31)	Richard Dreyfuss (29 years, 156 days, *The Goodbye Girl,* 1977)
Supporting (M)	Justin Henry (8 years, 352 days, *Kramer vs. Kramer,* 1979)	Timothy Hutton (20 years, 227 days, *Ordinary People,* 1980)
Leading (F)	Isabelle Adjani (20 years, 276 days, *The Story of Adele H,* 1975)	Marlee Matlin (21 years, 218 days, *Children of a Lesser God,* 1986)
Supporting (F)	Tatum O'Neal (10 years, 148 days, *Paper Moon,* 1973)	Tatum O'Neal

Shirley Temple is the youngest person to receive an Oscar: A special Award in 1934, when she was 5 years and 10 months.

5: ACTORS NOMINATED FOR OSCARS IN THEIR FILM DEBUTS

[Note: *indicates winner.)

Best Actor in a Leading Role

Lawrence Tibbett	(*The Rogue Song,* 1929–30)
Orson Welles	(*Citizen Kane,* 1941)
Montgomery Clift	(*The Search,* 1948)

Best Actress in a Leading Role

Greer Garson	(*Goodbye, Mr. Chips,* 1939)
Martha Scott	(*Our Town,* 1940)
Shirley Booth	(*Come Back, Little Sheba,* 1952)*
Julie Harris	(*The Member of the Wedding,* 1952)
Maggie McNamara	(*The Moon Is Blue,* 1953)
Julie Andrews	(*Mary Poppins,* 1964)*
Elizabeth Hartman	(*A Patch of Blue,* 1965)
Barbra Streisand	(*Funny Girl,* 1968)*
Jane Alexander	(*The Great White Hope,* 1970)
Diana Ross	(*Lady Sings the Blues,* 1972)
Julie Walters	(*Educating Rita,* 1983)
Whoopi Goldberg	(*The Color Purple,* 1985)
Marlee Matlin	(*Children of a Lesser God,* 1986)*

Best Supporting Actor

Robert Morley	(*Marie Antoinette,* 1938)
Sydney Greenstreet	(*The Maltese Falcon,* 1941)
John Dall	(*The Corn Is Green,* 1945)
Richard Widmark	(*Kiss of Death,* 1947)
José Ferrer	(*Joan of Arc,* 1948)
Don Murray	(*Bus Stop,* 1956)
Victor Buono	(*Whatever Happened to Baby Jane?,* 1962)
Terence Stamp	(*Billy Budd,* 1962)
Michael Dunn	(*Ship of Fools,* 1965)
Mako	(*The Sand Pebbles,* 1966)
Jack Wild	(*Oliver!,* 1968)
Jason Miller	(*The Exorcist,* 1973)
Lee Strasberg	(*The Godfather,* 1974)
Chris Sarandon	(*Dog Day Afternoon,* 1975)
Mikhail Baryshnikov	(*The Turning Point,* 1977)
Justin Henry	(*Kramer vs. Kramer,* 1979)
Howard E. Rollins, Jr.	(*Ragtime,* 1981)
Adolph Caesar	(*A Soldier's Story,* 1984)
John Malkovich	(*Places in the Heart,* 1984)
Haing S. Ngor	(*The Killing Fields,* 1984)*

Best Supporting Actress

Maria Ouspenskaya	(*Dodsworth,* 1936)
Gale Sondergaard	(*Anthony Adverse,* 1936)*
Miliza Korjus	(*The Great Waltz,* 1938)

Patricia Collinge	(*The Little Foxes,* 1941)
Teresa Wright	(*The Little Foxes,* 1941)
Katina Paxinou	(*For Whom the Bell Tolls,* 1943)*
Angela Lansbury	(*Gaslight,* 1944)
Mercedes McCambridge	(*All the King's Men,* 1949)*
Lee Grant	(*Detective Story,* 1951)
Colette Marchand	(*Moulin Rouge,* 1952)
Eva Marie Saint	(*On the Waterfront,* 1954)*
Jo Van Fleet	(*East of Eden,* 1955)*
Diane Varsi	(*Peyton Place,* 1957)
Maureen Stapleton	(*Lonelyhearts,* 1958)
Mary Badham	(*To Kill a Mockingbird,* 1962)
Grayson Hall	(*The Night of the Iguana,* 1964)
Jocelyn LaGarde	(*Hawaii,* 1966)
Lynn Carlin	(*Faces,* 1968)
Sondra Locke	(*The Heart Is a Lonely Hunter,* 1968)
Catherine Burns	(*Last Summer,* 1969)
Tatum O'Neal	(*Paper Moon,* 1973)*
Ronee Blakley	(*Nashville,* 1975)
Lily Tomlin	(*Nashville,* 1975)
Leslie Browne	(*The Turning Point,* 1977)
Quinn Cummings	(*The Goodbye Girl,* 1977)
Cathy Moriarty	(*Raging Bull,* 1980)
Glenn Close	(*The World According to Garp,* 1982)
Oprah Winfrey	(*The Color Purple,* 1985)

6: MOST CONSECUTIVE ACTING NOMINATIONS

Five Consecutive Nominations:

Bette Davis	(1938–42)	Greer Garson	(1941–45)

Four:

Marlon Brando	(1951–54)	Jennifer Jones	(1943–46)
Al Pacino	(1972–75)	Thelma Ritter	(1950–53)
Elizabeth Taylor	(1957–60)		

Three:

Ingrid Bergman	(1943–45)	Richard Burton	(1964–66)
Glenn Close	(1982–84)	Gary Cooper	(1941–43)
Jane Fonda	(1977–79)	William Hurt	(1985–87)
Deborah Kerr	(1956–58)	Jack Nicholson	(1973–75)
Gregory Peck	(1945–47)	Meryl Streep	(1981–83)
Spencer Tracy	(1936–38)		

7: ROLES THAT HAVE WON MORE THAN ONE ACTING NOMINATION

[Note:* indicates winner.]

"Pa Baxter":	Gregory Peck (*The Yearling,* 1946)
"Marsh Turner":	Rip Torn (*Cross Creek,* 1983)
"Vicki Lester":	Janet Gaynor (*A Star Is Born,* 1937)
	Judy Garland (*A Star Is Born,* 1954)

"Arthur Chipping":	Robert Donat* (*Goodbye, Mr. Chips,* 1939) Peter O'Toole (*Goodbye, Mr. Chips,* 1969)
"Max Corkle":	James Gleason (*Here Comes Mr. Jordan,* 1941) Jack Warden (*Heaven Can Wait,* 1978)
"Michael Corleone":	Al Pacino (*The Godfather,* 1972) Al Pacino (*The Godfather Part II,* 1974)
"Vito Corleone":	Marlon Brando* (*The Godfather,* 1972) Robert De Niro* (*The Godfather, Part II,* 1974)
"Cyrano de Bergerac":	José Ferrer* (*Cyrano de Bergerac,* 1950) Gérard Dépardieu (*Cyrano de Bergerac,* 1990)
"Fast Eddie Felson":	Paul Newman (*The Hustler,* 1961) Paul Newman* (*The Color of Money,* 1986)
"Henry II":	Peter O'Toole (*Beckel,* 1964) Peter O'Toole (*The Lion in Winter,* 1968)
"Henry V":	Laurence Olivier (*Henry V,* 1946) Kenneth Branagh (*Henry V,* 1989)
"Henry VIII":	Charles Laughton* (*The Private Life of Henry VIII,* 1932–33) Robert Shaw (*A Man for All Seasons,* 1966) Richard Burton (*Anne of the Thousand Days,* 1969)
"Norman Maine":	Fredric March (*A Star Is Born,* 1937) James Mason (*A Star Is Born,* 1954)
"Father O'Malley":	Bing Crosby* (*Going My Way,* 1944) Bing Crosby (*The Bells of St. Mary's,* 1945)
"Joe Pendleton":	Robert Montgomery (*Here Comes Mr. Jordan,* 1941) Warren Beatty (*Heaven Can Wait,* 1978)

8: NOMINATIONS FOR FOREIGN-LANGUAGE PERFORMANCES

[Note: * indicates winner.]

1961	Sophia Loren,* *Two Women* (Italian)
1962	Marcello Mastroianni, *Divorce Italian Style* (Italian)
1964	Sophia Loren, *Marriage Italian Style* (Italian)
1966	Anouk Aimée, *A Man and a Woman* (French) Ida Kaminska, *The Shop on Main Street* (Czech)
1972	Liv Ullman, *The Emigrants* (Swedish)
1974	Valentina Cortese, *Day for Night* (French) Robert De Niro,* *The Godfather, Part II* (Italian)
1976	Marie-Christine Barrault, *Cousin, Cousine* (French) Giancarlo Giannini, *Seven Beauties* (Italian) Liv Ullman, *Face to Face* (Swedish)
1977	Marcello Mastroianni, *A Special Day* (Italian)
1978	Ingrid Bergman, *Autumn Sonata* (Swedish)

1986 Marlee Matlin,* *Children of a Lesser God* (American Sign Language)
1987 Marcello Mastroianni, *Dark Eyes* (Italian)
1988 Max von Sydow, *Pelle the Conqueror* (Swedish)
1989 Isabelle Adjani, *Camille Claudel* (French)
1990 Gérard Dépardieu, *Cyrano de Bergerac* (French)

C: Directors

1: DIRECTORS WITH THREE OR MORE NOMINATIONS

Twelve

William Wyler	(3 wins)

Eight

Billy Wilder	(2)

Seven

David Lean	(2)
Fred Zinnemann	(2)

Six

Frank Capra	(3)

Five

Woody Allen	(1)
Clarence Brown	(0)
George Cukor	(1)
John Ford	(4)
Alfred Hitchcock	(0)
John Huston	(1)
Elia Kazan	(2)
George Stevens	(2)
King Vidor	(0)

Four

Francis Ford Coppola	(1)
Michael Curtiz	(1)
Federico Fellini	(0)
Stanley Kubrick	(0)
Sidney Lumet	(0)
Joseph L. Mankiewicz	(2)
Mike Nichols	(2)

Three

Ingmar Bergman	(0)
Richard Brooks	(0)
Bob Fosse	(1)
Norman Jewison	(0)
Stanley Kramer	(0)
Frank Lloyd	(2)
Ernst Lubitsch	(0)
Leo McCarey	(2)

Lewis Milestone	(2)
Arthur Penn	(0)
Sydney Pollack	(1)
Carol Reed	(1)
John Schlesinger	(1)
Martin Scorsese	(0)
Steven Spielberg	(0)
Oliver Stone	(2)
William Wellman	(0)
Robert Wise	(2)
Sam Wood	(0)

2: DIRECTORS TO HAVE WON TWO OR MORE OSCARS

Four

John Ford	*The Informer,* 1935
	The Grapes of Wrath, 1940
	How Green Was My Valley, 1941
	The Quiet Man, 1952

Three

Frank Capra	*It Happened One Night,* 1934
	Mr. Deeds Goes to Town, 1936
	You Can't Take It with You, 1938
William Wyler	*Mrs. Miniver,* 1942
	The Best Years of Our Lives, 1946
	Ben-Hur, 1959

Two

Frank Borzage	*Seventh Heaven,* 1927–28
	Bad Girl, 1931–32
Milos Forman	*One Flew Over the Cuckoo's Nest,* 1975
	Amadeus, 1984
Elia Kazan	*Gentleman's Agreement,* 1947
	On the Waterfront, 1954
David Lean	*The Bridge on the River Kwai,* 1957
	Lawrence of Arabia, 1962
Frank Lloyd	*The Divine Lady, Weary River* and *Drag,* 1928–29
	Cavalcade, 1932–33
Leo McCarey	*The Awful Truth,* 1937
	Going My Way, 1944
Joseph L. Mankiewicz	*A Letter to Three Wives,* 1949
	All About Eve, 1950
Lewis Milestone	*Two Arabian Nights* (comedy), 1927–28
	All Quiet on the Western Front, 1929–30
George Stevens	*A Place in the Sun,* 1951
	Giant, 1956
Oliver Stone	*Platoon,* 1986
	Born on the Fourth of July, 1989
Billy Wilder	*The Lost Weekend,* 1945
	The Apartment, 1960

Robert Wise	*West Side Story,* 1961
	The Sound of Music, 1965
Fred Zinnemann	*From Here to Eternity,* 1953
	A Man for All Seasons, 1966

3: OLDEST AND YOUNGEST NOMINATED/WINNING DIRECTORS

Oldest Nominee	John Huston (aged 79)
	Prizzi's Honor, 1985
Oldest Winner	George Cukor (aged 65)
	My Fair Lady, 1964
Youngest Nominee	John Singleton (aged 23)
	Boyz N the Hood, 1991
Youngest Winner	Norman Taurog (aged 31)
	Skippy, 1930–31

4: DIRECTORS NOMINATED FOR THEIR DEBUTS

[Note: * indicates winner.]

1941 Orson Welles, *Citizen Kane*
1955 Delbert Mann, *Marty**
1957 Sidney Lumet, *Twelve Angry Men*
1959 Jack Clayton, *Room at the Top*
1961 Jerome Robbins, *West Side Story**
1962 Frank Perry, *David and Lisa*
1966 Mike Nichols, *Who's Afraid of Virginia Woolf?*
1978 Warren Beatty/Buck Henry, *Heaven Can Wait*
1980 Robert Redford, *Ordinary People**
1983 James L. Brooks, *Terms of Endearment**
1984 Roland Joffé, *The Killing Fields*
1989 Kenneth Branagh, *Henry V*
1990 Kevin Costner, *Dances with Wolves**
1991 John Singleton, *Boyz N the Hood*

5: BEST PICTURE WINNERS NOT NOMINATED FOR DIRECTION

1927–28 *Wings* (William Wellman)
1928–29 *Broadway Melody* (Harry Beaumont)
1931–32 *Grand Hotel* (Edmund Goulding)
1989 *Driving Miss Daisy* (Bruce Beresford)

6: BEST PICTURE AND BEST DIRECTOR WON BY DIFFERENT FILMS

1927–28	*Wings* (dir: William Wellman)
	Frank Borzage, *Seventh Heaven*
1928–29	*Broadway Melody* (dir: Harry Beaumont)
	Frank Lloyd, *The Divine Lady, Weary River* and *Drag*
1930–31	*Cimarron* (dir: Wesley Ruggles)
	Norman Taurog, *Skippy*
1931–32	*Grand Hotel* (dir: Edmund Goulding)
	Frank Borzage, *Bad Girl*

1935 *Mutiny on the Bounty* (dir: Frank Lloyd)
John Ford, *The Informer*
1936 *The Great Ziegfeld* (dir: Robert Z. Leonard)
Frank Capra, *Mr. Deeds Goes to Town*
1937 *The Life of Emile Zola* (dir: William Dieterle)
Leo McCarey, *The Awful Truth*
1940 *Rebecca* (dir: Alfred Hitchcock)
John Ford, *The Grapes of Wrath*
1948 *Hamlet* (dir: Laurence Olivier)
John Huston, *The Treasure of the Sierra Madre*
1949 *All the King's Men* (dir: Robert Rossen)
Joseph L. Mankiewicz, *A Letter to Three Wives*
1951 *An American in Paris* (dir: Vincente Minnelli)
George Stevens, *A Place in the Sun*
1952 *The Greatest Show on Earth* (dir: Cecil B. de Mille)
John Ford, *The Quiet Man*
1956 *Around the World in 80 Days* (dir: Michael Anderson)
George Stevens, *Giant*
1967 *In the Heat of the Night* (dir: Norman Jewison)
Mike Nichols, *The Graduate*
1972 *The Godfather* (dir: Francis Ford Coppola)
Bob Fosse, *Cabaret*
1981 *Chariots of Fire* (dir: Hugh Hudson)
Warren Beatty, *Reds*
1989 *Driving Miss Daisy* (dir: Bruce Beresford)
Oliver Stone, *Born on the Fourth of July*

7: DIRECTORS NOMINATED FOR FOREIGN-LANGUAGE FILMS

[Note: * indicates winner of Best Foreign Film.]
1961 Federico Fellini, *La Dolce Vita*
1962 Pietro Germi, *Divorce Italian Style*
1963 Federico Fellini, *8½**
1965 Hiroshi Teshigahara, *Woman in the Dunes*
1966 Claude Lelouch, *A Man and a Woman**
1968 Gillo Pontecorvo, *The Battle of Algiers*
1969 Costa-Gavras, *Z**
1970 Federico Fellini, *Satyricon*
1972 Jan Troell, *The Emigrants*
1973 Ingmar Bergman, *Cries and Whispers*
1974 François Truffaut, *Day for Night**
1975 Federico Fellini, *Amarcord**
1976 Ingmar Bergman, *Face to Face*
Lina Wertmuller, *Seven Beauties*
1979 Edouard Molinaro, *La Cage aux Folles*
1982 Wolfgang Petersen, *Das Boot*
1983 Ingmar Bergman, *Fanny and Alexander**
1985 Akira Kurosawa, *Ran*
1987 Lasse Hallström, *My Life as a Dog*

D: Writers

1: ORIGINAL SCREENPLAY: MOST NOMINATIONS/WINS

12 nominations	(3 wins)	Billy Wilder
8	(2)	Woody Allen
	(1)	John Huston
	(0)	Federico Fellini
7	(3)	Charles Brackett
6	(2)	Ben Hecht
	(1)	Carl Foreman

2: WRITERS WITH THREE WINS

Charles Brackett	(7 nominations)
Paddy Chayefsky	(4)
Francis Ford Coppola	(5)
Billy Wilder	(12)

E: Music

1: BEST SCORE: MOST NOMINATIONS/WINS

43 nominations	(9 wins)	Alfred Newman
26	(4)	John Williams
26	(2)	Max Steiner
19	(1)	Victor Young
18	(3)	Ray Heindorf/Morris Stoloff
16	(3)	Miklos Rozsa
15	(3)	Dimitri Tiomkin
14	(1)	Jerry Goldsmith
	(0)	Alex North

2: BEST SONG: MOST NOMINATIONS/WINS

26 nominations	(4 wins)	Sammy Cahn
18	(4)	Johnny Mercer
16	(3)	Paul Francis Webster
14	(4)	James Van Heusen
	(2)	Alan and Marilyn Bergman
11	(3)	Harry Warren
	(2)	Henry Mancini
10	(2)	Sammy Fain
	(1)	Leo Robin
	(1)	Jule Styne
	(1)	Ned Washington

F: Most Honored Individuals in Other Categories

(Male):
Walt Disney is the all-time Oscar champ, with 32 awards in all, including 12 for Best Cartoon, plus numerous other Oscars in such categories as Short Subjects, Documentaries, Special Effects and several Honorary Oscars.

(Female):
Edith Head won 8 Oscars for Costume Design out of 35 nominations between 1948 and 1977.

G: Oscar Trivia

Films in Which the Entire Cast was Nominated for Oscars
Who's Afraid of Virginia Woolf? (1966)
Sleuth (1972)
Give 'em Hell, Harry (1975)

The Only Films to Win Oscars for Best Picture, Director, Actor, Actress and Screenplay
It Happened One Night (1934)
One Flew over the Cuckoo's Nest (1975)
The Silence of the Lambs (1991)

The Only Films to Win Both Best Actor and Best Actress
It Happened One Night (Clark Gable and Claudette Colbert, 1934)
One Flew over the Cuckoo's Nest (Jack Nicholson and Louise Fletcher, 1975)
Network (Peter Finch and Faye Dunaway, 1976)
Coming Home (Jon Voight and Jane Fonda, 1978)
On Golden Pond (Henry Fonda and Katharine Hepburn, 1981)
The Silence of the Lambs (Anthony Hopkins and Jodie Foster, 1991)

The Only Actors/Actresses to Win Consecutive Oscars
Luise Rainer (1936–37)
Spencer Tracy (1937–38)
Katharine Hepburn (1967–68)
Jason Robards (1976–77)

The Only Person to Direct Himself to an Acting Oscar
Laurence Olivier, *Hamlet,* 1948

The Only Tie for Best Actor
Wallace Beery *(The Champ)* and Fredric March *(Dr. Jekyll and Mr. Hyde),* 1931–32

The Only Tie for Best Actress
Katharine Hepburn *(The Lion in Winter)* and Barbra Streisand *(Funny Girl),* 1968

The Only Year Two Oscars Given for Best Director
Robert Wise and Jerome Robbins won for codirecting *West Side Story* in 1961.

The Only Actor Nominated Twice for the Same Performance
Barry Fitzgerald was nominated both as Best Actor and Best Supporting Actor for

his performance in *Going My Way,* 1944. (He won the Supporting Oscar.) The rules were changed to prevent it from happening again.

The Only Actor to Win Two Oscars for the Same Performance

World War II veteran Harold Russell was voted Best Supporting Actor *and* received an Honorary Oscar for his performance in *The Best Years of Our Lives,* 1946.

The Only Consecutive Double Oscar-Winner

Joseph L. Mankiewicz won Directing and Screenplay Oscars for *A Letter to Three Wives,* 1949, and *All About Eve,* 1950.

All-Time Losers

The record for most acting nominations without a single win—seven—is jointly held by Richard Burton and Peter O'Toole.

Most Nominated Movies Not to Win a Single Oscar

The Turning Point (1977), 11 nominations
The Color Purple (1985), 11 nominations

Best Picture Winners that Received No Acting Nominations

Wings (1927–28)
All Quiet on the Western Front (1929–30)
Grand Hotel (1931–32)
An American in Paris (1951)
The Greatest Show on Earth (1952)
Around the World in 80 Days (1956)
Gigi (1958)
The Last Emperor (1987)

The Only Silent Film to Win Best Picture

Wings (1927–28)

The First Sound Film to Win Best Picture

Broadway Melody (1928–29)

The First Film in Color to Win Best Picture

Gone With the Wind (1939)

The Last Black-and-White Film to Win Best Picture

The Apartment (1960)

The Only Sequel to Win Best Picture

The Godfather, Part II (1974)

The Only Animated Feature Nominated for Best Picture

Beauty and the Beast (1991)

The First Non-American Film to Win an Academy Award

The Private Life of Henry VIII (1932–33), in which Charles Laughton won Best Actor.

The First Non-American Film to Win Best Picture

Hamlet (1948), produced by, directed by and starring Laurence Olivier, financed and filmed in the U.K.

The First Foreign-Language Performance to Win an Oscar
Sophia Loren, Best Actress for *Two Women* (Italy), 1961

The First Film to Be Released on Video and Cable Before Winning Best Picture
The Silence of the Lambs (1991)

The Only Television Play to Be Made into a Feature Film that Won Best Picture
Marty (1955)

The First Posthumous Oscar-Winner
Sidney Howard, for the Screenplay of *Gone With the Wind,* 1939

The Only Posthumous Oscar-Winner in an Acting Category
Peter Finch (Best Actor) *Network,* 1976

The Only Person to Win a Supporting Oscar in a Title Role
Vanessa Redgrave *(Julia,* 1977)

Husbands and Wives Nominated for Acting in the Same Year
(* denotes winner)

1931–32	Alfred Lunt	*(The Guardsman)*	Leading Role
	Lynn Fontanne	*(The Guardsman)*	Leading Role
1953	Frank Sinatra*	*(From Here to Eternity)*	Supp. Role
	Ava Gardner	*(Mogambo)*	Leading Role
1957	Charles Laughton	*(Witness for the Prosecution)*	Leading Role
	Elsa Lanchester	*(Witness for the Prosecution)*	Supp. Role
1963	Rex Harrison	*(Cleopatra)*	Leading Role
	Rachel Roberts	*(This Sporting Life)*	Leading Role
1966	Richard Burton	*(Who's Afraid of Virginia Woolf?)*	Leading Role
	Elizabeth Taylor*	*(Who's Afraid of Virginia Woolf?)*	Leading Role

Three Husband-and-Wife Teams Nominated in Each Writing Category in the Same Year (1950)

Motion Picture Story

*Edna Anhalt and Edward Anhalt for *Panic in the Streets*

Screenplay

Frances Goodrich and Albert Hackett for *Father of the Bride*

Story and Screenplay

Ruth Gordon and Garson Kanin for *Adam's Rib*

The Only Married Couples to Win Acting Oscars
Laurence Olivier, 1948, and Vivien Leigh, 1951
Joanne Woodward, 1957, and Paul Newman, 1986

The Only Brother and Sister to Win Acting Oscars
Lionel Barrymore (1930–31) and Ethel Barrymore (1944)

The Only Sisters to Win Acting Oscars
Joan Fontaine (1941) and Olivia de Havilland (1946, 1949)

The Only Brothers to Win Consecutive Oscars
James Goldman and William Goldman (Best Screenplay, 1968–69, for *The Lion in Winter* and *Butch Cassidy and the Sundance Kid*)

The Only Twins to Win Oscars
Julius J. Epstein and Philip G. Epstein shared the Screenplay award with Howard Koch for *Casablanca,* 1943.

The Only Mother and Daughter Nominated in Same Film
Laura Dern (Best Actress) and Diane Ladd (Best Supporting Actress) in *Rambling Rose,* 1991

The Only Oscar-Winner Whose Parents Both Received Oscars
Liza Minnelli (Best Actress, *Cabaret,* 1972), whose father, Vincente Minnelli, won Best Director for *Gigi,* 1958; and whose mother, Judy Garland, was awarded an Honorary Oscar in 1939.

The Only Family with Three Generations of Oscar Winners
Walter Huston (Best Supporting Actor, *The Treasure of the Sierra Madre,* 1948)
John Huston (Best Director, *The Treasure of the Sierra Madre,* 1948)
Anjelica Huston (Best Supporting Actress, *Prizzi's Honor,* 1985)

The Only Woman Ever Nominated as Best Director
Lina Wertmuller *(Seven Beauties,* 1976)

The Only Person to Win an Oscar Playing a Member of the Opposite Sex
Linda Hunt *(The Year of Living Dangerously,* 1983)

The Longest Gap Between Nomination and Victory
Jack Palance *(Sudden Fear,* 1952; *City Slickers,* 1992*)

The Only Person to Win an Oscar for Playing an Oscar Loser
Maggie Smith *(California Suite,* 1978)

The Only Oscar Ever to Win an Oscar
Oscar Hammerstein II (Best Song: 1941, 1945)

(Oscar Lagerstrom, Oscar Homolka, Oscar Brodney and Oskar Werner have all been unsuccessful nominees.)

The Longest Oscar Ceremony
April 9, 1984: 3 hrs 45 mins

Oscar TV Ratings

	Year	*Channel*	*Rating*	*Audience share*	*Est. homes watching*
First televised show	1953	NBC	42.1	76%	6.4 million
Highest rated show	1959	NBC	46.1	80%	19.3
Lowest rated show	1986	ABC	27.3	43%	23.4
Recent comparison	1991	ABC	28.4	48%	26.4

Source: Nielsen Media Research

Acknowledgments

Much of the research for the historical section of this book was conducted in the Margaret Herrick Library of the Academy of Motion Picture Arts and Sciences in Los Angeles, both before and after its move from the Academy's headquarters on Wilshire Boulevard to the new Center for Motion Picture Studies on La Cienega. I am grateful to the library's very courteous and helpful staff; to the Academy's historian, Patrick Stockstill; and to its public relations officials, Bob Werden and Monika Young Moulin of Ruder, Finn. I must also thank the Academy's president, Karl Malden, for a helpful meeting, and the chairman of the Academy's public relations committee, Dale Olson, for his help in both this and his other role as a leading Hollywood publicist.

Although Academy officials have been aware of this book throughout the three years I have spent researching and writing it, there has been no official sanction beyond the granting of various interviews, access to the library, and a pass for the Academy Awards ceremonies of 1990 and 1991. The Academy makes a policy of distancing itself from all such books and of jealously protecting the copyright of the very word "Oscar." It is thus appropriate for me to emphasize here that this is in no way an official or authorized study of the Academy Awards, and that nothing herein can be regarded as having received official endorsement from the Academy of Motion Picture Arts and Sciences.

My thanks are also due to the libraries of *Daily Variety,* the *Hollywood*

Reporter and the British Film Institute; to the newspaper libraries of the *Los Angeles Times,* the *San Francisco Chronicle, The New York Times, The Atlanta Constitution* and *The Times* of London; and to Nielsen Media Research. I am especially grateful to Entertainment Data Inc. of Beverly Hills for permission to use statistical material from their annual publication *Academy Award Handicap.*

Among those who have generously shared of their expertise, I have especial reason to thank, in alphabetical order, Elkan Allan; Sir Richard Attenborough; Lauren Bacall; Alan Bates; Henri Bollinger, president of the Publicists Guild of America; Don Boyd; Melvyn Bragg and Alan Benson of London Weekend Television; Tina Brown, former editor-in-chief of *Vanity Fair* and now of *The New Yorker;* Michael Caine; Pauline Collins; Guy East, Majestic Films; Fred Engels; Philip Garfinkle, Entertainment Data Center, Beverly Hills; Nicholas Fraser, Panoptic; Helen Friedmann; Caroline Graham, *Vanity Fair;* Gayle Hunnicutt; Ruth Jackson; Howard W. Koch; Irving "Swifty" Lazar; Joe Lustig; Rick McCallum; Ali MacGraw; Walter Matthau; Julian Myers; Wolfgang Puck, Spago; David Puttnam; Henry Rogers, Rogers & Cowan; Jane Sarkin and Wendy Stark of *Vanity Fair.*

The best time to corner Hollywood stars is at the plethora of pre-Oscar parties, at the Oscar ceremony itself and at the Governors Ball which follows, where you meet on terms as equal as they ever get. Those I have managed to pin to the wall for an Oscar conversation at such occasions include many of the nominees and winners at the 1990, 1991 and 1992 Academy Awards, plus former nominees or winners who happened to be among the presenters: Danny Aiello; Kathy Bates; Warren Beatty; Annette Bening; Michael Blake; Kevin Costner; Hume Cronyn; Billy Crystal; Geena Davis; Bruce Davison; Daniel Day-Lewis; Jodie Foster; Morgan Freeman; Brenda Fricker; Andy Garcia; Whoopi Goldberg; Richard Harris; Anthony Hopkins; Anjelica Huston; Jeremy Irons; Jessica Lange; Jack Lemmon; Sophia Loren; Jack Nicholson; Nick Nolte; Edward James Olmos; Al Pacino; Noel Pearson; Joe Pesci; Michelle Pfeiffer; Martin Scorsese; Oliver Stone; Jessica Tandy; Denzel Washington; Irwin Winkler.

My thanks also go to Michael Korda, Chuck Adams, Emily Remes, Andy Hafitz and Phil James of Simon & Schuster (U.S.); to Alan Samson, Krystyna Zukowska, Helga Houghton and Linda Silverman of Little, Brown (U.K.); to Cynthia Good of Penguin (Canada); and to my agents and friends Hilary Rubinstein (London), Ellen Levine (New York) and Lucinda Vardey (Toronto).

My wife, Cynthia, and my sons, Sam, Joe and Ben, have, as always, offered their unique personal blend of patient forbearance and dynamic support. All are movie buffs, whose voluminous knowledge has proved invaluable. Between them, at times without knowing, they have seen me through many a dark moment. They are, in short, my best friends—in return for which, all I can offer is my unconditional love.

Source Notes

Full publication details of books cited will be found in the Bibliography that follows.

Chapter 1. Arrivals

PAGE

17 "My God, they've thrown in everything": *Entertainment Weekly,* March 22, 1991.

18 "If you're lucky enough to win an Oscar": *Premiere,* April 1991.

19 "We don't mind whose creation they wear": Fred Hayman, "Academy Clamors for Glamour," *USA Today,* March 25, 1991.

19 "If you can go past those awful idiot faces on the bleachers": Chandler, *Atlantic Monthly,* quoted in Peter H. Brown, *The Real Oscar.*

21 "Why do we watch this nonsense with such rapt attention?": *New York Times,* April 17, 1983.

Chapter 2. Left Foot Forward

PAGE

23 "an unlikely showing in an unlikely location": Mary Jane Owen, M.S.W., *Horizons,* Washington, D.C., March 1990.

24 "Noel and Jim really spent a lot of time in L.A.,": *Variety,* December 31, 1990. In a genial exchange in Beverly Hills, March 1991, after being pursued for over a year, the head of Miramax, Harvey Weinstein, declined to be interviewed for this book. When the author asked if any of Mr. Weinstein's lieutenants might speak for him, the reply was: "If they talk to you, I'll kill 'em." Hence, to my relief as much as theirs, the reliance here and elsewhere on previously published quotations.

27 Cruise's own box-office takings in the previous seven years: *Academy Awards Handicap,* Entertainment Data Inc., Beverly Hills, 1991. E.D.I. also compiled the table on page 32. The author is grateful for permission to reproduce it.

28 "Any actor knows that comedy is more difficult": Fields, *W. C. Fields, A Life on Film.*

30 "How else are they going to hear about Henry V": Elkan Allan, "Left Foot Forward," *The Independent on Sunday,* London, April 1, 1990.

33 "The nature of the Academy membership is elderly": *Premiere,* April 1991.

33 "It's like the last vestige": Andy Marx, "Who Are These People?" *Los Angeles Times,* March 29, 1992.

37 "These two ritualistically dumpy men": David Mamet, "Oscars," reprinted from *Gentleman's Quarterly* in *Writing in Restaurants.*

38 "This year, as in the past, you will be importuned": "An Important Note from the Board of Governors of the Academy of Motion Picture Arts and Sciences," *Voting Rules for the 62nd Annual Academy Awards of Merit,* AMPAS, 1990.

39 "There are a lot of special mailers": *Premiere,* April 1991.

39 "Thanks, but no thanks. You don't stand a snowflake's chance": Dale Olson, interview with author, Beverly Hills, 1990.

39 Collins quietly complied: Pauline Collins, conversation with the author, London, September 1991.

40 "just a bunch of slobs": Streep, quoted in Levy, *And the Winner Is . . . .*

41 British representation had ranged from 11 percent in the 1950s . . . : Levy, *And the Winner is. . . .*

42 "stories whose power does not depend on high body counts": Sean Mitchell, "The State of the Movies," Calendar, *Los Angeles Times,* March 25, 1990.

43 "All five of the [Best Picture nominees] are aberrations": Stone quoted by Mitchell, "The State of the Movies," *Los Angeles Times,* March 25, 1990.

45 "a real film about real people": Karl Malden, interview with the author, Beverly Hills, June 1990.

45 "Anything that tugs at your emotions": Zanuck quoted by Mitchell, "The State of the Movies," *Los Angeles Times,* March 25, 1990.

45 "Now we've all got one": Karl Malden, interview with the author, June 1991.

46 "On paper, these two films have a lot in common": Jack Mathews, "Analysis: It's A Long Road for Miss Daisy," *Los Angeles Times,* March 25, 1990.

47 "production numbers that are genuinely innocent in their awfulness": Owen Gleiberman, *Entertainment Weekly,* March 23, 1990.

47 "Somewhat to the embarrassment of the traditional dignity of the Academy": *Academy Newsletter,* 1940.

49 "I saw someone up there doing something I could not do myself": The author was a member of the audience for the 62nd Oscar ceremony in the Dorothy Chandler Pavilion, Los Angeles, in March 1990, and attended the Governors' Ball afterward.

Chapter 3. Bogie and the Art of Oscar Maintenance

PAGE

53 "The process was not something I could live comfortably with": Harbinson, *George C. Scott.*

53 "What's really in that box, Walter?": widely told story confirmed by Walter Matthau in conversation with the author, Beverly Hills, March 1991.

54 "lots of people who win the award don't deserve it": Agan, *Robert De Niro.*

54 Any contest between actors is "meaningless": Bacall, *By Myself.*

54 "to have all the nominees don black tights": Hyams, *Bogie.*

54 "If you have no hope of getting one": Silverman, *David Lean.*

54 "jogged up onto the stage and took the Oscar": Benchley, *Humphrey Bogart.*

54 "When push came to shove, he did care . . .": Bacall.

55 denouncing the awards as "fake": *New York Times,* March 21, 1962.

55 "He stormed out of the room": Cottrell and Cashin, *Richard Burton: Very Close Up.*

55 "The way to survive an Oscar": Hyams, *Bogie.*

55 "Prizes are nothing. My prize is my work": Higham, *Kate.*

55 "Prizes are given. Prizes are won": Osborne, *Sixty Years of the Oscar.*

56 "I'm afraid I'm not going to win": Silverman.

56 "It's insane to have winners and losers": Pfaff and Emerson, *Meryl Streep.*

56 Confessing to feeling "freaked out": Streep, *On Cable,* December 1982.

56 "You can't eat awards": Shepherd and Slatzer, *Duke: The Life and Times of John Wayne.*

56 All his life Wayne claimed: Carpozi, *The John Wayne Story.*

57 "The Oscar is a beautiful thing": Tomkies, *Duke: The Story of John Wayne.*

58 "there's only one place that does it right": Bogdanovich, "The Oscar at Fifty," *Esquire,* April 1978.

58 "I don't honestly believe I've earned it": Freeland, *Dustin.*

59 "awards are very silly": Lenburg, *Dustin Hoffman.*

60 "offensive, barbarous and innately corrupt": New York *Daily News,* Parade, October 27, 1985.

61 "You were nominated by a vote of your fellow actors": *New York Times,* March 6, 1962.

61 "Life isn't a race": Scott to David Lewin of the London *Daily Mail,* quoted in Harbinson.

62 "nor will any legitimate representative": *Los Angeles Times,* February 24, 1971.

62 "I have no objection to awards as such": Scott interviewed by Bridget Byrne, *Los Angeles Times,* March 28, 1971.

62 "Maybe he's scared he won't win": *Newsweek,* March 8, 1971.
62 "Frankly, I resent being put on show like a buffoon": Scott interviewed by Morley Safer on *60 Minutes,* CBS Television, April 13, 1971.
64 "I don't give a damn about [the Oscar]": *Time,* March 22, 1971.
64 "it's given by a blue ribbon jury of [my] peers": Scott to Army Archerd, *Daily Variety,* April 30, 1971.
65 "He should have been there himself": Hall, *Raising Caine.*
66 "That's a part of the sickness in America": *Saturday Night with Connie Chung,* CBS Television, 1990.
66 "I don't care about the Oscars": Biographies of Jane Fonda by Davidson, Guiles, Kiernan, and Cole/Farrell.
67 "If you win an Oscar": Andersen, *Citizen Jane.*
68 her own father had not voted for her: Andersen, *Citizen Jane,* and Fonda, *My Life.*
68 "I've been at too many private parties": Fonda.
68 "The two most famous left-wing women of the seventies": Andersen, op.cit., and Robert Lindsey, "Oscars Stirs Redgrave Dispute Anew," *New York Times,* February 1, 1978.
71 "I'm sick and tired of people exploiting": McClintock, *Indecent Exposure.*
73 "There are two things that bother me about the Academy Awards": Lax, *Woody Allen.*
74 "I may have lost my body": Andersen.
75 "They felt it was a great film despite its racism": Aljean Harmetz, "Oscar-Winning 'Deer Hunter' Is Under Attack as 'Racist' Film," *New York Times,* April 26, 1979. See also: "How Much Is That Oscar on the Mantel?" from Lees and Berkowitz, *The Movie Business.*
76 "a rustle of embarrassment": *New York Times,* April 26, 1979.
78 "The Academy is essentially a trade union": "Tinsel," in Dunne, *Quintana & Friends.*
79 "a man with a mission": Malden, interview with author, Beverly Hills, June 1990.

Chapter 4. "A Pat on the Back"

PAGE

83 "a pat on the back": *New York Times,* March 28, 1982.
84 "the little gold-plated man in the palm of my hand": Davis, *The Lonely Life.*
84 "It wasn't a case of 'give our child a name' ": Skolsky, *McCall's,* April 1962.
84 "The little gold-washed statuette": Marion, *Off With Their Heads!*
84 For Guido Nelli's studio: Academy Awards file, AMPAS (Center of Motion Picture Studies, Beverly Hills).
85 He would build his family a house at the beach: Wiley and Bona, *Inside Oscar;* and A. Scott Berg, "Louis B. Mayer," *Architectural Digest,* Academy Awards Collectors Edition, April 1990. ("MGM discovery Peter Lawford eventually bought his former boss's Santa Monica House, and it became a favorite vacation spot for his brother-in-law President Kennedy.")
86 more than five hundred feature-length films a year: Osborne, *Sixty Years of the Oscar.*

86 a "mutually beneficial" organization: The best concise account of the Academy's foundation and early years is in Shale's brief foreword to *The Academy Awards: An Ungar Reference Index.*

87 "seemed exciting, not to mention flattering": Crowther, *Hollywood Rajah.*

88 two hundred and thirty-one of them . . . adding their names to its membership: Frank Woods, *Academy Annual Report,* 1929.

88 "The Academy will take aggressive action": Osborne.

89 "Even the Oscar was just another way": Gabler, *An Empire of Their Own.*

89 "the League of Nations for the motion picture industry": *Academy Bulletin,* April 22, 1928.

90 "There was little exaggeration in Equity's claim": Ross, *Stars and Strikes.*

90 "Studio owners, sensing a new era of labor militancy": Ceplair and Englund, *The Inquisition in Hollywood.*

93 "unglamorous, against the studio's image": "Long Live Vidor, a Hollywood King," *New York Times,* September 3, 1972.

94 "neither jealousy nor persiflage in Gloria's make-up": Marion.

95 Janning's Oscar was the first thing he showed: Shipman, *The Great Movie Stars,* Vol. 1 *(The Golden Years);* Klaus Mann, "Emil Jannings and Life After Hitler," *Los Angeles Times,* June 8, 1945; and "German Leaders Grew Wealthy on Favoritism," *New York Times,* August 5, 1945.

95 "America's sweetheart": Shipman, Vol. 1.

96 "that would be admitting the original decision was a mistake": *Los Angeles Times,* Calendar, March 24, 1991.

97 "Hollywood was just one big family": *New York Times,* March 28, 1982.

98 "free of the shackles of playing cute little girls with curls": Eyman, *Mary Pickford, America's Sweetheart.*

99 "If you looked around at the elegantly gowned women": Marion.

100 "The most valuable award a worker can get": *Academy Bulletin,* May 12, 1929.

104 "Regardless of which ones of the selected nominees": *Academy Bulletin,* August 11, 1930.

105 "Tell [the losers] that in a conflict": Academy *Annual Report,* 1930.

106 "What do you expect?": Jacobs and Braun, *The Films of Norma Shearer.*

107 "You have no idea what it means to me": Thomas, *Thalberg.*

107 "I admired him greatly": Garbo quoted in Fowler, *Goodnight, Sweet Prince.*

107 "I'll never play another scene with you": Thomas, *Thalberg.*

108 "The studio bosses—most of them great lechers": Brown, *The Real Oscar.* See also: Fowler; Alpert, *The Barrymores;* and Kobler, *Damned in Paradise.*

110 "crap like *Madelon Claudet":* Thomas, *Thalberg.*

110 "The time lapse made the second award": *Los Angeles Times,* November 19, 1932.

113 "The intensive struggle within the industry": *New York Herald-Tribune,* April 21, 1933.

113 "most heartening and inspiring result": *Academy Emergency Bulletin 3,* April 12, 1933.

113 "marked the beginning of the end of the usefulness of AMPAS": Ross.

113 "finally shattered the Academy's moral and professional stature": Ceplair and Englund.

115 "the motion picture companies have not been bankrupted": *Screen Player,* May 15, 1934.

115 "it was the only safe place to go": Wiley and Bona.
117 "If there is anything that moves the ordinary American": *Pare Lorentz,* quoted in Halliwell, *Halliwell's Film Guide.*
118 "In the interim between the nominations and the final voting": Capra, *The Name Above the Title.*

Chapter 5. The Capra Years

PAGE
123 "That French broad likes money": Capra, *The Name Above the Title.*
123 "Sure, you've got some good comedy routines": Capra.
125 "the air was thick with rumors": Davis, *The Lonely Life.*
126 "a Tammany-like organization": *New York Times,* February 24, 1935.
126 Audiences would "hate it": Considine, *Bette and Joan: The Divine Feud.*
126 "My bosses helped them by sending instructions": Davis, *The Lonely Life.*
126 "You'd have to be some kind of ninny": Crawford, *A Portrait of Joan.*
127 "one of the most entertaining films": *Halliwell's Film Guide,* 7th edition, 1989.
128 "It was either that or give the group some tacit recognition": Cagney, *The Authorized Biography.*
128 "The odds were ten to one": Capra.
130 "Dear Bette, what a *lovely* frock!": Considine, *Bette and Joan: The Divine Feud.*
130 "defiled the Academy": Davis, *The Lonely Life.*
133 "Last year the Screen Actors Guild": *New York Times,* January 24, 1937.
134 "huge inflated gas-blown object": Greene, *The Pleasure Dome.*
135 "good antennae for professional gossip": Swindell, *Screwball.*
136 "The principal trouble with the Academy Awards": "Hollywood from A to Z," *New York Times,* March 14, 1937.
138 "I was in Hollywood too early": *Los Angeles Times,* August 15, 1989.
138 "All I can see is the pain in my eyes": *Los Angeles Times,* April 28, 1987.
139 "surprised, even apologetic": Swindell, *Spencer Tracy.*
141 "It's an insult for them to offer me any honor": Holroyd, *Bernard Shaw,* Vol. III: *The Lure of Fantasy.*
142 "no longer the spunky little colonial": Davis, *The Lonely Life.*
142 "This is the last time Davis will win": Fontaine, *No Bed of Roses.*
142 jealousy "was understandable among the women": Marion, *Off With Their Heads!*
144 "only a few votes": *New York Times,* March 10, 1940.
145 "an insult to President Abraham Lincoln and the Negro people": Resolution of the American Labor Party, Jan. 18, 1940 (quoted from the Selznick Papers in Jackson, *Hattie).*
145 "I sincerely hope": Jackson, *Hattie.*
145 "this benefit for Selznick": Thomas, *Selznick.*
147 "a soap opera about a shopgirl": Higham, *Kate.*
147 "one-time Interstate Circuit hoofer": *New York Daily Mirror* quoted in Rogers, *Ginger.*

147 *"should* bring you the highest honors": Rogers, *Ginger.*
148 "For me to have won it with my first good role": Fontaine.
148 "I voted for Henry Fonda": Fonda, *My Life.*

Chapter 6. The Oscars Go to War

PAGE
151 "That Oscar can be a jinx": Fontaine, *No Bed of Roses.*
151 "I never imagined that I would hold this exalted post": Davis, *The Lonely Life.*
152 be referred to as a "dinner": *New York Times,* February 8, 1942.
153 "convinced there was no God": Jackson, *Hattie.*
154 "You have to be there": Fontaine.
156 "Winning an Academy Award": Fontaine.
156 "They failed in what they believed in": Kael, "Raising Kane," *The New Yorker,* reprinted in *The Citizen Kane Book,* 1971. Also good on this episode, apart from the Welles biographies by Leaming and Brady, is Swanberg, *Citizen Hearst;* and Guiles, *Marion Davies.*
159 "legal, artistic and moral right": Brady, *Citizen Welles.*
160 "More works of conjecture have been written": Cotten, *Vanity Will Get You Somewhere.*
162 "propaganda worth a hundred battleships": Carey, *All The Stars in Heaven.*
163 "provided a beacon of morale": Halliwell, *Halliwell's Film Guide.*
164 a "professional againster": Cagney, *The Authorized Biography.*
166 "I guess it'd have to be the Cohan picture": Bogdanovich, "James Cagney," *Esquire,* July 1972, reprinted in *Pieces of Time.*
167 "to a roomful of weary listeners at midnight": Osborne, *Sixty Years.*
169 "couldn't believe it was happening": Wallis and Higham, *Starmaker.*
171 "Did I get an Academy Oscar?": Bankhead, *Tallulah.*
171 "This is the only country where an old broken-down crooner": Thomas, *The One and Only Bing.*
172 "I'm afraid if I went on the set tomorrow": Bergman, *My Story.*
172 their gold-plated splendor: *New York Times,* December 9, 1945.
172 how the resulting total: Wiley and Bona.
172 "Me direct that temperamental bitch!": Thomas, *Joan Crawford.*
173 "Call Hedda Hopper": Henry Rogers, *Walking the Tightrope.* The author is very grateful to Mr. Rogers for the gift of a copy of his entertaining book—never published in England and now out of print in the United States.
175 "all the dames [were] 'oohing' and 'aahing' ": Behlmer (ed.), *Memo from David O. Selznick.*
176 "more awards than I knew existed": Milland, *Wide-Eyed in Babylon.*
176 "Henry, I can't do it": Thomas, *Joan Crawford.*
177 "She bounded out of bed and took a shower": Christina Crawford, *Mommie Dearest.*
177 "coiffed, perfumed, resplendent, radiant": Henry Rogers.
177 "This is the greatest moment of my life": Thomas, *Joan Crawford.*
178 "more of a popularity contest than a talent contest": Henry Rogers.
179 "with a free conscience": Thomas, *Selznick.*

180 "Hollywood is not producing enough *significant* pictures": Marx, *Goldwyn.*
182 "his Oscar in one hand, his Thalberg in the other": Berg, *Goldwyn.*
182 Special Oscar voted to Laurence Olivier: Holden, *Laurence Olivier.*
184 "dozed" his way through much of the film: Henry Rogers.
186 " 'Always a bridesmaid' ": Russell, *Life Is a Banquet* (Brisson foreword, 1979).

Chapter 7. Television to the Rescue

PAGE
189 "the finest ever given on the American screen": Huston, *An Open Book.*
191 "The basis for the Academy Award": Head, *The Dress Doctor.*
191 "There was no doubt in my mind": Head (with Calisto), *Edith Head's Hollywood.*
193 "A certain amount of bias": Wood, *Mr. Rank.*
194 "It's incredibly generous of Hollywood": Holden, *Laurence Olivier.*
194 "These statuettes are visible evidence": *New York Times,* April 17, 1949.
201 "Much that was in the script seemed comparable": "Do Not Forsake Me, Oh My Darlin'," *High Noon (1952),* from Behlmer, *Behind the Scenes.* See also Foreman, "High Noon, The Script," reprinted in Malvin Wald and Michael Werner (eds.), *3 Major Screenplays.*
203 "Fuck her," said Cohn: Considine, *Bette and Joan: The Divine Feud.*
204 "a familiar story": Linet, *Alan Ladd.*
206 Garland's uncomfortable local history: Edwards, *Judy Garland.*
207 "He and I had much in common": Davis, *The Lonely Life.*
207 "Fuck the Academy Awards, baby": Frank, *Judy.*
207 "the biggest robbery since Brink's": Frank.
207 "prinking herself up": Mason, *Before I Forget.*
210 "Take, for example, The Ten Commandments": Wiley and Bona, *Inside Oscar.*
212 "a kind of central clearing-house": Ceplair and Englund, *The Inquisition in Hollywood.*
213 "the intellectual rutting season": Navasky, *Naming Names.*
213 "It was all Sam's idea": Silverman, *David Lean.*
215 "experience has proven [it] to be unworkable": *New York Times,* January 14, 1959.
216 "You've won what they call an Oscar, sir": Guinness, *Blessings in Disguise.*
216 "I won't go the Awards": Kelley, *Elizabeth Taylor: The Last Star.*
217 "I seldom went to the ceremony unless I had been nominated": Leamer, *As Time Goes By.*
220 "Joanne Woodward has set Hollywood glamour back": Oumano, *Paul Newman.*
220 "You oughta win the Oscar for *Raintree":* Kelley.
220 "a nine-foot, two-ton marble replica of the Oscar": Walker, *Elizabeth.*
221 "LANA RETURNS WITH MOB FIGURE": Crane, *Detour.*
221 "I certainly wasn't going to appear": Turner, *Lana.*
222 "Nah. That was too early": Oumano.
222 "Everyone at the party seemed to have voted for me": Niven, *The Moon's a Balloon.*

223 "I think Academy members vote": Russell, *Life Is a Banquet.*
223 "angry letters from housewives all over the United States": Maddox, *Who's Afraid of Elizabeth Taylor?*
224 "at the mercy of public opinion": Kelley.
224 "The honor accorded Ingrid Bergman": For further details on Bergman's rejection by and reconciliation with Hollywood, see Bergman (with Alan Burgess), *My Story.*
225 "The men with the keys to the executive washroom": Brown, *The Real Oscar.*
226 "he had paid his debt to society": Preminger, *Preminger.*
226 "It's not my money, I assure you": *New York Times,* March 25, 1960.
227 "Just before Susan read it off": Heston, *The Actor's Life.*

Chapter 8. Politics and Sentiment

PAGE
229 "These are perilous times": Wayne interviewed by Louella Parsons, the *Los Angeles Examiner,* October 23, 1960. Press accounts of this episode are here supplemented, as detailed below, by the accounts of several Wayne biographers: Mike Tomkies; George Carpozi, Jr.; Maurice Zolotow; Donald Shepherd and Robert Slatzer (with Wayne's associate and friend Dave Grayson).
230 Everything he owned: Carpozi, *The John Wayne Story.*
231 "This is not the first time *The Alamo* has been the underdog": Zolotow, *Shooting Star.*
231 "dripping with sugary adjectives": Brown, *The Real Oscar.*
232 "What right has he got": Tomkies, *Duke: The Story of John Wayne.*
233 "one of the most persistent pressure campaigns": Shepherd and Slatzer, *Duke: The Life and Times of John Wayne.*
234 "outbirded Mr. Birdwell's": Zolotow.
235 "as if someone had taken a bucket of fecal matter": Zolotow.
236 "the battle raging around *The Alamo*": Carpozi.
236 "Keep praying, cousins!": Shepherd and Slatzer.
237 Elizabeth Taylor was "gravely" ill: Distilled from the accounts of Taylor biographers Kelley, Sheppard, Walker; of Bragg *(Rich);* and of Taylor herself.
238 " 'I'm Mummy collecting her Oscar' ": Kelley, *Elizabeth Taylor.*
238 "Play Gloria [Wandrous] and you'll get the Academy Award": Maddox, *Who's Afraid of Elizabeth Taylor?*
239 "Liz was the sole nominee": Brown.
239 "I had come within a breath of dying": Taylor, *An Informal Memoir.*
239 "I lost to a tracheotomy": Maddox.
239 she charged Twentieth Century Fox a *second* million: Kelley.
240 Elvis Presley as Tony, gang leader of the Jets: Sackett (ed.), The Hollywood Reporter *Book of Box Office Hits.*
240 "I am not just a sexy pot": Wiley and Bona, *Inside Oscar.*
240 "Oscar is a funny brute": Shipman, *The Great Movie Stars,* Vol. 2.
241 "a slap in its gold-plated face": *New York Times,* March 6, 1962.
241 "His attitude really doesn't make any sense": *Newsweek,* March 8, 1971.
241 "What do I have to do to prove I can act?": Bosworth, *Montgomery Clift.*

242 "I decided that I could not bear the ordeal": Hotchner, *Sophia: Living and Loving.*
244 "I'm not falsely modest about it": Freedland, *Gregory Peck.*
244 Bette Davis "versus" Joan Crawford: The shooting of *Baby Jane* is wonderfully chronicled by Shaun Considine in *The Divine Feud;* here supplemented by Thomas, *Joan Crawford;* and Davis, *This 'n That.*
244 "I wouldn't give you a dime": Considine.
244 "Bette comes first. She plays the title role": Hedda Hopper, New York *Sunday News,* September 16, 1962.
245 Davis "almost dropped dead": Considine.
248 "How he rejoices in the mastery of his craft!": Oumano, *Paul Newman.*
249 "it would be good for black people": Poitier, *This Life.*
249 "residual benefits for other Negro actors": Bergman, *Sidney Poitier.*
249 "I speak for two generations of black actors": George Christy, *The Hollywood Reporter,* March 17, 1992.
251 "two emasculated gentlemen": Ustinov, *Dear Me.*
251 "If he'd kept his mouth shut": Evans, *Peter Sellers.*
251 "blazing mad": Windeler, *Julie Andrews.*
254 "It is good for the soul": Osborne, *Sixty Years of the Oscar.*
254 "I was a victim of typecasting": Windeler.
255 "What I'd like one day": Shipman, Vol. 2.
255 "This is the most wonderful thing on earth": Callan, *Julie Christie.*
256 "When *The Sound of Music* gets an Academy Award": Baker and Firestone, *Movie People.*
258 "Leaving Richard alone in Paris": Bragg, *Rich.*
259 "It's outrageous!": Capote to the *Los Angeles Times,* quoted by Rex Reed in "The Academy Awards," *Women's Wear Daily,* April 12, 1968, reprinted in *Conversations in the Raw.*
260 "a near-fatal body-blow to Twentieth Century Fox's finances": Harrison, *Rex.*
260 "As a result of meetings today": Dunne, *The Studio.*
262 "A very nice film and a very good film": Halliwell.
263 the ten percent or so of Best Actor nominees: Levy, *And the Winner Is . . .*
263 declared himself "depressed": Lenburg, *Dustin Hoffman;* Freedland, *Dustin.*
264 "the first upset": Reed, *Conversations in the Raw.*
265 "I suspect my award": Edwards, *Katharine Hepburn.*
265 "I'm enormously touched": Edwards.
266 "I was scared to death, and couldn't work": Baker and Firestone.
267 "After the Oscar I was convinced": *TV Guide,* January 15, 1983.
268 "I went to the Philippines": *New York Times,* July 16, 1972.
269 Alan Bates heard the news: Alan Bates, conversation with author, July 1991.
272 "a profound crisis of the soul": Zolotow.
274 " 'You should have this, not me' ": Bragg.
274 Touched enough apparently, to stay up getting drunk: Dave Grayson's evidence in Shepherd and Slatzer.
274 "If I get an Oscar": Siegel, *Jack Nicholson.*
275 "So many people who have been nominated": Los Angeles *Examiner,* April 12, 1952.
275 "a lifeline for a drowning man": *New York Times,* April 26, 1970.

275 "What he was aching for": Eells, *Final Gig.*
275 "The vicissitudes of being hot and cold": Los Angeles *Herald-Examiner,* October 27, 1978.

Chapter 9. Scott, Brando and the Art of Rejection

PAGE
277 "No one should have a chance to see": *The Times,* London, March 30, 1992.
278 Scott's torpedo first hit Hollywood: Harbinson, *George C. Scott.*
278 "Although I have received no official notification": *Los Angeles Times,* February 24, 1971.
279 "a bloody bore": *Time,* March 22, 1971.
279 shared with a man he never met: Cowie, *Coppola.*
280 "I'm voting for myself": Siegel, *Jack Nicholson.*
280 "Sure, I'd like to win an Academy Award": Lenburg, *Dustin Hoffman.*
281 "a little like Margo Channing": Woodward, *Glenda Jackson.*
281 "a machine run by people who are serving an idea": Clive Irving, *McCall's,* July 1971.
282 "I felt disgusted, as though I was watching a public hanging": *The Times,* London, March 30, 1992.
282 "too much makeup and on too long": Mills, *Up in the Clouds, Gentlemen Please.*
283 "God A'mighty, free, free at last": Harbinson.
284 But Koch was undeterred: Koch interview, Beverly Hills, 1990.
284 "an indictment of American values": Andersen, *Citizen Jane.*
286 "the most emotional moment in the history of the Oscars": Karl Malden hosting the official Academy video *Oscar's Greatest Moments 1971–1991* (Columbia TriStar, 1992).
288 "I've got two words to say about the Oscars": Taraborrelli, *Call Her Miss Ross.*
289 "a hard thing for her to say": Freedland, *Liza with a "Z."*
291 "If he had something to say": *New York Times,* December 30, 1973. See also: "Sacheen Littlefeather: A Profile," *San Francisco Chronicle,* March 30, 1973.
291 "When they laid down their arms": Brando's undelivered speech was printed in full in *The New York Times* on March 30, 1973.
292 "No such logical connection between belief and action": Schickel, *Brando: A Life in Our Times.*
292 "thinking back to his first run of success": Downing, *Marlon Brando.*
293 "Not getting our own Academy Award": Siegel.
293 King of Thailand in a previous life: Freedland, *Jack Lemmon.* See also "Jack Lemmon: The Long Wait Before Oscar," by Charles Powers, *Los Angeles Times,* April 7, 1974.
294 "a male Esther Williams": Brown, *The Real Oscar.*
294 "the perfect chemical combination": Phillips, *You'll Never Eat Lunch in This Town Again.*
295 "the hardest work I have ever done": McCambridge, *The Quality of Mercy.*
297 "a proper set of bookends": Charles Marowitz, "The Honesty of a Suburban Superstar," *New York Times,* January 23, 1975.

299 "The Academy Awards are obscene": Freedland, *Dustin.*
299 "ugly and grotesque": Lenburg.
301 virtually alone in defending Schneider: Cowie.
301 Astaire apparently "did not think much": Satchell, *Astaire.*
302 "I'm happy one of my boys made it": Agan, *Robert De Niro.*
302 "Not since Ray Milland guzzled his way to an Oscar": Siegel.
302 "primarily for another reason": Bergman, *My Story;* Leamer, *As Time Goes By.*
304 "After you've been chosen one of the five best": Siegel.
305 "I'd like to have subpoenas": Kaye and Sclavunos, *Michael Douglas and the Douglas Clan.*
305 "They blew it": *New York Times,* March 31, 1976.
305 "a director's movie": Mott and Saunders, *Steven Spielberg.*
308 "a perversion of the natural human instinct": Wiley and Bona, *Inside Oscar.*
309 "Howard Beale was *not* a supporting role": Dundy, *Finch, Bloody Finch;* Faulkner, *Peter Finch.*
312 "No less acute [an] observer of American politics": Goldman, *Adventures in the Screen Trade.* (Writing in 1982, Goldman confidently predicted that *E.T.* would win Best Picture: "There's nothing else.")
314 "I couldn't let down the guys": Lax, *Woody Allen.*
314 "just not coming across as funny": Agan.
315 "I achieved exactly what I wanted": Iain Johnstone, "A Star Is Reborn in Beverly Hills," *The Sunday Times,* London, May 26, 1991.
316 "I told Howard": Redgrave, *Vanessa Redgrave.*
317 "you can see how meaningless this Oscar thing is": Lax.
318 "I knew I wouldn't like it": "How Much Is That Oscar on the Mantel?" in Lees and Berkowitz, *The Movie Business.*
318 "The picture would die if we opened it cold": Aljean Harmetz, "Movie Angling for an Accolade," *New York Times,* November 23, 1978.
320 "I can see a communications revolution": Cowie.
322 "Warren has an interesting psychology": Thomson, *Warren Beatty;* Moor, *Diane Keaton.*
323 "My dress had sweat marks": Pfaff and Emerson, *Meryl Streep.*
324 "incredible . . . I can't put it together": *New York Times,* April 4, 1979.
324 "I still think it's my clincher": Evans, *Peter Sellers.*
325 "Hey, someone left an Oscar in here!": Emerson and Pfaff.
325 "May I have the envelope, please?": Goldstein, *Sally Field.*
327 "Burt really thinks I went out after that Oscar": Bonderoff, *Sally Field.*
327 Martin Sheen had taken over: Cowie.
328 "silly . . . they hurt a lot": Lenburg.
328 "thrilled and shocked": Clinch, *Robert Redford.*

Chapter 10. History vs. Popcorn

PAGE
332 "deeply disturbed": Agan, *Robert De Niro.*
333 "Since the judge seemed determined": Polanski, *Roman.*
334 "the woman who gave me all that hair": Emerson and Pfaff, *Country Girl.*

336 "It was in the wind": Andersen, *Citizen Jane.*
337 "the greatest compliment I ever got": Siegel, *Jack Nicholson.*
338 "high perversity: only a shell-shocked showman": Thomson, *Warren Beatty.*
338 "The Academy has been a little reticent": Parker, *The Joker's Wild.*
339 "What the heck were our costumes?": David Puttnam, interview with author, London, 1991.
340 "I want to name Mr. Barry Diller": McClintick, *Indecent Exposure.*
342 *Reds* proved another commercial failure: Thomson.
344 "I think about the Oscars constantly": Jerry Lazar, *California* magazine, June 1983, supplemented by Brown & Pinkston.
346 "Privacy is very hard to come by": Pfaff and Emerson, *Meryl Streep.*
347 "To say that I'm not interested": Oumano, *Paul Newman.*
348 "I have never seen someone": Jeffries, *Jessica Lange.*
349 "*E.T.* and *Tootsie* are films": *New York Times,* April 12, 1983.
350 "I have Oscar": Wiley & Bona.
351 "I think you've got to have nutty goals": Siegel.
351 "the American Olivier": Slawson, *Robert Duvall.*
352 he thought he was going to win: Michael Caine, conversation with author, London, 1991.
353 "If I fail": Considine, *Barbra Streisand.*
355 Swifty Lazar's Oscar-night party: Irving "Swifty" Lazar, interview with author, New York, 1990. The author is also grateful to Mr. Lazar for an invitation to his Oscar-night party at Spago, Beverly Hills, 1990.
356 "Even the experience of India": Billington, *Peggy Ashcroft;* Silverman, *David Lean.*
358 "one of the most dramatic in Academy Awards history": Kipps, *Out of Focus.*
360 "I guess Olivier was lucky": Puttnam interview with author.
361 "I have dined with kings": Osborne, *Sixty Years of the Oscar.*
362 " 'If people are going to honor you' ": Goldstein, *William Hurt.*
363 "The biggest risk for me": Mott and Saunders, *Steven Spielberg.*
366 "Just wanted one for Toots": Rick Reilly, "Wild in the Seats," *Sports Illustrated,* March 11, 1986.
366 "dropped a lot of dead weight off Anjelica's psyche": Grobel, *The Hustons.*
369 "When you look down the pike": Oumano, *Paul Newman.*
370 "It was only the supporting award": Caine, conversation with author, 1991.
370 "I've seen it a dozen times": Eberts and Ilott, *My Indecision Is Final.*
373 Kirkland had been the beneficiary: Dale Olson, interviews with author, Beverly Hills, 1990–91.
375 Streep had become "disillusioned" with Nicholson: Parker.
376 "Winning the Oscar made me a player": *Los Angeles Times,* March 29, 1992.
378 "Those who made the film": Kipps.
379 "Couples, Costars, Companions, Compadres": Paul Rosenfield, "The Oscar Show and the Exercise of Power," Calendar, *Los Angeles Times,* March 26, 1989.
380 "Women have been portrayed as the second sex": Sam Kiley, "Fatale Attraction," *The Sunday Times,* London, May 12, 1991.
381 "Predicting next year's nominees": Jack Mathews, "Clear the Stage for the 1989 Oscars," Calendar, *Los Angeles Times,* March 26, 1989.

Chapter 11. Whoops, We Forgot You

PAGE

383 "When they sign you up for one of those": Crawford, *A Portrait of Joan.*

383 "If you win, by the end of May": *Los Angeles Times,* March 30, 1992.

385 "they'd always treated him as second": Oumano, *Paul Newman.*

386 "merely shrugged her shoulders": Frances Marion, *Off With Their Heads!*

389 "Okay, turn it on": familiar anecdote retold in Brown, *The Real Oscar.* (Shipman tells the same story, in *The Great Movie Stars,* Vol. 1, with the Luise Rainer punch-line, about Raymond Chandler and his wife).

389 "They were probably correct": Spoto, *The Life of Alfred Hitchcock.*

394 "Ray Stark would kill for an Oscar": Kipps, *Out of Focus.*

397 "out of cold storage": Brown.

397 "the sheer excitement might prove too much for her": For a different view, see Mike Royko, "So Mary Pickford Has Grown Old, So What?" *Los Angeles Times,* April 2, 1976: "Many say they would rather remember her as she once was. Why? She's not dead. She may be old, but she is a living, breathing human being. She has thoughts and emotions and, I'm sure, experiences happiness. That's what I thought I saw on her face when the camera came in close. There was even a tiny teardrop in her eye."

398 "represents the ultimate in acting": Holden, *Laurence Olivier;* Spoto, *Olivier.*

400 "God, I mucked that up": *Hollywood Reporter,* March 30, 1992.

403 "deepened his inveterate sense of being an outsider": Wansell, *Cary Grant.*

405 "Kramer the director": *New York Times,* October 23, 1966.

406 "although he was being paid this tribute": Huston, *An Open Book.*

406 at the suggestion of Fredric March: *New York Times,* September 10, 1949.

412 "The Oscars have been more fair": Kay & Sclavunos, *Michael Douglas and the Douglas Clan.*

Chapter 12. Who's Afraid of Dancing with Wolves?

PAGE

415 "Whether Hollywood likes it or not": Henry Rogers, *Walking the Tightrope.*

416 long been written off as a movie genre: The definitive study is Philip French, *Westerns,* 1974. See also Anthony Lejeune, "Bad Days at Black Rock," *The Times* Saturday Review, London, December 22, 1990; and Peter Guttridge, "The Western Rides Again," *The Sunday Times,* London, February 3, 1991.

417 an enterprising British distributor: Guy East, conversation with author, Beverly Hills, 1991.

419 This was "hindsight talking": Geoff Brown, *The Times,* London, January 22, 1991.

419 "With gifts not found in the average Western American historian": Patricia Nelson Limerick, *USA Today,* March 25, 1991.

420 a cold and windy night in Wilmington: Kevin O'Sullivan, *The Sunday Times,* London, April 7, 1991.

421 "Men's salaries are preposterous": Glenn Paskin, *Time Out,* London, January 2–9, 1991.

422 Typed on pink paper: An original copy of Diane Ladd's letter was passed to the author by an Academy member wishing to remain anonymous; but a request for permission to quote it was refused by Ladd via her lawyers. The reader must thus rest content with a paraphrase within the laws of copyright.
423 "The only rule in filmmaking": Capra, *The Name Above the Title.*
428 "Shirley didn't even get a nomination": Dale Olson, interview with author, Beverly Hills, March 1991.
429 "If *Sporting Life* was my *Hamlet":* Richard Harris, conversation with author, Beverly Hills, March 1991.
431 "the worst side of prescriptive American liberalism": *The Observer,* London, March 31, 1991.
433 "Be prepared, be singular, be brief": Gil Cates; this and other quotes come from Nominees' Lunch, attended by the author, at the Beverly Hilton Hotel, Beverly Hills, March 1991.
434 "like being caught up in a Fellini movie": "On View," *Los Angeles Times,* March 29, 1992.
438 "I'm carrying a lot of people with me": Nominees' Lunch, Beverly Hills, March 1991, attended by the author.
439 Backstage he recalled: The author was among those backstage at the 1991 Oscar ceremony at the Shrine auditorium.
441 "All of us practice our Academy Award speech": Matt Wolf, *The Times,* London, May 1, 1991.
443 "not the filmography of one anxious for glory": Geoff Brown, *The Times,* London, March 27, 1991; and Iain Johnstone, *The Sunday Times,* London, March 31, 1991.
444 "alcoholism is rife": Sam Kiley, *The Times,* London, April 1, 1991.

Chapter 13. Silence Is Golden

PAGE
447 "he didn't want his stars to be seen": *New York Times,* March 15, 1992.
448 "not a very reassuring statistic": Anne Thompson, *Film Comment,* March/April 1992.
449 "greenlighting too many iffy products": Thompson.
449 "This adversity may be the best thing": David Robinson, "Keep It Cheap and in the Family," *The Times,* London, January 7, 1992.
450 a "vintage year for flops": Shaun Usher, *Daily Mail,* London, January 4, 1992.
452 "Here to present our Showmanship Award": For the fourth consecutive year, the author was a guest of Mr. Bollinger (to whom many thanks) at the annual luncheon of the Publicists Guild of America.
454 "seeing the people that I've worked with": *TV Guide,* March 28, 1992.
455 "sixteen tons of rocks": Kevin O'Sullivan, *The Sunday Times,* London, February 25, 1992.
456 "I don't work for rewards": Joey Berlin, *SV Entertainment,* March 1992.
456 "It's all a matter of perspective": Baz Bamigboye, *Daily Mail,* London, February 25, 1992.
456 "I have some difficulty with the Oscars": Berlin.

456 "Hollywood politics, not talent": O'Sullivan.
457 "Nick's already won it": Peter Usher, *Daily Mail,* London, March 6, 1992.
457 a huge $591.5 million: figures provided by *Academy Award Handicap,* Entertainment Data Inc., Beverly Hills.
457 "It's anyone's ball game": *Hollywood Reporter,* March 30, 1992.
458 "A curious week": Peter Bart, "Sexist Snub?" *Weekly Variety,* February 24, 1992.
460 "Nineteen ninety-one was the kind of movie year": "Oscar Predix: Beauties and Beasts," *Film Comment,* March–April 1992.
461 "a snivelling hypocrite": *Vanity Fair,* August 1991.
461 "Everything's so repressive now": *Premiere,* April 1992.
461 "Our sexuality is used": *Sunday Times,* London, March 22, 1992.
461 "arrogance: a smug faith": Richard Schickel, *Time,* March 23, 1992.
461 "The protesters give the film credit": *People,* March 30, 1992.
462 "vocal public demonstrations": *Variety,* March 27, 1992.
462 "a moment of film history": *Hollywood Reporter,* March 26, 1992.
462 "They deserve an Oscar": Army Archerd, *Variety,* March 26, 1992.
463 "a complete and honest look": *Variety,* March 29, 1992.
463 "In his three-hour lie": "Reshooting of the President," Saturday Review, *The Times,* London, January 18, 1992.
464 "Could any director, from Scorsese to Spielberg": *The Sunday Times,* London, December 15, 1991.
465 "revelling in its own transgressiveness": Angela McRobbie, *Sight & Sound,* March 1992.
466 "I feel really privileged": Phil Reeves, "A Blockbuster on the Never-never," *The Independent on Sunday,* London, December 15, 1991.
466 "the master of cinema is exiled": Richard Combs, "A Prisoner in Neverland," *The Independent on Sunday,* London, March 28, 1992.
467 "It was my father's idea": Calendar, *Los Angeles Times,* March 29, 1992.
467 "not of his own volition": *USA Today,* March 30, 1992.
468 "It's a grave oversight": Calendar, *Los Angeles Times,* March 29, 1992.
468 "it must have been galling": *Time Out,* London, January 15–22, 1992.
469 "Oscar's been courting me": *People,* March 30, 1992.
470 "Actors I've never met before": Mason Wiley and Damien Bona, "Puh-Leez, Academy," *Entertainment Weekly,* March 27, 1992.
471 "Not only has no consensus emerged": *Los Angeles Times,* March 29, 1992.
473 "it's a silly bingo game": *USA Today,* March 30, 1992.
475 "I always learn a part": Divina Infusino, *Vis à Vis,* March 1992.
476 "Only a younger membership": Andy Marx, "Who Are These People?" *Los Angeles Times,* March 29, 1992.
477 "a kind of medicine the public don't want to take": *Variety,* March 16, 1992.
477 "Christmas scheduling crunch": *Variety,* March 23, 1992.
477 "the more categories the better": Calendar, *Los Angeles Times,* March 29, 1992.
477 "In an ideal world": Peter Bart, "The Paranoia Pageant," *Weekly Variety,* March 23, 1992.

Bibliography

My main source of secondary material has been the huge library of volumes written by and about (or sometimes in spite of) film actors, directors, producers and their work.

Direct quotations from presenters and recipients at Oscar ceremonies, often garbled in other books, have gratefully been confirmed—as from life—from a highly entertaining videocassette, *Oscar's Greatest Moments,* made available by the Academy via Columbia TriStar in 1992. Details of earlier ceremonies are available in extenso in the Center for Motion Picture Studies. Contemporary critical comments have been culled from the indispensable *Variety Movie Guide* (London: Hamlyn, 1991), and financial figures from the equally useful Hollywood Reporter *Book of Box Office Hits* (New York: Billboard Books, 1990).

Most previous Oscar books are primarily photographic histories, some with more extended captions than others. The most authoritative is Robert Osborne's official history to mark the Awards' sixtieth birthday in 1988, *Sixty Years of the Oscar,* which superseded this veteran commentator's many previous books on the subject. An entertaining, opinionated study is Peter H. Brown's *The Real Oscar,* first published in 1981, revised (with Jim Pinkston) as *Oscar Dearest,* 1987. A meticulous academic treatise is Professor Emanuel Levy's *And the Winner Is . . . ,* first published in 1989 and revised for a softback edition the following year. Most comprehensive of all is *Inside Oscar* by Mason Wiley and Damien Bona, a vast panoramic survey that details every film in contention, captures the suspense of the awards shows and adds voluminous detail on each year's aftermath. Wiley and Bona have subsequently become the ex-officio experts on the Oscars, presiding with due authority over the predictions incumbent on publications ranging from *Premiere* to *TV Guide*. To them and all of the above I express my thanks for pointing me in the right directions. My own attempt at a sustained narrative account is, I hope, distinctive enough to live side by side with their more overt reference books.

There follows a select list of these and other books consulted, which may prove of further interest to either the general or specialist reader in search of greater detail or further information. The edition cited in each case is that consulted by the author. Material drawn directly from these books is acknowledged either in the text or in the source notes that precede this bibliography. In a work involving research on this scale, I hope that I may be forgiven any inadvertent errors or omissions, which will be corrected in future editions.

Agan, Patrick: *Robert De Niro: The Man, the Myth and the Movies* (London: Robert Hale, 1989)

Alpert, Hollis: *The Barrymores* (London: W. H. Allen, 1964)

Andersen, Christopher: *Citizen Jane* (New York: Holt, Rinehart & Winston, 1990)

Bacall, Lauren: *Lauren Bacall by Myself* (New York: Knopf, 1979)

Bainbridge, John: *Garbo* (London: Frederick Muller, 1955)

Baker, Fred, and Firestone, Ross: *Movie People* (London: Abelard-Schuman, 1973)

Bankhead, Tallulah: *Tallulah* (London: Gollancz, 1952)

Barry, Iris: *D. W. Griffith* (New York: Museum of Modern Art, 1965)

Bart, Peter: *Fade Out: The Calamitous Final Days of MGM* (New York: Simon & Schuster, 1990)

Baxter, John: *Hollywood in the Thirties* (New York: Paperback Library, 1970)

Baxter, John: *Hollywood in the Sixties* (San Diego: A. S. Barnes, 1972)

Behlmer, Rudy: *Behind the Scenes* (Hollywood: Samuel French, 1990)

Behlmer, Rudy (ed.): *Memo from David O. Selznick* (New York: Viking, 1972)

Behlmer, Rudy (ed.): *Inside Warner Brothers 1935–51* (New York: Simon & Schuster, 1987)

Benchley, Nathaniel: *Humphrey Bogart* (Boston: Little, Brown, 1975)

Berg, A. Scott: *Goldwyn* (London: Hamish Hamilton, 1989)

Bergman, Carol: *Sidney Poitier* (New York: Chelsea House, 1988)

Bergman, Ingrid (and Alan Burgess): *Ingrid Bergman: My Story* (London: Michael Joseph, 1980)

Billington, Michael: *Peggy Ashcroft* (London: John Murray, 1988)

Bogdanovich, Peter: *Pieces of Time* (New York: Delta, 1974)

Bonderoff, Jason: *Sally Field* (New York: St. Martin's Press, 1987)

Bosworth, Patricia: *Montgomery Clift* (New York: Harcourt Brace Jovanovich, 1978)

Brady, Frank: *Citizen Welles* (London: Hodder & Stoughton, 1989)

Bragg, Melvyn: *Rich: The Life of Richard Burton* (London: Hodder & Stoughton, 1988)

Braun, Eric: *Deborah Kerr* (London: W. H. Allen, 1977)

Brown, Peter H.: *The Real Oscar* (Westport, Conn.: Arlington House, Westport, 1981) revised (with Jim Pinkston) as *Oscar Dearest* (New York: Harper & Row, 1987)

Brownlow, Kevin: *Hollywood, The Pioneers* (London: Collins, 1979)
Buñuel, Luis: *My Last Breath* (New York: Knopf, 1983)
Cagney, James (with Doug Warren): *Cagney: The Authorized Biography* (London: Robson Books, 1986)
Callan, Michael Feeney: *Julie Christie* (London: W. H. Allen, 1984)
Capra, Frank: *The Name Above the Title* (New York: Macmillan, 1971; Vintage, 1985)
Carey, Gary: *Brando* (New York: Pocket Books, 1973)
Carey, Gary: *All the Stars in Heaven: Louis B. Mayer's MGM* (London: Robson Books, 1981)
Carey, Gary: *Katharine Hepburn, A Hollywood Yankee* (New York: St. Martin's Press, 1983)
Carpozi, George: *The John Wayne Story* (New York: Dell, 1972)
Ceplair, Larry, and Englund, Steven: *The Inquisition in Hollywood* (New York: Doubleday, 1980)
Chaplin, Charles: *My Autobiography* (New York: Simon & Schuster, 1964)
Clinch, Minty: *Robert Redford* (London: New English Library, 1989)
Cole, Gerald, and Farrell, Wes: *The Fondas* (New York: St. Martin's Press, 1984)
Considine, Shaun: *Barbra Streisand* (New York: Delacorte, 1985)
Considine, Shaun: *Bette and Joan: The Divine Feud* (London: Sphere, 1989)
Cotten, Joseph: *Vanity Will Get You Somewhere* (London: Columbus Books, 1987)
Cottrell, John and Cashin, Fergus: *Richard Burton: Very Close Up* (New Jersey: Prentice-Hall, 1972)
Cowie, Peter: *Coppola* (New York: Scribner's, 1989)
Crane, Cheryl (with Cliff Jahr): *Detour—A Hollywood Tragedy: My Life with Lana Turner, My Mother* (London: Michael Joseph, 1988)
Crane, Robert David, and Fryer, Christopher: *Jack Nicholson* (New York: M. Evans, 1975)
Crawford, Christina: *Mommie Dearest* (New York: Morrow, 1979)
Crawford, Joan (with Jane Kesner Ardmore): *A Portrait of Joan* (New York: Doubleday, 1962)
Crowther, Bosley: *Hollywood Rajah: The Life and Times of Louis B. Mayer* (New York: Holt, Rinehart & Winston, 1960)
Davidson, Bill: *Spencer Tracy* (London: Sphere, 1989)
Davidson, Bill: *Jane Fonda, An Intimate Biography* (London: Sidgwick & Jackson, 1990)
Davis, Bette: *The Lonely Life* (New York: Putnam, 1962; revised edition, Berkley, 1990)
Davis, Bette (with Michael Herskowitz): *This 'n That* (New York: Putnam, 1987)
de Mille, Cecil B.: *Autobiography* (Englewood Cliffs, N.J.: Prentice-Hall, 1959)
Downing, David: *Marlon Brando* (London: W. H. Allen, 1984)
Dundy, Elaine: *Finch, Bloody Finch* (London: Michael Joseph, 1980)
Dunne, John Gregory: *Quintana & Friends* (New York: Dutton, 1978)
Dunne, John Gregory: *The Studio* (New York: Limelight Editions, 1985)
Eastman, John: *Retakes* (New York: Ballantine, 1989)
Eberts, Jake, and Ilott, Terry: *My Indecision Is Final: The Rise and Fall of Goldcrest Films* (London: Faber & Faber, 1990)
Edwards, Anne: *Judy Garland* (New York: Simon & Schuster, 1974)

Edwards, Anne: *Vivien Leigh* (London: W. H. Allen, 1977)
Edwards, Anne: *Katharine Hepburn* (London: Hodder & Stoughton, 1985)
Eells, George: *Hedda and Louella* (New York: Warner, 1973)
Eells, George: *Final Gig: The Man Behind the Murder* (New York: Harcourt Brace Jovanovich, 1991)
Elley, Derek (ed.): *Variety Movie Guide* (London: Hamlyn, 1991)
Emanuel, Itzhak: *A Descriptive History of the Academy of Motion Picture Arts and Sciences' Annual Awards: The TV Productions 1953–70* (UCLA MA thesis, available for inspection in the Academy's Center for Motion Picture Studies, Beverly Hills)
Emerson, Mark, and Pfaff, Eugene E., Jr.: *Country Girl: The Life of Sissy Spacek* (New York: St. Martin's Press, 1988)
Evans, Peter: *Peter Sellers: The Mask Behind the Mask* (London: New English Library, 1980)
Eyman, Scott: *Mary Pickford, America's Sweetheart* (New York: Donald I. Fine, 1990)
Faulkner, Trader: *Peter Finch* (London: Angus & Robertson, 1979)
Fields, Ronald J.: *W. C. Fields: A Life on Film* (New York: St. Martin's Press, 1984)
Finler, Joel W.: *The Hollywood Story* (London: Mandarin, 1992)
Fischer, Erika J.: *The Inauguration of "Oscar"* (Munich: K. G. Saur, 1988)
Fonda, Henry (as told to Howard Teichman): *Fonda: My Life* (New York: New American Library, 1981)
Fontaine, Joan: *No Bed of Roses* (New York: Morrow, 1978)
Fowler, Gene: *Goodnight, Sweet Prince* (New York: Viking, 1944)
Frank, Gerold: *Judy* (London: W. H. Allen, 1975)
Freedland, Michael: *Fred Astaire* (New York: Grosset & Dunlap, 1977)
Freedland, Michael: *Gregory Peck* (London: W. H. Allen, 1980)
Freedland, Michael: *Jack Lemmon* (London: Weidenfeld & Nicolson, 1985)
Freedland, Michael: *Liza with a "Z"* (London: W. H. Allen, 1988)
Freedland, Michael: *Dustin* (London: Virgin, 1989)
French, Philip: *The Movie Moguls* (London: Weidenfeld & Nicolson, 1969)
French, Philip: *Westerns* (New York: Viking, 1974)
Gabler, Neal: *An Empire of Their Own* (New York: Anchor, 1988)
Goldman, William: *Adventures in the Screen Trade* (New York: Warner, 1983)
Goldstein, Toby: *William Hurt* (New York: St. Martin's Press, 1987)
Goldstein, Toby: *Sally Field* (New York: Paperbacks, 1988)
Graham, Sheilah: *Confessions of a Hollywood Columnist* (New York: Bantam, 1968)
Graham, Sheilah: *Hollywood Revisited* (New York: St. Martin's Press, 1985)
Greene, Graham: *The Pleasure Dome* (London: Secker & Warburg, 1972)
Grobel, Lawrence: *The Hustons* (London: Bloomsbury, 1990)
Guiles, Fred Lawrence: *Marion Davies* (New York: McGraw-Hill, 1972)
Guiles, Fred Lawrence: *Jane Fonda* (New York: Doubleday, 1982)
Guinness, Sir Alec: *Blessings in Disguise* (London: Hamish Hamilton, 1985)
Hall, William: *Raising Caine* (London: Sidgwick & Jackson, 1981)
Halliwell, Leslie (ed.): *Halliwell's Film Guide,* 7th edition (London: Palladin, 1989)
Harbinson, W. A.: *George C. Scott* (New York: Pinnacle, 1977)
Harrison, Rex: *Rex* (London: Macmillan, 1974)
Head, Edith: *The Dress Doctor* (London: Gollancz, 1940)

Head, Edith, & Calisto, Paddy: *Edith Head's Hollywood* (New York: Dutton, 1983)
Hepburn, Katharine: *Me, Stories of My Life* (New York: Knopf, 1991)
Heston, Charlton: *The Actor's Life* (New York: Dutton, 1978)
Higham, Charles: *Celebrity Circus* (New York: Dell, 1960)
Higham, Charles: *The Celluloid Muse* (New York: Signet, 1969)
Higham, Charles: *Kate* (London: W. H. Allen, 1975)
Higham, Charles: *Charles Laughton* (New York: Doubleday, 1976)
Holden, Anthony: *Laurence Olivier* (New York: Atheneum, 1988, rev. 1989; London: Weidenfeld & Nicolson, 1988)
Holroyd, Michael: *Bernard Shaw,* Volume III: *1918–50, The Lure of Fantasy* (London: Chatto & Windus, 1991)
Hopper, Hedda: *From Under My Hat* (New York: MacFadden, 1960)
Hopper, Hedda: *The Whole Truth and Nothing But* (New York: Pyramid, 1963)
Hotchner, A. E. (with Sophia Loren): *Sophia: Living and Loving* (London: Michael Joseph, 1979)
Houseman, John: *Front and Center* (New York: Simon & Schuster, 1979)
Huston, John: *An Open Book* (New York: Knopf, 1980)
Hyams, Joe: *Bogie* (London: W. H. Allen, 1971)
Hyams, Joe: *Bogart and Bacall* (New York: David McKay, 1975)
Jackson, Carlton: *Hattie: The Life of Hattie McDaniel* (New York: Madison, 1990)
Jacobs, Jack, and Braum, Myron: *The Films of Norma Shearer* (San Diego: A. S. Barnes, 1976)
Jeffries, J. T.: *Jessica Lange* (New York: St. Martin's Press, 1986)
Kael, Pauline: "Raising Kane" (*The New Yorker,* reprinted in *The Citizen Kane Book,* New York: Bantam Books, 1971)
Kanin, Garson: *Tracy and Hepburn* (London: Angus & Robertson, 1970)
Kaye, Annene, and Sclavunos, Jim: *Michael Douglas and the Douglas Clan* (London: W. H. Allen, 1989)
Kelley, Kitty: *Elizabeth Taylor: The Last Star* (New York: Dell, 1982)
Kent, Nicolas: *Naked Hollywood* (London: BBC Books, 1991)
Kiernan, Thomas: *Jane Fonda: Heroine for Our Time* (New York: Delilah Books, 1982)
Kipps, Charles: *Out of Focus: David Puttnam in Hollywood* (London: Century, 1989)
Kobler, John: *Damned in Paradise: The Life of John Barrymore* (New York: Atheneum, 1977)
Koch, Howard: *As Time Goes By* (New York: Harcourt Brace Jovanovich, 1978)
Korda, Michael: *Charmed Lives* (New York: Random House, 1979)
Lax, Eric: *Woody Allen* (London: Jonathan Cape, 1991)
Leaming, Barbara: *Orson Welles* (London: Weidenfeld & Nicolson, 1985)
Lees, David and Berkowitz, Stan: *The Movie Business* (New York: Vintage, 1981)
Lenburg, Jeff: *Dustin Hoffman: Hollywood's Anti-Hero* (New York: St. Martin's Press, 1983)
Levy, Emanuel: *And the Winner Is . . .* (New York: Continuum, 1990)
Likeness, George: *The Oscar People* (Mendota, Ill.: Wayside Press, 1965)
Linet, Beverly: *Alan Ladd* (New York: Arbor House, 1979)
Maddox, Brenda: *Who's Afraid of Elizabeth Taylor?* (London: Granada, 1977)
Mamet, David: *Writing in Restaurants* (New York: Viking, 1986)

Marion, Frances: *Off With Their Heads!* (New York: Macmillan, 1972)
Marx, Arthur: *Goldwyn, The Man Behind the Myth* (London: Bodley Head, 1976)
Mason, James: *Before I Forget* (London: Hamish Hamilton, 1981)
Mast, Gerald (ed.): *The Movies in Our Midst* (Chicago: University of Chicago Press, 1982)
McCambridge, Mercedes: *The Quality of Mercy* (New York: Times Books, 1981)
McClintick, David: *Indecent Exposure* (New York: Morrow, 1982)
Milland, Ray: *Wide-eyed in Babylon* (New York: Morrow, 1974)
Mills, John: *Up in the Clouds, Gentlemen Please* (London: Weidenfeld & Nicolson, 1980)
Milne, Tom (ed.): *The* Time Out *Film Guide* (London: Penguin Books, 1989)
Moor, Jonathan: *Diane Keaton* (New York: St. Martin's Press, 1989)
Mott, Douglas R., and Saunders, Cheryl McAllister: *Steven Spielberg* (Boston: Twayne, 1986)
Navasky, Victor: *Naming Names* (London: John Calder, 1982)
Niven, David: *The Moon's a Balloon* (London: Hamish Hamilton, 1972)
Niven, David: *Bring on the Empty Horses* (London: Hamish Hamilton, 1975)
Norman, Barry: *The Hollywood Greats* (New York: Franklin Watts, 1980)
O'Brien, Tom: *The Screening of America* (New York: Continuum, 1990)
Osborne, Robert: *Sixty Years of the Oscar* (New York: Abbeville, 1989)
Oumano, Elena: *Paul Newman* (New York: St. Martin's Press, 1989)
Parker, John: *The Joker's Wild: The Biography of Jack Nicholson* (London: Anaya, 1991)
Perry, Louis B. and Richard S.: *A History of the Los Angeles Labor Movement* (Berkeley, Ca.: University of California Press, 1963)
Pfaff, Jr., Eugene E., and Emerson, Mark: *Meryl Streep* (Jefferson, N.C.: McFarland, 1987)
Phillips, Julia: *You'll Never Eat Lunch in This Town Again* (New York: Random House, 1991)
Pickard, Roy: *Hollywood Gold* (New York: Toplinger, 1979)
Pickford, Mary: *Sunshine and Shadow* (New York: Doubleday, 1955)
Poitier, Sidney: *This Life* (New York: Knopf, 1980)
Polanski, Roman: *Roman* (London: Heinemann, 1984)
Preminger, Otto: *Preminger* (New York: Doubleday, 1977)
Redgrave, Vanessa: *Vanessa Redgrave* (London: Hutchinson, 1991)
Reed, Rex: *Conversations in the Raw* (New York: World Publishing, 1969)
Robinson, David: *The History of World Cinema* (New York: Stein & Day, 1981)
Rogers, Ginger: *Ginger: My Story* (New York: HarperCollins, 1991)
Rogers, Henry: *Walking the Tightrope: The Private Confessions of a Public Relations Man* (New York: Morrow, 1980)
Ross, Murray: *Stars and Strikes* (New York: Columbia University Press, 1941)
Russell, Ken: *A British Picture* (London: Heinemann, 1989)
Russell, Rosalind (and Chris Chase): *Life Is a Banquet* (New York: Grosset & Dunlap, 1977)
Sackett, Susan (ed.): The Hollywood Reporter *Book of Box Office Hits* (New York: Billboard Books, 1990)
Sands, Pierre Norman: *A Historical Study of the Academy* (New York: Arno Press, 1966)

Sarris, Andrew: *Hollywood Voices: Interviews with Film Directors* (New York: Avon, 1967)
Sarris, Andrew: *Politics and Cinema* (New York: Columbia University Press, 1978)
Satchell, Tim: *Astaire* (London: Hutchinson, 1987)
Schary, Dore: *Heyday* (Boston: Little, Brown, 1970)
Schickel, Richard: *Brando: A Life in Our Times* (New York: Pavilion, 1991)
Shale, Richard: *The Academy Awards: An Ungar Reference Index* (New York: Ungar, 1978)
Sharif, Omar (with Marie-Therese Guinchard): *The Eternal Male* (New York: Doubleday, 1977)
Shepherd, Donald, and Slatzer, Robert, with Dave Grayson: *Duke: The Life and Times of John Wayne* (New York: Doubleday, 1985)
Sheppard, Dick: *Elizabeth* (New York: Warner, 1974)
Shindler, Colin: *Hollywood Goes to War* (London: Routledge & Kegan Paul, 1979)
Shipman, David: *The Great Movie Stars*, Volumes 1, 2 & 3 (London: Futura, 1989–1991)
Shipman, David: *The Story of Cinema* (New York: St. Martin's Press, 1982)
Siegel, Barbara and Scott: *Jack Nicholson* (New York: Avon, 1990)
Silverman, Stephen M.: *David Lean* (New York: Abrams, 1989)
Sklar, Robert: *Movie Made America* (London: Chappell, 1975)
Slawson, Judith: *Robert Duvall* (New York: St. Martin's Press, 1985)
Spoto, Donald: *Stanley Kramer, Film Maker* (New York: Putnam, 1978)
Spoto, Donald: *The Life of Alfred Hitchcock: The Dark Side of Genius* (London: Collins, 1983)
Spoto, Donald: *Laurence Olivier* (London: HarperCollins, 1991)
Steele, Joseph Henry: *Ingrid Bergman* (New York: Popular Library, 1959)
Swanberg, W. A.: *Citizen Hearst* (New York: Bantam Books, 1961)
Swindell, Larry: *Spencer Tracy* (New York: World Publishing, 1969)
Swindell, Larry: *Screwball: The Life of Carole Lombard* (New York: Morrow, 1975)
Taraborrelli, J. Randy: *Call Her Miss Ross* (New York: Birch Lane, 1989)
Taylor, Elizabeth: *Elizabeth Taylor, An Informal Memoir* (New York: Harper & Row, 1964)
Taylor, Elizabeth: *Elizabeth Takes Off* (New York: Putnam, 1987)
Taylor, John Russell: *Hitch: The Life and Work of Alfred Hitchcock* (Boston: Little, Brown, 1978)
Thomas, Bob: *King Cohn* (New York: Bantam, 1967)
Thomas, Bob: *Thalberg* (New York: Doubleday, 1969)
Thomas, Bob: *Selznick* (New York: Doubleday, 1970)
Thomas, Bob: *Walt Disney* (New York: Pocket Books, 1976)
Thomas, Bob: *The One and Only Bing* (New York: Grosset & Dunlap, 1977)
Thomas, Bob: *Joan Crawford* (New York: Bantam, 1978)
Thomson, David: *Warren Beatty* (London: Secker & Warburg, 1987)
Tomkies, Mike: *Duke: The Story of John Wayne* (London: Arthur Barker, 1971)
Turner, Lana: *Lana* (New York: Dutton, 1982)
Ullmann, Liv: *Choices* (New York: Knopf, 1984)
Ustinov, Peter: *Dear Me* (Boston: Little, Brown, 1977)
Vickers, Hugo: *Vivien Leigh* (London: Hamish Hamilton, 1988)
Vidal, Gore: *Hollywood, a Novel* (London: Andre Deutsch, 1989)

Walker, Alexander: *Peter Sellers* (London: Weidenfeld & Nicolson, 1981)
Walker, Alexander: *Vivien* (London: Weidenfeld & Nicolson, 1987)
Walker, Alexander: *Elizabeth* (London: Weidenfeld & Nicolson, 1990)
Wallis, Hal (with Charles Higham): *Starmaker: The Autobiography of Hal Wallis* (New York: Macmillan, 1980)
Wansell, Geoffrey: *Cary Grant: Haunted Idol* (London: Collins, 1983)
Wiley, Mason, and Bona, Damien: *Inside Oscar* (New York: Ballantine, 1987)
Windeler, Robert: *Julie Andrews* (New York: St. Martin's Press, 1983)
Wood, Alan: *Mr. Rank* (London: Hodder & Stoughton, 1952)
Wood, Michael: *America in the Movies* (New York: Columbia University Press, 1989)
Woodward, Ian: *Glenda Jackson: A Study in Fire and Ice* (London: Weidenfeld & Nicolson, 1985)
Yule, David: *David Puttnam: The Story So Far* (London: Sphere, 1988)
Zeffirelli, Franco: *Zeffirelli* (London: Weidenfeld & Nicolson, 1986)
Zolotow, Maurice: *Shooting Star: A Biography of John Wayne* (London: W. H. Allen, 1974)

Index